The Soul of the American University
Revisited

The Soul of the American University Revisited

From Protestant to Postsecular

GEORGE M. MARSDEN

OXFORD
UNIVERSITY PRESS

OXFORD
UNIVERSITY PRESS

Oxford University Press is a department of the University of Oxford. It furthers
the University's objective of excellence in research, scholarship, and education
by publishing worldwide. Oxford is a registered trade mark of Oxford University
Press in the UK and certain other countries.

Published in the United States of America by Oxford University Press
198 Madison Avenue, New York, NY 10016, United States of America.

Library of Congress Control Number: 2021904220
ISBN 978-0-19-760724-4 (pbk.)
ISBN 978-0-19-007331-2 (hbk.)

DOI: 10.1093/oso/9780190073312.001.0001

1 3 5 7 9 8 6 4 2

Paperback printed by Marquis, Canada
Hardback printed by Bridgeport National Bindery, Inc., United States of America

Contents

Acknowledgments   vii

Introduction   1

Prologue I: God and Buckley at Yale (1951)   9

Prologue II: Henry Sloane Coffin's Yale (1897)   17

Prologue III: Yale Embattled: Noah Porter versus
                 William Graham Sumner (1880)   21

PART I   THE ESTABLISHMENT OF PROTESTANT
             NONSECTARIANISM

1. The Burden of Christendom: Seventeenth-Century Harvard   29

2. The New Queen of the Sciences and the New Republic   43

3. Two Kinds of Sectarianism   63

4. A Righteous Consensus, Whig Style   73

5. The John the Baptist of the German University Ideal   89

PART II   DEFINING THE UNIVERSITY IN A
              SCIENTIFIC ERA

6. The Christian Legacy in the Age of Science   101

7. Back to Noah Porter's Yale   109

8. Daniel Coit Gilman and the Model for a Modern University   121

9. Liberal Protestantism at Michigan   137

10. Harvard and the Religion of Humanity   151

11. Orthodoxy at the Gentlemen's Club   163

12. The Low-Church Idea of a University   175

PART III   WHEN THE TIE NO LONGER BINDS

13. The Trouble with the Old-Time Religion   193

14. The Elusive Ideal of Academic Freedom   215

15. The Fundamentalist Menace   241

16. The Obstacles to a Christian Presence   255

17. Outsiders   279

18. Searching for a Soul   291

19. A Church with the Soul of a Nation   309

20. Liberal Protestantism without Protestantism   329

21. The Twenty-First-Century Postsecular University   351

Epilogue: An Unexpected Sequel: A Renaissance of
Christian Academia   365

Notes   391
Index   459

Acknowledgments

This volume, which is a revision and updating of *The Soul of the American University: From Protestant Establishment to Established Nonbelief* (1994), has benefited from the work of many contributors, mostly from about three decades ago. The Pew Charitable Trusts funded a multi-year study of the topic. That helped provide research assistance from quite a number of graduate students and others listed in the acknowledgments to that volume. I'll just mention again the three who contributed the most: Bradley Longfield, Darryl G. Hart, and Paul Kemeny. I also benefited from comments on the original text from ten distinguished reviewers, acknowledged in that volume.

For this revised and updated edition I am particularly indebted to Rick Ostrander, who read the entire text and provided many comments and suggestions, many of which I have followed. I am also grateful to Todd Ream, Bill Ringenberg, Benjamin Wetzel, and Tom Jones, who read and commented on the principal new parts of the volume, the introduction and two concluding chapters.

I also owe a debt once again to the editors and staff at Oxford University Press for their always excellent help. I especially want to thank my longtime editor, Cynthia Read, who suggested a revision such as this and has been an invaluable contributor to the project.

Introduction

American higher education has changed in some striking ways since the publication of *The Soul of the University* more than a quarter century ago. That is especially true if one is seeking to understand its "soul" in the sense of some sort of essence growing out of a common story that shapes its identity and purpose.[1] In light of such changes, I am offering a new and more concise version of the history that brings the story up to date and also recasts its concluding interpretive theme.

One telling indicator of the differences between the prevailing outlooks toward religion and culture in the twenty-first century and those of the preceding era is the fact that today one of the widely accepted characterizations is to say that we are in a "postsecular"[2] age. "Postsecular" does not mean that secularism is dead or dying or necessarily that religions, including traditional religions, are making a comeback. Rather, "postsecular" is a paradigm for understanding our era that contrasts with the old widely used twentieth-century "secularization" paradigm that saw human history as inexorably heading toward a secular era. According to that old paradigm, as modern, industrialized, technological, scientific-minded societies advanced, traditional religions would have to give way much in the same ways as would traditional medicine or modes of agriculture. Such assumptions about secularization involved a variety of Western imperialistic thinking that assumed that the patterns of secular development in the West would become the template for the rest of the world. Marxism provided a strong version of such assumptions.

Even in mid–twentieth century America, when religions of all sorts were flourishing, many academics were dedicated to variations of the "secularization thesis" that projected inevitable decline, especially of old-fashioned, "prescientific" religious beliefs. Such ideas that related secularization to progress were among the reasons that many universities and colleges put their religious heritages aside in order to keep up with the forefront of American education. And for similar reasons many would-begatekeepers

The Soul of the American University Revisited. George M. Marsden, Oxford University Press. © Oxford University Press 2021. DOI: 10.1093/oso/9780190073312.003.0001

in mainstream higher education characterized traditional religious perspectives as unscientific and "unprofessional."

My subtitle for the original version, "From Protestant Establishment to Established Nonbelief," was designed to point out the irony involved if the mainstream academy would allow only essentially secular views. For centuries Protestantism had been virtually the established religion even in state-run American higher education, a monopoly that sometimes involved injustices to those with differing viewpoints. But by the later twentieth century it was advocates of purely naturalistic viewpoints who aspired to have their views established as the norm for truly professional higher education. In my "Concluding Unscientific Postscript" I argued that, instead of assuming that higher education should become increasingly secular, a more genuinely pluralistic alternative would be to encourage a diversity of religious as well as secular points of view.

By now, well into the twenty-first century, the situation has changed, and I have reframed the concluding narrative in light of such changes. For one thing, as was already apparent in the late twentieth century, purely naturalistic viewpoints (that is, those that would exclude traditional religious perspectives) were hopelessly divided against themselves. Broadly speaking, there are two major types of anti-religious naturalism. First, there is the old-fashioned mid–twentieth century positivistic naturalism, which seeks objective or universally valid truths based on scientific models. Second, becoming much more prominent since the 1960s, has been what can be called subjectivist naturalism. Such views reflect modern or postmodern celebrations of the sacred self and of the communities that shape the self's identities. Such celebrations typically reject enlightenment attempts to find common philosophical ground for all. Instead, they involve liberationist narratives for individuals and groups that previously had been discriminated against. Claims to knowledge, accordingly, can be best understood as matters of power.[3] Although such narratives may have a religious basis, as they do in some more liberal versions of Christianity, much more often in academia they have been exclusively naturalistic, rejecting most traditional religious beliefs as sources of oppression.

Aside from the question of how one might evaluate these viewpoints, one can recognize the historical phenomenon that subjectivist forms of naturalism have done much to undermine the authority of the old positivistic objectivist naturalism. Science itself is now often seen as shaped in part by the assumptions, values, and power interests of the communities that practice it.[4]

One reason why the American academy of the twenty-first century might be fairly called "postsecular" is that there is so much room for diversity of opinion that, while secular viewpoints continue to dominate, various religious outlooks can still find room for expression. Even though there are plenty of documented examples of prejudice against religiously based viewpoints,[5] religiously based scholarship that meet the usual standards of academic merit is likely to find a place among the varieties of accepted perspectives. Even some quite traditional religious perspectives, though they may remain unpopular, have proved themselves to be intellectually viable. Thus, while a diversity of viewpoints that includes various religious viewpoints is not as often encouraged in mainstream academia as it might be, neither are religiously based academic outlooks entirely ruled out.

One side effect of my subtitle, "From Protestant Establishment to Established Nonbelief," was that it led some readers to view the history as essentially both a secularization story and a declension narrative. It is, of course, in part a story of secularization in the strict sense of the removal of an activity from church influence. And it concluded with what could be construed as a declension narrative in that I expressed my disapproval of the degree to which more traditional Christian perspectives had been largely marginalized from mainstream academia.[6]

Still, even if the story of American higher education inevitably involves a secularization narrative, it is important to recognize, as this history emphasizes, that secularization is a complex and often paradoxical process. Sociologist David Martin has shown through the study of comparative secularization that the process takes many forms, depending largely on the nature of the religious establishment, and that, by itself, the term carries little clear meaning.[7] Such observations are especially relevant to the United States, where the religious establishment was almost wholly Protestant and still so bewilderingly diverse. Further, one prominent feature of secularization in the United States, where voluntary religion has been especially strong, has been that when a religious dimension is reduced or removed from one sort of activity, it will reappear in compensating ways in others. The clearest illustration of that phenomenon is that the population of the United States is in many respects more religious than was its antecedent counterpart in the colonial era, even though there is much less formally established religion today. So in my telling of this story, I have tried to take into account that what may seem like secularization often involves the shifting of the locus of religious activity rather than its disappearance.

Furthermore, one of the main lessons of this history is that religious establishments are inherently problematic. So disestablishment, whatever its downsides, brings benefits even to the principal religion involved. That is certainly the case in the history of Protestantism and American higher education. There was no golden age from which there was a simple decline. Rather, a leading theme that emerges from this narrative is the inevitably flawed character of trying to maintain a de facto national religious establishment. The most evident problem with religious establishments is that they are discriminatory. In the mid-nineteenth century, for example, even state universities typically had all Protestant faculties, had clergymen as presidents, and required Protestant chapel services. By the mid-twentieth century it was becoming evident that principles of equity demanded the ending of such Protestant privilege if leading institutions were to serve a diverse citizenry.

A less obvious consequence of the informal Protestant establishment, but a major motif that emerges in this history, is its negative impact on the quality of Protestant intellectual life. The assumption that Protestant Christianity should be, at least informally, the American established religion, meant that that most leading academics took for granted a broadly Christian cultural ethos. Rather than regard Christianity as a distinct point of view at the heart of the entire educational enterprise that ought to challenge the idols and ideologies of the age, they tended to treat it as supplemental to the more general and religiously neutral education that was suitable for gentlemen. At the time, they had understandable reasons for this approach. They were heirs to a long tradition, inherited from medieval Christendom, of reverence for the Greek and Roman classics, and so they viewed Christian teachings as largely supplemental to secular learning, which comprised the heart of higher education.

In the eighteenth century, in places where Protestantism was still the established religion, the new "enlightened" thought of the era could be regarded in much the same way: It could be appropriated as an updating of the best of human inquiry based on reason alone. Theology and biblical revelation might be necessary to understand the full picture, but "natural" revelation, or aspects of God's creation that could be understood by objective reason and science, was fully reliable so far as it went. So Christian teachings continued to be seen as largely supplemental to the learning suitable for all educated persons.

To make a long story short, such assumptions regarding the harmony of Christianity and modern thinking remained strong through the mid-nineteenth century but collapsed under the pressure of the second scientific revolution of the late nineteenth century, of which Darwinism became the symbol. In the context of a rapidly modernizing industrial society, "science" came to be equated with "natural science," and leading thinkers insisted that true rationality demanded consideration of natural phenomena exclusively. In part, such exclusively naturalistic ideologies were used to undermine the authority of residual religious establishments. Darwinism was an especially effective weapon in the resulting warfare, since it seemed to provide for the first time a plausible explanation as to how a universe that included intelligent beings might arise without the agency of a higher intelligence. Furthermore, Darwinism, together with rising biblical criticism based on naturalistic assumptions, seemed to undermine the authority of the Bible.

By the beginning of the twentieth century, therefore, it was no longer feasible simply to add traditional Christianity to the best of modern learning. One prominent response was to conclude that Christianity had to be modified to meet the modern standards, as liberal Protestants did. At the other end of the spectrum were conservative Christians who declared war on much of modern thought and developed their own teachings and institutions, as did fundamentalists and traditionalist Roman Catholics. Though there were many more moderate shades of opinion, these extremes often seemed to define the conversation through the first half of the twentieth century.

In the past generation, however, a very different picture has emerged. As is described in the concluding chapter of this volume, learning that is based on explicitly Christian perspectives yet engaged with the intellectual mainstream has been prospering in its new outsider status. One of the benefits of disestablishment is that thoughtful Christians are forced to see their outlooks as distinctive minority points of view in a world where there is not going to be a majority consensus. Such flourishing could be illustrated in some of the varieties of outlooks among a wide range of Protestant and Catholic thinkers. But as a historical phenomenon, perhaps the most unexpected development has been the blossoming of explicitly Christian scholarship among more traditional Protestants. That is surprising because in the mid-twentieth century, their academic progenitors had been largely written off by the mainstream establishment as hopelessly obscurantist. In the twenty-first century, by contrast, traditionalist Protestant scholarship, both in America and around the world, has developed substantial and intellectually impressive interdisciplinary communities. The story of that development is hardly one of simple success. Serious scholars typically represent only a tiny minority in any community, so often there are large gaps between outlooks of academics and their more populist church constituencies. Nonetheless, in recent decades traditional Protestants have developed a substantial community of accomplished scholars who can hold their own in mainstream academic settings and also provide alternatives to forms of anti-intellectualism that continue to persist in many of their own communities.

I have presented much of the principal history through the stories of elite institutions. That is because when doing cultural history there are advantages in looking at the most influential leaders and institutions in the cultural mainstream. Nonetheless, one must always bear in mind that, given America's bewildering religious and ethnic diversity and opportunities for local initiatives, there are many alternative stories that are important in their own right.[8]

In telling the stories of America's leading educators and their schools, I also tend to focus on the relationships of Christian teachings to intellectual and moral concerns. Higher education, like Western intellectual life generally, has long included searches for meaning. And young people of college age have often been engaged in personal quests for meaning. Until recent decades, that was commonly considered to be one of the major goals of undergraduate education, and it is still considered so by a minority.[9] In a nation where many people have had some degree of religious training, religious questions have often been involved in such searches. So it is worthwhile to reflect, as this volume does, on the degree to which explicitly religious perspectives may have helped shape what was taught in the classrooms, what was published for the edification of the public, and how institutions were defined. Other scholars might choose to address the role of religion in universities by focusing on student life, chapels, revivals, and the many voluntary religious organizations on American campuses. Those are also important parts of the story that I try to keep in view. But my primary inquiries concern how Christian perspectives were related to the intellectual inquiries that were essential to the enterprise.

Though I write this history with a general audience in mind, it is important to recognize that I speak as one who has long been part of religious-intellectual communities that have built their educational institutions around the conviction that Christianity should offer distinct perspectives. If one truly believes, as Christians profess, that everything in the universe is part of God's ongoing creation and that human history centers around God's plan of salvation in Jesus Christ, such claims are so radical that they ought to change the contextual framework for thinking about just about everything. Such perspectives, shaped by our loves (as St. Augustine suggests), should influence our commitments and priorities, including those surrounding education and scholarship. One's approach to learning may be in practical ways much the same as that of people working from other perspectives, since Christians see themselves as part of a common humanity living in a universe that is ordered in the same way for everyone. Yet even in their most technical research and scientific learning, Christians seek to self-consciously view the purpose of what they are doing through the lens of their commitments to a loving God who mandates love to others and cherishing of creation.

Even though many Christian educators through the centuries have informally viewed their vocations in such ways, it has not been until relatively recently that such approaches have been widely articulated as the ideal for distinctly Christian higher education.[10] This history helps us understand why such efforts to integrate faith and learning, now the stock in trade of many Christian thinkers and institutions, were not more fully developed earlier. The short answer, as suggested previously, is that so long as higher education was a privileged dimension of Christendom, it was difficult for educational leaders to see Christianity as a radically distinct point of view.

Finally, in this new edition I have edited and abbreviated the main historical narrative. Specifically, I have reduced the number of schools whose histories I recount in the formative transitional era of the emergence of modern universities in the late nineteenth century.[11] I have also abbreviated some of the other accounts in that and other eras and reframed a few of the interpretive themes. Overall, the result is that, even with the new twenty-first-century materials, the volume is similar in length to the original. Most of the essential history, of course, remains the same. Nonetheless, with the view that historical interpretation is properly meant to illumine one's own times, this study is updated for a twenty-first-century audience.

Prologue I

God and Buckley at Yale (1951)

"I was somewhat concerned," wrote McGeorge Bundy (Yale '40) in the *Atlantic* of November 1951, "lest my readers refuse to believe that so violent, unbalanced, and twisted a young man really existed."

Bundy, a professor at Harvard but speaking on behalf of his alma mater, treated William F. Buckley Jr. as an upstart who had failed to know the rules at a gentlemen's club. Buckley's infraction was that he had been so ungrateful as to write a scathing attack on the school from which he had just graduated, alleging that it was a hotbed of atheism and collectivism. This ingratitude was compounded by Buckley's failure to recognize that, as a Roman Catholic, he was something of a guest at Yale. "Most remarkable of all," said Bundy near the beginning of his review of *God and Man at Yale*, was that Buckley, while not even mentioning that he was "an ardent Roman Catholic," should attempt to define Yale's religious tradition. "Yale has thousands of Catholic alumni and friends," said Bundy, "who would not dream of such a course."[1] The Rev. Henry Sloane Coffin (Yale '97), chairman of a blue-ribbon committee to report on the spiritual and political condition of Yale, wrote to one inquirer, "Mr. Buckley's book is really a misrepresentation and distorted by his Roman Catholic point of view. Yale is a Puritan and Protestant institution by its heritage and he should have attended Fordham or some similar institution."[2]

God and Man at Yale would have caused a sensation even without the religious issues. Senator Joseph McCarthy was on the loose, and at the height of his influence, the United States was in the midst of the Korean War, and at other universities professors had lost jobs over accusations of communism. Buckley did not allege that there were communists on the Yale faculty, but his accusations that traditionally conservative Yale was promoting "collectivism," even if this amounted to little more than New Deal liberalism, threatened to test the loyalty of some of the Old Blue.

The Soul of the American University Revisited. George M. Marsden, Oxford University Press. © Oxford University Press 2021. DOI: 10.1093/oso/9780190073312.003.0002

In retrospect, however, the religious dimensions of the controversy are the most remarkable, since they are the least remembered. Even a generation later it would seem almost inconceivable that there could have been a national controversy involving the question of whether a major university was sufficiently Christian. Yet not only the responses of Yale, but also those of the reviewers, make it clear that it would have been news to admit that Yale had drifted loose of its Christian moorings.

To be sure, the task of assessing the role of religion in the controversy is complicated by Buckley's conflation of the economic and religious issues. At one point in the book, Buckley even affirmed, "I believe that the duel between Christianity and atheism is the most important in the world. I further believe that the struggle between individualism and collectivism is the same struggle reproduced on another level." Years later Buckley remarked that the words "the same struggle reproduced on another level" were not originally his own but were suggested by one of his conservative mentors. Nonetheless, he let them stand because there was "a nice rhetorical resonance and an intrinsic, almost nonchalant suggestion of an exciting symbiosis."[3] Though Buckley, always the debater, thus acknowledged that his fondness for rhetoric overrode his concern for precision of argument, the explicit equation was implicit throughout the book.[4]

In any case, a substantial section of Buckley's essay dealt solely with the state of Christianity at Yale, and this provides us with a revealing account of both the extent and limits of religious influences at the middle of the twentieth century. Buckley's evidence, as well as Yale's responses, offers clues as to how it was that many American universities of this era could still see themselves as Christian and yet simultaneously, especially from an outsider's point of view, seem essentially subversive of Christianity.

One of the things Buckley was so impolite as to point out was a sizable gap between Yale's rhetoric and reality. His lead quotation was from President Charles Seymour's 1937 inaugural: "I call on all members of the faculty, as members of a thinking body, freely to recognize the tremendous validity and power of the teachings of Christ in our life-and-death struggle against the forces of selfish materialism. If we lose that struggle, judging from present events abroad, scholarship as well as religion will disappear."[5]

The statement was typical of the public philosophy of many universities of the time. Spokespersons could routinely identify Christianity with the very future of civilization and with what separated the United States from totalitarianism. Nonetheless, at a university, especially a university that served a free nation, these teachings could not be taught by indoctrination and were accepted only by "a thinking body, freely."

On such grounds, Yale claimed to score well. Yale was reputed to be more religious than many universities, and Seymour had in the same address called for "the maintenance and upbuilding of the Christian religion as a vital part of the university life."[6] Not only did it have a strong religious heritage, a divinity school, a university chapel, and campus religious programs, but its undergraduate program could also point to its large religion department and to many influential faculty who were strongly pro-Christian.

Buckley presented a formidable case that none of these amounted to much and that a Yale education was more likely to shatter a person's commitment to Christianity than to fortify it. The most popular religion course, taught by the university chaplain, was popular because it was easy. Moreover, the professor, despite his personal religious faith, made a concerted effort to teach *about* Christianity, rather than to teach Christianity. The next most popular course, taught by T. M. Greene, a philosopher of religion, though explicitly Christian, was a course in "ethics, not religion." By this Buckley meant that it did not do anything to affirm the essentials of traditional Christianity, such as belief in God and in " 'Jesus Christ as Divine Lord and Saviour.' "[7]

Another well-attended religion course was taught by a man who told his students he was "80% atheist and 20% agnostic." A few other courses were taught by avowed Christians, in Buckley's sense, but were not well attended. In fact, religion, although an option to fulfill some core requirements, enrolled less than 10% of Yale students in any given year; its influence thus would not have been pervasive, even if it had been laudable.

Turning from the low Christian influence in religion courses, Buckley documented strong anti-Christian influences in the rest of the curriculum. He did note a few exceptions. A course in European intellectual history and another course in Shakespeare each had avowed Christian perspectives. Professor Robert Calhoun of the Divinity School occasionally taught an undergraduate course on the history of philosophy but kept most of his religious views to himself. Church historian Kenneth Latourette was openly a traditional Christian, but his undergraduate courses were not popular.

Such influences were more than offset by others. In the History Department was a "vigorously atheistic . . . professional debunker . . . who has little mercy on either God, or on those who believe in Him." Two of the leading figures in the Philosophy Department, Brand Blanshard and Paul Weiss, were, respectively, "an earnest and expansive atheist" and "a confirmed debunker of the

Christian religion." In the social sciences, where disbelief in God seemed almost a faculty prerequisite, one of the most cynical reputedly declared that "a cleric today is the modern counterpart of the witch doctor" and suggested to Jesuits that they could convert the world overnight if they could "submit the wine to a chemical analysis after consecration and then see if you've gotten hemoglobin out of grape juice."

Noting that most of the texts used in the university were either hostile or indifferent to religion, Buckley summarized the problem at Yale and elsewhere as the triumph of "relativism, pragmatism and utilitarianism," in the spirit of philosopher John Dewey. "There is surely not a department at Yale," Buckley observed, "that is uncontaminated with the absolute that there are no absolutes, no intrinsic rights, no ultimate truths."[8]

Defenders of Yale invariably dismissed any anti-Christian influences in the curriculum as defensible as matters of academic freedom and pointed to the extracurricular religious influences at the university. Catholics had the St. Thomas More Club, Jews had the Hillel Foundation, and Baptists, Methodists, Congregationalists, Lutherans, and Episcopalians had campus ministries, but by far the most important campus organization was Dwight Hall, headquarters of the Yale University Christian Association. This venerable institution began in 1881 as the Yale YMCA when both Yale and the Y were strongly evangelical institutions and still carried considerable social prestige. It sponsored religious retreats, book clubs, and considerable social work in New Haven.

Buckley insisted, however, that "the *religious* influence of Dwight Hall is in no way commensurate with its general importance on campus." Much of its work was not distinctly Christian, and Christianity seemed to be regarded by the association as an option (as it would have been at YMCAS generally by this time). In 1949 the editors of Dwight Hall's magazine, *Et Veritas,* stated that they "choose the Christian" philosophy as a matter of "personal conviction" rather than editorial policy. Editors in succeeding years were not even Christian, one being an "avowed agnostic." The Yale Christian Association attitude that Christianity was purely a matter of preference, said Buckley, turned Christianity into " 'my most favorite way of living.' "[9] Buckley's point was that the extracurricular religion promoted at Yale was so bland that, except in rare instances, it had little chance of counteracting the combination of indifference and hostility toward religion displayed in the curriculum and by many professors.

Identifying this problem was easier than proposing a plausible cure. Buckley attacked the ideology of modern universities at a vulnerable point, subtitling his polemic "The Superstitions of Academic Freedom." Academic freedom, he argued, could not be the sacred absolute its proponents were claiming. Universities already ruled out any number of teachings, such as extreme racism. So the question was not whether there were limits on what might be taught, but only what those limits were. The problem remained, however, of how to change those limits.

Buckley's proposed solution was the most heretical part of his essay. Applying principles of free enterprise, he reasoned that if Yale's principal supporters were its alumni and if the alumni were predominantly traditionally Christian and conservative economically, it would be reasonable for alumni to withhold their support until Yale was providing the product they desired. This was a variation on his point about academic freedom. Since Buckley surmised that alumni pressure already limited what might be taught at a university, he was asking only for the more rigorous application of an existing principle.

The idea of substantive external control of universities was, of course, anathema to most educators. McGeorge Bundy dismissed it as simply alien, intimating that Buckley's views reflected "the pronounced and well-recognized difference between Protestant and Catholic views of education in America." The Protestant cultural establishment still cultivated the long-standing view that Catholicism was associated with absolutism while Protestantism had brought the world democracy and freedom.[10] Some Catholic complicity with fascism during the World War II era had reinforced this view. Freedom of academic institutions from direct control of either church or state was one of the things many educated Americans saw themselves fighting for in the war. As Randolph Crump Miller, a liberal Christian educator, put it, "This is more than an attack on Yale; it is an attack on all liberal education. It is not a plea for more religion, but for a religion of external authority."[11]

Buckley's Catholicism was critical to the debate.[12] Though mainline Protestant leaders frequently condemned Catholic authoritarianism, they also often made special efforts to be tolerant of individual Catholics, especially if they were willing to act like tolerant Protestants. Buckley, however, saw jarring contradictions in the two religious worlds. From his ardent Catholic perspective he could see traits that establishment Protestants took for granted. From his more rigorous religious viewpoint, their easy tolerance of unbelief seemed naive, if not hypocritical.

From the inside the claims that Yale was still Christian did not appear hypocritical at all. Mainline Protestantism could genuinely be considered to be flourishing at mid-century and to be holding its own on college campuses. In response to Buckley the standing "Committee on Religious Life and Study" at Yale offered a candid but optimistic internal assessment. Despite religious indifference and "a very active secularism," which celebrated "objectivity" and attempted to exclude value judgments of any sort, Yale was maintaining "a Christian atmosphere which has been accepted as traditional through many college generations." "Students," the committee argued, "are not antagonistic to religion." Even though they were " 'ecclesiastically illiterate,' " the committee had been assured that "they believe in God and in the moral and ethical teachings of Christ." Moreover, "they are eager for service which is in the broad sense Christian."[13]

William Buckley and the Yale establishment differed so widely regarding the Christian character of Yale because they were using vastly different definitions of Christianity. Buckley was measuring the religion at Yale against something like traditional Catholicism. Much of the Protestant establishment, on the other hand, was talking about Christianity as "service," "morality," or "high values in living," which was more or less equivalent to faith in God or "religion" and for which formal religious observance was desirable but not absolutely necessary.[14]

So throughout the first half of the twentieth century, despite some obvious decline of Christianity in public life, mainline Protestant religion[15] could plausibly be said to be holding its own, even in the universities. World War II, in fact, had sparked a widespread religious revival. In the 1950s college students were still as likely as the rest of the population to be members of churches and to express religious beliefs.[16] What was not always taken into account in assessing this religious interest, although it was debated among the theologians, was that the low-voltage religion in many of the churches and on the campuses often did little more than impart a warm glow to the best moral ideals of the culture at large. So the disappearance of explicit Christian influences in public culture might be imminent, but at the same time it was possible with the broadened definition of religion to see the situation as the spread of religious enlightenment. Protestantism, also known as "religion," could face the future with confidence.

In response to the furor created by Buckley's book, Yale's president A. Whitney Griswold appointed a committee of distinguished alumni, chaired by the Rev. Henry Sloane Coffin, '97, to review the charges. Not surprisingly, the committee gave Yale a clean bill of health. As to the accusation that Yale was encouraging irreligion or atheism, it was flatly "without foundation." While the committee did not mention Christianity, it affirmed that "there is, today, more than ever, widespread realization that religion alone can give meaning and purpose to modern life." Students particularly needed the wholeness and sense of direction that religion provided. "It is by faith that man sees all things working together in the light of God and gives himself to work with them. To supply such light and truth Yale was at birth dedicated, and to this high aim the University continues." In fact, said the committee, "religious life at Yale is deeper and richer than it has been in many years."[17]

Prologue II

Henry Sloane Coffin's Yale (1897)

The Rev. Henry Sloane Coffin, '97, who chaired the blue-ribbon committee that in 1952 answered William F. Buckley Jr. with the categorical conclusion that "religious life at Yale is deeper and richer than it has been in many years," could recall more distant student days when Yale's religious life was deeper and richer still. Coffin was a renowned preacher, was the president of Union Theological Seminary in New York City (he had once been a leading candidate for the Yale presidency), and had done as much as anyone to shepherd mainline Protestantism from evangelicalism to theological modernism.[1] At Yale he had first come to prominence in his senior year as president of the Yale Christian Association, or Dwight Hall.

To be president of Dwight Hall was reputedly to be only a little lower on the campus scale of being than football captain.[2] This status was remarkable, particularly because Yale was known at the time for the "the professional spirit in . . . athletics," which cynics contrasted with "the amateur spirit . . . in Yale scholarship."[3] Yale was one of the first campuses to make football into a major religion. Yet this was also an era of "manly" Christianity, when many of the brightest and the best were revitalizing campus Christianity as a first step toward transforming the nation and the world. The Dwight Hall presidency was particularly significant since Yale was a training ground for American elite leadership and the Yale Christian Association was the largest of the burgeoning YMCAs where the campus renewals typically centered. The Yale Christian Association prided itself on being the "conservator of democracy" where "the millionaire and the man who is making his way through college [are] working side by side."[4] Fervent evangelical religion, while far from universal in its influence on Yale students,[5] was, nonetheless, the dominant religious force and was eminently respectable. Henry Coffin was duly elected to Yale's preeminent secret society, Skull and Bones, and rumor had it that the leaderships of the two powerful organizations were closely linked.[6]

The Soul of the American University Revisited. George M. Marsden, Oxford University Press. © Oxford University Press 2021. DOI: 10.1093/oso/9780190073312.003.0003

One clue to the character of this respectable campus religion was that the person who did most to lend prominence to the Yale Christian Association was the leading evangelist of the day, Dwight L. Moody. During his student days Henry Coffin cultivated the Moody connection, and in later years he still spoke fondly of the evangelist. The Protestant religious situation in the 1890s did not yet include the sharp differentiation between revivalist evangelical missionary fervor and advanced theological opinion, humanitarianism, and social concern. All of these could march hand in hand in the heady days when American Christianity, closely allied with its British counterparts, promised to transform and civilize the world. Each summer Yale would send the largest delegation, typically a hundred or more, to Moody's famed college conferences in Northfield, Massachusetts. At Northfield in 1886 Moody had inspired students to form what soon became the Student Volunteer Movement pledged to "the evangelization of the world in this generation."[7] Yale's missionary efforts were so widespread that John R. Mott, chairman of the Student Volunteer Movement, could remark in 1899 that having visited some thirty countries, "I am pained to say I have even been in a country where I did not find the American flag; but I have never been where I did not find the Yale flag."[8]

Moody had first come to Yale in 1878 when he sparked the revival that led to the organization of the campus YMCA. He returned to the campus regularly, and he was instrumental in two other notable revival harvests, in 1890 and in 1899, the year of his death. In that last revival he appeared with biblical critic George Adam Smith, and the revival was seen as one point at which "conservatism and higher criticism united in bringing from the same platform the message of Christ to Yale."[9] Henry Drummond, a Scotsman controversial for his progressive views, also made a profound impact both at Northfield and on the Yale campus. The broad-minded Drummond was, like Moody, legendary among Yale Christians. Yale men, however, also fondly recalled preachers at Northfield who would later be thought of as progenitors of fundamentalism, such as Reuben A. Torrey, Arthur T. Pierson, Charles G. Trumbull, and A. J. Gordon.[10] They saw such evangelism as perfectly compatible with "social service," such as proudly evidenced by the Yale mission to the "Bowery of New Haven," founded by Yale sports hero Amos Alonzo Stagg in 1888. In both the goal was "soul saving."[11]

Everyone seemed to agree that the nondoctrinal, activist, accommodating evangelicalism of the day was the best hope for humanity, "an influence that makes for righteousness, and the highest type of civilization."[12] Sectarianism was considered wholly out of place. An effort to found a separate Methodist campus organization was short-lived and tagged as clearly "un-Yale."[13] If Protestants could stand united, proclaiming the best in religion along with the highest ideals of civilization, there were few limits on what they could do for humanity.

Christianity at Yale had become healthier over the past generation by following a familiar American pattern: disestablishment and a shift to a voluntary basis. Lyman Beecher had remarked after formal state religion was terminated in Connecticut in 1818 that it was *"the best thing that ever happened to the State of Connecticut,"* since it threw Christians "on their own resources and on God."[14] Yale Christians at the end of the century could say much the same thing. In the mid-nineteenth century, religious coercion lingered longer in colleges, where the belief was that boys had to be disciplined, than in most other parts of American Protestantism. Yale in 1850 had two required chapel services daily, the morning one before breakfast. In addition, students were required to attend two lengthy preaching services on Sundays that served as a virtual course in theology. Professors and tutors attempted to enforce strict social discipline.

By the end of the century only one chapel service was required, and it remained reasonably popular. Every senior class from 1894 to 1909 voted to perpetuate compulsory service. Aside from the question of piety, the daily services had come to be regarded as important symbols of Yale traditionalism and community.[15] The religious center of the university, however, had shifted from the chapel to Dwight Hall.[16] This was part of the general rise of a semiautonomous student culture, of which the cult of football was the most prominent manifestation. Although campus life was far from predominantly religious, vigorous young men across the country, like Stagg, Mott, Coffin, and many others of equal abilities, had taken command of their own activities and were promising to change the world for Christ. Yale remained, as it always had been in the nineteenth century, the flagship school of interdenominational Protestant evangelicalism. Nevertheless, the progressive evangelical atmosphere among students at Yale was only an accentuation of what could be found on campuses throughout the country.

Observers at the time agreed that respect for Christianity among collegians had increased notably just in the past two decades. During the 1870s and early 1880s, agnosticism, fortified by Darwinism and the rising popularity of biblical criticism, had fostered an atmosphere of doubt on college campuses. By the end of the century that era seemed over. Henry Davidson Sheldon, in a general account of *Student Life and Customs*, published in 1901, could remark:

> The idea so prevalent in the eighties among undergraduates that all forms of aggressive religious endeavour were superannuated survivals of medievalism, out of place in the present enlightened age, is fast giving way either to appreciation or to acute dislike. The movement has stimulated the churches, aroused the religious societies of the colleges to their responsibility, and has extended its influence to foreign countries. Its success in the present age in reviving the ideals of militant Christianity in the same institutions that by subjective criticisms were undermining the foundations of religious belief, is one of the striking signs of the complexity of modern social forces.[17]

Dwight L. Moody, speaking of Yale during 1897–1898, could put it more simply. He was entirely pleased with the broad energetic spirit of Yale's evangelicalism and was happy that his sons studied there. "I have been pretty well acquainted with Yale for twenty years," he remarked, "and I have never seen the University in so good a condition religiously as it is now."[18]

While Moody's enthusiasm for the vigor of the voluntary religion of young men at Yale was understandable, the winds were already blowing that would eliminate Christianity as an effective force at the centers of American academic life. During the next sixty years these winds of modernity would reach gale force, so that even a generation of men dedicated to "evangelization of the world in this generation" could only ride the storm. As a Christian institution, Yale College had originally been designed for far different conditions. The fledgling university had inherited, so far as the interests of Christianity might be concerned, what would prove to be deep structural defects in the face of the forces of modernity. If we step back just a few more years into the history of Yale, to a pivotal contest over its Christian character, we can glimpse some of the obstacles to keeping education at Yale, or other leading American schools, long on a distinctly Christian course.

Prologue III

Yale Embattled: Noah Porter versus William Graham Sumner (1880)

"Yale as a Battleground" was the title of the first of two front-page stories in the *New York Times* of April 4 and 5, 1880. The newspaper offered extensive revelations of the recent efforts of Yale's President, Noah Porter, to stop William Graham Sumner, one of the college's best-known younger teachers, from using as a text in his senior course Herbert Spencer's *The Study of Sociology*. As the *Times* put it, Spencer was well known as the "White Czar of Agnosticism," and his iconoclastic book classed Christianity with "the superstitions of the Mohammadans and South Sea Islanders" as the sort of bias that true scientists needed to be rid of. This controversy, the paper proclaimed, divided the Yale faculty down the middle and "involves the whole issue between science and religion and its final settlement will decide the attitude of the college toward the modern spirit of inquiry, which proposes to be guided by reason rather than by faith."[1]

The *Times* followed its accounts with a satirical editorial that, imitating Spencer's tone, granted that "no intelligent man in this age of the world will for a moment maintain that there is any truth in Christianity," but that since Christianity still had a strong hold on "the ignorant masses," Yale's giving it up would cause a great outcry. After all, the editorialist sarcastically suggested, if Spencer is right, and everything is relative, then it does not matter whether Spencer and Comte's positivism or Christianity is "the recognized faith to be taught to Yale students." It is all "mere prejudice," so we might as well "rid ourselves of prejudice as well as religion" and let Yale continue to be Christian.[2] At Yale this was all quite an embarrassment. However divided the Yale faculty might be, they agreed that such matters should be settled privately, among gentlemen.

The Rev. William Graham Sumner had before teaching at Yale been an Episcopal rector in Morristown, New Jersey, and he had been already very much part of the Yale family. Porter had prized him as one of college's

The Soul of the American University Revisited. George M. Marsden, Oxford University Press. © Oxford University Press 2021. DOI: 10.1093/oso/9780190073312.003.0004

promising recent graduates ('63), and Sumner, after a tour in Europe, had served as a tutor at Yale before going to Morristown in 1867. In 1872 he was appointed to the Yale faculty in the chair in political science. At the time he was still a traditional, though broad-minded, Christian who affirmed the full divinity of Christ versus Unitarianism and considered the Bible "a true revelation of spiritual and universal truths."[3]

Early in his Yale tenure, Sumner's religious views began to change rapidly. Although he remained an Episcopal priest all his life, he dropped the "Rev." from his title.[4] Later he made the famous and revealing remark, "I never consciously gave up a religious belief. It was as if I had put my beliefs into a drawer, and when I opened it, there was nothing there at all."[5]

Sumner's conversion to scientific naturalism came in the mid-1870s through the influence of Charles Darwin, T. H. Huxley, and Herbert Spencer, whose work he had not earlier been able to accept.[6] As he explained in a letter to Yale officials in June 1881, "Four or five years ago my studies led me to the conviction that sociology was about to do for the social sciences what scientific method has done for natural and physical science, viz.: rescue them from arbitrary dogmatism and confusion."

Of the few texts available, Spencer's seemed the best, though it was unsatisfactory in some respects. Sumner did not think, however, that Spencer's religious views were even relevant to the question: "Mr. Spencer's religious opinions seem to me of very little importance in this connection, and, when I was looking for a book on sociology, the question whether it was a good or available book in a scientific point of view occupied my intention exclusively."[7]

Since Sumner was a gifted teacher, known for his brusque and forceful manner, his new views that science was the only relevant intellectual authority and religion was at best irrelevant had soon come to President Porter's attention. Recognizing the threat to his Christian humanist citadel, Porter attempted to hold off the alien forces by exercising his presidential authority.

In December 1879, Porter wrote to Sumner that the use of Spencer's *The Study of Sociology* had created "a great deal of talk." Even though Porter himself had used another of Spencer's works in a graduate course, he considered *The Study of Sociology* to be much less solid, "written very largely in a pamphleteering style." He especially objected to "the freedom and unfairness with which it attacks every Theistic Philosophy of society and of history, and the cool and yet sarcastic effrontery with which he assumes that material elements and laws are the only forces and laws which any scientific man can recognize, seem to me to condemn the book as a textbook for a miscellaneous class in an undergraduate course."[8]

Porter, who in such a small college setting knew the reputations of his teachers, was not confident that Sumner would do anything to correct numerous statements by Spencer that, indeed, dismissed Christianity as an option for a modern intelligent person. Accordingly, Porter concluded that since "I am presumed to authorize the use of every textbook, I must formally object to the use of this."[9]

At the Yale gentleman's club Porter's ambiguous conclusion left the door open for compromise. Sumner took the point and met with Porter privately to air their differences. The result was that Porter allowed the course to go on in the spring term, still using the Spencer text. However, the publicity in the newspapers in the spring of 1880 meant that the matter would now come to the attention of the Yale Corporation. When the corporation met in June, shortly after Porter's Wellesley speech, former Yale president Theodore Dwight Woolsey was prepared to offer a resolution confirming that presidents did, indeed, have veto power over texts. Porter, however, calmed the waters by assuring the corporation that part of the understanding in December had been that Sumner would not use the text again. Both Woolsey and Porter held the view that discipline of an erring faculty member should be dealt with by the faculty, meaning the president, rather than the corporation.[10]

Again the matter was kept quiet, so quiet, in fact, that it was not until the next December, when the time for offering the course again was near, that Sumner was informed of this resolution. When he learned of it, he was furious that Porter had claimed that he had agreed not to use the text again, when he himself did not think he had endorsed any such agreement. Still the gentleman, however, he was eager to avoid more sensational publicity. So he decided that it would be better for his students to have no course in sociology than to be exposed to such emotionally charged discussion. At the end of the term in June 1881 he addressed his letter to his colleagues and to the corporation, somewhat bitterly detailing his discontent and announcing his intention to seek other employment.

The controversy was then successfully kept from the public eye and eventually died down. Sumner was an important asset of the school and was prevailed upon not to resign. In a sense, a compromise had been reached, while the point at issue was left unresolved. Sumner had, on the one hand, stopped using the Spencer text. On the other, he had not conceded that administrative interference in the choice of texts was acceptable.

Most important, just at the moment when its principal competitors were proclaiming themselves scientific research universities, the Yale Corporation could not afford to lose one of its few modern thinkers over what could be construed to be a matter of doctrinal orthodoxy.[11] Sumner's conservative economic views helped secure his position as well. His chief expression of his scientific naturalism was in his advocacy of an unsentimental "survival of the fittest" free enterprise. (For our story it is a nice irony that the agnostic Sumner, who remained at Yale until 1910, taught many who would be among the economically conservative Yale alumni whom William Buckley would try to enlist on Christian grounds.)

The crucial point in 1880, however, was that no matter how much a mainstream academic leader such as Noah Porter might be dedicated to defining the academic life of a college as "Christian," there was no way both to retain such a stance and to remain as a leading center of American higher learning. At flagship Protestant schools such as Yale that aspired to be universities, commitments had already been set that would inevitably free academic life from the distinctive qualities of its Christian heritage.

PART I

THE ESTABLISHMENT
OF PROTESTANT
NONSECTARIANISM

During the seventy years between the William Graham Sumner crisis and the William F. Buckley crisis, leading American schools were transformed almost beyond recognition. Regarding the issue that Noah Porter and William Buckley agreed was pivotal to Christian education, however—that teaching and scholarship should not undermine Christian perspectives—the matter had already been all but settled in principle by 1880. At least to his many of his contemporaries who were shaping the new universities, Porter's way of protecting Christianity in the classroom seemed outdated. The university builders were not, however, opposed to Christianity as such. Rather, the great majority of them were happy both to broaden its definition and to encourage the solution that proved so successful at Yale by the 1890s. Essentially there would be a division of functions. Most, even if not all, of the highest academic pursuits would soon be defined in such a way that the intrusion of specifically Christian concerns would seem irrelevant or prejudicial. Nevertheless, the whole enterprise could be regarded as broadly Christian so long as there was some room for morally uplifting undergraduate teaching and for voluntary commitment as an extracurricular activity.

Such solutions could work for a time, trying to balance three strong tendencies—trust in scientifically defined academic models that sought objectivity, a desire to serve the public by honoring a variety of viewpoints, and concern to be nonetheless spiritual. By the 1950s, however, as Buckley was pointing out, these dimensions in higher education were drastically out of balance. The substance of the education undermined rhetoric claims to cherish the Christian heritage. Soon even the semblance of such a balance would give way, and, despite some vestiges at a number of divinity schools, it would seem deeply out of place for mainstream universities to bill themselves as "Christian."

One thing that this glimpse at the latter days of the Protestant establishment suggests is that there never was a halcyon time in the relationship between Christianity and mainstream American higher education. Rather, we find an often-contested history of efforts to cope with some essential inbuilt problems. The greatest of these problems was inherited from the long history of universities in Christendom, dating back to the Middle Ages, which is that universities were to be established to serve simultaneously both the church and the whole society. That seemed a natural arrangement in the medieval era when there were a strong church and assumptions that the whole society should be effectively Christian. After the Reformation, various Protestant or Catholic universities could likewise see their task as to foster Christian learning within their confessional understanding of what Christendom ought to be like.

The earliest American colleges would be founded with state support as distant outposts that reflected those ideals. Harvard and Yale were established to help promote the Reformed or Calvinist ideal of Christendom. William and Mary was an integral part of Virginia's Anglican establishment. In all these cases, the assumption was that the interests of the state and of the church were to go hand in hand. Yet that ideal, which was becoming increasingly problematic in the Old World, soon would be even more so in the New. The colonies and then the states would become bewilderingly diverse in religion, and thus formal state establishments would no longer be viable, even eventually in New England. Nevertheless, some of the assumptions about the proper relationship of Christianity to the culture remained in an informal Protestant establishment. And nowhere more than in most of the new nation's standard-setting colleges and universities, whether private or public, was the idea of Protestant privilege more taken for granted. That relationship, even while becoming increasingly anomalous and contested, would persist into the mid-twentieth century.

The dual commitments to church teachings and to the service of the state and larger society extended to the curriculum. What did Christian learning mean? Typically it would mean that there were some Christian teachings, particularly in theology and in ethics, that for a complete education should be added to purely secular subjects. But then, as the nation became increasingly diverse, the question arose as to which brand of Protestant Christianity should be presented. Was there a meaningful "nonsectarian" Christianity?

How might it relate to the scientific ideals that were increasingly setting the standards for intellectual inquiry? Could Christianity be equated with the best of American cultural ideals? Further, what of the place of students, especially in state schools, who did not profess to be Christian, or were of some other faith? How could they be fairly treated if Christianity were essential to the enterprise? These are the sorts of issues that shaped the twists and turns in the history that follows and provided the challenges that, into the mid-twentieth century, Protestant educators were trying to negotiate.

1

The Burden of Christendom

Seventeenth-Century Harvard

One of the remarkable facts of American history is that only six years after their settlement in the Massachusetts wilderness, the Puritans established what soon became a reputable college. Higher education was for them a high priority in civilization building. During its early decades New England had one of the highest per capita concentrations of university-educated men anywhere in the world. By establishing a college so early (in the southern colonies it took a century to do the same) the Puritans laid the foundation for New England's dominance in American higher education for the next three centuries. As late as the era when Americans founded modern universities or transformed their colleges into universities, few of the key leaders lacked New England connections.

The Puritans' commitment to higher education and the tensions that it created for such an intensely spiritual movement must be understood in the context of a long history of the often uneasy relationship of Christianity to advanced learning. The Puritans of the 1630s, it is helpful to recall, were living closer to the era of Thomas Aquinas than we are to theirs. So while we inevitably refract our understanding of them through what has happened since, we will gain a more balanced appreciation of their own concerns if we think in terms of their own history. They were still in many ways people of the Middle Ages. Their medieval outlook had, indeed, been modified by what we call the Renaissance, and more by the Reformation, and they had been touched as well by glimmers of what was to become modernity. Nonetheless, the problems they addressed were still largely those of medieval Christendom. How could they set Christendom back on its proper course?

So far as university education was concerned, they took for granted some deeply entrenched patterns that for several centuries had defined advanced learning in the Western world, but as reformers they were also ready to bend the patterns to suit their purposes.

The Soul of the American University Revisited. George M. Marsden, Oxford University Press. © Oxford University Press 2021. DOI: 10.1093/oso/9780190073312.003.0005

Christian and Pagan Learning: The Medieval Pattern

The preeminent theoretical issue inherited from the Middle Ages was the question of how to relate Christian truths to pagan learning. This debate went back to Christian antiquity. Christianity inherited the intellectual standards of the ancient world, and for a millennium and a half its thinkers stood in the shadow of the classical achievement. A few could reject the relevance of Athens for Jerusalem, but it was virtually impossible to ignore Athens entirely. Yet the danger was that to honor the pagans for their unparalleled intellectual achievement would seem to dishonor the preeminence of the wisdom revealed in Christ. The rise of the universities within the vigorous medieval civilization of the twelfth century signaled a determination to deal with this paradox. The classical learning had to play a leading role; that was essential to intellectual respectability. The scholar was practically defined as the guardian of ancient wisdom. At the same time, leading scholars of each succeeding generation had to address the major intellectual challenge of the epoch. How could they reconcile the pagan authorities with the authoritative theological dogma of the church?[1]

The intellectual dilemma was paralleled by the institutional definition that emerged for the universities. Christian scholars, who earlier had been situated primarily at cathedral schools, established themselves in the twelfth century as self-governing guilds. They were licensed by the pope to grant degrees, meaning that only they could determine who was qualified to be a master, or teacher. Despite the major achievement of some autonomy, these scholars' guilds or universities were ultimately under the control of the church. Masters had to take holy orders as clerics and, hence, were subject to church control. Their conduct could be a matter of church concern and, very important, their teachings could be condemned.[2]

In this context of limited autonomy Christian scholars perennially debated the relation of reason to faith. No one could seriously challenge the preeminence of faith; the issue was the degree to which the philosophy or science (roughly, knowledge) of the pagans might be of value toward salvation. Did one need to believe in order to understand, as Anselm, following Augustine, had maintained? Or could one say, as Thomas Aquinas did in the thirteenth century, that reason could point toward divine truths, even though it needed to be supplemented by truths known only by faith? In either case, it was taken for granted that pagan knowledge of mundane affairs was true knowledge, so far as it went. Education was not conceivable without the pagans. Latin and

Greek were the very languages of education. All the practical elements (the trivium of grammar, rhetoric, and logic and the quadrivium of arithmetic, music, geometry, and astronomy) had been established by the ancients.

So, from its beginnings Western university education involved a fusion of pagan and Christian elements. The trivium and quadrivium defined the basic liberal arts. Moreover, the consensus prevailing through the early centuries of the universities was that a proper arts education involved substantial study of Aristotle, especially on logic, metaphysics, and natural philosophy (natural science). While some questioned elements in Aristotle's ethics or metaphysics that contradicted Christian dogma, virtually all recognized a pinnacle of intellectual achievement that must be mastered.

The most practical way of counteracting the prominence of the pagan elements in the curricula was to surround them with a Christian atmosphere. First of all, the studies were surrounded liturgically. Christian worship began and ended the university day, signaling that all was to be dedicated to the glory of God. Furthermore, the role of clerics in education inevitably provided Christian perspectives even on pagan authorities. Higher education in this era involved primarily the mastery of texts (as it usually did until the nineteenth century). These texts were presented in the context of commentary or lectures by the university masters, hence providing at least the potential for dealing with issues where Christian and pagan authority conflicted. Since the pagans could not respond, this method of synthesis worked well for centuries. Christian dogma retained its official dominance in academia.

The medieval pattern of surrounding pagan elements with a Christian environment allowed most of university education to be freed from the direct concerns of theology. The half-dozen or so medieval universities that shaped Western education included four distinct faculties: the arts, theology, law (canon and civil), and medicine (although each of the universities typically lacked one of the latter three). A master's degree in the arts was normally prerequisite to the study of theology, law, or medicine. Theology, then, although queen of the sciences, did not directly rule the other sciences but was instead a separate, specialized discipline.[3]

Reformation Learning

Within this framework there were many variations over the centuries and many internal debates, but an essential continuity prevailed. Even the Reformation only modified some of the basic structures and emphases. Nevertheless, since the Puritans were, first of all, a battalion of the international movement for Protestant reform, the Reformation modifications of higher learning were especially relevant to establishing American precedents.

Early in the Reformation, Martin Luther had railed against the universities. "What else are the universities," he complained in 1520, "than . . . 'Places for training youth in Greek glory,' in which loose living prevails, the Holy Scriptures and the Christian faith are little taught, and the blind, heathen master Aristotle rules alone even more than Christ? In this regard my advice would be that Aristotle's [philosophical works] be discarded altogether."[4]

Luther's attack on the Aristotelianism of the Scholastics was not an anti-intellectual attack on universities but, rather, a critique from within. Luther, after all, was a university man, a doctor on the theological faculty at Wittenberg. The spark that touched off the Reformation thus came from within the university and was, as E. Harris Harbison suggested, a combination of a spiritual struggle and "*a scholar's insight.*"[5] In part, this insight arose out of long-standing traditions of intellectual tensions between the Aristotelianism of the Scholastics and the Augustinianism in which Luther had been tutored. In any case, the initial base of the Reformation was a university, and one of its first fruits was a curricular revision, increasing the emphasis on Greek and Hebrew in the curriculum.[6]

During the next generations universities remained major centers for the Protestant challenges to Catholic authority. Protestantism was, after all, vulnerable to the accusation that it would open the door to an anarchy of individual opinions. The principal Protestant leaders deeply feared such anarchy. In order to counter it they recognized that it was essential to back up their appeals to the authority of Scripture alone with the firmest scholarship so as to determine what Scripture actually said. In fact, education at all levels was crucial to the Protestant program. Challenging the exclusive clerical dominance in the church, the Protestant doctrine of the priesthood of all believers encouraged the cultivation of an educated laity, well catechized and instructed in Scripture.

Luther himself was interested primarily in biblical and theological scholarship as they would directly serve the church,[7] but as a professor he recognized the importance of universities to the Protestant program. Philip Melanchthon, who joined Luther at Wittenberg in 1517, was especially important in establishing the models for Protestant universities during the next forty years. The Protestant university curriculum as established by Melanchthon was a mix of progressive and conservative elements. Despite Luther's earlier strictures, Melanchthon persuaded him by the 1530s that Aristotle was useful to the university curriculum, even if not a reliable guide in theology or ethics. At the same time, more humanistic classical authors of literary and historical works were being added to the curriculum, as was greater emphasis on the sacred languages (Greek, Latin, and Hebrew) and the study of the church fathers.[8]

Important to understanding the impact of the Reformation on higher education is that the Reformation took place while another critique of scholasticism was already gradually influencing the universities from another direction. Renaissance humanists embraced and revered the classics, but instead of the philosophy of Aristotle their preeminent classics were literary works, like those of Cicero or Virgil, which they saw as God's gifts, useful for enriching life in this world. In their view literary texts exemplifying rhetoric, rather than those exemplifying logic, should be foundational in the arts curriculum. Several of the Reformers, including Melanchthon, Zwingli, and Calvin, were well educated in such humanism.[9]

Though the Lutherans under Melanchthon's tutelage established the most important models for Protestant universities,[10] Calvin and Calvinists also played a significant role. Calvinist models would also have the more direct influence in America. Calvin followed Luther in emphasizing the importance of the study of the biblical languages, including Hebrew. Though Calvin did not hold an academic position, one of his major accomplishments was the establishment of an academy in Geneva that functioned as a university for training Protestant leaders. The academy reflected humanist influences in its emphasis on the study of ancient languages and employed texts from Cicero, Virgil, Livy, and Xenophon in teaching grammar, rhetoric, logic, and history.[11]

More generally, Calvin helped develop the broadly Augustinian rationale for the importance of higher learning. Attributing all that is good to God, Calvin's principle of common grace justified learning at least limited truths from the ancients. Though Calvin, like Luther, thought reason of no value on its own in attaining salvation, he considered it competent in things "earthly."[12] Moreover, the Calvinist doctrine of the calling emphasized that the vocations of Christians were to serve God in whatever their occupations, not just in special "religious" vocations. Hence, university learning, even apart from theological preparation, could be a means of glorifying God.

While there were, indeed, broad and humanist tendencies in Protestant higher education, these were always tightly fenced in by dogmatic confessionalism. By the middle of the seventeenth century the Western world was sharply divided into cold war camps that followed largely confessional lines. The exigencies of such battles meant that Protestant institutions of higher learning were also militant agents of confessionalism and defenders of the faith, and that their faculties of theology sometimes served as substitutes for the pope and councils as the definers of orthodoxy.[13] Until at least the mid-seventeenth century (longer in Puritan New England), the tensions among the claims of the inherited medieval curriculum, humanism, and theologically oriented confessionalism were the major motifs in Protestant education.

Looking for the broad significance of these developments, we can see that, while the curriculum and methods of education evolved more than they were revolutionized under Protestantism, the Reformation brought important changes in the social *function* of education. Protestantism promoted a well-educated clergy, which quickly became the backbone of the international revolutionary movement. Very early in the Reformation, Zwingli and Luther began wearing the scholar's gown for preaching and, although not all Protestant clergy had university training, "the scholar's gown was *the* garment of the Protestant minister."[14] In villages throughout Protestant lands for centuries to come, the clergyman would be the best-educated citizen, and education would be a key to his authority.

In the Protestant setting the classicist humanist education particularly made sense. In a day before natural science gained intellectual eminence, the key to intellectual expertise and authority was mastery of languages. The claims of the Reformers hinged on the interpretation of texts and on a science of textual interpretation sufficient to challenge church authority. Each Protestant clergyman, accordingly, should ideally have linguistic expertise that would establish him as an authority in the most essential science of the day. Knowledge of the classics helped establish social and intellectual authority, but not for arbitrary reasons. It was an expertise necessary for the highest science of the day. Ultimately, linguistic expertise served the cause of theology, still the queen of the sciences in the Protestant (as much as in the Catholic) world and the capstone of Protestant education.

This professionalization of the clergy gave Protestants some advantage over their Catholic rivals. In the Middle Ages clerical education had largely been by apprenticeship and sometimes was minimal. On the eve of the Reformation only about one-fourth of clergy had any university training.[15]

After the revolt Catholics countered with more attention to clerical educa-tion, including the establishment by the Council of Trent of the innovation of theological seminaries dedicated solely to theological training.

This rivalry contributed to what Lawrence Stone describes as the "as-tonishing growth" from the mid-sixteenth century to the mid-seventeenth century in which "a staggering number of students were pouring into the uni-versities." At Oxford in England, which Stone investigated, the burgeoning student body of the early seventeenth century was made up of two distinct classes. Most of the growth came from the influx of students from plebeian families, often preparing for theological study for the ministry, for which an arts degree was prerequisite. Others were aristocrats, preparing some-times for other professions, or more often gaining some university education as a sort of gentleman's finishing school, but not taking a degree. After the English civil wars, the disruptions of the 1640s and 1650s, and subsequent disillusion with religious struggles, English universities hit a prolonged slump in enrollment, with the numbers of plebeians in attendance dropping off dramatically.[16]

Harvard College

It was in the context of the post-Reformation boom that the most impor-tant precedents for American higher education were set with the founding of Harvard College in 1636. The remarkable establishment of a reputable col-lege on the frontier of Western civilization is more understandable in light of the importance of education to the whole structure of authority in the on-going Reformation movement. By 1646, 140 university men had emigrated to New England. Of these, the majority were from Cambridge, and fully one-fourth were from a single Cambridge College, Emmanuel. About thirty other New Englanders had been educated at various Oxford Colleges and a few had been educated abroad.[17]

The two English universities had developed as degree-granting federations of colleges. Each college was self-contained, maintaining its own faculties of masters and tutors as well as residential facilities. Hence, in practice the colleges were more important than the university, at least for the actual con-duct of education.

Oxford and Cambridge colleges had been particularly important to the Puritan movement since the multiple-college system allowed de facto religious pluralism, following the indecisive English Reformation. Puritans, who wished to push the English settlement to a more Calvinistic conclusion, could gain influence in individual colleges or, as in the most important case of Emmanuel, found their own college.[18]

To overstate the case only slightly, in New England the college was the parent of the colony. The New England experiment was largely the product of an old-boy network of Emmanuel graduates, including John Harvard himself, with their close Puritan allies from a number of other colleges. When the founders decided to settle their college in Newtown, the new name they chose for the town was Cambridge.

The essential role of the college in the colony would have been even more conspicuous had the brightest star of Puritan higher education, William Ames (1576–1633), been able to emigrate to the colony as he had intended. Had he lived, Ames almost certainly would have become the head of the new college. One of the most militant of the Puritans, Ames had been suspended from his position at Christ's College in Cambridge in 1609 for refusing to wear a surplice and for delivering a sermon condemning frivolous entertainments. Too uncompromising a Puritan for his bishop to allow him a pastorate in England, Ames found a position in Holland, where he eventually became professor of theology and rector at the University of Franeker. His great prestige in New England can be measured by the fact that his *Medulla Theologica* (Marrow of Theology) became *the* textbook on theology at seventeenth-century Harvard. Symbolic of Ames's influence is one of the early mottoes on the Harvard seal, *Christo et Ecclesiae*—the motto of Franeker University and the text of Ames's inaugural as rector there in 1626.[19]

While the college was, first of all, in the service of the church, it also was a public institution in the service of the civil government. While this relationship might seem ambiguous in our own terms, it made perfect sense according to the conventions of the time. The church was as much a public institution as was the civil government. "Public" referred simply to the minority who, because of rank, land ownership, or other status, had a part in running society. The British usage of "public" for schools that Americans would call "private" suggests something of the older usage.[20] So in seventeenth-century Massachusetts, as in seventeenth-century England, a college trained leaders for both church and civil society. In Puritan New England the cooperative relationship between the two was indicated by the fact that Harvard College was created by the civil government and governed by a board of overseers, or trustees, made up equally of clergy and magistrates.

Although universities had served both church and larger society since their beginnings, this specific arrangement represented not the medieval model for universities, which had been created by scholars who gained civil recognition as a guild and degree-granting rights from the pope, but, rather, the Reformation model, which was one step more secular in the sense of being less directly under church control.[21] The Reformers, who depended on the princes for their success and followed the principle that the state should support one true religion, thereby granted the magistrates greater authority in religious affairs, including higher education. Typically, the princes created the new schools of the Reformation, universities, or close equivalents (some Calvinists thought degrees were Romanist trappings), but these were governed by external boards of trustees. For the colonists this was a convenient arrangement, since in English law a charitable trust did not require a royal charter.[22] The balance between clergy and magistrates on the board also reinforced the long-standing point that a college was a distinct entity, not a department of either church or state, though ultimately subject to both.

This Protestant arrangement had several implications for the subsequent history of American higher education. In a strict sense it was more secular because some control was shifted from church to state. It thus created a deep ambiguity for American church-related education, since typically it was state related as well. However, the picture was complicated by the priority in the colonies of Calvinist models. Calvinists stressed the sacral character of all of life, of the state as well as the church. Hence, no major gap was perceived between being a public trust and being under church control. For the first three centuries of American higher education, the dominant view was that such dual functions were easily compatible.[23]

Early Harvard College, in fact, operated within strict limits set by both church and state. So, for instance, although there was no formal theological test for those who taught at the college, that was only because such a test did not need to be stated. Like other Reformation schools, Harvard served the interests of confessionalism and of the corresponding political principle that an orderly realm should tolerate one religion, the true one. So in 1654 when Harvard's very successful early president, Henry Dunster, questioned the practice of infant baptism, there was no choice but for him to resign. As Samuel Eliot Morison observes, endorsing the views of the radical Baptists in the mid-seventeenth century would be like a Harvard president announcing that he was a communist in the mid-twentieth.[24] Or, in the twenty-first century, it would be like a Harvard president coming out as a climate change denier.

In the seventeenth century theological authority was a mainstay of male social authority. The most striking illustration is that 1636 was the year not only of the legislation establishing Harvard College but also of the turmoil over the Anne Hutchinson case.[25] These two famous events were related since they dealt with two sides of the question of authority. They were establishing who would be allowed to speak publicly in the model Christian society. Anne Hutchinson challenged the leadership's ideas of good order on several counts. First, she was a woman and therefore was regarded as having no right to teach or exercise authority over men in the church. Second, she addressed theological issues (accusing most of the clergy of preaching works rather than grace) and thus defied the principle that formal university education (closed, of course, to women) was the normal prerequisite for exercising theological authority. Third, and ultimately most alarming to the authorities, Hutchison was what we would today call a charismatic Christian who appealed to the direct voice of the Holy Spirit. As a woman, that was her only court of appeal higher than that of the men who legitimated their own authority as the only proper interpreters of Scripture. Had Hutchinson's appeal to a direct voice from God been allowed to stand, the whole Puritan system of hierarchical authority would have collapsed. Anyone, male or female, however unqualified they otherwise might be, would be able to challenge the biblical and theological principles on which the society was being built.

Higher education was thus a keystone of the edifice of social authority. Not only did it separate men from women, but just as important, it also identified those men who were called by their spiritual and intellectual qualifications to be the interpreters of Scripture and thus those who would maintain the fundamental principles on which the community would run. In 1636 it was urgent not only to eliminate charismatic dissent that challenged the established authority but also to set up the educational link essential for the perpetuation of the system. The primary purpose of Harvard College was, accordingly, the training of clergy.[26]

Nonetheless, as the sacred and the secular were not sharply differentiated in this hyper-Protestant society, the Puritans had no difficulty in maintaining the traditional dual purposes of Christendom's university, serving the temporal as well as the ecclesiastical order. Just over half (52%) of Harvard graduates in the seventeenth century became clergy.[27] Though the dual function of the college was comparable to that of English universities, the Puritan emphasis that all vocations were sacred was evident in the religious character that was to pervade. "Every one," said the first college laws of 1646, "shall consider the main End of his life and studies, to know God and Jesus Christ which is Eternal life. John 17:3." Not only did the college have communal religious exercises, but also each student was to give himself to secret prayer (Proverbs 2:2, 3 etc.) and twice a day to reading Scripture (Psalms 119:30.).[28]

While the founders emphasized that spiritual principles should pervade the life of the college, most of the actual curriculum inevitably followed the rather traditional lines of the liberal arts. Patterned after that of Emmanuel College (which was also founded primarily for training clergy), the Harvard curriculum in formal respects reflected the amalgam of the theological and the secular that had always characterized Western university education. Latin, the international scholarly and ecclesiastical tongue, was the language of instruction and of formal disputations. In addition to Latin, students had to master Greek. Regular disputations balanced the rote learning of much of the curriculum and offered the opportunity to apply basic skills studied in grammar, rhetoric, and logic. Students also read some ancient and some modern authors as parts of their studies of mathematics, geometry, astronomy, physics, metaphysics, history, and geography.[29]

One counterbalance against the strongly classicist patterns was that Saturday and Sunday were, in effect, devoted to theology. Saturday was for formal study of biblical exposition and theology, principally from Ames's *Medulla*. The Sabbath day of "rest" included two lengthy sermons, each of which had to be repeated to the tutors later in the day. During the week, Hebrew was added to the other ancient languages, since for the Puritans the Old Testament was as authoritative as the New. The twice daily Bible reading was reinforced by a twice daily "logical analysis" of a biblical passage, breaking it down into its major and minor premises and expounding its arguments.[30] The Word might be perspicuous in Protestant eyes, but it also took a sound logical training to be qualified to interpret it plainly.

All this was only part of the regular arts program, which by the 1650s was expanded from three to four years (thus setting a pattern that subsequent Americans accepted as unassailable). Those training for the clergy took a master's degree, which required an additional three years. This was a far more informal course of reading theology in which residence was optional. A few of the theological students served as the tutors at the college. Others resided at the college, or at home, or occasionally at the home of a clergy mentor.[31]

Christianity and Pagan Learning

Given their commitment to sanctifying every moment of life, New England's Puritans were acutely aware of the issue created by having a major portion of the Christian arts curriculum devoted to the study of pagan authors. The way in which to glorify God in all things, the Puritans argued, was to strictly follow biblical principles. Some radicals challenged them to be consistent with this claim when it came to education. "Humane learning," said these critics, was of the Devil and universities were Antichrists. The Bible alone should be the only basis for education.

Charles Chauncy, successor to Dunster in 1654 as president of Harvard, answered such critics directly in his commencement sermon of 1655. If, said Chauncy, the radical critics of universities (who were proliferating in Cromwell's Commonwealth in England) meant by "humane learning," which they condemned, simply any study of the arts and science, their position was absurd, since the Bible itself taught principles of ethics, politics, economics, rhetoric, and astronomy, as well as the ancient languages. If, on the other hand, by "humane learning" critics meant "all that learning that the heathen Authors or philosophers have delivered in their writings," then also the critics had failed to note that the Scriptures occasionally cite such humane authors. Moreover, "who can deny but that there are found many excellent and divine moral truths in *Plato, Aristotle, Plutarch, Seneca, etc.?*"[32]

Chauncy was appealing to the familiar Calvinist principle of common grace, which tempered the radical biblicism of their movement. So in typical Calvinist fashion Chauncy appealed to a common light of nature, quoting I Corinthians 11:14: "*Does not nature it self teach you etc.?*"[33]

Such common grace ideals, which in principle said that pagan learning could be sanctified, in practice amounted to much the same thing as the Catholic natural law tradition of Aquinas. In each case there was an assumption that classical learning could be made subservient to the cause of Christ. The resulting tension was, in other words, inherent even in the most successful efforts at maintaining fully Christian learning while still doing justice to pagan science. The biblically informed ideals could well be the dominant first principles, providing the context into which pagan learning was interpreted. Yet the pagan learning was often taken at face value so that it easily could take on a life of its own as the dominant partner. Even though pagan shortcomings on matters pertaining to salvation were often cited, much of pagan thought that implicitly challenged Christian first principles was nonetheless revered. Thus, a balancing act was maintained between a strict biblicism and openness to recognizing that mundane aspects of God's truth were revealed in nature or the created order and therefore could be learned from nonbiblical sources.

The seventeenth-century Puritans resolved this dilemma essentially by surrounding pagan learning with biblical and theological subjects. Unlike some precedents in which the arts curriculum had been more detached from the higher study of theology, the Puritans saturated the arts program with as much Bible and theology as it could contain.[34]

Some Puritan educators, most notably William Ames, wanted to go further and integrate theology into the curriculum, rather than just add it. If Ames had had his way, as he likely would have had he come to America, both metaphysics and ethics would have been treated as subdisciplines of theology in the arts curriculum. One consequence would have been to remove Aristotle from these parts of the curriculum. Plato, on the other hand, would still have been studied since Ames, following Augustine, believed that Plato's teachings could be absorbed into Christian faith. Ames's curricular puritanism was not dominant, however; at least it did not prevail at early Harvard, where Aristotle was a major text.[35]

Seventeenth-century Harvard inherited all the tensions inherent in Christian higher learning in the West. Perpetuating the medieval ideal of a unified Christendom, American Puritans retained the inevitable tension built into the assumption that the church and the civil state can have common interests. In higher education, where they adopted the Protestant pattern of primary authorization from the state, they accentuated the potential for future conflicts between theological and civil interests. They were also living with tensions that they themselves better recognized, between biblical and pagan authorities. For the time being, in their isolated and strictly controlled environment, they could resolve most of the resulting dilemmas and build a model of Christian learning according to their own standards.[36] Nevertheless, the cost of sustaining such an achievement was maintaining a tightly closed environment.

By the end of the seventeenth century total Puritan autonomy in Massachusetts was no longer possible. While clerical influence was still immense by most standards, the long process of adjusting purist biblicist ideals to a gradually more open social and intellectual setting had begun.

While the Puritan legacy set a standard for Christian education, there were major fissures even in these structures. When shaken by the vicissitudes of a less stable sustaining social environment, these fissures would open and reopen as major gaps. Succeeding generations of American educators would live with these gaps, typically plastering them over. Beneath the surface, however, remained perennial faults that would not disappear. How could educators fully serve the church with its particular theological commitments while at the same time serving the whole of society? Closely parallel, how could they be true to the Protestant principle that the Bible alone was the supreme authority yet at the same time gain the respect of the world by being open to the highest other intellectual authorities of the day, whether ancient or modern? As the inherited assumption in Christendom had been that the interests of church and state should coincide, so it was assumed that the truths of Scripture would not contradict the best of science or knowledge that humans had gained on their own. As ideas of Christendom faded, though only slowly even in America, these assumptions were put under increasing strain.

2

The New Queen of the Sciences and the New Republic

God's Way in Nature

For what is still one-fourth of the era of English-speaking people in America, from the mid-seventeenth to the mid-eighteenth century, Harvard and eventually its Connecticut counterpart, Yale, were almost all there was to American higher education. Only toward the end of the period was the Anglican college in the South, William and Mary, fully functional. With a head start of nearly a century, New England thus achieved the dominance it would long maintain.[1]

The unresolved tensions between the realms of common grace and the realms of theology in Puritan learning helped stimulate the major developments in the content of Puritan college education during this first century. The American colonies were still marginal outposts of European culture. On the one hand, this gave colonists the freedom to preserve much of their distinctive traditions. On the other hand, it also meant a provincial mentality in which they were always reassuring themselves that they were keeping up with British and European standards, particularly those that accompanied the scientific revolution.

Puritanism was congenial to the study of the natural order. The Reformed emphasis that the creation could be known through reason, combined with the broader Protestant ideal that one could serve and glorify God in the mundane as well in special spiritual vocations, stimulated scientific study. Certainly there was no intimation of a warfare between science and religion in New England. Rather, the Puritans assumed that natural philosophy (natural science) would serve the interests of religion and point toward the glories of God in creation.

It is not surprising then that the curriculum of early Harvard kept somewhat up to date in natural philosophy, considering its location in a distant province. The principal issue in the seventeenth century was not natural

The Soul of the American University Revisited. George M. Marsden, Oxford University Press. © Oxford University Press 2021. DOI: 10.1093/oso/9780190073312.003.0006

science versus the Bible; rather, it was the new natural philosophy versus the "peripatetic" philosophy of Aristotle. By the end of the century Aristotle's long dominance in Western university education was finally being ended in all fields, including natural philosophy. So at Harvard President Increase Mather could commend the students in a commencement address because they "seem to savour a liberal mode of philosophizing, rather than the Peripatetic." After a few swipes at Aristotle for his pagan denials of creation, resurrection, and immorality of the soul, Mather ended with a tribute to the new philosophy, while honoring the old: "You who are wont to philosophize in a liberal spirit, are pledged to no particular master, yet I would have you hold fast to that one truly golden saying of Aristotle: *Find a friend in Plato, a friend in Socrates* (and I would say a friend in Aristotle), *but above all find a friend in* TRUTH."[2]

Shortly after the turn of the century, Mather's control of Harvard was displaced by a rival faction, slightly more progressive. The champion of the new party, John Leverett, elected president in 1707, enunciated in the 1711 commencement what would be the prevailing opinion in most eighteenth-century American college education:

> In philosophical [scientific] matters, Harvardians philosophize in a sane and liberal manner, according to the manner of the century.... [After a nod to Aristotle and others] For what is Natural Philosophy, unless a system in which natural things are explained; and in which that hypothesis is certainly the best by which the greater part of natural phenomena are most fully and clearly explained; these things are to be sought and acquired. Without any manner of doubt whatever, all humane matters must be tested by Philosophy.
>
> But the same license is not permissible to Theologians....[3]

A number of points are significant in such resolutions of the issues of Christianity and higher learning as the Western world shifted to the modern era of scientific dominance. First, in both Mather and Leverett, there is a general shift to the "liberal" spirit of truth seeking, rejecting (though still respecting) the ancients as authorities in favor of the modern scientific method. Nonetheless, the new learning like the old is still to be surrounded by Christian liturgical, behavioral, and theological dictates. Theology is still assumed to be the queen of the sciences and the crucial component added to the arts curriculum. Even while Harvard was determined to keep up with the currents from abroad, theology there was still based on the authority of the ancient texts and assumed to serve the interests of a particular church group.[4]

This emphasis on dogma was appropriate since dominant New England opinion was that their theological tradition embodied universal truth. The traumatic events of the 1680s, the reorganization of the colonies under the Crown, and the enforcement of religious toleration even after "the Glorious Revolution" of 1688 had undermined some of the institutional support for such dogmatism. Yet the spirit of the theological age persisted in New England. The idea of the modern age that a church was a denomination, just one among many equal religious groups, had not yet blossomed. In higher education theological exclusivism was firmly entrenched institutionally throughout the Western world. As a matter of course, schools were defined by church loyalties. In England, one had to subscribe to the Thirty-nine Articles in order to matriculate in Oxford and Cambridge universities, so that members of dissenting churches, such as Congregational, Presbyterian, and Baptist, were effectively barred. Confessional exclusivism, therefore, did not set New England apart from the rest of the Western world, even if theological dogmatism was particularly strong there.

Relating faith and science was a matter of relating two approaches to universal truth within this dogmatic context. The truths learned from Scripture and those learned from nature were assumed to be complementary. Christians who had long learned from the pagans could learn even more from their own natural philosophers. And since the creator of heaven and earth was also the author of Scripture, truths learned through the methods of philosophy and those learned from biblical authority would supplement each other and harmonize in one curriculum

Yale College

When Connecticut clergy founded their own college in 1701 it was in the context of, even though not explicitly a response to, a perceived decline in theological orthodoxy at Harvard.[5] That was the year that Increase Mather was ousted from his post at Harvard, and for Increase and his son Cotton, at least, the change in the Harvard presidency signaled the demise of Massachusetts orthodoxy.[6] In letters of advice to the Connecticut college founders, the Mathers indicated that they were ready to support their

Connecticut brethren in taking a firm stand for orthodoxy. They suggested that they follow a continental rather than an English model for Reformed colleges by requiring faculty to subscribe to the confessions of the church as a guarantee of orthodoxy. Increase had failed to get such a provision approved by the Crown in a proposed Harvard charter, but he hoped for better in Connecticut, where the college, despite local government support, was doing without a charter.

Connecticut clergy, despite the concern for orthodoxy that often characterizes those in outlying provinces, were at first disinclined to demand formal subscription to creeds.[7] The issue, however, was soon forced on them. In 1722, Timothy Cutler, the capable rector who had recently brought stability to the fledgling college, declared himself Anglican. This was truly shocking for a Connecticut clergymen. It was as though an elder in a Mennonite community had announced he was joining the army. Anti-Anglicanism had been an integral part of the definition of the Connecticut colony. Anglicanism signaled broad-mindedness and "Arminianism," the code word for the increasingly popular optimistic views of human nature as opposed to strict Calvinism. Further, Cutler was not alone among Connecticut clergy in his apostasy, a fact that sent up choruses of laments from the orthodox. The Yale trustees promptly dismissed Cutler and an offending tutor. To ensure continued orthodoxy, they now required all officers of the college to subscribe to the Westminster Confession of Faith, as stated in the Congregational Saybrook Platform. They even asked Cotton Mather to take over as rector, but Mather, who spent his life compulsively writing tomes proving that he was not a provincial, was not ready to leave Boston for the Connecticut hinterlands.[8]

Concern for orthodoxy, however, was set as part of the early Yale's identity. The young Jonathan Edwards is a well-known example of the early orthodox spirit. Edwards's father, Timothy, was of the orthodox party, and young Jonathan was a student at Yale under Cutler. Though one should not be blamed for one's traits as a teenager, Edwards as a student may have been a little too good to be true. Most college students in the eighteenth century found release from the strict discipline of the campus by occasionally raising hell. Young Edwards, always in the throes of strict Puritan self-discipline, would have none of it. He complained of "Unseasonable Nightwalking, Breaking People's windows, playing at Cards, Cursing, Swearing, and Damning, and Using all manner of Ill Language." At age fifteen (younger than average, but not unusual for college students of the time) Edwards wrote to his father about a fellow townsman, Isaac Stiles, aged twenty-one. Stiles had joined in a rebellion protesting the quality of the college food. "As soon as I Understood him to be One of them, I told him that I thought he had done exceedingly Unadvisedly, and told him also what I thought the Ill Consequences of it would be, and quickly made him sorry that he did not take my advice in the matter," wrote Edwards. Edmund Morgan may be correct that most students thought young Edwards "a hopeless prig."[9] On the other hand, Edwards was brilliant and admired at least by adults and perhaps by some of his peers as well. Shortly after the Cutler defection he was named tutor and served for a year, no doubt firmly defending orthodoxy, even as he was privately developing some of his breathtaking insights into orthodoxy's implications for the modern era.

Edwards aside, Yale College was set on a path of sectarianism that would characterize it until the American Revolution. The most notorious sectarian was Thomas Clap, an exact contemporary of Edwards (though Clap graduated from Harvard) who became rector in 1739 ("president" after Yale received its charter in 1745). Clap's tenure at Yale illustrates most of the hazards of taking a strict sectarian stance, especially for a school that had a monopoly on higher education. Clap himself, of course, saw the issue as a simple one of maintaining a traditional orthodox basis for a responsible state establishment of religion.

The issue was being much debated in Great Britain and its colonies. The presumption still was that colleges were established state religious organizations. Since Oxford and Cambridge excluded members of dissenting sects, Nonconformists in England were forced to found "dissenting academies" for the equivalent of college training. In the Anglican colony of Virginia, the Oxbridge pattern was followed, though only in a general way. The College of William and Mary—chartered in 1693, opened in 1707, and only gradually becoming a full-fledged college—was an integral part of the Anglican establishment. Seated facing the state house in Williamsburg, it was supported by state revenues while its faculty were required to be Anglican and were almost all clergymen. By mid-century William and Mary was comparable to the New England colleges and included as well a divinity school for the training of Anglican clergy.[10]

Thomas Clap and most of Connecticut took for granted that Yale should have the equivalent privileges in Congregationalist Connecticut. Just about half the college's graduates had become Congregationalist clergy, and it seemed sensible that such a vital function should be governed as strictly as the church itself.

The issue became complicated almost immediately after Clap took office as the convulsions of the Great Awakening shook New England. George Whitefield was welcomed at Yale during his grand tour of 1740, but his more extravagant successors and imitators, including the most extreme, James Davenport, a Yale graduate, began to disrupt Congregationalist unity. Soon it was one orthodoxy versus another.

At a crucial juncture in the controversy, at the commencement of 1741, Jonathan Edwards, already renowned for his account of the revival in Northampton, was brought in to preach. Many of the audience had heard James Davenport preaching in the vicinity the night before his "indecent mad and blasphemous religion," as the Old Lights typically put it. Edwards, preaching on "The Distinguishing Marks of the Works of the Spirit of God," made clear that extravagances such as Davenport's were not necessarily evidence of the Spirit of God, but he made just as clear (as only he could) that emotion and enthusiasm were no signs of the lack of the Spirit either.[11]

David Brainerd was a Yale student at the time and a great admirer of Edwards. Young Brainerd, following the pattern set by some of the less cautious New Lights such as Presbyterian itinerant Gilbert Tennent, was quick to make dogmatic pronouncements about the spiritual condition of those in the establishment who were cool to the awakening. Already at commencement time in 1741 the trustees had passed a college law forbidding students to call college officers "carnal" or "unconverted." When Brainerd soon remarked that one of the Yale tutors "has no more grace than the chair I am leaning upon," he was expelled. Yale was now firmly in the Old Light camp. In 1742 the commencement speaker was Isaac Stiles, who accused Edwards and company of leaving "the Pole-star to follow Jack with a Lanthorn."[12]

The awakeners were claiming that New England's colleges were already hopelessly secularized (which underscores the point that it just depends on the standard one is measuring from). The most notorious accusations came from George Whitefield. In 1740 the Grand Itinerant had been warmly welcomed both at Harvard and at Yale. Whitefield, however, was keeping a journal of his travels. Relying on the characterizations of his New Light informants,[13] Whitefield characterized the schools as "not far superior to our Universities in piety." This was a scathing insult, especially since in the same journal Whitefield wrote that Oxford and Cambridge were "sunk into *meer Seminaries of Paganism. Christ or Christianity* is scarce so much as named among them." Whitefield, who was not a private man, soon published his journal. His former hosts at the New England schools were in a rage.

Harvard, though still professing orthodox Calvinism, was more vulnerable than Yale since it was slightly more open to fashionable British opinion. Whitefield claimed that discipline there was at a low ebb and that students and teachers were reading latitudinarians such as John Tillotson and Samuel Clarke rather than the old evangelical Puritan authors. In 1744, when Whitefield was back in New England, the Harvard faculty replied indignantly, characterizing Whitefield as "an uncharitable, censorious and slanderous Man," and, worst of all, an "*Enthusiast*," meaning he claimed direct guidance from the Spirit of God. "Enthusiasm" had been a damning accusation in Massachusetts since Anne Hutchinson's time. Indeed, the issue was similar. Some New Lights were suggesting that persons might be called to preach directly by the Holy Spirit, without the benefit of a classical education. Harvard professors and their clerical supporters correctly perceived that Whitefield was a threat to their whole system of social authority.[14]

Though the Yale faculty also issued a rejoinder, Whitefield's characterizations of spiritual laxity were less plausible there. While Harvard was combating the Awakening from a moderate Calvinist position, Thomas Clap's Yale opposed it from a position of strict orthodoxy. Clap was an imposing and domineering character who hoped to ride out the turmoil by standing firm against the pluralism of the age. The extent to which he was willing to go was suggested in 1744 when Clap expelled two students, John and Ebenezer Cleveland, because while home on vacation they had attended a New Light church service conducted by a lay exhorter, rather than attending the Old Light church in their town.[15]

By the 1750s, however, Clap had forged a political alliance with the New Lights, who he may have decided were, in the long run, less prone to tolerance than some of the moderate Old Lights. Yale was also now in competition with the new College of New Jersey (Princeton), which was New Light.[16] In any case, Clap successfully resisted any trend of his time to see tolerance as a virtue. In 1753 he denied the request of New Haven's recently settled Anglican minister to allow his sons to attend their own church instead of the college services. In reply to the irate Anglican's rejoinder, Clap spelled out the case for the old order of narrow religious establishments. First of all, alluding to the exclusions of dissenters at Oxford and Cambridge, he remarked that while Yale College "does not come up, to the Perfection, of the Ancient Established Universities," it still "would endeavour to Imitate them in most things." And, said Clap, "Religious Worship, Preaching, and Instruction on the Sabbath, being one of the most important Parts, of the Education of Ministers," were the part of education that should be most under the authority of the college. No outside agency, whether parent or church, should be controlling the part of education that the college was set up most to preserve. And if students were simply required to attend the worship of their choice, what would happen, asked Clap, if "there may be an Assembly of *Jews*, or *Arians*, in *New Haven*"? Then, the college would be requiring "such a Worship, as they esteem, to be *worse than none*."

As to the objection that since Anglicans, such as Bishop Berkeley and Eli Yale himself, had made large contributions to the college, they should have some influence over college laws, Clap had an answer that probably every college president since would have appreciated: "If it were so; it seems, as if they intended to *Buy* the College rather than to make a *Donation* to it."

To the more difficult objection that Anglicans paid taxes to support the college, Clap had a feebler reply. Anglicans, he said, were free to send their children to the college so long as they abided by its rules; furthermore, Yale had trained enough Anglican clergy (Clap did not mention that these were mainly Cutler and his friends) to make their tax donations a bargain.[17]

During the next decade, Clap's narrow partisanship managed to alienate almost everyone. He insisted that anyone having to do with the corporation be subjected to tests of orthodoxy. He alienated former Old Light allies and never gained the full confidence of New Lights. He fired tutors on suspicions of heterodoxy. He refused a contribution of books because it contained some heretical volumes. Meanwhile, the legislature was threatening to cut off funds, the college was losing students, tuition was rising, and the food was bad. Only the unusual force of Clap's personality kept the college running. Finally in 1765, the situation collapsed. A mob of students and townspeople rioted and damaged his home. Student dissension, rebellion, and calls for Clap's ouster continued through the next year. Finally in 1766, exhausted and in ill-health, Clap resigned.[18]

New Light and Enlightenment

The intensity of such mid-eighteenth-century controversies should help us to understand the religious dimension of the founding of the other colonial colleges. Most of these colleges—The College of New Jersey (Princeton, 1746), Brown (1764), Queen's (Rutgers, 1766), and Dartmouth (1769)—were founded by the activist New Light clergy, respectively, among Presbyterians, Baptists, Dutch Reformed, and Congregationalists. The two exceptions were King's (Columbia, 1754) in New York City and the College of Philadelphia (Pennsylvania, 1755), more broadly supported by non–New Light coalitions with Anglican leadership and Presbyterian support.

Of the New Light colleges the College of New Jersey located at Princeton proved to be the most significant, especially since Presbyterians would be the chief college founders during the next century and their college became the only major rival to the older New England colleges as a national model. The Princeton charter, granted in 1746 and revised in 1748, originally designated as trustees only New Side Presbyterian ministers, but to ease public unrest, the sympathetic royal governor persuaded the trustees to add the governor and four members of his council and three Presbyterian laymen to the board, though the board remained overwhelmingly Presbyterian and clerical and was self-perpetuating. More notably, the charter guaranteed that students "of any religious Denomination" could enjoy the full privileges of the college, regardless "of his or their Sentiments in Religion, and of his or their being of a Religious profession Different from the said Trustees of the College." Princeton was founded immediately in the wake of the exclusions of the New Lights at Yale and the connections were close.[19] Gilbert Tennent and Aaron Burr, Jonathan Edwards's son-in-law, were on the original Princeton board. In New Jersey, where there was more diversity, there was also greater sensitivity to the rights of dissent.

With the exception of Queen's College, where ethnicity sharpened Dutch Reformed standoffishness, all the colonial colleges founded in this period resolved the problem of interdenominational rivalries by allowing minority denominations some representation on their boards.[20] Also, with the exception of Yale, all the boards were or became mixes of clergy and laymen, even if clergy usually retained their traditional dominance. Most had the colonial governor and members of his council as ex officio members, but unlike the first three colleges, they received little, if any, tax support. Interdenominational rivalries were again the crucial factor. Politics and religion were inextricably linked in the mid-eighteenth century. Despite growing tolerance forced by the public functions of the colleges, they were still essentially under the control of a dominant religious group.

Even the College of Philadelphia, the most secular of the schools, and the only one with an entirely lay board, was beset by rivalries between Anglicans and Presbyterians for control. Similarly, King's College in New York City, the only other new college not a direct product of the Awakening, was the focus of intense rivalries between the Anglicans, who by charter held the presidency, and the powerful Presbyterians, who countered any Anglican sectarianism. Samuel Johnson, the first president, was himself no friend of sectarianism. He had been one of the tutors who joined Cutler in defecting to Anglicanism and were forced to leave Yale. In 1754 he formulated for Protestant colleges serving the public the creed that in substance would be repeated at almost every such college for the next two centuries. It is so typical as to be worth italicizing: *As to religion, there is no intention to impose on the scholars, the peculiar tenets of any particular sect of Christians; but to inculcate upon their tender minds, the great principles of Christianity and morality in which true Christians of each denomination are generally agreed.*[21]

Maintaining a moral order was a major challenge for eighteenth-century British society, as it is in every era. So far as young people were concerned, the traditional way to promote habits of good behavior was coercion. At King's College, for instance, monetary penalties were used. Absence from chapel brought a fine of two pence, one pence for tardiness. Students caught at fighting cocks, playing cards, or dice were fined up to five shillings. The lesser offense of "fighting, maiming, slandering, or grievously abusing any person" drew a three-shilling penalty.[22] Traditional methods of controlling youth by strict regulation and discipline often fostered between faculty and students a cold war atmosphere, punctuated by student rowdiness and occasional riots.

Those in control seldom questioned the well-tried authoritarian methods, but one trend in the eighteenth century was to look more to the individual as a self-regulating force. Inner discipline could supplement external authority. Puritan and other religious disciplines anticipated this emphasis on internalizing a moral order. The problem for Protestantism, however, was how to apply this to entire societies.

The two major eighteenth-century solutions to this problem were those associated with pietism and the Enlightenment. Despite some striking parallels between these movements (such as individualism, challenging

old authorities, and concern with morality), they moved in essentially opposite directions regarding the crucial question of human nature. Pietism
and the associated revivals emphasized the need for a dramatic change in
the individual through conversion experience, suggesting a fundamental
gap between the saved and the lost. So far as the social order was concerned,
the redeeming feature was that revivalism offered the hope that vast numbers might be saved, thereby infusing society with Christian virtue.[23] The
Enlightenment approach, on the other hand, emphasized human commonality and ability to internalize the findings of a universal moral science, once
people correctly apprehend them.

For the next century, these two programs, the revival and moral philosophy, were the chief collegiate supplements to traditions of regulated worship, required church services/theological study, and discipline of personal
behavior. The tension between the Christian particularism of the revival
and the scientific universalism of the Enlightenment was a source of potential conflict between the two outlooks. Remarkably, in the late eighteenth
and the early nineteenth centuries, however, these two programs generally
were not seen as in conflict, but more often as complements in the task of
Christianization.

The experience that bonded these two disparate trends was the American
Revolution. Protestant dissenters, among whom New Lights were the most
vigorous party (as their college founding illustrates), gained cultural influence in alliance with more broadly enlightened opponents of the Anglican
and British establishment. Enlightenment moral philosophy, which British
dissenters for over a generation had been using to challenge Anglican and
royal authority,[24] provided the common language for the revolutionary enterprise. Hence, moral philosophy became a fixed part of the American New
Light or evangelical tradition.[25]

The Scottish Connection

American colonial educators were provincials intellectually dependent on
sophisticated Great Britain. Their primary models in the eighteenth century were the Scottish universities. While Anglican gentlemen's education at
Oxford and Cambridge had fallen into the doldrums, the Scottish universities suddenly blossomed into a golden age of the Scottish Enlightenment.
The Enlightenment in Scotland was as brilliant as anywhere in the world,

boasting scholars such as Francis Hutcheson, Thomas Reid, David Hume, and Adam Smith, as well as a formidable second rank almost as well known in their day. Unlike its more renegade French counterpart, the Scottish Enlightenment was situated primarily in the universities. In part this was possible because the Scottish universities were dominated by Presbyterian Moderates who combined Presbyterian zeal for learning with a determination to demonstrate the compatibility of Christianity with the latest cultural and scientific trends.[26] Their prestige virtually guaranteed that they would set the standards for the fledgling American schools.

Scottish universities were especially important to American dissenters because they stood at the apex of the vigorous network of non-Anglican education in Greater Britain. To combat the Anglican monopoly dissenters in England had developed "dissenting academies," which provided precollegiate and collegiate education. The Scotch-Irish in Ireland, many of whom were migrating to America, had built similar Presbyterian academies and soon imported the system to the colonies. The most famous of these was William Tennent's "Log College" at Neshaminy, Pennsylvania, founded in 1727, out of which eventually grew the College of New Jersey. During the next seventy-five years at least sixty-five other academies were founded by Presbyterian minister-teachers, largely in new settlements of the West and South. These provided mostly precollegiate work but also some college-level instruction, and the ministers might also tutor some college graduates reading divinity. A few such schools evolved into colleges.[27]

So extensive was the Presbyterian educational program that it is not much of an exaggeration to say that, outside of New England, the Scots were the educators of eighteenth-century America. Even Thomas Jefferson, who studied at William and Mary, found the one stimulating teacher to be a Scotsman, William Small. Small, the only layman at the school, was professor of mathematics but also taught the moral philosophy of Francis Hutcheson. Jefferson attributed to Small his own intellectual awakening to modern science and learning.[28]

By the end of the Revolutionary era, Scottish moral philosophy was well on the way to becoming the integrating crown of American collegiate education. In the New England and New Light colleges that still used Saturdays and Sundays for theological study (which was as integral as anything else in the curriculum, since there were recitations but no grades), moral philosophy might share its rule with theology. In the less sectarian schools that did not have a fixed theological program, the emerging science could already stand alone as the chief embodiment of the best of modern, scientifically based, and broadly Christian ideals.

A Dissenting Alternative

The total autonomy of morality as a science did not go entirely uncontested, especially by some New Englanders. Particularly, a number of Christian thinkers recognized the tension between the exclusivism of conversionist theologies and the universal claims of the new moral science. Most formidable were Jonathan Edwards's attacks on Arminianism, a catch-all term he used to designate most of the theological and ethical trends of the era. In his most purely philosophical work, *The Nature of True Virtue*, for instance, he attacked Francis Hutcheson's view of a reliable universal moral sense. As an ardent Calvinist and a luminously clear thinker, Edwards recognized that modern claims to establish a universal ethics rested on optimistic views of human nature that denied the severity of original sin and affirmed the free ability of persons to choose the good simply by putting their minds to it. Such moral systems, he argued, would ultimately undermine a sense of total dependence on God.

In 1757 Edwards became president of the College of New Jersey, at Princeton, already a contender for the position of leading colonial college. Early in the next year he died from complications following a smallpox inoculation. We can only speculate as to what his rigorous challenge to the autonomy of the new moral philosophy would have done for Presbyterian collegiate education.

Perhaps it would not have been much different from what happened at Yale, where a similar stance by Thomas Clap simply slowed the transition to the new philosophy for a generation or so. Clap's ethical principles, though less brilliantly argued, were not far from Edwards's. In Clap's lectures to Yale students he insisted that moral philosophy was learned not by examining human nature, but from the perfections of God. Moreover, "the divine Revelation is the only Way and Means whereby we can know what the Perfections of God are, and what Dispositions and Conduct in us, are a Conformity to these Perfections." Clap summarized and refuted each of the contenders for alternative moral foundations, such as self-interest and happiness, moral taste or sense, or conformity to reason. He conceded, for instance, that humans had a moral sense but then pointed out in rigorous

Calvinist fashion that "since the Fall, his Understanding is darkened, his judgment is perverted, his Taste and Relish is defiled. . . ."[29]

Edwards and Clap, seeing that the orthodox Puritan heritage was going to be out of step in the modern world, were raising the disturbing theoretical issue that Christian education must be distinctive, not only in theology, but also in the most crucial practical philosophical understandings of human behavior and morality. Theoretically this argument looked formidable; in practice it created the huge problems, already considered, of sectarianism for essentially public institutions. It implied also a practical moral rigor in college that would be difficult to sustain. Clap's efforts almost killed Yale and eventually led to an uprising that effectively ended his presidency. Edwards, for all his theoretical brilliance, was not known for his tact when it came to enforcing the moral order. If the good citizens of Northampton ran him out of town, one wonders how long he would have lasted with the students of Princeton had he lived into the Revolutionary era.

Since Aristotle's ethics had until the eighteenth century played a large role in Western education for so many centuries prior to the eighteenth, it is fair enough to ask what was new in the challenge posed by the new science of morality. The difference may be compared to the difference between Aristotelian and Newtonian physics. In Aristotelian physics, qualities like impetus, levity, or gravity could be acquired dispositions of objects. So one can impart impetus to a stone, but when the impetus wears out, it will come to rest. The Aristotelian physical universe was thus wide open to the interposition of external personal agencies, including supernatural miracles. The Newtonian universe, on the other hand, despite the piety of Newton and most of his immediate heirs and despite assumption that there was a creator, was for practical purposes a closed system of universal physical laws. The differences in ethics were similar. In Aristotle virtue was conceived as an acquired skill, developed by practice. Hence, one could benefit from the wisdom of Aristotle in the principles of acquiring the habits of virtue, but the door was wide open for adding Christian content in defining the content of the virtues. Aristotle's ethics thus could be presented with Christian commentary that would correct his misconceptions, for instance, concerning the human soul or immortality.[30] The new moral philosophy, on the other hand, could be conceived of as a closed rational system, which eventually would make special revelation superfluous, at least for ethics.

Add to this an advantage that the new moral philosophy had over Aristotle: like Newton's physics, it was a broadly Christian philosophy in the sense of arising out of Christian civilization. In its earliest forms, such as in the Cambridge Platonism originated in the mid-seventeenth century, the Christian dimensions of the enterprise were quite explicit. Already by the 1690s such texts replaced Aristotle at Harvard. By the mid-eighteenth century broadly Christian moralists such as Samuel Clarke, Francis Hutcheson, and the third Earl of Shaftesbury were well known to virtually every educated American.[31] One implication that some were drawing was that the new moral philosophy provided a rationally based Christianity that could supersede the contending theological authorities of previous generations. As Samuel Clarke put it in 1708, "Moral Virtue is the Foundation and the Summ, the Essence and the Life of all true Religion; For the Security whereof, all positive Institution was only designed; For the Restoration whereof, all revealed Religion was ultimately intended."[32] Or, as an admirer of Shaftesbury and Hutcheson put it in 1740, "religion and virtue are the same thing."[33]

As Jonathan Edwards observed in *The Nature of True Virtue*, such advocates of the autonomy of moral philosophy still, nonetheless, typically mentioned the Deity as ultimately the source of the moral systems that they might discover by rational means alone. "If true virtue consists partly in respect for God," Edwards retorted, "then it doubtless consists *chiefly* in it."[34] So for Edwards, even while he could incorporate some of the insights of the new moral philosophy into his thinking, it was essential to start first with what we knew about God's purposes as revealed in Scripture and then to determine our moral duties within that framework.[35]

Moral Philosophy in the Service of the Republic

Though Edwards had many admirers during the next generations, few followed him in his radical challenge to the autonomy of the new moral science. Rather, even the most orthodox typically made peace with the modern philosophy, much as their predecessors had incorporated Aristotle's ethics into their thinking. The new philosophy offered them an up-to-date means of supporting a moral system applicable not only to dedicated Christians but to all of society. For instance, Francis Alison, the leading figure among the theologically conservative but antirevivalist Old Side Presbyterians, was also the most influential early proponent of Francis Hutcheson's views in America. Alison was educated at Scottish universities, in part by Hutcheson himself.

In America he founded one of the more advanced Presbyterian academies in Chester County, Pennsylvania, in 1742. Alison was highly regarded by most of the colonial intellectuals, including Benjamin Franklin, and with William Smith became cofounder in 1755 of the College of Philadelphia. He participated in some of the practical and scientifically oriented educational reforms of the Pennsylvania college and taught Hutcheson's moral philosophy there until 1779. That Alison was no theological liberal is suggested by the fact that in 1755 Clap's Yale awarded him an honorary doctorate.[36]

Alison's principal influence on Yale, however, came through his close friendship with Ezra Stiles, with whom he corresponded for years. Stiles was a tutor under Clap and eventually served as Yale's president from 1778 to 1795. Alison helped foster in Stiles an appreciation of Scottish universities and methods, and Stiles, in fact, obtained an honorary doctorate from Edinburgh in 1765.[37]

Even though Stiles was a model of the broad intellectual of his era, interested in mastering all human learning and sciences and of a tolerant, open spirit, he was a conservative in his religious allegiances. When, for instance, in 1792 some state officials were made ex officio members of the Yale Corporation in exchange for tax support, Stiles reflected on the disaster it would be to the religious interests of the college if the Corporation ever became all laymen. First, he said, there would be terrible fights for balance among all the religious sects. Then they would have to drop all religious tests for the board and admit "Deists & enemies to all Sects of Xtians." Soon even theistic tests would be removed for the faculty. "In short," Stiles concluded (in a dim prophecy of God and Man at Yale), "the Religion & that good Order which arises from the Religion of the original Institution must be laid prostrate."[38]

Stiles, nonetheless, managed to synthesize strong concerns for a continuing Christian identity with the catholic spirit of the Enlightenment.[39] So on the one hand, out of respect for his mentor, he continued to include Clap's text as a brief part of his senior course on moral philosophy. Nonetheless, by 1790 he had added to the senior requirements William Paley's Principles of Moral and Political Philosophy and Montesquieu's Spirit of the Laws. Theology was still a formidable presence at Yale, but what was most significant in these changes was that the subject of political philosophy had now risen to prominence as part of moral philosophy. Following the Revolution and facing the traumas of nation building, the overwhelming priority in collegiate education was shaping good citizens.[40]

The most dramatic shift, however, came at Princeton. Within less than a generation its atmosphere seemed vastly different than when it was a New Light and New Side stronghold with Jonathan Edwards as president.

Crucial to the change was the Scotsman John Witherspoon, who served as president of the College of New Jersey from 1768 to 1794. The Princeton trustees, having suffered one after another early death of New Light presidents, had turned abroad to find Witherspoon, who might offer some added prestige. Although Witherspoon had been an outspoken opponent of liberal tendencies among Scottish Presbyterians, in American categories he turned out to be closer to moderate Old Lights than to the New Lights. Francis Alison in Philadelphia and Charles Chauncy (an old opponent of Edwards) in Boston took delight in discovering that they suddenly had an ally at Princeton. As Chauncy put it, "He is no friend to the grand and distinguishing Tenets of Mr. Edwards wch. have been almost universally imbibed in that part of the Country."[41]

Upon arriving in Princeton, Witherspoon immediately took the situation in hand: he cleared out the tutors who were champions of Edwardsean philosophy and introduced the principles of Francis Hutcheson. Disagreement with Hutcheson's moderate theology was to Witherspoon no reason to reject his philosophy. Witherspoon's lectures, in fact, followed Hutcheson closely with little real criticism. Ethics, he emphasized, must be a natural human science. The foundational facts could be discovered by examining human nature. "The principles of duty and obligation must be drawn from the nature of man." So human consciousness became a source of scientific data. Such self-examination led to a moral sense of good and evil, principles from which a universal ethical system could be derived. Witherspoon, like the other Scots, was hopeful that "a time may come when men, treating moral philosophy as Newton and his successors have done natural, may arrive at greater precision." Though Witherspoon spoke of his views as a Christian philosophy and backed them with appeals to Scripture, he regarded them as ultimately part of an inductive science.[42]

Scientific method could thus both confirm Christianity and support the moral foundations necessary to the republic. Science and religion were in no way seen as in conflict. Witherspoon, accordingly, like Alison in Philadelphia or Stiles in New Haven, took pride in acquiring scientific equipment and adding doses of practical natural philosophy to the classical curriculum.[43]

One striking index of the change was that from the early years of the presidency of John Witherspoon (1768–1775) to his last years (1784–1794) the number of the college's graduates entering the ministry fell from nearly one in two to little more than one in eight. Clearly this was a reflection of the revolutionary times. Princeton was particularly susceptible to the political fervor; nearby Philadelphia, where some of its best known trustees resided, was the center of American national political life. The College of New Jersey itself, which boasted the largest building in the colonies, even served as the seat of the Continental Congress for five months in 1783. President Witherspoon, the only clergyman to sign the Declaration of Independence, was among the most active leaders in organizing the new government. His student James Madison was a leading figure in drafting the Constitution. During the national era Princeton produced so many leading public officials that it eventually characterized itself as "the school of statesmen."[44]

Service to the Republic had emerged as the preeminent goal. For this there was hardly any distinction between the benefits of religion and the benefits of the science of morality. The two supported each other. As Witherspoon's successor, President Samuel Stanhope Smith of Princeton, put it in a conventional statement, "the truths of religion . . . [are] the surest basis of public morals." "Every class of the people" needed to be trained in their "moral and social duties."[45]

Dr. Benjamin Rush of Philadelphia, a Princeton graduate and friend of the college, with sincere though broad Christian sensibilities, made a similarly conventional point in 1798, saying that "the only foundation for a useful education in a republic is to be laid in Religion." Rush was one of the principal champions of educational reform, including the establishment of a national university. Like most leaders of the American Enlightenment, he favored more practical scientific education, but moral education was the most practical subject of all. Education was crucial to the republic because citizens needed to be shown their moral duty in order to act upon it.[46]

Christianity was crucial to the equation that led to republican virtue. Rush admitted that rather than no religion, he would prefer "the opinions of Confucius or Mohamed inculcated upon our youth." Christianity, however, according the old "real Whig" or British dissenter tradition of the American revolutionaries, had unique civil benefits. The Old Testament teaching of a common creation was "the strongest argument that can be used in favor of a natural equality of all mankind." In fact, Rush insisted, in a revealing summary of how Gospel and republic had been fused,

A Christian cannot fail of being a republican, for every precept of the Gospel inculcates those degrees of humility, self-denial, and brotherly kindness, which are directly opposed to the price of monarchy and the pageantry of a court. A Christian cannot fail of being useful to the republic, for his religion teacheth him, that no man "liveth to himself." And lastly, a Christian cannot fail of being wholly inoffensive, for his religion teacheth him, in all things to do to others what he would wish, in like circumstances, they should do to him.[47]

3

Two Kinds of Sectarianism

The "ambition and tyranny" of the Presbyterians, Thomas Jefferson fumed to his friend Thomas Cooper in 1822, "would tolerate no rival if they had power." Jefferson's contempt for the Presbyterians assumed Voltairian proportions: "Systematical in grasping at the ascendancy over all the sects, they aim, like the Jesuits, at engrossing the education of the country, are hostile to every institution which they do not direct, and jealous at seeing others begin to attend at all to that object."[1] Presbyterians, Jefferson was convinced, yearned to reinstitute a Protestant inquisition that would, as Calvin had done to Servetus, "exterminate all heretics to Calvinistic Creed." As it was, they controlled by manipulating "public opinion, that Lord of the universe." Jefferson was convinced, nonetheless, that he had reason on his side. Despite Presbyterian "fulminations against endeavors to enlighten the general mind, to improve the reason of the people, and to encourage them in the use of it," he assured another correspondent, "the liberality of this State will support this institution [the University of Virginia] and give fair play to the cultivation of reason."[2] The aging revolutionary had cause to resent the Presbyterians. For over forty years he had been attempting to found a first-rate nonsectarian university in Virginia, a step he considered essential for the health of the republic. By now, however, the Presbyterians had emerged as the principal rivals to his republican dreams for higher education. Demanding an educated clergy, the Presbyterians, although no longer as numerous as the more populist Baptists and Methodists, were the leaders in American higher education and gaining in strength. Although Jefferson persisted in his plans to found a revolutionary university and the Jeffersonians were holding on in educational influence, Jefferson had reason to fear that Presbyterians might prevail.

On the eve of the American Revolution, the major contenders for control of American higher education (outside of New England) had been the Anglicans and the Presbyterians. Schools, however, were not solely church organizations but also quasi-public institutions that depended on the colonial governments for the privilege of charter and sometimes support. In the

South Anglicans controlled William and Mary; in New Jersey Presbyterians controlled the more private College of New Jersey. In the pivotal cities of New York and Philadelphia, the two parties had vied for control, debating the issues of the propriety of government favoritism to one sect over all others. In New York, King's College was Anglican but had to make concessions in the face of constant Presbyterian accusations of public favoritism. The College of Philadelphia, the most nonsectarian of the colonial schools, balanced interests by having an Anglican provost and a Presbyterian vice provost.

Since the Presbyterians had been overwhelmingly on the side of the Revolution, whereas the Anglicans were badly divided, independence gave the Presbyterians the advantage. Although dependent on a primary Scotch-Irish ethnic base that made them something of outsiders, they were now in a position to play insiders' roles in shaping the ethos of the new republic. Especially important was that some Presbyterians cultivated a continuing alliance with Calvinist Congregationalists of New England, primarily Connecticut, and in 1801 established a formal alliance, the Plan of Union, for joint work in frontier settlements, primarily in New York State. They were thus part of the oldest and most sophisticated American educational network. In the Northern states, as New Englanders moved west, that alliance was especially important in promoting their ambitions for higher education.

While the Revolution had strengthened the Presbyterian hand and weakened the Anglican, it had also brought onto the scene a new major contender for shaping American education—liberal Christian and Deist champions of freer thought. The American Revolution had been supported primarily by an alliance of Calvinists and such enlightened liberal Christians. Since American revolutionary theory had grown largely out of the dissenter tradition, which traced its lineage to the Puritan Revolution and Commonwealth, these two heritages were related and had much in common. Each opposed Anglican establishments, and each believed that scientific thinking could discover universally valid first principles of morality. Nonetheless, once the smoke had cleared from the Revolution, it soon became apparent that they also had sharply opposed visions for the new nation.

Agreeing that the new nation should not have an established church, both sides saw education as crucial to founding common values and beliefs. The Jeffersonians, who had worked to make the federal government largely secular in definition, envisioned secular government, either federal or state, as the best agent for organizing a common educational system. Often, especially immediately after the French Revolution, this was based on French models and involved a recognition that, as Rousseau had pointed out, without an established church the state would have to provide some sort of common moral teaching. During the first years of the Republic the Jeffersonians wrote much about the necessity of state educational programs, and through the Jeffersonian era there were regular proposals to found a national university.

Although the involvement of the states in education was nothing new, the initial enthusiasm for such ideals in the revolutionary era soon ran into the related questions of how centralized and how secular such systems should be. Church groups, especially the Presbyterians and the Anglicans (who were down but not out), inevitably were to be the chief opponents of such state educational schemes—unless, of course, they saw prospects of taking them over.

New York State provided an early example. In the wave of revolutionary enthusiasm, the legislature in 1784 established a state "university," meaning a centralized board of regents who would establish schools and colleges in the state. The legislature also changed the name of King's College, the only actual college in the system, to the appropriately patriotic Columbia. At the reorganized college, no "preference" would be given to any religious group. Each religious denomination could name a regent, but they would be considerably outnumbered by representatives of the state's counties and major cities. In order to establish a theological faculty, any "religious body or Society of Men" could endow a professorship for the "Promotion [of its] particular religious Tenets." The progressive outlook of the reorganizers is suggested by their committee's initial nominees for president, Joseph Priestley, Richard Price, and John Jebb, three Englishmen known for their liberal religious views. These presidential nominations were quickly tabled, ostensibly because of financial concerns. In fact, the whole system was unwieldy and unrealistic and soon collapsed in the face of widespread opposition. In 1787 control of colleges was returned to local hands. In New York City this meant a resumption of control of the college by competing religious interests. By 1800 Columbia once again had an Episcopal clergyman as president, though it also had a cross section of laity and clergy of other denominations, especially Presbyterian and Dutch Reformed, on its faculty and board.[3]

Jefferson ran into similar dynamics in Virginia. In 1779, when he was governor of revolutionary Virginia, Jefferson had proposed that the state take over William and Mary as part of a general system of public education. In Jefferson's view, since the church college always had been a state agency anyway, it now should conform to revolutionary principles. Jefferson's bill was not adopted. Nonetheless, in 1780 he did manage to get the college to drop its two professorships of divinity. The school, however, remained in Episcopal hands, and by about 1800 it was clear to Jefferson that he would make no more progress in deflecting it from its ecclesiastical course.[4] In the meantime, the Presbyterians were in the midst of their own campaign to educate the republic. In Virginia they founded their own college, Hampden-Sydney (1783), as well as a couple of academies, making centralization of education under the state even less likely.[5]

South of Virginia, in states that previously had been largely innocent of institutions of higher education, it was easier for governments to move to fill the gap. Georgia (1785), North Carolina (1789), and South Carolina (1805) each established a state university. Even in such instances, the Jeffersonian liberal program was not unopposed. In North Carolina, for instance, Scotch-Irish Presbyterians took the lead in founding the state school. The two most influential trustee organizers were both Princeton graduates, although one of them, William Davie, was a Deist and a rationalist while the Rev. Samuel F. McCorkle was an orthodox Presbyterian. The curriculum and regulations were patterned closely after Princeton, and in 1799 another Princeton graduate, Joseph Caldwell, became head of the school. The original regulations provided for morning and evening prayers, "divine Services" each Sunday, and Sunday evening examinations "on the general principles of morality and religion," all strictly required.[6] Caldwell used the Bible as a text, and the senior course in moral and mental philosophy followed closely Witherspoon's syllabus of lectures.[7] In Georgia, after a more liberal start, Presbyterians soon became entrenched on the board of trustees, and that school also was run by a succession of men with Princeton connections. The strongest of these was the Rev. Moses Waddell, who became president in 1819. Waddell was dedicated to communicating "to the system of public education *the spirit of Christianity*" and insisted on "the Bible as the source and fountain of all true wisdom and government."[8]

By the early 1820s, when Jefferson was complaining about the influence of the Presbyterians, an all-out war was going on over whether American higher education would follow the Jeffersonian revolutionary model of liberal Christian leadership or be controlled by more traditional denominational interests.[9]

The most celebrated instance was the Dartmouth College case. Dartmouth had been founded in 1769 under the control of Congregationalists. In 1799 John Wheelock, the son of the founder, became president. The younger

Wheelock moved away from his father's conservative religious views, and in 1815 the Board of Trustees took the drastic step of removing him and appointing a Congregational minister in his place. Wheelock's Democratic political views were apparently also at issue, and Democrats hurled accusations that the old-guard Congregationalist minority was wielding unfair power by preserving the college for their own interests alone. In retaliation the state legislature, which had recently gained a Democratic majority, voted to revoke Dartmouth's charter and to make it into a "university," following the Jeffersonian revolutionary model. Jefferson himself wrote to William Plumer, the Democratic governor, congratulating him on the act. In Jefferson's view, "The idea that institutions established for the use of the nation cannot be touched nor modified, even to make them answer their end . . . may perhaps be a salutary provision against the abuses of a monarch, but is most absurd against the nation itself."[10]

The suit went to the United States Supreme Court, where Daniel Webster (Dartmouth '01) pleaded his first case before the high court. Webster concluded his defense with the famed oratorical flourish: "It is, Sir, as I have said, a small College. And yet *there are those who love it.*" More to the point, Chief Justice John Marshall was a Federalist and his court ruled against the Jeffersonians. "Is education altogether in the hands of government?" Marshall asked rhetorically. "Does every teacher of youth become a public officer, and do donations for the purpose of education necessarily become public property, so far that the will of the legislature, not the will of the donor, becomes the law of the donation?" While the distinction between public and private colleges would not be fully clarified for another generation, Marshall's landmark decision was a major step in establishing the immunity of charitable corporations from state control and struck a blow in an ongoing contest for sectarian versus state higher education.[11]

The contest was proceeding on other fronts with more openly partisan religious dimensions. In Kentucky, Transylvania University at Lexington, founded in 1799, had long been the focus of an open battle between Presbyterians and liberals for control. In 1817 Presbyterian dominance came to an end with the election of Horace Holley, a Yale graduate who, however, had become a Unitarian minister. Under Holley the institution flourished, but the Presbyterians, who represented only a small minority of the state's population, were in the midst of a fierce campaign (eventually successful in 1827) to drive the Unitarian (who had an even smaller ecclesiastical constituency) from office.[12]

Thomas Jefferson and Thomas Cooper were painfully aware of what such campaigns involved. Since his retirement from national politics, Jefferson had been carefully shepherding Virginia toward accepting a state university. He began by establishing Central College; although it existed on paper only, the organizing board in 1817 invited Thomas Cooper to be its first professor. When in 1819 the Virginia legislature finally adopted Jefferson's plan to take over Central, the question of the status of Cooper immediately arose. Though questions were raised about his drinking habits and temperament, the substantial issue was Cooper's religious beliefs. Cooper, English by birth, was a friend and protégé of Joseph Priestley and was known for his skepticism regarding traditional theology. As editor of Priestley's *Memoirs*, he had remarked, "The time seems to have arrived, when the separate existence of the human soul, the freedom of the will, and the eternal duration of future punishment, like the doctrines of the Trinity and transubstantiation, may no longer be entitled to public discussion."[13]

The Presbyterians, led by the Rev. John Rice, raised such an outcry against Cooper's beliefs that, much to Jefferson's embarrassment, they forced Cooper's resignation from the promised post. Cooper in the meantime had taken a temporary position at the University of South Carolina, which was eager to keep him on. The destruction of the keystone in his effort to build a university faculty, however, brought Jefferson's anti-Presbyterianism to full boil.

Joseph Cabell, who was Jefferson's right-hand man in the legislature, managing the efforts to build a university, attempted repeatedly to explain to Jefferson that the Presbyterian objections to Cooper were not part of a general opposition to the university. What the Presbyterians were objecting to was the virtual establishment of Jefferson's own Unitarian religious views. "They believe," Cabell wrote in a letter, "that the Socinians are to be installed at the University for the purpose of overthrowing the prevailing religious opinions of the country."[14] Jefferson had difficulty seeing this point. From his perspective liberal religious views appeared objective and scientific and only traditional ones appeared sectarian. Hence, he saw nothing wrong with using the state to enthrone his objective scientific views.[15]

In Jefferson's principal blueprint for the university, the Rockfish Gap Report of 1818, he and his associates, while alluding to a room that might be used for worship (presumably by approved religious groups), had stated that at the state school a professor of divinity would be constitutionally inappropriate, since that would be inevitably sectarian. The report did allow, however, that principles which they regarded as common, such as proofs for the existence of God and for moral obligations "on which all sects agree," could be taught by the professor of ethics. Study of Hebrew, Greek, and Latin would also be useful to all religious groups.[16]

Cabell explained to Jefferson that these provisions also were raising the ire of Presbyterians against what they saw as an unfriendly establishment, since their own more particular theological views were being specifically excluded.[17] Jefferson, who did believe that each religious group should have the freedom to promote its own views, was apparently more sympathetic to this objection. Eventually he agreed to what he thought would be a constitutionally acceptable solution. In 1822, the report of the university's Board of Visitors suggested that each sect might build a divinity school "on the confines" of the university. Divinity students could then take courses in other disciplines at the university as well as enjoy specialized training from their sectarian theological professor. Divinity faculty could also lead worship for the various denominations within the university facilities. According to Jefferson, this remedy, "while it excludes the public authorities from the domain of religious freedom, would give to the sectarian schools of divinity the full benefit of the public provisions made for instruction in other branches of science."[18]

This solution, though not taken advantage of by the denominations, was much like that later adopted in Canada[19] and had much to recommend it in resolving the dilemma of how to have public education without either having discriminatory sectarian religious teaching or excluding religion entirely and thus discriminating against all religious views. It did nothing to address the problem of sectarian or anti-sectarian bias in undergraduate training, except that it did provide for some denominational worship. However, it did recognize that theology was among the sciences that belonged at a university and provided a means for its practitioners to enjoy benefits of the state-supported academic center without being directly supported by the state.[20]

The proposal to have theological seminaries on the grounds was in tune with one of the latest developments in American higher education. Prior to the nineteenth century theological training beyond what everyone received on Saturdays and Sundays at colleges had been largely a matter of informal study or apprenticeship. By the end of the revolutionary era, however, many colleges were no longer attracting and graduating ministerial candidates. Moreover, the broadening religious sentiments of the era were creating tension between the beliefs of the orthodox and what was being taught in some of the colleges. The most celebrated case was at Harvard where Henry Ware, a Unitarian, was elected Hollis Professor of Divinity in 1805. Orthodox Congregationalists of Massachusetts responded by establishing Andover Theological Seminary in 1808, dedicated by its charter to be forever committed to orthodox Calvinism. At Princeton the struggle was more subtle. The college at the turn of the century, under Samuel Stanhope Smith, was still firmly in Presbyterian control but fused Presbyterian doctrine with an enlightened spirit. The students were riotous (in 1802 they burned down the great Nassau Hall, and a rebellion in 1807 brought the suspension of most of the student body), and the number of ministerial candidates was down alarmingly. In response, some of the more orthodox trustees in 1812 established a theological seminary, located at Princeton, but separate from the college, and under the auspices of the Presbyterian Church.[21] Thus, an important pattern of division of labor was established or re-established. Theological seminaries could perform distinctly ecclesiastical functions, thereby making it easier for the colleges to continue in their more problematic dual role as both denominational and public institutions. During the next decade or so Episcopalians, Lutherans, Presbyterians, Congregationalists, and Unitarians all founded additional seminaries or college-related divinity schools.[22]

When the plan to encourage denominations to found seminaries on the premises of the state university was suggested to Jefferson by some "pious individuals," he adopted it both as a constitutionally viable compromise that might pacify religious opponents and with the hope that it might help neutralize sectarianism. In his letter reporting the development to Thomas Cooper in 1822 he prefaced the report with his tirade against Presbyterian aggressiveness, quoted at the opening of this chapter. Then, after describing the plan to Cooper, he reassured his friend that the arrangement might alleviate sectarianism, "by bringing the sects together, and mixing them with the mass of other students: we shall soften their asperities, liberalize and neutralize their prejudice, and make the general religion a religion of peace, reason and morality."[23] Jefferson never lost confidence that reason would triumph over prejudice.

The tide, however, was turning against him. Thomas Cooper found this out in South Carolina in the years following Jefferson's death. Cooper, who had become president of the College of South Carolina in 1820, kept up his mentor's bitter attacks on Calvinism, differing from Jefferson only in making them fully public. In 1830 he published a pamphlet titled *An Exposition of the Doctrines of Calvinism*, alleging of Presbyterian doctrine that there was not "from ancient or modern times, a set of tenets so absolutely, so unprovokedly cruel, blasphemous, and devilish." The Presbyterians, he said, echoing Jefferson's sentiments, were an arrogant priesthood, much like the Jesuits, who were attempting to control all the educational institutions of the land and thus become the established religion.[24]

Presbyterians and other Protestants responded true to form by organizing a campaign in 1832 to oust Cooper from the college on the charge of infidelity and undermining the faith of Christian students. Cooper answered with an eloquent plea for academic freedom, arguing that the freedom of speech guaranteed by the constitution of the South Carolina should not cease at the college doors. Moreover, he argued forcefully, it was unconstitutional for the state to impose a religious test on its college president. No doubt, he admitted, his views were unpopular with much of the school's constituency, but similar objections had been raised to the teachings of Socrates, Jesus, Wycliffe, Galileo, and others.[25]

Politics was involved as well. Cooper was proslavery and for state's rights and the South Carolina nullification movement. For the moment, his political allies in these locally popular stands saved him from dismissal.[26] Nonetheless, because of the adverse publicity, enrollment at the college declined sharply, and the next year Cooper, now seventy-four, resigned. Technically he was a winner but, in fact, the religious climate in the South had so turned against the Jeffersonian outlook that a stance of open hostility to Christianity could not be sustained. As Richard Hofstadter observed, "It is perhaps significant that the boldest and most advanced argument for academic freedom to be made in the United States during the pre–Civil War period should have been made by a man in his seventies."[27] And, it might be added, by a slaveholder. The skeptical Enlightenment's hopes for an age of reason seemed near an end.[28]

Jefferson's prediction that the work of revolutionaries might last only one generation also proved more prescient than he would have liked at the University of Virginia. Within two decades of the founder's passing, the best-known professor at the university was a stalwart Presbyterian, the Rev. William H. McGuffey, elected professor of moral philosophy in 1845. McGuffey was known for his *Eclectic Readers*, which in their early editions taught explicitly Protestant principles to the nation's schoolchildren. His election at Virginia had been in response to continued attacks on the school for alleged infidelity, including objections to hiring both a Catholic and Jew. Also by this time the university was facing competition for students from seven church colleges in the state, which together enrolled a total of 550 students to the university's 122.[29] So the university was capitulating to a trend. Much as Jefferson had feared, once the Presbyterians had a firm foothold on the faculty, they could back up their stance with the weight of a strong supporting constituency in an increasingly conservative society. McGuffey instituted a successful voluntary morning prayer meeting to supplement the voluntary chapel services. In 1849, the Presbyterian chaplain for that year organized a series of lectures by an impressive group of Presbyterian divines on the scientific evidence for Christianity, in what became an important volume on the subject. For the generation of Stonewall Jackson and his ilk the Presbyterians had thus successfully placed their batteries on the high ground of Virginia infidelity. In 1859 the Presbyterians scouted the prospects for consolidating their position by being the first to establish a theological seminary on the premises. The War between the States, however, interrupted the cultural scrimmages, and, for the time being, left the university simply a desolated enterprise.[30]

The cases of Thomas Cooper and of the University of Virginia epitomize the roadblock that the Jeffersonian version of American public education faced. The Jeffersonians had on their side the revolutionary principles of freedom from public religious tests, even though these had not been at all consistently applied to states. Yet as opponents of the Jeffersonians were successfully pointing out, champions of enlightened religion were not any less a religious party than were conservative Presbyterians.[31]

4

A Righteous Consensus, Whig Style

By mid-century Jeffersonian "infidelity" was being outgunned across the entire front of American higher education. One index was that the most formidable intellectual strongholds of the day were theological seminaries. These schools were in the forefront of American professional education and offered about the only American opportunity for anything resembling graduate education. The leading seminaries, especially those in the Presbyterian–Congregationalist axis, published redoubtable and well-edited theological quarterlies that were the forums for most of the nation's major academic debates. The momentous struggle over Calvinism and its various modifications overshadowed everything else and preoccupied most of the ablest academic minds of the era.

Despite the strengths of the theological enterprise, the perennial debates over Calvinism nonetheless signaled an intellectual sea change. Except within the Reformed (Calvinist) denominations themselves, it seemed as though everyone from Unitarians to populist revivalists was trashing Calvinist doctrines as absurd and unreasonably harsh in an enlightened and benevolent age.[1] Even within the Reformed churches the shifting cultural sentiments were taking their toll by mid-century. The tradition's most exclusivist versions, which had emphasized the totality of God's sovereignty, were under widespread attack and beginning to give way to modifications more congenial to democratic ideals of free choice and moral responsibility.[2] Some critics were challenging the theological profession as such. Harriet Beecher Stowe is a striking example. Tied to the theological heritage by birth and by marriage, yet as a woman excluded from formal theological education, Stowe did more than anyone to establish the novel as an alternative forum for religious debate. In *The Minister's Wooing* (1859), for instance, she directly attacked not only Calvinism but also any teachings that tied eternal salvation to correct theological belief. Like many of the middle class of her generation, she was becoming convinced that the essence of Christianity was moral character, not divisive doctrines.

The Soul of the American University Revisited. George M. Marsden, Oxford University Press. © Oxford University Press 2021. DOI: 10.1093/oso/9780190073312.003.0008

The proliferation of American colleges during this era can be better under-stood in the context of such theological debates and debates about theology's place. For one thing, the professionalization of theology in theological semi-naries and divinity schools helped free colleges to emphasize other concerns, such as morality. This trend was reinforced by American social realities. While most of the new colleges were church related, each typically had to serve a public beyond its own denomination. The very religious diversity of the American context thus was pushing American collegiate education in seemingly contradictory directions. On the one hand, the decentralized at-mosphere was conducive to free enterprise and sectarian rivalry. Each de-nomination started its own colleges. At the same time this centrifugal force toward fragmentation was always being countered by centripetal forces that fostered a degree of uniformity. No matter what the denominational identity and the theological issues in its background were, each Protestant college had to deal with more or less the same American market. In such a free enterprise system a strong emphasis on theological distinctions could limit a college's constituency and be a competitive disadvantage. Hence, each college was more likely to emphasize the socially unifying aspects of its Christian tradi-tion, especially its moral benefits, rather than theological peculiarities.

The pace of American college founding during this era was phenomenal. Many of the new enterprises were like the seed that fell on rocky ground in the biblical parable, which sprouted quickly but soon withered in the sun. Fledgling colleges or collegiate institutes were planned everywhere. In the pre–Civil War era over five hundred were founded or at least founded on paper, although perhaps only two hundred survived into the twentieth cen-tury. Determining what to include in a count of colleges is difficult, since some of the schools offered primarily, or sometimes exclusively, precollegiate training. Still, the total by 1860 was remarkable when compared with the nine colonial institutions. Probably two-fifths of the surviving institutions were founded under either Presbyterian or Congregationalist auspices. In Jefferson's day, such Calvinist schools had been well over half, but since then the larger Methodist and Baptist denominations had advanced socially and were taking an interest in higher education, adding to the craze for college founding, which accelerated sharply after 1830. Catholics also became active founders, especially after 1850.[3]

The typical educational patterns that emerged fit the unique American situation. Free enterprise was triumphing over earlier efforts toward cen-tralization. In part, the predominant decentralization was a matter of

geography and the frontier conditions in the vast, new, and sparsely settled nation. Transportation was poor, and colleges were objects of local
community pride. Every town, it seemed, wanted one. Churches were well
prepared to move into this vacuum, performing their traditional functions
as educational leaders, providing community service, and accruing some
advantages to their denomination. As was traditionally the case, colleges
did not have religious tests for their students, and the lines between
church-private and public were not clearly drawn. This broader inter-
Protestant nonsectarianism was necessitated by localism. Denominational
identifications, in fact, may have become more significant later in the century as transportation improved and each school could cultivate wider regional loyalties from its own group.[4]

Though oriented to community as well as to church, the schools clearly
were religious institutions. In 1840 four-fifths of the college presidents of
denominationally related colleges were clergymen, as were two-thirds of state
college presidents. Other faculty and tutors might be clergy as well, although
clerical dominance was not nearly as overwhelming as in colonial days. The
professoriate had only begun to be differentiated as a distinct profession.
Natural sciences were being added to curricula, and some specialists were
appearing in those fields. Most faculty members, however, were expected to
be generalists who could teach almost anything. Even if they were not clergymen, they were expected to be pious. Faculty members, particularly residential tutors, were supposed to keep a close eye on the students since the
college was expected to act in loco parentis in maintaining Christian behavior among its charges. The most explicitly religious requirements were attendance at daily chapel and Sunday religious services.[5]

Broadly Christian concerns were also worked into parts of the curriculum.
The natural sciences, for instance, were typically taught "doxologically,"
emphasizing the design in nature for which one should praise the creator. Students typically learned "evidences of Christianity" or "natural theology," which reinforced this point. William Paley's Natural Theology (1802),
containing the famous argument that if we discovered a watch we could be
sure there was a watchmaker, was a popular text. Since belief in the deity was
essential to establishing a moral order, such apologetic concerns were closely
related to courses in moral philosophy, taught usually by the president in the
senior year. Moral philosophy now was firmly established as the capstone
of the program, providing without apparent sectarian bias a moral base for
Christian civilization building.[6]

The moral philosophy courses were attractive, wide-ranging, and long-lived. One of the most vivid accounts comes from the latter days of their dominance, from a survey of American colleges by G. Stanley Hall, published in 1879:

> The most vigorous and original philosophical instruction is almost every-where given in ethics, though like nearly all other subjects it is taught from text-books. . . . The work with text-books is commonly supplemented by lectures where ethical principles are applied to law, to trade, art, conduct, &c., in a more or less hortatory manner. The grounds of moral obligation are commonly deduced from Revelation, supplemented by the intuitions of conscience, which are variously interpreted.

Many teachers of philosophy, Hall observed, were trained only in theology "and their students are made more familiar with the points of difference in the theology of Parks, Fairchilds, Hodges, and the like, than with Plato, Leibnitz, and Kant."[7] While moral philosophy had established its popularity in American collegiate studies in the first half of the nineteenth century, the classics still made up most of the curriculum. The rationale for this contin-uing emphasis was consistent with broadly Christian moral concerns. The classics were useful for development of human faculties, both intellectual and moral.

This ideal was definitively expressed in the famous Yale Report of 1828. Not only was Yale one of the oldest colleges, but its several hundred students also made it one of the largest. During the national era it had emerged as the leading model for colleges with evangelical ties.

The premise of the Yale Report was that the human personality was made up of various faculties of which reason and conscience were the highest.[8] These faculties could be developed by exercise, much like physical strength. At the same time, the development of these faculties must be balanced. So the goal of education was "to maintain such a proportion between the different branches of literature and science, as to form in the student a proper *balance* of character." Drawing on the analogy to physical development, the report argued that "as the bodily frame is brought to its highest perfection, not by one simple and uniform motion, but by a variety of exercises, so the mental faculties are expanded, and invigorated, and adapted to each other, by famil-iarity with different departments of science."

The classics formed the core of this balanced character-building education. While they needed to be supplemented with modern natural science and
moral science, they contained wisdom, elevated tastes, and exercised a variety
of mental faculties. "It must be obvious to the most cursory observer," the report argued, "that the classics afford materials to exercise talent of every degree, from the first opening of the youthful intellect to the period of its highest
maturity. The range of classical study extends from the elements of language,
to the most difficult questions arising from literary research and criticism."[9]

Most American college builders, however, were heirs to the Great
Awakening as well as to classicism, Enlightenment moralism, and formal
Christian practice. In the New Light tradition colleges were also part of a
larger missionary and evangelistic enterprise. So it was natural for evangelical clergymen at these colleges to seek revival among their students, and
during the era from the Revolution to the Civil War many college revivals
took place. These revivals, however, were not routine. Even at the institutions
where they were most frequent, they were likely to occur no more than once
in a given student's career. When they did, classes might be canceled for days
as the time of prayer and renewal continued. Annual days of prayer, however,
were common parts of the college year, always with the hope for spectacular
spiritual outpourings.[10]

Yale was also the leading model of this New Light missionary spirit
in American collegiate education. In 1802 President Timothy Dwight,
grandson of Jonathan Edwards and successor to Ezra Stiles, preached a series
of sermons refuting Enlightenment infidelity. Unexpectedly, a major revival
broke out, in which a third of the Yale students professed conversion. The
Yale revival had symbolic importance for sparking the New England wing
of what became known as the Second Great Awakening. During the next
decades Yale and Connecticut became major staging grounds for organizing
a formidable phalanx of agencies, missionary and reform societies, that set
out to evangelize and transform the nation.[11] Such efforts were closely related to Yale's strategic social position. Connecticut Yankee emigrants were
in the forefront of settling western New York State and the upper Midwest.
Not only did they take with them the New England Puritan heritage; they
also did so with a missionary zeal to shape the West in their own image.

In such efforts New Englanders were in close alliance with like-minded
Presbyterians. Many New Englanders, in fact, became Presbyterians when
they moved west. New York City, where Congregationalism had long since

merged into Presbyterianism, was also a center for many of the national agencies. By the 1830s the combined budgets of the agencies of this "united evangelical front" rivaled that of the federal government. In an era when voluntarism reigned, New Englanders and their allies had appropriated for themselves the role of chief religious and moral agents in civilizing the nation.

Educational leadership was one service that New Englanders had to offer the new settlements, and college revivals were crucial to producing and motivating educated leaders for the missionary enterprise. Conversion of young men was, in fact, one of the common rationales for promoting and sustaining colleges. For instance, the Society for the Promotion of Collegiate and Theological Education at the West (SPCTEW), which with its founding in 1843 became the principal agency in the Presbyterian–Congregational network for college founding, always kept the well-documented benefits of college revival prominent in its promotional literature.[12]

The larger mission of the colleges was the civilizing task of spreading Protestant Christendom into the untamed wilds. Lyman Beecher, a protégé of Dwight's and a founder of the SPCTEW, is justly famed for articulating this motive in his *Plea for the West* of 1835. Noting that the millennium was likely to start from America, Beecher urged that "if this nation is, in the providence of God, destined to lead the way in the moral and political emancipation of the world, it is time she understood her high calling, and were harnessed for the work." The West was the key to the American empire and hence the territory to which its religious and civil ideals must be transmitted. Specifically, what the West most needed was "universal education, and moral culture, by institutions commensurate to the result." Education, Beecher argued to audiences who were facing the uncertainties of the Jacksonian revolution, was essential if republican institutions were to survive universal suffrage. Moreover, the education of the West could not be achieved simply by sending an army of teachers from the East. It must be accomplished through Western institutions themselves, colleges and theological seminaries. Schools such as Lane Theological Seminary in Cincinnati, where Beecher was president, would train the most talented men in the region.[13] Educational institutions, in Beecher's view, would determine who controlled the West.

The great fear, the flames of which Beecher did his best to fan, was that Catholics would take over the West. Much of his *Plea* was a fervid effort to document a conspiracy of the alliance of Catholic ecclesiastical power and Romanist European despots to capture the American West through massive Catholic immigration, fortified by Catholic centers for higher education. Disclaiming any intention to discriminate against Catholics, Beecher assured that he would welcome them if they just acted like other American denominations: "Let the Catholics mingle with us as Americans, and come with their children under the fell action of our common schools and republican institutions, and we are prepared cheerfully to abide the consequences." The problem with the Catholics, Beecher insisted, was political. They were determined to unite church and state into a single antirepublican despotism.

Recognizing that some Americans had alleged similar ambitions for Presbyterian and Congregationalist Calvinists (even comparing them to Jesuits, he might have added), Beecher argued that the record demonstrated the opposite. Calvinists, he said, had since the Reformation and the days of the Puritans always been on the side of liberty. Catholics, on the other hand, were almost invariably associated with tyranny and opposed to republicanism. One only had to look at the antirevolutionary, antirepublican Catholicism of contemporary Europe to confirm this. On the other hand, so long as Americans retained separation of church and state, said Beecher, it was impossible that they had anything to fear from Calvinists.[14]

The Whig Ideal

Beecher's outlook was a typical expression of the Whig cultural ideal of mid-nineteenth-century New England. Such "conscience Whigs," who played an important role in the Whig political party and in later Republicanism, were both heirs to the Puritan heritage and builders of modern civilization. Civilization building, in their view, was as much a moral task as a material one. It required both principled leadership from government and the training of strong, disciplined individuals.[15]

This outlook was closely related to their Protestant and republican heritage. In New England republican and Whig rhetoric dating back to the American Revolution, Protestantism was identified with the advances of civilization and the cause of freedom. The term "Whig" was borrowed from the party in eighteenth-century England that wished to limit the powers of the king. American Whigs saw themselves as standing for the original moral principles on which the American nation was founded. Freedom in their outlook meant not only political freedom and personal liberties derived from higher moral law but also the free inquiry necessary for modern science. Catholicism, by contrast, represented absolutism, suppression of individual development, and suppression of free inquiry.

The advance of morally responsible education was accordingly part of the Protestant and Whig program, so that Whigs became the educators of the nation. Such New Englanders, Unitarians as well as Trinitarians, wrote most of the nation's textbooks, championed public schools, and with a missionary spirit helped carry the zeal for founding colleges to towns and hamlets through much of the nation. Next to religion, education was the best means of taming an unruly populace and assimilating diverse peoples into a common culture with shared ideals. Education would develop the individual sense of duty and a national conscience.

Science and Protestant religion went hand in hand, since both stood for free inquiry versus prejudice and arbitrary authority. Francis Bacon, the seventeenth-century progenitor of the ideal, was high among the saints in the American Protestant hierarchy. Praise for Bacon's nonspeculative, non-metaphysical, down-to-earth methods knew few bounds.[16] Neither the natural order nor the moral order was a matter of sectarian doctrine; rather, both were of divine creation, open for all to see. The candid inquirer had nothing to fear from a disciplined search for the truth.

What is fascinating is that Calvinist educators like Lyman Beecher, who embodied this Whig outlook, insisted just as much as had the Jeffersonians before them that they were not a sect. They represented, rather, in their own view, simply the essence of Americanism, combining its highest political, moral, and religious ideals to which others might be fairly expected to conform.[17]

Whig educators could thus take over the Jeffersonian agenda of building a public educational system. In the Midwest, for instance, there was much discussion, for many of the same reasons that Beecher had raised, of the need for the states to organize educational systems to help bring order to the frontiers. State colleges or "universities" were to be the capstones of such state systems. Between 1828 and 1848 Indiana, Michigan, Kentucky, Missouri, Iowa, and Wisconsin chartered such publicly supported institutional higher learning. With the secular Jeffersonian ideology by this time battered and on the defensive, and the Methodists and Baptists still seen as poor relations just beginning to value education, the obvious, experienced, and well-qualified candidates for leadership in such state-sponsored enterprises were the moderate Presbyterians and Congregationalists.

In Michigan, for example, the founders of the new university addressed the question of sectarianism directly, and in a way that would hardly have pleased the Jeffersonians. Rather than exclude Christian teaching, they decided to try to rotate professorships among the major Protestant denominations.[18] This they saw as fairer than establishing irreligion. By this time it had become commonplace to point out, as the Presbyterians had in Virginia, that, as the Michigan Regents put it in 1841, "Attempts made to exclude all religious influence whatever from the college, have only rendered them the sectarian of an atheistical or infidel party or faction." Since, on the other hand, "the great mass of the population profess an attachment to Christianity," there "is common ground occupied by them, all-sufficient for cooperation in an institution of learning, and for the presence of a religious influence, devoid of any sectarian forms and peculiarities." All that was needed was "men to be found in all different Christian sects of sufficiently expanded views, and liberal spirit, and enlightened minds, devoid of the spirit of bigotry and narrow prejudices of sect." The guarantees would have to be informal. Such men of open-minded spirit would "furnish the best and only true guarantee against the evils of sectarianism."[19]

The statement was drafted by the Rev. George Duffield, a prominent Presbyterian pastor in Detroit. Duffield was typical of the shapers of American education. He was from among the first families of Presbyterians, being the grandson and namesake of the chaplain to the Revolutionary Army. He was also a "New School" Presbyterian. New School Presbyterianism had been shaped largely by its alliance with Congregationalists in the campaigns to create a nonsectarian Protestantism that could serve to shape the national ethos.

In 1837 and 1838 the New School had separated from the Old School Presbyterians, resulting in two denominations of comparable size, each claiming the same name, the Presbyterian Church in the U.S.A. Duffield, along with Lyman Beecher and others, had been prominent in the bitter controversies that preceded the schism. Though a number of points had been at issue, they all involved the question of how American as opposed to how distinctly Presbyterian the denomination would be. The New School, which had its strength in the Yankee alliance with the Congregationalists, prided itself on representing "American Presbyterianism." It softened Calvinist doctrines and had built the empire of agencies that were to evangelize, reform, and educate the nation. The Old School, predominantly Scotch-Irish in constituency, insisted on maintaining distinctive Presbyterian traditions, regardless of American trends. They brought New School leaders to trial on charges of heresy and insisted that the only proper agency for missions, education, and reform was the denomination itself. The Old School, which had much more strength in the South than did the New School, resisted especially cooperation in antislavery societies. Most Old Schoolers were Democrats; most New Schoolers were Whigs. Politics, however, was far from the only divisive issue. Americanism, of the New England Whig variety, was at stake. And in 1841 New School leaders like Duffield could see themselves as having resisted sectarianism, thus putting themselves in the forefront for building a broad Protestant America.

Common Sense

Such a "nonsectarian" public philosophy required an intellectual rationale. This was essential to an age that revered science and reason. And such a rationale could be found in the peculiar American revolutionary synthesis of evangelical Christianity, the Enlightenment, science, republican principles, and morality. The moral science of the eighteenth century had emerged as fundamental dogma built on appeals to self-evidence. This outlook, taught in college moral philosophy courses, was closely tied to the broader development of Scottish philosophy, known collectively as the philosophy of Common Sense. This philosophy was considered supremely scientific and universal and hence ideally suited to producing good citizens whose fundamental beliefs went beyond sectarianism. "Common sense" was also a revolutionary slogan and so could be popularized as an appeal to democratic sentiments. By 1830 Common Sense philosophy seemed to have swept everything before it in American intellectual life.

The character of the American Revolution, which wed Enlightenment ideals and dissenting Protestantism, best accounts for this triumph. The revolutionary principles, to which all major parties in America were in one way or another dedicated, were viewed as embodying the epitome of human morality grounded in universal self-evident, or commonsensical, principles. These principles were not only seen as supremely rational or scientific; they were also assumed to be congruent with true Christian morality. Behind such assumptions was the premise that God's revelation in Nature and Nature's law must be consistent with any true revelation in Scripture.

In postrevolutionary America, then, it was a widely shared article of faith that science, common sense, morality, and true religion were firmly allied. Various parties disagreed on exactly how the argument concluded. All the major Protestant parties agreed that commonsensically based scientific understanding of God's revelation in Nature confirmed His revelation in Scripture. They disagreed sharply, however, on how much weight to give to reason and to Scripture when there was apparent conflict. Nonetheless, everyone, it seemed, from Campbellites to Unitarians, from Old School Presbyterians to Jeffersonians, was in the same debate. Moreover, all were convinced that in fair controversy universal truth would eventually flourish.

The first principles for this scientific worldview were derived largely from the Scottish Enlightenment, especially in its later, more intellectualist formulation provided by Thomas Reid (1710–1796). Reid, in answering David Hume's skepticism, emphasized that there were a host of foundational beliefs, such as one's personal identity, the existence of other minds, consistency of nature, verifiable empirical data, and beliefs based on reliable testimony, as well as necessary truths of mathematics and logic, that all normal people (i.e., except philosophers and the insane) could not help believing. A firm science of human behavior could be founded on such unquestionable principles, and eventually, through careful inductive reasoning, all philosophical disputes should simply be settled.[20]

Such views found fertile soil in the new nation. For one thing, they appealed to the practical and antimetaphysical bent of popular American thought and conceptions of science. For another, since the new nation was cut off from England and suspicious of France after its revolution, Americans found in Scotland the most congenial resources for defining a national outlook. This dependence on Scotland was strongest until about the 1820s, after which a few younger Americans began looking to Protestant Germany for alternatives. By that time, however, Scottish models had a firm hold on American higher education.

In the colleges, Common Sense philosophy, combined with celebrations of the inductive methods of Bacon, was especially useful as a tool of apologetics. Those who won the battle to dominate American higher education had won against the forces of the skeptical Enlightenment.[21] In their own view, this victory was through force of argument. Modern science and rationality, they argued at length to their students, were really on the side of Christianity and the Bible. Scottish epistemology reinforced strategies that had already taken firm hold. The two most common texts were Bishop Joseph Butler's *The*

Analogy of Religion, Natural and Revealed (1736) and William Paley's *Natural Theology* (1802). Both authors were ardent empiricists. Each argued, as was common to the era, that empirical questions must be settled by accumulating evidences that, like the many strands that make a rope, would establish an inescapable probability that amounted to virtual certainty.[22]

Mark Hopkins, famed teacher at Williams College in Massachusetts, provides a classic compilation of such arguments in his own textbook on *Evidences of Christianity* (1846). "If God has made a revelation in one mode," he says, echoing Bishop Butler, "it must coincide with what he has revealed in another." If Christianity was true, it would harmonize with the other facts of the universe. Standing on this ground, Hopkins claimed to show that "the Christian religion admits of certain proof." Human sinfulness, which creates a moral resistance to Christianity's claims, can blind us or at least incline us toward skepticism, but such prejudices can be put aside if we look at the evidence "in the position of an impartial jury." "This course alone," says Hopkins in typical Baconian rhetoric, "decides nothing on the grounds of previous hypothesis, but yields itself entirely to the guidance of the facts properly authenticated."[23]

Hopkins proceeds with a long series of arguments, both from Nature and from Scripture, cumulatively strengthening the case for Christianity. The moral nature of humans, for instance, makes it as unlikely that the Creator would not provide a revelation that speaks to our moral needs as it would be to create an "eye without light." So, says Hopkins, just as a key is adopted to a lock, the wing to a bird, or a fin to a fish, "Christianity, I hope to show, is adapted to man." Such proofs are confirmed by evidences such as the miracles of Scripture, prophecy fulfilled, and the high moral character of the patriarchs and Apostles who witnessed these things. These proofs, and much other evidence, creates a "moral certainty" of the truth of Christianity, that is, a conclusion based on empirical grounds as compelling as those that could settle matters of life and death in a court of law.[24] Objective science, then, was the best friend of the faith.

Few collegians could sit in a classroom with Mark Hopkins, but many would learn much the same lessons from the most influential textbook writer of the era, Francis Wayland. President of Brown from 1827 to 1855, Wayland was another of the quintessential moral philosophers of the era. His textbooks included *The Elements of Political Economy*, *The Elements of Intellectual Philosophy*, and *The Elements of Moral Science*, our best source detail on the typical capstone courses on moral philosophy.

Wayland was a Whig prophet for economic growth and for practical education suitable to technologically advanced modern times, but he also emphasized that these were worth nothing without an increase in virtue. So he wrote in the era's most popular college text on *Political Economy*, "intellectual cultivation" will only "stimulate desire, and this unrestrained by the love of right, must eventually overturn the social fabric which it at first erected." Religion, then, was necessary to the equation. "No nation can rapidly accumulate or long enjoy the means of happiness, except as it is pervaded by the love of individual and social right; but the love of individual and social right will never prevail, without the practical influence of the motives and sanctions of religion; and these motives and sanctions will never influence men, unless they are, by human effort, brought to bear upon the conscience."[25]

A New England Baptist and president of Brown University, Wayland was thoroughly connected with the network of Presbyterian and Congregational educators. A graduate of Andover Theological Seminary, he had earlier studied at the "Presbygational" Union College in New York under the tutelage of the legendary Eliphalet Nott. Nott, who served an incredible sixty-four years as president of Union, from 1802 to 1866, was renowned for his extraordinary influence as an advocate of college reform. At Union he pioneered the idea of developing a parallel science-oriented track for the Bachelor of Arts degree. Wayland, as a protege of Nott, likewise championed more practically and scientifically oriented options in the curriculum.[26]

Wayland combined science and revelation in the way that was typical of the era, as complementary avenues to truth. Scientific observation was reliable, but truths of special revelation needed to be added. Wayland connected these through repeated reminders that all truth, as well as our ability to apprehend it, came from the Creator. The laws of the universe, whether physical or moral laws, were simply matters of cause and effect, "sequences connected by our Creator." From careful science, therefore, we could derive principles, not only for personal morality, but for sciences like political economy. Personal industry, for instance, should be rewarded. Laws of the market should be allowed to operate freely, rewarding people duly for their labor. Such economic laws, which bore a striking resemblance to those formulated by Adam Smith,[27] could be discovered simply by scientific observations, that is, "on merely economical ground." Ultimately, however, the reason our science could discover such truth was that both our minds and the economic laws were part of a created order.[28]

Wayland had, as was common in this era, great confidence in science, technology, and progress, yet he saw these as confirming rather than threatening his biblicist Protestant faith. As Daniel Walker Howe has pointed out, Protestantism was, in the view of Wayland and many of his peers, one of the great engines driving the amazing advances of civilization. In the case of the United States, the combination of Protestant promotion of literacy with innovation of technology, especially for mass print culture and in transportation, was raising standards of living on a wide scale. In contrast to Catholic countries that suppressed modern ideas, Protestant educators had the opportunity and the duty to promote the "means for elevating universally the intellectual and moral character of our people." Protestant American ideals of freedom and self-development ultimately came from the Bible. The United States thus had a destiny to become a leader in promoting the advance of civilization throughout the world.[29]

In the short run, the Whig Protestant synthesis of science, universal common sense, cultural progress, and moral advance, and the authority of biblical revelation, proved something of a triumph in the intellectual life of mid-nineteenth-century America. Evangelical Protestants had effectively taken over the Jeffersonian claims to scientific authority and had also captured the initiative in shaping national educational standards. Biblicist Protestantism and enlightenment, they boldly affirmed, went hand in hand.

This intellectual stance fit exactly with evangelical Protestant efforts to Christianize America. In the absence of state establishments of religion, evangelicals were entrenching themselves as a voluntary religious establishment. Standing for republican values, for Christian morality, and in the forefront of industrial and economic progress, they presented a cultural outlook to which all Americans might be expected to assimilate. With objective science seemingly on their side, their case could be overwhelmingly persuasive. Science, moreover, promised to be a powerful force for cultural unity, since eventually all educated persons should agree with its conclusions.

In the long run, however, the claims to ground the distinctive aspects of biblicist Christianity on science and a universal commonsense epistemology put traditional Protestantism in a most vulnerable position. While evangelical Christians controlled much of the culture's intellectual life, they also confidently proclaimed that they would follow the scientific consensus wherever it would lead. Yet the Western European intellectual community was fast-moving in reaction to the hegemony of Christian establishments.[30] Once natural science took the step of operating without the implicit assumption of a creator, its findings would be as uncongenial to traditional Christianity as were its new premises. The American evangelicals' faith in the objectivity of empirical science provided no preparation for such a shift. While in the 1850s a Mark Hopkins or Francis Wayland could make compelling statements about how scientific findings would always confirm biblical revelation, within a generation such claims would look like bravado.

5

The John the Baptist of the German
University Ideal

Francis Wayland's outlook, representative as it was of many of the leading educators of the era, stood solidly in the British common-sense tradition. Yet the mid-nineteenth century was also an era of romanticism. American romanticism bloomed later than most of its European counterparts, and in Wayland's era its most prominent representatives, such as transcendentalist Ralph Waldo Emerson and other literary figures, operated outside the traditional Protestant collegiate circles. Yet there were some romantic strains, not only in the philosophies of some of the educators, but more broadly in their immense faith in cultural and spiritual progress. Many of them were "postmillennialists," believing that human history would culminate in a golden age that was the "millennium" spoken of in Scripture, after which Christ would return to institute a "new heaven and a new earth." That teaching fit with more popular optimistic American outlooks, such as America's "manifest destiny," which justified its vast territorial expansion during the era. In all, their faith in the American spirit, including its accompanying material advances, might be seen as a sort of homegrown Hegelianism without Hegel.

Even though such ideas of progress were already in place, the transformation of American colleges into modern universities that would transpire in the next generation was inspired, in part, directly by the romantic German university idea. It is difficult to measure the exact impact of German models on American higher education. One thing that most interpreters agree on, however, is that neither German ideals nor educational models were imported without major adjustments to the American setting.[1] Americans stood in awe of the German universities. Eighteenth-century German universities had taken the lead on the European continent, and, especially after the establishment of the University of Berlin by Prussia in 1810, had moved to world preeminence. For Americans, who in university building were behind just about every European country, an appeal to a German precedent could be an intimidating argument.

The Soul of the American University Revisited. George M. Marsden, Oxford University Press. © Oxford University Press 2021. DOI: 10.1093/oso/9780190073312.003.0009

The most direct influence was that in the days before America had modern universities German universities served as their graduate schools. Between 1815 and 1914 about nine to ten thousand Americans studied in Germany. In the mid-nineteenth century that trend was only beginning, but it would soon accelerate. Throughout the rest of the nineteenth century it would be rare to find either a university leader or a major scholar who had not spent some time studying in Germany.[2]

Early nineteenth-century romantic German outlooks celebrated original creative "discovery." Influenced by Immanuel Kant's "Copernican Revolution," they saw the mind as an active creator more than a passive receiver, so the "research ideal" that came to be associated with the German universities developed not simply in the natural sciences but largely in the humanities. In the late eighteenth and early nineteenth centuries the flagship scientific discipline was philology, which explored the history of ancient languages. This emphasis, in turn, reflected a growing historical consciousness, or a sense that things could be understood best in terms of their development.[3] The broad implication was that intellectual inquiry was not directed primarily to the discovery of fixed verities but, rather, to ideals as they developed in a cultural context. As in the influential philosophy of Hegel, history might be seen as driven by progressing spiritual ideals that could be realized by evolving cultures and individuals.

The German version of the scientific research ideal, accordingly, was not a celebration of cold abstract analysis. Rather, German science, or *Wissenschaft*, was to take place within the context of philosophical idealism and could contribute to the larger humanistic goal of *Bildung*. Sometimes translated as cultivation, *Bildung* suggested the ideal of education as building character or "untrammeled personal development of personal powers and faculties to some kind of transcendental fulfillment."[4]

The new learning and the universities that embodied it were thus truly to be liberating to the race. They were seen as the keys to the progress of humanity, especially spiritual progress. In the new idealist philosophy learning took on a redemptive quality. Johann Gottlieb Fichte, the most influential of the university theorists associated with the model university established at Berlin in 1810, made this implication explicit:

The University . . . is the institution . . . where each generation hands on . . . its highest intellectual education to the succeeding generation. . . . All this, however, is solely with the intention that the divine may ever appear in the human in fresh clearness. . . . Now if the university is this, it is clear that it is the most holy thing which the human race possesses. Since the education given there preserves . . . and hands on everything divine that ever burst forth in mankind, the real nature of mankind lives there in its uninterrupted life, far above everything transitory; and the University is the visible representation of the immortality of our race.[5]

In the United States, Henry P. Tappan (1805–1881), president of the University of Michigan from 1852 to 1863, has been rightly called "the John the Baptist" of the age of the American university.[6] Although Tappan did not see all his ideals realized in the fledgling State of Michigan, he did establish the university as a leader in the American West.

Tappan had the full pedigree of the dominant circle of educational leaders of his era. He was, like Wayland, one of the distinguished protégés of Eliphalet Nott at Union College. He was also a graduate of Auburn Theological Seminary, and an ordained New School Presbyterian minister. Though an advocate of Common Sense philosophy, Tappan was a representative of the popular mid-century variant, which fused trust in Common Sense with idealism. Like many American thinkers of his day, Tappan rhapsodized about Scotland's Sir William Hamilton, who had forged what was thought to be a compelling synthesis of Scottish and German thought, especially that of Kant.[7] Tappan's own major scholarly work was a treatise attempting to refute Jonathan Edwards's on *The Freedom of the Will*. Tappan was relatively optimistic about natural human powers, and human freedom was a central motif of his thought.[8]

Tappan described his educational goals, which he contrasted directly to Wayland's practicality, as "philosophical and ideal."[9] Rather than "fitting our colleges to the temper of the multitude,"[10] education needed leadership from wise men at the top, who could cultivate the best of human potential. He wrote, "This conception of education is not that of merely teaching men a trade, an art, or a profession; but that of quickening and informing souls with truths and knowledges [sic], and giving them the power of using all their faculties aright in whatever they choose to exert them."[11] Or even more ideally, and seeming to echo Fichte, "the true end of Learning, the genuine fruit of knowledge is the development of the human soul that it may become wise, pure and godlike—that it may reach that perfection which is the ultimate ground of its existence."[12]

Another lesson that Tappan brought from Prussia was that educational reform should come from the state. German universities were strongly controlled by the various German states. Rather than being restrictive, state control could be seen as a way of guaranteeing a measure of academic freedom, that is, freedom could be limited by the interests of the state, rather than by more local or sectarian interests. In Prussia, for instance, professors, by being designated as civil servants, gained an immunity against arbitrary dismissal, which amounted to academic tenure. An enlightened state ministry could also promote excellence in universities and hence promote the interests of the state, by appointing distinguished professors who would attract students. In Prussia, idealism played a role in this state leadership. The state existed for the development of the culture, or of the spiritual essence of a people. Universities symbolized this grand cultural ideal. Such idealism ultimately was not impractical. The universities strengthened the state by training bureaucrats, professionals, and researchers who would serve society.[13]

Tappan had spent time in Europe studying the German universities, and he had an almost mystical reverence for the Prussian model, which he hoped would be applied to Michigan. The current American four-year college degree, he thought, was roughly equivalent to the German gymnasium course and should be so designated. This preliminary education ought to be completed by three more years of true "university" study in which students attended the lectures of advanced faculties, who were truly specialists in their fields. The analogy to Prussia could hardly be made exact in the American setting, but Tappan did establish a foothold for the ideal in Ann Arbor.[14]

While Tappan's proposals for major structural reforms met many obstacles, he did succeed in planting at Michigan the ideal that he saw as the key to European universities—a great university was made up of a great faculty. "What is needed for a great university?" asked Tappan. "There is but one reply—scholars and books. . . . Of all mere human institutions there are none so important and mighty in their influences as Universities; because, when rightly constituted, they are made up of the most enlightened, and the choicest spirits of our race."[15] Tappan had a great man view of history and thought that he was one.[16] He also worked hard at bringing other scholars to Michigan. The essential criterion was that they had to be professionals. This was the most fundamental lesson that Americans absorbed from studying in Germany, and Tappan was one of the first to attempt to implement it consistently: "However amiable his character, however pure his religious or political creed according to the judgement of any sect or party, if he have not the requisite literary or scientific qualifications, he is of no account."[17] Though Tappan did not immediately make Michigan into a great university, his ideals had wide influence. Four of his faculty later became college presidents. The best known is Andrew Dickson White, whom we shall soon meet again as the founder of Cornell University and who attributed many of his views to Tappan's influence.[18]

The University of Michigan under Tappan also had striking success in attracting students. By the eve of the Civil War well over six hundred were enrolled, tripling its size from when he had arrived and making it one of the largest schools in the nation.[19]

Tappan had definite ideas about the relation of religion to the university. Essentially a broad-minded evangelical, Tappan assumed that the university would be broadly Christian and even Protestant, as was his Prussian model. He supported the university requirement that all students attend a Sunday service, he regularly led the required daily university chapel, and he offered voluntary Sunday afternoon lectures, open to the public, on moral philosophy or natural theology. He supported voluntary student religious organizations at Michigan,[20] which had one of the nation's first collegiate YMCAs, then evangelical organizations. Tappan further hoped that various denominations would establish theological faculties in Ann Arbor, since he believed that theological faculties were integral to a true university and denominational differences at the state school itself could be avoided in this way.[21]

Tappan was vehemently opposed to any sectarianism at the university. When he arrived at Michigan he was appalled to discover that there was an informal agreement among the leading Protestant denominations to keep a balanced representation on the faculty by having various "chairs" that should be filled from each denomination. This arrangement was apparently an effort to compensate for the fact that the state, reflecting some earlier Jeffersonian influences, attempted to discourage the proliferation of sectarian colleges by not granting them the formal power to grant degrees. Tappan agreed that there was no need for sectarian colleges. The American majority, he argued, should be consistent in its educational views. Since they were insisting against Catholics that the common schools could be nonsectarian, how could they turn around and demand that they must have sectarian higher education? University policy should be consistently nonsectarian. So Tappan brought an end to the denominational chair scheme, pointing out that Catholics, Unitarians, Universalists, and others would soon be claiming chairs as well.

In his view, except where there were theological faculties, sectarian teachings simply had no place in a university.[22]

Tappan held a two-realm view of scientific and biblical truth. He was a believer in the Bible, but he also emphasized that scientific thought demanded complete freedom of inquiry. Like most of the evangelicals of mid-century, he assumed that the conclusions of free science and of proper biblical interpretation would eventually harmonize. In the meantime one could live with some apparent differences.[23] The overriding point in his mind was that neither the Bible nor theological dogma should be the starting point for philosophical or scientific inquiry. Nonetheless, he reassured, Christianity could still come into the college experience in less formal ways. It could appear "by graceful and apt episodes in the class room when the subject naturally suggests them; by employing scientific truths to illustrate natural theology; by the easy familiarity of daily converse opened by the relation of the teacher to the pupil; . . . [various displays of personal concern or counseling;] . . . and by the exercise of all those tender charities which are as remote from sectarian bigotry, [as] they are near the vital heart of Christianity."[24]

Tappan's opposition to sectarian bigotry was reinforced by historical analysis, always a prominent aspect of his educational discourses. Tappan had been originally recommended to the Michigan regents by George Bancroft, the first major American historian with German training. Like Bancroft's celebrations of the rise of democracy in his *History of the United States*, Tappan's educational history was the story of the rise of freedom. "Freedom," he proclaimed, "—this is the grand characteristic of University Education, as it is the essential attribute of manhood."[25]

Universities, particularly Protestant universities, played a leading role in the history of human freedom. The "Scholasticism" of the founders of European universities "was really a struggle of the human mind for freedom and enlargement of thought against the authorities of the Church and the State." But they did not go far enough. "The great error of the Schoolmen lay in receiving both their religious dogmas and their philosophical systems upon authority." The evils of scholastic dogmatism survived even to the present day. For instance, the English universities were still "paralyzed by high-church influence" and "still feel the incubus of the old Scholasticism, and reap the effects of the changes introduced by the Chancellorship of Laud."[26]

Where universities had succeeded, on the other hand, was primarily in the Protestant lands. In "Protestant Germany" and to some extent Scotland, "freedom and independence" were coming to prevail.[27] Although Luther was a contributor to freeing people from the tyranny of church dogma, Protestantism by itself did not press the principle to its conclusion. Rather, it was one great man, Francis Bacon, who was at first the solitary prophet of the new ideal. Just as "the divine religion made its advent in the solitary Jesus of Nazareth," so Bacon's views progressed from a few admirers to the current era of "the beginning of association preparatory to the universal diffusion of knowledge." A great new era of intellectual freedom was about to dawn: "The third period is that in which association will be perfected, and the universal diffusion of knowledge take place. In Universities we have the association which in the end creates common schools, or schools for the people."[28] The Kingdom of God was at hand.

Though Tappan's fate was not as dramatic as John the Baptist's, his demise as an educator was almost as sudden. The state regents had long been struggling with the chancellor for control. On June 24, 1863, they caucused secretly and the next day in regular session voted Tappan's dismissal. Tappan's pretensions to greatness apparently had alienated many people. The Democratic press relentlessly accused him of being an elitist, which he was. The religious denominations resented him because he had attacked their influence in the university. To make matters worse, Tappan, true to his European tastes, served wine with meals and did not object to students drinking beer (thus anticipating one of the most lasting components of the modern university). This stance, in days of ardent temperance sentiments, lost him Republican friends. The result was that he had few allies. Tappan accepted his defeat quietly and retired to Europe, where he spent his last two decades in exile. His last words to the Michigan regents were: "The pen of history is held by the hand of Almighty Justice, and I fear not the record it will make of my conduct."[29]

PART II

DEFINING THE UNIVERSITY
IN A SCIENTIFIC ERA

The Protestant colleges of the mid-nineteenth century would have been readily recognizable to the founders of Harvard two centuries earlier. Chapel services were still regular parts of the day. Classical texts shaped much of the curriculum. Clergy dominated college leadership. Professors and tutors taught a variety of subjects. They were concerned for student piety and attempted to control student behavior largely by coercion. Almost all colleges were for white boys only.

Despite these striking continuities, American collegiate education had also evolved in substantial, though subtle, ways. The subtlety of these changes within the inherited institutional framework hid the potential for the quantum leap from old-time college to modern university within one generation following the Civil War. Pressured by a changing environment, the potentiality for transformation into a whole new species had been building for at least a century within the apparent equilibrium of the old system. During that time, gradual but momentous shifts taking place in their essential commitments made the modern colleges of the 1850s far different from their premodern, almost medieval, Harvard predecessor two centuries earlier.

With respect to religion, the most obvious modification was that the training of future clergy had been the strongest reason for maintaining colleges in early New England, but by the mid-nineteenth century concern for clerical education no longer was a primary defining feature. By far, the majority of collegians were preparing for other professions, and ministerial education itself had been shifted to divinity schools or separate theological seminaries.

The other more subtle major changes all had to do with accommodations to the demands of Enlightenment thought, emerging romantic ideals, and to the culture of the first modern nation. The reverence for scientific authority was the major intellectual manifestation of the new commitments. The corollary was that moral philosophy had replaced theology as the primary locus for defining collegiate Christian intellectual life. Theology, while never well integrated into collegiate curricula, long had played an important role in defining intellectual boundaries and in providing a point of reference for some intellectual inquiry. By the late colonial era, however, the demands to serve several Protestant constituencies had brought pressures against theological definitions of the enterprise. Theology remained a point of intellectual reference at most colleges, but often in a residual capacity. So the potential was already there for the distinctly Christian aspects of the intellectual enterprise to be jettisoned, or broadened into vestigial platitudes, without threatening any of the fundamental functions of the educational enterprise.

The intellectual changes were thus intimately related to the colleges' commitments to the American public. Colleges had to serve their immediate communities or regions and be responsive both to popular American ideologies and to practical needs. They were competitors in a free market economy in which by mid-century the struggle for survival was fierce.

While American colleges always had served both church and community, the character of public life had changed. In the seventeenth century the distinction between church and community was not always clear. An established church was part of public life, and a college was an extension of the church's public role. In nineteenth-century America such assumptions persisted among collegiate leaders, but, in fact, the constituencies that they were expected to serve were far more diverse than those of any one supporting church. Churches were only one component in an increasingly market-oriented cultural ethos in which the churches' public role was becoming superfluous.

The institutional framework that contained these potentialities and commitments—the so-called "old-time college"—was ready to give way to dramatic change. The old classicist education was outmoded and served a limited constituency. Not even all the presidents of the United States were college graduates. Americans were eager to be practical and up to date, and the colleges were scrambling to keep up, adding this and that scientific or practical offering into the cumbersome classicist curriculum. Only so much could be added, however, within the old structures. Little in the old system allowed for professional or specialized development. For graduate training one had to go abroad. The German university ideal shone especially brightly as an alternative to the parochial American realities.

The American Civil War released the energies necessary for these potentialities that had been building in American higher education, toward a dramatic metamorphosis. The Southern Secession and the war cleared the way
for the dominance of Republican reformers who combined commitment to
industrial expansion with moral idealism. A generation of younger men, almost all from the Northeast, had visions of replacing colleges with universities as the dominant structure of American higher education.

As in many American developments, there was no central plan. Although
the founders of the major universities knew each other well, each of their
universities had its distinctive character. Typically these schools reflected the
personalities of their founders, the "captains of erudition" as they were later
called. By surveying the outlooks and motivations of the foremost architects
of American universities, their schools, and leading faculty, as do the ensuing
chapters, we can piece together the crucial traits that converged in the dominant university culture that emerged by the twentieth century. In retrospect,
we can see at this pivotal moment in history just how vulnerable the traditionalist Protestant educational establishment had become. And it is a vul-
nerability all the more striking in the light of the extravagantly confident
rhetoric that often accompanied it. Such dramatic turning points, marking
the demise of an old regime and the rise of a new, can also be especially instructive for modern observers.

The old regime in American collegiate education had some admirable
qualities, but also some severe limitations. Sometimes students were
greatly inspired by a Mark Hopkins, a Francis Wayland, or other legendary
teachers. But by and large, ways of relating Christianity to the enterprise
were coercive and superficial. Colleges were small and elitist. Such faults
were, of course, characteristic of most of the institutions of the age. As in
most human arrangements, they were a mix of admirable and not-so-ad-
mirable qualities.

While most of the particular qualities of the old-time colleges disappeared
with the era, one of their important paradoxical qualities survived, even if
in changing forms. This is that most leaders of higher education who were
concerned with its religious character did not make much of a distinction
between the notion of a Protestant and that of an ideal American. Such an
outlook was justified, in part, by seeing a leading part of their duty as helping
provide the needed moral dimensions to the national enterprise. Antebellum
educators saw that America's amazing economic growth ought to be tempered by charity. And though academic leaders were seldom radical, they

favored moral reforms. Francis Wayland, for instance, argued eloquently for gradual abolition of slavery.[1]

What they did not see clearly was just how much the pact they were making with the spirit of American progress was costing. True, Protestant leaders might help shape mainstream American culture, and it seems laudable enough that they saw it as their duty to do so. In fact, mainstream Protestantism, dependent as it was on the voluntary assent of its constituents, needed some accommodations to prevailing values if it was to continue to thrive. Yet at the same time, the values, assumptions, economic pressures, and national aspirations of middle-class capitalist and enlightened America were reshaping Protestant outlooks at least as much as distinctly Christian concerns were infusing American growth. The two sorts of influences were, indeed, so intertwined, or, perhaps one might say, like tares sowed among wheat, that they were impossible to sort out clearly. In any case, as might be expected, mainstream Protestant educational leaders, many of whom were, indeed, clergymen, were more likely to play priestly rather than prophetic roles amid their surrounding culture.

6

The Christian Legacy in the Age of Science

In December 1869 Andrew Dickson White, the young president of the new Cornell University, delivered a memorable address at the Cooper Union in New York City. That venue was famed as that at which Abraham Lincoln had in 1860 presented the most decisive speech of his presidential campaign. Lincoln's Cooper Union Address proved to be a precursor to terrible warfare. White, speaking after that war, titled his address "The Battlefields of Science" and used the metaphor to announce that another sort of war had long been going on, that of religion against scientific inquiry. This war was being fought "with battles fiercer, with sieges more persistent, with strategy more vigorous than in any of the comparatively petty warfares of Alexander, or Caesar, or Napoleon."[1] White, who had declared that Cornell would be "an asylum for science" and, indeed, was fending off some criticisms for opposing religious tests for his faculty, was depicting such critiques as just the latest in the assaults of religious dogmatists against free inquiry. In retrospect, White and his allies, especially the new Darwinians in England, were constructing a version of history as an intellectual warfare. White's friend Andrew Greeley published the address the next day in *The New York Tribune*. The metaphor caught on. In England Thomas H. Huxley, "Darwin's bulldog," pressed the image, and in 1874 Thomas Draper offered his *History of the Warfare between Religion and Science*. White himself spent the next quarter-century developing the theme in a series of publications culminating in *History of the Warfare of Science and Theology* (1896). By that time the warfare metaphor had been established as one of the principal ways to see the relationship between modern science and traditional Christianity.

In the American Protestant collegiate world, as we have seen, such a construction was a dramatic reversal of the way the history had been understood. Whiggish Protestants taught that their religion had been the chief engine in challenging Catholic dogmatism by unleashing the spirit of free inquiry, modern science, and progress. White and others were turning the tables on that construction. They were throwing dogmatic biblicist versions of Protestantism on the defensive. Protestants who aspired to maintain their cultural leadership would have to broaden their understandings of Christianity to remain in touch with the progressive spirit of the age. White himself, an Episcopal in affiliation and professing to stand for the true spirit of Christianity, remarked, "The very finger of the Almighty has written on history that science must be studied by means proper to itself, and in no other way."[2]

What made the new assaults on dogmatism especially effective was, of course, the advent of Darwinism. In England, the appearance of *On the Origin of Species* in 1859 came just at a moment when forces were already building against the traditional religious establishment. Resentments concerning the injustices of traditional church privilege were especially strong regarding the leading universities, Oxford and Cambridge, where assent to the Thirty-nine Articles was required for matriculation and university positions were limited to Anglicans. Meanwhile, while the university reforms that would dislodge that conservative regime were ongoing, within the Church of England itself, progressive Broad Church clergy had been pressing for liberal biblical criticism highlighted by the controversies over the notorious *Essays and Reviews* of 1860. Other prominent thinkers were moving beyond Christianity. Freethinkers such as Thomas Huxley, who coined the word "agnostic," were especially eager to push the battle against the "Bibliolaters." Those who were most enthusiastic in endorsing Darwinism welcomed it as a weapon in these ongoing battles against the entrenched conservative religious establishment. As Huxley put it in a review of *Origins* in 1860, "Every philosophical thinker hails it as a veritable Whitworth gun in the armoury of liberalism."[3]

In the United States, such forces for change had been inhibited in the antebellum era by the strength of Biblicist evangelicalism, and then debates over Darwinism were delayed by the Civil War itself. Yet the war, fought on both sides in the name of the biblical God, had in the victorious North a decidedly secularizing effect. While in the South defeat sealed Antebellum-style evangelical Christianity as integral to the cult of the lost cause, in the North the efficient wartime mobilization helped accelerate an era of economic growth. And the extravagant rhetoric of wartime righteousness soon came to look hollow in light of the stark conditions of industrial and urban society. The Republican Party, which had originated in part to represent the conscience of the nation, now was the party of the giant corporations. In short, the evangelical golden age gave way to the industrial Gilded Age.

Simultaneously, a number of major cultural forces were converging that would bring the end of the old biblicist evangelical colleges and the transition to the era of the modern universities. One of the most significant of these was economic expansion that was accelerating during the war era, through the Gilded Age, and beyond. Such expansion fueled the demand that higher education serve not just the professions but also the state in its scientific, technological, agricultural, and corporate cultures, hence the founding by the federal government of practically oriented land grant universities as a result of the Morrill Land Grant Act of 1862. As in the case of Andrew White's Cornell, that base could be expanded into building a broader scientifically based institution.

Economic changes were accompanied by demographic changes. During this era, the United States was becoming a less Protestant nation. That was already apparent when Catholic immigrants began surging in during the mid-1800s. After the Civil War in an increasingly urban America, that current would become a flood. In part because Catholics had their own colleges, immigration did not immediately have a great impact in mainstream American schools of the later nineteenth century. Jewish presence and also that of freethinkers occasionally had to be taken into account. Protestant and sectarian varieties were always increasing. State schools, while still broadly Protestant, had to at least consider how to deal with this growing cultural diversity. Prestigious private schools that were not strictly denominational but aspired to serve the whole culture also had to consider the implications of diversity that went beyond varieties of Protestants and unbelievers.

Henry Tappan, who had a good eye for talent, had brought Andrew Dickson White to teach at Michigan in 1857. White, in turn, always revered Tappan as the founder of the modern American university and honored some of his ideals. Particularly, he was, like Tappan, intensely dedicated to science and saw it as opposed to sectarianism and as the key to human freedom. White viewed Tappan as having been destroyed by sectarian attacks at Michigan, and the younger man would be preoccupied throughout his career by the menace of sectarianism.[4]

White, like Tappan, opposed sectarianism in the name of Christianity, but with an important difference. While Tappan was a more or less orthodox New School Presbyterian, White always had a broader conception of Christianity. Reared in the Episcopal Church, White retained something of the High Church disdain for evangelicals. Yet he rejected Episcopal sectarianism just as firmly. His father had insisted that he attend tiny Geneva College (now Hobart) in New York State. Andrew found the churchly atmosphere intolerably stifling. Early in his sophomore year he walked out of Geneva and soon transferred to Yale. Though he was more satisfied with Yale, he viewed it as far from ideal educationally and essentially sectarian. Rather than reject Christianity, White adopted a liberal version of it, crediting Unitarians William Ellery Channing and Theodore Parker with strengthening his faith.[5] Parker taught, for instance, that whereas the external forms of religion might change, a permanent essence of pure religion and pure morality underlay all particular dogmas.

As a gentleman with no clear plans upon graduation in 1853, White settled on accompanying his Yale friend Daniel Coit Gilman as an unpaid attaché to the American diplomatic mission in Russia. While abroad, White enrolled for lectures in history, art, and literature at the University of Berlin, thus sampling the renowned German universities, an enterprise that was becoming almost mandatory for aspiring American scholars. The experience was sufficient for him to decide on a scholarly career.

Apparently hoping to improve his chances for employment at Yale, White returned to New Haven to receive a Master of Arts degree, which was still a perfunctory degree granted after three years to virtually any graduate who paid a fee.[6] While there he was inspired by a remark by the visiting Francis Wayland (who by then had been largely frustrated in his attempts at grand reforms in the East) that the future of American education lay in the West. White applied to Tappan's Michigan and was hired.

In the fall of 1863, during a long leave of absence from Michigan to care for his health, White was elected to the New York Senate. He immediately took an interest in education in New York, his home state, and especially hoped to implement a long-standing dream of building a model university. In the New York Senate White found a congenial spirit in the wealthy Ezra Cornell. Cornell, a self-made man, had drifted from the Quakerism in which he had been reared and developed a sort of homegrown deism that limited his formal religious options to the Unitarian Society, which he attended as a nonmember. He had, if anything, more antipathy than White to evangelical religion, which he considered the height of unreason. Nonetheless, he also believed in a deity who guaranteed and affirmed human progress. "I have no doubt," he wrote in a letter to his wife, "that God's first and unalterable design was good will to man." "But the gospel as it is preached," he wrote in another letter, "falls more like a mildew upon a benighted world, and tries to shield the deformities of the dead and putrid carcass of 'the Church' from the penetrating eye of advancing science and humanity. . . . The steam engine, the railroad and the electric telegraph are the great engines of reformation, and by the time we enter upon the twentieth century the present will be looked back to as we now look back to the dark ages. . . . A new era in religion and humanity will have arrived."[7]

White and Cornell found the opportunity to join their somewhat disparate ideals for the modern university as a result of the momentous Morrill Land Grant Act of 1862. This act represented the culmination of popular agitation for higher education in the mechanical and agricultural arts, a proposal that promised to help make the United States competitive in economic and industrial development. The cause was part of the emerging Republican agenda to develop the nation industrially and morally. "We want a seminary," inveterate reformer Horace Greeley declared in 1858, "which provides as fitly and thoroughly for the education of the Captains of Industry as Yale or Harvard does for those who are dedicated to either of the Professions."[8] In 1858 the act had been passed by Congress but vetoed by President Buchanan as an unconstitutional infringement of the federal government. With the Southern states absent in 1862, the way was cleared for passage of the act, which was signed by Lincoln on July 2, 1862. The act provided for the proceeds from large tracts of public land to go to the establishment and support of colleges of agricultural and mechanical arts.[9]

Initially it was not at all clear precisely how the funds should be distributed, whether they should go to one or to several institutions, or whether they should go to existing schools or to newly established ones. Nothing prevented the funds from being used at schools with liberal arts programs as well as the more utilitarian ones. States handled the issue in various ways, many eventually establishing a separate state agricultural and mechanical school, typically the "state" university, such as Ohio State, Michigan State, or Iowa State. Some states also used the funding to support or expand existing programs or scientific schools.

Andrew White was convinced that New York needed to concentrate its university-building energies in one place and persuaded Ezra Cornell to fund such a school in Ithaca. The new university would have both liberal arts and practical programs. By 1868 it was ready to open with over four hundred students. White had designed multiple degree tracks for practical subjects, such as agriculture, mechanical arts, engineering, mining, and medicine. There also was a general track, with or without classics. All programs were treated as equal. Under some pressure from Catharine Beecher and others to prove their liberality, White and Cornell agreed to include women on a regular basis beginning in 1872.[10]

From the outset, opposition to sectarianism was a major theme of the university. As soon as the Cornell plan was formulated, denominational colleges led the opposition in the New York legislature, hoping to gain the public funds themselves. When Cornell announced its opening they quickly tagged it as "godless." White immediately counterattacked, claiming the now venerable distinction between Christian and sectarian. "We will labor to make this a Christian institution," he proclaimed in his inaugural, "—a sectarian institution it may never be." In what was to become his characteristic manner, White recounted the evils of sectarianism. As was already common in Massachusetts, White used the evils of the Puritan heritage to batter sectarianism. "From the days when Henry Dunster, the first president of the first college in America, was driven from his seat with ignominy and with cruelty because Cotton Mather declared him 'fallen into the briars of anti-paedo-baptism,' the sectarian spirit has been the worst foe of enlarged university education." Anticipating words later enshrined as the shibboleth of the movement by Harvard's Charles Eliot at the Johns Hopkins inaugural in 1876 ("A university can not be built upon a sect"), White proclaimed, "I deny that any university fully worthy of that great name can ever be founded upon the platform of any one sect or combination of sects."[11] Ezra Cornell made the same point with succinct railroad imagery: "It shall be our aim, and our constant effort to make true Christian men, without dwarfing or paring them down to fit the narrow gauge of any sect."[12]

White seldom missed an opportunity to point out that Cornell University was indeed a Christian institution. Concerns about public relations no doubt provided the immediate motives for such expressions, yet they were not entirely alien to White's personal outlook. Although he was never confirmed, White attended Episcopal services and often professed a broad religious commitment. He wrote in a private letter, for instance, that "whatever my heterodoxies I do believe in a higher power who controls human affairs for good."[13]

This broad identification of Christianity with humanism, in the sense of whatever promotes human welfare, was reflected in university policy. Chapel was not required at Cornell (though, as at all land grant colleges, military training initially was), but White was proud to point out that religious services were held daily. Moreover, he welcomed the Christian Association and gladly accepted a gift to build a substantial chapel on campus and to introduce the novelty of filling the pulpit with leading preachers from a variety of denominations. In 1872 White offered a pamphlet, "The Cornell University: What It Is and What It Is Not," in which he argued at length for its Christian character. Again the definition was broad. "The Cornell University is governed by a body of Christian Trustees, conducted by Christian Professors, and is a Christian Institution," wrote White, "as the Public School system of the State is Christian."[14] The analogy in the last clause was revealing.

There were limits to what public relations could stand. In 1874, the university accepted a gift for the purpose of hiring Felix Adler to teach Hebrew and Oriental literature. It was, indeed, a progressive move to hire a Jew, though there had been precedents at American colleges for the teaching of Hebrew. Adler, who founded the Ethical Culture Society in 1876, however, was a different case. Adler used his courses directly to attack religious beliefs. In 1877 his contract was not renewed, ostensibly on the grounds that the university did not want to be controlled by donors who endowed chairs. In fact, whatever the sympathies of the university administration toward Adler, it could not afford to allow the accusation of harboring skepticism to be so openly confirmed.[15]

White regarded the university as having a moral mission and regarded "the sickly cynic" as the "most detestable" product of college life. To his friend Daniel Coit Gilman he wrote in 1884, "Why is it not possible in this country to have the great fundamental principles of . . . ethics . . . presented simply and strongly, so that we can send out into the country men who can bring simple ethical principles to bear upon public instruction everywhere?" Early in 1886 he received the endowment of a professorship from Russell Sage, which included the provision that the teacher "shall instruct students in mental philosophy and ethics from a definitely Christian standpoint." White did not object to Christianity being represented in the university, only to traditional Christian dogmatism. In his 1885 *Annual Report* he remarked, "Even error honestly arrived at will do more for religion and for science, than truth merely asserted dogmatically. . . . No talk about the *tendency* of any man's teaching should have any weight against him if he be capable and honest."[16]

By insisting that Cornell was Christian, nonsectarian, dedicated to high moral values, yet free, especially free for scientific inquiry, White was effectively taking over the rhetoric of the evangelical establishment. White particularly emphasized a Whiggish version of the rise of science, free inquiry, moral advance, and human betterment. In insisting on the importance of free inquiry for scientific progress White sounded essentially like his mentor, Henry Tappan. But in White's version nonsectarian Protestantism had been quietly dropped from the story and replaced by a broader Christianity or religion of humanity. White was a great admirer of Thomas Jefferson and, without saying it, brought the broad spirit of Jefferson to upstate New York.

7

Back to Noah Porter's Yale

The emerging ideals of the modern scientifically based university that Andrew Dickson White represented can be nicely contrasted with those of Noah Porter, one of the ablest defenders of preserving the essentials of the old order. By looking more closely at Porter's rationale for retaining the expressly "Christian" character of Yale College, we can understand better why, whatever the virtues of his arguments, there was little way that he could banish William Graham Sumner or the sorts of positivist scientific ideals Sumner and his ilk stood for and still keep Yale near the forefront of American higher education.

The announcement in the late 1860s that Yale's president, Theodore Dwight Woolsey, would retire in the spring of 1871 sparked excited speculations as to who would succeed him. Yale was the flagship evangelical college. It was near the center the network of Congregationalist and Presbyterian educators who were shaping much of the higher education in the West. It had been long in the forefront of national trends. Now Cornell had opened its doors in 1868, and in 1869 Harvard inaugurated President Charles Eliot, a relatively young man clearly in the progressive camp. Some Yale alumni started a "Young Yale" movement centered in New York[1] and called for a similar choice at their alma mater. The leading progressive candidate was Daniel Coit Gilman,[2] a Yale graduate, the principal administrative officer at Yale's Sheffield Scientific School and a close friend of Andrew Dickson White. Gilman had already turned down two college presidencies and was known to favor transforming the college into a true university. The conservative Yale Corporation, still virtually all Connecticut clergymen, chose instead Noah Porter, the college's professor of moral philosophy. Porter, aged sixty when he assumed the post, had been one of the leading figures during the recent decades of Yale's preeminence, was one of the preeminent clergymen moral philosophers, was a champion of the classical curriculum, and promised to preserve the old-time college ideal.

While in 1871 Porter looked like a conservative, he had been at midcentury among the New Haven scholars who were promoting moderately

The Soul of the American University Revisited. George M. Marsden, Oxford University Press. © Oxford University Press 2021. DOI: 10.1093/oso/9780190073312.003.0011

progressive reforms. As was becoming almost requisite, he had studied in Germany, most of his two years at the University of Berlin. Somewhat like Henry Tappan, Porter hoped to reconcile some German romantic ideals with an essentially orthodox Congregationalist Reformed theology. In the 1850s and 1860s, he and his colleagues at Yale had also introduced a degree of professionalization and specialization and established the Sheffield Scientific School, and Yale had even granted a few PhDs.

The Yale scholars also reflected the modern Whig ideals so prominent in mid-century New England.[3] They were forward-looking in favoring the advance of industry and science, yet they emphasized balancing material advance with simultaneous efforts to develop American character, both individually and communally. They could fuse that heritage with the German ideal of "Bildung." Shaping civilization was, as much as anything, a moral task. Morality, in turn, was essentially a matter of duty. So when Noah Porter taught moral science, he organized it around the subject of duty, including coverage of theories of duty and practical subjects such as various duties of self-discipline, and duties to others, to friends, to family, to the state, and even to animals and to the physical world, and of course, duty to God.[4]

The Idea of a Christian College

In 1869, as the frontrunner for the Yale presidency, Noah Porter published what amounted to his campaign platform in a series of lengthy articles in the *New Englander*, titled "The American Colleges and the American Public," later to be offered as a book. Although some disagreed with Porter's curricular conservatism, he was widely respected as a leading philosopher. He has even been characterized by one historian of American philosophy as "in many ways the greatest and most erudite of the professors of philosophy" of his day.[5] His reflections offer, then, the most sophisticated articulation of what it would mean for an institution to remain Christian as it faced an emerging new era of modernization and scientific authority.

Porter's principal concern was to preserve what he thought was excellent about the American undergraduate college as it was exemplified at mid-century Yale. So, for instance, he defended the classicism of the Yale Report of 1828, arguing on the broad grounds that the primary purpose of college education was "to give power to acquire and to think rather than to impart special knowledge." College was a place to learn valuable habits that would foster growth in later life. It would promote cultural development. Specialized information concerning physical or practical sciences had proper places in preparatory and graduate education. But there was a danger that these would crowd out the character-building purposes of undergraduate training. By now, he said, most colleges had made sufficient—"perhaps excessive"—concessions in the direction of the immediately practical.[6]

In his culminating essay Porter defended the proposition that "American Colleges should have a positively religious and Christian character." Some persons, he noted, said that since the goal of education is to inculcate culture, religion should be relegated to an indirect and incidental role. At the opposite extreme, others argued that religion was supreme, and culture might therefore be sacrificed to religion. Porter insisted that there need be no such tension. Religion and culture were perfectly complementary.

Porter characterized the contributions of Christianity to enlightened, tolerant, and civilized culture, essentially summarizing the Whig ideals. Christianity contributed to "*industry*," it was "*truth-loving*," and it was "*refining*" of culture. Culture could, indeed, refine Christianity also, but "culture itself is exposed to certain excesses for which Christianity is the only adequate counterpoise and remedy." It was needed "as a corrective against the one-sidedness, the Philistinism we might call it, of modern science and literature."

On the subject of modern science Porter seemed to be responding particularly to his former student Andrew Dickson White. In his recently published inaugural address White had depicted the evils of Christian dogmatism and proclaimed that no university "fully worthy of that great name can ever be founded upon the platform of any one sect or combination of sects." Porter, however, turned the tables on White by quoting the Cornell president's *Report on the Organization of Cornell University*, in which White mentioned that science itself had sectarian divisions. Porter, who emphasized that the sort of Christianity he stood for was "nonsectarian," suggested that such Christianity could help scientists rise above the narrow perspectives of their specialized disciplines. So to the claim that science was the highest road to nonsectarianism, he retorted that, in fact, "Christian science furnishes the natural and most efficient prophylactic and cure for ... sectarian narrowness and embitterments."[7]

Like other evangelical apologists Porter could proclaim that Christians had nothing to fear from modern science. Since truth seeking was all they were interested in, they could affirm open inquiry.[8] Such assurances grew out

of the evangelicals' experience of having been part of a cultural and intellectual establishment. It was an optimistic mood related to their Whig heritage
of cultural reform and their assurance that Christianity would lead to cultural progress.[9]

Porter, however, was sounding a more ominous note as well. He was well
enough informed about British and German trends to recognize that modern
culture might be turning against Christianity. The world of the 1840s and
1850s, when for Americans evangelicalism seemed to hold firm intellectual
sway, might be disappearing. Christianity therefore had to play a new kind
of defensive role. "Religious influences and religious teachings," he wrote in
his *New Englander* essay, "should be employed in colleges, in order to exclude
and counteract the atheistic tendencies of much of modern science, literature, and culture." Powerful currents from the international community of
which Yale was just an outpost were threatening to overwhelm the comfortable consensus. "Every educated man now a-days," Porter warned, "must either accept or reject the ill-disguised materialism of Huxley, the cerebralism
of Bain, the thin and vacillating metaphysics of Mill, the evolutionism of
Herbert Spencer, with its demonstrated impossibility of a positive theism,
and the serene fatalism of the devotees of Nature or of the Absolute."

Faced with the practical atheism of much of modern culture, there could
be no middle ground. These teachings, Porter pointed out, were not neutral
regarding religion but took definite theological positions. "The question is
not whether the college shall, or shall not, teach theology, but what theology
it shall teach,—theology according to Comte and Spencer, or according to
Bacon and Christ, theology according to Moses and Paul, or according to
Buckle and Draper."

The question of the openness of higher education looked entirely different
in this light. "The plea of freedom and tolerance is put in on every quarter,"
said Porter, but if that meant that these atheistic views were to be presented
without Christian refutation, the plea was deceptive. Not to answer atheistic
views was practically to promote them, which was beyond the pale of the
Christian college.

Surely advocates of anti-Christian outlooks should not be teaching impres-
sionable young people. "If all opinions should have a hearing, as they ought,"
Porter suggested, still claiming to stand for openness, "let theistic teachers
be selected who will represent fairly all the atheistic and anti-Christian
objections and difficulties, but let not atheism or anti-Christianity be taught
in any of its chairs, either directly or indirectly." This raised a question "of the

greatest delicacy." What should be the religious tests for teachers? The inability to resolve this issue was the point on which Porter's presidency would founder in his famous encounter with William Graham Sumner.

In May of 1880, the month after the *New York Times* had exposed Yale's controversy to the public view, Porter found an opportunity to reiterate his views in another sort of manifesto on "The Christian College." The talk was soon well circulated as a pamphlet.

The occasion was the ceremonies celebrating the laying of a cornerstone for the second building of Wellesley College. Wellesley had been founded in 1870 by Henry and Pauline Durant, ardent evangelical Christians. Henry Durant, who ran the college personally, made sure that everything about the institution proclaimed that, as its first announcement said, "The institution will be Christian in its influence, discipline, and course of instruction."[10] Extensive required Bible study supplemented the regular curriculum. Each of the professors, all women, would have to be able to teach such courses in addition to her regular offering.[11] Dwight L. Moody, a friend of the Durants who shared their religious style, in 1878 had joined the distinguished board of trustees, made up mostly of leading clergy and clergy-educators, who, like the faculty, were required to be members of an "Evangelical Church."[12] Noah Porter himself was president of the board.

Since the advent of women's college education in mid-nineteenth-century America, ardent evangelicals had been among those in the forefront, even if far from alone, as its advocates. In fact, proponents of women's collegiate education covered the spectrum of religious views. In 1837 Mary Lyon opened Mt. Holyoke Female Seminary, which was largely a Christian training center for teachers and missionaries, emphasizing religious conversions and service. The same year Oberlin College, headed by the ardent reform-minded evangelist, Charles Finney, became the first college to allow co-education. Catharine Beecher, one of the strongest advocates of equal education for women, spoke from a liberal Christian perspective. The University of Michigan under Henry Tappan had resisted co-education but adopted it in 1870, partly in response to prodding by the state legislature. Cornell and Andrew Dixon White came around in 1872. Meanwhile, a number of other Western schools had become co-educational. In general, openness to co-education was greater where there was not a long tradition of male-only higher education. In the East it was more common to found separate colleges for women. Between 1861 and 1875 Vassar, Smith, and Wellesley were founded with varying degrees of explicitly Christian emphasis.

All emphasized that women's education should be equivalent to men's. Wellesley, though, was the most evangelical. Henry Durant, who had served on the Mt. Holyoke board, was particularly influenced by that model. He wanted Wellesley to be a true college, but with the Holyoke missionary spirit.[13]

Porter thought that women's colleges should be Christian in the same way men's schools should. He shared the dominant middle-class views of his era concerning the two sexes. While on the one hand he affirmed that it was now proven that women were as able in every field as men, on the other he noted that in religious matters their greater sensibilities made them "superior to men." However, "these special endowments of the sex expose them, perhaps more, to unreasoning fanaticism and tenacious bigotry for any cause which they ardently espouse." Hence, for Porter the best Christian education for women, even more than for men, should be that which built habits of sound discipline.[14] Porter had long advocated that Christian education should build character.[15]

The real interest in Porter's address, however, was in what he might say that would bear the now-public controversy at Yale, and in that he did not disappoint. Responding implicitly to those such as Andrew Dixon White or "Darwin's bulldog," T. H Huxley, who declared that there was a warfare between Christianity and science, Porter proclaimed once again that Christians were, indeed, engaged in a warfare, not with science, but with secularism. The secular view was that education "must be free of all alliances with religion." It was crucial, therefore, that "Christianity must control the college in order to exclude its antagonist, or rival, in the form of some false religion." Atheism and the recently popularized agnosticism "are religious creeds as truly as are theism and dogmatic Christianity."

In this warfare there could be no neutrality. "Ethics, politics and social science suppose a decisive position to be taken one side or the other in respect to both theism and Christianity: even elementary treatises on these subjects teach a positive faith or as positive a denial." Similarly, instructors could not be neutral. Even if they claimed an objective stance, agnosticism might be taught "indirectly by gentle or sarcastic insinuation" or even "unconsciously . . . in subtle ways of impression even by an instructor who may honestly strive to withhold the slightest suggestion of his faith or his feelings."[16]

We can understand the limitations built into Porter's position if we see that he was caught between his two views of the relationship of Christianity to culture. On the one hand lay his Protestant-Whig view that there was no conflict between Christianity and the highest culture and that Protestantism stood for openness and free scientific inquiry. This was the establishment side of the ruling New England culture. To retain hegemony it had to be open enough to embrace and absorb all relevant views. On the other hand, the ominous turn that Porter saw advanced culture taking suggested that Christians would have to hold a more closed sectarian stance if they were to retain their distinctiveness.

Another way of putting it is that Porter was faced with a latter-day version of the Puritan dilemma of how to live in the world but not of it.[17] On the one hand, he had inherited the establishmentarian side of Puritanism, which assumed that Christians should dominate the culture. In the republican context of the nineteenth century such tendencies had merged with Whiggish ideals of liberty, moral reform, free scientific inquiry, and progress. On the other hand, Porter was heir to the sectarian side of Puritanism, which was still vigorous in New England theological debates. This side of the heritage emphasized the distinctiveness of Christian thought in opposition to all rivals. On this reading of the tradition New England provided a haven of purity against the corruptions of old-world rivals. The sectarian side of the heritage said that colleges should be bounded by doctrinal orthodoxy; the establishmentarian side said that they could not.

Porter attempted to resolve this dilemma by maintaining that there should be religious tests, but that they should be informal, left to the discretion of the college president who did the hiring. Sometimes the teacher with "honest doubts" would be preferable to the overbearing orthodox dogmatist. In some chairs, Porter thought, the religious views of the incumbent could not affect the teaching. In others, however, "an anti-Christian sophist or a velvet-footed infidel might pervert [it] to the most disastrous uses."

By thus making religious tests a matter of judgment of character more than of creed, the New Haven scholars could retain their stance of having moved beyond dogmatism. They could also claim to be "nonsectarian," meaning that the college should not stand narrowly for the views of one Protestant denomination as opposed to the others. They remembered well bitter controversies with rock-ribbed conservatives who insisted on creedal tests.[18] So they could hardly turn around and impose such tests, even if Christianity itself became culturally beleaguered. The only checks on infidelity would be the power of personal influence. That power, it seemed, would serve well enough for a time, so long as the right individuals remained in control.

Porter correctly recognized that the campaign for transformation from college to university threatened the maintenance of such personal control. The ideal of freedom, even if vague in its implications, was essential to the university. Porter, shaped in part by his time at the University of Berlin, conceded that wider room for free inquiry might be appropriate for a true university. However, he called for a sharp distinction between colleges and universities. Much of the current confusion in America, he thought, came from conflating the two and applying university standards to colleges. Colleges like Yale were for the training of "immature" boys."[19] Porter had devoted one of his 1869 articles to the college as a community, an ideal threatened by the individualism of university freedom. Even in a university, Porter was not prepared to concede that every shade of opinion and "antireligious philosophy" should have a chair to represent it. At a Christian college, however, it was entirely inappropriate to hire people to teach anti-Christian viewpoints.[20]

Porter, one of the ablest defenders of the centrality of positive Christianity in America's influential nonsectarian colleges, thus backed himself into a corner. It was a corner that advocates of distinctly Christian education could defend, but only temporarily. Even though they proclaimed that Christianity stood for freedom, the only way they could retain a semblance of free inquiry without opening the door to atheism was by maintaining a setting in which they could hold close personal control. They could defend what they already had, the disciplined undergraduate college as a haven against secular intrusion, but they had no real plan for the university as a graduate, professional, or specialized scientific institution. This line of defense thus had momentous implications in that it simply failed to address the issue of the relationship of Christianity to the emerging universities.

Porter was also implicitly tying the defense of Christian higher education to the continued dominance of the clergy. One of the articles in his 1869 series argued that colleges should be built around teachers rather than researchers. The ideal scholar in his view was a renaissance person who had developed a specialty but still was essentially a well-rounded gentleman. It fit the mid-nineteenth-century model of the gentleman-scholar or the clergyman-scientist. Porter and the New Haven scholars might be promoting professionalism, but they were still doing it largely as clergy

Why William Graham Sumner Could Stay

The crisis precipitated in 1879 by Porter's attempt to stop William Graham Sumner from using Herbert Spencer's *The Study of Sociology* brought these principles to the test and proved that ideals that might have seemed viable in the middle decades of the century were not going to survive its later years. The forces of professionalization and scientific ideals that Porter and his generation had helped nourish in America now had emerged with the self-assurance of adolescence. Long-held standards of submission to duly consti- tuted authority were crumbling, and proclamations of individual autonomy were taking their place. William Graham Sumner's rugged "dog-eat-dog" so- cial Darwinist laissez-faire sociology not only fit the economic realities of the day but was just one expression of the watchword of "freedom" heard on every front. In practical terms for higher education it meant that the rules that had prevailed among clergy, where boundaries were set on the basis of doctrinal orthodoxy, would no longer apply. Science would be the new or- thodoxy. Whatever the theoretical concerns, the institutional realities were that colleges were becoming universities and universities were being defined as scientific institutions, free from traditions. The newest institutions were on this basis threatening to displace the old colleges. In addition to Andrew Dickson White's Cornell, the intellectually formidable Johns Hopkins University opened in 1876, headed by Porter's principal progressive rival for the Yale presidency, Daniel Coit Gilman. In the contest between Sumner and Porter, time was on the side of Sumner.

Science and Christianity

Had the issue been purely intellectual, Porter's emphases on the threats to Christian distinctiveness might have received wider hearing. It was not a question of a warfare between science and clerical dogmatism as Sumner, Andrew Dickson White, and others represented it.[21] Nor was it, as is often thought, primarily a debate over Darwinism; Yale, like almost all leading colleges in the North, was teaching biological evolution by 1880.[22] Rather, the crucial issue was the assumptions on which natural scientific inquiry would be founded. As Charles Cashdollar has shown, the underlying chal- lenge to Christian thought in this era was the challenge of positivism.[23] Positivism, arising from the views of Auguste Comte (1798–1857), the founder of the field of sociology, asserted that true science precluded religious considerations. In Comte's construction of history, humans were rising from a religious stage in which questions were decided by authority, through a metaphysical stage in which philosophy ruled, to a positive stage in which empirical investigation would be accepted as the only reliable road to truth.[24]

Noah Porter, like some other thinkers of the era influenced by idealism, recognized that the question concerned the assumptions that would determine the context in which science would take place. In his substantial text, *The Human Intellect* (1868), he concluded with a purely philosophical (that is, not directly Christian or biblical) argument for "the absolute." Belief in the absolute, Porter argued, was a presupposition necessary to explain how we can know anything:

> We assume that this absolute exists, in order that thought and science may be possible. We do not demonstrate his being by deduction, because we must believe it in order to reason deductively. We do not infer it by induction, because induction supposes it; but we show that every man who believes in either, or in both, must assume it, or give up his confidence in both these processes and their results. We do not demonstrate that God exists, but that *every man must assume that He is.*[25]

The objection to Spencer was that he a priori excluded any absolute and asserted that observable phenomena are all we can know about. As Porter put it in a sharply worded review of Spencer's *The Study of Sociology* in the midst of the Sumner controversy, Spencer's iconoclasm was based simply on arguing in a circle. Having defined science in such a way as to exclude all absolutes, he then triumphantly concludes that science shows there are no absolutes: "And so he ends this long discussion with the assumption with which he begins, that in social phenomena we can only recognize natural causation, because, forsooth, if Sociology is a science it cannot admit any other agencies."[26]

In retrospect, Porter does not appear obviously to have had the worst of the argument, as sometimes is assumed.[27] He recognized, as is largely granted today, that both natural science and sociology always take place within a framework of assumptions. Sumner's view that religion could not be relevant to social science seems, indeed, to be built on uncritical acceptance of the Comtean positivist claim that science must be defined outside any theistic context. Clearly both natural science and social science investigations could take place either within or without theistic assumptions. In fact, in Porter's day Sumner represented a tiny minority of American academics who explicitly rejected the relevance of theism. Even many American sociologists for the next generation attempted to relate their sociology to their Christianity, at least to Christian ethics.

The significance of the episode, however, is that even on the limited ground of undergraduate education Porter could find no acceptable way to establish effective institutional safeguards against Christian theism being undermined in the name of positive science. Sumner remained at Yale and continued there into the twentieth century as a formidable alternative to popular evangelical influences. Given Yale's history of commitment to serve the public as well as the church, there was much to be said for this solution. Porter looked like an obscurantist because he was attempting to impose standards of the church on an institution that had more than church loyalties. The higher loyalty was to the nation, as the famous concluding line of Henry Durand's 1881 song put it, which became the Yale motto, "For God, for Country, and for Yale."[28]

And for the time being there was little danger that Yale as a whole would lurch off into agnosticism. In the short run it had enough ties to its evangelical past to absorb some diversity of opinion and to be all the more stimulating a place for it. During the next generation most Christian academics came to believe that wide freedom of expression for faculty and opportunities for students to encounter representatives of a variety of viewpoints were essential to the best education. Despite the evident merits of these considerations, however, Porter should be credited with recognizing that there was a dilemma involved. In the long run Porter was correct that the Sumners would win. Standards drawn from science that would preclude traditional considerations of faith would become the norm in higher education. Porter's outlook would be viewed like other things from the horse-and-buggy era, and it would become difficult to remember what the question of the relationship of traditional Christianity to collegiate academic life had been all about.

8

Daniel Coit Gilman and the Model for a Modern University

Rather than warfare, the typical motif in the transition from the old-time colleges to the new universities was peaceful revolution. Few of the old guard were willing to take a stand, as Porter did, that would risk looking sectarian. On the other side, most of the revolutionaries were sons of the evangelical college tradition and wished to emphasize that they were the true heirs to its ideals. While they were well aware of a need for a break from the past, they also took care to emphasize the continuities between the old colleges and the new universities.

As the founding president of the new Johns Hopkins University in 1876, Daniel Coit Gilman emerged as the preeminent leader in shaping the American idea of a modern university. Even though Gilman's closest friend was probably Andrew Dixon White, their views regarding religion were not identical. Gilman and White had both been members of the Skull and Bones secret society at Yale, and after their graduation in 1852 they had traveled to Europe together. While White was Episcopal and broadly Christian, Gilman had deep New England Congregational roots. Gilman did share with White a distaste for all sectarianism and a faith in free scientific inquiry as essential for the progress of humanity, but he combined these with conventional enough Christian concerns to fit in at Congregationalist Yale. In 1854 during his travels in Europe he had spent three days with Noah Porter and had discussed going into the ministry.[1] In 1860, while working at Yale, he attended Porter's lectures on theology and obtained from the Congregationalist Association a license to preach. Though he did not pursue this avenue any further, he retained active lifelong religious interests and saw leadership in education as a Christian calling.

Gilman's religious outlook, however, was broad in the mid-century Congregationalist context. He considered the progressive Congregationalist theologian, Horace Bushnell, the great "theological emancipator."[2] And notably absent from Gilman's later theological pronouncements was any

The Soul of the American University Revisited. George M. Marsden, Oxford University Press. © Oxford University Press 2021. DOI: 10.1093/oso/9780190073312.003.0012

reference to Christ, except as "the Master" and moral teacher. Gilman typically talked of religion as a promoter of morality and character. In this respect, his gospel of science and education was fully compatible with his understanding of the Christian Gospel. Both had the goal of uplifting humanity.[3]

In 1870 the fledgling University of California offered its presidency to Gilman. Citing his interest in Sheffield College and also noting that his wife had recently died and his two young daughters could be better cared for by relatives in New Haven, he nonetheless kept the door open, mentioning his strong interest in the prospect of shaping almost from its start a university in California. Two years later, after Porter had won the Yale appointment, the Californians renewed their offer and Gilman accepted.

The origins of the University of California are a striking example not only of how closely church and state interests in higher education might be tied, but also of the emerging new directions regarding how the religious issues might be negotiated when the state is in charge. The College of California had been founded in 1855 as a preparatory school and emerged in Oakland in 1860 as a typical Presbyterian-Congregationalist New England–oriented four-year college under clerical leadership. Though it aspired to be "the Yale of the West" and billed itself as nonsectarian, the school faced some opposition from other religious groups and struggled to find enough students.

The Morrill Land Grant Act of 1862 had an effect something like the promised gift that set the whole town to fighting in Mark Twain's "The Man That Corrupted Hadleyburg." In a state where education had not been a high priority, contenders for the government funds scrambled to demonstrate that they were great friends of the agricultural and mechanical arts. The College of California, numbering its students only in the dozens and unsuccessful in finding a major benefactor, very quickly announced the creation of a "Mining and Agricultural College" as a department within the institution and informed the state that it would be quite happy to accept the Morrill endowment. Since the mining and agricultural division existed only on paper, and the College of California was self-evidently a typical classicist and, in the minds of most Californians, impractical enterprise, the offer, though taken seriously, was not accepted. In 1866, the state itself, in order to secure the funds, created its own Agricultural, Mining, and Mechanical Arts College, which also existed only on paper.

As the prospect increased that the state would soon establish an actual college in the Bay Area, in 1867 the trustees of the already struggling

College of California took the extraordinary step of donating their entire enterprise to the state with the "earnest hope and confident expectation" that the state would establish on the site "a University of California, which shall include a College of Mines, a College of Agriculture, and an Academical College, all of the same grade, and with course of instruction equal to those of Eastern Colleges."[4] One of the chief attractions of the College of California was that it owned a magnificent tract of land in the area near Oakland that they had named Berkeley, after the British philosopher. They assumed that the existing college would, in effect, become the arts college of the new university.

Almost immediately their plan began to go awry. The union of the College of California and the state university had been based, in part, on the assurances of the Republican governor, Frederick Low, who envisioned a school modeled on the University of Michigan. Low, however, was replaced the next year by Henry Haight, a Democrat. Political tensions remained high after the war. Haight had supported McClelland against Lincoln in 1864 and was an Old School Presbyterian, a group highly critical of New England Republican pretensions. Democrats were also open to some Southern sympathies. The new regents appointed under Haight included a remarkably diverse group, including a Jew, a Catholic, a Unitarian, and some who were regarded as "indifferents and skeptics."[5] The two centerpieces of the new university faculty were Southerners from the University of South Carolina, John and Joseph Leconte, fleeing carpetbaggers. The first choice of the new trustees for the university presidency was George McClelland. The General (never known for taking chances) turned down the honor. John LeConte temporarily assumed the post. The only carryover from the former faculty was Martin Kellogg, a thoroughly tolerant friend of the university ideal, who would teach the classical courses at the university.[6]

Coming into this remarkably diverse and often contentious setting, Daniel Coit Gilman showed some concern for the question of the university's religious character. Other state schools, such as Michigan, spoke of themselves as distinctly "Christian." And at the University of Illinois, a land grant school opened in 1868, one year before the University of California, not only was daily chapel required but students were also expected to attend Sunday morning worship services and required to attend a Sunday afternoon worship and a lecture by the president on such topics as: Is there a God? Is the human soul immortal? Is the Bible of divine authority? Was Jesus more than a man? Is Christianity true?[7]

In his inaugural, citing California's remarkable religious pluralism, Gilman attempted to assure that at least a broadly Christian character might be maintained. One suggestion, which was apparently never implemented, was that faculty and students voluntarily "daily assemble of their own accord to acknowledge their dependence upon divine wisdom, to chant the psalms of David, and to join in the prayer which the Master taught his disciples.[8] Another solution was that various surrounding houses of worship might provide religious training in houses in which students might reside. This was a variation on the Jeffersonian proposal of surrounding theological faculties and seemed a promising practical approach to the same issues.

Despite this recognition of sectarian interests, when Gilman got down to it, he saw little to distinguish the role of a university from the civilizing role of Christianity itself. So he suggested in his California inaugural that a university "must show how Christian civilization has overcome pagan practices and beliefs, and has purified the home, the state, and the relations of nations, modifying laws, usages, manners and languages, establishing charities, reforming prisons, securing honesty, virtue, and justice."[9]

While broadly Protestant, the University of California was committed to a nonsectarian course. The state political code stated directly that "no sectarian, political, or partisan test must be ever allowed . . . in the selection of Regents, faculty, or students . . . nor must the majority of the Board of Regents be of any one religious sect or of no religious sect." Gilman had this statement printed in the university catalog.[10]

Critics, of course, continued to snipe at the supposed irreligion of the university. In response, Gilman assured that Christian prayers of clergymen opened and closed public events. He pointed out, furthermore, that he was on record as encouraging denominations to found residential houses for their students. Moreover, his own remarks to the students had invoked "the blessings of Almighty God" and had warned them against "dishonesty, selfishness, and sloth." While the university, he argued in summation, "is so conducted that neither Protestant, Catholic, nor Jew can claim that it is a 'sectarian' or 'ecclesiastical' foundation; it aims to promote the highest development of character."[11]

At California Gilman soon discovered that he did not have a free hand. He was spending much of his time defending the university from critics on all sides. As he confided to Andrew Dickson White, "The University of California is . . . nominally administered by the regents, but it is virtually administered by the legislature."[12]

Gilman found his way out when an opportunity to found a university without financial or political constraints presented itself in 1874. The will of Johns Hopkins, a Quaker businessman, provided funding for such an enterprise in Baltimore. Gilman let it be known to his friends in the East that he would be interested in the presidency and quickly accepted it when offered.

Hopkins

The Johns Hopkins University opened its doors in 1876 and remained under Gilman's leadership until his retirement in 1901. Unlike his situation in California, Gilman had almost complete control over the institution. One of the legacies of the old-time colleges that the founders of the new universities typically retained was the wide discretionary power of the president. With a relatively free hand to implement his dream for a university, Gilman quickly built Johns Hopkins into America's leading graduate university, setting the standards for others to emulate.

Johns Hopkins is often thought of as a thoroughly secular institution and in many respects it was. Yet Gilman's background of religious concerns, both at Yale and in California, cast a light on the character of that secularity. Gilman was, as we have seen, a liberal Congregationalist who had studied theology and seriously considered the ministry. He always remained active in Christian concerns, and he approached what D. G. Hart calls his "academic ministry"[13] at Hopkins with a New Englander's sense of Christian calling.

The question of what role religion would have at the new Johns Hopkins University was relatively open. Seven of the original twelve trustees were Quakers, as had been Johns Hopkins (d. 1873). Three of these were also on the board of Haverford College,[14] suggesting serious Quaker educational concerns. To Gilman they affirmed that there should be a spirit of "enlightened Christianity" at the university, an ideal with which he could readily concur.[15] The only provision was for "the absence of all sectarian bias, and of political spirit on the part of the President of the University," a point especially important to the Quaker trustees because of "the position of our community during the troubles of the war, and its sensitiveness even to this day, in relation to those issues." Such sentiments, received in 1875, must have been music to Gilman's ears, when he was still reeling from attempts of the

California legislature to run the university via public opinion. In responding, he eloquently set forth his own credo:

> The Institution we are about to organize would not be worthy of the name of a University, if it were to be devoted to any other purpose than the discovery and promulgation of the truth; and it would be ignoble in the extreme if the resources which have been given by the Founder without restrictions should be limited to the maintenance of ecclesiastical differences or perverted to the promotion of political strife.
>
> As the spirit of the University should be that of intellectual freedom in pursuit of the truth and of the broadest charity toward those from whom we differ in opinion it is certain that sectarian and partisan preferences should have no control in the selection of teachers, and should not be apparent in the official work.[16]

In Baltimore Gilman's efforts to take a stand for a thoroughly nonpartisan quest for truth soon drew sniper fire from the religious orthodox, similar to that which he had experienced in California. The East Coast version of the controversy, however, became much more celebrated, especially because of interest in the auspicious beginning of the new university and the notoriety of the participants.

In conjunction with the opening of the university to students, Gilman had invited Thomas Huxley, then on tour in the United States, to deliver a public lecture during September 1876. Huxley was notorious not simply as a leading proponent of Darwinism but as a militant in using the prestige of Darwinism to champion the recently invented concept of "agnosticism." This idea that a scientific thinker was, in principle, unable to settle questions about God was currently making a major intellectual stir in Britain and the United States and contributing to skepticism among some college students. Huxley was also a leading champion in the campaigns to combat Anglican dominance in English academic life. While Gilman did not share all of Huxley's views, he considered that having Huxley speak represented just the sort of openness in the scientific search for truth to which the university was most dedicated. The lecture was presented to a packed house at the Baltimore Academy of Music. Contrary to Gilman's suggestion, the trustees felt the event should be kept professional and not opened by prayer.[17]

The predictable happened. As usual, the Presbyterians were first into the field. The Presbyterian *New York Observer* accused the university of opening

with honor to "evolutionism" while "honor . . . was refused to the Almighty."
Gilman, they surmised, must have been well aware of this anomaly.
They wrote, "But if the neglect was due to the unchristian or materialistic
sentiments of the authorities, then we can only say, God help them, and keep
students away from the precincts of the young institution."[18] The Methodist
Christian Advocate followed with similar sentiments, suggesting that "if
reports are correct, the Johns Hopkins University has started wrong." The
Methodist editors, in good evangelical form, suggested the Hopkins board
should perhaps "retrace their steps, repent of their sins, make their peace
with God and give their university a Christian management."[19]

Reports, however, were not entirely correct. The religious journals had
mistakenly assumed that Huxley's speech constituted the opening of the
university and hence that the enterprise was begun without prayer. Huxley's
speech had sometimes been referred to as an "opening address," but, in fact,
the university had been formally opened with ceremonies the previous
February when Gilman had been inaugurated as president. At that time there
had been the full requisite of prayers and a good bit of talk about the religious
character of the enterprise. The critics were forced to publish corrections.
Nonetheless, in the considerable controversy that surrounded the event, the
image of a godless institution was what stuck. As one New York clergyman
put it, in the best remembered quip from the controversy: "It was bad enough
to invite Huxley. It were better to have asked God to be present. It would have
been absurd to ask them both."[20]

Gilman, however, was sincerely convinced that one could have both. In
his dealings with the religious questions, he was, of course, also dealing with
a public relations crisis, so it is sometimes difficult to distinguish the two.
Yet Gilman had raised the religious issues in California when he probably
did not have to, and his efforts to relate his religious interests to university
life were substantial enough to indicate that they were not only for public
consumption.

The most conspicuous expression of Gilman's Christian interests in his administration of the university was his establishing voluntary chapel, which
he himself conducted for many years. He also encouraged the presence of
the YMCA and often spoke at its meetings as well as at voluntary assemblies
instituted for undergraduates in 1883. His taking on these tasks suggested
the seriousness with which Gilman took the ideal of preserving what he saw
as the best of the old Christian college heritage. He still was willing, at least
for undergraduates, to play something of the role of the old-time college

president. Yet he did so in a way that could hardly offend the sensibilities of the Quaker trustees or anyone else (except, perhaps, some theological hard-liners). When he spoke to the assembled undergraduates, he spoke on topics such as "Bodily Discipline," "The Training of the Will," or "A Lesson on Truth" (against lying). These were consistent with one of the expressed aims of the new university, "to develop character—to make men."[21] On this front, the old-college ideal persisted.

Yet if we look at the university as a whole, it becomes clear that such efforts had little to do with the heart of the enterprise. Crucial to the revolution that was being effected was the sharp distinction that Gilman made between the undergraduate college and the university as a whole. The college, in his view, was still a steppingstone to the perfect freedom of the university. Vestiges of in loco parentis might still be appropriate to it,[22] and hence there was direct concern to provide for spiritual and moral welfare. The college, for instance, included a course called "Logic, Ethics, and Psychology," that is, moral philosophy. Gilman and the trustees apparently made genuine efforts to ensure that this course would be taught by a person of faith who was not a philosophical materialist. The first to hold the position, George Emmott, used as a textbook Noah Porter's Elements of Moral Science.[23]

What made Johns Hopkins immediately famous among American universities, however, was that it was the first school to make graduate and professional education the center of the enterprise. Gilman, in fact, initially wanted to make it purely a graduate and professional institution, including a projected medical school, but added the undergraduate college as a concession to the local Baltimore constituency.[24] At the graduate and professional level, he wanted freedom to prevail. Freedom was essential to the scientific search for knowledge, which was the overarching function of the university. The natural sciences and methodologies patterned after the natural sciences were therefore emphasized in the early design of Hopkins. The Baltimore university was renowned for following German models, for instance, in the introduction of graduate seminars. Such models were always translated and modified in American settings, but the appeal to German precedents served as a powerful symbol of an ideal of value-free scientific inquiry.

The symbolic meaning of the German model had thus shifted somewhat since Henry Tappan's day. Idealism and the humanistic shaping of character were still essential to the educational outlook; but since mid-century in Germany, meticulous research had become increasingly important to defining educational ideals. At the same time, the number of

American students traveling to Germany for graduate education was rapidly increasing by the 1870s. What they most often brought back with them was a reverence for the "German method," by which they meant rigorous empirical investigation. As the Americans appropriated it, in fact, it bore the deep impress of their own traditions of British empiricism[25] and of the Baconian rhetoric that had dominated earlier American science. German *Lehrfreiheit*—the freedom for the guild of professors independently to pursue its inquiries, publications, and teachings—became a symbol for an emerging ideal of academic freedom.[26] This ideal, in the minds of American reformers such as Gilman, was inextricably mixed with the simple ideal of pure scientific investigation, or the pursuit of truth. The graduate seminar was an important forum in which such investigation could take place. The seminar had developed in Germany as a model of how the research ideal and the humanistic ideals could be combined. It simultaneously stressed individual attention from professors, original scientific research, individual creativity, and honing of critical skills.[27]

Just as important as any specific model or technique was a broader assumption borrowed primarily from the German experience. Longstanding in Germany was the tradition of freedom for university students, or *Lernfreiheit*. Such freedom was premised on a strong distinction between preparatory education in the gymnasium and university education. The gymnasia, in which the abilities were "exercised," much as in the old American college ideal, were known for their discipline. Universities, on the other hand, were places for the expression of student freedom. Students, who were now adults, had freedom both in how they regulated their own lives and in what they learned. American colleges, which had developed their style when many of the boys they educated were only in their midteens, had retained the disciplinary model, both in regulating personal life and in what was learned. As a clearly new level of education emerged, with the introduction of graduate education and the expansion of professional education, especially medicine, almost all American educators accepted the child-versus-adult distinction, including the idea that the higher levels of education (except in theology) should be freed from the old restrictions, including theological concerns.

This definition of the theoretical basis for graduate and professional education marked a momentous step in American higher education. Given its immense repercussions, it is especially revealing to realize that the step was taken almost without dissent or criticism. Even Noah Porter, as we have seen, acknowledged essentially this same distinction between graduate and undergraduate education. While Porter recognized theoretical differences between Christian and non-Christian thought, his institutional conservatism extended only to preserving the Christian undergraduate college. For graduate education "freedom" seemed a compelling ideal, and in light of the cultural dominance of Protestantism there was little reason to suppose that Christianity would be discriminated against in a free exchange. It was so commonplace for Protestants to claim that science was on the side of non-sectarian Christianity that even someone like Porter seems to have seen no threat to his ideals in defining the methodology of graduate education as value-free science.

Rather, the Porters as much as the Gilmans seemed oblivious to the broader theoretical issue of what would be central to universities, while concentrating on the more immediate and personal question about the religious and moral welfare of undergraduates. As important as that issue might be, it almost totally distracted attention from the innovations, and the assumptions behind them, that would determine the soul of the university. Not only graduate education, but also professional education and technical institutes were being established on a new professionalized basis with almost no reference to religious concerns. The value-free ideal declared religion irrelevant to scientific inquiry. At the same time, however, administrators could refer religious supporters to their concern for the morality and even the religious life of undergraduates. So far as the denominations were concerned, though a few experimented with universities, none seriously challenged the undergraduate versus graduate and professional distinction. Rather, their overwhelming response was to concentrate on undergraduate colleges and perhaps on university divinity schools. For constituents who might be deeply concerned about religious issues, church colleges provided an alternative that further could allay concern about the larger trends in higher education.[28]

Thus, even though the story of religion and higher education continued long after the days of Gilman and his peers, its basic trajectory was settled from day one of the design of the modern American university. Religion would have virtually nothing to do with the vast majority of the enterprise, including graduate, professional (except theology), and technical education. Since virtually all university professors eventually would be trained in graduate schools built on the purely naturalistic assumptions of the new science and professionalism, the forces eroding Christian influences even in the undergraduate classrooms were destined to be immense as well.

Christian scholars were hardly likely to see such developments as a threat to the faith, not only because of the assumptions most of them shared concerning the objectivity of the scientific method, but also because of educational precedents. In the longer history of universities, theology had seldom been well integrated with the arts or the other professional faculties. Similarly, the old-time colleges had treated most of the sciences as well as the classical arts as essentially autonomous disciplines, even though working within a broad framework of theological assumptions and tying together some theological and practical issues in moral philosophy. For the first generation of the universities, much the same practice continued, so that there was a transitional period when there was enough continuity with the past not to cause alarm. In philosophy itself, and in the various fields growing out of moral philosophy such as psychology, sociology, and economics, some religious or at least moral concerns persisted. The study of literature also picked up some of the functions of moral philosophy, encouraging students to explore the deeper issues of life.[29] Since the college and the graduate schools had the same faculties, some of these concerns survived for a time in graduate education and in professional publications as well. Nonetheless, given the scientific-technical definition of the professional scholar, such functions were vestigial and soon disappeared.

The bottom line was that the new universities were designed to serve an emerging industrial technological society. The professionalization of the universities was part of the much larger process of differentiation and specialization necessary for industrial and commercial advance. As Burton J. Bledstein argues at length, "By and large the American university came into existence to serve and promote professional authority in society." In the new middle-class society, which the universities were designed to serve, "success increasingly depended on providing a service based on a skill, elevating the status of one's occupation by referring to it as a profession."[30] Such emerging professions were legitimated on a technological or scientific basis. Technical specialization almost inevitably meant that there would be vast realms separated from direct religious influences. American universities emerged just when these cultural processes were taking place on a massive scale and were an integral part of these processes. That meant that the universities themselves, as well as the vast majority of their disciplines, were defined according to the new professional scientific basis for which religion was considered irrelevant.

Religions themselves might be studied as objects of scientific inquiry. And religious faith and practice themselves might be regarded as a specialized leisure time activities to which universities might give their blessings as healthful options for individuals.

Methodological Naturalism

Why pious Christians, like Gilman and his counterparts in business, the professions, science, and technology, did not see such developments as threats to the faith can be explained in terms of a larger tendency of modernity sometimes called "methodological naturalism." By that is meant simply the removal of specific religious reference from a task without necessarily making a judgment as to whether religious concerns *could* be relevant to the task. In philosophy a distinction is often made between "methodological naturalism," as in considering only natural phenomena in scientific experimentation, and "metaphysical naturalism," which would be the claim that natural causes are all there are or are all we can ever know about.[31] Whatever terms we use, one of the major dynamics of complex modern societies arises from the principle that many tasks are done most efficiently by isolating and objectifying them.

Such methodology works particularly well in technical tasks, both those that demand large-scale organization and those that demand intensive analysis. In effect, one creates a mechanism for addressing the issue and applies this to a practical problem. Religious considerations play little if any role in the mechanism itself. Hence, if one is considering how to improve the efficiency of the steam engine, information derived from religious belief would not be expected to affect the construction of the mechanism. In the late nineteenth century this scientific-technological principle, which paid momentous dividends, was being extended to almost all areas of life. The new universities were especially devoted to the service of this technological ideal and were among its major proponents. Thus, pious Christians were expected to leave at the laboratory door any explicit theoretical considerations of religious beliefs, even if they had prayed God to bless their work and came from their discoveries praising God for his work. Diversities of religious beliefs also made it particularly important for scholarly cooperation that substantive religious considerations be kept out of the laboratories. Since the laboratory became a key metaphor and model for all advanced intellectual work, this ideal was extended throughout the university, often even to speculative and evaluative questions that might not, in fact, be settled by natural scientific considerations alone.

Pious Christians had little reason to protest most instances of methodological naturalism, especially since, regarding most concrete and technical issues, the methodology demonstrably improved human ability to discover the truth. Since scientific activity might take place within the context of piety and be an expression of the highest moral ideals of service to humanity, there was nothing about the method in and of itself that seemed inherently antagonistic to Christianity. Moreover, if serving humanity was, indeed, the goal, then the scientific-technological method could unquestionably be a good, since it provided unprecedented means to help one's neighbors, ease their lives, and help them to better understand themselves, their culture, and their environment.

Liberal Christians like Gilman were deeply convinced, as he said at his Johns Hopkins inaugural and often repeated, "Religion has nothing to fear from science." "Religion," he explained, "claims to interpret the word of God, and science to reveal the laws of God." "The interpreters may blunder," he continued, implying that theologies may change, "but truths are immutable, eternal, and never in conflict."[32] If Christians took seriously the antebellum dictum that science and religion must necessarily harmonize, how could Christians fear the scientific advance of truth?

Gilman thus saw his work at Johns Hopkins as essentially a Christian ministry. This is suggested further by an invitation he accepted in 1887 from the Evangelical Alliance, a leading mainstream Protestant group, to address them on the role of the universities in the evangelical mission to the nation. Indeed, Gilman was one of the signers of the call for this special ecumenical gathering of evangelicals on "National Perils and Opportunities" faced by the increasingly industrialized and urbanized world.

After rehearsing how universities had long served the churches, Gilman justified their continuing service exactly on the grounds of the virtues of methodological naturalism, arguing that the methods of science were the best means to advance the goals of Christianity:

> The methods they [the universities] employ are particularly directed to the ascertainment of truth and the detection of error; and these methods are those which all men everywhere can make use of. Moreover, the end in view—the ultimate end of all educational and scientific effort, as well

as of all legislation and statesmanship—is identical with that at which
Christianity aims . . ., "Peace on earth, good will to men."

Gilman illustrated this point by enumerating the recent discoveries in
universities that had benefited humanity in "the age of electricity." Such
discoveries had benefited commerce, diplomacy, missionary efforts, medicine, understanding human behavior, and even theology itself. All this
achievement should assure us that "in the long run, in the progress of centuries, even in the progress of decade after decade, the world grows better."
Gilman was convinced that "as misery, vice and sin grow less, religion has
a freer field, and Christianity extends its invigorating and uplifting influence." So he said that he often asked which branch of the church would be
the first to "assert everywhere that Science is the handmaid of Religion, that
every effort made to extend the domain of human thought, and to interpret
the plan of creation, is an effort to extend the reign of righteousness and
truth."[33]

Gilman's appropriation of such broadly postmillennial language of spiritual and material progress was to some extent rhetorical flourish, yet at the
same time there is no reason to think that he did not believe what he said. In
his view science simply *was* an expression of Christianity. As far as the design
and conduct of the university was concerned, this meant that, although he
had to be solicitous of the spiritual and moral welfare of undergraduates and
to keep some regard for public opinion, by far the overwhelming duty was to
follow the scientific method wherever it led.

For the generation of university builders reared during the heady days
of antebellum and Civil War millennialist evangelicalism, it was important
to insist that methodological naturalism in the universities did not mean
the universities were being secularized or removed from religious concerns.
Rather, what they were doing illustrated the principle that secularization
often proceeds at first not by the contraction of areas that religion touches
but by what may be regarded as their expansion. Mid-century evangelical
orthodoxy had anticipated this sacralization of science, celebrating its theories as discoveries of the revelations of God and its applications as signs
of the millennium. University reformers typically extended such rhetoric
to maintain that scientific investigation simply was a Christian enterprise.
Hence, its autonomy could not be challenged on either rational or religious
grounds.

The degree to which commitment to this principle would lead to separating traditional Christianity from mainstream intellectual life was also obscured, as we shall see, by the simultaneous liberal Protestant redefinition of Christianity as broad ethical ideals or even as just the highest principles of civilization. In such form explicit Christianity might linger in the curriculum, especially in the humanities and social scientific disciplines that were the successors to moral philosophy.

9

Liberal Protestantism at Michigan

In 1888 the Rev. Francis Horton, a Presbyterian clergyman in Oakland, attacked the University of California for its religious heterodoxy, and the contrast he cited was the University of Michigan: "That institution does not teach religion any more than does ours, but its prevailing sentiment is favorable to revealed religion, as here it is against it."[1] Horton's comment reflected lingering resentments that Presbyterians and Congregationalists felt betrayed twenty years earlier when they lost what they had thought was promised control after they donated their College of Californian to the state. Unitarians had more influence at the university, and the recently elected president of the university was a Unitarian. One local Unitarian pastor had even recommended the controversial novel *Robert Elsmere*, by British writer Mrs. Humphrey Ward. The novel told of a young man's loss of faith and openly ridiculed evangelicalism.[2]

Whatever the merits of Horton's complaints about the University of California, his reference to Michigan as more favorable to Protestant orthodoxy was typical. Michigan was often mentioned hopefully as a model for the future of religion in higher education. The Ann Arbor example showed not only that a state school could be openly sympathetic to Christianity—the same could be said of most state universities[3]—but also that such sympathy was, in fact, displayed by a leader among the new research universities.

In this era when presidents ran institutions almost single-handedly, Michigan's reputation as a Christian university was closely related to the overt Christian piety of James Burrill Angell, president from 1871 to 1909. Angell was from Rhode Island and had studied at Brown under Francis Wayland and subsequently taught there. Like most university reformers, he had been ardently pro-Lincoln. During the Civil War he edited a Republican newspaper. He then served as president of the University of Vermont before going to Michigan. As a student he had thought seriously about a ministerial career and clearly carried that sense of calling into his work in higher education. When Angell was being considered for Michigan, Professor George P. Fisher of Yale described him as "a religious man, without the least taint of

The Soul of the American University Revisited. George M. Marsden, Oxford University Press. © Oxford University Press 2021. DOI: 10.1093/oso/9780190073312.003.0013

bigotry."[4] In Angell's case, this was no pro forma stance. Unlike some of his peers, who largely kept their piety under wraps, Angell made Christianity in the university a major cause. He spoke about it, conducted surveys on it, wrote articles and edited a book on Christianity, facilitated the growth of campus ministries, and continued through the first decade of the twentieth century to preach Christ to Michigan.

Angell liked to quote Article III in the Northwest Ordinance: "Religion, morality and knowledge being necessary to good government and the happiness of mankind, schools and the means of education shall forever be encouraged." At his inauguration Angell interpreted "religion" to mean explicitly Christianity, announcing that "the Christian spirit, which pervades the law, the customs, and the life of the State shall shape and color the life of the University, that a lofty, earnest, but catholic and unsectarian Christian tone shall characterize the culture which is here imparted."[5]

Michigan as a state school had always faced some criticisms in that it always claimed to be broadly Christian and nonsectarian but, in fact, was run by the New England "Presbygational" network, who were the preeminent leaders of higher education in the whole region. Methodists earlier had complained the most.[6] And by the post-Civil War era, others, especially secularists, were insistent that the university was *too* Christian and thus violating the separation of church and state.

Angell's explicit Christianity brought the latter issue to a head. In 1873 Stephen B. McCracken of Detroit made a formal complaint about the statement in the inaugural and Angell's expressed intent to hire faculty "whose mental and moral qualities will fit them to prepare their pupils for manly and womanly work in promoting our Christian civilization." McCracken pointed out that the population of Michigan included Jews, spiritualists, and various types of freethinkers and alleged that treating Christianity as an "exclusive or privileged opinion" violated the state constitution. He also observed that claims to be nonsectarian were hollow when everything but Protestantism was excluded. Angell's university, he argued, intimating Celtic resentments against New England imperialism, really stood for "puritan sectarianism."[7]

The state senate, after some reluctance to take the complaint seriously, appointed a committee to visit the university and investigate. Similar issues had surfaced in California, but this was an early instance of the question of religious diversity, beyond just diversity among Protestants, at a state school and was addressed in a formal way. The investigating committee asked some probing questions, and the answers of Angell and his lieutenants are revealing of what could still pass as both Christian and nonsectarian in a state setting.

Asked by the committee to explain what he meant by "religious or denominational sectarianism," Angell replied that sectarianism referred 'to a spirit of special devotion to some one denominational system of belief in some branch of the Christian church." But when asked whether he construed sectarianism "to mean denominationalism and Christianity generally, as the opposite of infidelity, materialism, spiritualism, or any other unorthodox 'isms,' Angell replied that it referred only to differences among Christians, 'not going outside of Christian beliefs."

The committee pressed further, asking: "Do you inculcate Christianity as a system of religious belief as a teacher and professor in the University? And, if so, do you regard that as sectarian?"

Angell replied:

To the first part of the question I should say indirectly, Yes; to the second, No. I will explain as to the first answer that I believe it to be necessary for any Christian to state, if he is honest, what his beliefs are, and to honestly state opposing beliefs, if he knows what they are; for example, I don't think you can teach the History of the Reformation without stating your beliefs, while stating the opposing ones also, and, if a man of any power over your students, without impressing them besides. But I have never tried to enforce my beliefs.

The answers of the other principal witness, Dr. Benjamin Cocker, Professor of Intellectual and Moral Philosophy, are even more revealing as to the limits of how far professors might go in promoting Christian faith. When asked specifically whether he taught Christian theology, Cocker answered that "If by 'theology' you mean the doctrine concerning God,—yes." But when pressed as to whether that included "the theological basis of ordinary Christianity," he answered "Yes" but then emptied his meaning of Christianity of any theological content. "My definition of Christianity," he affirmed, "is 'to yield one's heart to the teachings and spirit, and to follow the example of Jesus Christ, who went about the world doing good.' I urge all the boys to follow Christ as hard as they can in that way."

The committee pushed hard on whether that was all he meant by theology as the teaching about God. "Do you, or do you not," they asked, "teach the miraculous birth, and redemptorial office of Christ as a necessary part of the 'Christian Theology,' and do you, or do you not teach, the 'Christian Theology,' so called, as the true religion?"

Cocker responded, "I have never made an allusion to that subject since I have been in the university. I believe it. It is my private view, but I don't teach the doctrine in my class."

So what did he mean by "Christianity in the university"?

"I mean," replied Cocker, "the spirit which pervades the University as Christian; there is Christianity in the observance of the Sabbath, in the date of the year, in the intercourse of the professors, in the repetition of the Lord's Prayer in chapel, in the bricks and mortar of the walls, in everything connected with the institution."

The senate committee cleared the university, concluding:

> The teachings of the university are those of a liberal and enlightened Christianity, in the general, highest and best use of the term. This is not in our opinion sectarian. If it is, we would not have it changed. A school, a society, a nation devoid of Christianity, is not a pleasant spectacle to contemplate. We cannot believe the people of Michigan would denude this great university of its fair, liberal and honorable Christian character as it exists today.[8]

President Angell and his lieutenants, such as Benjamin Cocker, had resolved the question of Christianity in the university in the way that Christian leaders of the era typically did. While they supported evangelical Christianity personally, in the classroom they limited what they said to essentially Unitarian Christianity, advocating the ethics of Jesus and celebrating a "Christian spirit" within the civilization. At the time, that seemed like a reasonable enough solution at a state university even from a traditional Protestant perspective. They apparently recognized that it would be unfair to make the specific theology of one denomination normative at a state university. Yet promoting the highest ideals of a "Christian spirit" of the civilization was a standard part of public life. And as the Rev. Francis Horton later pointed out, the leaders of the school were known to be sympathetic to a more orthodox Christianity that students could pursue in local churches or student societies on a voluntary basis. At the same time, as Angell and Cocker assured the state senate committee, they also allowed a Radical Club where students could investigate whatever they wished.

James Angell also recognized that the Christian spirit in a modern state university would have to be cultivated differently than Christianity had been sustained in the old colleges. One of the first things he did was to shift chapel, which had been required for undergraduates, to a voluntary basis. When Angell arrived, the rebellious student spirit of the old-time college survived in a tradition of creating bedlam before, after, and sometimes during chapel. During his first weeks, Angell managed to quiet the multitude, but by the next year he had permanently resolved the issue by dropping compulsion. He also made moral philosophy and history of philosophy electives.[9]

Angell further moved to broaden the university's religious base. Early in 1873, while the agitation over McCracken's complaint was at its height, he proposed appointing a Roman Catholic, E. W. Hilgard, to the faculty. He felt, however, that he had to solicit the approval of the regents before taking such a step. Their reactions were mixed. One said an orthodox Catholic would be preferable to an infidel; another said that one moderate Catholic might be acceptable, another was not sure what the people would think. In general, however, they approved and Hilgard was appointed.[10]

Angell saw these moves to temper the Protestant establishment as of a piece with his efforts to build Christianity at the university on a healthier voluntary basis. In 1890, responding to a request from the editors of the *Andover Review*, an influential progressive Congregational journal, Angell attempted to disabuse Easterners of the impression that because "we have such a complete separation of church and state," the state universities were "devoid of the religious spirit." The evidence proved the contrary, Angell argued. For instance, in a survey he had conducted of 24 state schools of learning, chapel services were held at 22 and at 12 were compulsory for undergraduates. The old type of chapel requirements enforced by a monitor, he suggested, were inappropriate when, as at Michigan, the entering age for freshmen was nineteen-and-a-half years. Besides, he pointed out, those who were so solicitous about required chapel for undergraduates made no objection when such services were typically neglected at scientific schools in the East, such as the Massachusetts Institute of Technology or the Sheffield Scientific School at Yale.

More important than formal requirements was the general Christian spirit that pervaded institutions. The faculty was, of course, crucial. Of the schools surveyed, 71% percent of the teachers were church members, and many others were actively religious despite not having formally joined churches.

Angell did not mention it, but these church membership figures were far above national averages, especially for men. True, there were a few teachers at state schools, as at others, who might undermine Christian faith, but the majority were models of earnest and reverent men. In fact, in cities where state universities were located one could find members of university faculty teaching Sunday schools, conducting Bible classes, and engaged in every other sort of exemplary Christian activity.

Angell, no doubt, had his own faculty in mind as a model of such activity. He himself took care, especially in the fields that were replacing moral philosophy, to seek Christian teachers. "In the chair of History," he wrote to Daniel Coit Gilman in 1885, "the work may lie and often does lie so close to Ethics, that I should not wish a pessimist or an agnostic or a man disposed to obtrude criticisms of Christian views of humanity or of Christian principles. I should not want a man who would not make his historical judgments and interpretations from a Christian standpoint."[11]

At the University of Michigan, Angell could also point out as well that opportunities for extracurricular religion were growing. Michigan, like every other state, university had a Christian Association or the equivalent. These usually were affiliated with the YMCA or the YWCA. The university provided rooms for meetings and faculty spoke regularly at them. Dwight L. Moody had recently conducted revival services at the University of Michigan, and Angell pointed with pride to the number of missionaries the university had sent to the foreign field. State universities, of course, did not have the percentages of ministerial graduates that denominational colleges had. But this was because denominational colleges typically offered scholarships for students preparing for ministerial study. It would be a mistake, Angell felt, however, if denominations neglected state schools, where they could have considerable influence as well.

In fact, with Angell's encouragement Ann Arbor was becoming the model for denominational work at state schools. In 1887 Episcopalians and Presbyterians had established student centers or guilds near the university, and they were very soon followed by the Methodists, Catholics, and Unitarians. The Tappan Presbyterian Guild, for instance, had a library of some four thousand volumes, a gymnasium, social rooms, and study rooms. Guilds offered courses of lectures on religious topics and sponsored prominent religious speakers.[12] Eventually denominations imitated this Ann Arbor model in most state universities' towns, although it took several decades for denominational centers to emerge as the typical pattern.

Religious Thought at the University of Michigan (1893)

While recognizing that Christianity would not play much of a role in the classroom of a modern state university, James Angell wanted to make sure that the voluntary religion proclaimed by the surrounding institutions could offer the same benefits as had moral philosophy at the old colleges. One evidence that this concern was widely shared was a volume published in 1893 by the Student Christian Association, *Religious Thought at the University of Michigan.* The volume contained twenty addresses, two by Angell and the rest by university faculty members, delivered on Christian themes at the Sunday morning services of the Christian Association. The reason for the lectures, the editors explained, was that it had been pointed out to them that "most of the University instructors . . . were interested speculatively as well as practically, in matters of religion." However, most of what went on intellectually was "a great deal of quiet but active thinking about religious questions . . . of which students had but occasional intimations."[13]

The lectures touched on a wide range topics, including assurances that Darwinism did not challenge essential Christianity, discussions of the impact of Christianity on history and society, and questions of the relationship of Christianity to teaching, medicine, music, and missions.

The overwhelming impression offered by these lectures is of an aggressively liberal Christianity. Repeatedly the lecturers urge students that the way to resolve the apparent tensions between faith and learning is to see that Christianity is in essence simply a life of morality that science can only enhance. Thus, in addressing the much discussed topic of "How Has Biological Research Modified Christian Conceptions?," Professor V. M. Spalding assured his audience that the essence of Christianity was the "absolute unselfishness of Christ," which presented us with a "sublime gospel" that we could know to be eternal. "Has the onward march of scientific discovery," he asked, "has the development of philosophical thought in any form affected by so much as a shadow the great central figure of Christianity?" Nothing had "come to light that prevents any one of us from being his disciples, learning of him, catching his spirit."

On the other hand, said Spalding, the "venerable structure" of theology offered a great heritage of "men who walked with God." "Yes, but of *men!*" he immediately added, "And no work of man has ever stood unchanged through any long period of time." So, the entire history of Christian theology, much as it should be revered, would be dismissed. There would be, "to use Prof.

LeConte's expression, the necessity of a complete reconstruction of Christian theology," based on scientific principles. Most important, Scripture as a dogmatic authority would have to go: "An increasing number of the most conscientious and intelligent leaders of Christian thought are looking upon the Bible simply as the lamp through which the light of God shines." So the Bible was "a book written for men and by men, but full of sublime, holy and divine truth." Regarding the Bible "as an infallible oracle," on the other hand, "tends directly to encourage indolence and superstition." More and more thinkers were coming to recognize that "the search for truth is God's ordained means of obtaining it." Christians were "coming to understand that religious truth is no exception to this rule."

The search for truth, then, brought Christianity down to its spiritual essence, which, of course, was not susceptible to scientific refutation. "The stripping off of traditions has only brought into clearer relief the Divine Presence."[14] As Professor Francis W. Kelsey, in a lecture on "Primitive and Modern Christianity," put it, "The history of the church as a whole is an illustration of the law of the survival of the fittest. Christianity has shown a constant tendency to take the place of inferior beliefs. In its own inner life there has been a marked tendency to pass from lower to higher forms. . . . Christianity was not primarily a system of government, a ritual, or a theology; it was a life."[15]

The treatment of Christianity as a life and not a doctrine, as something caught more than taught, as "the Fatherhood of God and the brotherhood of man,"[16] resolved a multitude of problems. First of all, it was a genuinely grand moral vision, an attempt to recover and apply the selfless ethics of Jesus, which had often been obscured by theological dogma and ecclesiastical ambition. The grandeur of these ideals explained the otherwise intellectually embarrassing assertion of the superiority of Christianity to other religions, and hence the superiority of Western cultures to others that it was dominating. James Angell himself, who had served as the U.S. minister to China, made this the theme in one of his lectures, listing the ways in which Christian civilization was morally superior, especially in its regard for individuals, for charity, for international law, for the dignity of women, and for truth seeking.[17]

Justifying Christianity in Lincolnesque fashion solely by its moral teachings, which seemed to bring freedom, and justice, resolved an even more trying problem that plagued almost every thinking Christian of the generation—was Christianity true? Particularly, could Christians still believe the Bible? The generation had been reared on the most profound reverence for the authority of the Bible, not only in doctrine, but also in history. In the pre–Civil War era, America's most advanced academic debates, those in the great theological journals, had been built on the premise of biblical authority and reliability. The next generation, especially the swelling numbers of academics who took their graduate work in Germany after 1860, found this premise almost impossible to accept.

The historical criticism of the Scriptures that these academics learned in Europe was already far advanced. While Cambridge and Scotland offered some models of more moderate criticism, Americans who studied in Germany seemed more often impressed by more radical continental views. Scholars such as Ernest Renan and David Friedrich Strauss had, in effect, demonstrated a flaw in the fusion of Enlightenment and evangelical Protestant ideals that seemed to have worked so well in America. If Christianity was supported and confirmed by objective science, then the Bible should be able to be subjected to the same historical analysis as the documents of any other religion. Scientific naturalism thus became the starting point for historical inquiry into the Bible. From that point of view, of course, the Scriptures looked very different than they did if viewed with the premise that they were revealed by God. The miracle stories, for instance, became embarrassments, rather than evidences. By modern critical standards historical reporting in Scripture looked inaccurate and fabricated. Particularly, the Old Testament narratives, as well as many of the claims to authorship and dating, appeared implausible if the writings were viewed as simple products of the evolving faith of an ancient primitive people.

Darwinism, which was built on the same purely naturalistic premises, only added a dramatic point to this more basic erosion of biblical authority. Darwinism reinforced already strong challenges to the historicity of the narratives of the early chapters of Genesis, which included not only the creation narratives, but also accounts of the Great Flood and the Tower of Babel. Darwinism was especially important in that it offered a plausible alternative to biblical creation accounts of how humans originated. The biblical accounts, rather than standing as the best answer to an otherwise unsolvable question, could be relegated to the realm of myth.

John Dewey, one of the stars on the Michigan faculty, took the new point of view as his starting point in his address on "Christianity and Democracy" to the Christian Association. Religious beliefs, he said, may appear to be in a special category of human experience. "Research into the origin and development of religion destroys the appearance," however. "It is shown that every religion has its source in the social and intellectual life of a community or race." Dewey did not mention that this outlook was the premise of the research as well as its conclusion. "Every religion," he said simply, "is an expression of the social relations of the community," to which he added somewhat more affirmatively, "its rites, its cult are a recognition of the sacred and divine significance of these relationships."[18]

Dewey is especially fascinating because his spiritual and intellectual journey, spanning the whole era of the rise of the American university, almost perfectly mirrors the changing dominant academic opinion. Born in Vermont in 1859 and reared in the evangelical Calvinism of his mother, Dewey soon learned moderate Calvinist theology from his pastor and as a student at the University of Vermont. In his early twenties he had a conversion experience and became an active member and frequent Sunday school teacher in the Congregational church. From 1882 to 1884 Dewey was a graduate student at Johns Hopkins University, and, under the influence of the philosopher George Sylvester Morris, adapted his Christianity to Hegelianism. This put him in the camp of liberal "progressive orthodoxy," which was revolutionizing Congregationalism, most notably at Andover Theological Seminary.[19] During this era, especially among philosophers and theologians, a progressive philosophical idealism that could explain spiritual progress in divine terms, and was not dependent on the historical claims of Scripture, was the major academic substitute for the old biblically based dogmatics and history.

When Dewey spoke to the University of Michigan Christian Association in 1892 the Hegelian elements in his outlook still shone through. Nonetheless, even though he was still active in the local Congregational church, the distinctly Christian elements of his thought were eroding, an erosion covered in part by idealist rhetoric. God, said Dewey, is not the sort of being who makes certain fixed statements about himself. Rather, "The one claim that Christianity makes is that God is truth; that as truth He is love and reveals Himself fully to man, keeping back nothing of himself; that man is so one with the truth thus revealed that it is not so much revealed *to* him as *in* him; he is its incarnation." This is what Jesus meant by "The Kingdom of God is within us." God is therefore revealed in all search for truth in the human community. Democracy thus is an expression of God's spirit in that it allows freedom, including the freedom to search for the truth: "If God is, as Christ taught, at the root of life, incarnate in man, then democracy has a spiritual meaning which it behooves us not to pass by. Democracy is freedom. If truth is at the bottom of things, freedom means giving truth a chance to show itself, a chance to well up from the depths." This spirit of freedom and truth embodied in democracy provided not only intellectual freedom, but also practical freedom in ending slavery and breaking down class and social barriers that were dividing humanity.[20]

Other speakers to the Michigan Christian Association in 1892 and 1893 suggested, as did Dewey, an emerging social gospel as yet another justification for the redefinition of Christianity as the highest democratic morality. Here was another immense set of challenges that the shift to the ethics of Jesus could address. Those ideals, such as from Jesus's "Sermon on the Mount," could, indeed, be compelling challenges for Christians to speak in more effective ways concerning the prevailing social conditions. Industrialization, powerful trusts, labor troubles, urbanization, and immigration all tested revived verities about economic and social relations. The new social sciences that were emerging out of the old unspecialized moral philosophy and political economy were attempts to address the far more complex and differentiated social and economic realities that were emerging. Christians, still inspired by millennial dreams of moral and material progress going hand in hand, hoped to temper social strife with an ethic of love. During the first generation of the rise of the social sciences many Christians, including many social scientists, assumed that the sciences would be allies of the faith.

So at Michigan, Professor Henry C. Adams, an economist, in his address on "Christianity as a Social Force," insisted that one "must assume the ethical teachings of Jesus as an unalterable premise in the discussion of every social, political, industrial, or personal question." Adams considered it blasphemy for some persons to quote Scripture to argue that in either national affairs or business one should look out only for one's own interests in disregard of the interests of others. Adams admitted this was "a hard saying" for those who wished to be competitive in American business. He argued that a person should work within the present rules of what the law calls honest but take "as the highest aim in life, the task of doing what he may to so change laws and modify customs that the old Christian conception of a just price, and the modern Christian conception of equal opportunities for all, may become a realized fact."[21]

Such challenging social gospel views, not unusual among leading economists and sociologists of the generation, were not popular with some of the business supporters of the universities. In 1886, the year of the Haymarket riots, Adams himself had been denied a permanent professorship at Cornell because of the reaction of the university's conservative Christian benefactor, Henry W. Sage, to a pro-labor speech in 1886. Adams's case was one of the first of such tests of academic freedom during the latter years of the century.[22]

James Angell, who, much more than Adams or Dewey, retained the conventional language of the New England theological tradition, nonetheless interpreted that heritage in a strongly ethical way, so that the example of Jesus was always a prominent theme.[23] In preaching to students he typically applied the ideals of Jesus in urging them to cultivate traits of personal character, such as chastity, honesty, purity, and self-control, but he also taught that the message of love had world-changing social implications with respect to the way one should treat strangers, outcasts, and the less fortunate.[24] Though Angell himself did not tread into social controversy, he was sympathetic to a social Christianity and clearly encouraged his faculty openly to express their Christian ideals.

In his 1890 essay on religion at state universities Angell celebrated the expansion of voluntary religion: "I doubt whether a really better state of religious life has ever existed in our principal colleges and universities than now exists." The recent remarkable response of students to Moody's call for missionaries, resulting in the Student Volunteer Movement, was evidence of this trend.[25] Keeping his hand on the religious pulse of the university, Angell conducted another survey of state universities in 1896 and gained further support for this claim. Of nearly five thousand students concerning whom he gained information at five state universities (Indiana, Kansas, Michigan, Washington, and West Virginia), 55% were church members, and the total rose to nearly 90% if one included those who claimed to be affiliated with or to attend a church. The membership figures, also far above the national average, appeared to be rising,[26] perhaps because liberalized Protestant church membership was easier to attain. The universities were also overwhelmingly Protestant, far more than the nation as a whole. Only 165 students (or about 3%) were identified as Catholics, and only 44 (less than 1%) were Jews.[27] A notable feature of these statistics is that everywhere the percentage of women students who were church members was substantially higher than the percentage of men. At Michigan, for instance, the figure was only 52% for men and 70% of women. Growing numbers of women students were a significant force in the growth of voluntary religion.[28]

The dominant attitude toward religion in the 1890s was probably well reflected in a student address by Mary Hawes Gilmore at the commencement at the University of California in 1894. Religion, said Gilmore, was all influence that is uplifting "from the sordid, the partial, the insignificant [toward] the absolute, be it called Beauty, Truth or Goodness." "The fundamental idea of a University," in turn, "is universal truth-seeking, fair-mindedness, and impartial reception and scrutiny of all views—the enforced acceptance of none." It followed then, she argued, that to "enforce religious doctrines by direct methods would be subversive to its very nature—would be a return to medievalism." None of this, however, entailed opposition to traditional religious teaching. "Direct inculcation of divine truth and of practical moral precepts is necessary indeed, but the proper instrument and institution for that duty is surely the church."[29]

Such a division of labor, which did not differ much from Angell's approach at Michigan, seemed to resolve the issue, at least for those of the dominant social classes and religious sentiments. The universities could be practically Unitarian with lots of room for liberal Christian opinion, religious indifference, or skepticism. The specifics of traditional Christianity could also flourish, but as an encouraged voluntary activity. From the dominant Protestant perspective, the university then should hardly look subversive to Christian interests. As one Berkeley professor pointed out in 1900, church membership at the university was actually higher than in the state generally. So he could argue that "of all the forces which make for righteousness as Christian forces, I think a strong case might be made out for our state institutions of higher education."[30]

Such policies, then, simply operated side by side and largely independently of the research ideals that were defining most of the disciplines of the modern universities. Those research ideals were increasingly being shaped by scientific models that were considered neutral and objective,

Ironically, then, what Angell and his generation of predominantly New Englander educators achieved, often in the name of Christianity, was much like the Jeffersonian ideal for the university. In this respect, Michigan was not much different from the University of California. It was scientific at its center, open to broad humane ideals, and welcomed voluntary and sectarian religion on its periphery. The only difference was that Angell spoke more openly of the unifying philosophy and moral ideals as "Christian." Whatever Angell's personal beliefs, the type of Christianity that actually played a role in the conduct of the university would hardly have displeased Jefferson. It was an informally presented nonsectarian ethics of Jesus, combined with a total commitment to truth seeking and to the scientific method as an unassailable sacred enterprise. "We may learn from our Lord," said Angell, "that the quest after truth, after all truth, is justified. . . . So all learning, all science, is in its proper sense sacred."[31] Angell might emphasize that all such science must serve humanity,[32] but so had Jefferson. The specifics of science and philosophy had shifted in developmental and idealist directions, but the prevailing spirit was still that of a nation founded on Enlightenment principles. After a century of resistance from more traditional Christians, the dominant educational ideals were defined by a synthesis of Enlightenment ideals and an enlightened Christianity, or a religion of humanity.

It would not be a long step from such informal ethical Christianity to recognition that explicit Christianity was not essential to the enterprise. Since Christianity was being defined by high moral ideals of a civilization dedicated to freedom, science, and service, why not state directly that these latter were practically your defining principles?

John Dewey saw this point presciently and thus became a leading spokesperson for the academic consensus of the next half-century. At Michigan Dewey was on the verge of dropping both his philosophical idealism and his Christianity as unnecessary baggage. When he went to the University of Chicago in 1894 he let his church affiliation lapse. One of his last contributions to the University of Michigan was an essay that argued that "because science represents a method of truth to which so far as we can discover, no limits whatsoever can be put, . . . it is necessary for the church to reconstruct its doctrines of revelation and inspiration, and for the individual to reconstruct, within his own religious life, his conception of what spiritual truth is and the nature of its authority over him."[33]

In 1892, when speaking to the Michigan Christian Association, Dewey had anticipated these sentiments, ending his address with a stirring appeal to turn away from supposed revelation in "the older formulation, inherited from days when the organization of society was not democratic," to the scientific method of the university, which will not "isolate religious thought and conduct from the common life of man." Dewey ended with almost an altar call to turn from past religion to a scientific future: "Remember Lot's wife, who looked back, and who, looking back, was fixed into a motionless pillar."[34]

10

Harvard and the Religion of Humanity

Once we have seen the extent to which the rest of New England's higher education establishment moved in a functionally Unitarian or even Jeffersonian direction as it adjusted to the demands and promises of a complex modern society, we can see one reason why by the end of the century Harvard could readily reclaim its national leadership. Of course, its superior age and wealth, as well as the literary prominence of many of its graduates, guaranteed Harvard's eminence. During the first half of the nineteenth century, however, Harvard's Unitarianism had isolated it somewhat from the evangelicalism of national trends and from the leadership that Yale and similar New Englanders were enjoying. But in the age of the university, as the winds of liberalism blew strong, the fact that Harvard had already tacked in the direction of liberal Christianity helped it to regain its position as a flagship setting the pace for a national educational ideology.

Nowhere was the metamorphosis from old-time religious college to modern university more rapid or more dramatic than at Harvard. To paraphrase Henry Adams, Harvard in 1850 was in many ways closer to the Middle Ages than to the Harvard of 1900.[1] At mid-century many of the forms of seventeenth-century Harvard—the tutors, the recitations, the discipline, the strong clerical presence, daily chapel, the high regard for the Bible, and the classical curriculum—were still in place. The professoriate was largely Unitarian, drawn predominantly from the local eastern Massachusetts aristocracy and their descendants. By the final decade of the century only a fifth of the professoriate were Unitarian. Among the others, Catholics and Jews had at least token representation. Perhaps most significant, over a fourth were of no easily identifiable religious persuasion.[2] At turn-of-the-century Harvard, in the "golden age" of William James, Josiah Royce, George Santayana, Hugo Münsterberg, and others, religion could still be an issue, but old questions of orthodoxy seemed as far away as the Dark Ages.

It was not at all an accident that in Massachusetts, where the formal establishment of the church had lasted longest (until 1833) and the Puritan heritage had been most formidable, the reaction of dedication to freedom

The Soul of the American University Revisited. George M. Marsden, Oxford University Press. © Oxford University Press 2021. DOI: 10.1093/oso/9780190073312.003.0014

for liberal religious expression was most intense. California might be comparable in its openness, but its freedom prevailed in the far West largely because the area lacked a heritage of Protestant establishment and hence was open to pluralistic tolerance and indifference. At Harvard, by way of contrast, acceptance of the ideal of individual freedom was the culmination of a long-standing crusade. Charles W. Eliot, Harvard's renowned president from 1869 to 1909, had a faith in self-development that was most clearly manifested in his insistence on a radical elective system that gave undergraduates virtually complete freedom to choose their own courses. A corresponding freedom from religious restraints facilitated Harvard's ability to prevail in the late-nineteenth-century competition to assemble professional faculties. For a time it easily surpassed its longtime rivals.

The early Massachusetts Unitarian liberalism, which emerged in the oldest and most cosmopolitan parts of Massachusetts during the Revolutionary era, was an adaptation of the Puritan heritage to the demands of moderate Enlightenment ideology. Above all, it was reasonable and moralistic. Without rejecting biblical revelation, it argued that the Bible should be interpreted in light of modern rational standards of morality. Unitarians were optimistic about human abilities and hence were, even more than evangelical Protestants, enthusiasts for common sense, specifically for Scottish Common Sense epistemology and moral philosophy.[3]

During the first half of the nineteenth century, then, moral philosophy was as close to the essence of the collegiate mission at Harvard as it was anywhere in the country. The goal above all else, as Henry Ware Jr. put it in a highly successful 1831 tract, was shaping "Christian character" by internalizing habits of moral discipline that would build character, help liberate the individual, and improve society.[4] Having liberated themselves from Calvinism, mid-century Unitarians thought of themselves as in the forefront of the human quest for intellectual freedom. Like other American Protestants, they saw what they were doing as simply an extension of the Reformation. In the *History of Harvard University* (1840), President Josiah Quincy deplored the medieval times when "religion and learning were taught by the same masters. "After the Reformation," Quincy continued, "a more liberal system was introduced." Even so, the Protestant states did not progress far from the Church of Rome's traditional goal of bringing "the general mind into subjection through the instrumentality of education." Only in recent times were attempts being made "to rescue the general mind from the vassalage in which it has been held by sects in the church, and by parties in the state." Only as science and learning were recognized as community values in their own right was the mind beginning to be liberated from "subserviency to particular views in politics or religion."[5]

Harvard was the first American school to feel the impact of the ideal presented by the rising eminence of the German universities. Even before 1820 two of its graduates, Edward Everett and George Bancroft, as well as George Ticknor, who joined the Harvard faculty in 1819, had already led the way in what would later become a flood of American gentlemen-scholars studying in Germany. What the Harvard contingent, like their other American counterparts, brought back from Germany were not exact German models so much as admiration for German scholarship and increasing openness to idealist and romantic modes of thought. This new spirit added to the Americans' Enlightenment reverence for science a celebration of the life of the creative mind or the individual's intellectual quest. The "Copernican revolution" of Immanuel Kant in the eighteenth century had shifted the paradigm of human intellectual activity from a model of discovery of the fixed principles to a model of the intellect as an active agent imposing its categories on reality. Idealist philosophy recognized that this revolution made truth to some degree relative to the individual and to time and place and celebrated truth seeking as a process. Concern for understanding historical development also began to emerge, but the accompanying romantic idealism insulated it against the negative implications of relativism. God and the entire universe could be understood in terms of the analogy of the mind progressing toward truth. The highest human activity was to participate in this ongoing, creative, self-fulfilling, and ultimately divine truth-seeking process. Intellectual inquiry was thus deified.[6]

Prior to the presidency of Eliot, such trends were only emerging, as Harvard remained largely provincial and parochial. But the era of Unitarianism *had* cleared the way for rapid modernization without the religious restraints seen at other schools. As the Rev. Frederic Henry Hedge of the Harvard Divinity School reassured an alumni group, even though the college had shifted from its original emphasis on training clergy, "the secularization of the College is no violation of its motto, *'Christo et Ecclesiae.'* For, as I interpret those sacred ideas, the cause of Christ and the Church is advanced by whatever liberalizes and enriches and enlarges the mind."[7] In effect, Hedge was declaring that whatever Harvard does simply *is* Christian.

Other schools would soon arrive at similar rationales. The beauty of the argument was that secularization of the universities could be presented not as the diminishment of Christian influences but, rather, under the banner of the expansion of its Christian mission.

Charles Eliot and Freedom

Charles Eliot initiated practical reforms at Harvard as a means of implementing religious ideals. Eliot's religion, which has been well described as "Unitarianism raised to the *n*th degree,"[8] reflected his Unitarian background as modified by both the evolutionary-scientific and idealist-romantic ideological currents of his era. Harvard, because it was already free from the constraints of Calvinism and popular evangelicalism, could with little inhibition absorb the latest intellectual trends from abroad and translate them into an American context. At the same time in New England, even more than in the rest of the country, reform had to be justified by appeal to an ultimate ideal. That was what Eliot, thoroughly a son of Harvard, could provide. The cause of education was ultimately the cause of a higher religion.

In one sense Charles Eliot's career at Harvard might be seen as mobilizing the forces of professionalism and modern technique. His academic field was chemistry, and he was chosen for the Harvard presidency because of his reputation as a practical organizer. In his inaugural he announced his aspirations to apply to higher education the modern methods of technological organization, declaring: "The principle of divided and subordinate responsibilities, which rules in government bureaus, in manufactories, and all great companies, which makes a modern army a possibility, must be applied in the University."[9] By the latter part of his career, in the age of efficiency, he described himself as an apostle of "the expert."[10]

This theme of rational efficiency might be seen as reflecting the practical commercial-materialist side of the Unitarian heritage (Eliot's father was a businessman who had studied theology), but in Eliot, as for many in his generation, it was harmonized with an equally basic motif of romantic individualism. Eliot came of age in the era when young men and women of the Protestant elite, especially in Massachusetts, were enthralled by romantic ideals of self-reliance and spiritual inspiration, as championed, for instance, by Ralph Waldo Emerson. The "Sage of Concord" provided a popular and non-technical American version of the German idealist celebration of self and creativity.[11]

One did not have to adopt Transcendentalism wholesale, nor did one have to be an impractical romantic, to appropriate these inspiring ideals. Rather, Eliot's generation, of which he was so typical, resolved the tensions of modernity by allowing two themes to counterbalance each other. On the one hand, they could have the passion for order, systematizing, efficiency, scientific principle, personal discipline necessary for modern warfare, business, or professional and social organization.[12] At the same time, they filled the void left by the collapse of older theologies with their celebrations of a new idealism that not only ascribed redemptive qualities to the modernizing processes themselves, but at the same time deified individual freedom as the ultimate end that justified modern progress.

Eliot's presidency is best remembered for the controversial elective system that by the 1880s allowed Harvard students free choice in course selection. The beginnings of an elective system were already evolving at Harvard and elsewhere at the time Eliot took office, but Eliot's reforms offered students virtually free rein. The new system was, of course, the quickest way to break the hold of old college traditions. One justification for the revolution was practical. Almost none of the two hundred courses offered at Harvard in 1885, Eliot pointed out, could have been offered in its present form at the beginning of the century, so it was impractical to say that a few timeless courses were essential for all. Growth, change, and development were fundamental categories for Eliot and his generation, so while he saw the necessity of keeping touch with the past, "not neglecting the ancient treasures of learning," one could not be bound to it, lest one miss what is important in the present.[13]

The more essential rationale, however, was moral. The moral purpose of the college of the new university, as that of the old colleges, was to build character. The theories of how that was best done, however, had evolved. Character was best shaped not by constraints from without, but voluntarily from within. Still, there was continuity with the old mental and moral philosophy. Eliot, like his predecessors, talked about training the mental faculties. A major component of the rationale for the elective system, in fact, was that mental growth came through exercise of the mind, so that particular subjects did not matter a great deal. Learning the uplifting habits of freedom of thought gave this exercise a moral quality. One could meet great minds at work, seeing how they applied the principles of free inquiry, equally in any discipline.[14]

Preeminent among the faculties to be cultivated was the individual will, in which personal freedom was paramount. In the old colleges the pedagogical theories reflected still older ideals of constraint from without, or even trying to break the will; hence, they were constantly contending with overt and covert rebellions of willful students. The nineteenth century, however, had put increasing emphasis on the freedom of the will as essential to what is human. So now freedom and choice were to be cultivated and turned toward the interests of effective pedagogy. As Eliot argued,

> The moral purpose of a university's policy should be to train young men to self-control and self-reliance through liberty. It is not the business of a university to train men for those functions in which implicit obedience is of the first importance. On the contrary, it should train men for those occupations in which self-government, independence, and originating power are preeminently needed.[15]

Some critics viewed Eliot's emphasis on student freedom as Germanizing; in fact, it was at least as much homegrown.[16] Eliot did note in his 1885 defense of electives that continental universities long had allowed student freedom in course selection and that Oxford and Cambridge recently had instituted it. Nonetheless, he also insisted, as he had put it earlier, "When the American university appears, it will not be a copy of foreign institutions, or a hot-bed plant, but the slow and natural outgrowth of American social and political habits."[17] Although the very idea of evolving ideals embodied in a national spirit reflected the influence of German idealism, even in this framework the American heritage was the only relevant one. So Eliot, while appropriating international intellectual trends, saw what he was doing as in continuity with the New England religious past, which, in turn, had contributed to American ideals of liberty. "The elective system," he proclaimed, "is in the first place, an outcome of the spirit of the Protestant Reformation. In the next place, it is an outcome of the spirit of political liberty."[18]

The counterpart to this vast expansion of the spirit of Protestantism was a constriction of its formal regime. At Harvard compulsory chapel was the principal issue. Eliot moved cautiously on this front, apparently motivated by an administrator's concern not to offend conservative opinion. By 1886 they abandoned compulsion. Distinguished preachers addressed the continuing voluntary services, which in subsequent decades continued to be reasonably well attended.[19]

Freedom was the principle that tied everything else together. Evolutionary naturalism, which was one dimension of Eliot's outlook, may have seemed to rest on deterministic principles, but not if the highest product of evolution was the ideal of freedom itself. Similarly, the scientific method might have been thought to rest on deterministic premises, but on a higher plane it could be seen as teaching the lofty principles of free inquiry by which mind triumphed over matter. For the individual, freedom was the principle that allowed one to transcend local and parochial limitations and to reach one's full potential. And, of course, freedom was essential to American national spirit.

It was fitting that Harvard's most famous professor of the era was William James. James's philosophy, like Eliot's outlook, addressed the question of how to deal with an intensely religious heritage in the new scientific era. James, who was seventeen years old and studying science at Harvard when Darwin's *Origin of Species* appeared, came to see Darwinism as leading to an abyss of determinism that would destroy individual freedom and meaning. The dread of this prospect was one of the causes of a profound personal crisis that reached its peak in 1870. James resolved this by adopting a variation on the Kantian view of the primacy of the active powers of the mind in supplying categories necessary to make reality meaningful. Hence, free will could legitimately be a first principle, based on faith. So, as James wrote in his diary the day he resolved his crisis, "My first act of free will shall be to believe in free will."[20]

In 1872 Eliot hired James to teach at Harvard. During the next decades James led the way in developing the field of physiological psychology. Since psychology was not yet clearly separated from philosophy James could develop his more speculative philosophical interests at Harvard, emerging by the end of the century as the leading exponent of new philosophy that he called "pragmatism." James's pragmatism was essentially an extension of his psychological work, taking the active powers of the human mind as the object of scientific inquiry. Since our minds provided the only access to reality and, indeed, structured what we knew, the proper philosophical questions were those such as "How does the mind come to hold the beliefs it does?" Or, given evolutionary premises, "What are the functions of the mind in adjusting us to reality?"

Although James rejected the prevalent systems of cosmic idealism as too speculative, his more down-to-earth emphasis on the creative powers of minds had a similar function, providing a generation with a basis for broad religious belief as an alternative to traditional Christianity on the one hand and materialism on the other. James was careful, therefore, in his famous analysis of *Varieties of Religious Experience* (1902), to affirm the reality of the "more" to which religious experience pointed, even if we could not know about it as exactly as most particular religions claimed.

Moreover, even though James disagreed with cosmic idealism, he was not entirely adverse to it. He was instrumental in bringing to Harvard in 1882 its other great philosopher and America's leading idealist, Josiah Royce, who became his next-door neighbor and close friend.

James's leading concern was to preserve human freedom while giving natural causes their due in an age of increasing scientific determinism. Emphasizing the creativity of the individual mind, one of his major concerns became that the field of philosophy and, indeed, the entire the academy was becoming too much defined by the ideal of professional expertise.[21] Late in his career, in 1903, he lamented bitterly how the "Ph.D. octopus," or the demand of many colleges that every teacher, no matter how talented, must earn a Ph.D., was eliminating the creative amateur thinker. America, he thought, was in danger of suffering terribly from "the Mandarin disease" if this "grotesque tendency" continued.[22]

Ultimate Nonsectarianism

During this transitional era, philosophy was not the only contender to fill the spiritual and moral void created by the demise of moral philosophy and conventional Protestantism. Indeed, fields like economics and sociology emerged as separate disciplines, often including strong agendas to advance "Christian" social concerns. History, too, was seen as a source of moral insight. Even the natural sciences might be regarded as sacred expressions of moral integrity and truth seeking. Under these circumstances Eliot's radical elective system seemed less threatening to the moral integrity of the college program.[23]

The emerging fields of literature and the arts were especially conspicuous in taking over a spiritual and moral role. Again Harvard was a pioneer. Countering the trend toward the imposition of scientific models, the study of literature began to shift from philological approaches toward a view of great literature both as a source of enduring moral insight and as part of an inspiring "liberal culture" into which every educated person ought to be initiated. Great literature, such as Homer, Dante, Chaucer, Shakespeare, and Milton, thus became the canon for a popular cultural idealism. Human spiritual growth in the highest culture could be a complement to or a substitute for the Christian drama of the biblical canon. By the latter decades of the century this inspiring view of "liberal culture" was the prevailing curricular ideal for literature.[24] Classical culture also took on a new life as a major component of this ideal heritage, a point that was underscored by the continuing dominance of classical architectural models for the expanding universities.

The fine arts also emerged as a significant curricular component of the new cult of high culture. Here again Harvard was in the forefront. In 1874 Eliot appointed his cousin Charles Eliot Norton to teach art history. During the next two and a half decades at Harvard, Norton became the dominant spokesman and even symbol of American education's commitment to inspiring cultural ideals. As one student summarized Norton's influence, "Beauty became not aesthetic satisfaction merely but took her place high among Moralities."[25]

President Charles Eliot's views on religion in the university can be understood in this framework of liberating idealism, which provided the spiritual counterbalance to evolutionary naturalism. To Eliot the divine was simply the name we give to the essential spirit of the universe. As he wrote in 1886, "the life-principle or soul of that organism for which science has no better name than God, pervades and informs it so absolutely that there is no separating God from nature, or religion from science, or things sacred from things secular."[26] Hence, any entirely free and honest inquiry into any dimension of reality simply *was* part of true religion. Speaking at the inaugural of his friend Daniel Coit Gilman at Johns Hopkins, Eliot took the opportunity to meet head-on the issue of religious criticisms of the new universities. Some had spoken as though open-minded study of humans and of nature led to impiety. Eliot retorted, "On the contrary, such study fills men with humility and awe, by bringing them on every hand face to face with inscrutable mystery and infinite power. The whole work of a university is uplifting, refining, and spiritualizing."[27]These infinitely broad sentiments provide the context for understanding Eliot's most frequently quoted remark, which immediately followed: "A university cannot be built upon a sect. . . ." Just as Harvard served Christ and the church by doing anything that Harvard did, so universities were by definition the cathedrals of the most catholic of all religions, transcending every pettiness of sect.

True to his patriotism, Eliot framed this new universalism in terms of the nation. The complete sentence of his remark was "A university cannot be built upon a sect, unless indeed, it be a sect which includes the whole of the educated portion of the nation." This, in turn, simply echoed a phrase from his own inaugural in 1869, "A university is built, not by a sect, but by a nation."[28] The sentiment was one that spoke to the post–Civil War generation. Nations were sacred and must be united on the highest principles. In the new age nations would no longer have established churches; they would establish universal truths in other ways. Yet they must have a morally superior elite leadership who would bring unity out of diversity. Sectarian divisions among that class would be disastrous. Rather, "the whole educated portion of the nation" should guide the nation intellectually. Though free individuals, each with creative insights, they could speak as though with one voice because they were united by one divinely sanctioned scientific quest for truth. Thus, they could be the ministers of unifying cultural ideals in an increasingly diverse nation.

This was, it is worth noting, also an era that saw a resurgent American populism. Most Americans were not looking to the educated elite for spiritual and cultural guidance. How that issue might be resolved in the long run would be an ongoing story. Nonetheless, in this heady time of intellectual innovation it could be an inspiring grand ideal for some of the best minds in the nation. It was still, after all, the Victorian era, when deference was sometimes valued. And, in fact, middle-to-upper-class white Protestants ran most things. So the idea of a nation led by "a natural aristocracy," as John Adams had put it, was still a worthy and plausible ideal.

Near the end of his career, Charles Eliot, in fact, participated in an effort to disseminate the ideal beyond just the few who could gain a college education. The publishing house of P. F. Collier and Son persuaded him to lend Harvard's name and his own as editor of the Harvard Classics. "Dr. Eliot's five-foot book shelf" was highly promoted and remarkably successful. Into the mid-twentieth century it was common to see this set of Western and American classics in middle-class homes as at least a symbol of regard for new canon for the religion of humanity.[29]

So far as our story of the transformation of American universities is concerned, the significant fact is that a similar set of humane ideals would become the heart and soul of just about every liberal arts collegiate program through the first two-thirds of the twentieth century. American higher education would include much more in the practical, technical, and scientific realms, but something like these ideals would provide the spiritual center for those looking for more than just to learn a skill.

Nor would every school that adopted such ideals have to be as progressive as Harvard on the religious question. Such humane outlooks of "the best in the West," as they sometimes were later called, would be adopted by those of just about every religious or secular persuasion. And by the later twentieth century, when the ideal was fading elsewhere, often it would be institutions with more traditional Christian outlooks that would do most to preserve that version of the liberal arts ideal.

Still, it is instructive to see that at Harvard, one of the places where these ideals most impressively first bloomed, they appeared as spiritual human-istic ideals that were seen as potentially leading the human race beyond any-thing specifically Christian. Charles Eliot at the time of his retirement from Harvard in 1909 quite explicitly championed a "Religion of the Future" as an alternative to traditional Christianity. In this higher unifying religion "the best knowledge of God" quite simply "comes through knowledge of the best of the race."[30]

11

Orthodoxy at the Gentlemen's Club

At Harvard's 250th anniversary celebration in 1884, the aging Oliver Wendell Holmes Sr., of "One-Hoss Shay" fame and one of the great debunkers of the Puritan heritage, read his poem exalting how "Harvard's beacon shed its unspent rays" to benefit other American colleges. Among Harvard's beneficiaries was the College of New Jersey: "O'er Princeton's sands the far reflections steal, Where mighty Edwards stamped his iron heel...." According to the Harvard story, Princeton's president James McCosh left the festivities early in protest.[1] McCosh, indeed, admired Edwards and saw his own work as continuing that of his most famous forerunner.[2] In any case, Princetonians hardly welcomed being told that they were beneficiaries of Harvard's "unspent rays."

James McCosh had come from Scotland to the Princeton presidency in 1868, following the path taken by John Witherspoon a century earlier. Born in 1811, McCosh was the most distinguished academic to fill the college's presidency since Witherspoon, perhaps since Edwards. He had established himself as a significant interpreter of the central Scottish philosophical debates, while the tradition of Common Sense realism was being modified in a Kantian direction by William Hamilton and attacked by the empiricism of John Stuart Mill. Like many foreign-born intellectuals, McCosh was revered by Americans, who were still severely conscious of their provincial status. Unlike Noah Porter, McCosh could not be written off as a local reactionary. A leading philosophical realist, McCosh also did some work as a naturalist, kept up with the latest scientific ideas, and caused a mild sensation in American Presbyterian circles by being an early advocate of a theistic version of Darwinism. He was also a reformer, desirous of turning the College of New Jersey into a university.[3]

One of the things that made Princeton unique among leading schools was that it had close ties to confessional traditions Old School Presbyterians, who were renowned for their militant defenses of a strict Calvinist heritage. Following the Revolutionary era, the college, renowned as it was as a cradle for statesmen and jurists, struggled with so serving the nation's elite and maintaining standards of the church. As a partial solution, in 1812 some

The Soul of the American University Revisited. George M. Marsden, Oxford University Press. © Oxford University Press 2021. DOI: 10.1093/oso/9780190073312.003.0015

board members helped established Princeton Theological Seminary as a separate entity next door. While the college was chartered by the state to serve the public but controlled by a predominantly Presbyterian board, the seminary was strictly an agency of the Presbyterian Church in the U.S.A. Despite this separation, as at other colleges, the religious identity at Princeton grew stronger by mid-century. In Princeton's case, that meant strengthening informal ties with the seminary, which overshadowed the college intellectually. Princeton Seminary had played a leading role in the denominational division of the Presbyterian Church in 1837–1838, separating their Old School party from the New England influences of the New School. *The Princeton Review*, one of the most formidable American academic journals of the day, edited by theologian Charles Hodge, continued to fulminate against fine points of New England doctrinal innovations. At the time that McCosh was called to the Princeton presidency, seven of the ten faculty members were clergy and all were strongly Calvinist.[4]

McCosh's arrival at the College of New Jersey coincided then with a general effort to broaden its outlook so as to recapture its position of national leadership without abandoning its heritage of doctrinal vigilance. McCosh was a biblicist and theological traditionalist, but he was also to a degree an open-minded innovator, particularly regarding the issue of biological evolution. In contrast to Princeton Seminary theologian Charles Hodge, who argued that Darwinism was "atheism" because it was derived from a nontheistic premise, McCosh argued that the real threat was nontheistic "positivist" philosophy, but not necessarily the biological mechanisms for development that Darwin proposed. These, McCosh believed, could be God's way of creating particular species out of potentialities built into the original creation. So biological evolution could be compatible with Genesis, so long as one allowed for some special creation of humans as spiritual beings. In that setting McCosh's view won support from many conservative Presbyterians at Princeton and elsewhere. The leading Princeton theologians of the generation that succeeded Charles Hodge, including Francis Patton, Benjamin B. Warfield, and Hodge's own son, Archibald Alexander Hodge, all accepted McCosh's viewpoint.[5] Even Andrew Dickson White in his *History of the Warfare of Science with Theology* hailed the Scot as a deus ex machina who appeared at Princeton just in time to save it from the obscurantism of Charles Hodge and others.[6]

Like other academic reformers of the day, McCosh introduced more diversity into the faculty. During his first twelve years, 13 of the 17 professors he brought in had no previous affiliation with the college or the seminary. At the same time, however, he affirmed that he would not appoint anyone who "is not known to be a decided Christian." While, in fact, there may have been a couple of exceptions,[7] McCosh was adamant that "religion is not to be abolished from College teaching." To reinforce the point, he added to the existing chapel and Sunday service requirements mandatory biblical instruction on Sunday afternoons, taught for years by himself, on which students were examined.[8] While McCosh was attempting to modernize the college, as in improving its science offerings and teaching, and even was eager to transform it into a full-fledged university,[9] he insisted that it would be a Christian university, in a traditional sense.

It is not surprising, then, that Princetonians would become the most prominent critics of Charles Eliot's efforts to modernize the university on a higher post-Christian spiritual basis. The first to take on Eliot was the Rev. Francis L. Patton, who had joined the seminary faculty in 1881 and was about to take up the pivotal role of professor of ethics at the college. Patton was a skilled debater and renowned as a conservative Presbyterian polemicist for his role as accuser in the much publicized Chicago heresy trial of the Rev. David Swing.

Eliot, as one of his educational reforms, had in 1883 proposed changing the education of clergy from an authoritarian to a scientific basis. "The divine right of the minister," said Eliot, "is as dead among Protestants in our country as the divine right of kings." Like other progressives, Eliot in urging reform pointed to a changing national spirit. In the United States, "the people in these days question all things and all men, and accept nothing without examination." Ultimately this national spirit was expressed in the scientific ideal: "A new method, or spirit, of inquiry has been gradually developed, which is characterized by an absolute freedom on the part of the inquirer from the influence of prepossessions or desires as to the results." Clergy were suspected by laymen of violating this sacred rule if they relied on external authority or theological tradition.[10]

Patton responded that it was absurd to suggest, as Eliot had, that theology should be made to conform to the political system. Moreover, Americans did not seem often to apply the new spirit of inquiry that supposedly questioned everything to the work of lawyers, physicians, bankers, or scientists. The real conflict was not between a new spirit of honest inquiry and accepting authority. Rather, it was between agnostic science and positive religion. "If men can oppose Christianity only by saying that we do not know whether anything is true and therefore do not know whether Christianity is true [or false], we need no modification of the minister's traditional training to remedy this condition of affairs."[11]

Far more widely celebrated were the subsequent debates between President McCosh himself and Eliot. In 1885 the Nineteenth Century Club in New York staged the gentlemanly showdown concerning Eliot's controversial elective system.[12] In response to Eliot's arguments on the values of freedom, McCosh argued that freedom must always exist within limits. Just as in medicine or engineering there was a body of requisite foundational studies to be mastered, so it was also in the arts. It was incongruous, said McCosh, to have a college curriculum in which a student might study music, French plays and novels, or whatever captured his fancies, but which omitted not only the classics but also mathematics, logic, ethics, political economy, or the sciences. Particularly, he was alarmed that one could gain a Harvard education without being taught anything of either morality or religion. Rumor had it that Harvard was close to giving up required chapel as well. McCosh culminated his presentation by suggesting that since the future of religion in colleges was such a crucial issue, a second debate should be held just on that subject.

The second debate, held before a large crowd on a stormy evening in February 1886, was also highly publicized in the newspapers. Eliot presented his arguments that a national college could not be founded on a sect. If it were, it would have the undesirable effect of dividing the educated classes so that they could not effectively stand together against materialism and hedonism. He thus alluded to a powerful motive for the liberalization of Protestantism: in an ethnically changing country, the dominant class should not be divided. Moreover, said Eliot, tolerance of all religion did not imply indifference. Voluntary religion should be encouraged both out of respect for family ties and because no one had found an effective way to teach morality without religion. Yet colleges could also teach catholicity, so that every classroom would point to the candid spirit that illustrated the unity of all truth seeking and that science was creating a truly spiritual idea of God.[13]

In reply McCosh argued first that the sectarian issue was a red herring. Princeton and most other religious colleges exempted students from religious instruction if it was a matter of conscience for their parents or (if they were of age) themselves. Hundreds of colleges had also demonstrated that one could have nonsectarian college worship. So it did not make sense to say that, just because of alleged sectarianism, one of the greatest forces in the shaping of modern civilization should be excluded from higher education.

At places like Harvard, McCosh suggested, the motto over the gates should read "All knowledge imparted here except religious."

Differing views of human nature separated the Calvinist from the Unitarian institution, and McCosh felt that he had the empirical evidence on his side. "If religion is not honored in a college, any one acquainted with human nature," he alleged, "and with the present tendencies of opinion, can easily perceive what will be the prevailing spirit among the students." They will drift into "idleness or dissipation." Religion that is merely tolerated will soon come to be regarded as antiquated superstition and agnosticism will flourish. Students were asking, more earnestly than at any time since the declining days of the Roman empire, "Is life worth living?" Harvard students were wrestling with this question, whether their president knew it or not. "Agnosticism has no answer to it, and I know that many a heart in consequence is crushed with anguish till feelings more bitter than tears are wrung from it."

Closing with a bit of rhetorical flourish, McCosh repeated several times with his own elaborations Eliot's remark that "nobody knows how to teach morality effectively without religion." It followed, did it not, that a college that neglected religion was neglecting morality?[14]

In rebuttal, Eliot observed that he meant something different by religion than did McCosh. What Eliot meant was the cosmic religion suggested in the phrases "In him we live and move and have our being" and "Beneath are the everlasting arms." Such religion, he affirmed, *was* taught at Harvard, and hence was the basis for a higher morality.

McCosh pressed what he sensed to be his advantage among those interested in the topic. He closed by urging that the two papers be published together. When Eliot declined McCosh published his own side of the debate, noting that Eliot had declined publication and that "unless Christian sentiment arrest it, religion, without being noticed, will disappear from a number of our colleges, that is, from the education and training of many of our abler and promising young men."[15]

Princeton in the next quarter century provides a most instructive case of trying to negotiate the tensions between a more or less traditional Protestant heritage and the expectations for an emerging modern university. That story is especially intriguing because of the succession of the school's presidency. When McCosh retired in 1888, he was followed by the theologically conservative Francis Patton. Then, in something of a palace coup, when by 1902 faculty dissatisfaction with Patton had reached a peak, the more progressive elements succeeded in getting Patton replaced by Woodrow Wilson, one of their own. Wilson remained in the position until 1910, the year he was elected to be governor or New Jersey.

The story of the three distinct ways this succession of presidents dealt with the religious issues at Princeton has been well told in Paul Kemeny's *Princeton in the Nation's Service*, and the detail does not have to be repeated here.[16] Still, the major themes and outcome provide a particularly nice summary of how to understand why traditional Protestantism would be unable to retain its established place in mainstream American universities.

The College of New Jersey, though founded by revivalist Presbyterian clergy with predominantly religious motives, had ever since the Revolutionary era under John Witherspoon defined itself as having a dual role of serving both the church and the nation. The confessional Presbyterians, who throughout the nineteenth century still controlled the Board of Trustees, were relatively adept at drawing distinctions between church and nation. One instance of making the distinction was when in 1812 they established Princeton Theological Seminary as a separate and purely ecclesiastical institution (others would found divinity schools as part of the college or university). James McCosh likewise recognized that the standards for the college were not the same as for the church. At the same time, if the college was to serve the church as well as the nation, its teachings should not undermine those of the church. Faculty, accordingly, should be Christian, and that should be relevant to their teaching. But their teaching should not be sectarian. Further, though chapel was required, it, too, was to be broadly Christian, and exemptions from the requirement might be made in cases where there were religious scruples.

Francis Patton, if anything, made an even sharper distinction between the college and the church without much attention to the nation as such. In the church he insisted on strict biblicism and doctrinal purity. But in everything else he was congenial, liberal, and lax. Wilson, whom he hired in 1890, described Patton to a friend as "a man of most liberal outlook in his whole mental attitude, outside of church battles."[17] Similarly, James Mark Baldwin, professor of philosophy and psychology, observed that there were "two Pattons—a Calvinist of the most thorough stripe in the pulpit, but a person of immense charity among the 'sinners' of the world the rest of the week."[18]

Patton's reputation for distinguishing between the college and the church rested, in part, on his direct resistance to the complaints in 1897 by some irate Presbyterians that a number of Princeton faculty had joined in a successful petition to grant a liquor license to the Princeton Inn so that beer and wine could be served. They defended this on the grounds that it would promote temperance by allowing student drinking in a controlled environment, rather than in the local saloons. Total abstinence, however, was becoming a virtual article of faith in many denominations, and some Presbyterians expressed outrage that Princeton was operating a "university rumshop" and leading students toward "the calamity of the cup."[19] Patton, however, held that demanding total abstinence went beyond the Presbyterian confession and assured a crowd of alumni at Delmonico's in New York that "I will do what in me lies to keep the hand of ecclesiasticism from resting on Princeton University."[20]

That promise soon turned out to have its limits. Woodrow Wilson found that out when in 1898 he invited his friend and renowned historian of the frontier, Frederick Jackson Turner, to apply for a position at Princeton. When Turner, a Unitarian, asked whether there were any doctrinal tests at Princeton, Wilson replied, "I think I can say without qualification that no religious tests are applied here. The president and trustees are very anxious that every man they choose should be earnestly religious, but there are no doctrinal standards among us."[21] This was the standard Patton line, and Wilson was no doubt convinced it applied in this case. Much to Wilson's chagrin, it proved otherwise with the conservative Presbyterian trustees with whom Patton sided. Like McCosh, Patton had the view that the college teaching should at least not undermine essential nonsectarian Protestant doctrine. Unitarianism seemed to be crossing some sort of line and so they rejected Turner.[22]

The issues that brought down Patton's administration four years later were not those of such specific policies but, rather, the general laxity of his administration. He did not, for instance, have an "office," but a "study." Before 1901 he did not even have a secretary. He answered the vast majority of his letters by hand and, in true gentlemanly manner, responded to even the most trivial inquiries.[23] His style seemed to be based on the principle that the university, being composed of free individuals, should run itself without much presidential interference or systematic planning.

Patton's gentlemanly manners were part of his personal charm and helped set the tone at Princeton, which was rapidly developing into an elite gentleman's club. The students, forbidden on religious grounds from having fraternities, created members-only eating clubs, which during Patton's years developed into an elaborate system of elitism that dominated campus social life. Patton was reputed to have boasted that he presided over the finest country club in America.[24] He did not believe in rigorous student discipline, either socially or academically. He also welcomed the violent cult of football that gripped schools at the time, believing it a basis for cultivating friendships and future loyalty to the school.

The men's club atmosphere that Patton permitted might not have been offensive to the faculty had it not carried over to academics. At the turn of the century, as college education was increasingly becoming a status symbol in the emerging consumer culture, there were complaints at many leading schools of low levels of academic performance. Princeton was reputed to be second to none in such lack of rigor. Patton frankly encouraged the trend. A native of Bermuda, he retained his British citizenship and wished Princeton to be based on an English model, which he regarded as implying the recognition that only a select few students would be truly serious about the life of the mind. To force others into such a commitment would be artificial. Students who chose to take the many "pipe" courses the college offered were free to do so.

Patton did as little for graduate education as he did for undergraduate rigor. Although he oversaw the name change to Princeton University at the time of the sesquicentennial in 1896, he did little else to fulfill his promises to establish a true graduate school. In 1900, after years of frustration, the faculty took matters into its own hands and succeeded in getting the board to inaugurate a graduate school with a dean, independent of the president's authority. Similar intransigence regarding undergraduate reforms led to faculty demands that the school be run by an executive committee, with Patton as the nominal head. Patton rejected the plan, and after being assured that his substantial salary and professorship would be continued offered his resignation. Always the gentleman, he immediately nominated Wilson to be his successor. Patton moved to the presidency of Princeton Theological Seminary.[25]

Woodrow Wilson had already explicitly built on the existing distinction between the school serving the nation rather than the church in his famous speech at the sesquicentennial celebration in 1896, "Princeton in the Nation's Service." The eloquent young professor emphasized that the founders of the college "acted without ecclesiastical authority, as if under obligation to society rather than to the church." Central to sealing the character of the school, Wilson emphasized at length, was the American Revolution. The college was always a "school of duty," and its close ties to the Revolutionary cause gave it a central role in its mission to the nation. Specifically, the college served the nation by training its leaders. It cultivated character and an ideal of service. Religion was important to this public task: "There is nothing that gives such pith to public service as religion. A God of truth is no mean prompter to the enlightened service of mankind; and character formed, as if in his eye, has always a fibre and sanction such as you shall not easily obtain for the ordinary man from the mild promptings of philosophy."

This public influence of religion, however, should come only indirectly from the churches. "Churches among us," Wilson declared, "as all the world knows, are free and voluntary societies, separated to be nurseries of belief, not suffered to become instruments of rule." That principal was crucial to Wilson's own heritage as the son of a Southern Old School Presbyterian pastor. Churches served the spiritual realm, but they were purely voluntary societies, not agencies to rule over people with differing standards.

Wilson himself was loyally Presbyterian and indelibly religious, so he could use these principles to modernize the university in the service of a national idealism that had a genuinely religious dimension, but resembled the cultural idealism of the other university leaders of the time. "It is the business of a University," he proclaimed, "to train men in . . . the right thought of the world, the thought which it has tested and established, the principles which have stood through the seasons and become at length part of the immemorial wisdom of the race." Hence, university study should be built around history and, especially, the best literature of the race. "In short," Wilson declaimed, "I believe that the catholic study of the world's literature as a record of spirit is the right preparation for leadership in the world's affairs, if you undertake it like a man and not like a pedant."

Wilson also argued presciently that too much reliance on the scientific method was "working in us a certain great degeneracy." While the immense benefits of scientific and technological advance should be duly celebrated, the successes of applied science, he argued, had created an illusion that was leading many people to forget the defectiveness of human nature. Here an essential component of his Augustinian and Calvinist heritage showed through. Science, said Wilson, in what might be taken as a prophecy of the twentieth century, "has not freed us from ourselves. It has not purged us of passion or disposed us to virtue." Rather, the quick wealth and "incredible improvements of the physical setting of our life" create the illusion that we can forget the past and create a new better humanity through the processes of experiment.[26]

While as university president Wilson did much to put Princeton education on a more professional basis, he continued to insist that mere knowledge, then, whether scientific or even humane, could not be the ultimate purpose of education; rather, that goal had to be a transformation in moral character that would result in right action.[27] Religion, Wilson believed, was a great contributor to that end, but in the public setting of a university, the religion he preached was a religion of moral action. Wilson, in fact, preached often at Princeton, at the student Philadelphian Society, at chapel, at Sunday services, and at baccalaureates. As president he also selected visiting preachers and essentially filled the role of "university pastor."[28] While he set his moral emphases in a general Christian framework and sometimes emphasized that selfless action must be a response to God's love, he preached moral ideals that would be unexceptionable among liberal Protestant preachers of the day.[29]

Wilson essentially toned down the religious emphases that had prevailed under the Patton regime. He dropped the required Sunday afternoon service, though not the Sunday morning requirement or daily chapel. More dramatically, upon assuming the presidency, Wilson immediately terminated Bible instruction as part of the curriculum. Required introductory Bible courses had been offered by Francis Patton, who had recently hired his son George to supplement the offerings. George Patton was promoted to offering upper-level options in ethics, as his father continued to do. After three years, electives in biblical studies were reintroduced under new auspices. Wilson also signaled the end of religious tests for the faculty by hiring the first Jew to teach at Princeton in 1904 and the first Roman Catholic in 1909. In 1906 he had the university formally declared nonsectarian.[30]

The subtext, especially for the elimination of required Bible courses taught by the Pattons, was that the Presbyterian Church in the U.S.A. was in the midst of a protracted struggle between strictly conservative forces, most strongly represented at Princeton Theological Seminary, and liberalizing theological interests. Much of the controversy was built around the question of the authority of the Bible. Was it an infallible standard that should be the principal lens through which one views all other knowledge, or was it a book of ancient spiritual wisdom that should be honored as a profound early source of evolving Christian ideals but studied as a fallible cultural product much like other books? Francis Patton was one of the leading champions of the former position. His personal presence in teaching not only ethics but also the required Bible courses had been a vestige of the old college ideal of the clergyman-president. And even in his son's hand, the Bible courses signaled an alliance to Princeton Theological Seminary and the conservative party in the Presbyterian Church. Keeping such controversial views of conservative clerics as essential to a Princeton education was out of step with the nonsectarian, if broadly Protestant, moral ideals that were to serve the whole nation by training its elite public-spirited leaders.[31]

It is important to notice that during this time of disestablishment of sectarian conservative Presbyterian privilege, religious life among Princeton students flourished in many respects. The ethos in the first decade of the century was similar to that of Yale in the days when Henry Sloan Coffin was a student. At Princeton the Philadelphia Society, a fashionable affiliate of the YMCA, flourished during the Wilson era, growing from some five hundred to over eight hundred members. In the early twentieth century lines were not yet strictly drawn between evangelical-conservative and evangelical-liberal-progressive, especially at the student level. So the society could help generate enthusiasm for evangelism, overseas missions, and personal piety, and also broader and more socially oriented Christianity.[32]

That flourishing points to a principle found throughout the history of Protestantism and the American universities. Though the various changes can sometimes be described as "secularization" in the strict sense of removing a privileged form of religion from a particular activity, it is almost always more accurately seen as a repositioning or relocating of religious or spiritual interest from one place to another. Often, and characteristically in the era of the rise of the modern university, the repositioning involved a redefinition as to what was at the heart of the Christian message. And at the same time, any emphasis that might be displaced from the classroom could be seen reestablishing itself on a voluntary basis somewhere within the increasingly diverse university community. And as institutional diversity increased, so would voluntary religious diversity.

12

The Low-Church Idea of a University

If the emerging turn-of-the-century outlook was that there need be no conflict between the inherited spirit of Protestantism and the ethos of modernizing capitalist America, that was nowhere better illustrated than at the University of Chicago, founded by William Rainey Harper in 1892 and funded by John D. Rockefeller Sr. While older schools, such as Yale and Princeton, had to negotiate what to do with their Calvinist, Scottish common sense, and old-time college clerical heritages, Harper faced no such obstacles, other than perhaps concerns of his benefactor that there be sufficient expressions of piety and sobriety. And, unlike earlier founders such as White and Gilman, for whom the religious issue was primarily one of reassuming pious constituents, Harper put his positive Bible-centered religious interests right at the center of a thorough modern university.

Harper was an accomplished Hebrew Bible scholar himself, having taught at Yale prior to his work at Chicago. His larger mission, beyond his strictly academic work, was to educate Americans more widely in the English Bible and hence help sanctify the nation on biblical principles. That interest had in the 1880s brought him to a leadership position in the Chautauqua movement. Chautauqua was a broad program, originated by Methodists, to bring lay education, comparable to collegiate offerings, to Victorian Americans. Although biblical and theological studies were offered as part of the program, the whole enterprise was regarded as religious on the basis that "all knowledge, religious or secular, is sacred."[1] The task of restoring the Bible to its foundational place in American life was a mission not primarily against paganism but against Christian superstition, particularly biblical superstition. Popular Protestantism's benighted prescientific readings of Scripture were discrediting Christianity and had brought it to the precipice of a vast cultural disaster. One of Harper's most frequently reiterated themes was that traditional Bible teaching was an embarrassment, unworthy of the faith of modern educated persons. Such naive "bibliolatry" opened up Christianity to "the sneers of an Ingersoll."[2] "It is the misinterpretation of the Bible that furnishes the occasion of all skepticism," he wrote in an editorial in

The Soul of the American University Revisited. George M. Marsden, Oxford University Press. © Oxford University Press 2021. DOI: 10.1093/oso/9780190073312.003.0016

his academic journal, the *Biblical World*, in 1894: "The friends of the Bible have been its worst enemies. A faith in the Bible constructed upon a scientific basis will be acceptable to everyone who will take the pains to look at it."[3] The University of Chicago arose out of the concern of Baptists that they were falling behind in the educational race in the West. Congregationalists and Presbyterians had, of course, disproportionate influence in education, but even the Methodists, who had been rising socially at about the same rate as the Baptists, had twenty-one colleges outside the East and five times as many students as the Baptists. While the Methodists could point to their Northwestern University near Chicago, the Baptist effort to sustain its "University of Chicago," begun in 1857, had never amounted to anything, and it finally closed its doors in 1886.

In their efforts to rebuild, the immense breakthrough for the Chicagoans, of course, was convincing John D. Rockefeller Sr., that their city was the place to build a great new university. Rockefeller, a pious Baptist layman of a traditional sort, in typical American fashion saw competitive individualism as an expression of Christian calling and thus apparently had little trouble reconciling Standard Oil's ruthless business practices with his sincere Christian belief. Moreover, he professed to see his money as a trust given by God for Rockefeller to administer for the benefit of God and fellow humans. A Christian university was wonderfully suited to such altruistic ambitions. Using one's fortune for founding a university was in vogue, for example, at Cornell, Johns Hopkins, Vanderbilt, and, more recently, Stanford and Clark. Unlike the others, Rockefeller did not attach his family name to his money and apparently saw a university as a way to serve both the church and the society on a broad basis.[4]

William Rainey Harper, likewise a Baptist, even more than Rockefeller, embodied the American spirit of the time that almost anything was possible with creative and efficient organization, scientific methods, education, individual advancement, and technological innovation. His German contemporary, Max Weber, would have needed to look no further for illustrating a current link between the Protestant ethic and the spirit of capitalism. And in Harper's case it was quite explicitly guided by a religious zeal to serve the wider community. The Chicago Baptists knew him in part because he had taught briefly at their local Morgan Park Theological Seminary, which was to be absorbed into the new university as its Divinity School.

Indefatigable and driven by a work ethic, Harper had a passion for innovation. Although not all of his schemes worked, his university anticipated many of the traits of the twentieth-century multiversity. In addition to the Graduate School and Divinity School, the university in its early decades included a College of Commerce and Administration, a College of Education, a Medical College, a Law School, and a College of Religious and Social Service. The undergraduate program was divided into a Junior College and a Senior College and was to be fed by affiliated high schools and lower schools. The university also introduced a summer school and was widely known for conducting an elaborate extension and correspondence program to broaden the base of higher education. Moreover, it moved toward affiliation with existing colleges around the country that were to become part of the Chicago system.

Not everyone was impressed by the religious idealism that underlay Harper's enterprising spirit. Soon it became commonplace to make commercial comparisons, referring to Chicago as a "department store," "a factory," "Ye Rich Rockefeller University," or, of course, "Harper's Bazaar."[5] Thorstein Veblen, who had been a junior member of Harper's original faculty but was soon asked to resign because of poor teaching and an unorthodox lifestyle, used Chicago as his number one example in *The Higher Learning in America: A Memorandum on the Conduct of Universities by Business Men*. Veblen drafted his polemic early in the century but out of respect delayed publication until long after Harper's death from cancer at age fifty in 1906. Veblen, celebrated for his earlier critique of the "conspicuous consumption" of the American dominant leisure class, now complained that the operation of universities by businessmen on business principles was corrupting higher education as much as had the tyranny of clerical control. "Captains of erudition," of whom Harper was the prototype, were creating huge bureaucratic structures, based on principles of efficiency and promoted by crass advertising. All the innovations were oriented toward the practical, which threatened to replace true learning and scholarship. "Business house" universities were designed to indoctrinate citizens with the spirit of capitalism. "Through indoctrination with utilitarian (pecuniary) ideals of earning and spending, as well as engendering spendthrift and sportsmanlike habits, such businesslike management diverts the undergraduate students from going in for the disinterested pursuit of knowledge."[6] Scholarship itself had been preempted by "matter-of-fact" specialization and had become primarily a means of the advertising by which a university trumpeted its own prestige.

Upton Sinclair followed Veblen's bitter attack with a better-documented and even more scathing critique of his own, *Goose-Step: A Study of American*

Education, published in 1922. Sinclair, writing from an explicitly socialist perspective, argued that the vaunted freedom of American universities was a hoax. University professors were free to say anything just so long as it did not offend the plutocratic business interests that ran the institution. "Interlocking directorates" of universities were indistinguishable from those of the businesses that financed them. "The University of Standard Oil" under Harper was only one of many such instances in Sinclair's account, and not the worst.[7]

The image of Harper's Chicago as manifesting the application of business principles to universities has persisted. In Laurence Veysey's classic 1965 study, *The Emergence of the American University*, this framework provided the dominant interpretive grid. Veysey divided the rise of the American university into two eras. First was the age of idealist pioneers, lasting until about 1890. Then came an era of rapid expansion, rising prestige for university education, correspondingly large business support, and proliferation of university-related structures. The dominating theme of the later era is the bureaucratization of the enterprise, related to its expansion. Although only 4% of Americans in the appropriate age group were attending colleges or universities in 1900, the function of universities for socializing the Northern European Protestant elite was becoming increasingly important. Moreover, the expanded and diversified universities were designed to serve a wider constituency and thus anticipated a time in the later twentieth century when academic policy would be even more openly market driven. Dependent on social, economic, and market forces, universities soon became remarkably alike and could not be guided by abstract ideals. The alienated academic intellectual who still stood for humane values was an unhappy byproduct of this inexorable American tendency to run a university like a successful department store. At the top of such enterprises emerged, inevitably, managers replacing the earlier presidents, who had been men of vision.[8]

Veysey's approach has much to recommend it, especially as a reminder that religious interests, however sincere, always operate in the context of a host of other factors, many of which run at cross purposes. That is, in fact, the invariable nature of religious history. Religion as a historical force often works at most, as a leaven, or more often a salt, among this mix of other human interests and propensities, themselves a perplexing mix of good and evil. So even if we extend the era of significant idealism among university leaders (such as Wilson or Harper) into the twentieth century, those impulses were often and, perhaps, usually compromised by others, often by those who did the financing.

Seeing universities as emerging bureaucracies serving the interests of capitalist culture can do much to clarify our understanding of the magnitude of the practical forces shaping their development. Yet to see those forces as solely shaping their essence is probably to impose too much of a materialist/bureaucratic interpretive grid on enterprises that did include genuinely idealist aspirations as well. Nowhere is this more evident than in Veysey's treatment of William Rainey Harper.

According to Veysey, Harper epitomizes "charisma without ideology." Moreover, Harper is representative of the other managers. His personality "meaningfully if at times almost comically caricatures the traits of the rising new group of academic executives." He had a fondness for organizational charts and "structural embellishments," so that his university was "unmistakably *over*-organized during its early years." Harper's mind was "basically untouched by the power of abstract ideas," so that "Chicago never clearly 'stood for' anything in the sense that Cornell had stood for democracy and Johns Hopkins had stood for research." Though Veysey recognizes the strongly Baptist origin of the university, he dismisses it by pointing out that the dominating Baptist views were of a liberal sort, that the university had token representation of Jews on the board and faculty from the beginning, and that the administration did not want to emphasize "the Baptist side" of their work. More telling traits, according to Veysey, are revealed by observing that "the University of Chicago represented a blending of the small-town promotional spirit of the adolescent Middle West with big-city standards of sophistication." Although the university had a talented faculty that made it "one of the liveliest, most creative academic establishments of the day," it nonetheless "was indeed rather like a factory in many respects."[9]

Harper was, indeed, a quintessential organizer in the turn-of-the-century age of efficiency,[10] yet there is no reason to assume that building a more efficient or bureaucratic organization is incompatible with a religiously based idealism.[11] One can find countless examples of the union of the two impulses in free enterprise, specifically, religious organizations. We can better understand the obsessive energy behind this relentless preoccupation with organization if we see it as driven by a sense of religious calling. As he wrote to a correspondent in 1905, "All my work is in a very fundamental sense missionary work."[12]

So at the same time that we can correctly see Chicago as an early proto-type of what eventually became the bureaucratic multiversity, we should also understand it as a quintessential *Protestant* institution. Not only was it Protestant, but, more particularly, it was also *low-church* Protestant. This fact has to some extent been successfully obscured by Gothic or classical archi-tecture. Nonetheless, the low-church Protestant background is a basic clue as to why American universities took on some of their characteristic traits. In fact, we can generalize more broadly by observing that because the United States is the only modern nation in which the dominant culture was substan-tially shaped by low-church Protestantism, we should expect the institutions of that dominant culture to bear indelible marks of that heritage. So with re-spect to American universities, their pragmatism, their traditionlessness, their competitiveness, their dependence on the market, their resort to adver-tising, their emphasis on freedom as free enterprise for professors and indi-vidual choice for students, their anti-Catholicism, their scientific spirit, their congeniality to business interests, and their tendency to equate Christianity with democracy and service to the nation, all reflect substantial ties to their low-church Protestant past. Of course, Protestantism is always one among many sources of most of these traits, and the relationship between Protestantism and modernity is complex. Nonetheless, the low-church Protestant heritage is a most revealing clue for understanding the shape of American universities.

William Rainey Harper was particularly explicit (though otherwise not widely different from most of his contemporary university builders) in attempting to build the university on principles of a broad new Christianity that was a way of life that permeated everything, rather than a narrow set of doctrines. The university conducted daily chapel services, but it soon made attendance voluntary, partly because of the lack of a place for all to assemble. Later in Harper's administration weekly chapel was required for various divisions of the university, including a Thursday chapel for graduate students. The massive Rockefeller Chapel was not built until the 1920s, one of the clearest cases of a building erected in memory of a fading religious spirit.[13] During Harper's day, the situation was the opposite. A building was not a high priority because Christianity was not to be confined to one locus but was to pervade academic life.

The university itself was to be like a church community. Harper apparently regarded the YMCA and YWCA as too narrowly evangelical in 1892 and in-stead instituted a Christian Union. A remarkable and revealing aspect of this agency was that all members of the university were automatically nominal members of it. The original university faculty of about one hundred included three Jews, as well as a dozen without ecclesiastical ties, though no Roman Catholics.[14] The student body, although also overwhelmingly Protestant, included some Catholics and Jews as well.[15] The university chaplain, Charles R. Henderson, explained that although Christians led worship at university services, "this does not exclude other dialects of the common faith of the world, and the freedom to voice the deeper feelings of the soul in any form hallowed by reverence and family associations is permitted and encouraged."[16] In 1901 Christian Union membership was made voluntary, though it remained open to all.

Harper's zeal for community was reflected as well when in 1896 he added to the university governance a body known as the Congregation, composed not only of all administrators and faculty, but also of Ph.D.s of the university, various other alumni, and representatives of affiliated institutions. Major policy decisions were to be discussed by the Congregation, thus integrating the university community with the wider constituency it was to serve. Having no real authority, this unwieldy structure proved superfluous and faded from prominence.[17]

Religious education, in Harper's view, was analogous to physical education and should be included in the university curriculum for comparable reasons. Both sought to develop a crucial aspect of human experience that was now becoming much better understood through scientific study, but in which practice was essential. A similar analogy could be drawn to the study of medicine. There was room for pure research, but always with an eye to applications. Such an outlook fitted Harper's characteristic combination of the scientific and the practical. Though he revered the Johns Hopkins research ideal, he shared some of the suspicions of other turn-of-the-century critics regarding specialized research for its own sake. Practical applications were essential. So with respect to religion, he declared in 1904, "The university in its laboratory of practical religion should encourage the development of the altruistic spirit, for this is an essential part of the religious spirit. . . . In settlement work and in a thousand other ways, opportunity is open. This is a real part of the religious life which may not be neglected, and for which the university should make ample provision."[18]

Sports themselves were also integral to the university and at Chicago had an explicitly Christian rationale. In the Victorian era collegiate sports were typically seen as building character and community. Harper saw them in these respects as extensions of the practical work of the church. Consistent with this philosophy, Harper hired as his director of athletics, with full faculty status, the prototype of the Christian collegiate athlete, Amos Alonzo Stagg. When Harper was at Yale in the 1880s Stagg was at the center of the new cult of Yale athletics. The sports star also established the strong link between athletics and evangelical religion at Dwight Hall. He began divinity studies and had taken a course from Harper, but he came to believe he could do more to serve the cause of Christ in Christian athletics than in the ordained ministry. When he was invited to Chicago he feared that Harper might be too much of an intellectual to support sports, but he was immediately assured that the president saw the value of winning teams who could go "around the country and knock out all the colleges." His work, Stagg reflected, would not only create "college spirit," "best of all, it will give me such a fine chance to do Christian work among the boys who are sure to have the most influence. Win the athletes of any college for Christ, and you will have the strongest working element attainable in college life."[19]

Football could do for the universities much of what liberal Christianity hoped for and in the long run did it more effectively. Far more than chapel, it could bring the whole community together in one place and unite them in a cause. It could also serve better than the church for enlisting the loyalties of the surrounding community. It could be viewed also as a way, on a voluntary basis, to domesticate student rowdiness. Student uprisings did not entirely disappear, but football could be one way of channeling the energy in a voluntary society.[20] The problem, of course, was to keep football from making matters worse. The problem of violence on the field in the era before elaborate protective gear was a serious one and eventually had to be addressed. Moreover, the sports life could be associated with the vices that were a large part of the free and leisurely style that was so attractive in collegiate life. The abstemious Stagg (who lived to be one hundred) worked hard to clean up this image, encouraging athletes to shun smoking and drinking. He also helped invent and regulate modern football, bringing to the game innovations such as the forward pass, which helped his Chicago teams become major powers in the Big Ten.

Stagg viewed his calling, not just as coach but also as head of the University of Chicago Department of Physical Culture and Athletics, as fully in sympathy with Harper's liberal Protestant vision. In his autobiography, Stagg quoted approvingly the great liberal preacher Lyman Abbot's summary of the Harper vision: "The distinguishing characteristic of the German university is scholarship. The spirit of the English university is culture. President Harper has built a university in terms of service." While Harper's university valued scholarship, it was always "as a preparation for active American life."[21] As for many liberal Protestants, the United States was, in effect, Harper's church. This was consistent with his ultra low-church principles. So in his Presidential Report of 1902, reviewing the first ten years, Harper could emphasize that "the position of the University of Chicago religiously has been definitely and professedly Christian." This was so, he noted, despite substantial Jewish contributions, and the presence of Jews on the board, on the faculty, and in the student body. Moreover, it did not make any difference that there were no religious tests and that the faculties were drawn from people of almost every religious communion, and "many who were not members of any church." Nonetheless, "as the country of which we are citizens is a Christian country, so the University of Chicago is a Christian institution."[22] Furthermore, the university provided the foundation for America's mission to the world. In a talk to students on "America as a Missionary Field," Harper proclaimed that the world is approaching "the American period." These would be "the best days for civilization." Later generations would recognize the insights of this age as "new revelations of God." Such insights would come through science, and especially through recognition of "the paramount dignity of the individual." Harper virtually equated individual self-development with Christianity: "The question of individualism as a whole is still on trial; the real test of Christianity's success is still in the future." Christianity would have achieved final success only when "her founder Jesus Christ has been everywhere recognized." But America would be where "the great trial" of this faith "shall be conducted." The old countries, with their traditions and institutions which obstruct their performance of full human functions by the masses, cannot work at the problems that confront us.

Advanced Christianity and America, which was freed from "dead institutions and deadly traditions" (that is, Catholicism and monarchy), were both on trial. But traditional evangelicalism by itself would not meet the test: "The gospel as it is commonly understood . . . is not sufficient. It will free men from vice and impurity, but when thus freed the converts would better be permitted to die, unless they are provided with an education which will free them from narrowness, prejudice, and dishonesty." Traditional evangelization without education was worse than nothing: "Education will be the watchword [of] the new Christianity." Here was America's Christian mission to the world: "It is a call to establish here at home the foundations for the evangelization of the world; for if the world is to be evangelized, America must do it."[23] Harper made the equation of Christianity, Democracy, and the goals of university education in what became his best-known discourse on the nature and destiny of the university, "The University and Democracy," delivered at Founders' Day ceremonies at the University of California in 1899 and assigned first place in his 1905 collection, the *Trend in University Education*. Drawing on his Old Testament studies and on an analogy to the familiar formula that Jesus Christ was a prophet, priest, and king, Harper summarized his message: "Democracy has been given a mission to the world, and it is of no uncertain character. I wish to show that the university is the prophet of this democracy, as well, its priest and its philosopher; that in other words, the university is the Messiah of the democracy, its to-be-expected deliverer."[24]

This democratic religion was frankly humanist, but still Christian. "Its god is mankind, humanity; its altar, home; its temple, country." It creed was "brotherhood," its ethics "righteousness." At the same time, "In this religion there is much of Judaism, and likewise much of Christianity." It was "Jeremiah of olden time who first preached the idea of individualism, the idea that later became the fundamental thought in the teaching of Jesus Christ, the world's greatest advocate of democracy. [25]

John Dewey and the Religion of Democracy

Once we notice Harper's tendency to conflate Christianity and democracy, it becomes apparent that his view was not functionally much different from that of John Dewey, eventually the best known of the early Chicago faculty members. When Dewey was being considered for the position for which he was to leave Michigan for Chicago in 1894, James F. Tufts, who had earlier made the same move, assured Harper in a letter of recommendation that Dewey was "a man of a religious nature, is a church member, and believes in working with the church. He is, moreover, actively interested in practical ethical activity, and is a valued friend at the Hull House in this city."[26] Dewey himself had proclaimed, in sentiments much like Harper's, that a democracy is "a society in which the distinction between the spiritual and the secular has ceased, and as in Greek theory, as in the Christian theory of the Kingdom of God, the church and the state, the divine and the human organization of society are one."[27] The major difference was that Dewey concluded that in such an equation the church was superfluous. So when he arrived in Chicago, Dewey, who was also abandoning the Hegelian idealism that had sustained his theism, took the occasion to allow his church membership to lapse. At the same time, he was a board member of Jane Addams's Hull-House and, as Robert Crunden argues, Dewey, like Addams, was prototypic of that generation of progressives who, as their traditional theological beliefs receded, compensated with a corresponding increase in social idealism and activism.[28]

At the University of Chicago, where he remained until 1904, Dewey was the head both of the Department of Philosophy and of a new Department of Pedagogy (later Education), in which he established his experimental school, where he tested his progressive theories of education. Both in developing what became his instrumentalist philosophy and in his accompanying action-oriented educational theory, Dewey proved himself a kindred spirit to Harper. Dewey and Harper both believed in the redemptive functions of education. Dewey viewed the public schools as virtually the new established church, teaching the values of American democracy. Though Dewey had worked out the theory further than Harper, each believed that science was the key to finding unifying communitarian values, because only through science could one eliminate superstitions and sectarian differences and thus build an inclusivist "community of truth."[29] Dewey's talk, presented to the students at Michigan, "Christianity and Democracy," and Harper's "Democracy and the University," despite some differences, were two of a kind.

In this context of mutual concern to build a democratic or Christian community, it made little practical difference that Dewey had jettisoned his own church life and at Chicago spoke less explicitly of the Christian side of the equation. Just as at the convention of the Progressive (Bull Moose) party as late as 1912 the delegates could unite to sing "Onward Christian Soldiers,"[30] regardless of their personal beliefs, so at the progressive University of Chicago, Christian service, not theology or church practice, was the test of faith.

Sociology as the Last Flowering of Moral Science

Although one could find the functional equivalent of Protestantism playing a role in a variety of academic disciplines at the turn of the century, the academic field most closely matched to what the University of Chicago stood for was sociology. In fact, when it opened in 1892 Chicago was the first university to include sociology as a full-fledged separate discipline. To head the new field, Harper brought to Chicago Albion W. Small, president of Colby College in Maine. Small, who had studied at Johns Hopkins and in Germany, was the principal founder of the discipline of sociology in the United States. In 1896 he began the *American Journal of Sociology*, and he secured Chicago's place as a leader in the discipline.

Small was a man after Harper's own heart. He was a serious Baptist with ministerial training and dedicated, above all, to establishing a practical Christianity.[31] His continuities with the ideals of the old moral philosophy were direct; he had taught "Mental and Moral Philosophy" to the seniors at Colby. Concerned to reach a larger audience, he readily involved himself in Chautauqua work, coauthoring his first book, *An Introduction to the Study of Sociology* (1894), with George E. Vincent, Chautauqua's founder, for use in the summer programs. Sociology for Small had a practical moral purpose and was a means of inspiring people to take part in understanding and re-solving society's problems, especially through charitable institutions such as Hull-House. At the same time, Small was eager to establish the discipline on a scientific basis. In Germany, where he married the daughter of a general, he acquired a taste, typical of the sociological reformers, for German versus the more conservative British classical economic approaches to understanding society. Small regarded the German views, based on evolutionary models of a progressing community of ideals, as more scientific than classical economics. Thus, the high calling to research was of one piece with progressive moral re-form. "The first commandment with promise for graduate schools," declared Small, mimicking the *Westminster Shorter Catechism* on the Sabbath com-mandment, "is: Remember the research ideal, to keep it holy!"[32]

Small was part of a circle of social scientists who viewed their disciplines as means to promote progressive social causes. Small's mentor had been Richard T. Ely, who stood at the center of that circle. Others in the circle included John R. Commons, Edward A. Ross, Albert Shaw, Thoms Nixon Carver, Frederic C. Howe, and Edward Bemis. Ely is well described, as his principal biogra-pher puts it, as "a missionary and an evangelist to the American public."[33] In 1885 Ely was a principal organizer of the American Economics Association to promote his anti-laissez-faire views of a "practical Christianity."[34] He believed the state should be a principal agency for implementing Christian principles.

At Chicago, Albion Small, like a good many of his academic contemporaries, combined moral idealism (often explicitly Christian idealism) with a positivist faith in scientific progress, based on an "objective" research ideal that would guide the evolution of society.[35] Dorothy Ross, in her account of the origins of American sociology, attributes its distinctive qualities to the need to justify American exceptionalism. Accepting Ross's insight, we should go one step further and recognize that at the heart of American exceptionalism for these elite men was their Protestantism. As the republican and Whig traditions of earlier eras had taught, what made the United States exceptional were traits of its Protestant heritage related to freedom, free inquiry, morality, individual and communal values, and democracy.[36] Such ideals might be grounded in specifically Protestant rationales or, as the case of John Dewey provides an early instance, could take on vigorous lives of their own without the support of formal religious teachings.

PART III

WHEN THE TIE NO
LONGER BINDS

Harper's Chicago represents the high-water mark of liberal Protestant university building in which Christianity played an explicit role. Harper was more outspoken in his statements of Christian purpose than were most other university leaders, and he was a pioneer in giving the Bible a place in the curriculum. Yet his outlook had many parallels. The evangelical Yale of Henry Sloane Coffin and of Dwight L. Moody's missionary volunteers was another claimant to be the model Christian university. And Harper did not differ greatly from his presidential peers in his broad Christian outlook. James Angell, who still presided at Michigan throughout Harper's Chicago years, was just as explicitly Christian. Woodrow Wilson was attempting to implement something comparable to Harper's ideals for university-as-community in the less expansive Princetonian context. Daniel Coit Gilman, though less often explicitly Christian in his academic rhetoric, paralleled Harper in many of his interests and motivations. Eliot at Harvard could be viewed as a broader counterpart. Even Andrew Dickson White saw Christian and national interests as one, if Christianity was properly understood. And none of these interests were proposing a program for the university that contradicted the proviso, popularized by White, that modern intellectual life must follow the dictates of value-free scientific inquiry. Christian moral ideals would supplement and counterbalance such demands for scientific professionalism, not undercut them.

The quest to define the moral purposes of American higher education as it moved into the twentieth century has, indeed, become one of the prominent interpretive themes regarding that era. Julie Reuben's *The Making of the Modern University: Intellectual Transformation and the Marginalization of Morality* (1996)[1] has been especially influential in defining this agenda. Reuben divides her account into three overlapping stages. The first was the religious stage, lasting from about 1880 to 1920. University leaders were not hostile to religion, but they were redefining it by emphasizing its constructive moral qualities, and separating it from theology and church authority. In the second phase, from about 1900 to 1920, emphasis shifted more to science itself as a source of values. The social sciences, seen as successors to the old moral philosophy, were to be the chief bearers of moral teaching in the curriculum. By the 1920s, however, many in a new generation were insisting that science, including social science, must be value free. Hence, in this third era, or "humanistic and extracurricular phase," the humanities rise as the major surrogates for religion and bearers of the ideals of beauty and truth in Western civilization.

More recently, Andrew Jewett, in *Science, Democracy, and the American University: From the Civil War to the Cold War* (2012),[2] has argued for a more persistent place for the social sciences as bearers of morality. Rather than "value neutral" ideals simply triumphing in the 1920s, those ideals continued to be challenged through the mid-twentieth century by a "consequentialist" camp, in the spirit of John Dewey, that emphasized the use of science for more constructive social guidance. Christian Smith, in *The Sacred Project of American Sociology* (2014), argues more pointedly that the long-standing dedication of American sociology to promoting ideals of liberating human autonomy amounts to a functionally religious devotion.[3]

Further, as Julie Reuben noted, already by the late nineteenth century, debates over what the moral mission of the universities was were complicated by the simultaneous emergence of two impulses, the rise of the professionalized research ideal and a revolutionary reconstruction of undergraduate student culture. Roger L. Geiger develops this theme prominently in his *History of American Higher Education* (2014). He writes that "whereas research and Ph.D's were the hallmarks of the academic revolution, football and fraternities were the hallmarks of the collegiate revolution." School spirit, sports, and a host of student-led activities characterized the new campus atmosphere. Yale was a preeminent example. In such settings, voluntary religion could also flourish. Geiger notes that in the latter decades of the nineteenth century the YMCA "grew like wildfire." By 1900 its 559 chapters claimed 32,000 members, 31% of all male college students."[4] Women's higher education was emerging at this same time, both in women's colleges and in coeducation in most state schools and newer universities. Educators typically justified women's education in terms of what Andrea Turpin designates as a "new moral vision." Women tended to be more likely to be active in religious organizations than men. The YWCA counted as many as half of women collegians in its ranks by the early 1900s.[5]

Such analyses are helpful reminders that when we are inquiring specifically about the role of religion in the emerging universities of the twentieth century, we need to keep in mind the several distinct issues in modern higher education we are talking about. One question has to do with the roles of specifically religious outlooks in research or the production of knowledge, including the moral purposes for such work. Another is the role of religion in student life. That topic includes both voluntary religion, which seems to have reached something of a peak in this era, and vestiges of more formal recognition of institutional religious heritages, as in continuing chapel requirements. A further matter, related both to scholars' ideals and students' interests, is the role of specifically religious considerations in the curricula. That might show up in the content of what was being taught and also in attitudes of professors. And it might range from conventional pieties to open hostility to traditional religious belief.

Complicating all these issues, even when talking about a relatively homogenous white Protestant middle-to-upper class ethos, is the question of "whose religion?" Do we have in mind the traditionalist theologically oriented Protestantism of a Francis Patton, the evangelical piety of a Dwight L. Moody and the Y's, or the broadly "Christian" moral ideals of serving society or of building moral character among students? For mainstream institutions of the early twentieth century, there were evident advantages in focusing on broadly Christian moral ideals, which could be shared by traditionalists, ardent evangelicals, liberal or modernist Protestants, and in many cases even by atheists. Unlike specifically theological perspectives, broadly Christian moral concerns allowed ample latitude for faculty. Even the most materialist researchers could see themselves as serving the nation and the race and offering knowledge that could improve individual lives. In effect, the emphases on morality and service meant that the more troubling and divisive religious issues could be set aside. And champions of such nonsectarian moral ideals—or of pure scientific ideals, for that matter—could point out that there was plenty of room for voluntary evangelical religion on campuses. Furthermore, one of the striking features of the American cultural landscape was that there were hundreds of church-sponsored colleges that were free to be as sectarian as they liked. Those who were looking for a strongly religious atmosphere could find something to match their denominational proclivities in the higher education marketplace.

One further perspective for viewing all these questions is as largely internal debates among a privileged and often exclusive white Protestant community. Even though Catholics were the largest single religious group in the nation, they constituted only a small part of the university population and were a rarity among faculty. Catholics, in turn, maintained their own highly sectarian colleges in recognition of the strong Protestant biases of the mainstream. Prejudices against Jews, especially in most elite colleges, were also strong and helped keep their numbers small. African-Americans, despite the Protestantism of most, were a rarity in the mainstream. Often they were systematically excluded, and for most, any opportunities for higher education were confined to their own segregated colleges. Social class had much to do with all these instances. The dominant American universities were not only white Protestant; they were also elite institutions serving only a small portion of the population.

So even in this era that was in some ways a high point in fostering religious and moral concerns in mainstream American higher education, there were significant shortcomings. The largest underlying problem was that serving the particular concerns of any one religious faith was not the same as serving a rapidly diversifying nation. Genuinely high-minded moral idealism might obscure that reality, but ultimately it could not change it. So at the one extreme were secularist critics, such as Thorsten Veblen or Upton Sinclair, who might plausibly complain that the whole show of piety at mainstream universities was a facade that papered over capitalist business interests that funded and thus controlled the universities. Though universities might include some socially progressive interests, conservative economic interests always ensured that more radical ideas were excluded. At the other extreme were Protestant traditionalists who believed that the progressive moral ideals were undermining biblicist teachings that had once been dominant and were still the essence of true Christianity.

13

The Trouble with the Old-Time Religion

"Blasting at the Rock of Ages"

In May 1909 *Cosmopolitan* magazine published the first in an announced three-part series on what was being taught at American colleges. The sensationally written articles paid secondary attention to controversial economic views, but the revolution in religion was the major theme. The first of the essays, "Blasting at the Rock of Ages," immediately created a stir in pulpits around the country. The editors, sensing that they had hit on something, extended the series for two additional months, devoting the last two essays entirely to religious questions.

The author, Harold Bolce, followed the typical muckraking conventions. After visiting a number of campuses, sitting in on classes, and interviewing professors, he adopted an attitude of consternation in disclosing his discoveries. The editors, borrowing a number of Bolce's phrases, summarized both the content and the breathless tone of the message:

> Those who are in not in close touch with the great colleges of the country, will be astonished to learn the creeds being foisted by the faculties of our great universities. In hundreds of class-rooms it is being taught daily that the decalogue is no more sacred than a syllabus; that the home as an institution is doomed; that there are no absolute evils; that immorality is simply an act in contravention of society's accepted standards; that democracy is a failure and the Declaration of Independence only spectacular rhetoric; that the change from one religion to another is like getting a new hat; that moral precepts are passing shibboleths; that conceptions of right and wrong are as unstable as styles of dress; . . . and that there can be and are holier alliances without the marriage bond than within it.[1]

Despite the hyperbole, Bolce correctly identified the direction in which higher education was heading and the revolution that already had taken place regarding traditional Christianity. He acknowledged that by no means

The Soul of the American University Revisited. George M. Marsden, Oxford University Press. © Oxford University Press 2021. DOI: 10.1093/oso/9780190073312.003.0017

did all professors agree with the most progressive views, but he quoted many of the best-known and most influential academics throughout the country—William James, Josiah Royce, George Howison, William Graham Sumner, Edward Ross, Albion Small, Shailer Mathews, Andrew Dickson White, and many others. President David Starr Jordan of Stanford, who compared the way "men lose their reason and self-control" in a religious revival to drunkenness, was only one of many prominent figures who deplored conversionist evangelism. Even at Northwestern, a Methodist school, George A. Coe opposed most traditional evangelistic methods. At Syracuse, another Methodist school, Professor Edwin L. Earp taught that sociology showed that moral beliefs were evolutionary products of experience and it was therefore "unscientific and absurd to imagine that God ever turned stone mason and chiseled commandments on a rock." As for the University of Chicago, Bolce summarized: "This institution is nominally a religious seat of learning, but if it were dedicated to free thought and agnosticism it could not be more outspoken in its arraignment of many things in our orthodox theology." Chicago's Professor Herbert B. Willett, for instance, maintained that the Old Testament needed editing to raise its moral tone. At Syracuse, Chicago, and elsewhere, Bolce pointed out, teachings on the social origins of religion and morality led to the view that all moral rules were merely "mores" and that traditional institutions, particularly marriage, were not sacred.

Bolce was clear, however, that the progressive views seldom reflected mere secularism. Rather, he pointed out, although the professors to whom he listened thought orthodox Christianity unscientific and preposterous, they believed that "what is needed in this age is not less of God, but more." The professors, he correctly saw, "believe that the mightiest movement the world has witnessed is now under way—a movement destined to sweep away the mass of ritual which has kept man from a clear vision of God." Their views, which dominated all the leading philosophy departments, were evolutionary idealist, affirming scientific progress but opposing materialism. Bolce suggested an analogy between their views and those of Christian Science. Although the analogy was not exact, each, indeed, suggested a genteel and literate route to a new age of a higher religion and a higher morality. Each embodied a missionary zeal. "If we move our students," economist Simon Patten (a friend of Ely) of the University of Pennsylvania was quoted as saying, "we move the world."[2]

Orthodox clergy, including many in mainline Protestant pulpits, were disturbed by such revelations, and in his fifth essay Bolce sympathetically recounted some of their reactions. Their consensus, according to Bolce, was that "no greater calamity could befall civilization than the academic destruction of the old gospel that there is but one name given among men whereby humanity can be saved." Whereas "the unequivocal teaching of orthodox Christianity" was that "man is ransomed by the blood of Christ," the college professors repudiated that doctrine, "declaring that the fall of man is a myth; that it was a Judean peasant, not a God, that was crucified on Calvary; and that shameful tragedy had absolutely nothing to do with remission of sins and the reconciliation of an erring race to an outraged God."[3]

Although Bolce was pointing out an ever-widening chasm between what was typically taught in America's pulpits and what was taught in its universities, only a minority of church people or even of clergy were ready to sound an alarm. The strength of American Protestantism was largely in its activism and elevating sentiments. Even though most American Christians formally adhered to traditional doctrines, most of that same rank and file agreed that the real tests of the faith were in one's sense of personal reverence for the deity and in living according to moral principles. Liberal Protestant theology said much the same and in doing so employed much traditional Christian language. Evolutionary idealism might be more theistic than Christian, and pragmatism might base more action on scientific concerns alone, but all the positions could be blended together and united behind the high cause of a moral culture. In the dominant Anglo community of the mainline churches, the impulse was strong to emphasize commonalties with, not differences from, other Protestants.

Besides, those who were unhappy with the religion taught at the universities had other options. There were still hundreds of denominational colleges, and in many of them traditional Christianity still played a prominent role. Approximately half of all undergraduates attended church-related schools. Although the better-known colleges were reshaped by the same spirit that formed the universities, so that an Oberlin or an Amherst shifted dramatically from evangelical to progressive religion by the World War I era,[4] many more local and parochial colleges remained as havens for distinctive denominational emphases. So for those who remained strictly traditional in their religious sensibilities, the denominational colleges provided an important safety valve while the universities got on with advancing modern technical civilization.

Another factor mitigating criticism of the liberal trends was that most Americans did not go to college. By 1910 the total had risen to only about one in twenty.[5] For white middle-class Protestants, the percentage was much higher but was still a decided minority. Thus, there was not as yet much of a social base for a religiously populist critique of university trends.

Most of what criticism there was could be deflected by universities by the standard pieties regarding their service to industry and to the nation, their contributions to building student character, and the freedom and opportunities they provided for students to worship as they chose. A survey of state university campuses in 1905 indicated that about 60% of students were church members and that the percentage had risen slightly since the previous decade. An estimated 35 to 50% of students attended churches on an average Sunday at state campuses, and something like 20% of men and 50% of women belonged to the YMCA and YWCA, respectively. It was still plausible to claim that "the atmosphere of our state universities is preeminently Christian."[6] Moreover, by the second decade of the century the much-discussed idea of denominational houses to offer varieties of ministries was at last being realized, increasing opportunities for voluntary religious expression.

For university administrators, of course, a major concern was always that any controversial religious teaching might stir up constituents. In 1916, President Benjamin Ide Wheeler of the University of California wrote to Henry Morse Stephens, chair of the History Department, about Preserved Smith, a liberal Protestant interpreter of the Reformation. Wheeler wrote that, while he much admired Smith's work, "I am afraid it would never do to make him a professor in the University outright because of the very ticklish character of his subject. In spite of the utterly scientific method of his procedure, one denomination or another would surely take exception, if not to the facts, at least to his balance. . . . We are going on very comfortably now and perhaps it is better not to kick a slumbering dog."[7]

Catholic Authoritarianism

There were, of course, many Catholic colleges and universities. These, however, were all small, having a total collegiate enrollment of less than seven thousand in 1907. The great majority were under complete clerical control and were run and staffed by members of religious orders. Prior to World War I the Catholic colleges still had not adjusted to American curricular patterns; rather, they typically offered six- or seven-year courses, for boys only, combining preparatory and collegiate courses on a European gymnasium model. The curricula of these schools resembled those of the American Protestant old-time colleges. They were built around readings of Greek and Latin classics, with a capstone year devoted to Thomistic philosophical studies. Graduate education generally was still limited to the M.A., which was a beefed-up B.A. awarded after two additional years of study. The most notable effort to bring Catholic education somewhat more in line with current American university trends was the founding of the Catholic University of America in 1889. Originally exclusively a theological school, Catholic University soon offered doctoral degrees under Catholic auspices in a variety of subjects.[8]

The founding of Catholic University[9] was, however, part of the ill-fated Americanist movement. The university's first rector, John Keane, was one of the principal leaders of that progressive Catholic movement. The outlook of the Catholic Americanists reflected an attempt to synthesize Catholic teachings with cautious versions of the attitudes typical of American university founders. Not radicals, the Americanists' would be far closer in their views to moderate traditionalist Protestants such as a James McCosh or a Woodrow Wilson than to a William Rainey Harper or a George A. Coe. They could affirm traditional theology, but they wished to be open to reconciling it with modern science, reverent biblical criticism, and, especially, with the tolerance of liberal culture. These attitudes went hand in hand with a deep faith in American culture and American destiny and hence an eagerness to see Catholics assimilated into American life. One of the early professors at Catholic University, for example, argued against the common Catholic belief that in America the government was too un-Christian to offer acceptable public education. Rector Keane was an outspoken champion of the temperance crusade, a cause identified with the Protestant establishment. He also joined his liberal Protestant counterparts in participating in the Parliament of World Religions held in conjunction with the Columbian Exposition in Chicago in 1893. All this brought sharp criticism from conservatives, especially from Germans, who were more zealous than the Irish leadership to retain ethnic identity, Catholic schools, and Catholic theological distinctives.

The intra-American debates, however, were soon preempted by the pope, who had complete authority over the American church, still officially a missionary enterprise. Pope Leo XIII viewed the Americanist developments of the 1890s with increasing alarm. In 1895 he issued an encyclical addressed to the American church, warning that American separation of church and state should not be thought of as the desirable model for the church everywhere. The next year he fired a more forceful warning shot against the innovators by removing Keane from his rectorship of Catholic University.

The Americanizers' zeal for American political freedom went hand in hand with their faith in free inquiry. The most conspicuous issue was Darwinism. Conservative Catholics had condemned biological evolution as incompatible with Christian faith. In America, notably, the formidable Orestes Brownson, famed Catholic convert of the previous generation, had declared the Darwin doctrines in the *Descent of Man* irredeemably materialistic and incompatible with belief in a Creator. A few progressive Catholic scholars, however, argued along with many Protestant counterparts that biological evolution need not be *necessarily* materialistic but could be guided by God's creative providence. Keane and Archbishop John Ireland attempted to appoint one of the best known of such theistic evolutionists, the British zoologist St. George Mivart, to a chair at Catholic University, but their efforts were blocked by conservatives in the American hierarchy. The progressives did appoint a lesser-known defender of theistic evolution, Joseph Pohle.

The controversy came to its crisis in 1896 when John Zahm, professor of physics at Notre Dame in Indiana and a close ally of Keane, published *Evolution and Dogma*, detailing the compatibility of biological evolution, church teaching, and Scripture. In 1898 Zahm's volume was placed on the Index of Forbidden Books, and he was forced to withdraw it from its publisher.[10] The tense situation was not helped by the American defeat of Catholic Spain in 1898 in which the Americanists supported their nation's cause. Early in 1899 Pope Leo issued another encyclical, this time directed against the heresy of "Americanism." Although the doctrines condemned may have gone beyond what the progressive American leaders actually held, the Vatican critics of American culture pointed out that American emphasis on freedom as a central organizing cultural principle begged the question of "freedom for what?" and opened the door for building social values around human material desires and interests alone. Moreover, the prevailing intellectual trends threatened the authority of Scripture, church tradition, and centralized church control. Confronted with the dominant outlook in American culture running counter to its interests, the principal solution that Rome had to offer was a heavy-handed one. Not only did it reassert its own authority over the entire church, but it also wedded itself to very conservative views in politics and, especially, in doctrine, preempting all progressive efforts to reconcile church teachings with the spirit of the age.

The Roman Catholic Church in America was thus forced to retain its identity and its distinctiveness, but at the price of accepting Roman authoritarianism and severe restraints on its intellectual life. During the following decade the limits of permissible Catholic inquiry became increasingly restricted. In 1906, much to the consternation of a number of Catholic biblical scholars, the Pontifical Biblical Commission declared that the settled church position was that Moses was the substantial author of the first five books of the Bible and that one could not teach otherwise. The next year Pope Pius X issued a sweeping condemnation of "modernism" directed at a wide variety of efforts to reconcile Catholic teaching on theology and Scripture and on society and politics with the assumptions of nineteenth-century historicist methodology.

The result in America was that a "siege mentality" and an "inquisitorial spirit" prevailed within the intellectual community.[11] At Catholic University a professor of Scripture, Henry A. Poels, was dismissed in 1910 because he held, contrary to the Biblical Commission's declaration, a multi-authorial view of the Pentateuch. A complicated controversy, extending over several years and involving direct intervention by the pope, came down to the point that Poels would be required to sign an oath stating not only that he would not *teach* views on the Pentateuch that contradicted those of the Biblical Commission, but also that he did not *hold* contrary views. Poels could not sign such a statement in good conscience and his contract was not renewed. None of the influential Americanists, who in earlier years had spoken out for freedom, now took a strong stand in Poels's defense. Cardinal James Gibbons, for instance, was instrumental in his dismissal.[12] After the papal condemnation of modernism in 1907, in fact, other faculty members at the university who had endorsed positions that might have been interpreted as modernist quickly repudiated any such positions.[13]

While in retrospect few observers find attractive such suppression of even the mildest of dissenting views, overall evaluations of the long-term impact of the Americanist controversies will differ widely depending on what one thinks the ideal relationship between Catholic faith and prevailing American ideals ought to be. Sometimes the story is told simply as one of Americanist champions of freedom and enlightened progress versus benighted forces of repression. Yet others have observed that an assimilationist strategy of the most progressive Americanists may have involved a faith in the modern ideals of the American way of life that might be seen as, in its way, just as much a blind faith as was the support of conservative American Catholics for Roman authority.[14]

Much the same can be said of the intellectual crisis. Catholic conservatives, whatever the merits of their reasons, were among the few major groups in America to dissent substantially from viewing liberal American culture as virtuously neutral and from promoting a universal triumph of such ideals under the rubric of "progress." Conservative Catholics recognized, at least in selected areas, the fundamental materialism that underlay American claims to idealist progress. Moreover, they questioned whether philosophies that constantly celebrated innovation, openness, and individual choice could, in fact, provide the moral basis for a higher civilization, as was claimed by progressive Protestants and secularists. Most fundamentally, they questioned the claim that the application of modern scientific standards to all area of inquiry provided the basis of universally valid claims about the essential nature of reality.

The constructive counterpart to the restrictions on American Catholic intellectual life was the rise of neo-Thomist philosophy. This Thomist revival was almost entirely the result of an effort by the papacy to standardize Catholic thought and to provide it with a viable basis for resisting the inroads of modernity. In 1879 Leo XIII declared Thomism the official philosophy of the church. In America, where other philosophies had been taught, it took some time for Thomism to gain a foothold. At first the revival of Scholasticism appeared to some progressives as providing a basis for raising the level of Catholic intellectual life. At Catholic University a School of Philosophy was opened in 1895 dedicated to St. Thomas. The head of the school was Edward A. Pace, a well-trained Thomist but also a progressive, notable for bringing an experimental psychological laboratory to the university. With the papal reactions to Americanism and modernism, however, the shift toward Thomism became increasingly a method of maintaining papal control and a new conservatism. In 1914 Pius X admonished Catholic teachers of theology and philosophy that "if they deviated so much as a step from Aquinas, especially in metaphysics, they exposed themselves to grave risks."[15]

The strength of Thomism was that it provided a formidable alternative to prevailing twentieth-century naturalist and historicist assumptions, particularly in asserting an alternative basis for scientific knowledge grounded in divinely created natural law. It could thus counter contemporary claims that modern science established universally valid objective truths with its own version of the same claim. As Thomism was generally interpreted, the natural law philosophy provided the functional equivalent of an eighteenth-century Enlightenment claim for a human ability to discover objective truth. An orderly universe with theistic origins was, in fact, presupposed, as it was by most Enlightenment thinkers, but science was presented as established based not on prior faith claims but on objective foundations discovered by reason. Thus, a historicist positivism was countered with a natural law positivism, which within the Catholic community could hold the line in an era when the universal validity of science was widely taken for granted.[16]

In Europe the imposition of Thomism sparked something of a renaissance in Catholic thought, evidenced by such impressive scholars as Etienne Gilson, Jacques Maritain, and Christopher Dawson. In America the intellectual achievement was far more modest.[17] Near the end of the era of intellectual isolation Catholic scholars could assume, as John Tracy Ellis put it in 1955, "general agreement as to the impoverishment of Catholic scholarship in this country."[18]

Nonetheless, given impressive Catholic intellectual achievements abroad, this impoverishment appears to have had far more to do with massive problems inherent in the American immigrant Catholic situation than with the imposition of Thomism and the limits placed on academic freedom. As Ellis points out in his analysis of the situation, Catholics in America had no sustained intellectual tradition. When Catholic University was founded in 1889 John Keane, in recruiting his first faculty, hired six foreign-born and two American-born converts. With so much of the community consisting of first-generation immigrants of peasant origins, priorities were elsewhere, financial resources were limited, and anti-intellectualism was strong. Throughout the first half of the twentieth century Catholic colleges sent far smaller percentages of their students on to graduate school in either the sciences or the humanities than did their Protestant equivalents. As late as 1947 not one of the American Catholic hierarchy of bishops and archbishops had college-educated parents. Protestant prejudice and monopolies on America centers of power combined with the ongoing disadvantages of immigrant communities to perpetuate vastly disproportionate patterns of leadership in all aspects of American life. In 1927 Who's Who in America listed more than half, again, as many Unitarians as

Catholics, even though Catholics outnumbered Unitarians three hundred to one in the general population.[19]

All this is not to argue that intellectual repression from abroad was not a contributor to the conspicuous limitations of Catholic colleges and universities during the first half of the twentieth century. Rather, it is to suggest that a significant trade-off was involved. Catholic colleges and universities, in fact, made major gains by almost every measure during this era. The problem was that they also had such a long way to go. The intellectual restrictions of neo-Thomism limited the range of their intellectual inquiry, but it also provided a base for building an alternative worldview by a community that was threatened with melting-pot absorption into an alien culture with highly appealing claims.[20] Without dependency on European Catholic guidance, American Catholic intellectual life, impelled by a zeal to gain respectability, almost certainly would have developed a far greater dependency on the dictates of contemporary American intellectual fashion.[21] Whatever the weaknesses of Catholic higher education during this era, and they were many, Catholics emerged from this era with one thing Protestants did not: universities with substantial religious identities.[22]

In the short run, however, the Catholic repression combined with the second-class character of their universities confirmed all the worst Protestant prejudices. For mainstream Protestant universities, such authoritarian repression of academic freedom along with the seemingly medieval ethos of Vatican I Catholicism, which shaped its academic communities, was unthinkable. That is not to say that theologically defined boundaries were unthinkable in every Protestant context. Numerous mainline Protestant smaller denominational colleges retained at least some informal boundaries. Further, countless sectarian groups, immigrant groups, and conservatives in almost every denomination who were resisting absorption of their tradition into the larger national culture favored strict doctrinal and behavioral standards, and, when possible, imposed them on their colleges.[23] Most of the schools in the South, where sentiment never to yield to Yankee imperialism was still strong, routinely accepted formal and informal restraints regarding religious teaching. Where such repression was becoming unthinkable was, rather, among *mainstream* Protestants, who aspired to shape and lead a unified, technologically advanced, and morally superior American culture. For them, the Catholic example underscored the point that any religiously defined university would be a contradiction in terms.

The Perils of Methodist Success

The development of Methodist universities provides some telling examples of the difficulties in building a Christian university. Methodists, unlike other major Protestant denominations, founded numbers of significant universities. Schools with Methodist origins include Boston University, Drew, Duke, Emory, Northwestern, Southern California, Southern Methodist, Syracuse, and Vanderbilt. Several factors contributed to Methodism's greater propensity to university building. Older denominations, such as Congregationalist and Presbyterian, could point to distinguished universities that shared their heritage and concentrate any continuing efforts to preserve denominational identity on colleges. Methodists, however, were just emerging on the educational scene during the years of university building. By the Civil War era they had many colleges, but none was especially distinguished. Methodism's elaborate systematic organization also made it possible to build schools for whole regions, rather than being forced (as the Baptists, for instance, usually were) to rely on more local and more limited support.

Especially important for understanding the development of Methodist universities is that in the era following the Civil War Methodism was making the transition from the periphery to the center of dominant Protestant culture. In the early nineteenth century Methodism grew rapidly among the less educated classes and showed little interest in higher education. However, by the 1840s they had become the nation's largest Protestant denomination and were shedding most of their sectarian image. Many Methodists were now middle class and accordingly were building their own colleges. In the post–Civil War era evangelism still remained a high priority, and most Methodists were close enough to their sectarian roots to be proud of their pietistic heritage. Interest in founding Methodist universities reflected the continuing rise of some of their number in social class. It also signaled that they wanted both to participate fully in the cultural mainstream and to remain faithful to at least the essence of their distinctive doctrines and practices. As with other denominational traditions in this era of rapid cultural and intellectual transition, that would often prove to be a challenge.

In higher education the most dramatic struggle was at Vanderbilt University. The Methodist Episcopal Church, South, which had separated from its Northern counterpart in 1844, had been talking about establishing a university in Nashville since before the Civil War. In 1873 the local Methodist bishop succeeded in convincing Commodore Cornelius Vanderbilt to fund a university. Vanderbilt's young wife had a strongly Southern Methodist background, though the Commodore himself was neither a church member nor much interested in such matters. Nonetheless, he saw an opportunity to endow not merely a university but, as Paul Conkin puts it, "an educational mission in a benighted land."[24] Vanderbilt offered half a million dollars, sufficient to allow the opening of the university in 1875, and brought his total contribution to approximately a million before his death in 1877.

Despite its financial advantages, Vanderbilt University during its first two decades was little more than an undistinguished Methodist college and a few fledgling professional schools. As both a Methodist and a regional school, it had to contend with a lack of a well-developed educational tradition. Southern Methodists never offered much support financially and students were hard to find. In 1884–1885, a low point, there were only 176 students. Fifty of these were in the "Biblical Department," a separate school so named because of Methodist suspicion of professional theological training.

The college also ran into early suspicions that it would undermine orthodoxy. Alexander Winchell, a geologist, was the most accomplished member of the faculty and the only Northerner. Winchell's credentials as a loyal Methodist were strong. In 1873 he had moved from a faculty post at the University of Michigan to Syracuse University, another new Methodist enterprise, where he had served briefly as chancellor. In 1875, not having found administration agreeable, he returned to Ann Arbor but took a part-time position lecturing each spring at Vanderbilt.

Winchell was among the pious defenders of Darwinism, and in 1875 he published his efforts to reconcile evolution with traditional views of Scripture. Where he ran into difficulty was not with Darwinism as such but with his view, published in 1878, of races of humans who preceded the biblical Adam. This theory raised the sensitive question of the biological evolution of humans and also seemed to contradict the plain reading of Scripture. Though Winchell claimed the Bible did leave room for these unmentioned pre-Adamites, he was attacked in some Southern Methodist publications. Without mention of these issues, the Vanderbilt board meeting in the spring of 1878 summarily terminated Winchell's lectureship. They thereby eventually gained the dubious honor of being memorialized along with the opponents of Galileo and others in the final 1896 edition of Andrew Dickson White's *A History of the Warfare of Science with Theology in Christendom*.[25]

Early Vanderbilt remained in most respects a strict Methodist institution, much like an old-time college in its authoritarian style of government and strict ideas of discipline. In 1878 a popular professor of modern languages, Edward S. Joynes, an Episcopalian, was dismissed for drinking, though he claimed that the basis was only one much exaggerated incident several years earlier and he was not allowed a hearing or an appeal.[26]

The students, who were in a buyer's market, were more difficult to keep under tight rein. The student body was predominantly Methodist, but it was also all male and restless to free itself from strict Methodist social restrictions. Probably the most significant student victory was in establishing fraternities, despite administration efforts to ban them. By the mid-1880s fraternities dominated campus life and had defied Methodist mores by sponsoring dances and even, it was rumored, encouraging consumption of alcoholic beverages. During the same era, students had instituted intercollegiate sports teams despite some old Methodist opposition to such games as frivolous. As usual, the rise of the national student culture of volunteerism also brought with it an active YMCA on campus to supplement required chapel and Sunday services.[27]

By the 1890s Vanderbilt was beginning to look more like other fledgling American universities. This transition was effected particularly under the leadership of James Hampton Kirkland, who in 1893 began what was to be a lengthy chancellorship. Kirkland, the son of an upcountry Methodist itinerant, was a fully pedigreed 100% loyal Methodist. He was, however, typical of most of the turn-of-the-century leaders in higher education in holding to a broad view of what was essential to his denominational heritage. As Conklin observes, "He always tended to translate 'Methodist' into 'Christian.'" Moreover, he often translated Christian into "liberal Christian," or the "upbuilding of Christ's kingdom," a phrase that could encompass everything constructive in modern civilization.[28] Having taken his doctoral work in Germany, Kirkland also had modern views of scholarship and was determined to make Vanderbilt into a high-quality national institution.

Old-style Southern Methodists were not happy about this trend toward absorption of higher education into a national culture. They correctly recognized that their deeply held religious values would no longer be an influence. In 1901 came the first faint rumbling of what was to build into a massive controversy. Bishop Warren Candler was one of a number of archconservatives on the Vanderbilt board. In 1901 he introduced a resolution that the university should give preference to hiring Methodists, all else being equal. The motion passed without opposition, since this had, in effect, always been the position of the university. They would look for good Methodists but, since candidates were seldom equal, hire the best man from any Protestant denomination.

Three years later, however, the resolution became a serious issue when Candler nearly persuaded the board to postpone the appointment of Frederick W. Moore as academic dean. Moore was a devout Baptist. Chancellor Kirkland was irate and took steps to end the bishops' dominance over the board, on which they served as ex officio members. That led to a bitter controversy between the chancellor and the bishops that dragged on for nine years. Kirkland insisted that the university, even if predominantly Methodist, at the same time be nonsectarian. That stance became particularly attractive financially after 1905 with the establishment of the Carnegie Foundation, which offered attractive retirement programs for faculty members of colleges and universities, but only if the institutions were non-sectarian.[29] The bishops continued to claim the right to controlling representation on the university board. In 1910 the Southern Methodist General Conference claimed final say over the university, including the right to name board members as well as oversight by the bishop's board. The Vanderbilt board, meeting in the summer of 1910, defied the General Conference and refused to seat new trustees elected by the conference. Compromise was no longer possible and the issue went to the courts. A lower court ruled in favor of the General Conference, but in 1914 the Tennessee Supreme Court reversed the decision. Amid great rejoicing among the student body and the faculty, Vanderbilt was declared entirely separate from the denomination.[30]

In the meantime, to take up the slack from the Vanderbilt defection conservatives established two new universities with theological seminaries, Southern Methodist in Dallas and Emory in Atlanta. The latter was funded by the Coca-Cola magnate Asa Candler, brother of the conservative bishop. Predictably, after a generation or so, these schools, too, drifted into the national mainstream.[31]

The developments at Vanderbilt differed from what was going on elsewhere at Protestant denominational universities only in explicitness and dramatic quality. Because Vanderbilt was located in the South, conservative church forces were strong enough to force a showdown. In the North the same forces were present but had less strength, so that traditionalists' efforts to restrain the trends collapsed earlier. For instance, at Northwestern University, the largest of the Northern Methodist institutions, Charles W. Pearson, a professor of English for thirty years, was dismissed in 1902 for publishing in a local newspaper an article that said the Bible contained myths and errors. Evanston, Illinois, had a large Methodist population and local residents demanded Pearson's resignation. The school was between presidents, so the board handled the matter itself. In a rare case in which sanctions regarding religious views were brought against a professor outside a school of theology, the board supported the local sentiments. The firing, however, brought much negative national publicity, and the incoming president made clear that he would steer a broader Christian course, even though he would steer carefully. "It is vitally important," he told the board in 1908, "that an institution like Northwestern should not be misrepresented in its character in such a way as to offend either the denomination which gave it birth or the great community which is becoming interested in it without respect to denominational considerations."[32]

Northern Methodist universities were all moving in a similar direction, though with similar caution not to arouse a large, usually tolerant, conservative constituency. At Boston University, early in the century, charges of heresy were brought against two of its professors. One of these, Borden Parker Bowne, was the best-known figure at the university. Bowne had served as head of the philosophy department and as dean of the graduate school. He was the principal progenitor of the philosophy that came to be known as Boston Personalism, one of the most influential efforts to counter the materialism of modern science by putting it into the framework of a theistic universe that was ultimately personal. Bowne's theology was by no means orthodox, and he was accused of denying traditional views of the Trinity, of miracles, the Atonement, future life, and salvation. After a trial before a local Methodist conference, the charges were dismissed in 1904.

The case of Bowne's colleague, Old Testament professor Hinckley G. Mitchell, however, went much differently. One reason may have been that Mitchell was teaching in the School of Theology, where orthodoxy was regarded more as a direct concern of the church. Moreover, since 1895 students had initiated several petitions complaining of Mitchell's teaching higher critical views of the Bible. Faculty appointments to the School of Theology were reviewed every five years by the bishops of the Methodist Episcopal Church (North). In 1900 Mitchell was reappointed with a warning not to violate church teachings. In 1905, however, his contract was not renewed. In the wake of the ensuing controversy over his dismissal, however, the Methodist General Conference of 1908 decided that the church bishops should no longer act as guardians against theological heresy, thus effectively removing the likelihood that the church would

intervene in university affairs. Conservatives continued to complain bitterly for years, but the fact of the matter was that the leadership of the denomination was coming under the firm control of the more liberal party.
In 1916 the General Conference abandoned a conservative test for membership and adopted a book list in its "Course of Study," used for training
clergy, that included some decidedly more liberal texts than had previously
been used. After that point, the issue of church control, so far as traditional Methodist theology was concerned, was moot. The denomination
had followed its educational institutions on their liberal Christian path and
hence was not likely to attempt a reversal.[33]

In the meantime the Methodist universities were being further pressured
by almost all the forces shaping them to put aside their traditionalist ties.
Many of these forces, such as technological concerns, broad ideological
trends, and changing student mores, were informal. Others were more
explicit.

The most dramatic explicit pressure came from the Carnegie Foundation
for the Advancement of Teaching, founded in 1905. Andrew Carnegie, an
immigrant from Scotland, had no traditional religious training and acquired
his religious views eclectically. He was, in effect, an Emersonian. "It is a
growing belief with me," he told theology students at St. Andrews University
in 1902, "that in the not distant future increasing importance will be attached
to one truth until it overshadows all others and proves the center around
which religious sentiments will finally gather—the declaration of Christ, 'The
Kingdom of Heaven is within you.'" This kind of religion taught that "the
worship most acceptable to God is service to man" and had faith in "science
which has revealed an illimitable, indestructible and constantly expanding
universe under the reign of law, and also the divine law of his being which
leads man ever steadily upward, thus assuring him that all is well, since all
grows better."[34]

In setting up a foundation to benefit higher education Carnegie turned
to Henry Smith Pritchett, president of the Massachusetts Institute of
Technology (MIT). Pritchett, the son of a Missouri frontier Methodist
preacher, held an essentially secular faith in the same things as did Carnegie.
"His 'faith' was science," wrote historian Ellen Condliffe Lagemann, "his
church the university; and, with the new power to know the natural order
that science provided, he believed a new possibility existed for achieving
human harmony." Secular and religious were not meaningful distinctions in
the context of this faith in science and humanity. Pritchett was a close friend

of President Charles Eliot, who was chair of the foundation board when it called Pritchett to its presidency in 1905.

Pritchett, perhaps true to his Methodist roots, was one of the leading proponents of the gospel of efficiency, so popular at the turn of the century. Not surprisingly, William Rainey Harper, whose illness cut off his work with the new foundation, was one of those who strongly urged Pritchett to take its presidency. In his inaugural at MIT, Pritchett had talked about "The Educated Man and the State," emphasizing specialized training along with character and patriotism to serve the state.[35] As the United States was moving from its agricultural basis to become a leading industrial power, he proclaimed in a typical statement, "every human being should become an effective economic unit."[36] He brought similar goals for shaping a national higher education to the Carnegie Foundation. His goal, he wrote to Carnegie, was to make the foundation "one of the Great Agencies not only in dignifying the teacher's calling but also in standardizing American education."[37]

With the blessings of Carnegie and of a board made up of virtually every major university president, including Charles Eliot, Nicholas Murray Butler of Columbia, Arthur T. Hadley of Yale, David Starr Jordan, and Woodrow Wilson, Pritchett designed the Carnegie Pension Fund in 1906 with the explicit purpose of providing monetary leverage for standardizing American higher education.[38] Much as William Rainey Harper had been, Pritchett was concerned about the unregulated and often backward state of American higher education. Sectarian control was an obvious culprit. Accordingly, among the fund's earliest and most explicit goals was an effort to eliminate denominational affiliations whenever possible. To help do so, it set up a generous pension fund for college and university teachers, making it available only to those private institutions not owned or in any formal way controlled by a denomination and at which there were no denominational tests for trustees, students, or faculty and no "distinctly denominational tenets or doctrines [were] taught to students." In an initial survey of schools in the United States and Canada only fifty-one qualified.[39]

Pritchett, apparently not afraid to play the role of lion in a den of Christians, presented a strongly argued and revealing defense of the foundation's policy in a speech in Atlanta before the Conference on Education of the Methodist Episcopal Church, South, in 1908, when the Vanderbilt controversy was in full bloom. Pritchett offered a number of arguments against denominational control. Teaching sectarian tenets and having religious tests, he argued, led to inferior education that "goes against the very spirit of intellectual freedom for which a college or university stands." Further, having hundreds of competing denominational institutions, as in the United States, was an inefficient use of resources that could better be concentrated in universities with common standards that served the whole public. Churches should concentrate on being churches and not also being in the business of education. And if churches did expect to run their own sectarian schools, they should be willing to pay them themselves. "No denomination can in the future expect to control a college," Pritchett announced, "and at the same time call on the public to support it."[40]

Pritchett's strongest argument was that he controlled a lot of money, so that the foundation's policy was having the predicted result. Within the first four years of the Carnegie pension program twenty additional schools had severed their vestigial denominational ties and so qualified for the funding. Moreover, the Carnegie agents discovered that when those who did have denominational ties were asked what difference denominational affiliations made, they responded "almost without exception that such connection played little, if any, part in the religious or intellectual life of the student body."[41]

No one was unhappier about his school being disqualified as "sectarian" by the Carnegie Foundation than Chancellor James R. Day of Syracuse University. Syracuse was founded as a Methodist university, and the majority of university's trustees were named by Methodist conferences. On the other hand, already in 1872 its first chancellor, Alexander Winchell, had declared, "The University is not sectarian. It is an institution founded in the interest of truth, which knows no sect, no sex, no color, no contrasts."[42] Despite continued affirmations that it was nonsectarian, Syracuse had a reputation as a strongly religious school and the location was popularity known as "Piety Hill," a characterization that contrasted it with its longtime rival, Cornell.[43] When James Day assumed the chancellorship in 1894, he had been a successful Methodist preacher of the upwardly mobile sort. In a prominent New York City pulpit he had already gained a reputation for cultivating the wealthy. At Syracuse, where he presided for close to three decades, he was known for his powerful chapel preaching, for his domineering presence, for his autocratic rule, and for raising the funds necessary to turn the school into a major university.

At Day's inaugural in 1894 he made the point that, although Syracuse was Methodist, it was to be far more Christian than denominational. . . . It will be a university Christian enough to make a Hebrew as much at home as a Christian, to afford equal facility to Catholic and Protestant. There is no creed in mathematics or in natural science. Syracuse University will be a brain manufactory, taking its material from all sources of usable brains. It will be Christian not by exclusion, but by inclusion; not by magnifying a sect, but by magnifying human learning and contributing to the same.[44]

The Carnegie Foundation's test, however, was not that of the spirit but of the letter of church control. In its initial evaluations the Carnegie Foundation first informed Day that since Syracuse "has stood so consistently and so vigorously before the country as a distinctly Methodist institution," it did not qualify for the pensions. Chancellor Day, however, would not take no for an answer and in an exchange of correspondence pressed the point that the Methodist conferences did not have to choose Methodists as trustees, that the chancellor did not have to be a Methodist, and that there were no denominational tests for faculty. Unable to convince the foundation by such arguments, Day explored whether it would help if the Methodist conferences chose only 5 of the 33 trustees. The foundation refused to draw such a line and replied that *any* church control constituted ineligibility. Day also protested to Pritchett against the presumption of the Carnegie Foundation in acting as an accrediting agency and publishing reports evaluating and comparing institutions. Finally, after years of fruitless protests, Day settled the matter in 1910 by publishing a bitter defense of Syracuse and denunciation of the foundation. He concluded:

> Other colleges may do as they please. If they wish to crawl in the dirt for such a price, that is their privilege. But no university can teach young people lofty ideals of manhood and forget its self respect and honor or sell its loyalty and faith for money that Judas flung away when in remorse he went out and hung himself. It is an insult for such a proposition to be made to a Christian institution. "The Money perish with thee," is the only answer to it.[45]

Chancellor Day's righteous indignation against mammon may have rung hollow to some observers, since he was known for his books and articles defending big business. Critics supposed that these were related to his zeal for fundraising. He had attacked not only the muckrakers for their criticisms of business interests, but also even President Theodore Roosevelt for attempting to break the trusts. Unrestrained capitalism, Day insisted, was the only source of the nation's prosperity, and there was no reason for the pious to be worried about tainted money, a point he had put into practice by successfully cultivating the Rockefellers.[46]

Nor was he unwilling to modify the relationship to the denomination when funding was involved. In 1919 when he was attempting to bring the New York State College of Forestry to the Syracuse campus, he was denied funding by the state on the grounds that the university was "sectarian." This time (as he had earlier proposed to the Carnegie Foundation) he did have the charter amended to ensure that the Methodist conferences could elect only a minority of board members. The strategy worked and the funding was granted.[47]

Chancellor Day was probably as much as any of the university builders attempting to steer a middle course and discovering how difficult that was. The Methodist and Christian identities were important to him, and he was not willing to abandon them entirely. At one point in 1913 in response to an alumni request to increase board representation he told the trustees, "This body is not sectarian, but it is important that some Christian body should be responsible for this organization. This [proposal] simply opens the way to throw this institution out of the hands of the church that founded it within five years. . . . We cannot afford that." Day wished to be as open as possible, but he also recognized that there were deep problems in attempting to remain generically Christian. A year later he sent a communication to his dean regarding faculty appointments, noting that "we are running pretty largely to other denominations," and urging that no one forget that Syracuse was a "Methodist School." This was not precisely what he said to the foundations. To John D. Rockefeller Jr., he wrote in 1916, "We know no man after flesh or sect or nation here. We welcome Jew, Gentile, Protestant and Catholic. We will not have atheists and free thinkers on our faculties to sow seeds of infidelity in young minds, but we are no sectarian propagandists."[48]

Despite his efforts to hold some balance, the effect of Day's chancellorship was to remove Syracuse from any effective Methodist control. This seemed almost essential to his goal of building a "great university." As one of his associates wrote approvingly of his work, "Syracuse is like most of the church-founded institutions—each of them was forced to make a choice—either to remain a small denominational college with formal religion very much in the foreground, or to endeavor to play a larger part in the intellectual world without great emphasis on the outward expressions of religious interest." Chancellor Day "chose the latter course."[49]

James Day, like his counterparts elsewhere, led the university toward the increasingly standardized national and professional standards, but he was particularly explicit in calling the university "Christian" and in invoking God as his ultimate guide. This stance, which might not have caused comment in a strictly ecclesiastical setting, invited criticism the more the school moved toward being a national institution. With respect to Day, the most biting criticism came near the time of his retirement in 1922, with the publication of Upton Sinclair's polemic *Goose-step*. According to Sinclair, Syracuse was the "University of Heaven." Its board members, of whom the president of Standard Oil was only the most conspicuous, were the most pure plutocracy in the nation. "Never has there been such a series of grand dukes and duchesses as at this university," wrote Sinclair. Chancellor Day, Sinclair claimed, apparently on the basis of conversations with faculty, ruled as a total autocrat, "unassisted save by God." For Sinclair, of course, Day was the chief of sinners because he had invoked God's name for the trusts and against strikes and labor unions. Sinclair alleged, however, that Day's disregard for workers extended to the faculty at the university as well. There was no faculty tenure, claimed Sinclair. Rather, Day hired and fired people at will and sometimes for petty religious offenses, such as endorsing Sunday baseball, or deviations from doctrinal orthodoxy, such as denying the verbal inspiration of the Pentateuch. While acknowledging that scientists might teach evolution, Day told them at least to "be as pious as you can."[50]

Some of this, such as the charges concerning Sunday baseball and the Pentateuch, was probably apocryphal or exaggerated. Nonetheless, even the official history of the university reveals that Day was an autocrat, who had (as was still common at the time) his own way in hiring and firing. In 1916 he assured John D. Rockefeller Jr., "We will allow no wild-eyed socialism in economics or kindred subjects, while giving liberty of investigation to sound minds." When he was accused in 1920 by a socialist of having had a bill introduced in the New York legislature to ensure that he could fire without redress, Day replied only that this was nonsense since the power already lay with the trustees, which was to say that the chancellor already had virtual control. The most notorious case at Syracuse had been back in 1899 when the position of John R. Commons, one of the socially progressive Richard T. Ely circle, was mysteriously terminated. Although Commons did not claim that he was fired specifically because of his progressive economic views, he did later remark that "it was not religion, it was capitalism that governed Christian colleges."[51]

Here was still another problem for those who would maintain an explicit Christian identity for a university trying to serve a wide public. Political disagreements among Christians can be just as much the source of sectarianism as can theology. So even if the doctrinal disagreements that divide Protestants might be toned down, strong political-economic differences may be just as divisive, or more so. Ideally a university might be a place for, as Alastair McIntyre later put it, for "constrained disagreement" within a tradition. But often allowing such a plurality of viewpoints on contested political issues is difficult to sustain. In the case of Syracuse, the combination of an autocratic leader and the political outlooks of those who finance the institution preempted internal debate on a variety of Christian political-economic views, even as the meaning of being a "Christian" university was otherwise broadening.

In the long run, so far as the relationship to Methodism was concerned, there was not a great difference between James Kirkland of Vanderbilt and James Day of Syracuse. Kirkland shepherded his university to independence from church ties while Day retained a formal relationship with Methodism but removed the possibility of formal church control. Each was insistent that his university not be classed with Roman Catholic or other close-minded schools. The simple fact was that once a college expanded its vision to become a university and to serve a broad middle-class constituency, the days were numbered when it could be substantially shaped by its distinctive denominational tradition. In the cases of Vanderbilt and Syracuse, the less the student body and then the alumni were predominantly Methodist, the less they would stand for Methodist traditions. Perhaps even more important, if the financial support for the university was to come from largely non-Methodist sources, as it did in each case, it was virtually inevitable that the religious stance of the school would be determined by a broader consensus of middle-class polite opinion, whether secular or religious. It was still appropriate on occasion to call this consensus "Christian," but as new generations took over and informal traditions of distinctiveness faded, that term took on an increasingly ceremonial function.

14

The Elusive Ideal of Academic Freedom

While concerns of the modern market, represented by business supporters, students, and public opinion, were sometimes blindly pushing emerging universities away from their distinctive Christian emphases, the persons most explicitly seeking a rationale for freedom from religious restraints were the progressive professors. By the early decades of the twentieth century professors were beginning to emerge from under the shadow of administrators and to set their own professional standards for academic culture.

The rumors were true that on matters religious the most prominent professors were also likely to be the most outspoken progressives at a university. What Harold Bolce had expressed with alarm to *Cosmopolitan* readers in 1909, James Leuba documented with approval in 1916. Leuba, a professor of psychology at Bryn Mawr College, had been a student of G. Stanley Hall, and his 1916 volume *The Belief in God and Immortality: A Psychological, Anthropological and Statistical Study* was both an early effort to apply the scientific uses of statistics and a pragmatist tract for scientifically created religion.

As a tract, Leuba's study may be seen as an early effort not only to bring out of the closet the widespread academic skepticism regarding traditional Christianity, but also to proclaim skepticism's intellectual superiority and domination. Leuba's essential thesis was that as intelligence and education increase traditional religious beliefs will inevitably decrease. This was a thesis that Thomas Paine, Thomas Cooper, or Thomas Jefferson would have subscribed to, but in the United States its proclamation had been muffled for nearly a century as evangelicals and their immediate heirs had held much of the field in academia. Now armed with the prestige of the new evolutionary sciences and with the reassuring idealist versions of a Jeffersonian Sermon-on-the-Mount civil religion, the cause could re-emerge in an irrepressible form. Often hidden behind the pious and patriotic rhetoric of academic administrators, the renaissance of this enlightened skepticism was already well advanced. Much had happened even since the 1890s when the vestiges

The Soul of the American University Revisited. George M. Marsden, Oxford University Press. © Oxford University Press 2021. DOI: 10.1093/oso/9780190073312.003.0018

of orthodoxy had been routed in most leading schools. And if James Leuba's statistics meant anything, the future was bright for a new era guided by science and high ideals.

Leuba's most striking findings, and those that told the most about the future, were the marked differences in attitudes toward traditional beliefs among those who were leaders in academic fields compared with the rank and file. Beginning with scientists, he chose randomly from *American Men of Science* three hundred in the ordinary listings and two hundred others who were categorized as "eminent" scientists. He sent each of these a brief survey, on which he received approximately 75% answered returns. The first set of three questions regarded belief in God and offered three choices:

1. I believe in a God to whom one may pray in the expectation of receiving an answer. *By "answer," I mean more than the subjective, psychological effect of prayer.*
2. I do not believe in a God *as defined above.*
3. I have no definite belief regarding this question.

Although Leuba recognized that this question about God was limited to a very specific dimension, he argued that this dimension of a personal relationship between God and humans was essential to a traditional Christian view. The point of so limiting the question was to find a very brief way to distinguish traditional Christian views from those views (often also called Christian) in which "the traditional Christian God is exchanged for a God-belief in agreement with present knowledge."[1]

A second set of questions attempted to make a similar discrimination by offering the same three choices regarding belief in personal immortality of persons in another world.

Of the "lesser" scientists answering, 45.5% affirmed belief in a God in the sense specified, nearly as many disbelieved, and the rest had no opinion. For the "greater" scientists, however, a startlingly lower number, only 27.7%, affirmed the belief, while just over half expressed disbelief, with the rest not sure. Regarding personal immortality the percentage of believers was 52.8% for "lesser" scientists, but only 35.2% for "greater" scientists.[2]

Leuba also conducted smaller surveys of other major fields. Philosophers, of course, could not be evaluated since they were unable to answer survey questions without adding their own provisos. Of the rest, Leuba found that historians were the most likely to affirm the beliefs in question, about half of them doing so. On the other hand, sociologists and psychologists were even more likely than biologists to be skeptics, with only about a quarter of their whole number believing in a prayer-answering God (see figure 14.1). Leuba explained these differences by noting that physicists might "recognize the presence of invariable law in the inorganic world only," and that for historians, who still often see the hand of God in human affairs, "the reign of law is not so clearly revealed in the events with which history deals as in biology, economics, and psychology."[3]

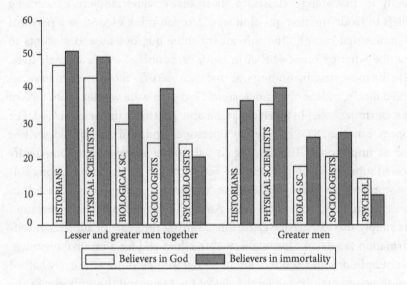

In each field, however, the surveys yielded similar patterns of greater skepticism among those who were identified as eminent in their fields than those were not. Leuba had a clear explanation: "I do not see any way to avoid the conclusion that disbelief in a personal God and in personal immortality is directly proportional to abilities making for success in the sciences in question."[4]

Whatever the assumptions behind Leuba's conclusion and the limits of his questions, he did seem to be finding striking differences between likelihood of belief among those most prominent in their fields compared with the less prominent. One explanation for this might be self-selecting mechanisms within disciplines in which persons with similar assumptions about the universal orderliness of things were controlling the disciplines and helping the likeminded rise to the top. In any case, Leuba was probably correct that something like these assumptions was correlated with academic success. His conclusion also was basically correct: "The essential problem facing organized Christianity is constituted by the wide-spread rejection of its two fundamental dogmas—a rejection apparently destined to extend parallel with the diffusion of knowledge and the intellectual and moral qualities that make for eminence in scholarly pursuits."[5]

Not surprisingly, the beliefs of students were influenced by those of their mentors. To measure student responses Leuba had distributed to students at nine "colleges of high rank" and at one normal school (teacher's college), mostly in psychology classes, a short-answer questionnaire concerning beliefs in God. The first question was "Do you think of God as a personal or impersonal being?" The subsequent three questions asked students to describe what difference belief in God, or nonbelief, made in their lives. Here the most striking finding was that men were far more likely to have accepted modern ideas of an impersonal God than were women, with 56% of men affirming belief in a personal God and 31% in an impersonal God. For women, however, 82% believed in a personal God, and only 11% described God as impersonal. This finding fit with other surveys that consistently showed substantially higher rates of active church participation among college women than among college men or, for that matter, among American women generally, compared with American men. Leuba's interpretation was simply that, for whatever reasons, "during the years of adolescent self-affirmation the desires for intellectual freedom and for a rational organization of opinions and conduct are in young women more effectively balked than in young men by the tender ties of the home and the authority of the church."[6]

Since responses in these student surveys were short answers, they were difficult to classify neatly. Leuba did find that rate of belief was considerably higher in the one teacher's college than it was in the leading colleges, so he was tempted to throw out the data from the normal school. One of his general conclusions, nonetheless, pointed to a substantial trend, once we discount its overt bias: "The deepest impression left by these records is that, so far as religion is concerned, our students are groveling in the dark. Christianity, as a system of belief, has utterly broken down, and nothing definite, adequate, and convincing has taken its place."[7]

Leuba also documented, on the basis of a more limited sample, some change in students' religious beliefs through their college careers. Here he surveyed all the students at only "one college of high rank and moderate size," presumably Bryn Mawr. "The spirit of this institution," he observed, "is assuredly as religious as that of the average American college." This time he asked about belief in personal immortality and found 80% believers among freshmen, 76% among sophomores, 60% among juniors, and 70% among seniors. Leuba could not accept the greater belief of seniors compared with juniors as evidence of a pattern of "a return to a 'saner' view after a brief iconoclastic period." Rather, true to his biases, he was convinced by a suggestion, confirmed by several observers, of the "intellectual superiority of the junior class." This conclusion he thought was demanded, since his investigation of professors provided "incontrovertible evidence of a decrease of belief corresponding to an increase of general mental ability and, perhaps, of knowledge."[8]

Based on his larger student survey, Leuba felt that he could generalize that most young people enter college "possessed of the beliefs still accepted, more or less perfunctorily, in the average home of the land," but that at the better colleges about 40 to 45% had abandoned some cardinal Christian beliefs. This he attributed to the maturing of their mental powers, to achieving greater independence of thought, and (somewhat paradoxically) to "study under the influence of persons of high culture."[9]

A self-reliant, independent quality, Leuba affirmed, was the principal characteristic distinguishing eminent men of science in all fields from lesser persons in the field. The leaders had to be willing to break, sometimes even with a certain callousness, from family and social pressures that would otherwise control their opinions. Lesser professors, either temperamentally, or as a result of social constraints of local communities on local schools, less often achieved this independence. Greater academics were more often from more eminent families in which they were able to achieve habits of personal freedom earlier. Moreover, they could more often establish themselves in major academic communities in which "intellectual freedom is honored far above orthodoxy."[10]

Academic Freedom as a Sacred Concept

When the American Association of University Professors (AAUP) was organized in 1915, its founders proclaimed an ideal of academic freedom as essential to the definition of a university. At first some academic administrators resisted aspects of the due process in hiring and firing that the AAUP insisted their ideal implied, but within the next two decades academic freedom, more or less as the AAUP had defined it, it was widely accepted. By 1940, when an important restatement of the AAUP principles was widely adopted, the ideal had become a standard assumption in American academic thought.[11] Certainly by the end of the era of McCarthyite repression of the early 1950s, academic freedom had attained sacred status among the professoriate and was often spoken of as though it were an ancient absolute, associated with universities since time immemorial.

The fact of the matter was that, although aspects of the concept of academic freedom could be found among the Jeffersonians and at nineteenth-century German universities, the phrase, as well as most of its twentieth-century applications, was hardly older than the century itself.[12] Some aspects of the modern concept, of course, had a longer history. Thomas Jefferson talked about liberty in education as the ideal for the University of Virginia, but at the time the American educated elite was sufficiently divided for his program to be widely recognized for what it was: a substitution of boundaries of inquiry consistent with Unitarian Christianity for the older conventional boundaries set by orthodox Protestantism.[13] By the late nineteenth century, however, an updated version of the Jeffersonian ideal of a neutral science had become sufficiently dominant in the academic community to rout the remaining opposition. In this regard the intellectual naiveté of faith in the neutrality of science now often attributed to the Enlightenment was much more prevalent in early-twentieth-century America than it had been in the eighteenth or early nineteenth centuries.[14] Prevailing academic opinion now accepted, almost without dispute, that since a university was defined as a scientific institution it was a neutral territory in which all views would have an even chance to be judged on their intellectual merits alone. Marxists, Catholics, conservative Protestants, and others who complained that their views did not get a fair hearing were dismissed as lacking in intellectual merit.

The direct inspiration for the modern American conception of academic freedom came, however, from Germany, or at least from the romanticized impressions of Germany that the many thousands of American academics who studied there brought back with them. Particularly important for the American organizers of the academic profession after 1890 was the German *Lehrfreiheit*, referring to freedom for university professors. In Germany this freedom included, first, the rights for professors to teach whatever they chose with a minimum of administrative regulations and, second, the freedom to conduct one's research and to report one's findings in lectures and publications without external restraint. At the heart of *Lehrfreiheit*, as

Americans typically understood it, was the modern ideal that truth is progressive and that for science to advance it must be freed from tradition and preconception. In nineteenth-century Germany this outlook was associated with the term *Wissenschaft*, which meant more than just the English word "science," suggesting instead the "sanctified" moral ideal of a scientific search for truth.[15] During the nineteenth century, German Protestant universities only gradually won full recognition of such professorial autonomy, including freedom from occasional ecclesiastical interference. Nonetheless, they were always far in advance of American schools, and by the time of the establishment of the German Empire *Lehrfreiheit* was solidly enshrined. The peculiarity of the German freedom, however, was that it was guaranteed by the autocratic state, which controlled the universities and so protected them from direct interference of other interests. In a society far more hierarchical and more conscious of status than the United States, *Lehrfreiheit* was not an extension of any general commitment to freedom for all citizens, but one of the prerogatives of professorial status, suggesting the precedent of much more limited professorial immunities going back to the Middle Ages. Once the wider applications of modern *Lehrfreiheit* were accepted, however, they were proclaimed by their Protestant advocates as essential to any institution calling itself a "university."[16] While the German ideals of *Wissenschaft* and *Lehrfreiheit* converged with and were translated into American Whig or republican ideals and so transformed had important influences as *ideals* for the academics who defined American universities, the Americans never followed German precedents very closely.

In the 1890s the cases that precipitated the American formulations of "academic freedom" were a series of dismissals, or calls for dismissals, of politically progressive activist professors with pro-labor and mildly socialist views. Most of these were social scientists broadly within the orbit of Richard T. Ely, founder of the American Economics Association, and like Ely combined Christian moral idealism with their progressive views. Ely himself survived such attacks at the University of Wisconsin. In 1895 Edward W. Bemis, a former student of Ely, did not have his contract renewed at Chicago. William Rainey Harper claimed that Bemis's s pro-labor views were not the reason for the dismissal, but Ely and friends believed otherwise. Even more certainly, they were convinced that the 1899 dismissal from Syracuse of John R. Commons, a more distinguished economist, was due to his political views. At Stanford, Edward A. Ross, another of the same circle, was dismissed in 1898 quite frankly for his political views, after extensive pressure from Jane

Lathrop Stanford, widow of the founder, railroad tycoon Leland Stanford. Ross's dismissal sparked some strong protests, and in 1900 the American Economics Association appointed an investigating committee that anticipated, including some of the same persons, the formation of the AAUP fifteen years later.[17]

The major question of the 1890s, which was still not resolved late in the Progressive Era at the time of the founding of the AAUP, was what rights professors had to speak *in public*, particularly on political issues. In Germany, professors were not assumed to have a right to take partisan political stands, especially if they favored socialism.[18] In the United States, however, when progressive professors with mildly socialist leanings were dismissed for political activities or public presentations of their views, an outcry was raised about freedom of speech. Could professors have less freedom than other American citizens? Freedom for public speech thus was a major component rolled into the American version of "academic freedom."

Academic freedom in an elusive concept because it is not a simply matter of affirming freedom of inquiry and expression but always also involves the question of what the limits are on such freedom. Freedom is never unbounded. So in academia there are always some restrictions on what may be advocated publicly, such as obscene, scandalous, cruel, inflammatory, fraudulent, and illegal teachings. Exact standards regarding such matters are always contested, change over time, and may differ in regard to institutional circumstances and purposes. So there is no simple formula for settling the hard cases.

John Dewey, who became the first president of the AAUP, was the leading early proponent of what became the orthodox view. Writing on "Academic Freedom" in 1902, he enunciated all the essentials of the standard twentieth-century American definition of a university. There are two types of institutions, he said. "An ecclesiastical, political or even economic corporation holding certain tenets," he affirmed, "certainly has a right to support an institution to maintain and propagate its creed." These "teaching bodies, called by whatever name" were not to be confused with "the university proper." While professors at partisan institutions might deplore the narrowness of such schools and work to speed their transformation into true universities, in the meantime they would have to accept that schools had a right to limit free inquiry, so long as their standards were clearly stated.

Universities, on the other hand, were constructed for the scientific investigation of the truth: "To investigate truth; critically to verify fact; to reach conclusions by means of the best methods at command, untrammeled by external fear or favor, to communicate this truth to the student; to interpret to him its bearing on the questions he will have to face in life—this is precisely the aim and object of the university."[19]

Dewey regarded this principle as beyond dispute but recognized problems in its application. The major one was that in many fields science had not yet reached the mature state it had attained in mathematics, astronomy, physics, and chemistry. In part this was simply a problem of lack of full public acceptance of scientific findings, as when popular prejudices limited teaching about biological evolution at some smaller colleges. In some other disciplines, such as sociology and psychology, and those aspects of history and literature having most to do with religion, the almost total public ignorance of the scientific character of such inquiries was compounded by some backwardness in the sciences themselves. This meant, on the one hand, that there must be total freedom to educate the public in the findings of these sciences. On the other hand, it demanded care on scholars' parts not to speak dogmatically on subjects on which they were not scientifically expert.

This latter point was an important proviso in the AAUP founders' early definitions of academic freedom. Freedom of expression was limited to areas of scientific competence. So Dewey quoted approvingly a statement of President William Rainey Harper in 1900 that declared that professors abused academic freedom if they propounded opinions not accepted by the community of scientists, if they preempted scientific inquiry with partisan politics or sensational methods, or if they spoke on controversial issues beyond their subject or their competence. Dewey emphasized as well his enthusiasm for Harper's affirmation that enduring the dangers of abuse of such liberty "is not so great an evil as the restriction of such liberty." Even though Dewey welcomed Harper's reassurances on this crucial point, he saw dangers in the centralization that the expansion of the universities had brought. Presidents had assumed increasing power at the expense of faculties. This tendency should be systematically corrected.[20]

Ultimately the question for Dewey was how the university was to serve the public. Just as his New England predecessors of the John Adams ilk had seen the necessity of a natural aristocracy to check an unruly democracy, so Dewey believed that the cacophony of conflicting and nonsensical voices in modern America called for leadership of men of science. "There has never been a time in the history of the world," he wrote, "when the community so recognized its need of expert guidance as to-day. In spite of our intellectual chaos, in spite of the meaningless hullabaloo of opinion kept up so persistently about us by the daily press, there is a very genuine hunger and thirst after light. . . . With the decay of external and merely governmental forms of authority, the demand grows from the authority of wisdom and intelligence."[21]

In 1904 Dewey moved from the University of Chicago to Columbia in New York City, where Nicholas Murray Butler, another of the great academic entrepreneurs of the era, presided. Bringing Dewey to Columbia was part of Butler's program to build the New York school into a leading American university. Butler was conservative in many ways, and his views may be taken as representative of the more cautious administrative opinion at the time the concept of academic freedom was emerging. In a succinct statement, published in the Philadelphia *Public Ledger* in 1914, Butler pointed out some necessary limits to academic freedom. These limitations were "those imposed by common morality, common sense, common loyalty, and a decent respect for the opinions of mankind." Most abuses of academic freedom, he observed, were cases in which mildly controversial opinions that might have been tolerated otherwise were combined with "lack of ordinary tact and judgment." At Columbia there was therefore one simple rule, "to behave like a gentleman." Being a gentleman meant to have due regard for the opinions of others, for the impressionability of the young, and for the wisdom of earlier eras. Despite urging such voluntary limits, Butler as much as the progressives accepted the standard formula that freedom from "shackles of political, religious, or scientific beliefs and opinions" was essential to the definition of a university: "If preconceived views must be taught and if certain preconceived opinions must be held, then the institution whose teachers are so restricted is not a university."[22]

As in the 1890s most of the controversies regarding academic freedom were political. Typically they involved accusations by political progressives and by increasing numbers of Socialists (Eugene Debs received nearly a million votes as the Socialist party candidate for the presidency in 1912) that academics were muzzled by the business interests who paid their bills. That big business would now be seen as the primary threat to free expression was understandable, not only because of the conspicuous power of vast wealth, but also because of the shift from clerical to lay control of higher education. In 1860–1861 nearly 40% of the board members of private colleges were clergymen, and these were often the most prominent, the best educated, and the most influential trustees. By 1900–1901 less than a quarter of board members were clergy, and for the first time they were outnumbered by businessmen and lawyers. The percentage of clergy representatives continued to drop precipitously, especially at schools without close church ties.[23] Clergy presidents might still be found at small colleges and at denominational schools but were becoming rare at major universities. At most of the leading schools overt restriction of religious belief was not an issue so long as one was a gentleman. Jews, of course, might be thought not very gentlemanly and were discriminated against in hiring, especially in the humanities, but that was not necessarily a question of religious belief. Pentecostals, Mormons, and sectarian revivalist evangelicals would not likely have been hired at most universities either. Despite these blind spots, the official policy was, as Nicholas Murray Butler put it in his 1914 article, that "the tenure of office of a university teacher must ... be quite independent of his views on political, religious, or scientific subjects."[24]

Controversial religious views and most traditional theological views were often virtually excluded at leading universities by being either disparaged or ignored. Remarkably, one of the few founders of modern academia to make this point and to recognize that the universities might not be as free as they claimed was Charles Eliot. The Harvard president was a rugged individualist of the mid-nineteenth-century type and hence had a more jaundiced view of modern organization than did most of the more entrepreneurial university presidents of the next generation. Speaking to the Cornell Phi Beta Kappa society in 1907, Eliot pointed out the subtle censorship that could occur even at places like Cornell: "To be sure, there is another mode of preventing free teaching on dangerous subjects, which is quite as effective as persecution and much quieter, namely, the omission of all teaching on those subjects, and the elimination of reading matter bearing on them. Thus, the supreme subject of theology has been banished from the state universities, and from many of the endowed universities."[25]

Most of the early twentieth-century shapers of the American ideal of academic freedom sidestepped that irony. For John Dewey and his allies, their positivist-progressive paradigm dictated that any decline in traditional religious privilege was an advance for freedom. Even if they did recognize that freedom for one thing often means exclusion of something else, they typically viewed the exclusion of religious restraints on intellectual inquiry as self-evidently justified.

Even if while traditional religious perspectives in teaching were fading at most universities, the battle was ongoing in academia as a whole. Many professors taught at church-related colleges where such questions were still very much alive. Questions of religious restrictions, moreover, had more to do with precipitating the founding of the AAUP than is recognized in the usual historical accounts. In fact, just at the time in January 1914 when the *Philadelphia Ledger* was publishing President Butler's views on academic freedom, the Philadelphia area was agitated by a controversial case of religious restraint. The question, fought bitterly at Lafayette College in Easton, Pennsylvania, was in effect whether the academic profession would any longer even tolerate old-time college religious standards in Northern colleges that hoped to compete in the respectable mainstream. For the first time, professional organizations of the professoriate played a major role in the controversy, and the case was intimately involved with the organization of a professorial union.

Warfare at Lafayette

The president of Lafayette College was Ethelbert Warfield, who was probably best known as the younger brother of Benjamin Breckinridge Warfield, the leading conservative Presbyterian theologian of the era. The brothers were from the Union side of the famous Breckinridge family of Kentucky and were loyal to the rigorous Old School Presbyterianism in which they had been reared. Ethelbert had studied in Germany and at Oxford, practiced law briefly, and served as president of Miami University in Ohio before becoming president of Lafayette in 1891 at age thirty. Benjamin, who joined the faculty of Princeton Theological Seminary in 1887, had helped forge the Princeton formulation of the "inerrancy" of Scripture and had been a leading opponent of Charles Briggs for deviation from that standard. In 1899 Ethelbert was ordained to the Presbyterian ministry, and in 1904 he became the president of the board of trustees of Princeton Theological Seminary, which remained a fortress of Presbyterian orthodoxy. Originally chartered in 1826, Lafayette College was a classic instance of a college founded, as its name suggested, under liberal auspices. The original charter stated clearly "That persons of every religious denomination shall be capable of being elected trustees, nor shall any person, either principal, professor, tutor or pupil, be refused admittance into said college or denied any of the privileges, immunities or advantages thereof for or on account of his sentiments in matters of religion." Nonetheless, as often happened to colleges of the mid-nineteenth century, Lafayette soon came under the sway of Presbyterian educational imperialism.

Militant Old School Presbyterians were largely responsible for the early success of the college, and in 1854 its charter was amended to give the Old School Synod of Philadelphia power to nominate or to dismiss trustees or faculty. In 1885, however the Synod's power was reduced to a nominal oversight that was commensurate with the Synod's lack of financial support for the college. During Warfield's presidency the catalogs stated that the school was "under the general direction of the Synod of Pennsylvania" and that the instruction was to be "within the lines of general acceptance among evangelical Christians."[26] Any more specific controls would be informal.

Before the case that came to the attention of the founders of the AAUP, President Warfield had been involved in an extreme, though aptly symbolic, illustration of the problem of lack of formal professorial recourse against autocratic presidents and their boards. In 1897 the position of George Herbert Stephens, a Princeton College and Seminary alumnus who taught logic and ethics, had not been renewed. Stephens responded by burning down the principal college building in hopes of thus discrediting Warfield. No ideological issue was overtly involved, and Stephens was judged mentally unstable.[27]

In 1905 Warfield filled a new endowed chair in the pivotal old-time college subject of mental and moral philosophy by turning to an outstanding young man, John Mecklin. From Warfield's perspective Mecklin had the correct pedigree. The son of an orthodox Presbyterian pastor from Mississippi, he had been educated in Presbyterian schools, had a degree from Princeton Theological Seminary, was distinguished by a German doctorate, yet remained solidly in the Presbyterian orbit.

Once at Lafayette, Mecklin very soon became absorbed with the pragmatism of William James as a philosophical guide. Warfield, who taught a brief senior course in Christian evidences, expected the chair in mental and moral philosophy to be used to defend traditional Christianity against the challenges of modern thought. Mecklin, however, was moving rapidly away from his strict Presbyterian heritage and saw philosophy as an ongoing and ever-changing human quest. His job, as he viewed it, was to reconcile the Christian heritage to modern thought. He did so, for instance, by suggesting that Jesus, Paul, Athanasius, and Augustine were all ultimately pragmatists who valued their experience of knowing and obeying God more than mere doctrine. Mecklin was an intellectual leader on the faculty and quickly became far more popular among the students than was Warfield himself.[28]

Despite repeated efforts by Warfield to have the board of trustees formally constrain Mecklin's teachings or the texts he was using (including

John Dewey and James Tufts on ethics and a number of other pragmatists on psychology and psychology of religion), the young professor successfully defended himself on the grounds that he was only teaching students to *think* and that such honest intellectual inquiry could not be a threat to the faith. In the meantime, however, he was quite explicitly teaching that religious beliefs were products of social evolution and illustrating such views by references to higher critical interpretations of the Old Testament.[29]

The controversy between Warfield and his board versus Mecklin smoldered over a four-year period, finally bursting into flames in the spring of 1913. Mecklin sent Warfield copies of exams from his course on theism, which Mecklin apparently believed would reassure the president of the good he was doing. The exams had the opposite effect, confirming Warfield's suspicions that Mecklin's teachings were undermining traditional Protestantism. Warfield, like other conservative Princetonians, had no objection to biological evolution being taught in science classes, since that could be reconciled as a mode of divine Providence. On the other hand, he believed, quite correctly from his point of view, that theories of social evolution of religion were far more threatening to traditional Protestantism. Particularly, higher critical theories of the social evolution of Judaism and Christianity threatened the claim, foundational for biblicist Protestantism, that Christianity originated in divine revelations, supernaturally revealed in the Scriptures. While Warfield did not insist on inerrancy as a test of the faith at the college, he was convinced that theories of social evolution would destroy any version of the traditional Protestantism for which the college professed to stand.

At the June board meeting, just before commencement in 1913, Warfield finally persuaded most of his board that Mecklin's views did, indeed, threaten the religious stance of the college. Calling Mecklin in, the board confronted him with the possibility of a vote on his dismissal. Sensing that there probably was no other recourse, Mecklin offered his resignation, which the board accepted.

The case, however, was far from closed. When the graduating seniors, gathered at a baseball game, heard of Mecklin's resignation they immediately demonstrated in protest. For years Warfield's star had been setting so far as popularity with the students was concerned. Dissent had been expressed most directly during daily chapel exercises when the students, all boys (as they were called—not always inappropriately), would regularly show disrespect any time Warfield or one of his sympathizers was speaking by simultaneous tapping, fits of coughing, or with standard chapel pranks such as setting a series of alarm clocks to go off during the service. At the graduation ceremony the day after Mecklin's resignation, the students behaved in a similar fashion, tapping loudly whenever Warfield spoke and falling silent otherwise. After the graduation ceremony the class marched to a commencement room chanting what they called their "pirate cheer," ending with a forceful "to hell with Warfield." After repeating their cheer three additional times at the door for the benefit of the assembled alumni and faculty, they entered the room, but when Warfield rose after the meal they gave a cheer for "Johnny Meck" and exited en masse. To add a little weight to their protest they adopted a formal petition stating that they were "thoroughly convinced that President Warfield has demonstrated his incapacity to fill the position of president of Lafayette College" and that they would withhold their class gift until there was a new administration. Needless to say, the board of trustees was alarmed by what looked like an old-time student rebellion, and they were worried about the threat to their student constituency. In a special meeting they appointed a committee to investigate.[30]

Thus far the story was not so different from that of the ouster of President Clapp from Yale in the eighteenth century, except that in the twentieth century the issues seemed anomalous, even if the behavior was somewhat tamer. In the eighteenth century, it would have been the students who burned down the college building.

The added twentieth-century feature, however, was the professionalization of the professoriate. Academics were already organized into professional societies, and these provided annual meetings and journals for publicity and a base for further organization.

Mecklin sent letters to two professional journals explaining that it was not because his views were contrary to church standards, but because he used textbooks such as Dewey and Tufts on ethics and James R. Angell's *Psychology*. (Angell, son of Michigan's former president, was a Dewey student and later president of Yale.) These texts were used at some other Presbyterian colleges, and their use was opposed only by the more conservative Presbyterians, not by the church as a whole. So, in Mecklin's view, the case boiled down to the question of "whether a well-meaning but misguided loyalty to outworn theological beliefs is to take precedence over loyalty to approved scientific methods and well-attested facts."[31]

The presidents of the American Philosophical Association and the American Psychological Association acted quickly in appointing a joint committee of inquiry, headed by Arthur O. Lovejoy of Johns Hopkins University.

In November 1913 the committee addressed a letter to President Warfield inquiring via a lengthy list of questions as to the exact policies of the college and whether John Mecklin's published account was accurate. A month later they received an evasive reply from the executive committee of the board, not answering the specific questions but stating that the college was under the general direction of the Synod of Philadelphia and that the chair Mecklin occupied had been endowed with the express purpose of continuing Lafayette's tradition of providing "a foundation for conservative Christian thought and character."

Arthur Lovejoy responded on behalf of the committee, pressing Warfield "to let the committee have, from yourself personally, some more specific statement" in response to the questions asked. To this Warfield took the ground that colleges were still autonomous associations of gentlemen whose affairs were not open to the public. "I trust you will pardon me," he responded curtly, "if I say that your committee has no relation to me personally which would justify my making a personal statement to you with regard to this matter." Citing the confidentiality of board affairs, he concluded with the hope that the committee would "on reflection perceive the impropriety" of his discussing private board affairs with outsiders.

Such a response could only raise the ire of the committee and speed them in their resolve to create an organization through which professorial rights could be heard. In the meantime they could resort only to publicizing their views.

Their conclusion, as published in the *Journal of Philosophy, Psychology, and Scientific Methods*, was that "American colleges and universities fall into two classes." Institutions of one type enjoyed virtually complete freedom of inquiry, while the others were "frankly instruments of denominational or political propaganda." Since it was inevitable that such propagandizing institutions should continue to exist, the professional societies should publicize which institutions were which. They should also investigate and expose instances at either type of school, in which freedom had been infringed beyond declared limits. Most important for the propagandizing schools, professors should demand that exact limits on freedom be declared to prospective teachers publicly and *in advance* of their employment. One of the objectionable features in the Mecklin case, the committee argued quite convincingly, was that, whatever the merits of the Lafayette board's position, everything in the college literature was phrased so ambiguously as to make it impossible to know what the doctrinal rules of the college, in fact, were.[32]

John Mecklin himself astutely pointed out the inherent contradiction in Lafayette's policy, which was the same contradiction found in every explicitly Protestant institution we have looked at. On the one hand, Warfield was determined to keep the school's teaching at least compatible with orthodox Presbyterian doctrine. On the other hand, the school's charter still carried the provision against religious discrimination. Moreover, while the catalog declared that the aim of the school was "distinctly religious," and the school was under the "general" direction of the Synod of Pennsylvania, nonetheless it also assured that "religious instruction is carried on . . . within the lines of general acceptance among evangelical Christians, the points of agreement, rather than those of disagreement, being dwelt upon." The ambiguity was captured in a Synod visiting committee's report that recommended "this splendid institution as a safe and profitable one . . . for a liberal up-to-date education." According to Mecklin, "Our two-faced educational Janus said to the heretics, 'We offer you a liberal and up-to-date education.' To the minority of orthodox Presbyterians and so-called evangelicals this educational Janus said, 'Behold, I give your boys a safe and sound Christian education.' "[33]

In February 1914, within a few weeks of the publication of the findings of the investigators from the professional organizations, Warfield resigned his presidency at Lafayette. The Lafayette board, however, had been moving in the direction of seeking Warfield's resignation since before the intervention of the professional associations, and there is no way to measure the impact of the national publicity. John Mecklin was not restored to his position.[34]

The American Association of University Professors

The Lafayette case was directly tied to the organization of the AAUP. Already in the spring of 1913, in the spirit of progressive reform,[35] senior faculty members at Johns Hopkins University had issued a call for an organization of professors. Major universities sent representatives to a preliminary conference held in November 1913, which coincided with the efforts to investigate the Lafayette case. Arthur Lovejoy, chair of the Lafayette investigating committee, was the principal organizer and served as acting secretary. The group called for a larger gathering, which met January 1 and 2, 1915, and formed the AAUP. John Dewey was chosen president.[36]

In an opening address Dewey pointed out one of the major implications of professorial organization. National association provided a healthier

232 WHEN THE TIE NO LONGER BINDS

atmosphere for the progress of science. Truth, he said in a line of thought that Charles Peirce had suggested and Dewey had popularized, was defined by the convergence of views of scientific observers. It was what objective investigators would eventually agree on. For such pragmatic views, as much as for their Baconian predecessors, it was therefore crucial that local and parochial interests not hinder agreement. "The best way to put educational principles where they belong—in the atmosphere of scientific discussion," Dewey proclaimed, "is to disentangle them from the local circumstances with which they so easily get bound up in a given institution. The very moment we free our perplexities from their local setting they perforce fall into truer perspectives. Passion, prejudice, partisanship, cowardice and truculence alike tend to be eliminated, and impartial and objective considerations to come to the front."

Whatever the merits of such proposals, as cultural history we can see them as efforts to define, standardize, and control a national culture at the expense of local cultures. Professional societies were already accomplishing this to a degree; they were creating loyalties and self-definitions based on the scientific standards of national organizations, and thus undermining loyalty to particular institutions and their traditions. The AAUP would foster this nationalizing trend. Its ideals would be the apotheosis of nonsectarianism. Local and parochial traditions would be eliminated, not immediately by a decree of a ministry of education, but in the more democratic way of the "expression of a public opinion based on ascertained facts."[37]

In such a modern world the experts would rule. The AAUP accordingly was formed among the professorial elite. Membership was initially limited to full professors and was by nomination only. The original core organizing committee had consisted of representatives of nine leading research universities. These in turn nominated men of full professorial rank in their own institution and within each of their disciplines. At the first gathering of these academic leaders the understanding was confirmed that "the association shall be composed of college and university teachers of recognized scholarship or scientific productivity."[38]

We can presume that such a gathering of America's academic elite would have had just about the same attitudes toward traditional Christianity that James Leuba had discovered in his contemporaneous survey of "greater" men of science in all major disciplines. Enough of a distinguished minority of conservatives or those who had respect for conservatives would be present to ensure no frontal assault on traditional Christian education. Nonetheless, a disdain for the parochial past would be clearly visible as well.

This was the case in the classic Report of the Committee on Academic Freedom and Tenure presented at the end of 1915 and accepted and approved at the AAUP annual meeting. Following closely the formula of the report on Lafayette, the committee (which had two of the same members, including Lovejoy) noted that churches or businesses have a moral right to conduct a proprietary institution to be used "as an instrument of propaganda." "Concerning the desirability of the existence of such institutions," the committee remarked somewhat disingenuously, "the committee does not desire to express any opinion." Nonetheless, it was "manifestly important that they should not be permitted to sail under false colors." The hopeful sign, the committee suggested, was that "such institutions are rare, and are becoming ever more rare." Most denominational colleges were evolving toward uniform ideals of academic freedom in which their particular traditions did not substantially intrude.

Such institutions, the committee pointed out, were moving from a private proprietary status to being a "public trust." Consequently the defining characteristic of true institutions of higher learning was that they would serve the public, and academic service to the public was based on the premise that "education is the corner stone of the structure of society and progress in scientific knowledge is essential to civilization." Such a trust justified elevating the dignity of the professoriate, so that the best men would be attracted to it.

In serving the public the university had three major functions. First was "to promote inquiry and advance the sum of human knowledge." On this point the committee's allusion to religion was particularly revealing of the prevailing theory of knowledge: "In the spiritual life, and in the interpretation of the general meaning and ends of human existence and its relation to the universe, we are still far from a comprehension of the final truths, and from a universal agreement among all sincere and honest men." Such an assumption as to where all human knowledge would eventually lead demanded a freedom that by definition would preclude all claims to settled religious truths.

The second function of the university was "general instruction to students." Here freedom to say what one believed was essential to the integrity of teaching. At the same time the professoriate saw college education as disabusing students of outdated beliefs and recommended that, particularly for the immature students of the first two college years, "the instructor will introduce the student to the new conceptions gradually, with some consideration for the students' preconceptions and traditions." In general, however, it was "better for students to think about heresies than to not think at all."

The third function, to "develop experts for various branches of the public service," was likewise revealing of the underlying assumptions defining the modern academic profession. Here the document thoroughly reflected the spirit of progressive reforms. Democratic opinion needed to be guided by scientifically informed experts. Almost half the drafting committee were social scientists, including Richard T. Ely and the chair, Edwin R. A. Seligman of Columbia, another founder of the American Economics Association. Democracy, they pointed out, was both a check against tyranny and itself a potential source of tyranny through intolerant public opinion. Experts were desperately needed to keep democratic opinion from being swept by waves of irrationality. Such guardian experts must be free to examine and advocate positions contrary even to strongly prevailing opinion. Hence, it was essential that the universities protect freedom of scientific investigation even when its conclusions were unpopular. Professors should have the same rights as other citizens to speak out in public and even to campaign on controversial issues. Science provided the means whereby democracy could be saved from itself, and hence for the sake of society universities must be sacred preserves.

The theory was accompanied by proposals for needed practical reforms. The central idea that professors served the public and not private interests meant that college professors should no longer be treated as though they were simply employees. Faculty committees should participate in the processes of hiring and firing. Professors and associates should have permanent tenure. All faculty members should have rights to standardized judicial procedures involving peer review.

The AAUP committee recognized that academic freedom could not be unlimited but argued that there should always be a presumption in its favor, with no firm lines drawn around it. Restraints were sometimes necessary, of course, against extreme, scandalous, or irresponsible statements. But, as a rule, restraints should be voluntary.[39]

Critics were, of course, quick to point out difficulties in the revolutionary concept of freedom as a virtual absolute or presumption on which there were no formal restraints. Particularly, what if such freedom undermined the stated goals of an institution? Chancellor Day, for instance, argued that if professors have rights of conscience, so should trustees have rights of conscience and freedom to fire.[40] The Association of American Colleges, an organization that college presidents founded in 1915 and that included representatives of many church-related institutions, spoke specifically to the religious issue in a 1917 report: "A man who accepts a position in a college which he has reason to believe is a Christian institution and who, further, may properly infer that the canons of good taste forbid, perhaps, the asking when the contract is made, of intimate personal questions about his own religious belief, can scarcely assume that freedom of speech includes either the right privately to undermine or publicly to attack Christianity."[41]

This line of defense pointed to a critical weakness in the Protestant establishment in higher education. As at Warfield's Lafayette, even the more liberal Protestant administrators wanted to have it both ways. On the one hand, as they were attempting to attain more professional scientific standards and to serve an increasingly pluralistic public, propriety forbade that they ask about professorial candidates' religious beliefs. Those were "intimate personal" matters. On the other hand, many of the schools were sufficiently connected to their denominations that they did in effect have an implied doctrinal test, at least that professors were not allowed publicly to attack Christianity. The AAUP was demanding, reasonably enough, that if Christian institutions had boundaries, they should state them clearly. Before very many years, schools that aspired to a national standing would have to concede that particular religious traditions could not have normative standing in shaping academic policies.[42]

Loyalty as a Limit on Freedom

On the other hand, the inherent limits of the AAUP's position on the larger point of proclaiming the sacredness of freedom as though it were an absolute became apparent very quickly when the United States entered World War I in the spring of 1917. Patriotic hysteria swept through the elite professoriate as it did among many other types of Americans. The professors were predominantly Anglo and saw the ideals of Anglo-democracy as their heritage, well worth fighting for. President Wilson, who predicted the hysteria but did not prevent it, was one of their number, university professor and president turned progressive reformer. If the highest morality—some would say the highest Christian morality—was to serve democratic society, then no calling was higher than for professors as well as universities to put themselves at the nation's service. This was not a conservative-versus-liberal issue, because many of the liberal reformers saw in the war the ultimate progressive cause and were as ready as any conservative to defend the flag. Often with unrestrained enthusiasm, they offered their services to university and local war committees. They wrote books and thousands of articles in the massive propaganda effort to vilify Germany and to represent the war as the ultimate crusade for all that humanity held dear. The National Security League, which later was accused of patriotic excess, included among its propaganda writers leading progressive professors and organizers of the AAUP such as Richard T. Ely and Arthur Lovejoy. Shailer Mathews of the University of Chicago Divinity School, a center where patriotism was especially fervid, served as chair of a Committee on Patriotic Service established by the AAUP.[43]

Of the organizers of the AAUP Arthur Lovejoy was particularly enthusiastic in support of the war effort, though others, like John Dewey, shared similar sentiments with only minor qualifications. Those such as Dewey, who had during the early stages of the European conflict urged rational pacific solutions, came around to support American intervention once they were convinced of the high moral justification that the survival of democracy was at stake. Professorial opinion, of course, covered a spectrum, and a small minority was pacifist, pro-German, or otherwise opposed to the American war effort. Across the country at least twenty academics were fired for disloyalty, and the number whose contracts quietly were not renewed is impossible to estimate.[44]

At Columbia University AAUP leaders John Dewey and Edwin Seligman tried to play mediating roles as their university faculty was torn apart by the purge. The situation was aggravated by the allegedly dictatorial methods of President Nicholas Murray Butler. Already in 1916 the distinguished progressive historian Charles Beard, notorious for his irreverent *An Economic Interpretation of the Constitution* (1913), was accused of condoning a speaker who said "To Hell with the Flag." Beard survived the board's inquisition by denying that he condoned the statement. Once the United States entered the war the following April, heads began to roll. In October, after a protracted controversy, the trustees dismissed on the grounds of disloyalty two senior professors, J. McKeen Cattell and the pedigreed Henry Wadsworth Longfellow Dana. Within a week Charles Beard resigned, affirming his own support for the war but charging that the university "is really under the control of a small and active group of trustees who have no standing in the world of education, who are reactionary and visionless in politics, narrow and medieval in religion."[45]

While the AAUP leadership also deplored such unilateral procedures by trustees, they did not in principle oppose dismissals for disloyalty. In December 1917 the AAUP adopted a report on "Academic Freedom in Wartime," from a special three-man committee chaired by Arthur Lovejoy. The committee affirmed its own unqualified loyalty and that of the vast majority of academics to the American cause and deplored "the sinister forces which have involved humanity in the present unspeakable catastrophe." They further argued simply that freedom of speech and academic freedom had to be temporarily curtailed in wartime and that their only concern was that such necessities not be carried to extremes or allowed to subvert proper procedures in ways that would permanently threaten the very freedoms they were fighting for. Thus, although they urged that universities not dismiss all conscientious objectors or German sympathizers, they found it perfectly justifiable to do so if anyone taught or advocated draft resistance or publicly questioned the moral legitimacy of the American cause. Professors with German heritage might be "so blinded to the moral aspects of the present conflict" as to support the land of their origins, but they should remain silent.[46]

American professors typically were chagrined by the way the professors of the German universities seemed to have sold out to the cause of barbarism. At the outset of the war in 1914 ninety-three of Germany's most renowned professors, including liberal theologian Adolf von Harnack, had issued a manifesto defending Germany's role in the war. Many American scholars were appalled by this blatantly partisan departure from a scientific stance and by what seemed to the Americans a denial of the plain facts. The unprofessional attitude of the German academics was particularly galling to many of the American elite who had studied in Germany, and in retrospect many recalled autocratic tendencies deep within the German character. Already in 1914, Arthur Lovejoy called the German professors' statement "a scandalous episode in the history of the scholar's profession" and approvingly quoted a statement that it was "the greatest moral tragedy of the war." In 1918, Richard T. Ely used stronger terms, linking the cause directly to that of Christian civilization. We are at war with Germany, he explained, "because Germany has embraced a false religion, worships a false tribal god and practices false tribal ethics."[47] Demonstrating his total loyalty to the American cause, Ely was a leader in organizing a petition in 1918 signed by 90% of the Wisconsin faculty deploring what they described as the virtually treasonous disloyalty of Wisconsin senator Robert LaFollette.[48]

The vast majority of the American professoriate, seeing the cause of science and the highest morality so self-evidently on the side of American patriotism, found it difficult to recognize that they were guided by a virtually religious loyalty to their own nation not far different in kind from that of their German counterparts. Both sides proclaimed a new age of science that would be at once objective and consistent with the highest ideals of civilization. Once contrary idealisms clashed, armed with the destructive power of the latest technology, the same intellectual world could not be put back together again.

The Sequel

After the war many American professors eventually became chastened about the degree of their wartime patriotism, but it is not clear that many appreciated the dimensions of the intellectual crisis that was facing the Western world. Even if they did, they did not see in it any lesson that would modify their prewar faith in science, which made it possible to speak of academic freedom as almost an absolute.[49] Rather, soon after the war there were signs of reconciliation between the Association of American Colleges (AAC) and the AAUP, and by 1940 a widespread consensus on the subject led to a succinct restatement of the 1915 principles now jointly authored by representatives of the AAUP and the AAC and endorsed by many other academic associations. The 1940s report was thus canonized and became the basis for American case law regarding academic freedom.[50]

Academic freedom in the 1940 report was based, as in earlier formulations, on its being essential to "the common good."[51] Institutions that limited freedom for religious or other purposes could be exempted from the general rules so long as they stated in writing their restrictions as conditions for appointments.

What did not seem to be well acknowledged was that the ideal of the common good involved inbuilt restrictions on what one was free to say or teach. The blatant restrictions on academic freedom during World War I were simply accentuations of the sorts of limitations that always had prevailed. Ultimately it was not academic freedom but the common good that was the absolute. Freedom would be limited to that which was judged consistent with the prevailing concepts of the common good.

Who would judge what was the common good was another crucial question. In American academia it would be the elite professoriate. That group, as Leuba had shown, was more likely even than most other academics to be skeptical of traditional religious claims. Moreover, they typically were committed to the opinion that scientific viewpoints were the basis for finding the highest good in society, and to the orthodoxy that freedom from preconceptions was essential to the scientific method. In the light of such beliefs, traditional religious viewpoints had a negative effect on "the common good." They could be tolerated, but only as exceptions to the rule. In the universities themselves, they would be like grandparents in an upwardly mobile family, tolerated and sometimes respected because of their service in the past, even given some nice quarters of their own and celebrated on holidays, but otherwise expected either to be supportive or to stay out of the way and not say anything embarrassing.

15

The Fundamentalist Menace

Nothing did more to consolidate dominant academic opinion behind the cause of academic freedom than the fundamentalist attacks of the 1920s. While there might still be some religious traditionalists at major universities, almost no one, either administrator or faculty, would countenance the extreme demands of fundamentalists, which would have turned back the clock forty years.

Traditional teachings still prevailed in the vast majority of Protestant pulpits, and traditional belief was even stronger in the pews. This meant that as immense cultural changes proceeded on other fronts, the potential for an explosive showdown steadily increased. Within each of the major denominations there had already been scrimmages and minor wars over this or that change, often centered, as we have seen, on educational institutions. Not until after World War I, however, were the conservative forces effectively organized into a national campaign.

The war itself was the immediate precipitant of the sense of a national religious crisis among Protestant conservatives. Promoted as a moral crusade, it heightened consciousness of the issue of national righteousness and made it everybody's business. Preserving doctrinal purity was therefore not just a church concern, but a national issue as well. Under Wilson's guidance the Puritan ideal of a national covenant had re-emerged as a popular concept. It was a mixed blessing. One unexpected consequence was that the heightened national moral consciousness immediately raised the question for Protestant conservatives of why the liberals were setting the terms. Moreover, the example of the perceived moral monstrosity in Germany suggested to conservatives what happened to civilizations that forsook their Christian foundations. It was an easy step from that observation to another that pointed out the formidable German influences on America's educational elite and especially how Protestant liberals had been imbibing German theology for years.[1]

Fundamentalists found confirmation of the alarming consequences of the German and Protestant liberal influences in the dramatic changes in

The Soul of the American University Revisited. George M. Marsden, Oxford University Press. © Oxford University Press 2021. DOI: 10.1093/oso/9780190073312.003.0019

mores that followed the war. The rebellion against Victorian culture had been building for some time, but it took the war to bring it into the open. Despite the triumph of the enactment of Prohibition, the last major cause on which the conservative and the moderate-liberal wings of Protestantism had agreed, the moral foundations of the nation seemed to conservatives to be eroding. Women's suffrage, and especially the breakdown of taboos regarding sexuality, seemed to threaten the family, the bedrock of the republic.[2] Young people were, of course, a particular cause for alarm. The Jazz Age and the dance craze, women smoking, new openness about sex, and the whole new phenomenon of a youth culture with its own standards signaled a breakdown of traditional verities. Such behavior was the inevitable consequence of the spread of relativist and materialist philosophies and would undermine any Christian basis by which Americans could resist godless and radical solutions to their problems. The foreign-inspired Bolshevism that sparked the Red Scare immediately after the war was one manifestation of the threat, but homegrown atheism and materialism were more subtle and would be equally destructive.

Crucial to the fundamentalist countermovement was finding an issue that got to the heart of the matter, rather than merely attacking symptoms, and at the same time would have a popular appeal. Bolshevism and the German threat soon became too distant, materialism was too subtle, and admitted atheists were hard to find. The real culprits, after all, were those compromisers, the liberal Protestants, who in the name of Christianity had opened the doors to relativistic philosophies that ultimately would undermine Christian moral foundations.

Biological evolution proved to be the issue that tied everything together. Not only could Darwinism be shown to rest on materialist assumptions, but naturalistic evolutionary assumptions were part of every false philosophy of the day. Just as important, the hypothesis of the biological origins of humans could be contrasted to the Genesis account and thus raise the issue of the authority of the Bible. For Protestant conservatives, the displacement of the authority of the Bible was at the heart of the intellectual revolution of the past forty years. In the opinion-shaping centers of the culture the Bible was being judged and often discredited by evolutionary theories of cultural development and by supposedly higher moral ideals that had developed since biblical times. Most conservative Protestants saw the culture of the United States as implicitly Christian, resting on a moral foundation derived from the Bible. If the Bible's authority were undermined, as the Darwinist account of human origins seemed to them to do, then the very survival of American civilization was at stake.

What was more, the issue of biological evolution had a strong populist appeal, important for market-oriented American evangelicalism. At the democratic level the threat of Darwinism to the dignity of humans could be presented as the question of whether one's ancestors were apes and amoebas. In the South opinions on such issues were especially strong. One of the effects of World War I was to demonstrate that the South was coming back into the Union and to show that Southern pride could be expressed in the form of American patriotism. Southern patriotism, however, had this twist: concern for national morality still often translated into alarm at how secular culture imported from the North was corrupting Christian Southern ways. All over the nation—in ethnic communities of the Midwest, for example, and in many religious communities with distinct identities–there were comparable pockets of resistance to the dominant ideals of emerging national culture.

Education was the most concrete area where almost everyone had to face the issues. Particularly important was the rise of the high school. In 1890 fewer than 300,000 Americans were attending high schools; by 1930 the number was 4,800,000, representing a sixteenfold increase.[3] Compulsory high school education was a new invention of an industrial society that was moving away from the countryside. No longer did the economy depend on youth employed at home. Rather, it needed more literate and commercially skilled citizens. High school also helped create an independent culture among youth. Its designers, however, saw it as a way of promoting the same set of assimilating national cultural ideals that had been shaping the new universities. The vast growth of high schools also increased the constituency for colleges and universities, which by the 1920s were also firmly established as an essential component of the cultural machinery. Formal education had thus emerged as a much more pervasive part of the culture than ever before. Compulsory education laws meant that almost everyone would have to contend with national cultural ideals. For many conservative Protestants, the teaching of biological evolution came to symbolize the sinister dimension of this trend.

All the campaign needed was organization and leadership. Organization came largely from evangelists who created various independent agencies to combat the new cultural and religious trends after the war. The World's Christian Fundamentals Association, founded in 1919 by premillennialist[4] Protestants who insisted on literal biblical interpretation, was a prototype.

By 1920 antievolution had emerged as a leading issue in these circles, which were being tagged as "fundamentalist." At a preconvention gathering of the new fundamentalist coalition in the Northern Baptist Convention, premillennialist leader A. C. Dixon eloquently tied evolution to all the evil trends of the day, from the triumph of the "might makes right" philosophy of Nietzsche in Germany, to Bolshevism, to the decline of the family and moral values at home. At the annual meeting of the Northern Baptist Convention itself, the fundamentalists succeeded in appointing a committee to investigate alleged infidelity at Baptist-supported schools.[5] In the meantime, T. T. Martin, secretary of the Anti-Evolution League (and soon well known as the author of *Hell and the High Schools: Christ or Evolution, Which?* [1923]), had created a furor in North Carolina early in 1920 with an attack on William Poteat, the distinguished president of Wake Forest College, for his endorsement of evolutionary views.[6]

During 1920 antievolution grew from what was largely a church issue into a national concern when William Jennings Bryan took up the crusade. In the fall of that year Bryan spoke on the evils of evolution to a Sunday crowd of 4,500 at the University of Michigan. Some local clergy were outraged that Bryan was presenting false and simplistic alternatives that reopened an issue they thought had long since been resolved. Bryan responded by beefing up his argument and having five thousand copies of his speech printed and distributed. During the next two years controversy swirled around Bryan as he carried the antievolution torch on the Sunday school and lecture circuits.

Bryan was not a typical fundamentalist; he promoted a progressive social gospel that included women's rights as well as the literal interpretation of Scripture. His prominence and the dramatic character of the issues, however, depicted both by him and his opponents as the clash of two worlds, provided a field day for the press. The issue had practical importance as well. Bryan supported fundamentalist efforts to enact legislation prohibiting the teaching of biological evolution in states throughout the nation. He and his cohorts were especially threatening to state universities, which were the targets of such legislation. When early in 1922 Bryan used an invited speech at the University of Wisconsin to assail the teaching of evolution, President Edward A. Birge, a scientist himself, was furious. The two had a heated exchange after the speech and continued to hurl published polemics at each other for the next year and a half. Bryan suggested that the taxpayers should rid themselves of a president whose university undermined the majority of the people's Christian belief.[7]

Bryan's favorite evidence of the alarming state of universities and colleges was James Leuba's survey on belief in God and immortality among academics. Over half the prominent scientists and social scientists in fields dominated by evolutionary theory rejected traditional faith. "The evil influence of these Materialistic, Atheistic or Agnostic professors" was further disclosed by Leuba's studies of professorial influence on the beliefs of college students. Bryan reported stories he had been told of how professors at Wisconsin, Michigan, Columbia, Yale, and Wellesley taught classes in which they explicitly told students to give up their traditional beliefs about the Bible. A president of one of the largest state universities reportedly had told students that "if you cannot reconcile religion with the things taught in biology, in psychology, or in the other fields of study in this university, then you should throw your religion away." Such materialistic beliefs, Bryan warned, would undermine any basis for unselfish moral reform. The choice was between "Nietzsche's 'Superman'" and the biblical Prince of Peace. According to Bryan, "If the Bible cannot be defended in these schools it should not be attacked, either directly or under the guise of philosophy of science."[8]

Essential to Bryan's argument was that there were only two choices, the Bible or evolution. "Theistic evolution," which, especially in the North, was supported by some prominent Protestant conservatives as well as by moderates and liberals, was in Bryan's representation "even more demoralizing than atheistic evolution." It might be true that "*some* believers in Darwinism retain their belief in Christianity; some survive smallpox." Since Darwinism "*leads many astray*," students should be protected from it. "Theistic evolution," Bryan said dramatically, "is an anesthetic; it deadens the pain while the Christian religion is being removed."[9]

Bryan recognized that the either/or choice was essential to his populist campaign. In private the Commoner acknowledged that evolution of species other than humans would be compatible with biblical theism;[10] in public he would admit only a simple dichotomy. There was, after all, enough truth in what he said to make a plausible case. Even if some form of biological evolution could be reconciled with biblical ideas of a Creator, Darwinism *was* often used to undermine faith in literal interpretations of the Bible.[11] The pieties of theistic evolution tended to obscure that fact. Moreover, the assumption that made Darwinism's conjectures regarding evolutionary mechanisms so compelling in the scientific community—that there *had* to be a purely naturalistic explanation of how life forms developed—was parallel to that shaping every scientific discipline. Everything *had* to have a purely naturalistic explanation, and hence evolutionary theories were the best explanations of how change took place. Darwinism made it plausible to adopt this outlook as a universal view of things, and Darwinism's prestige was an essential component in the growing prestige of purely naturalistic worldviews.

There were, then, some significant theoretical issues that might have been debated. The proposal simply to ban the teaching of the biological evolution of humans, however, made constructive debate virtually impossible. It turned the issue into a political debate and assured that what was a complex and subtle issue would be vastly oversimplified.

The Battle of North Carolina

Some of the most dramatic antievolution agitation and campaigns against a state university took place in North Carolina. There, as in most of the South, traditional evangelicalism seemed to be everywhere, and biblical literalism was often taken for granted. In 1924, the governor of the state, Cameron Morrison, personally intervened with the State Board of Education to ban two biology textbooks that taught the evolution of humans. Virtually every major antievolution crusader, including Bryan, Billy Sunday, T. T. Martin, evangelist Mordecai Ham, the World's Christian Fundamentals Association, and A. C. Dixon, a native son, campaigned in the state to promote legislation banning the teaching of biological evolution. The battle in North Carolina was particularly fierce, however, because the forces of the New South were strong as well, especially in some of the colleges and the University of North Carolina at Chapel Hill.

In 1920 T. T. Martin's attack on President William Poteat of Wake Forest had sparked a lengthy controversy among North Carolina Baptists. Nonetheless, Poteat was an impressive figure, and his evident piety, together with some Baptist reluctance to enforce centralized control, helped him survive attacks in the North Carolina Baptist Convention.[12]

Among the Methodists, second in numbers to the Baptists, there was similar agitation against "unorthodox doctrines" taught in the denominational colleges. Of particular concern was Trinity College in Durham, headed by William Preston Few. Few was a pious Methodist, deeply committed to relating Christianity to higher education, but liberal in his theological leanings. He was also a champion of the New South, wanting to bring the South in general and Trinity in particular into the mainstream of

American culture. Despite conservative Methodist opposition, Methodists accepted practical piety as a test of the faith and were reluctant to enforce doctrinal tests. When in 1924, in the midst of the controversies, James B. Duke endowed Trinity as Duke University, liberal piety was conspicuous. The bylaws of the act of endowment were a classic encapsulation of liberal Protestant educational ideals, opening with the words "The Aims of Duke University are to assert a faith in the eternal union of knowledge and religion set forth in the teachings and character of Jesus Christ, the Son of God. . . ." Few had this statement inscribed on a plaque at the center of the campus, facing the huge Gothic chapel that dominated the lavish architecture of the new university. A School of Religion, for the training of clergy, stood next to the chapel. Although the first dean, Edmund D. Soper, a comparative religionist from Northwestern, was accused of being a modernist, Duke University could hardly be faulted for neglect of Christian concerns.[13]

The Presbyterians, the third largest denomination in the state, were the best organized against evolution. Since the dismissal of James Woodrow from the Presbyterians' Columbia Seminary in South Carolina in 1884, antievolution had been an article of faith among conservative Southern Presbyterians. William Jennings Bryan and Billy Sunday were Presbyterians, as was Governor Cameron. The Presbyterians' leading college, Davidson, was considered safe by the antievolution campaigners. The problem, however, was the University of North Carolina at Chapel Hill, in which the Presbyterians long had taken an informal proprietary interest.

In 1920 Harry W. Chase became the president of the University of North Carolina. Chase was from Massachusetts and had studied psychology with G. Stanley Hall. He titled his inaugural "The State University and the New South," thereby announcing a New South agenda to create a new civilization that synthesized "the best in both the old and the new." It did not help that Chase was a Yankee and that the university tolerated distinctly progressive views, including some on race. Nonetheless, Chase was making effective strides toward building the Chapel Hill school into being a respected institution by national standards.

By 1923 attacks on the university were building on several fronts. Late in 1922 A. C. Dixon had set off a new round of controversy in a well-publicized antievolution sermon at the First Baptist Church in Raleigh. William Jennings Bryan made two visits to North Carolina in 1923, presenting his standard antievolution views, citing the evidence from the Leuba study. Bryan berated professors who belittled him on the basis of their mere guesses and noted that a professor in Kentucky who had attacked him was now out of a job. While Baptists were ambivalent about the intrusion of religion into state institutions because of their principles of the separation of church and state, conservative Presbyterians had fewer such compunctions. They saw the republic as voluntarily Christian, or, as Governor Morrison put it to an Elks convention, North Carolina was an "old fashioned Christian state." Since 1921 Presbyterians had taken the lead in attempting to counter the secular drift with legislation that would have instituted Bible teaching, under church supervision, in public schools, including Bible offerings for credit at the colleges. President Chase was not adverse to courses on the Bible, but negotiations with the Presbyterians broke down in 1924 when it became clear that churches could not control how the Bible would be taught.

As efforts to guarantee positive Christian teachings in state schools faltered, the Presbyterians and their allies turned increasingly to the argument that had routed the Jeffersonians in the nineteenth century, namely, that teachings contrary to Christianity should not be taught either. The conservatives were particularly concerned about the McNair lectures, established in the nineteenth century by John Calvin McNair, a conservative Presbyterian, to address questions relating science to theology. Since 1915, the McNair lecturers had included John Dewey, Shailer Mathews, Roscoe Pound, and in 1922 Charles Dinsmore of Yale Divinity School, who had explicitly attacked conservative interpretations that taught the universe was only six thousand years old. William Poteat was announced as the lecturer for 1925. Although Poteat was a moderate and not a Yankee like the others, this again stirred up the cauldron of Baptist antievolution sentiments.[14]

In the meantime a storm of protest broke from conservatives in all the major white Protestant denominations in the state in response to what seemed an even more direct attack on traditional Christianity from the university. In January 1925 the *Journal of Social Forces*, edited by sociologist Howard W. Odum of the university and published by the university's press, published two articles that could not have better illustrated what the conservatives were warning about. The first, by L. L. Bernard of Cornell, on "The Development of the Concept of Progress," spoke of the gods "as having been created by the folk mind as the projection of their longing and desires" and included early Jewish belief in that category. Jesus, according to Bernard, suggested a more secular idea of progress, though he talked in mystical language, but he had been unable to formulate an abstract principle for social improvement without the "metaphysical and scientific categories yet to be developed."

Harry Elmer Barnes of Smith College was even more blunt. Referring to the belief that ethical values were derived from divine commands, Barnes stated that "Hebrew and Christian history, together with biblical criticism, have, of course, proved that these ideas have been but the product of the folkways and mores of the primitive Hebrews."[15]

The journal was swamped with requests for the January issue, which was immediately attacked by religious periodicals all over the state. One sympathetic observer remarked, "What I have long feared at last has happened. Somebody has read the *Journal of Social Forces*." The journal was, among other things, conspicuous in promoting new views of race and made a point of including in its pages works of African-American scholars. Howard Odum, who knew the existence of the journal was threatened, was determined not to back down to the "Ku Kluxers" and antievolutionists. He wrote to one sympathizer that his Christian faith had survived two Ph.D.s at supposedly "infidel institutions," but that current scurrilous attacks in the name of Christianity were now severely shaking his belief.[16]

By now, however, Bryan and others had so often made the point that biological evolution lay at the root of all the other dangerous evolutionary views that the controversy could not be focused on anything else. This became especially true after early January 1925 when a state representative, David Scott Poole, introduced a bill in the state legislature prohibiting any official or teacher in a tax-supported school from teaching "as a fact either Darwinism or any other evolutionary hypothesis that links man in blood relationship with any lower forms of life."[17] This raised the controversy to a fever pitch over the next six weeks as the bill was considered. The threat was real, as the success of a parallel bill in Tennessee that same winter was to prove. President Chase saw the very essence of a university threatened by allowing popular opinion to dictate what might be taught. "A real university," he told the student body at Chapel Hill, "is an ideal. It is a spiritual thing . . . and those of us to whom the preservation and perpetuation of that ideal are . . . entrusted . . . are obliged to feel that it lives in the realm of principle, where consideration of expediency can not enter."[18]

Much to the relief of the progressives in the state, after much public debate, the Poole bill was defeated in February by a vote of 67 to 46. The antievolution agitation, however, by no means ended. Poteat's lectures at the university in the summer of 1925 brought a new round of efforts by Baptists to oust him from Wake Forest. There was also an attempt to oust Chase from the university. In 1927 Poole introduced a second antievolution bill. All these efforts were defeated. Nonetheless, the fundamentalist gains were substantial. Some counties passed legislation banning the teaching of anything that called into question the inspiration of the Bible, and on the local level most teachers were intimidated from teaching evolution. The universities, however, survived with their independence. Although North Carolina had one of the most heated controversies, its most progressive schools, at least, survived with renewed zeal to defend their independence.[19]

The National Debate Trivialized

Resolve for academic freedom was similarly steeled throughout the country. During the 1920s legislation banning the teaching of biological evolution was considered in twenty states and adopted in five, all more or less in the South. More important for higher education were the dismissals taking place over the issue. The AAUP (American Association of University Professors), of course, took a strong stand. By the end of 1923 its president, Joseph V. Denny, noted a dozen or more dismissals, two at state universities. He declared that "fundamentalism is the most sinister force that has yet attacked freedom of teaching."[20] In Tennessee, for instance, a young professor of secondary education, J. W. Sprowls, was told that he should not use as a text James Harvey Robinson's *Mind in the Making* because of its evolutionary views. Sprowls objected bitterly, but the president of the university insisted on the grounds that antievolution legislation might be passed if the university should "soft pedal" the issue. At the end of the academic year 1922–1923, Sprowls was dismissed, ostensibly on grounds of incompetence as a director of fieldwork. In the controversy that followed, six others of the university faculty were dismissed, largely for their roles in defending Sprowls. The AAUP investigated and sharply criticized the university, primarily for its improper system for tenure and hearings. The investigating committee, however, did not find grounds for concluding that views on evolution or Protestant orthodoxy were at the heart of the issue, as some of the dismissed alleged, even though two of the dismissed were Unitarians and most of them were known for their liberal religious views.[21]

In the meantime many in the professoriate were looking with increasing alarm and disbelief at the antievolution campaigns across the country. The AAUP appointed a special committee on "Freedom of Teaching in Science," which reported early in 1925. The fundamentalist opposition, they observed, was "un-American" in that it attempted to control learning by popular vote, rather than rely on the leadership of qualified experts.[22] Significantly, the Association of American Colleges agreed. "The thing that America needs more than anything else from American colleges and universities," wrote one of their representatives with specific reference to religion, "is the type of leader who understands that the first requisite . . . is not the desire to know what the people want, but . . . to help the people want what they ought to have."[23] The Age of the Expert was dawning.

The consolidation of academic opinion was evidenced by a special gathering on Academic Freedom and Tenure held under the auspices of the American Council on Education, which included the AAUP, the American Association of Colleges, and several other higher education associations. The American Association of Colleges drafted a statement on academic freedom, which was slightly modified at the suggestion of the AAUP and then unanimously endorsed by all the representatives present. This statement, which in substance closely resembled the 1915 AAUP statement, represented a major step toward gaining almost universal recognition of the essential AAUP principles among the shapers of dominant American academia.[24]

The sequel to the dismissals at the University of Tennessee was, of course, the Scopes Trial of 1925. The two events were not unconnected. When John Scopes, a young high school teacher, was persuaded to test the state's new law banning the teaching of biological evolution, one of the dismissed professors, John R. Neal, from the university's Law School, was the first lawyer to volunteer his legal services.[25] Even though Scopes was convicted and prevented from effective appeal, the opponents of the law succeeded spectacularly in their objective of exposing it to public scrutiny. The huge publicity surrounding the trial's debates between Clarence Darrow and William Jennings Bryan solidified liberal opinion against Bryan's larger concerns. In the midst of Menckenesque ridicule, the serious issues that Bryan attempted to raise were widely dismissed.

Perhaps most important was that the populist attacks on biological evolution trivialized the old anti-Jeffersonian argument and thereby helped seal its doom. A central point in the campaigns for antievolution legislation was that if specifically Christian teachings were to be banned from tax-supported schools, then so also should teachings that attacked Christianity. Bryan, for instance, argued that

in schools supported by taxation we should have a real neutrality wherever neutrality in religion is desired. If the Bible cannot be defended in these schools it should not be attacked, either directly or under the guise of philosophy or science. The neutrality which we now have is often but a sham; it carefully excludes the Christian religion but permits the use of the schoolrooms for the destruction of faith and for the teaching of material-istic doctrines.[26]

Bryan here correctly identified a major problem in American democracy. If Christianity was no longer going to be the established religion, either of-ficially or unofficially, in the tax-supported schools, then what philosophy *would* be established? If doctrines of materialism prevailed and schools rou-tinely taught that all religion was an illusory human creation, then irreligion would be established. Darwin's own version of Darwinism was materialistic, and philosophies built on evolutionary analogies increasingly were given a materialistic bent. Such philosophies, whatever their merits, Bryan was pointing out, should hardly be permitted to travel under the colors of neu-trality toward religion, especially toward biblicist Protestantism.

William Allen White once said of Bryan that he was always right in diag-nosis and always wrong in prescription.[27] Bryan's remedy for philosophical materialism was another case in point. Although Darwinism was sometimes, indeed, part of a materialistic worldview and sometimes used to promote such a view, the situation was far more complicated. Liberal Protestants typ-ically affirmed biological evolution as explaining the mechanics of Creation but saw that as subordinate to a higher spiritual reality by which God was guiding the world toward establishing his kingdom. Consistent with this view, high school textbooks of the era typically pointed out that biolog-ical evolution did not preclude God's role in Creation.[28] When the AAUP recommended that professors take into account the tender sensibilities of younger college students, it probably had in mind allowing room for similar reconciliations of science and religion. Some conservative Protestants made similar accommodations, although with concerns to fit in the essentials of the biblical narrative. Only the most literalistic biblicists (of whom, of course, there were many) regarded the issue, as Bryan did, as a clear choice: *either* bi-ological evolution or the Bible.

So what might have been raised as a serious point of national educational policy was presented in such a narrow way that only true believers would be convinced by the argument. For others it could easily be held up for rid-icule as obscurantist and antiscience. Populist fundamentalist campaigners guaranteed this interpretation of their efforts. T. T. Martin, for instance, speaking to a North Carolina audience in 1926, with a massive flag-draped portrait of the recently deceased Bryan in the background, asked the crowd how they would like it if the state demanded that they pay taxes to have their children drilled on Tom Paine's *Age of Reason* and then sold their property if they refused to pay. "That is exactly the issue, except that evolution is far worse than Tom Paine's *Age of Reason*. God's word says that God created great whales; evolution teaches that is a lie; that whales used to have legs and walked around on the earth and got to going into the water more and more and after millions of years evolved into whales; here it is in school books."[29]

Walter Lippmann, who attempted to step back from the immediate prejudices of the day, was one of the few mainline opinion makers to acknowledge the genuine dilemma involved. In *American Inquisitors: A Commentary on Dayton and Chicago*, given as the Barbour-Page Lectures at the University of Virginia, Lippmann pointed out that Jefferson's Bill for Establishing Religious Freedom, adopted in 1786, stated that "to compel a man to furnish contributions of money for the propagation of opinions which he disbelieves, is sinful and tyrannical." Bryan, he pointed out to the heirs to Jefferson's university, was fair enough in asking why, if it was wrong to compel citizens to pay for the teaching of Anglicanism, it was not wrong to compel them to pay for teaching agnosticism.

Furthermore, the events at Dayton exposed the flaw in Jefferson's assumption that democratic rule would foster the reign of reason. Lippmann constructed a "Dialogue on Olympus" to make this point. On the sacred mount, Socrates quizzed Jefferson and Bryan on their first principles. Bryan's appeal to people's prejudices, Socrates pointed out, showed the danger of assuming, as Jefferson had, that the dictates of reason were fixed and that eventually a free people would discover them. In the twentieth century, however, Socrates argued, the conclusions of sciences were constantly changing. The populace could not be relied on to follow the latest view. Nor was there any ground for believing that they would typically follow reason at all, for that matter. Hence, he implied, education must be guided by a class of disinterested experts. Certainly it could not be guided by popular whims.[30]

The fundamentalist attacks on the teaching of biological evolution exposed the problem of the blending of Protestant religion, enlightenment principles of democracy, and modern scientific inquiry. Fundamentalists had grown up in a culture where Protestants had long taken for granted that being Christian and being American went hand in hand. Now they were confronted with a dominant public culture, dominated by alien outlooks of the great urban centers, that was undermining their religion and way of life. Liberal Protestantism could hold together the idea of compatibility of Christianity and modernity as the basis for civilization by becoming increasingly open to incorporating modern ideals into their faith. Fundamentalists, however, correctly perceived that the mainstream national culture, as represented, for instance, in universal public education was becoming a threat to their kind of Protestantism.

Turning the issue into a warfare to control the public domain, and making biological evolution the symbolic focal point for the battle, only trivialized the issues and so turned counterproductive in the long run. The issue of biological evolution had symbolic and emotional appeal as a populist cause, but it did not get to the heart of the issues involved. Rather, serious discussion of the deeper issues between traditionalist Protestantism and dominant twentieth-century cultural and intellectual assumptions was largely jettisoned by the accusation that traditionalist Protestants were obscurantists who were trying to impose their views on everyone.

The *Christian Century*, the leading mainline Protestant journal, for instance, expressed astonishment that repression, encouraged by Mr. Bryan, was occurring "outside the ranks of the Roman Catholic teaching fraternity, where dogmatic control of learning was supposed to have its sole abode." For Protestant America to turn in a similar direction, the *Century* warned, would be disastrous to American cultural progress: "The backwardness under the Roman Catholic system is a commonplace. The effect of a similar policy in the United States will be none the less pronounced if state universities or denominational colleges are not allowed a perfectly free quest for truth."[31]

For the time being, "fundamentalist" would become the most widely used term with which to designate any traditionalist Protestant. In America's cultural centers, mainline Protestants could maintain a role in cultural leadership by emphasizing that they were the party of tolerance. Recognition of the rights of conscience was, after all, one part of the Protestant tradition. Meanwhile conservative Protestants, having failed to control mainstream Northern denominations and widely discredited by the evolution furor, were branded as intolerant fundamentalists and forced to build their own institutions, including colleges and universities. They would have to develop a sense of being a distinct subculture, rather than being the true heirs and overseers of "Christian" America, before they could recover intellectually.

16

The Obstacles to a Christian Presence

Protestantism's New Initiatives

Despite their resolve not to sound like fundamentalists, moderate and liberal Protestant church leaders of the 1920s, including some university administrators, were still concerned with the most general question raised by the fundamentalists. Where was the place for Christianity in modern higher education? From their own experience, mainline Protestant church leaders were acutely aware of the massive revolution that had taken place in education over the past forty years. By the mid-1920s, moreover, it was much more difficult to be sanguine about these changes than it had been even fifteen years earlier. Staid liberal Protestants had almost as much reason as fundamentalists to be alarmed about the flappers, the dance craze, jazz, the automobile, bobbed hair, short skirts, women smoking, and both sexes drinking to excess in defiance of the recent Protestant triumph in the enactment of Prohibition. The consumer economy had produced a youth culture with its own rules, language, entertainments, and mores. As high school education expanded, college attendance also took a sudden upswing. Undergraduate enrollments tripled from 1910 to 1930 so that by the latter date the equivalent of one in every eight eighteen- to twenty-one-year-olds was in college.[1] The burgeoning college campuses became leading loci for declarations of youthful independence.[2]

The most perplexing question was how to maintain some countervailing Christian influence at state universities. While all higher education was expanding, state education was growing at a faster rate than was private education and by 1930 was threatening to displace private education as the dominant force on the university scene. This most tangible manifestation of secularization presented especially perplexing challenges to Protestant leaders because of the ambiguous relationship between Christianity and government. Arrangements varied from state to state. Not only were lines between church and state variously drawn, but the much more ambiguous issue of the relationship of Christianity to the state was not at all settled.

The Soul of the American University Revisited. George M. Marsden, Oxford University Press. © Oxford University Press 2021. DOI: 10.1093/oso/9780190073312.003.0020

Not surprisingly, thinking on the legal issues of relating Christianity to civil government paralleled the trends we have already seen in higher education. Until about the 1890s it was common to give open legal recognition to the preferential position of Christianity in American life. In 1892, for instance, Associate Justice Brewer, in presenting a unanimous decision of the Supreme Court, argued that the acceptance of Sabbath laws, prayers in government assemblies, legal oaths in the name of God, and simply the vast public support for Christian activities indicated that the United States "is a Christian nation." Much mainline Protestant opinion supported this conclusion.[3]

At the same time, many states during the era following the Civil War adopted legislation or constitutional provisions banning sectarian religious tests, sectarian instruction, sectarian books in classes or libraries in public schools, and use of state money for sectarian instruction.[4] The complex motives for such laws were largely related to the massive rise in the Catholic population. The increasing Catholic presence fostered a growing recognition, sparked by Catholic protests, of the problems of Protestant privilege and control of public education. Further, one of the principal motives for erecting a wall between church institutions and the state was fear that, otherwise, tax moneys might fall into Catholic hands in areas where Catholics were dominant.[5] With respect to higher education, some states, such as Wisconsin, attempted to be scrupulous in keeping sectarian teachings out of state colleges and universities, while others, such as Iowa, were more sympathetic toward explicitly Christian teachings. In the South, where the Catholic presence was the least, changes came most slowly. The University of South Carolina's revised statutes of 1873 provided for a moral philosophy course including "evidences of Christianity," and in 1890 an act of the state legislature declared that the president could not be an atheist or an infidel.[6] Into the early decades of the twentieth century most Southern state-supported schools had required chapel, whereas in the North chapel at state colleges was becoming more rare, though not unknown, especially at smaller schools and teachers' colleges.

In some places in the North, however, legislators and administrators had become sensitive to public outcry concerning anything that might appear to use tax money to support a particular religious viewpoint. The 1919 case in which it was ruled that the New York state school of forestry could not be on the Syracuse University campus because Syracuse was a "sectarian" institution illustrates the ambiguities of the situation. When Chancellor Day had the university's charter amended so that the Methodist Conferences would control the naming of only a minority of the trustees, the state was satisfied. In Northern state universities, the general disposition of administrators seems to have been to avoid the subject of religion, citing separation of church and state, except occasionally to issue reassuring statements about religion's importance on a voluntary basis.[7] There was no doubt, however, that by the early 1920s studies of religious subjects had become only a minute part of the curriculum.[8] Religious perspectives were absent from the vast majority of the courses students took, and study about religion was marginal in the mainstream of academia. It was not regarded as one of the humanities, and although often a topic of investigation by psychologists and sociologists, much of that attention had become hostile toward any belief in the supernatural.[9] The only place for substantial sympathetic academic study of Christianity was in divinity schools and theological seminaries.

While these pressures toward secularization of public life were rapidly increasing, so were concerns that Christianity retain at least some representation. The ambivalence of the national mood during the first decades of the twentieth century may be seen in the contradictory patterns of legislation concerning Bible reading in public schools. Between 1900 and the early 1920s five states joined Wisconsin in banning Bible reading or morning prayers in public schools. In the meantime, however, eleven states had joined Massachusetts in *requiring* such religious exercises.[10] At the university level there were comparably widespread concerns about finding some way to retain a place for Christianity, or at least for a more general civic religion, without violating either principles of separation of church and state or academic canons.

At the turn of the century William Rainey Harper's campaign to include academic study of the Bible in liberal arts curricula had borne some fruit, so that at least a few courses in the Bible were available at most of the better schools, including the state universities. Protestant leaders, however, regarded the offerings as woefully inadequate, since the vast majority of students did not elect these courses.[11]

The growth of the state universities in the early decades of the century was the principal factor in convincing the major Protestant denominations that they must change their strategy regarding higher education. Maintaining their own colleges was still important, but they increasingly realized that in addition they would have to minister to their many students on state campuses. As state university enrollments began reaching into the thousands, it was not unusual for the total Methodist, Baptist, or Presbyterian population of such a university to outnumber the respective denomination's constituency at one of its own colleges nearby. Through the first decade of the twentieth century, most of the work of campus ministry had been left to the Christian Associations (YMCA and YWCA). Denominations had welcomed such work and continued to do so. Nonetheless, by early in the century the major denominations were becoming convinced that they should take matters into their own hands, and by the second decade of the century they were rapidly building major networks of campus ministries.

The pattern soon became familiar at state universities. Each major denomination appointed a minister to the university. In an early recommendation the Presbyterians, for instance, compared the need as similar to that for military chaplains.[12] Methodists, Baptists, Congregationalists, Lutherans, Episcopalians, and Disciples adopted similar programs in a movement that accelerated around 1910. Denominational chaplains or university pastors typically would be associated with a denomination's church near the campus and would oversee a student center as headquarters for student religious activities. Modeled after the houses established by Presbyterians and others at the University of Michigan in the 1890s, these were centers for regular religious meetings, special lectures, and social activities that provided structures for ministering to students of each major denomination during their college years. While designed on the one hand to encourage denominational loyalties, these ministries reflected an ecumenical spirit as well. Most of the campus ministries were established in the era just following the founding of the Federal Council of Churches in 1908 and embodied a similar activist zeal for using denominations to mobilize a transdenominational Protestant activism. Roman Catholics' establishment of their own Newman Centers near university campuses closely paralleled the Protestant developments.[13] After 1920 the B'nai B'rith began establishing Hillel Foundations as well.

A major question for these early campus ministries was how they might compensate for the lack of opportunity for substantial religious training within the curriculum of the modern university. Typically the response was for the denominational centers to offer supplemental courses of study, especially in the Bible. One of the most promising solutions was for denominations to endow "Bible chairs" at their centers so that men with adequate academic credentials could offer courses in the Bible. The Disciples of Christ, whose tradition was especially strong on relying on "the Bible alone," were the early leaders in this movement and already by 1909 had established chairs at five state universities, Michigan, Virginia, Texas, Kansas, and Missouri. Other denominations followed suit, establishing additional chairs, often on an interdenominational basis. In the best cases, so far as the campus ministries were concerned, university administrations would be persuaded to grant academic credit for such courses when offered by academically qualified personnel. Eventually at least twelve state universities were giving credit for such church-sponsored courses. Elsewhere courses were offered on a noncredit basis.[14] Though such efforts were peripheral to the main business of the universities, they did represent a version of the Jeffersonian solution and helped reassure religious leaders and concerned constituencies that at least some state universities would not exclude religious voices entirely.

By the 1920s, the Bible chair ideal was expanding in some states into larger efforts to establish schools of religion within or associated with the universities. In 1922 Charles Foster Kent of Yale (which retained some of its zeal for educational missions) established a National Council of Schools of Religion (changed in 1924 to the National Council on Religion and Higher Education) to promote such enterprises. Kent was a leading liberal biblical scholar, eager to re-establish a substantial place for religion in the university curriculum. He saw schools of religion as the answer. His greatest success, partially realized before his death in 1925, was in helping to establish a model for such schools in the School of Religion at the University of Iowa. As early as 1908, responding to pressures from religious groups, the University of Iowa had begun offering credit courses in religion. The rationale was that, since the Northwest Ordinance of 1787 had declared that "religion, morality, and knowledge" were necessary to good government, "Public education was by this organic act to be Christian education." In 1924, inspired by ideas promoted by Kent and others, local religious leaders succeeded in persuading the State Board of Education to establish a School of Religion. The school, which opened in 1927, was financed in part by John D. Rockefeller Jr. Mainline Protestants, Catholics, and Jews were each allowed to nominate and finance a professor for the university program. During the next years the school offered a wide variety of courses on religious topics. In 1930 it also instituted a Commission on Religious Activities to coordinate campus religious programs of all campus ministries. The original purpose of the school was not simply the academic study of religion. Rather, the school was also explicitly to promote religious interests, to foster sympathy for religion among students, and to encourage students to go into religious vocations. In 1938 the university took over the full administrative costs of the school.[15]

Despite a great deal of talk about the schools of religion movement in the 1920s, no other school of religion emulated the Iowa model. The National Council of Religion in Higher Education did see the beginnings of schools of religion in ten other state universities in the region from Indiana to Montana;[16] typically these schools simply represented the coordination of efforts of campus ministries offering courses at their student centers. Some of these programs were recognized for credit at the universities, and others were purely voluntary.[17]

One of the more successful programs was started at the University of Illinois. There in 1919 clergy representing the campus ministries of the Methodists, Disciples, and Roman Catholics petitioned to have university credit offered for courses taught at their campus houses. Despite some faculty resistance, permission was granted and course offerings began in 1920. By 1936–1937 nine courses were being offered each semester under Catholic, Jewish, and combined Protestant auspices, enrolling some three hundred students per semester.[18]

Despite some such successes, the school of religion idea began to recede during the 1930s. Part of the rationale for the program had been that it would promote the development of "a scientific attitude and method in the study of religion."[19] This ideal not only suited the liberal Protestant agenda but also could justify religion courses to university colleges and administrations. In fact, the very success of the campaign to promote the academic study of religion was making sponsorship by outside religious groups superfluous. Increasing numbers of colleges and universities were now offering courses in religion and establishing their own departments of religion. When university administrators were responsive, as they often were, to demands for offerings in religion, it was in their interest to offer such courses within the university as scientific or literary studies, rather than have them administered by denominations whose primary purpose was to promote a religious cause. The result was a hybrid field that typically had Christian form and implicitly Christian direction, but in which specific Christian purposes were subdued.

The case at the University of North Carolina is illustrative. In 1923, as the antievolution furor was heating up in the state, Presbyterian and Methodist leaders petitioned the university for permission to offer courses that would be financed and staffed by the cooperating religious groups but recognized for credit by the university. A university committee considered the proposal but turned it down. Their reasons were revealing. First, they declared, "A state university . . . cannot owe its primary allegiance to anything less than the State: to any class, party, locality, or creed within its borders." Hence, they reasoned, "Men who give accredited instruction . . . cannot from the very nature of the case be men whose primary loyalties are to one or another special cause, no matter how worthy that cause may be." Furthermore, though they recognized the ambiguity surrounding separation of church and state, their own view was that Bible instruction by church employees was a matter for church colleges. The university, on the other hand, might offer courses on the Bible "from the literary or historical point of view." At the time, however, the antievolution agitation involving the university was gaining in intensity, and the proposed courses were not immediately forthcoming. Finally, in 1926, after lengthy agitation, the major Protestant ministries in Chapel Hill joined together to form their own School of Religion. When in 1928 students from this school petitioned to receive credit for their courses, the faculty responded by instituting its own program. The course offerings as they actually developed had a broadly Christian orientation, some dealing specifically with Christian ethics or theology or the Bible itself, as these bore on the search for God in the modern world. At the same time they were presented in academic frameworks that would soften partisanship.[20]

By 1940 not only did virtually all church-related colleges have departments of religion, but so did the vast majority of private colleges and universities, and even also 30% of state universities (excluding teachers' and technical schools). Only 27% of nationally accredited colleges had no formal offerings on religious topics. So great was the increase, especially after 1930, that Clarence Shedd of Yale, one of the leaders in the movement, could declare confidently in 1941 that "state universities are more concerned today about religion than they have been at any other time during the present century."[21] Although these gains appeared considerable, the statistics that Shedd reported could have been interpreted in a much more sobering light. In a typical year, only about 1 in 25 students at public universities was taking a religion course.[22]

Merrimon Cuninggim, a protégé of Shedd who shared his mentor's enthusiasms in interpreting the trends, nonetheless acknowledged that courses in religion were not all they might be intellectually. In many colleges they were considered "snaps" or "cribs," suitable especially for football players. As a writer observed in a 1941 Collier's essay, "How to Keep Football Stars in College," the "beef" had to be guided to courses such as Bible,

Psychology I, Astronomy, and Music Appreciation. "All were 'cripples' of the purest ray. Bible was taught by a lovable old gentleman who delivered lofty lectures and never bothered his sleeping class with details like questions or examinations." After quoting this passage, Cuninggim remarked that "at the present time the major problem concerning religious instruction is not, as in earlier days, to secure its introduction into the curriculum but rather to improve its quality."[23]

In the post–World War I era, those concerned with keeping at least some religious presence in the universities had been working on a number of fronts. Charles Foster Kent, for instance, in 1923 instituted through his National Council a program to appoint "Council Fellows." Typically these were to be first-rate graduate students concerned with relating religion to their academic vocations. By 1941 the council could point to 202 of these fellows, including 31 women, 5 blacks, 3 Catholics, and 3 Jews, most of whom had become professors or administrators at colleges, universities, and divinity schools, including many of the best throughout the nation.[24] Furthermore, a number of mainline Protestant organizations, including the Religious Education Association, founded by William Rainey Harper in 1903, the Council of Church Boards of Education, and the National Association of Bible Instructors, provided a steady stream of literature encouraging the movement to bring more religion to higher education. So did other organizations with broader focuses, such as the American Council on Education and the Association of American Colleges. The AAC was a particularly significant forum for religious discussion, and during this period college administrators affirmed the place of religion in higher education.[25] The YMCA continued to play a prominent role, though it was now only one of many organizations that sponsored major national conferences on the theme. Financial support was not a significant problem either. Rockefeller money had long been a major sustainer of the mainline Protestant establishment. Also important was the Edward W. Hazen Foundation, founded in 1925 and centered in New Haven, which supported many religious causes.[26] Religion in higher education was not going to disappear for lack of resourceful leadership.

The Larger Picture

The problems, however, ran much deeper. While the numerous campaigns of the interwar era succeeded in keeping and sometimes even building religious options in undergraduate liberal arts curricula, these very successes may have hidden the extent to which substantive aspects of Christianity were losing ground at the heart of the university enterprise.[27]

The great growth of higher education, including the doubling of the student population during the 1920s,[28] did not reflect a sudden upsurge in the love of learning among Americans but, rather, that higher education had at last become a major arbiter of success in modern America.[29] World War I gave a dramatic impetus to the idea that an increasingly complex society demanded trained experts and specialists. The growth of higher education therefore largely took directions that would fill practical needs. While curricula were relatively coherent and traditional by later standards and at the better colleges subjects touching on the larger meanings of life were sure to be part of an education, increasing numbers of students concentrated in practical areas that such concerns would not touch.[30] One evidence of this trend was the growth of junior colleges. In 1918 fewer than 1 in 50 college students attended a junior college. By 1938 more than 1 in 6 did.[31] Approximately two-thirds of these were public institutions. Often they were commuter colleges without the religious support surrounding residential schools. Moreover, fewer could afford the luxury of religion courses compared with the larger four-year schools. Normal schools for teacher training were being transformed into regular liberal arts schools during this era. Nonetheless, they were also directed toward practical preparation, and religion offerings were relatively rare, as they were in state agricultural and technical schools, where practical concerns also prevailed.[32]

Even in the largest schools with strong liberal arts offerings, where the campaigns for religion courses had their greatest success, expansion in other areas rendered such gains peripheral to the larger enterprise of the university. The expansion of professional schools, especially of medicine, law, and business, had virtually no religious dimension. This division of labor reflected long traditions, but it was also reinforced by the liberal Protestant belief that the technical dimensions of life had rules of their own to which religion might be added as a higher option. Just as the news magazines that first appeared in this era included a religion page somewhere in the back, so should a university keep a place for the option. At a dozen or so major private universities, divinity school provided a relatively substantial manifestation of this option, even if one that did not counter the effective irrelevance of Christianity to all but a small portion of the rest of the enterprise.

If the heart of an institution can be located by looking at its budget, the peripheral role of Christianity is apparent. During the era from 1900 to 1940, the budgetary story of the leading universities, aside from growth related to the vast increase in students and of buildings to care for them, was the comparably vast increase in funding of research. By the interwar years, leading universities, including California, Chicago, Columbia, Harvard, Illinois, and Michigan, were spending more than two million dollars per year on research, at a time when their yearly incomes were typically five to eight million dollars.[33] The principal special funding for such research, in this era before much federal government support, came from private foundations, particularly the network of Rockefeller agencies.[34]

How could Christianity relate to such institutions? The universities increasingly were becoming conglomerations of loosely related practical concerns without any particular center. They were "a collection of disparate interests held together by a common plumbing system."[35] Student bodies still seldom numbered over five thousand, but at the larger schools where the point had been passed the overall enterprise had a more or less unified rationale. Each unit was designed to serve the interests of business and society, thus endowing everything with a vague moral justification. Nonetheless, as elsewhere in American society, the effectiveness of the schools was associated with the absence of strong centralized control or a clear ideological center. Rather, universities flourished by allowing disparate interests to pursue independent initiatives.[36] In such a setting the specifics of Christianity seemed relevant to only one segment of university life, undergraduate education, and only to a fragment of that.

One compensatory strategy in the private universities was architectural. During this era when universities were particularly dependent on major business support,[37] business leaders were in the forefront in donating impressive chapels. Sometimes, as in the case of the Rockefellers, those who supported the diversified research also financed the unifying symbol, most notably the Rockefeller Chapel at the University of Chicago, completed in 1928. Although such buildings fostered important opportunities for worship and inspiration for parts of the communities and provided centers where the university itself might be worshiped on its high holy days, they were also, as Margaret Grubiak has nicely elaborated in *White Elephants on Campus*, monuments to a disappearing Christian ideal.[38]

The Indifferent Generation

Another major obstacle to those who wanted to build a substantial Christian outlook in the universities was a lack of student support. For one thing, as student populations burgeoned they became more diverse. Even where they remained largely homogeneous and of predominantly Protestant stock, a more strongly secular spirit was apparent by the early 1920s. Popular magazines were filled with articles, often alarmist in tone, on the new youth culture and its departures from the mores of earlier years.[39] F. Scott Fitzgerald's *This Side of Paradise*, published in 1920, had an important effect on popular conceptions of the new college life. Set in prewar Princeton, it suggested how far youth culture had moved from Presbyterian (or in Fitzgerald's case, Catholic) mores. Fast cars, heavy drinking, and petting parties were the order of the day. Students sat late into the night "talking of every side of life with an air half of earnestness, half of mockery, yet with a furtive excitement." "The cities between New York and Chicago," Fitzgerald's protagonist discovered, were "one vast juvenile intrigue."[40] Fitzgerald's image caught the imagination of the new college-oriented generation, and the image helped promote the reality. The place for Christianity in such an emerging youth culture was, to say the least, problematic.

As early as 1923 James Bissett Pratt of Williams College published a perceptive analysis of the widespread belief that the characteristic attitudes toward religion of college young people were far different from those of a generation earlier. The mood of the dominant groups of young people, who set the tone for most others, was not skepticism toward religion, but indifference. It was only a little exaggeration, Pratt explained, to say of today's generation that "their grandfathers believed the Creed; their fathers a little doubted the Creed; they have never read it." As a teacher of the history of religions for twenty years, Pratt reported that early in the century he had approached with great caution the comparisons between the Old Testament and the ancient religions of China, India, and Persia, lest he raise too many doubts about traditional Christianity. "Never a year went by," he reported, "but some of my students came to me after sleepless nights, wearied with inner struggle, sometimes with indignant voices to talk out, after class, the implications involved in Higher Criticism and in the attempt to deal with the Hebrew religion in the same historical light as we had studied Hinduism and Buddhism. All this is changed now."

The students of the 1920s, Pratt reported, were "as far removed from heresy as from orthodoxy." They did not worry about inspiration because they did not care about the Bible and, in fact, were largely ignorant of it. Recently, Pratt reported, a student had written that the ancient Hebrews were fairly moral considering their times, "though of course they did not have our Ten Commandments."

Looking back twenty years to the William Rainey Harper era, Pratt observed that there had been "glowing promises which we of the liberal movement made to ourselves . . . of a rationalized and newly vitalized Christian faith which should fill the masses with more spiritual religion and take the place of the old bondage of the letter." Instead, liberal religion had removed not only bondage to the letter of Scripture, but most of the reasons for paying attention to the Bible in the first place.[41]

Such new attitudes were not confined to New England, even if there the generational changes were most dramatic. In 1928 Robert Cooley Angell, a young sociologist at the University of Michigan, published *The Campus: A Study of Contemporary Undergraduate Life in the American University*. Based on his own close observations at the University of Michigan over a ten-year period, Angell's account provided the most astute portrait of the university student life of the era. On the subject of religion, he found himself in almost complete agreement with Pratt's more impressionistic observations.

While a majority of Michigan students were church members, that figure was deceiving. Only 20 to 25%, Angell estimated, attended church on Sunday. In Angell's judgment, most of them did so not because "of acceptance of unscientific dogma, but rather of whole-hearted participation in an institution which they believe to have value both for themselves and for society at large." While most students leaned in the direction of belief in a Supreme Being, only about a third had religious or philosophical views sufficiently formulated to provide a stable outlook that might shape their lives. A few more had attempted to find a guiding faith and failed. The majority, however, had not even attempted it. Perhaps a third of the students, Angell estimated, prayed; but many of them did so no more than about once a week. Regular reading of Scripture or adherence to an institutional creed was a rarity.

Nor did religious beliefs have much to do with student behavior on campus. "Young people, for instance, will dance or not dance according as their experiences of life suggest that dancing is good or bad. The fact that it is allowed or forbidden by their churches has almost no influence, except for a very small group."[42]

Campus drinking most conspicuously accentuated the gap between the students and their church heritages. Drinking on campus was increasingly a problem and did not seem to be appreciably slowed by the presence of large numbers of students who were at least nominally members of Protestant churches that supported Prohibition. More often, as Angell observed, Prohibition had "lent a glamour to drinking formerly quite unknown," and because liquor was sometimes scarce, a common view was that it should be readily used whenever it was available. As was commonly said, Prohibition seemed to reinforce the younger generation's attitude of disrespect for rules formulated by their elders. Even at a liberal Protestant bastion like Yale, a straw ballot taken in 1926 showed almost three out of four students favored repeal of the Volstead Act. Three-fourths said they thought there was no less drinking on campus since Prohibition. The only place on campus where the survey found almost universal sentiment for enforcement of the law was at the Divinity School.[43] At Methodist schools like Duke and the University of Southern Carolina, students not only enjoyed the heightened pleasures of illegal drinking but also agitated for the schools to abandon vestigial Methodist rules that banned dancing on campus as well.[44]

According to Robert Angell, a virtual holiday atmosphere was the prevailing spirit of campus life. On almost every campus, this mood was sustained by the dominance of fraternities and sororities. Though Greek letter houses had been common on American college campuses since the mid-nineteenth century, they reached their heyday in the 1920s. The numbers of fraternities and sororities grew dramatically. At Michigan over a third of the students belonged. As elite societies that chose potential campus leaders, the societies wielded influence disproportionate to their size. They were by far the best guarantees of social success on campus, they were prominent in sports and extracurricular activities, and they were recognized as steppingstones to success later in life.[45] Fraternities and sororities had always provided students with bases for resistance against some college (and hence sometimes church) control. In the 1920s they especially flourished since they were ideally situated as independent fortresses that could sustain independent youth culture in the emerging consumer society.

Fraternities and sororities also performed surrogate religious functions. Christian denominations had often spoken of having residential houses near campuses to serve their students, but nothing much ever came of such suggestions. In the meantime Greek letter houses provided churchlike functions as centers for brotherhood or sisterhood to which one gave a primary allegiance. Quasi-religious initiation rites and pledges of lifelong fraternal or sororital loyalty made the analogy explicit. Just as the Masonic order has long functioned quietly as a religious reality in American society, supposedly supplemental to Christianity but often superseding the churches by building alternative major loyalties, so fraternities and sororities helped guarantee youth cultures virtual independence to establish loyalties of their own. Although the societies might profess to be friendly toward Christianity, in fact, they were functionally Deist and in effect discouraged strong loyalty to a traditional religion.

Fraternities and sororities, of course, represented only one segment of campus life; there were a number of other substantial subgroups. "Independents" might remain outside of fraternities either by choice or because of failure to be selected. Poorer students who had to earn their way through college were less likely to be fraternity members and were also more likely to be regular church attendees.[46] "Grinds," or those who actually viewed college as an academic activity, were another largely outsider group. Jewish students were often put in the same class with grinds, and discrimination against them was taken for granted by the Greek letter houses. Otherwise, religious distinctions were usually not as conspicuous as social distinctions on campus. In retrospect, both in personal memoirs and in academic studies, campus life of the era was typically recalled as though religion had not been present at all.[47]

At the time, observers who were old enough to recall prewar days often commented on the changes. The decline of the YMCAS was the most dramatic. In the prewar era they had been a major force in campus life. By 1921 the YMCAS reached their numerical peak with 731 chapters on the approximately 1,000 campuses in the country; they had enrolled well over 90,000 members, or about 1 in 7 in a student population of about 600,000. By 1940 the number of institutions had climbed to 1,700, with 1.5 million students, but the number of Ys had fallen to 480, and their enrollments had dropped to some 50,000, or about 1 in 30. Y activities were changing dramatically also. During the peak year in the Bible study movement, 1908, a typical Y chapter could expect to enroll one-fourth of the men on campus in Bible studies, and the total national enrollment was some 50,000. In 1920 the enrollments (always larger than numbers of regular participants) were still at 30,000; by 1930 the number had plummeted to 5,000.[48]

In the meantime the YMCAS were rapidly adjusting their emphasis from evangelism to the social gospel. This was partly in response to changing student interests. Before the war the Ys had been closely associated with the Student Volunteer Movement and between 1899 and 1915 over three thousand of the American missionaries who sailed had been products of the YMCAS or the YWCAS. Shortly after the war, student interest in missions, as in Bible studies, dropped precipitously. By the end of the 1920s, student chapters were taking the lead in making social service the principal emphasis of the YMCAS. C. Howard Hopkins, historian of the movement, compared the disappearance of the old evangelistic theology and methods of the movements to the collapse of "The Wonderful One-Hoss Shay." In 1931 the YMCA dropped its evangelical basis altogether, describing itself rather as "a world-wide fellowship of men and boys united by a common loyalty to Jesus Christ for the purpose of building Christian personality and a Christian society."[49]

Despite the sacrificial efforts of many Y members in volunteer welfare work, the organization, which of course was "dry," was out of step with the self-indulgent spirit of the dominant student culture. Most students at the University of Michigan, Robert Angell explained, vaguely resented the YMCA's "holier than thou" attitude. While they thought Y activities were worthy, they did not think there should be a special class of people who were known for their good deeds. "There is also a subtle feeling," Angell added, "that a person who is meek, gentle, and unusually religious is in some sense effeminate and unfit to cope with the problems of full-blooded men." By contrast, he observed, "women generally look with more favor on the YWCA, probably because service has been felt in our civilization to be a peculiarly feminine function."[50] In fact, campus women remained more active in their religious practice and slightly more conservative in their religious and social views, but in the emerging hedonistic student culture men's dominance was still widely assumed, so that men were seen as setting the trends.[51]

In 1926 and 1927 the student department of the YMCAS for the Midwestern states commissioned a scientific study that confirmed that the influence of Ys on campuses was declining precipitously. "There is a serious trend toward failure and breakdown and even a complete wash-out of student YMCAS across the region," the report warned. Students were not clear on whether the Ys were supposed to be religious or social agencies, and in several schools students were "distinctly unfriendly to the Y." Some were put off by the fundamentalist-versus-modernist controversies. Others simply found the meetings unappealing. "I do not go to the Y. meetings," said one ex-attendee.

"They sing the same unlucky thirteen hymns every time and I know in advance the brand of moralizing piffle the speaker will spout."[52]

Required chapel services were under attack for similar reasons. The chapel tradition, which had been integral to university life since the Middle Ages, had persisted into the interwar era. Clearly at church-related and private institutions administrations had an interest in retaining this symbol of a venerable heritage, which ensured at least one place for Christianity in official university life. Even in 1940 the prevalence of chapel in the nation's colleges could seem reassuring. Of schools accredited by the Association of American Universities, 48% still had compulsory chapel, 20% had voluntary chapel, and only 32% had none. Even among state schools 27% still had chapel, usually voluntary. Smaller colleges were particularly likely to have chapel, and at schools for African Americans chapel was the rule, even in those that were not denominational.[53]

Nonetheless, religious observance had some relationship to social class, and at many of the wealthiest and most influential private schools required chapel had yielded to student assaults, particularly during the mid-1920s. Within a few years Amherst, Brown, Chicago, Dartmouth, Vassar, Williams, and Yale all yielded to demands for voluntary worship.[54]

The case of Yale, still a bellwether school, was typical. When in 1921 Arthur Twining Hadley, Yale's first lay president since 1899, retired, the Rev. Anson Phelps Stokes, secretary of the Yale Corporation since 1899, was a strong candidate to replace him. The fact that he was an Episcopal clergyman, however, closely identified with Dwight Hall, counted against him among some influential alumni. Another insider, the Rev. Henry Sloane Coffin, was rejected on similar grounds. Instead, the corporation turned to not merely a layperson but a non-Yale graduate, James Rowland Angell. Angell, the son of Michigan's former president, was a leader in the field of psychology at the University of Chicago. His thought had been influenced by James and Dewey but incorporated aspects of the liberal Protestantism of his upbringing as well.[55]

Yale's Dwight Hall heritage still ensured a strong representation of liberal evangelicalism on the faculty, but by the 1920s the definition of Christianity at Yale was increasingly emphasizing its formal functions.[56] From the 1890s until about 1910, Yale had been noted for its evangelical piety.[57] After that, however, Bible study and private piety had declined precipitously. Moreover, the younger generation did not seem to share the prewar generation's enthusiasm for sacrificial public service.

By the mid-1920s required chapel had become one of the victims of the new climate. In 1925 the *Yale Daily* led a persistent campaign against compulsion and through straw polls established overwhelming student and faculty opposition. Student editorials, of course, argued that religion would be healthier if it were voluntary, but the true sentiments of most may have been captured in a bit of doggerel titled "A Hymn: To Dear Old Mother Battell," referring to the venerable Battell chapel building and including such sentiments as:

> Though we're grown you still confine us
> Close beneath your musty wind,
> And with nosey voice you whine us
> Sappy songs you always sing.[58]

In bowing to student pressures, the Yale Corporation reassured concerned constituents that the shift to voluntary chapel was just an adjustment to the spirit of the times and would not lessen the university's intention to "uphold and propagate the Christian protestant religion."[59] President Angell likewise affirmed that the university remained in close contiguity with its religious heritage. "While the theological views of our generations are in many respects quite different from those of the founders of Yale and the later founders of the Church of Christ in Yale," he told the *Yale Daily* in 1927, "all are alike characterized by allegiance to the essential teachings of Jesus and to the promotion of those fundamental attitudes in private and public life which we call Christian."[60]

In the later years of his presidency, during the mid-1930s, Angell had to admit that at Yale, as elsewhere among American youth, "complete indifference to religion, colored at times with acrimonious hostility and ignorant contempt, is an altogether too common phenomenon." Nonetheless, he claimed comfort in other "large and influential groups of students" who showed "a deep and serious concern . . . for the essential religious and ethical values in life." In 1936 in one of his last baccalaureate services, Angell called for "a moral and spiritual renaissance." This awakening, however, would not be of "superstitions" or "outworn creeds" but instead "a vital reverence for the highest values in human life."[61]

Whatever the degree of genuine sympathy for the Christian heritage such statements indicated, even among its supporters religion was being reduced to vague platitudes. This was true not only of administrators, of whom such equivocation was to be expected. They, after all, had to communicate with a wide public and also prepare baccalaureates and other occasional remarks in which they had to say something pious yet offend no one. What is more telling is that such tendencies were increasingly typical of mainline Protestantism as a whole, especially when they addressed a wider public. The religious professionals most interested in restoring a place for Christianity on campuses were conspicuous in constructing a religion of no offense.

Searching for a Message

During the interwar era there was no lack of discussions, studies, symposia, journals, conferences, and programs about the restoration of Christianity to a place on campus. In almost all of these, however, one gets the impression that by the early 1920s the leadership in the Protestant establishment was desperately attempting to find a message that would reach the youth culture. One thing they were firmly convinced of was that they could not say anything that would make them sound like fundamentalists. The independent and rebellious mood of the youth, as they saw it—perhaps correctly—was in part a reaction against fundamentalism, or Puritanism, or outworn presci-entific creeds. In response they attempted to articulate a broader version of Christianity that would appeal to a more modern mentality. Unfortunately, among many youth in the 1920s such religious idealism was also passé. It was high-sounding rhetoric; the problem was that most of the young were going to regard it as just that, the platitudinous ideals of an older generation that, aside from Prohibition, lacked much of a substantive agenda.

A 1924 symposium on "The Place of Religion in Higher Education," conducted by the Association of American Colleges, provides a typical example. Throughout the era, the AAC published in its *Bulletin* discussions of the importance of retaining a place for religion in higher education, some-times recognizing how difficult the task was. The transcript of the opening remarks in the symposium by the president of the AAC, President C. A. Richmond of Union University, reveals the changed atmosphere of the day. Apologizing that he was a minister who was a college president, Richmond quipped,

Some of you may have found that the office of minister, and college president—are often incompatible (laughter), at least, in the popular

imagination they are supposed to be so, and when you ask a college president to talk about religion, well, it is like asking Mr. Bryan to talk about evolution. (Laughter). He is supposed to be unembarrassed by any knowledge
of the subject. (Laughter).

The most substantive discussion of the issues on this occasion was provided by President Marion L. Burton of the University of Michigan, in
remarks considered noteworthy enough to be reprinted in part in the *Bulletin
of the American Association of University Professors*. While universities were
successful in teaching their students of advances in science, President Burton
observed, they had failed to convey the advances to religion brought by scientific knowledge:

> Christ is no longer the center of metaphysical discussions about His person,
> but all of our thought, political, commercial, and economic, is increasingly
> Christlike. Man is no longer the wreck and ruin of a once perfect harmony,
> but he is a chaos, not yet reduced to order. Sin is not merely a taint of the
> past, but selfishness, pure and simple. Salvation is not saving the sinful soul
> from the fires of Hell, but the making of all men into good ones here and
> now. All things are not true, because they are in the Bible, but they are in the
> Bible because they are true.[62]

Yet the problem, said Burton, was that there was a "deep, abysmal, unfath-
omable darkness about religion" on college campuses as elsewhere in the nation. When people thought of religion, they still thought of categories from
the Dark Ages. What was needed was a religion that dealt with "character."
They must, Burton concluded, "send out a generation of students who understand religion in its largest terms, and know that we can only build a life with
an inner reality which matches the stern ineradicable order of truth that life
gives us."[63]

"Character" was the most prominent word in the literature on the role of
religion in higher education, since that was a worthy ideal to which religion
could contribute without offending modern sensibilities. Moreover, in an age
when the typical ambition of young people was to move from four years of
hedonism in college to the life of business profit, building character seemed
an especially urgent educational task.[64]

In *Christian Education*, published by the interdenominational Council of
Church Boards of Education in the United States of America, a symposium

on "Character Education" was headed by John D. Rockefeller Jr., who spoke out for honesty in business, obedience to law, and clean living. The standard formula for how to influence college students was enunciated by another speaker: "Character is caught, rather than taught."[65] The more common version was voiced by Henry Sloane Coffin at a conference of leading Eastern educators held at Princeton in 1928: "Religion is caught—not taught." The meaning was precisely the same. The consensus was that the key to conveying religious ideals in colleges was for leading persons, from administrators to professors, to be persons of high Christian character. Of course, as Coffin was quick to add, doctrinal tests were entirely out of bounds. Nonetheless, schools could informally provide worthy Christian models.[66]

With popular magazines as well as fundamentalists making as much of a sensation as they could out of the alleged laxity in morals on campuses, the liberal Protestant establishment more often affirmed that things were not really so bad after all. In a 1926 survey of college and university presidents, conducted by *Literary Digest*, the not surprising result was an almost unanimous belief that drinking was down since Prohibition, at least on their own campuses. An editorial in the *Christian Century*, "Are College Girls Bad?," acknowledged that changes in mores were taking place at a bewildering speed. Women smoking openly on campuses, for instance, was causing a great deal of consternation at the moment. Changes in sexual mores were particularly rapid. "The changes are sudden, but are they bad?," asked the *Century*:

> Everybody knows that an interpretation of conduct obtains in college class rooms from which the fixed absolutes of a generation ago have been eliminated. Is there any better word to say than that we are going from an old world to a new and that we may trust human nature—in our girls as well as in our boys and grown-ups—to right itself upon its own keel? We can trust it, if, with our trust, we lend them the support which sympathy and understanding and faith can give and which distrust and dark suspicions cannot give.

The key phrase was that "we may trust human nature."[67] While liberal Protestants might sometimes express alarm about campus trends, their principal strategy was to sympathize and offer supportive guidance. They recognized correctly that the student attitudes were in many ways only extensions of their own principles. They represented confidence in human nature, and hence confidence that increased freedom would lead toward the good.[68]

The counterpart was that they stood against authoritarianism. So did the students. There would be a period of adjustment, but with some spiritual guidance, there was little need to worry.

Faith in God, humanity, and moral progress were all rooted in confidence in the scientific method as the great revealer. To the question "What are the ruling concepts in modern education?" the *Christian Century* responded in a 1931 essay: "The ruling concepts of modern education are freedom of the individual from disciplines and patterns of conduct based solely upon tradition, the right of the individual to realize his own possibilities and to discover the best means of realization by his own experience, and the duty of both individuals and society to bring all codes and commands and prohibitions to the experimental test." This "application of the scientific spirit to the matters which most deeply concern human life" had the danger, the *Century* conceded—presumably with Prohibition in mind—that experiments sometimes went wrong. Nonetheless, most people thought the benefits were worth the risks. Advances might bring periods of confusion and painful adjustment. Yet that was not too high a price to pay for "the transition from a morality of accepted codes and ipse-dixit rules to a morality based on a scientific study of the observable results of conduct."[69]

At the end of the 1930s, religious liberalism was sometimes chastened by postliberal or neo-orthodox theological trends, which challenged their close identification with the culture. That theological critique of culture had little impact, however, on the largely positive assessments of what was happening on campuses. For one thing, the international threat of totalitarianism in the 1930s reinforced the point that Protestant colleges in America must stand first of all for freedom. Given this political context, it would, indeed, be difficult to deny that the very openness of campuses to diverse opinions, even to those antithetical to Christianity, were signs of health in a world of contagious absolutism.[70] Calls to strengthen Christian identity or separate the church from the world, therefore, would be inappropriate to campuses, even church-related campuses, since they would involve more restrictions, in contradiction to the quintessential cultural watchword of freedom. While Christian ministries saw themselves in a struggle against crass materialism, what they offered was nonetheless not confrontation with American culture but a voluntarily chosen spiritual dimension that could provide divine grounding for the highest cultural ideals.

On these terms it was still plausible, even at the end of the 1930s, to give an optimistic account of religion on campuses. So, for instance, T. T.

Brumbaugh after a tour of twenty-two colleges and universities concluded, "I am ready to state unhesitatingly not only that there is a growing concern for religion as such among students in this country but that in administrative circles in tax-supported and other schools there is enhanced appreciation of the spiritual interpretation of existence which is the specific province of religion." Brumbaugh cited the development of schools of religion and co-operative campus ministries, often encouraged by school administrations. Nonetheless, such ministries had to learn that "public institutions of learning can go no farther than to place due emphasis of learning upon the spiritual interpretations of life and the commonly acknowledged moral values im-plicit therein."[71]

Similarly, Merrimon Cuninggim, after extensive study of campuses just prior to World War II, could describe the forces of religion as gaining dramat-ically. On the one hand, he acknowledged that "the prevailing atmosphere in higher education today is secular," defining secularity as an "emphasis upon the material to the exclusion or denial of the intangible and upon nature to the disparagement of the supernatural." Nonetheless, Cuninggim, who had been a campus religious worker at Duke, saw the contest as more a friendly "two-sided game" than a warfare: "That it [higher education] has dealt so many cards to religion in recent years has made the game close, but has not yet made religion the victor. Secularism is too widespread for one to be able glibly to conclude that colleges are more Christian in attitude than in 1900."

What made such optimism possible was a broad definition of religion. Religion, said Cuninggim, is

> a knowledge of high values in living. It is, moreover, an appreciation of and a personal commitment to those values, a search for the eternal verities, a faith in God. A student may be said to "have religion" when, for example, he possesses personal integrity and, what is more, knows why; or when he respects selfhood in those around him, the rights and needs and joys of others; or when through personal experience he knows reverence and sym-pathy and goodness; or when he is sensitive to his obligation to society and acts upon it.[72]

When religion was defined in more traditional ways, however, then it was clear that it was on the periphery of student life and consciousness. Ruth Davies, a professor of English literature at Ohio Wesleyan University, observed in 1939 that she was often asked the question "Are students losing their religion?" She responded that students "cannot lose what they do not have." The realistic view was that "the average student today has very little religion of the type meant by the people who ask the question," that is, not religion as just a broad idealism but "the conventional conception of religion which has found expression in the creeds and practices of the church in America." As modern activities were increasingly defined by mechanism, Davies observed, "religion is simply not on the boards in the theater of modern American life." People talk about "religious consciousness," but "religious unconsciousness" might be the more appropriate term. "Generally speaking, we seem spiritually to be under the influence of an anesthetic."[73]

17

Outsiders

Despite attempts to define the university in terms of the inclusivist ideal of liberal Protestantism, some significant groups were, in fact, being left out. Two major reasons accounted for groups being underrepresented in the leading institutions of the dominant culture. At one end of the spectrum were those who chose to maintain their own cultural identity, usually supported by strong religious convictions. At the other end were those who, while cultivating cultural identities with religious roots, nonetheless aspired to become part of the mainstream. Most religious groups, however, fell somewhere in between, exhibiting various mixes of both tendencies.

Roman Catholics were the largest group whose outsider status had a large voluntary component. They maintained their own parochial school system, an extensive network of colleges, and a few modest universities. So while Catholics' 5 to 10% representation among student bodies and faculties of non-Catholic universities was much less than their representation in the population generally, the difference was attributable more to choice and social class than overt religious discrimination. Even at prestigious schools of the East there was little evidence of overt discrimination against Catholics, although there was always strong discrimination based on social class and alumni ties.[1]

The 5 to 10% representation in the nation's major universities reflected Catholic ambivalence and division on the question of separation from the dominant culture. A Catholic, after all, had been a viable candidate for the U.S. presidency in 1928, and many Catholics were pushing to become part of the mainstream. At Notre Dame, for instance, even though Thomas Aquinas might be preeminent in philosophy and theology, Knute Rockne's preeminence on Saturdays suggested another side of Catholic culture that aspired to be 100% American.

At the University of Illinois, the Catholic Foundation sparked a protracted controversy within the church. The Rev. John O'Brien, an able scholar and colorful personality, was the pastor and chaplain to Catholic students. He had been instrumental in instituting courses, taught under his auspices, for

The Soul of the American University Revisited. George M. Marsden, Oxford University Press. © Oxford University Press 2021. DOI: 10.1093/oso/9780190073312.003.0021

which the university agreed in 1919 to offer academic credit. A few years later O'Brien launched an ambitious campaign to build a magnificent building for the Catholic Foundation. He pointed out that there were more Catholics enrolled at the university than in all the Catholic colleges in the state and that the foundation presented a marvelous new educational and missionary opportunity.

O'Brien's campaign soon aroused stiff opposition. Influential members of the Illinois church hierarchy, supported strongly by the Jesuits all over the world, argued that O'Brien's ministry was an attack on Catholic universities. If O'Brien's scheme succeeded, it would only encourage more Catholic students to attend state universities. O'Brien retorted that many of the best students were attending state universities anyway, and that his foundation was playing an essential role in training Catholic lay leaders for the next generation. Finally, the controversy became so bitter that the Vatican stepped in and brought it to an end. O'Brien continued his work on the Catholic Foundation, but he had to scale down his plans because the opposition had weakened his sources of financial support.[2] The Catholic leadership that opposed O'Brien was asserting an ideal of Catholic separateness. O'Brien, on the other hand, was responding to the reality that, no matter what the church said, Catholics were being served and shaped by secular American institutions at least as much as by the church.

Protestants were also divided as to whether university culture should be regarded as a threat to the faith. In most mainstream denominations there were three major positions on this question. The largest group were those so used to Protestant hegemony that they could hardly conceive of a conflict between church and culture; as a matter of course they sent their children to universities without thought for their religious stances. Another sizable constituency supported the hundreds of denominational colleges. These offered a variety of religious outlooks, but the most common was a serious-minded evangelical liberalism, supported by required chapel, Bible courses, and restrictive campus moral regulations that preserved something of the Protestant mores that had been dominant before World War I. Rather than see themselves at war with the university culture, mainline denominational colleges saw themselves as offering the invaluable option of an added spiritual dimension.

The third group were the fundamentalists, who militantly opposed the cultural trends, were building their own institutions, and in some cases were seceding from the major denominations. After the mid-1920s, however, militant fundamentalism declined sharply in Northern churches and now seemed marginal so far as those denominations were concerned. In fact, however, new networks were developing to support Protestant higher education outside the mainstream. Fundamentalist breakaway groups joined many other sectarian groups, such as those in Pentecostal and holiness traditions, each of which supported its own institutions. Such groups founded more than a hundred Bible institutes, often patterned on the Moody Bible Institute in Chicago, which offered training in basic skills oriented toward learning to witness to the truths of biblicist Christianity in evangelism at home and in missions abroad.[3] Sectarian groups also supported many smaller four-year colleges. Protestant immigrant groups, such as the Missouri Synod Lutherans and the Christian Reformed, also founded their own colleges and cultivated a militant sense of separateness. Much of the white Protestantism of the South also had a mentality much like that of a separate ethnic group, and many of their colleges, especially those of Southern Baptists and Southern Presbyterians, were determined to preserve conservative theological and cultural views.[4]

Women's colleges presented an ambiguous case with respect to the insider–outsider question and religion. Women were excluded from undergraduate admission at some of the most prestigious Eastern universities. Elite institutions for women tended to be a shade more traditional in their religious observances than were their all-male counterparts.[5] Denominational women's colleges also emphasized religion a bit more than did men's schools and were certainly more protective regarding social behavior. In North Carolina even the state women's college at Greensboro had required chapel services into the 1940s, a decade after chapel requirements had been abandoned at the University of North Carolina at Chapel Hill. The conventional association of women with domesticity and religion contributed to a slight lag in secularization at women's colleges.

As Andrea Turpin has shown, the rise of women's education in the late nineteenth century typically had explicitly Christian motivations, and by the early twentieth century progressive and liberal Protestant ideals had generated a distinct "moral vision" for women's collegiate education. Women, like men, were to be trained to serve society, but usually in gendered forms of social service appropriate to their sex. By the 1920s men's education was becoming more oriented toward preparing for business success than toward serving society. Women collegians after the Progressive era were likewise finding fewer opportunities to engage in social reforms through service professions. At the same time their opportunities in the business remained negligible. So the purposes of women's higher education, beyond building character, were ambiguous.[6]

Far less ambiguous was the situation of African Americans. Formally or informally discriminated against in most American universities, they were largely left to make the best of poorly funded black colleges. After World War I, the number of blacks attending college increased dramatically, though by 1927 the total had reached only some fifteen thousand, nine-tenths of whom were at colleges with all-black student bodies. At predominantly white schools, blacks faced numerous obstacles. At Yale, which had a long record of support for education of African Americans, a few were admitted, though they faced informal racial discrimination, which was growing during this era.[7] At Harvard in the early 1920s a major stir was caused when President Lawrence Abbot Lowell ruled that African Americans would not be admitted to freshman dorms. Although alumni protest led the trustees to modify the rule, blacks still could be admitted to the dorms only if they could afford a single room or find a black roommate. At Princeton, which always had strong Southern ties, blacks were not admitted as undergraduates until after World War II, though they were admitted to the independent and theologically much more conservative Princeton Theological Seminary.[8] Qualified blacks could gain admission to state universities and, if they could afford it, to many private colleges in the North, but everywhere they faced social discrimination.

In most black colleges, biblicist Christianity played a major role. This emphasis was in part a reflection of the centrality of the churches in the black community. A survey conducted by Benjamin E. Mays in 1940 showed that an overwhelming majority of students at black colleges, usually well over 90%, were church members, and most professed conservative beliefs about God, prayer, and the Bible. Evidence of actual religious practice was, of course, mixed. One survey in 1945 showed that while 90% of black students attended church at least twice a month, only a third considered their classmates to be religious. Mays noted that black college students (like their white counterparts) often resented compulsory chapel and few attended when chapel services were made voluntary.[9]

Institutional support for Christianity was also strong at most black colleges. Over two-thirds were private colleges, most founded by Northern white missionary organizations or by churches. Most of these had compulsory chapel, as did even some of the state schools.[10] In this respect they did not differ much from all-white colleges in the South.

The persistence of biblicist Christian patterns was deeply mixed with the questions of African American identity in America. From one point of view the continuation of traditional Christian patterns, often with relatively strict social regulation of students, could be seen as a form of white control, since most black schools were still administered by whites. This issue was dramatically illustrated at Fisk University, where in the 1920s a strict disciplinary code was brought down by student protests. Fisk was considered academically the best of the black colleges. It was founded by the American Missionary Association and still had a white president. So the attack on the disciplinary code was in part an attack on white paternalism. On the other hand, the black community was divided just as was the white over how strict its colleges should be. Fisk's code was not as severe as that at Wilberforce, the first black school controlled by blacks, but which was run by the African Methodist Episcopal Church and hence had strict Methodist mores.[11]

Howard University, the only school for African Americans that was truly a university, with professional schools in law, medicine, and theology, presents an interesting case of the ambiguities of the role of religion. Howard was founded in Washington, D.C., after the Civil War with support from the Freedmen's Bureau and various church groups. By the 1920s, when its some two thousand students represented almost one-sixth of all blacks receiving higher education, its principal support came from yearly congressional appropriations.[12] Originally the school required evangelical church membership for faculty members. At the end of the nineteenth century attendance had been required at daily chapel services and at Sunday Bible classes and preaching services. The 1898–1899 catalog stated: "This institution is always emphatically Christian. Its instructors believe in Christianity as the only basis of true culture; but pupils here are given no denominational bias and no ecclesiastical or denominational instruction is given in any department."[13]

Like some other colleges of the era Howard experienced revivals among its students into early decades of the twentieth century.[14] By the 1920s the collegiate atmosphere had begun to change. The college catalog still described the school as "distinctly Christian in its spirit and work,"[15] and the president, James Stanley Durkee, one of a long succession of white Congregational clergymen to head the school, still described the purpose of the chapel as to encourage "life surrender to Christ."[16] Compulsory chapel, however, was becoming controversial at Howard, as elsewhere. Protests initiated by students in 1922 eventually resulted in capitulation to voluntary chapel in 1925. The variation at Howard from the pattern elsewhere, however, was that the chapel controversy was only one part of growing black student unrest about racism. Howard was not as strictly regulated as most of the smaller black colleges, but its regulations sparked broader protests. Students demanded the end of white control. Finally, in 1926, after enduring protracted criticism, President Durkee resigned to accept a pastorate. The trustees chose as its next president Mordecai W. Johnson, a young black Baptist pastor, who began a presidency that was to last until 1960.[17]

Under Johnson and his successors the process of secularization at Howard followed just about the same pattern as in mainline denominational colleges. The catalog statement that Howard was "distinctly Christian" remained until the 1960s, but the formal definitions of Christianity broadened. Since then the university has become essentially secular, although it still has a Christian divinity school.[18]

Christianity, then, played mixed roles in the outsider status of black schools. To some extent Christianity was used as a means of social regulation and was an expression of white control. On the other hand, Christianity played an even greater role in African American protests against white domination, and the demand for social justice was not a demand for secularization. As at denominational colleges of the era, there was some feeling that the religious character of the black colleges and universities was holding them back academically. E. Franklin Frazier, a Howard graduate of 1916 and later one of its most distinguished faculty members, encapsulated the problem in his famous remark that at black colleges there was "too much inspiration and too little information."[19] Other black educational leaders said the same. The fact of the matter was that in the dominant culture the great majority of those universities and scholars considered to be the best were those who dropped any reference to religion. Whatever the value of Christianity to the black community, the message they were being sent was the same one that was being sent to denominational colleges everywhere: if they wanted to be part of the serious educational enterprise, Christianity would have to go. Since there were compelling economic and social reasons for blacks to strive for full acceptance in the dominant culture, it was unlikely they were going to question its essential assumptions, except on the matter of race itself.

Judaism, Christianity, and Higher Education

Discrimination against Jews in the academy, though involving something of this same dynamic, had much more explicit implications regarding the place of religion.

From the point of view of our theme, a remarkable dimension of the Jewish experience in America is the paucity of explicitly Jewish institutions of higher learning. By the late nineteenth century, Reform, Conservative, and Orthodox Jews had established centers for the training of rabbis. Only in 1928, however, with the organization of Yeshiva College in New York as an Orthodox school that included teaching of secular subjects, was there opportunity for collegiate education from a Jewish religious perspective.[20] The founding of Yeshiva aroused considerable opposition from American Jews who deplored any voluntary Jewish segregation and the criticism of dominant American institutions that a Jewish college implied. After World War II Brandeis University in Waltham, Massachusetts, was founded on a broader basis as a "Jewish sponsored secular university." Brandeis followed a pattern much like that of denominationally related universities of the era. While providing a strong Jewish presence and opportunities for Jewish observance, Brandeis was careful to be nondiscriminatory, so that its initially strong Jewish identity was maintained primarily by self-selection and hence almost bound to fade.[21]

The nature of Judaism as an ethnic as well as a religious identity, its long history of being discriminated against and persecuted in Christian societies, and the dynamic of seeking acceptance and opportunity in American society all contributed to the predominant Jewish tendency to accept American higher education on its own terms. The most relevant question was how to get in. Jews were getting the same message from the universities that was being sent to outsider Christians, but it was underscored by religious differences. If persons were to be fully accepted in the academic community, they would have to keep their traditional religion out of the picture. Hence, American Jewish academics in the twentieth century were typically persons who had been reared in traditional Jewish practice but had abandoned their earlier religious practice and were ardent champions of thoroughly secular academic outlooks.[22]

On the other side, discrimination against Jews presented an embarrassing challenge to the broadly liberal Protestant self-definition of the American university that had emerged by the World War I era. Essential to the definition of the universities was that they stood for a universal cultural ideal to which everyone could be assimilated—at least in principle. The universal claims of science, together with the moral ideals of liberal democratic culture, provided a basis for this assumption. After World War I, such claims were less often identified explicitly with Christian civilization. During the 1920s and 1930s even foreign missionaries in the liberal Protestant camp were becoming reluctant to challenge other world religions in the name of Christianity and were talking, rather, about mutual learning of one religion from another. Yet at the same time that Christianity was being disestablished as the presumed highest religion of American culture, discrimination against Jews was on the rise. Such discrimination was particularly awkward to explain in the universities, which claimed to stand for freedom. Whether they still defined themselves as centers for promoting broad "spiritual value," or whether they spoke of themselves in more secular terms as essentially scientific, universities were still supposed to be inclusive.

A number of practical factors help explain why discrimination against Jews became a major issue in universities after 1920. The most immediate was that before the upsurge in popularity of collegiate education after World War I college admission had seldom been selective; even the best colleges took virtually anyone who applied and met the sometimes considerable entrance requirements. Jews, who made up only about 3.5% of the population, were disproportionately represented in student bodies. In 1918–1919 a survey of over a hundred institutions showed that Jewish students made up nearly 10% of the total number of students. The percentage was considerably higher in some Eastern schools and in New York City ran from one-third at a number of institutions to over two-thirds at the College of the City of New York.[23]

At the same time, although Jews were still only 3.5% of the total American population, that figure represented an immense increase over the past several decades—in 1881 Jews had numbered only a little over 0.5% of Americans. By far the largest part of this increase had come from Eastern European immigration. The character of the American Jewish population changed from predominantly German and relatively well-to-do to a predominantly foreign-born, Yiddish-speaking, initially poor immigrant population with all the problems that attend any such cultural transition. So the upsurge in the size and character of the Jewish population contributed to increasing anti-Semitism, which, of course, had always been present to a degree. Moreover, this was a time of a worldwide increase in anti-Semitism and racism. In the United States such attitudes were reflected in the post–World

War I resurgence of the nativism that led to restrictions on immigration. Many clubs, resorts, neighborhoods, and jobs were closed to Jews. American universities, although by no means as discriminatory as many other areas of American life, were nonetheless touched by these sentiments.

Most notorious in this respect were the elite Ivy League schools, which in the early 1920s devised various ways to set admissions criteria other than sheer academic ability so as to limit the percentage of Jewish students. At Harvard and Yale the percentage was kept at about 10%. The theory at these and other Eastern colleges was that higher numbers of Jewish students would change the character of the student body. Lingering ideals of the Christian establishment, that colleges were to cultivate Christian spiritual values and character, had something to do with this sentiment, and these schools were still occasionally spoken of as essentially "Christian" institutions. The stronger cause, however, was the social snobbishness of the elite schools, which would have been much more directly threatened by a predominance of any group of students without WASP pedigrees.[24]

Princeton offers an especially interesting case of the mix of these motives. During the first half of the twentieth century Princeton was notorious as the prestige university least hospitable to Jewish students. The percentage of Jewish students there was always much lower than at other Eastern universities, and Jews who did survive the selection process had to brave ongoing social discrimination.[25] During this era Princeton, unlike Yale and Harvard, continued to require chapel attendance and displayed a slightly more serious desire to maintain a Christian ethos. Nonetheless, the concern to preserve a preferential place for the Christian religion in the communal life at Princeton seems only a secondary factor in accounting for anti-Jewish discrimination. As Woodrow Wilson learned, nowhere was social elitism more firmly entrenched than at Princeton. Such elitism had something to do with Christianity, but so did much of the opposition to it. So it would be difficult to interpret the discrimination as reflecting specifically religious concerns nearly as much as social ones.

It is difficult to isolate specifically religious factors in the growth of American anti-Semitism in the interwar era. So far as colleges and universities are concerned, it is an intriguing irony that discrimination against Jews increased after 1920 as traditional Protestantism was rapidly disappearing at leading schools to be replaced by liberal Protestant and secular alternatives. Perhaps the timing reflects only the coincidence of social prejudices and traditional religious decline. At least it does not seem right to blame anti-Semitism on liberal Protestantism. At Yale the college chaplain, Sidney Lovett, in the 1930s took the lead in ministering to Jewish students, encouraging their own religious practice, and inviting a rabbi to preach each year in Battell Chapel.[26] What the record indicates is not that liberal Christian teaching promoted anti-Semitism but, rather, that church leadership did not have a major influence one way or the other in the universities when social and economic issues were at stake.

The role of religious discrimination in faculty hiring was similar but more subtle. From the late nineteenth century, most leading universities were not entirely closed to hiring Jewish faculty members, whose numbers gradually increased in the subsequent eras. However, Jews were much more likely to be hired in the sciences than in the humanities, and in professional schools rather than in undergraduate programs. This was the pattern at Yale, for instance. While Jews had some representation on the scientific, professional, and graduate faculties, and occasionally held junior positions at the college, before World War II no Jew received tenure on the Yale College faculty.[27] Not until after the Holocaust was anti-Semitism widely perceived as an embarrassment to the claims of liberal culture.

It was a telling symptom of the pattern of discrimination that at Yale, as at some other private colleges with Protestant lineage, the field of English literature was virtually closed to Jews until after World War II. This seems to have had something to do with the vestigial spirit, if not the substance, of the religious heritage. As James M. Turner has suggested, when traditional Protestantism faded in the late nineteenth century, English literature was one of the manifestations of a sacral ideal that arose to take its place.[28] This was one expression of a growing tendency to treat Western civilization as the bearer of the Christian heritage, broadly conceived. It was sometimes suggested that because this heritage of literature in Christendom grew in part out of the New Testament, it was inappropriate for Jews to teach it.[29] As literature was an important locus for teaching "character," it may have also been an area in which it was thought particularly appropriate to find the right sort of gentlemen, preferably those who used a familial middle name.

As much as any other factor, the continuance of anti-Semitism points to one of the deepest problems in maintaining a Christian identity at liberal Protestant institutions. As has been a persistent theme in this history, such schools had long viewed themselves both as Christian institutions and as serving the whole American public. During the nineteenth century, they resolved this dilemma by declaring themselves to be "nonsectarian" even while discriminating against Catholics and other smaller religious groups, such as the Jews. In the twentieth century, this nonsectarianism was broadened into the moral ideals of liberalism, democracy, and Western civilization. Protestant leaders saw such ideals as perfectly compatible with their efforts after World War I to reinstate an explicitly Christian presence at universities and colleges. At the same time that such efforts were gaining ground, however, so were the realities of a pluralistic culture. How could they promote ever-widening inclusivist liberal ideals and at the same time reassert an explicitly Christian identity?

In the years following the World War II and the Holocaust, the logic of the commitment to inclusivism would lead to speaking of the "Judeo-Christian" heritage as representing the highest ideals of Western civilization, which both liberal education and religious people "of all faiths" could stand for. That would allow for opening up even the humanities to Jewish presence. The postwar academy could thus still affirm its allegiance to its theistic heritage. At the same time, there was growing support in some disciplines for objectivist and positivist scientific standards that would effectively marginalize substantive religious concerns. How these two commitments might be reconciled was already a matter of debate that had not been resolved.

18

Searching for a Soul

In the interwar years American cultural leaders faced a new crisis of faith, not simply concerning Christianity but concerning liberal Western culture itself. This intellectual crisis, which emerged in the 1920s and heightened during the 1930s and the war years, undercut the ideological rationale for the universities as servants of democratic civilization. The universities were unreservedly committed to two things: science and the highest ideals of Western culture. Now a distressing realization began to dawn, although only a few prophets were willing to face its full implications, that these two ideals might be incompatible.

This crisis of cultural faith was sharply intensified by the general crisis of Western culture. By the early 1930s Americans were becoming aware of the dimensions of the worldwide crisis and at the same time facing the severest domestic challenges since the Civil War. The failure of democracies abroad and the rise of totalitarianism underscored the revived question of whether the American experiment would long endure. The unprecedented economic depression changed what had been previously a theoretical question into an engrossing concern, impossible to ignore. People were bound to ask what held American society together, or, for that matter, what would hold together any democracy. Was a democracy merely a pragmatic arrangement, or did it require a body of shared ideas in order to function?

American universities, which only recently had emerged as major players in the national culture, mirrored the national crisis. The painful economic constraints of the Depression era were, of course, the most immediate concern, but the questions debated at universities went deeper. Many of those who were used to looking for underlying explanations were becoming acutely aware that the cultural upheaval of the past half-century had undermined what had been thought to be the very foundations of Western civilization. Having been among the major promoters of these changes, intellectual leaders in the university had to face the question of whether the new culture for which they spoke had anything to offer in place of, or at least to shore up, the old verities.

The Soul of the American University Revisited. George M. Marsden, Oxford University Press. © Oxford University Press 2021. DOI: 10.1093/oso/9780190073312.003.0022

For humanists, who were most likely to be debating such issues, the fear of losing moral compass was exacerbated by recognition that the dominant forces shaping the universities were functional and mundane.

Universities had been built to serve the needs of modern industrial society.[1] Much of their money came from corporate America, which controlled their boards. Despite the sincerity of their professions to stand first of all for the humane, in fact, university organizations had far more to do with the insatiable demands of technological society. American universities succeeded in large part because they made themselves centers for scientific and technological research. In fact, their organizations were modeled throughout on the technological principle of looking for the most rational and efficient way to get the job done.[2] Academic life, accordingly, was compartmentalized. Rewards were given for increasingly specialized and technical research. In most fields this imitation of the principles of practical technique extended to the embrace of an objectivist scientific ideology as the highest road to truth. Courses in great literature and in Western civilization could be inserted as counterweights to the mundane trends, but the effort was remedial. It did not take a prophet to see that ultimately the practical would overwhelm whatever stood in its way. Ironically it was after 1929, when industry could no longer do its job efficiently, that the conflict of these ideals became most apparent. No longer could the theoretical questions be put aside on the ground that the system works.

The broadest goal of the university, as Theodore Francis Jones, New York University's (NYU's) centennial historian, put it in 1933, was to "spiritualize the machine created by an earlier age." By the 1930s, however, an urban university such as NYU was hard pressed to sustain such idealist rhetoric. To celebrate the NYU centennial in 1932, Chancellor Elmer Ellsworth Brown sponsored an academic conference on "The Obligation of Universities to the Social Order."[3] As historian David Hollinger describes it, the conference revealed the divided mind of the university. Much of the conference was "resoundingly technocratic and progressive: social engineering, it was said, must go forward immediately, casting aside anachronistic traditions."[4] Yet Chancellor Brown also included a section on "The University and Spiritual Values." Here the idealist themes continued to be sounded. President James Rowland Angell of Yale, while averring (former protégé of Dewey that he was) that universities must advance by constant adjustments to social and economic needs, at the same time affirmed the counterbalance of a tradition of gentility. The most advanced conception of the universities had "arisen in response to deep-seated social impulses seeking to integrate the highest institution of learning with the life of the people in ways which shall inspire and elevate and refine."[5] Or perhaps most revealing were the reflections of John Campbell Merriam, president of the Carnegie Institution, on "Spiritual Values" in relation to the sciences. "In addition to consideration of realities, their analysis and synthesis by scientific and other methods," Merriam declared, "the university must present the world of ideals, comprising the highest attainments of human faculties." Spiritual values, which had to do with ideals such as beauty and art and development of individual character, were thus contrasted by Merriam to "realities."[6]

The most troubling question of the day, however, was whether the "realities" of modern science were even compatible with the higher ideals that were supposed to supplement them. Mainline Protestant theologians, university administrators, and most humanists affirmed that naturalistic science and high ideals were compatible, but leading intellectuals were challenging such an assumption. Following the seemingly pointless horrors of World War I, literary figures such as Ezra Pound, the early T. S. Eliot, F. Scott Fitzgerald, Gertrude Stein, and Ernest Hemingway, instead of fostering lofty ideals, were exploring the implications of living in a morally empty universe. Joseph Wood Krutch, a journalist, expressed the underlying point well in his widely read *The Modern Temper* (1929). If one took seriously the pure naturalism of modern science, then the only honest view, said Krutch, was that "nature, in her blind thirst for life, has filled every possible cranny of the rotting earth with some sort of fantastic creature, and among them man is but one." It followed that all the high ideals of human religion, philosophy, or literature, including the belief that there were real distinctions between right and wrong, were illusions. Of the beings on the evolutionary ladder, the human was "perhaps the most miserable of all, because he is the only one in whom the instinct of life falters long enough to enable it to ask the question 'Why?'" "Both our practical morality and our emotional lives," Krutch summarized, "are adjusted to a world which no longer exists."[7]

Scholars on the cutting edge of the sciences and of related academic disciplines, as much as literary figures, were dynamiting the foundations of Victorian idealism and morality.[8] Whatever the field, the premise and the problem were the same: in a naturalistic universe, human beings were on their own. Human intellect was an evolutionary mechanism for survival, but it came with no guarantees. There was no reason to presume that its dictates corresponded to anything other than changing human perceptions of human needs. For many leading philosophers the only question left was, as one influential title put it, "The Meaning of Meaning." In such a universe "good" as a moral term had only an "emotive use."[9] Such conclusions were later canonized for a time in British and American academic thought in A. J. Ayer's *Language, Truth and Logic* (1936). Metaphysical as well as ethical statements were, strictly speaking, meaningless.[10]

In a series of brilliant lectures delivered at the Yale Law School in 1931 and published as *The Heavenly City of the Eighteenth-Century Philosophers*, historian Carl Becker summarized the implications of the outlook of the intellectual avant-garde. "Edit and interpret the conclusions of modern science as tenderly as we like," Becker declared,

> it is still quite impossible for us to regard man as the child of God for whom the earth was created as a temporary habitation. Rather must we regard him as little more than a chance deposit on the surface of the world, carelessly thrown up between two ice ages by the same forces that rust iron and ripen corn, a sentient organism endowed by some happy or unhappy accident with intelligence indeed, but with an intelligence that is conditioned by the very forces that it seeks to understand and to control. . . . What is man that the electron should be mindful of him!

Given this bleak portrait of the true implications of modern thought, Becker could argue his startling central thesis: that the Enlightenment was, in fact, closer to the outlook of the Christian Middle Ages than it was to modernity: "The *Philosophies* demolished the Heavenly City of St. Augustine only to rebuild it with more up-to-date materials." Enlightenment thinkers had, indeed, debunked the Christian superstitions of their predecessors, yet they themselves had an equally naive faith that in a universe governed only by the laws of nature; human reason would be able to find meaning beyond what they themselves constructed.[11]

For Becker, the principal acid of modernity, which dissolved even recent verities, was historicism. In all truly modern views, the world was in flux; change was the only constant. Meaning was only whatever interpretations humans, themselves the products of this flux, assigned to their experiences. Such historicist sensibilities, once their full implications were faced, placed an insurmountable gulf between twentieth-century thought and that of the era of the nation's founders.

In what became the best-known presidential address of the American Historical Association, Becker in 1931 made another major contribution to spelling out the academic implications of modernity. Giving his speech the title "Everyman His Own Historian," Becker argued that there no longer was any basis for viewing academic study as a scientific investigation of "the facts." Strictly speaking, he declared, "facts do not exist." All we have is interpretations. Historians thus did not have access to George Washington but only to interpretations about him, interpretations in the documents from his time refracted further through interpretations of the historians themselves. Such interpretations were controlled by the interests of the interpreters so that ultimately the job of historians was "the keeping of the useful myths" of a society.[12]

Relatively few academics followed Becker all the way in facing the implications of the purely naturalistic universe of modernity (which would come into academic vogue in their "postmodern" garb a half-century later). Many clung to scientific objectivism on the one hand and a wistful practical idealism on the other. Among historians, for instance, Becker and some kindred spirits, notably Charles Beard, were widely heralded but seldom followed to the bitter end of relativism. Comparatively few historians were philosophically minded, and few of them were ready to abandon the recently won authority of a discipline that used scientific methodology to sort out fact from mythology. Practical assumptions regarding objectivism persisted.[13]

In the social sciences, meanwhile, faith in the scientific method as definitive was hardly shaken at all. What Becker and the prophets of modernity in other fields did, however, was point out the deep internal flaws of modern intellectual life. Many intellectuals could recognize that the Enlightenment pillars on which their institutions rested were irreparably cracked and on the verge of collapse. Most, however, had little choice but to go on with business as usual.

Some looked for alternative scientific faith in the face of the internal contradictions of liberalism and its inability to guide modern life in any authoritative direction. For some forward-looking and secular academics of the 1930s Marxism seemed a promising and humane alternative. Marxism was another version of Enlightenment and nineteenth-century faith in science, but it at least took historicism and historical development into account. Claiming the authority of science, it offered a powerful explanation of why all other ideologies should be regarded as mythologies, constructed as legitimations of class and economic interest. For a generation reared on the hopeful idealism of the pre-World War I era, but now too sophisticated to accept the myths of Main Street, Marxism offered something in which to believe.

Protestant neo-orthodoxy offered quite a different sort of option, one that promised a way to reconstruct a chastened idealism. Like other movements responding to the widespread sense of cultural and intellectual crisis, neo-orthodoxy began to catch on among American theologians during the early 1930s. In the United States the best-known form was that articulated by the Niebuhr brothers, H. Richard and Reinhold. The leading American neo-orthodox spokesmen were not nearly as interested in the recovery of orthodox theological categories and biblicism as was the European progenitor of the movement, Karl Barth. What united the Americans was their rejection of modernist theologies, which they felt had been compromised by liberal cultural ideals. By reviving some traditional Christian categories, such as original sin or divine revelation, such theologians could wage an attack on the naive faith in humanity inherent in liberalism. So far as academic life was concerned, however, neo-orthodoxy had only a limited program to offer. During the next several decades it inspired the thinking of important individual academics here and there, but its outlook did not systematically challenge the essential scientific definitions of the academic disciplines as havens immune from theological critique.[14]

It was far more common for American academics to recognize the problem of relativism, but nonetheless to retain a faith in progress based on scientific achievement.[15] Representative of this outlook was Ruth Benedict's *Patterns of Culture*, published in 1934 and gaining a firm place in the academic canon during the next quarter-century. Benedict was one of a number of remarkable protégés of Columbia's Franz Boas, who set the standards for anthropology in America. Benedict saw less complex cultures, such as the Zuni and the Kwakiutl, as ideal laboratories for studying varieties of cultural adjustment that have separated humans from the beasts. To study such cultures scientifically, the elementary first step, she argued, was to abandon our illusions of cultural superiority. Every culture, we should recognize, makes such claims and typically supports them with religious teachings. Today, however, we should recognize that human achievement is not dependent on any force external to human culture: "If we inhabit one chance planet out of a myriad solar systems, so much the greater glory" for humans.

Modern persons, Benedict agreed with her readers, might feel a "justified superiority" over nineteenth-century Westerners who had assumed religious superiority in viewing other cultures. By now, she said, "we have accepted the study of comparative religion." At the same time, since Western culture was plagued by the irrationalities of race prejudice and nationalism, "we are justified in a little skepticism as to whether our sophistication in the matter of religion is due to the fact that we have outgrown naive childishness, or simply to the fact that religion is no longer the area of life in which the important modern battles are staged."

The overriding moral theme for Benedict was that the study of anthropology would encourage mutual tolerance and discourage racism. Once we saw that the widest human differences were social constructions we would have little reason to claim superior heredity. We could also learn to accept differing cultural mores, a point implicitly important for a pioneer in demonstrating that women need not be excluded from the scientific scholarship of universities.

Benedict's important concerns provided additional impetus for opposition to traditional Christianity, which was typically associated both with retaining traditional mores and with claims to cultural superiority. For the modern anthropologist or enlightened academic, the rule that all cultures should be treated equally did not apply to Western cultures that showed intolerance. The American Puritans were the most common symbol for such intolerance and, indeed, the Puritans came in for Benedict's most scathing criticism. "To a modern observer," she wrote, "it is they, not the confused and tormented women they put to death as witches, who were the psychoneurotics of Puritan New England. A sense of guilt as extreme as they portrayed and demanded both in their own conversion experiences and in those of their converts is found in a slightly saner civilization only in institutions for mental diseases."[16]

The troublesome problem for a secular liberal society, however, was how to establish the grounds on which the citizenry should accept progressive moral ideals. The answer, especially for those influenced by the social sciences, was to invest science with supreme cultural authority. Thus, reform-minded social scientists could speak, as Benedict did, as though science itself legitimated a worldview that all educated modern people would accept. Fundamentalists and others would disappear once education based on scientific principles was sufficiently widespread. John Dewey was the high priest of this faith. As he argued in his Terry Lectures at Yale, published in 1934 as *A Common Faith*, universal education could foster a rational humanistic religion dedicated to the healthy adjustment of humans to their social environments so as to promote "goods—the values of art in all its forms, of knowledge, of effort and of rest after striving, of education, and fellowship, of friendship and love, of growth in mind and body."[17]

The solutions offered by thinkers like Benedict and Dewey still left a major question unanswered. In a world where there were no longer self-evident first principles based on God-created natural laws, what happened when allegedly scientific definitions of the "good" conflicted? How could one argue, for instance, that all humans "are created equal" if one denied that humans were created?[18] In a world falling into totalitarianism, where "science" was rapidly being turned into an engine for propaganda, was there any court of appeal? Was American faith in science, social science, and experimentation just whistling in the dark of an empty universe?

Asking Hard Questions

The person who most successfully raised such issues and, in fact, made them the basis for national debate on the nature of universities was Robert Maynard Hutchins of the University of Chicago. Inaugurated in 1929 at age thirty as the fifth president of the university, Hutchins's meteoric rise in some ways resembled that of the school's founder, William Rainey Harper. Both were reared in Ohio, attended local colleges there, and came to Chicago after youthful successes at Yale. There were vast differences, however, so much so that Hutchins's career at Chicago may be seen as an effort to thwart the forces that Harper had set in motion.

One difference was that whereas Harper's father had been a storekeeper, Hutchins was the scion of pure-bred New Englander clergy. Both his grandfather and his father were Presbyterian ministers. The grandfather, Robert Grosvenor Hutchins, had been an abolitionist whose emotional evangelical style of preaching repelled his grandson. The father, Will Hutchins, on the other hand, was a model of the socially progressive evangelical liberalism of the early twentieth century. A graduate of Yale College and of Union Theological Seminary, Will Hutchins was an eloquent and well-known preacher, who in 1907 became professor of homiletics at the Oberlin School of Theology. Oberlin had just completed its transition from the revivalist evangelicalism of the Charles Finney era to a socially concerned liberalism.[19] Young Robert Maynard Hutchins attended Oberlin College for two years before joining the Army Ambulance Corp to serve in World War I. Oberlin at the time must have been at that seemingly idyllic (though transitory) stage at which a college has dropped many of the restrictive aspects of evangelical theology and piety yet retains an ethos in which it is still widely assumed that education involves relating eternal truths to contemporary concerns. Although Hutchins completed his college work at Yale after the war, he seemed to retain an assumption that true education should be something like what went on at prewar Oberlin.[20]

Hutchins went on to Yale Law School, from which he graduated in 1925. Only two years later, while still in his twenties, he was named dean of the Law School. Hutchins's reputation as one of the most brilliant men of the era was made. While at the Yale Law School Hutchins was enamored of the legal realism that dominated that institution. Following roughly the principles of Justice Oliver Wendell Holmes Jr., realism taught that the law should be regarded pragmatically as whatever the courts decide and so must be studied in the primary context of the social sciences, rather than with the illusory assumption that it reflected fixed truths.[21]

Hutchins's flirtation with the pragmatic social scientific spirit of the age was not to last long. By the time he arrived at Chicago in 1929 a deep reaction was setting in. This reaction was inspired primarily by his friendship with Mortimer Adler, a young Jewish philosopher who held the very unstylish view that philosophy should deal with questions of truth. Adler, whom Hutchins soon brought to Chicago, was a champion of the "Great Books" of the Western world, which he saw as revealing human thought at its best. Particularly, Adler was a champion of the tradition of natural law and human rationality as represented by Plato, Aristotle, and Aquinas. With them, Adler affirmed that true rationality pointed toward God.[22]

While Hutchins's new views resembled Adler's in his respect for natural law and human rationality in the tradition of the great thinkers, his idea of God remained vague. At the time of Hutchins's appointment, the chairman of Chicago's trustees, Harold Swift, still maintained that, although the university had dropped its Baptist affiliations, its president should be a member of a Protestant church since "it is the purpose of the board to insure the continuance of the University forever as a Christian institution." In his interviews Hutchins was quizzed at length by Swift and by Charles W. Gilkey, dean of Rockefeller Chapel. Swift was most concerned with his youth; Gilkey with his religion. "You will be surprised to learn," he wrote to his parents, "that I was able to give more satisfactory answers to Gilkey than to Swift. There is no answer to the charge of youth. You can lie about your religion."[23]

When he came to Chicago, Hutchins was still a Presbyterian church member and regularly attended Rockefeller Chapel for Sunday morning services. Hutchins had heard liberal Protestant preaching all of his life, some of the best of it from his father. He had an accordingly low tolerance when it lapsed into platitudes. The last straw was one Sunday when Gilkey opened his sermon, "Yesterday I was on the golf course and as I teed off I was reminded that we must follow through in life." After that, said Hutchins, he "acquired a weekend hideaway and never reappeared in the chapel of the University of Chicago."[24]

Although Hutchins's scathing attacks on modern conceptions of the university were directed primarily against its dependence on scientific, technological, and practical vocational models, he also excoriated the bland religious-moral ideals. These he regarded as palliatives used to make mindless pursuit of scientific models seem acceptable. In his convocation address in December 1933, which Hutchins used as a declaration of war on the current state of the university, he summarized with his typical cutting wit: "The three worst words in education are character, personality, and facts. Facts are the core of an anti-intellectual curriculum. Personality is the qualification we look for in an anti-intellectual teacher. Character is what we expect to produce in the student by the combination of a teacher of personality and a curriculum of facts."[25]

Those most outraged by the attacks were, of course, the champions of social scientific, empirical, and pragmatic ideologies who had built the University of Chicago into the nation's leading center for such outlooks. The new social science building at Chicago, completed in 1929, actually had the viewpoint of empiricist philosophy inscribed in stone over the entryway: WHATEVER EXISTS AT ALL EXISTS IN SOME AMOUNT.[26] Hutchins did his best to offend those who thus turned a methodology into a limiting worldview. "The gadgeteers and data collectors, masquerading as scientists, have threatened to become the supreme chieftains of the scholarly world," he declared in the 1933 convocation address. At a dinner for faculty and trustees a month or so later, Hutchins elaborated on the "anti-intellectual philosophy" that has "no principles." "The world is in a flux of events. We cannot hope to understand it. All we can do is to watch it. This is the conclusion of the leading anti-intellectuals of our time, William James and John Dewey."

The resulting furor, which divided the faculty, was highlighted by a dramatic debate between Anton J. Carlson, a noted physiologist, who defended empiricism and scientific naturalism, and Mortimer Adler, who insisted that for science to help humanity it must be located within a framework of metaphysical truths discovered by human rationality.[27] Hutchins and Adler were, however, swimming against the tide. Hutchins's attempt to institute major curricular revisions that would reflect his trust in the centrality of the great books was defeated in the spring of 1934, the first of a series of setbacks.

Undaunted, Hutchins next went to the public. In 1936 he published *The Higher Learning in America*, which became easily the most widely discussed book in higher education for the next decade. Combining his usual acerbic wit with keen analysis, Hutchins exposed the trends that were shaping the American university and driving it away from the search for truth. One of the most basic problems, he pointed out, was economic: "The people love money and think that education is a way of getting it. They think too that democracy means that every child should be permitted to acquire the educational insignia that will be helpful in making money. They do not believe in the cultivation of the intellect for its own sake."

American universities were thus constantly being distracted by the vocational. They were constantly pressured by a "service station mentality," which had led to the idea that "a state university must help the farmers look after their cows." Vocational concerns dwarfed everything else at private schools as well. Suggestions to establish schools of journalism, business, library science, social service, education, dentistry, nursing, forestry, diplomacy, pharmacy, veterinary surgery, and public administration typically were quickly implemented. Even in undergraduate work, it was becoming common to devote the last two years to preprofessional training. Most of university education was thus increasingly geared toward learning "tricks of the trade" that would soon be out of date.

Blindly following scientific models, universities had become organized into a bewildering array of specialized disciplines and subdisciplines with nothing to relate them. The result was that "the chief characteristic of higher learning is disorder." At the same time, freedom was urged as an end in itself. But utter freedom of choice could result only in "anarchy and the dissolution of the whole." The many sciences would turn up a myriad of facts, but universities provided no way of distinguishing the trivial from the timeless.

Hutchins's solution was to get rid of departments, provide only general education for the first two undergraduate years, and then divide university education into three parts: metaphysics or the science of first principles, social science, and practical sciences. Even in the latter two domains emphasis would be on a hierarchy of truths starting with the first principles regarding human relations or relations of humans to nature, especially as these had been discussed through the ages, and only then proceeding to more recent observations.

Metaphysics would thus be the heart of the enterprise. Theology had once served that purpose but could no longer. "We are a faithless generation and take no stock in revelation," wrote Hutchins. "Theology implies orthodoxy and an orthodox church. We have neither. To look to theology to unify the modern university is futile and vain." Therefore, as the ancient Greeks had done in the era of Plato and Aristotle, or as Thomas Aquinas had done insofar as he was a neo-Aristotelian metaphysician, we must use reason to determine the highest principles on which our civilization should be based. Otherwise our civilization would rush blindly after false ideas of progress and utility, guided only by our love of money and of things. A rationally ordered society, guided by rationally ordered universities, was our only hope.[28]

Like so many books of cultural criticism, Hutchins's tract gained wide attention on the strength of a compelling diagnosis, even while few were ready to follow its prescription. Some reviewers conceded that he had put his finger on some deep problems in American society and hence its universities, particularly the widespread love of money and attendant anti-intellectualism. On the other hand, except for the circle of Adler-Hutchins devotees, few were to find the solution plausible, let alone persuasive.[29] As Glenn Frank remarked in the Yale Review, "The metaphysics, which Mr. Hutchins substitutes for theology as the integrating force in the modern university, would, I fear, become but a secularized and denatured theology, a search for absolutes without revelation."[30]

The affinities of Hutchins's views to Catholicism were also a major strike against him. Catholics were in the midst of their neo-Thomist revival and were offering critiques of American education similar to those of Hutchins. While wishing that Hutchins would allow more room for revelation and theology, Catholic thinkers were likely to hail his critique. His proposals for a return to Aristotelian-Thomist metaphysics could be read as a sign of a cultural swing in their direction.[31] Catholic thinkers, however, were seldom given a serious voice in mainstream American intellectual culture, and most of those who controlled that culture were ready to dismiss Hutchins's views just because of their parallels to Catholicism. For secular progressive thinkers, the principal heirs to the old Whig rhetoric of freedom, older animosities were revived by the association of Catholicism with fascism. Catholic support of Franco in the Spanish Civil War aggravated such associations. Attacks on Catholicism by progressive intellectuals accordingly increased in the late 1930s. The New Republic, for instance, ran a series of articles in 1938 warning of Catholicism's characteristic opposition to political freedom. Sidney Hook, heir-apparent to Dewey as the leading philosopher of secular progres-sivism, in a typical statement of the era, wrote in the *Partisan Review* that Catholicism was "the oldest and greatest totalitarian movement in history."[32] Even if Hutchins disclaimed any interest in theology or the Roman Catholic Church, his views could still be dismissed as "medievalism."

As might have been expected, John Dewey himself was one of Hutchins's most severe critics. Dewey found Hutchins's underlying assumptions incred-ible in the modern era. Hutchins, he pointed out, believed in fixed truth "the same at any time and place" and in a fixed human nature that included an intellect to discover these truths. Hutchins was thus proposing to revive a concept of intellect divorced from experience. Hutchins's concept of a hier-archical set of first principles, already known, within which science should operate, said Dewey, was "authoritarian." "I would not intimate that the au-thor has any sympathy with fascism," Dewey remarked. "But basically his idea as to the proper course to be taken is akin to the distrust of freedom and the consequent appeal to *some* fixed authority that is now overrunning the world." Rather than follow the authority of Plato, Aristotle, and Aquinas and thus retreating to "monastic seclusion," higher learning, said Dewey, must come to grip with the science and society of our own age as Plato, Aristotle, and Aquinas had with theirs.

In his reply, Hutchins denied that he was advocating a simple return to the authority of the past or that he thought that truths were "fixed and eternal." Rather than arguing for any particular metaphysical system, said Hutchins, he was arguing that education should center on the quest for first princi-ples and that these should be pursued by the most rational means possible. University curricula centering on such metaphysics were inherently no more authoritarian than those that studied and taught only the natural and social sciences. As for fascism, it was "a consequence of the absence of philosophy. It is possible only in the context of the disorganization of analysis and the disruption of the intellectual tradition and intellectual discipline through the pressure of immediate practical concerns."[33]

Can This Civilization Be Saved?

Under the increasingly dark clouds of fascism the debates over first principles in American higher education took on an intensity and a seriousness they had never had before. Especially with the outbreak of World War II in Europe in 1939, many American intellectuals, as well as religious leaders, sought desperately for some cultural alternative to offer to the Western world.

The intensity of the feelings were dramatically illustrated in a storm that broke over a remark of Mortimer Adler in 1940. The setting was an auspicious gathering of leading American intellectuals supplemented by distinguished refugees from Europe. Initiated by Rabbi Louis Finkelstein, and held at the Jewish Theological Seminary in New York in September 1940, the conference was called by group of Jewish, Protestant, and Catholic leaders as the first of a series annual meetings to discuss the topic of "Science, Philosophy and Religion." The seventy-nine founding members included Franz Boas, Henry Sloane Coffin, Albert Einstein, Enrico Fermi, Harry Emerson Fosdick, William E. Hocking, Robert Hutchins, Douglas MacIntosh, John Mackay, Jacques Maritain, A. J. Muste, Allan Nevins, Pitirim Sorokin, and Paul Tillich. Van Wyck Brooks in the introduction to the published volume wrote that the conference

> recognizes that our failure to integrate science, philosophy and religion, in relation to traditional ethical values and the democratic way of life, has been catastrophic for civilization. We are aware of the perils that beset democracy, not only the obvious peril of national and racial despotisms, but the more insidious danger arising from the instability of our culture. We see the passing of ancient sanctions and the collapse of traditional loyalties. Having no basis for agreement regarding causes and remedies, we recognize these signs of cultural weakness.

In the face of such dire challenges, he concluded, "we are under a special constraint at the moment to realize a unity of thought and effort because of the growing threat to our way of life."

The conference agenda accordingly was, in effect, an extension of the liberal Protestant, interfaith, democratic outlook that would dominate much of American public thought during the next two decades. As Van Wyck Brooks explained it,

> It means that mankind is one, admitting of no fragmentation. Regarding this unity, the Conference seeks to bring out not only its negative basis, the fact that the freedom of the scientific spirit and of every philosophy and faith is threatened by totalitarianism, but also its positive basis, the belief in the value of personality, in the creative endeavour or unregimented culture,

in the brotherhood of man, and in the democratic way of life as a necessary means of sustaining these spiritual values.[34]

Mortimer Adler, a founding member of the conference, asked to present one of the papers at its first meeting. Adler agreed generally with the agenda of the conference but was convinced that its efforts would be undercut if it was essentially like other scholarly conferences in which people read papers to each other and there was no systematic effort to achieve consensus. When his efforts to establish a more unified agenda failed, Adler attempted to withdraw. He was finally dissuaded from doing so by Jacques Maritain and others and took the suggestion of Rabbi Finkelstein that he should present the essence of his critique to the conference.

Adler's paper, "God and the Professors," was a scathing attack on the American professoriate. The conference, Adler prophesied, was certain to fail because American professors were too inflexible to change their minds. This was proved by Robert Hutchins's "glorious, Quixotic failure" to achieve the reforms he sought at the University of Chicago. Had he succeeded, there would be no need for such a conference. The problem was that the great majority of American professors were positivists and naturalists. Their fragmented approach to learning, based on their illusions about the value of scientific models, prevented them from addressing questions of ultimate truth.

All this might have contributed to serious debate about the Adler-Hutchins agenda had not Adler been carried away by the logic of his own analysis. So convinced was he that a civilization could not survive without a way of searching for the truth and hence the real danger was from within that Adler reiterated his point with the most inappropriate hyperbole. "The most serious threat to Democracy," he declared, "is the positivism of the professors, which dominates every aspect of modern education and is the central corruption of modern culture. Democracy has much more to fear from the mentality of its teachers than from the nihilism of Hitler."[35]

This was an astonishing thing to say at the Jewish Theological Seminary in New York in 1940. That Adler was Jewish added to the incongruity. As he himself recalled, the audience received the remainder of the speech with icy stares. The press jumped on the unfortunate remark and gave it wide publicity. His serious points were forgotten. Adler had provided his progressive-positivist opponents an opening to discredit his campaign. Sidney Hook, for instance, made the most of the opportunity in an essay in the *New Republic* on "The New Medievalism."[36] The tag would be hard to shake.

As the remark illustrated all too well, the trust of Adler and Hutchins in intellect as the route to discover a metaphysical basis for modern civilization *was* quixotic. They had (as Dewey's attack on Hutchins in effect pointed out) much the same problem as did Dewey and Hook in establishing a scientific basis for civilization. In a pluralistic world, was there any adequate court of appeal to settle the questions of "Whose science?" or "Whose metaphysics?"

As America faced the prospect of a world at war, however, Adler and Hutchins versus Hook and Dewey represented only two of the major options in American intellectual life. Even among those who agreed on the responsibility of intellectual and religious leadership to find a basis for cultural consensus, only limited consensus was forthcoming. At the 1940 conference on "Science, Philosophy and Religion," almost every speaker took it as a premise that democracy was in danger of extinction unless some compelling rationale were provided to underwrite its basic values. Nevertheless, the points of view represented clearly contradicted each other. Rabbi Finkelstein, for instance, could approvingly quote Etienne Gilson to the effect that we must return to medieval concepts of the oneness of truth. Harvard sociologist Pitirim A. Sorokin, who had just issued his telling critique of modern "sensate" culture in *The Crisis of Our Age*, and Jacques Maritain could recommend similarly sharp critiques of modernity and the need to return to faith in God. Albert Einstein, on the other hand, suggested that the conflict between science and religion could not be resolved, and hence true unity cannot be achieved unless religious people give up the idea of a personal God and "avail themselves of those forces which are capable of cultivating the Good, the True, and the Beautiful in humanity itself." Liberal Protestant theologians, on the other hand, argued that such ideals were not incompatible with belief in a personal God. Throughout the war years the conferences on "Science, Philosophy and Religion" and similar themes continued annually, thus contributing to a degree of Protestant–Catholic–Jewish solidarity during and after the war, even if the intellectual and religious problems of finding a single ideological basis for the culture could not be resolved.[37]

Many secularist intellectuals were alarmed about this attempt to put religion into the same equation as science and philosophy. In 1940 and 1941, just about the time of the blowup over Adler, the New York intellectual and religious communities had been heated to a fever pitch over precisely such a point. Bertrand Russell, widely criticized in conservative circles for his criticisms of Christianity but especially for his open views on sexuality, was offered a visiting professorship to teach logic and mathematics at the College of the City of New York. City College was run by the city government, which Russell later described as "virtually a satellite of the Vatican."[38] Russell's appointment was sharply attacked by Episcopal Bishop William T. Manning, who long had been warning New Yorkers of the dangers of Russell's views. After considerable furor, Russell's appointment was sustained by the Board of Higher Education. Not satisfied, a layperson brought a civil suit. At the hearing Russell was described in one rhetorical flourish as "lecherous, salacious, libidinous, lustful, venerous, erotomaniac, aphrodisiac, atheistic, irreverent, narrow-minded, bigoted, and untruthful." The judge, a Catholic, ruled that Russell was morally unfit for the position and revoked the appointment.[39]

Many intellectuals, including some theists as well as nontheists, were outraged. A group of predominantly Jewish scholars, who were understandably alarmed at the ability of clerics to stir up popular animosity toward intellectuals, issued a scathing volume titled *The Bertrand Russell Case* in 1941. John Dewey, co-editor with Horace Kallen, compared it to the *Dred Scott* decision. Kallen evoked all the cases cited in Andrew Dickson White's *Warfare*, lamented Catholic prejudice, and deplored the zeal of clergy, with some Protestant exceptions, to "persecute."[40]

Such academics clearly felt beleaguered as World War II brought increasing talk of the importance of religion to civilization. In 1943 and 1944, progressive secularists, including many of the defenders of Russell, organized their own conferences. The first was titled similarly to its rival as "The Scientific Spirit and Democratic Faith." Its spokespersons directed their strongest polemics against the "new authoritarianism." Especially objectionable, participants insisted, was the claim that supernatural revelation provided the only proper foundation for the democratic way of life. They saw an ominous coalition emerging in the wartime religious revival. "The élite intellectuals with fine educational backgrounds" and great influence in the sphere of education were at the head of this coalition, the secularists warned, but the numbers of the supernaturalists were swelled by fundamentalists and Catholics. Max Otto, professor of philosophy at the University of Wisconsin, noted a passage by Jacques Maritain depicting civilization as locked in a struggle between God and the Devil and deplored that this passage was "not written by an untutored fundamentalist, but by one who is called the outstanding Christian philosopher of our time." Brand Blanshard, a philosopher at Swarthmore

College, quoted a passage from Cardinal Newman and observed that the objection to Catholicism and to other authoritarian religions was that their loyalties to democracy were expressly limited by a higher faith. Such loyalties, Blanshard suggested, led ultimately to the logic of the Inquisition.[41]

The title of the second such conference, held in New York in 1944, "The Authoritarian Attempt to Capture Education," made sure that nobody missed the point. John Dewey and Sidney Hook headed the list of speakers. Viewing education as more than just what happened in schools, several presenters decried what they saw as a conservative bias in the press and radio. In formal education itself, said Hook, the views of Monsignor Fulton Sheen, Robert Hutchins, Mortimer Adler, and others were particularly dangerous; further, the conservative press was all too ready to buy their line that the denial of eternal principles would lead inevitably to totalitarianism. The conference participants were convinced of just the opposite. The genius of American democracy was a spirit of freedom and tolerance. Authoritarianism, especially religious authoritarianism, was not only a superstitious denial of free inquiry but also ultimately incompatible with true tolerance. If the religious authoritarians gained control, the United States would be well on its way to its own brand of totalitarianism.[42]

19

A Church with the Soul of a Nation

The Spirit of Protestantism

The urgent wartime debates on the relation of educational philosophy to the survival of democracy[1] had their counterparts in institutional reassessments of what colleges and universities stood for. Many schools drafted a new statement of their purpose,[2] though, as usual, these typically considered broad goals for their undergraduate programs only. By far the most influential such statement was the Harvard Report of 1945, *General Education in a Free Society*. Written by some of the best-known scholars in the country, this two hundred–page volume set the standard for those seeking a middle ground among the contentious partisans.

The Harvard Report suggested that Americans had not yet faced up to their educational revolution. Between 1870 and 1940 the American population tripled, but the number of students enrolled in secondary schools increased ninety times and those in colleges thirty times. The day was long past when higher education could be directed simply toward producing gentlemen and ladies; it would now have to be geared toward educating the democratic masses. This tremendous growth, along with the increasing social diversity of the groups being served and the vast expansion and fragmentation of knowledge, complicated immensely the problem of reaching a consensus on the educational task.

The Harvard committee took for granted that higher education should serve democratic or free society but was acutely aware of the lack of a center for this enterprise. In fact, the committee pointed out, the ideal of a free democratic society accentuated the dilemma. How could a democracy promote both loyalty and liberty? "A free society . . . cherishes both toleration and conviction," the committee reflected. "Yet the two seem incompatible." Could they promote democracy without resorting to indoctrination that would undermine the very freedom that democracies held sacred?

The Harvard professors considered and rejected four possible models for filling the "supreme need of American education . . . for a unifying purpose and idea." Religiously based education was the first of these. The others were great books on education, education organized around contemporary problems, and education based on pragmatic scientific method. Each of these proposals had some merit, but each was inadequate by itself. The Harvard solution was to balance some elements from each.

The religious dimension of higher education was the most difficult for Harvard professors to incorporate into their proposals. Adopting a developmental view of society, they emphasized continuity with tradition, especially classical tradition, while affirming the need to serve contemporary democracy with current scientific method. The affirmation of tradition meant that they had to deal with the issue of the religious heritage. Accordingly, they noted that Protestant colleges until less than a century before had found unity through sectarian education. This was still the approach of Roman Catholic colleges. This solution, however, "is out of the question in publicly supported colleges and is practically, if not legally, impossible in most others." "Given the American scene with its varieties of faith and even of unfaith," Harvard did not feel justified in proposing religious instruction as such as part of an undergraduate curriculum.

Nevertheless, the committee hoped to keep the curriculum open to the benefits of religion through a back door. Acknowledging that "much of the best tradition of the West is to be found in the distillations of the prophets, in the homilies and allegories of an earlier age, and in Biblical injunctions," Harvard could retain the "moral guidance" of this heritage through the humanities. So the core curriculum that the committee proposed would include a humanities course on "Great Texts in Literature," including religious texts. Definitions of humanism, they advised, should be "careful . . . not exclude the religious ideal."

A canon of great books, the committee observed, "can be looked at as a secular continuation of the spirit of Protestantism." As Protestantism had rejected the authority of the medieval church, so Harvard was "rejecting the unique authority of the Scriptures" and placing "reliance on the reading of those books which are taken to represent the fullest revelation of the Western mind." The committee was satisfied that when thus oriented toward both human dignity and duty "the goal of education is not in conflict with but largely includes the goals of religious education, education in the Western tradition, and education in modern democracy."[3]

The Harvard reporters thus summarized the religious implications of one of the major curricular trends of the past half-century. In effect they were recommending a liberal Protestantism with the explicit Christianity removed. They were affirming, as liberal Protestantism had done, the religious value of the best in Western culture itself. If the culture defined the highest ideals, then the specifically religious dimensions were expendable. Though the Harvard Report tended to emphasize the humanities rather than empirical social sciences, from a religious perspective the committee's position was similar to John Dewey's. If religion was valued primarily for its civilizing moral ideals, then one could identify those moral ideals and determine how to promote them without directly resorting to Christianity.

This outlook was consistent with Harvard's own religious heritage, dating back to the days of Charles Eliot.

The Harvard Report reflected a curricular trend toward "general education" that had been developing for several decades. To counter the fragmentation of modern learning, educators had been searching for a way to establish a common core of beliefs for the dominant culture. The curricular expression of this ideal was a set of core requirements highlighted by some broad surveys. In the social sciences, for instance, the Harvard committee recommended a course called "Western Thought and Institutions," which would be a survey of the evolution of Western institutions with readings of selections from major Western thinkers, including, for example, "Aquinas, Machiavelli, Luther, Bodin, Locke, Montesquieu, Rousseau, Adam Smith, Bentham, and Mill." This course was explicitly patterned after a "Contemporary Civilization" course originated at Columbia during World War I as a "War Aims" course and was very successfully taught there to freshmen ever since. Such proposals did not go as far as a curriculum based entirely on "great books," such as Adler and Hutchins had proposed and was implemented at St. John's College in Maryland. Rather, the Harvard plan followed the much wider trend toward requiring a general core of subjects such as "Western Civilization," and surveys of sciences and social sciences, great literature, and the arts that would thus establish at least a minimal evolving Western canon.[4]

Planning the Technocratic Order

Such quasi-religious humanistic ideals probably reached the peak of their influence in the post–World War II era. Even then, however, they were being surpassed by other trends that were advancing even faster. American higher

education was once again expanding at a phenomenal rate. In the decade following World War II the college and university student population doubled.[5]
One implication was that the ethnically Protestant establishment that dominated the universities and provided the social basis for any consensus was in
its latter days. During the 1950s there was much talk of expanding the establishment into a Protestant–Catholic–Jewish consensus, but the fact was that
the United States was much more complicated than that. A further major
implication of the vast higher education expansion was an increasing orientation toward the practical and the vocational. Influential elite birthright
Protestants plus a few allies could still successfully promote literate humane
values in many institutions. Nevertheless, that was not the direction in which
American higher education was headed.

The most revealing barometer of the dominant cultural and intellectual
pressures that were reshaping American higher education was the influential
and widely discussed Report of the President's Commission on Education.
Appointed by President Truman in 1946, the commission issued a multi-
volume statement at the end of 1947, significantly titled *Higher Education for
American Democracy.*

One of the revolutions that the commission was announcing was the end
of higher education as an elite enterprise. The Harvard Report had said the
same thing, but the president's commission meant it. The commission repeatedly contrasted the democratic education it proposed to "aristocratic"
education that would be "the instrument for producing an intellectual elite."
From 1900 to 1940 the percentage of eighteen- to twenty-one-year-olds
attending college had risen from 4 to 16%. By 1947, with the huge influx of
veterans aided by the G.I. Bill, enrollments were well on their way to doubling again. Startlingly, the commission proposed to promote this postwar
expansion to the maximum. It estimated that about half the American population was qualified to complete at least two years of college and proposed
that by 1960 the educational system be expanded, including both four-year
and many new community two-year colleges, so that everyone who wanted a
college education could receive one. Federal and state funds should be used
to remove all financial barriers to such education. Moreover, racial barriers,
especially the massive discrimination against blacks and quotas for Jews,
should be eliminated.[6]

Together with this unreserved promotion of mass education came a pragmatic problem-centered educational philosophy. The commission called for
"education adjusted to needs," advised that leaders should "agree on common

objectives," emphasized above all "the social role of education," and emphasized education as an "instrument for social transition." The content of education should be "directly relevant to the demands of contemporary society."[7]
The spirit of John Dewey was evident on almost every page.

Robert Hutchins was, as one might expect, appalled. Speaking for many
humanists, his wit was at its best: "Every cliché and every slogan of contemporary educational discussion appear once more. Much of the report reads
like a Fourth-of-July oration in pedaguese. It skirts the edge of illiteracy, and
sometimes falls over the brink. And when the battle has ended, the field is
strewn with the corpses of straw men the Commission has slain." Moreover,
said Hutchins, "the Commission never misses a chance to communicate the
news that our educational institutions are far too intellectual." It attacked,
for instance, "the present orientation of higher education towards verbal
skills and intellectual interests." Though the commission disclaimed any
intention of subverting the liberal arts, it called for higher education to do
so many other things that such intellectual life would almost be incidental.
Given the fragmentation already present among disciplines, said Hutchins,
the commission's advice to diversify was like telling a drowning man to drink
lots of water.[8]

The report, reflecting the operating principles that were reshaping
American education, revealed the realistic prospects for religion in higher
education in the second half of the century. Despite the presence on the commission of clergy from the three major faiths (meaning a liberal Protestant,
a non-Orthodox Jew, and a Catholic), religion was hardly mentioned. When
it was, it was in the context of values that would make democracy work.
Morality, said the commission in defining the first of eleven desired "basic
outcomes," had been neglected in recent decades, as higher education had
been too exclusively concerned with intellect. Yet "in these troubled times"
people urgently needed "soundly based values," especially those of mutual
trust and tolerance. Where such values would come from the commission
was not quite sure, so it resorted to vagueness and use of the passive voice in
relation to religion:

> Ethical principles that will induce this faith need not be based on any single
> sanction or be authoritarian in origin, nor need finality be claimed for
> them. Some persons will find the satisfactory basis for a moral code in the
> democratic creed itself, some in philosophy, some in religion. Religion is
> held to be a major force in creating the system of human values on which

democracy is predicated, and many derive from one or another of its varieties a deepened sense of human worth and a strengthened concern for the
rights of others.[9]

Throughout the report the "democratic creed" was the absolute by which
all else was to be tested, just as the function of religion was to underscore
democratic values of a sense of human worth and concern for the rights of
others.[10]

According to the commission, loyalty to the democratic principle must
qualify all other loyalties:

Nor can any *group* in our society, organized or non-organized, pursue
purely private ends and seek to promote its own welfare without regard
to the social consequences of its activities. Business, industry, labor, agriculture, medicine, law, engineering, education . . . all these modes of association call for the voluntary development of codes of conduct . . . to
harmonize the special interests of the group with the general welfare.[11]

Religious groups were not mentioned in this list, but their educational
institutions certainly would be included. T. R. McConnell, chancellor of the
University of Buffalo and a commission member, responding to the frequent
criticism that the report had neglected religion, quoted with approval: "The
church-related colleges of America in the twentieth century must not be led
down the path of authoritarianism as opposed to freedom, nor up to the
heights of revelation as opposed to scientific knowledge. . . . They must not
separate themselves from the great goals of the society of which they are a
part."[12]

Many Catholic educators were incensed by the report and by its philosophy. They claimed it implicitly attacked some basic principles of Catholic
education, which usually was still frankly authoritarian. Two of the Catholic
members of the commission issued a Statement of Dissent, appended to
the report, objecting strongly to the recommendation that private schools
be excluded from the proposed funding of educational opportunity.[13]
According to Allan P. Farrell, education editor of the Catholic magazine
America, "almost everybody agrees" that the tone of the report was to say
"Farewell" to private education and to announce the era of government
control of education. Even more fundamentally, Farrell, along with many
other critics, was dismayed by the thoroughgoing secularism of the report.

Its underlying philosophy, said Farrell, was that youth should be trained for the democratic state and that "the democratic state is a sort of religion, with public education as its church."[14]

Sociologist Robert S. Lynd, a secular critic from the left, essentially agreed. "We non-Catholics," he wrote, "worry about the case of education forced to operate within the political goals of the organization ramifying from the Vatican. But we do not, in the main and in public, recognize the possibility that there are other constraints upon education no less coercive and determined to have their way within our own cultural system."[15]

The President's commission argued from the premise that democratic values were self-evident principles, both everlasting and evolving. These principles, they maintained, should form the basis for a cultural consensus, based especially on equality of opportunity and mutual tolerance. "It is imperative," they affirmed, "that American education develop a 'democratic dynamic' that will inspire faith in the democratic way of life."[16] In the wake of World War II, neither the left nor the right was to be allowed much of a voice in questioning the ideals of democracy for which so many had died. In such a setting the ideals themselves did not have to be placed on a rational basis. So, for instance, while the commission propounded democratic values as though they were self-evident, it denied that ethical principles needed to be final or based on any authority. Moreover, while the commission placed a premium on freedom for a diversity of opinions; it still wanted everyone to agree on democracy.

The President's commission was a prophetic voice announcing the advent of an era in which the federal government would be a major force in making the educational wilderness bloom through technique. During the war the universities had made an important contribution to national defense. Perhaps the most telling sign of the times was that the most momentous development during Robert Hutchins's tenure at the University of Chicago was not anything having to do with discussion of the humanities or natural law; it was that in 1942, under the Amos Alonzo Stagg football field, scientists at the university split the atom. That secret work was the iceberg of which many other university government contracts were the tip. The attitudes that emanated from such successful cooperation grew into a conviction among government leaders that the universities should continue to play a vital role in national defense during the Cold War era. By 1960 federal expenditures for university research had reached $760 million ($20 million each if distributed equally among thirty-eight top schools). Moreover, the National Defense

Education Act of 1958 declared that "the security of the Nation requires the fullest development of mental resources and technical skills of its young men and women." Accordingly, "This requires programs that will give assurance that no student of ability will be denied an opportunity for higher education because of financial need."[17]

While the American Protestant establishment could hardly be entirely pleased to see so much energy going into higher educational activities that had little direct relationship to their religious or humane goal, they had little ground for complaint about the premise on which such activities were based. Since at least Woodrow Wilson's day liberal Protestantism had been putting democracy and service to the nation first, in effect making the nation its church. During the first four decades of the century service to the nation had translated largely as service to the business community, which supplied most of the funds for the new universities. Some of the old classicist ideal of training for "citizenship" survived, but most of what was new in the universities was based on the technological model, and students were learning skills to be leaders in business or the supporting professions.

Now with World War II, "serving the nation" came to include, as in World War I, an additional commitment to national defense. Furthermore, rather than demobilize after World War II, throughout the Cold War the nation retained its military basis. The military draft was made virtually permanent, though the importance of college training was recognized by allowing for college exemptions. The G.I. Bill, which brought so many veterans to colleges after the war, was a sign of the government's interest in universities as a source of national strength. The federal government thus was a major player not only in financing universities during the Cold War but also in determining who attended them and when.

The educational establishment, still vestigially Protestant, raised few objections to this new development. Not only did the government's role ensure a healthy share of Cold War prosperity, but also the ideal of service to the nation was already so deeply ingrained that there was little ground for objection to expansion of that ideal. The humanists and the seriously religious might worry about some of its implications, but they had little reason to question the premise. Neither did those who were more secular, most of whom had nothing besides "democracy" to commit to.

The Revival of Campus Religion and Its Limits

Already in the years just before World War II, as Merrimon Cuninggim documented, there had been signs of growing religious interest on campuses. By the years after the war it was apparent that a national religious revival was gaining momentum, a momentum that reached its peak in the mid-1950s. The national revival covered a wide spectrum from sawdust trail, healing evangelists to the platitudinous pieties of the Eisenhower White House. Billy Graham rose to fame during this time, as did Norman Vincent Peale, Bishop Fulton J. Sheen, and Martin Luther King. Reinhold Niebuhr was practically the national theologian. Campuses were no exception to the religious resurgence. Campus ministries flourished. It was a sort of golden age for mainline campus ministries, and insurgent evangelical groups such as InterVarsity Christian Fellowship or Campus Crusade for Christ were gaining increasing influence. The college educated were as likely as other Americans to evidence religious commitments.[18]

Part of what made the revival seem nationally significant was that it was more respectable than it had been in the previous decades to discuss religious questions in public places such as campuses. The highlight of this discussion was the publication in 1949 by the English Student Christian Movement of Sir Walter Moberly's eloquent *The Crisis in the University.* Moberly, an Oxford philosopher highly placed in English academic life, argued that modern universities had become at least implicitly hostile to Christianity, because of their reverence for the supposedly value-free scientific method, from which followed their prejudice against religion and neglect of higher human values. Christians, he said, had two alternatives. Either they could resign themselves to being "a small Christian enclave within a predominantly pagan university," or, as he strongly advocated, they could play the role of a "creative minority" and win enough respect to restore at least a general sympathy to Christianity. The broadly Christian contours of the cultural heritage would be of aid in this task.[19]

Moberly's book, widely heralded on both sides of the Atlantic, was only the best known of an extensive literature on the topic during the postwar decade. Many writers followed Moberly in describing the Christian's task as intellectual. It became common to speak, as Moberly had, of challenging the underlying presuppositions of the universities and their pretensions to neutrality. The exponents of these views were part of a rapidly growing movement to reestablish a place for Christianity in the intellectual life of universities. Student ministries were expanding, and denominational and interdenominational agencies were building campus centers for religious activities at unprecedented rates. A number of research centers, such as the Christian Faith and Higher Education Center at Michigan State University, were founded. The National Council of Churches in 1953 established a Department of Campus Christian Life, which in turn created the Faculty Christian Fellowship and an attractive new journal, the *Christian Scholar*.[20] The numbers of religion departments, typically with an orientation to Christian theological and ethical concerns, continued to grow throughout this era.[21] Clarence P. Shedd of Yale Divinity School, who had long worked for such causes, may have been correct when he wrote in 1951, "Never in this century has there been so much serious and creative discussion of the problems of religion in higher education as during the past decade."[22]

This revival and the enthusiasm and activities it engendered were like a candle starved for oxygen, which burns more brightly before it flickers out. For the time being the gains were real and illuminating for many individuals involved, but they could not get to the source of the problem.[23] The commitment of mainline religion to "freedom" made any such gains necessarily dependent on the momentum generated by the revival of interest in things religious. Outside the churches themselves and their agencies, there were few institutional supports to sustain that momentum. Only in superficial ways could the renewed religious interests touch the structures of universities or redirect the dominant forces shaping those structures.

Clearly if Christianity was to have a significant role in universities it would have to be at least an option in the curricula, yet even in the most humane programs Christianity as such played no more than a token role. This was well documented in a study sponsored by the Edward W. Hazen Foundation, an agency that during and after World War II searched for ways to re-establish mainline Protestantism as a leading player in higher education. In 1948 the foundation issued *College Reading and Religion*, a collection of essays by some of the nation's top scholars—including Gordon Allport in psychology, Peter Bertocci in philosophy, Robert Calhoun in the history of philosophy, and Margaret Mead in anthropology—analyzing the treatment of religion in college texts normally assigned in each of their fields.[24]

The treatment of religion in the texts, the scholars found, ranged from indifference to implicit hostility. Several noted the power of what the editors called "the religion of science" and deplored the "materialist assumptions" of so much of modern academic writing. In the history of philosophy, texts could be dated according to their views of religion. Those written before World War I offered "critical appreciation"; those written between the wars reflected "active disparagement." Since World War II the treatment had brightened somewhat, although the most positive development, outside of Catholic publications, surprisingly, was a history by Bertrand Russell, who at least treated theology fairly. If Russell was on the positive side of the ledger, Christianity had, indeed, fallen on hard times in the world of scholarship. In American literature, a telling example was Vernon L. Parrington's popular three-volume *Main Currents in American Thought*, which gave lots of coverage to Puritan religion but with an unmistakably negative tone, valuing it as "merely one of the stages toward the growth of a secular democracy." Parrington's last volume, on the modern era, did not discuss religion at all. In the social sciences religion was usually ignored or, as in anthropology, seen as an aspect of "social mechanics." Social scientists, said one author, typically have only childish memories of religion, which they then contrast with the supposed "maturity and objectivity of the trained intellect" and conclude that religion should best be eliminated from modern life.[25]

One problem evident from the study was that the evaluating scholars themselves did not agree on what "religion" was and what role it ought to have in colleges. Theodore Spencer, writing on English literature, quoted an article by Margaret Mead in which the anthropologist had commented on the blandness of America's generalized religion and suggested that the quality of American religion was the source of its weakness within academia. More "impartial" teaching of religion would only be a sign of secularization, not an answer to it. Spencer contrasted the general texts to those written for Catholic colleges, in which religiously based viewpoints actually made a difference. One reputable Catholic anthology stated frankly that one of its themes was "a cordial hatred of the bourgeois ideal and a corresponding love of the spiritual."[26]

Here was one of the most troubling problems for those who worked for a return of religious influences in higher education. With many religious groups vying for influence, and with these groups representing vastly different and often opposed definitions of religion, it was difficult to see how religion could provide a basis for unifying culture. This was particularly so given that one of the highest goods for the Protestant establishment was that whatever religious influence there was must be entirely free. The Hazen Foundation, for instance, hailed "the liberal ideal" in higher education and ruled out coercion from any quarter, including the churches.[27]

The proportions of the impasse may be gauged by the inability of one of the most astute of mainline Protestants leaders, Reinhold Niebuhr, to find a way around it. Niebuhr in 1945 wrote *The Contribution of Religion to Cultural Unity* for the Hazen series on higher education. Niebuhr's statement is particularly significant because he was the chief spokesperson for the American neo-orthodox movement. While not rejecting the liberal Protestant commitment to science or to liberal democracy, Niebuhr advocated recovery of aspects of the Christian heritage that would temper any celebration of mere intellectual or cultural achievement. Particularly, Niebuhr emphasized that the Christian doctrine of original sin should chasten human celebrations even of such ideals as freedom and creativity, since the highest human achievements so often led to the greatest vices. During the postwar era, Niebuhr's "realistic" message became widely popular among intellectuals as an alternative to more optimistic religious liberalism and to unthinking celebrations of the American way.

Niebuhr started in his reflections on higher education in typically prophetic style: "The religious problem is the ultimate issue in education." Religion deals with "the meaning of the whole," so that attempting to find meaning to life in anything less than the divine amounts to the idolatry of promoting a partial interest or perspective as ultimate. This was the problem with the sciences. Making even democracy the center of education was idolatrous, because if democracy were an end it itself, that would amount to a political religion.

But what were the alternatives? The "orthodox portion of American Protestantism," especially as found in the South, Midwest, and West, was "culturally obscurantist" and "so irrelevant to religion in higher education that no policy in the academic program can hope to overcome that irrelevance." Liberal Protestantism, on the other hand, "is inclined to make so many concessions to the characteristic prejudices and presuppositions of modern culture that all unique emphases and characteristic insights of the historic Christian faith tend to become obscured." Liberal Protestants offered vapid and self-defeating religion courses that taught only "a Christian naturalism or humanism" or the Bible as "literature." What was needed then were religion courses that without proselytizing taught "the positive meaning of the Christian faith" and led to "commitment."

At this point, however, Niebuhr simply sidestepped a major problem. How would schools find teachers who would tread this fine line between proselytizing and inspiring? Particularly, how was this going to happen if, as

Niebuhr also made a point of emphasizing, there should be no religious test for faculty?

For Niebuhr, as for virtually every other Protestant writer on higher education, academic freedom was a sacred nonnegotiable. Moreover, he argued, such freedom was essential to Protestant Christianity. Protestant Christianity supported liberal culture in the best sense by insisting on criticism and self-criticism of the culture itself. However, as soon as the faith became official or dogmatic, the critical perspective so necessary to the faith itself was undermined: "While Catholicism may regard a secular culture as inimical to the highest values of Christianity, Protestantism at its best cannot make such an estimate of our liberal-democratic culture. Protestantism believes that faith must be achieved in freedom."[28]

Here surely was the Achilles heel of the mainline Protestant view of higher education, even when it was at its best in distinguishing between itself and the culture. The liberal ideal of freedom had become so essential to the faith that there was little way for the distinctive aspects of the faith to survive in the public institutions of a free society once the momentum of cultural dominance gave out. Christian realism of the Niebuhrian type had no plan for dealing with this concession to modern cultural ideals. Less critical liberal Protestants often did not even see the problem.

The corollary of the commitment to freedom was a commitment to science. Niebuhr was often sharply critical of the Deweyan reverence for scientific method as a basis for social planning. Niebuhr saw such faith in science as a typical example of the human tendency to turn a virtue into a vice. Nonetheless, as Douglas Sloan has tellingly demonstrated, Niebuhr and his mainline cohorts were so thoroughly committed to the academic scientific ideals that they could provide no alternative to the scientific and technical models that were increasingly shaping most academic disciplines. Granted, they did offer a transcendent perspective that would challenge human tendencies to absolutize the relative. As valuable as such perspectives might be, they would not deflect the scientific-technological juggernaut. According to Sloan, they hardly challenged it.[29]

The Limits of Freedom

The limits of the commitment to freedom in both the educational and religious establishments were painfully evident in their mixed reactions to

McCarthyism and anticommunism. On the one hand, university and main-line Protestant leadership overwhelmingly denounced the extremes of McCarthyism. Educational institutions and the Protestant National Council of Churches (which succeeded the Federal Council of Churches in 1949) were favorite targets of the right wing, for whom anything liberal was pink and anything pink was Red. Representatives of the accused groups were naturally outraged by the accusations, and they sharply denounced the McCarthyite tactics of guilt by association as well as the assumption that those who had sympathized with communism when that was in style in the 1930s but had since renounced it should be treated as though they were communists.

The counterbalance to liberal outrage over McCarthyite tactics was the liberals' own militant anticommunism. In the dangerous Cold War setting, Communist party membership involved not only authoritarian beliefs but also allegiance to a threatening and secretive international movement. Dedicated civil libertarians might defend rights for active party members, but much liberal opinion now saw the party as a threat to liberalism itself. Leaders of the American Association of University Professors (AAUP), for instance, typically saw membership in the Communist party as an exception to the rule that political affiliations should not be an academic concern. The reason was, as Arthur Lovejoy explained in 1949, that "the Communist Party has already extinguished academic freedom in many countries," so "no one who desires to maintain academic freedom in America can consistently favor" accepting as faculty members "persons who have voluntarily adhered to an organization one of whose aims is to abolish academic freedom." Sidney Hook, who in 1932 had signed a petition in favor of the Communist party presidential candidate, now strongly concurred. Party members were committed to professional misconduct, said Hook in "What Shall We Do about Communist Teachers?," an essay appearing in 1949 in the *Saturday Evening Post*.

President James Bryant Conant of Harvard said much the same thing, as did his peers across the nation: "In this period of a cold war, I do not believe the usual rule as to political parties applies to the Communist Party." Since members of the Communist party were committed to secrecy, dedicated to indoctrination, and subservient to foreign powers, said Conant, they were not so much a political party, as "something more akin to a fanatic religious movement."[30]

In line with such sentiments, the dominant academic leadership offered little opposition to efforts to formalize the anticommunist dimension of academia's commitment to the republic. Administrations routinely gave assurances that no Communist activities would be permitted on campus, speaker policies were tightened, and radical student organizations virtually disappeared. Almost every state passed laws requiring teachers at universities to sign loyalty oaths. Even when, at the University of California at Berkeley, some thirty liberal professors were dismissed for taking a stand and refusing on principle to sign California's oath in 1949, the AAUP did not take effective action. While academic opinion eventually stood solidly against the worst excesses of McCarthyism, it did so within the framework of a basic anticommunism that remained the order of the day.[31]

Whatever its merits, liberal American anticommunism illustrated the point that liberalism's attachment to freedom was always limited by higher allegiances, of which the highest was the survival of the American version of liberal culture itself. A real and present danger of overthrowing the government would, of course, necessitate some limit on freedom. Beyond that, however, the logic of American liberalism invited another limitation on freedom. Tolerance, above all, seemed necessary to make democracy work in a pluralistic setting. The one thing that could not be tolerated was intolerance. To many leaders of academic opinion, dogmatism of any sort appeared a threat to democratic institutions. In the debates between the pragmatists and the proponents of eternal verities, the pragmatists seemed to have captured the field. The genius of America, it seemed to many, was in its antidogmatism, a point reinforced by the widely admired pragmatism of New Deal politics.[32] Stalinist communism was heretical because it denied this principle. Although it was difficult to explain how severe restrictions of communist expressions were consistent with "freedom" or with "academic freedom," these measures were consistent if freedom was defined as the freedom to deny anything but freedom.

The appeal of this position obscured another paradox. Enforcing antidogmatism in the name of national welfare was itself dogmatic. Of course proponents of religious or political dogmatism were free to live in their own enclaves in America and their free speech was largely protected. One area, however, into which such protections did not fully extend was public or quasi-public education, including those institutions of higher learning that most celebrated their "academic freedom." Such institutions were considered so essential to the national welfare that they were inevitably limited by the dominant national viewpoints. Groups that were excluded, such as Marxists and fundamentalists, often raised the point that they were being excluded by liberal dogmatism, but they were seldom heard. In academic institutions where "free inquiry" was considered the very basis of the enterprise—the holy grail itself—the point that freedom always operates within the bounds of a dogmatic framework was not often acknowledged.

The Trouble with Catholics

The relationship of the intense commitment to freedom to the Protestant heritage of the liberal community that dominated American universities is most evident in the close parallel between postwar attitudes toward Catholicism and communism.[33] Totalitarianism of the right was to be deplored as much as totalitarianism of the left. Although Catholicism was far less plausibly a foreign threat than was the Communist party, the Roman Catholic Church remained the chief candidate for a takeover from the right. Nor were such fears exclusively the property of Protestant fundamentalists. In the outbreak of anti-Catholicism that grew out of the war, secularists and mainline Protestants took the lead. The 1944 conference on "The Authoritarian Attempt to Capture Education," which issued in dark warnings of the Roman threat, was sponsored by secularists and civil libertarians. Paul Blanshard's bestseller, *American Freedom and Catholic Power* (1949), which popularized fears of a Catholic takeover and warned that education would be the first thing to fall, was excerpted in *The Nation*.[34] *The Nation* also financed Blanshard's research for a second volume, *Communism, Democracy and Catholic Power*, which detailed the parallels between the two types of "totalitarianism."[35]

Attitudes toward Catholicism, of course, varied, but many of the most prominent leaders of mainline Protestantism joined in the liberal chorus of scathing attacks on Catholic intolerance and imperialism. Bishop G. Bromley Oxnam, for instance, perhaps the most influential Methodist leader of the era and a proponent of strengthening Christian identity in higher education, was a militant opponent of Catholicism. A person who takes his "religious thought from an authoritarian hierarch," Oxnam declared in one of his many postwar polemics, "is likely to be so conditioned that he may be willing to take his political thought from a dictator or his economic thought from a party." A close parallel could be drawn. "The American Catholic hierarchy," the Methodist bishop pontificated, "as well as the American Communist Party, is bound by directives from a foreign capital."[36]

The *Christian Century*, the leading journal of Protestant liberalism, was a major voice in mobilizing anti-Catholic sentiment. In late 1944 and early 1945 it ran an eight-part series by Harold E. Fey, titled "Can Catholicism Win America?," which warned of the menace of Catholic "totalitarianism." The series was then widely circulated as a pamphlet, advertised thus in the *Christian Century*: "Here is a carefully wrought study of the strategy by which Rome, weakened in Europe, hopes to make America a Catholic province, capturing Middletown, controlling the press, winning the Negro, courting the workers, invading rural America, and centralizing its power in Washington."[37]

Longtime *Christian Century* editor Charles Clayton Morrison followed up the Fey series with one of his own, which he expanded into a book, *Can Protestantism Win America?* (1948). Morrison warned that "three major forces are now bidding for ascendancy in the cultural and spiritual life of America." These were Protestantism, Roman Catholicism, and Secularism. Most Protestants, he felt, were complacent, taking their dominance for granted and not recognizing the urgency of the present cultural and spiritual crisis.[38] Such sentiments were one factor in strengthening mainline Protestant solidarity with the formation of the National Council of Churches in 1950.[39]

The most immediately alarming trend, according to the anti-Catholic authors, was Catholic inroads in education. One of their greatest fears, it seemed, was that public funds might be used to support Catholic schools. Court cases on such subjects were sending mixed signals. Oxnam and Morrison were among the leading founders of a movement to block any Catholic gains, Protestants and Other Americans United for the Separation of Church and State, established in 1948.[40]

Paradoxically, this revival of anti-Catholicism took place at a time when there was much call among the dominant voices in America for an end to bigotry. The revelations of the horrors of the Holocaust steeled resolve to end any discrimination against Jews. Anti-racist sentiments similarly had made great gains since the war, and there were calls for ending the segregation of African Americans. Anti-Catholicism thus placed Protestant and secular liberal leadership in an awkward position. Many prominent leaders accordingly were more reserved in their anti-Catholic expressions than were Oxnam and Morrison. Henry Sloane Coffin, for instance, was among a group of Protestant leaders who were concerned with the Catholic threat but explicitly wanted to avoid the appearance of "bigotry" that might come with association with Protestants United.[41] While Protestant leaders might deplore the dogmatic and authoritarian Catholicism that in their eyes had contributed to European fascism, they were also cultivating "the right sort" of Catholics for "three-faith" pluralism that included Protestants, Catholics, and Jews. This tame united front, however, would be established on Protestant terms. The price of full acceptance in American public life would be that Catholicism and Judaism would have to act like denominations; that is, claims to be the true church or a chosen people could make no difference in their behavior.[42]

The watchword for this attempted resolution was "pluralism." As Philip Gleason has shown, "pluralism" involved a verbal celebration of American diversity, but with an insistence that this diversity be limited by accepting basic American values. In other words, pluralism was a new name for the old melting-pot ideal. This was the message being sent to postwar Roman Catholics.[43] They were welcomed to America with open arms. Their unquestioned patriotism was deeply appreciated. Nonetheless, they should not expect something as un-American as their parochial school system to be accepted on equal terms with other forms of education in America. It was not just that Catholic schools were different. Rather, the religious authoritarianism at the heart of the enterprise was antithetical to free inquiry, which was the very basis of American education.[44] Paul Blanshard quoted a remark by John Dewey: "It is essential that this basic issue be seen for what it is—namely the encouragement of a powerful reactionary world organization in the most vital realm of democratic life with the resulting promulgation of principles inimical to democracy."[45] Harvard's president James Bryant Conant made the point a bit more politely. Contrasting America's education system favorably to those of England, Scotland, Australia, and New Zealand, Conant deplored the growth of American Catholic high schools. Public schools, he affirmed, were essential to unified national life. Religiously based criticisms of them were misplaced since "our tax-supported schools have had as a great and continuing purpose the development of moral and spiritual values."[46]

God and Buckley Revisited at Yale

In this atmosphere we can understand better the explosive reaction to Buckley's critique of Yale.[47] At the height of a revival of interest in religion, Buckley dared to say that university education was essentially not congenial to Christianity. Henry Sloane Coffin's committee was only echoing what leading religious educators were saying when it affirmed that "religious life at Yale is deeper and richer than it has been in many years." Compared with most front-rank schools Yale was relatively open to religious interests. Among themselves, Protestant leaders might admit that the situation was far from ideal. The Hazen volume on *College Texts and Religion,* published in New Haven, for instance, had recently documented the overwhelmingly secular slant of textbooks. Mainline Protestant speakers routinely decried the secularism, materialism, and scientism of universities. Yet when a Catholic pointed out the same things it was deeply offensive. To have a representative of their oldest ideological rival point out that the best of Protestant higher education was failing in its religious task was painful, especially so because the criticisms were largely accurate. As a number of the reactions suggested, his polemic against his alma mater was all the more outrageous because Buckley was a guest, one of the very beneficiaries of Protestant openness.

Buckley's dogmatic definition of Christianity was also offensive and deepened the inability of the two sides to communicate. Much of what the Protestant leadership long had counted as broadly Christian values Buckley regarded as wrongly baptized secularism.[48] Moreover, while the traditional Christianity for which Buckley spoke distinguished sharply between those who were in the church and those who were not, the Christianity believed suitable to a university centered on values that would bring people together. Ultimately, the Christianity that had survived at Yale, though it retained significant transcendent dimensions, had to meet the test of serving democracy.

Ironically, Buckley himself shared some of the premises that had helped define what religion would be tolerated in universities. He, too, had an establishmentarian's assumption that Christianity essentially involved a plan for a free American social order. Hence, his prescription for a return to God at Yale was inextricably wed to a social and economic agenda built around free enterprise. Buckley was not proposing to get rid of the American religious establishment but to refurbish it with conservative religion and economics.

Because Buckley's combination of religious and economic views differed so radically from those acceptable to the Protestant establishment, he was able to point out forcefully that their claims to "academic freedom" were "superstitions." Here was a point on which the Protestant establishment was most vulnerable, even on its own terms. What a believing Catholic could see clearly, but the Protestant elite were loath to admit, was that the Protestant establishment *was* an establishment. By weakening the distinction between church and nation it had claimed the whole nation as its church. Although its doctrines were thus blended with and often subordinated to the liberal ideals of the republic, they were still doctrines. Moreover, they were doctrines with a distinctly *Protestant* heritage.[49]

20

Liberal Protestantism
without Protestantism

In 1951 Robert Maynard Hutchins resigned as chancellor of the University of Chicago after years of frustration. Weary of having many of his most cherished proposals blocked by recalcitrant faculty Hutchins determined that he could do more for his educational ideals as an associate director of the Ford Foundation. Hutchins was, next to John Dewey, the best-known American educator of the era. Twice he was honored with the closest thing to canonization by the American hierarchy, a cover appearance on *Time* magazine. His resignation, however, may be taken as a signal that even a person of immense prestige and ability could not deflect the educational stream that was by now so firmly set in its course. As Hutchins put it, "The academic administrators of America remind one of the French Revolutionist who said, 'The mob is in the streets. I must find out where they are going, for I am their leader.'"[1]

"Civilization is doomed," Hutchins wrote in the *Journal of Higher Education* in 1947, "unless the hearts and minds of men can be changed, and unless we can bring about a moral, intellectual and spiritual reformation."[2] Modern Americans were never more open to such a reformation than in the postwar years. Western civilization had just survived the nightmare of Nazism and was faced totalitarian Stalinism. Religious leaders of all stripes were calling for return to first principles. Many of the ideals, such as liberty and equal justice for all, that Americans had just fought for seemed self-evident. Yet on what grounds were they based? On what basis could conflicts among such principles be adjudicated? Hutchins believed that the only hope for truly nonsectarian common ground was in natural law. Yet in recent generations any hopes for building a society on such enlightened ground had been dissolved. Americans were obsessed by practicality and technique, and pragmatic philosophies only articulated and systematized what most American educators already did anyway, which was to follow the trends. In Hutchins's view, almost all of American education was "not merely anthropocentric; it

The Soul of the American University Revisited. George M. Marsden, Oxford University Press. © Oxford University Press 2021. DOI: 10.1093/oso/9780190073312.003.0024

centers upon those aspects of human life least likely to elevate and ennoble the human spirit."[3]

In 1947 when Hutchins was calling for a "moral, intellectual, and spiritual reformation," many more conventionally Protestant leaders were proclaiming that it would have to be the spiritual reformation that led the way for the moral and intellectual renewal. Much of the revival of religious interest on campuses would involve such a hope. In addition to active campus ministries and opportunities for student worship and service, there was funding to encourage students to study for the ministry, increased interest in building religion departments and strengthening divinity schools, and an immense literature on how to promote religion on campus. Particularly, there was widespread concern that higher education promote higher values that would reflect the best in the Judeo-Christian and American heritages.[4]

As valuable as such programs undoubtedly were in changing the lives and outlooks of many individuals, it is worth pausing to consider why at this point in the history such religious renewal on campus could hardly touch the core issues shaping mainstream American intellectual life. As Hutchins was lamenting, that mainstream was controlled by practical concerns and scientific procedures that had little openness to spiritual or moral concerns. Furthermore, as he also recognized, if there were to be any substantial alternative it would have to be based on some widely shared common ground principles or natural law. Yet in the post-Darwinian Protestant world there was no realistic hope of reviving such an Enlightenment basis for consensus. And no particular brand of Protestantism, divided between liberals and conservatives as well into many denominations, could offer a realistic basis for an alternative spiritually based common ground.

One dimension of the problem had to do with the character of the dominant Protestant religious tradition that goes back to at least the eighteenth century. Again a Catholic observer helps us see what is distinctly Protestant. In 1845 John Henry Newman joined the Roman Catholic Church, a move that forced him to give up a position at his beloved Oxford University. Newman's renunciation of Protestantism was based in part on his perception of tendencies in it that he thought ultimately would undermine the intentions of the Protestant reformers. These tendencies were evident in the evangelical Protestantism of Newman's day and apparent in Protestant ideas of university education. Specifically they were tendencies to see the essence of Christianity as religious sentiment and practical morality. These emphases were suited to the public establishment of Christianity, as in higher education, since they moved any exclusive claims of Christianity, particularly theological claims, away from intellectual life. Christianity in academia was located either in the subjective lives of individuals or in ideals of service to humanity with which no one was likely to quarrel.

In contrast to the American trends, in Newman's *Idea of a University*, enunciated for his Catholic University of Ireland, of which he became the founding rector in 1852, theology was at the center. This did not mean that the university would be primarily a school of theology but, rather, that theology should have an integral place among the other sciences. Since universities claimed to teach universal knowledge and theology was a branch of knowledge, it did not make sense to exclude theology from the main business of the university as was being done in England. The tendency of each discipline is to aggrandize its approach to understanding reality. If theology were not guaranteed its own domain among the sciences, the other sciences would soon deny its relevance. The result would be attempts of the other sciences to understand reality without taking into account one of its most essential components.[5]

In American Protestant higher education, as we have seen, the trends militated against keeping theological principles part of the educational enterprise. Already in the eighteenth century, moral philosophy had begun to emerge as the central locus of Christianity in the curriculum, supplemented by periodic revivals intended to enlist student Christian commitment. Morality and sentiment, emphases that Newman criticized in Protestantism, were thus already prominent. Some reference to theological principles nonetheless persisted until the age of the universities. Early in that era, however, with many pressures working against theology and no formal provision for maintaining its presence, it was quickly banished to divinity schools, if not simply banished. Newman was correct that this development fit the logic of modernizing Protestantism. Most mainstream Protestants were in the process of declaring the whole nation their church, and with no strong institutional church in the picture the primary locations for Christianity lay in individual experience and in public morality. Neither of these provided any institutional basis for maintaining distinctive Christian theological principles as core factors in education.[6]

We can see this point in one notable example both of the extent and the limits of the renewed interest in religion. In 1953 Harvard inaugurated as its president Nathan M. Pusey, a devout Episcopalian. One of the first things Pusey did was accept an invitation to address the opening convocation of the Harvard Divinity School in 1953. Pusey noted that the last time the university's president had participated in a Divinity School exercise had been in 1909 when Charles Eliot had delivered what became a well-known address, "The Religion of the Future." Eliot had proclaimed that the religion of the future would be, in effect, all that is good, whether in performing surgery, building better schools or playgrounds, or cleaning up a slum. Pusey, in his own address, which was reprinted in *Harper's*, *Christian Century*, and other journals, took Eliot to task for thus reducing religion to social service. Pusey objected that Eliot falsely contrasted such good with metaphysical Christianity, which made traditional claims about God and Christ. Harvard's new president could even sound like at least a distant echo of Newman: "It is my very sincere hope therefore that theological studies can here be given a fresh impetus and a new life within this University.... Theology should not be thought of as a minor intellectual exercise among other intellectual exercises; certainly not only this. It is expected to carry an answer to our deepest hungers and needs." Having said that, however, Pusey closed with words that would have confirmed Newman's darkest suspicions of Protestantism. Quoting a Harvard Divinity School faculty member, Pusey affirmed that what was desperately needed was more of "faith [that] is the consciousness that moral values and spiritual experiences have sacred character."[7]

While Pusey did strengthen the Harvard Divinity School, he also was light years away from Newman in having no way of reintegrating Divinity with the rest of the university. Even his efforts to hire more committed theologians in the Divinity School met with opposition from other Harvard faculty.[8]

A dramatic confrontation brought out how difficult it was for the religious revival to make any headway if it was to involve anything distinctly Christian. In the spring of 1958 opponents of Pusey's efforts to strengthen Christianity at Harvard brought attention to the university's policy of regarding Memorial Chapel as a Christian place of worship and not allowing other faiths to hold services or even weddings there.[9] The policy itself was a remarkable example of one of the principal problems faced by champions of the religious renewal. Any strengthening of the place of Christianity on campus would be a strengthening of a residual cultural establishment[10] and hence was liable to attack simply on grounds of equity. The Memorial Chapel had been built in the early 1930s as a memorial to Harvard students who had died in World War I. Opponents of the Christians-only policy pointed out those who had died represented many faiths and perhaps none at all. A sharp controversy ensued, culminating in a distinguished group of faculty, including Perry Miller, Mark DeWolfe Howe Jr., I. Bernard Cohen, John H. Finley Jr., and Morton G. White, personally presenting Pusey a petition demanding that the chapel be open to all faiths. Perry Miller, an agnostic who thought that current Christianity at Harvard was a pale shadow of that of the Puritan founders, reportedly was outraged at the thought that he might not be buried from the chapel of his own university. The next week the corporation capitulated to the realities of Harvard pluralism and declared the chapel open to private services of all religious faiths.[11]

Pluralism was one of the major roadblocks whenever thoughtful religious leaders proposed ways of providing a substantive place for Christianity, or other religions, within university education. Will Herberg, a Jewish scholar and the era's most respected analyst of America's "three-faith" pluralism, observed in 1958 that "virtually all Americans who have given any thought to the matter are thoroughly dissatisfied with the present state of the relations between religion and education, particularly public education." Moreover, said Herberg, "the place that is granted to religion in the university scheme of things, at least on most campuses, does not correspond either to a sound conception of higher education or to the essential requirements of American religious pluralism."

Herberg backed his remark with a perceptive encapsulation of American educational history. "Nonsectarianism" of the nineteenth century had been translated into "nonreligious." Thus, American schools were not neutral with respect to religion but had opened the door for the dominance of "ideological secularism." Such "secularistic pseudo-religion, usually some brand of naturalism or positivism . . . soon began to acquire almost official status." In the meantime, "Catholics established their own institutions, and the Jews of the first or second generation who aspired to a higher education were even more secularist-minded than the rest." Few voices spoke for a genuine religious pluralism. "Pluralism" that welcomed religion only when it was another bland version of the "American Way of Life" was not a true pluralism. Religious philosophies, if they were to be treated fairly, would "be given the same rights and privileges in the academic world as are the secularist philosophies."[12]

Catholic social philosopher John Courtney Murray offered a parallel critique. Liberal society, he said, presented a "genteel picture" of itself as a peaceful development. This was particularly true of the universities, which claimed to be the havens of dispassionate reason. The fact of the matter was that the modern world had always been engaged in active ideological conflict, often having to do with religious questions about the fundamental nature of reality. The university should therefore "recognize its own spiritual and intellectual situation. The university would succumb to a special type of neurotic disorder if it were to cultivate an inflated image of itself as somehow standing in all serenity 'above' the religious wars that rage beneath the surface of modern life and somehow privileged to disregard these conflicts as irrelevant to its 'search for truth.'" To present this "genteel picture" of itself would be "to indulge in a flight from reality." American universities, rather, should be places where a student is free to "explore the full intellectual dimensions of the religious faith to which he is committed."[13]

Protestant observers, despite the rhetoric of some of their number, were inclined to hesitate if anything but mainstream Protestantism was thus related to the intellectual life of universities. Representing "the Protestant view" in the same forum addressed by Herberg and Murray, church historian Roland Bainton of Yale, for instance, saw a "quest for truth" as essential to the self-definition of modern universities. Bainton wondered, therefore, how Roman Catholics, fundamentalist Protestants, or Orthodox Jews could fully participate in the intellectual life of the university, as long as they held to the authority of sacred revelations that closed many intellectual questions. How could a Catholic fully participate in the intellectual community of biologists when the pope had ruled that Adam was a real person? "One may wonder whether Catholicism can be genuinely at home in any university other than a Catholic university."[14]

William Frankena, chair of philosophy at the University of Michigan, which hosted the conference, pointed out the particular problems of substantive religious teaching at a state university. Frankena, who was a more traditional Protestant than Bainton (a Quaker), pointed out that Herberg's proposal of separate ideologically oriented courses from the viewpoint of the three major faiths was itself a compromise, since American faiths were much more diverse than that. While apologizing for maintaining a "liberal" view when both Herberg and Murray were speaking of a "postmodern" age more open to religion, Frankena quoted approvingly John Stuart Mill's remarks: "The proper business of an University is . . . not to tell us from authority what we ought to believe, and make us accept the belief as a duty, but to give us information and training, and help us to form our own belief in a manner worthy of intelligent beings, who seek for truth." Frankena thus accepted the orthodox definition of a university established in America in the early twentieth century. Given this definition, yet agreeing with Herberg and Murray that mainstream Protestants were only confusing the issue by teaching the "bogus irenicisms [of] religions of the common denominator," Frankena concluded that at a state university one could do little more than teach *about* religion. The most that might be done would be to teach sympathetically, so as to suggest that such issues might be of personal importance to students. Specific religious teaching, however, was the responsibility of homes, churches, and religious ministries to universities; this could not be the business of the university as such. Frankena recognized that doctrinaire secularism might gain an advantage in the liberal university, but he saw no realistic way to promote religion within the boundaries of the public university itself.[15]

Despite the ambiguity as to their real purpose, the growth of religion departments during this era acted as a palliative that helped hide the inability to address the deeper issues. By 1950 some 60% of state universities and land grant colleges were offering courses in religion, and during the next decades the field continued to grow. For instance, more than three times as many doctoral degrees were granted during the 1950s than in the 1940s. Much of the immediate postwar growth was justified on the same grounds that sparked the general education movement to strengthen the humanities. As one of the humanities, religion was an important value-shaping dimension of the Western heritage. Religion department offerings in universities generally resembled the offerings at Protestant divinity schools,[16] where, in fact, many of the professors had been trained. Such offerings did provide some opportunities to sympathetically explore mainline Protestant and some other religious perspectives. Care was to be taken to avoid any dogmatism or indoctrination, especially at state schools, and technically the study was *about* religion. Nonetheless, in the 1950s such study was often conducted in an atmosphere that encouraged religious practice.[17]

During the 1960s, however, the predominant outlook in the field changed rapidly. Most important was the impulse to professionalize religious studies. Because of its ties to the residual Protestant establishment, its staffing by seminary graduates, and its associations with Bible requirements at church-related schools, the academic field of religion was often regarded as a second-class discipline and seldom taken seriously among the humanities. The response was to define the field increasingly in scientific terms. Thus, religious studies would have a methodology more like the social sciences. The new trend was to study religion "phenomenologically," so that the object of study was the abstraction "religion," the common traits of which could be exemplified by looking at particular religions. Another manifestation of the professionalizing impulse was the formation in 1964 of the American Academy of Religion, which grew principally out of the National Association of Bible Instructors (which had long lived with this less professional name). While the AAR embraced both the humanistic and the social scientific impulse, the latter signaled the dominant direction for the future.[18]

A most important parallel was a growing consciousness of the legal difficulty of maintaining a residual Protestant establishment, even of the blandest sort. In 1963, in a landmark ruling, *Abington Township School District v. Schempp*, the Supreme Court outlawed formal religious exercises in public schools. At the same time, however, the majority of the court proposed a way for dealing with the touchy issue of religion in public education. Religion should be studied with objective detachment. In fact, said Associate Justice Tom Clark in his majority opinion, "It might well be said that one's education is not complete without a study of comparative religion or the history of religion and its relationship to the advancement of civilization." Such sentiment cleared the way for accelerating the expansion of the study of religion in higher education during the next decade.[19]

By this time the field of religious studies was also being changed by counterculture critiques of Western civilization, Western values, and hence Western religion, thus adding impetus to the trend away from the dominance of the liberal Protestant heritage. During the anti-Vietnam War era many liberal Protestant academics largely sympathized with such critiques and became sensitized toward intruding into their work anything that might be construed as establishmentarian. One result was that religion programs increasingly provided a place for non-Western religions and increasingly looked for nontraditional ways to study Western religions.

Catch-22

These changes reflected an increasing uneasiness within the liberal Protestant community about asserting a distinctly Christian identity at all. One strong sensibility that had developed by the 1950s was fear of any appearance of cultural imperialism. The immediate postwar concern to strengthen the Western heritage soon was overwhelmed by the new phenomenon of American internationalism. Educated Americans, including much of mainline Protestant leadership, increasingly warned against claims of Western superiority. For mainline Protestants such concerns accelerated the trends already growing by the 1930s, to question the whole idea of traditional Christian missions, premised as they were on the assumption of Christian superiority.[20]

Much the same was happening in the face of increasing sensitivity to the challenges of pluralism at home. During the late 1950s and the 1960s the overwhelming social concern of the mainline Protestant churches was the attack on racial discrimination. Thus committed to an integrationist society, churches' public stances naturally gravitated toward opposition to discrimination of any sort, including religious discrimination. The fact that, among white Americans, more traditional religious views often correlated with racist views underscored the point that in public places religious privilege was dangerous. Hence developed the catch-22 of liberal Protestantism: the more it identified itself with a social mission, the less prominent should be its own identifiable social influence.

This was apparent in traditionally Protestant colleges. Having defined themselves increasingly in terms of their service to the public, they were now rapidly divesting themselves of the specifics of their Christian heritage. The reasons for this were a mix of principle and necessity. One important factor was economic. In the era of expansion, smaller colleges were having difficulties keeping up. One solution was to broaden constituencies. Inevitably this meant toning down religious emphases. Furthermore, such colleges were under pressure to conform to national academic standards if they were to retain prestige or even respect. David Riesman in 1956 described American academia as a "snakelike" procession, in which parts that were behind the leader, especially those in the middle, constantly try to follow the changing direction of the head.[21] Keeping up meant hiring faculty with loyalties to national academic standards more than to church concerns. It also meant dropping anything that might be interpreted as religious indoctrination. Measures of academic success emphasized evidence that students were being taught to think for themselves, as opposed to "conformism" or submission to "authoritarianism."[22] All these factors added to the impulse for mainline church-related colleges to define themselves in terms less and less distinct from their secular counterparts.

During the 1960s a number of well-funded studies examined what church-relatedness meant for a college.[23] As David Riesman and Christopher Jencks commented in 1968, "Organizations like the National Council of Churches as well as individual denominations are constantly commissioning investigations aimed at defining a unique mission for those colleges which remain Protestant, but the very idea that such questions require research is a tribute to the triumph of academic over clerical values." They concluded, "Very few Protestant colleges admit that the substance of what they teach is influenced by ideological considerations."[24] By the end of the 1960s, mainline Protestantism's own studies were saying little more than that their colleges should learn from the universities.[25]

Much the same trends were influencing Christian faculty at secular institutions. While during the 1950s a number of significant voices were still talking about the role of the Christian in the university, by the mid-1960s such concerns were sounding passé. The history of the *Christian Scholar* exemplifies the changing times. In 1953 the Commission on Higher Education of the National Council of Churches launched a Faculty Christian Fellowship and established the *Christian Scholar*, a well-edited and attractive journal. In its inaugural issue the *Christian Scholar* affirmed the remarkable claim that "the twentieth century is the greatest age in theology since the thirteenth." The journal would explore the whole range of academic implications of Christian faith, in the context of this theological renaissance. "*The Christian Scholar,*" it avowed confidently, "will be motivated by the assumption that Christian faith is not only relevant to, but actually indispensable for, the tasks of the academic community and the vocations of those who serve within it in their common search for meaning and truth."[26]

In 1967 the *Christian Scholar* announced its impending demise. The problem was not primarily financial, but ideological. The Department of Higher Education of the National Council of Churches no longer thought such a journal appropriate. Subscribers would receive a new journal, *Soundings: A Journal of Interdisciplinary Studies*. While this journal was published by the Society for Religion and Higher Education, the closest its initial announcement got to suggesting a religious perspective was that it would fill the gap of discussion regarding "engagement of the Scholar with issues of value, meaning and purpose"; "The focus will be on themes of genuine relevance to scholars both as academicians and as men engaged by the common human concerns of our day." The Faculty Christian Fellowship was officially declared dead a few years later.[27]

The dramatic shift toward dropping distinctive Christian identity had an ideological counterpart in the popularity during the mid-1960s of "secular" theologies. While the "Death-of-God" slogan of a few of this movement's theologians drew some sensational attention, a more typical expression of the mood of mainline Protestant spokespersons was Harvey Cox's widely popular *The Secular City*. Within less than a year of its publication in 1965 it had already sold over a quarter million copies. Cox, a professor at the Harvard Divinity School, had initially designed his book as lectures to the National Student Christian Federation, an alliance of mainline campus ministries. In a chapter on "The Church and the Secular University," Cox celebrated the secularization of the university and pronounced the attacks on secularization during the 1950s, when books like Moberly's were popular, to have been "a mistake."

Cox's most biting criticism was reserved for any vestigial idea of Christian higher education. The churches' first response to the rise of secular universities was to establish its own colleges and universities:

> This of course is medievalism. The whole idea of a "Christian" college or university after the breaking apart of the medieval synthesis has little meaning. The term *Christian* is not one that can be used to refer to universities any more than to observatories or laboratories. No one of the so-called Christian colleges that now dot our Midwest is able to give a very plausible theological basis for retaining the equivocal phrase *Christian college* in its catalogue.

What Cox was attacking was primarily what he characterized, accurately enough, as the vestigial establishmentarianism of mainline Protestantism in American higher education. The mainline campus ministries were, in his view, hardly any better than the so-called Christian colleges. The whole effort to keep a Christian presence in higher education was a "cumulative catastrophe." Established Protestantism was so entrenched socially that, despite the intentions of some of its leaders, it was essentially conservative in its cultural views and hence unable to facilitate real change. In contrast, Cox especially admired the YMCA and YWCA, which, in dropping their distinctive Christian heritage in favor of broader social concerns, had anticipated Dietrich Bonhoeffer's theology of "religionless man." Even though Ys were dying off as campus ministries, they had during the 1950s at least "survived the acute period of psychopathic confessionalism."

Cox's alternative to fighting the secularism of the university was to join it. The task of the Christians was "to discern where God's reconciliation is breaking in and to identify themselves with it." The church was not testifying to "some kind of common world view" or even to one worldview among many. Rather, the Gospel taught reconciliation in the world. "It frees people to live with each other *despite* radically conflicting ideologies, theologies, and politics, as men with men." Affirming that the "religious" stage of history had come to an end, Cox proclaimed that "man must now assume the responsibility for his world. He can no longer shove it off on some religious power."[28]

Leading mainline Protestants were thus already beating a retreat for their conventional ministries when the counterculture arrived on the scene.[29] Their own principles of dedication to serving the best interests of society meant, ironically, that they had to abandon some of the very institutions through which they had attempted to influence society. Nowhere was this more true than in higher education, where demands to keep up with the latest cultural trends were becoming overwhelming.

In the short run, the new stance could be seen not as a retreat at all, but as an advance. As Dorothy Bass points out, already by the early 1960s campus student organizations were increasingly turning to politics, particularly to issues of racial justice. With the eruption of the Free Speech movement in 1964, ever-deepening involvement in Vietnam, and increasingly violent urban disorders, politics overwhelmed everything else. Moreover, the imperative if churches were to "stay where the action is" was increasingly radical. Opposition to "the establishment" became a political fundamental. The comfortable campus ministry buildings with which religious groups had surrounded the universities were now an embarrassment when the poor were crying out for justice. Theological discussion was a cop-out if it did not lead to action. Traditional worship smacked of the staid and complacent middle class that was now so much despised. Even the guitars, balloons, and informality of the early sixties could hardly keep pace with the experiential standards of antiestablishment campus culture of the end of the decade.[30]

Politics set the agenda, and even on that front it was impossible to keep up. In 1966 the ecumenical National Student Christian Federation reorganized as the University Christian Movement (UCM). During its initial year the UCM president sent a "fraternal" letter to the radical Students for Democratic Society (SDS) pledging to stand in solidarity for equality and justice. The UCM was still funded by the Danforth Foundation, headed by Merrimon Cuninggim, and still the principal promoter of much of the work in religion in higher education. The UCM itself became increasingly radical. Its expressed purpose was "to work for the termination of American economic and cultural exploitation at home and abroad." Early in 1969 the meeting of the General Committee of the UCM broke down in acrimonious debate over a task force recommendation to work "only in terms of total dismantlement of that [American] society." With matters already at a seemingly hopeless impasse, members of the black caucus demanded that in the name of justice the UCM should turn over $50,000—most of the UCM budget—to their control. The next morning the UCM leadership voted the organization out of existence.[31]

The story of the University Christian Movement is an especially dramatic instance of what was happening to ecumenical and mainline denominational ministries generally. Committed to international and social justice, looking for God's action in what was happening in the secular society, they instinctively responded to the counterculture movement by trying to keep up with it. That, however, was becoming increasingly difficult as the counterculture became more fragmented and divided between ideals of reforming society and simply dropping out. Protestant leaders could still call for a prophetic political voice, as Kenneth Underwood did in a major Danforth study of campus ministries published in 1969. The difficulty, however, was that by 1969 there was little reason for students to think of campus ministries if they were looking for political advice.[32]

However justifiable the stance for peace and justice and the attack on the establishment may have been in the short run, in the long run there was little left of the mainline and ecumenical campus ministries by the 1970s. Once the war was gone as a unifying cause, the radical political movements fragmented even further into special interest groups. With the political issues changed and interest in political questions waning, there was little basis for retrieving a student constituency. The mainline Protestant churches were experiencing alarming numerical declines, attributable especially to their inability to retain the loyalty of the younger generation. By the 1970s a substantial gap had developed between Americans who had gone to college and those who had not with respect to religious belief and practice. In the 1950s surveys had found no significant correlation between college education and religious belief. By the 1970s the college educated were far less likely than other Americans to attend religious services regularly or to hold traditional Christian views.[33]

The Soul of the Multiversity

As for the universities themselves, whatever their myriad concerns, religion was very low on the list. The 1960s was another era of huge growth. The vast majority of this growth came in state-sponsored education. Whereas in 1950 private four-year institutions enrolled slightly more students than did public ones, by 1970 the enrollments at public schools outnumbered the private by well over two to one.[34] Virtually none of this growth, furthermore, had anything directly to do with religion, although an increase in the study *about* it, even at state schools, may have allayed potential complaints. So much else was happening to the universities, however, that the mainline Protestant withdrawal was hardly noticed. The university had become, as California Chancellor Clark Kerr had characterized it in 1963, a "multiversity."[35] Increasingly looking to the government for funding, its technical and research concerns were expanding in bewildering ways, so that any hopes to find a center to the enterprise were increasingly illusory. Expansion was also fueled by the cultural revolution that has been described as the shift from "mass to universal higher education."[36] With higher education now regarded as a right available to virtually anyone who desired it, further proliferation of programs oriented toward preparation for the job market contributed to the decentralized ethos.[37]

In modern America, technological expansion has always been accompanied by countermovements demanding more concern for human values. In the 1960s the most effective voices making such counterdemands were students at the multiversities. They attacked the depersonalization of the technological society and established alternative lifestyles. The intellectual counterpart was what Theodore Roszak well characterized as the attack on "the myth of objective consciousness," the premise, on which university education had been built, that detached observation was the most accurate and effective way of looking at things.[38]

Students also questioned the basic premises of American politics and economics, especially the partnership of business and government in technical, commercial, and international (and hence military) expansion. In pointing out that the universities served the political needs of the society, they were saying nothing new, but with the Vietnam draft hanging over the heads of many, students were not inclined to honor the idea of education as *preparation* for service. In local campus insurrections they briefly brought the educational process to a stop; henceforth change in university policy would be most effectively initiated by organized interest groups who could threaten to paralyze the rest of the enterprise if their demands were not heard.

While the counterculture movement was too diverse to characterize neatly, one thing that was often noted at the time was that the student demands had characteristics of a religious quest.[39] Part of the impulse was a demand for meaning in universities and a society that had little to offer on that front. Search for experiential and spiritual fulfillment in an otherwise depersonalized environment was a major part of the impulse as well. Eastern religions, new religions, and the occult gained unprecedented followings as well. Such movements, as well as the drug, communal, and rock cultures, provided alternatives, or complements, to political activism. The rise of the Jesus People movement by the early 1970s provided a Christian alternative, as did a broader resurgence of campus evangelicalism generally.

The principal responses of the universities were on the political front. American universities had always in some sense been political entities, but more than ever they would have to be directly responsible to their constituency. Or perhaps it would be more accurate to say that they would have to be responsive to a wider set of constituencies. On the one hand, their dedication to producing knowledge for industry and government persisted; on the other, their stated goals now had to include strong counterbalancing affirmations concerning social justice.

Perhaps typical of the thinking about the university that emerged from the 1960s were the conclusions of the Carnegie Commission on Higher Education and the Carnegie Council on Policy Studies in Higher Education arrived at after extensive studies between 1967 and 1979. In 1980 Clark Kerr summarized the findings of the many Carnegie reports, emphasizing that the main point that had given universities credibility was that they were *oriented toward the national welfare first and the welfare of all of higher education second.* In other words, "they were aimed at the advancement of American society through higher education and not the other way around." With this in mind the commission had identified five goals for higher education:

> (1) . . . the education of the individual student and the provision of a constructive environment for developmental growth; (2) advancing human capability in society at large through finding and training talent, developing new ideas, and enhancing understanding; (3) educational justice for the postsecondary age group; (4) pure learning—by supporting intellectual and artistic creativity; and (5) evaluation of society for renewal through individual thought and persuasion.[40]

Such statements would be duplicated many times over with little variation in particular institutions' definitions of their missions. They speak of educating students first, add the production and dissemination of knowledge, and emphasize ethical ideas of inclusive justice and of service to the community.

A typical formulation is the "mission statement" of Duke University developed for its self-study in 1988. Duke (which is appreciatively acknowledged as the primary venue for the first version of this work) is an institution well attuned to contemporary university trends, particularly since it has been self-consciously moving away from the more regional and parochial aspects of its heritage, toward establishing itself as a major national university. Its stated goals thus express a characteristic set of contemporary university ideals:

> Duke University shall endeavor to accomplish these missions: to educate students for meaningful, ethical and productive lives, to discover and interpret significant new knowledge; to promote the spirit of free inquiry on moral and intellectual issues; to foster the exchange of ideas and information within and across traditional disciplinary boundaries; to enrich the lives of the residents of our region by producing a variety of educational, medical, cultural and recreational services; and to support diversity and mutual tolerance throughout the university.

Duke's statement, however, offered a small uncharacteristic variation alluding to the Protestant heritage that in the South still needed to be acknowledged. After a paragraph elaborating on the goals already enumerated, the report adds: "Duke cherishes its historic ties with the United Methodist Church and the religious faith of its founders, while remaining non-sectarian."[41]

This delicately stated formulation suggests that, so far as the university's purposes are concerned, Christianity (not mentioned by name) is a thing of the past, yet at the same time the church connection is to be revered. In fact, the university has a predominantly Methodist and distinctly Christian Divinity School, privileges regular Christian services in its chapel, and retains pro forma ties between its board and the North Carolina United Methodist Conference. At the same time, as the statement of purpose indicates, Christianity as such is peripheral to the main business of the university.

The role of Christianity in Duke's 1988 mission statement contrasts strikingly with that adopted in its founding bylaws in 1924, only two generations earlier. That mission statement begins, "The aims of Duke University are to assert a faith in the eternal union of knowledge and religion set forth in the teachings and character of Jesus Christ, the Son of God."[42]

One implication of this historical narrative, however, is that these two statements are more closely connected than they might seem. The 1924 statement, originally drafted earlier in the century for Duke's predecessor, Trinity College, is a classic example of the liberal Protestant vision of a unified culture under Christ. Knowledge and religion are united in the ethics of Jesus. The implication is that all the university's goals are expressions of that unifying ethic. These goals are, the statement continues, "to advance learning in all lines of truth; to defend scholarship against all false notions and ideals; to develop a Christian love of freedom and truth; to promote a sincere spirit of tolerance; to discourage all partisan and sectarian strife; and to reach the largest permanent service to the individual, the state, the nation, and the church. Unto these ends shall the affairs of this university always be administered."

The ideals that universities typically were proclaiming in the late twentieth century were much the same as these, the difference being that the references to the ethics of Jesus and to the church had become superfluous. Liberal Protestant theology had already located salvation primarily in social advance and so had removed any basis of maintaining a distinction between church and society. The rest of the twentieth century saw the working out of the inevitable implication of that fusion. As the inclusive and tolerant social-ethical ideals became standard parts of progressive liberal culture, theological justification and churchly promotion of them became less necessary. And inclusiveness involved no longer giving the old Protestant establishment special standing. The universities still saw their ethical mission as involving the ideals of service to society and of enriching human life. These are high ideals, and liberal Protestantism should be recognized as being among their progenitors.

The Cultural Triumph of Liberal Protestantism?

One intriguing way of interpreting the ideological development of mainstream American higher education since about the 1970s is that it can be seen as in some sense shaped by the cultural triumph of many of the ideals of liberal Protestantism despite the sharp decline of the Protestant mainline as an institutional force. That thesis was proposed by sociologist N. Jay Demerath in 1995 and has been advanced by some other interpreters, including sociologist Christian Smith and historian David Hollinger. The argument is not focused on campuses as such but, rather, on a broader cultural acceptance of liberal ideals. Specifically, Demerath mentions individualism, pluralism, emancipation, tolerance, free critical inquiry, and the authority of human experience.[43] Mainstream university campuses are among the places where liberal versions of such ideals have most clearly prevailed. The dominance of such ideals has relatively little to do with specifically religious practices on campus.[44] In fact, one part of the argument is that in parts of the culture where these liberal ideals are taken for granted, institutional liberal Protestantism becomes redundant. One does not need to go to church to hear about tolerance and acceptance.

Christian Smith finds confirmation of this thesis in his interviews with twenty-first-century emerging adults, whether in universities or not. "Their dominant discourse about religion, faith, and God," he observes, " . . . often clearly reflects the basic cultural values, and sometime speech modes of liberal Protestantism." These cultural values include "individual autonomy, unbounded tolerance, freedom from authorities, the affirmation of pluralism, and the centrality of human self-consciousness, the practical value of moral religion, epistemological skepticism, and an instinctive aversion to anything 'dogmatic' or committed to particulars." In Smith's view, these characteristic outlooks of American young adults come close to matching H. Richard Niebuhr's famous characterization of Protestant liberalism as being "a God without wrath [who] brought men without sin into a kingdom without judgment through the ministrations of a Christ without a Cross."

Interestingly, the one area in Smith's observations concerning which the emerging adults did not share early-twentieth-century liberal views regarding religion was optimism regarding historical and moral progress. Twenty-first-century young people tend to be dubious regarding the future of society, politics, and the state of the world, despite being optimistic about their own futures.[45]

The most evident problem with this thesis regarding the triumph of liberal Protestant ideals is that it is virtually impossible to sort out the influences of liberal Protestantism from the influences of American liberalism in general—even when we characterize "liberalism" rather specifically, as does Demerath, as involving individualism, pluralism, emancipation, tolerance, free critical inquiry, and the authority of human experience—or with Smith's additions. Distinguishing Protestant influences from liberal influences is an interpretive problem throughout American history. One can find some of the roots of each of these liberal traits in Protestantism. In the nineteenth and early twentieth century, for instance, interpreters such as Ernest Troeltsch saw much of liberal cultural progress as an outgrowth of Protestantism. Max Weber connected Protestantism to the rise the spirit of capitalism. Some have credited Protestantism with the rise of modern scientific inquiry. In the mid-twentieth century, there was a considerable literature on the relationship of Protestantism to democracy. Protestantism has often been related to the rise of individualism. In the twenty-first century, some conservative Catholics writers see most of what has gone wrong in fragmented contemporary liberal culture as ultimately having origins in Protestantism.[46] All of these interpretations contain elements of truth, but the whole truth is more ambiguous. Protestantism is surely deeply intertwined with the rise of Western modernity. Typically, though, we find Protestants and Protestant outlooks on both sides of most developments. Also, Protestantism is constantly adapting itself to and reinforcing cultural trends that have a host of other origins.[47]

Assessing the degree of cultural influence of twentieth-century mainline liberal Protestantism is an especially a difficult task. The "modernist impulse" that shaped a good bit of the early-twentieth-century mainline Protestantism affirmed that an immanent God was acting in history, so the best of cultural progress was part of God's continuing revelation. Liberal Protestants typically saw that revelation as in continuity with biblical revelation centered in Christ. Yet the best modern liberal ideals were to be incorporated into the Gospel message. So even beyond the degree that most of American Protestantism was already shaped by characteristic American cultural assumptions, liberal Protestantism was frankly celebrating many of the more progressive liberal values. The relationships were reciprocal. Progressive liberal values were directly shaping mainline Protestantism. And in its heyday, as in the mid-twentieth century, liberal Protestantism played a considerable role in reinforcing and promoting such values. That can be illustrated in its substantial support of the civil rights movement, for instance. But other forces were also influential in promoting these same liberal values. Many of the most influential progressive liberal voices were frankly secularist. All the identified liberal ideals (individualism, pluralism, emancipation, tolerance, anti-dogmatism, free critical inquiry, and the authority of human experience) have not only Protestant origins but also long secular histories going back at least to the eighteenth-century Enlightenment.

So how does one assess the extent of liberal Protestant influence on the survival of these ideals into the twenty-first century when liberal Protestantism itself was shaped by more broadly liberal ideals and is no longer much of a direct influence? Even recognizing that the influences of liberalism and

Protestant are reciprocal, liberal Protestantism can be credited as one among the historical sources for the current ideals. That is especially true regarding mainstream higher education, where, until the 1960s, liberal Protestantism was typically one of the explicit forces shaping the moral ideals of the enterprise. Particularly, what became transformative ideals of tolerance, anti-discrimination, gender equity, inclusiveness, pluralism, globalism, peacemaking, and concerns for racial and other sorts of social justice, all had among their direct antecedents liberal Protestant teachings. American universities and mainstream colleges continue to celebrate that they are places that promote such ethical agendas.

Yet, while giving credit where it is due for the emergence of these ideals, from a twenty-first-century perspective there are good reasons to question whether these cultural influences should be characterized as a "cultural triumph." Part of the problem is that one of the ideals is that of individual self-fulfillment. As David Brooks has argued, in the twenty-first century "hyper-individualism is the reigning ethos of our day."[48] Individuals or groups construct emancipation stories of the self or of one's identity group freeing itself from the constraints of society. The hyper-individualism then tends to lead toward tribalism. Such tendencies, most manifest in identity politics, tend to undermine the universalism of the liberal tradition. The early civil rights movement was all about "integration" or full acceptance of particular groups into the larger society. And Martin Luther King Jr., emphasized the "brotherhood" among the races that should be the result. Or as David Hollinger later put it, the "postethnic concern involves widening 'the circle of the we.'"[49] It was a quest for a common humanity. But as Brooks points out, while global consciousness and genuine efforts to welcome inclusion and diversity certainly persist in liberal communities, the simultaneous cultivation of tribal identities often leads to fear and distrust of others. According to Brooks, therefore, not only on the religious and political right, but also on the left, anger becomes a dominant mode. Broader relational virtues are largely forgotten.[50]

As is often argued,[51] tribalism is a stronger natural human instinct than is universalism. So without religious influence, or some comparable universalist ideology, even while pluralism and tolerance are widely lauded, the various tribes that are seeking their emancipation revert to framing the world largely into "us" versus "them." In other words, as Robert Putnam and some other sociologists have concluded, it appears that the experience of greater exposure to diverse groups, if not embedded in a common ideology or set of commitments, is likely to create greater distrust rather than greater solidarity.[52]

Liberal Protestantism is not to be blamed for this contradiction that seems to be built into the inclusivist moral legacy; it is a legacy of secular liberalism as well. The problem involved is a classic example of the sort of ironies that Reinhold Niebuhr, arguably the most profound of the liberal Protestants, identified as characteristically found even in the best of ethical ideals. Liberal values such as inclusivism, tolerance, pluralism, and social justice surely ought to be valued in a diverse society. Yet, particularly in recent decades, when such secular liberal values have been largely divorced from liberal Protestantism itself or some other source for establishing moral standards, those values have not been able to overcome the self-interested tribalism that seems to be built into human nature and that can turn these very ideals into sources for division.

21

The Twenty-First-Century
Postsecular University

Whatever the achievements of mainstream American higher education in the first two decades of the twenty-first century, it is safe to say that few observers[1] are happy about its overall direction, identity, and purposes. Even if the preceding historical account shows that the religious dimensions of mainstream higher education were rarely more than mixed blessings, universities could still point to their moral purposes. They were providing education that might foster principled understandings that would help shape individual lives and serve the common purposes of the nation. Today such rhetoric rings hollow. The consensus seems to be that universities are driven even more than ever by economic interests.[2] While they do attempt to honor a moral imperative to maximize diversity and they serve a valuable practical function of enhancing future economic prospects for their constituents, those laudable goals often undermine other common moral purposes. The most common descriptors for the direction mainstream university education has been heading are terms such as "fragmenting," "splintering," "disrupting," "politicization," "commercialization," and "commodification.[3]

One could easily fill a couple of bookshelves with twenty-first-century declension narratives on such themes.[4] I will not attempt another such analysis here but, rather, review some of the most helpful of those laments from those who have been close to the scene. One of the most prominent themes in this literature is the demise of the humanities in providing something like a soul for university education. As Harry Lewis, a former dean of Harvard College, put it in 2006 in one of the most perceptive statements, *Excellence without a Soul*, "Universities have lost the sense that their educational mission is to transform teenagers . . . into adults with the learning and wisdom to take responsibility for their own lives and for civil society." Drawing on his own experience, Lewis sees Harvard's leaders as having "allowed the school's mission to drift from education to consumer satisfaction." Parents and students are consumers looking for return on their investments. Faculty members

The Soul of the American University Revisited. George M. Marsden, Oxford University Press. © Oxford University Press
2021. DOI: 10.1093/oso/9780190073312.003.0025

are as specialists hired and promoted almost solely based on scholarly reputation and see their university position as primarily a way for advancing
their careers. Undergraduate education is a duty but not a priority. Scientific
ideals and pressures for globalization help subordinate the humanities and
concerns for what it means to be human.[5]

Similarly, in another eloquent plea, Anthony Kronman, former Dean of
Yale Law School, laments that colleges and universities "have given up on the
meaning of life." Kronman, like Lewis, is of the generation that could look
back to more consensus-oriented elite humanistic education that was the
ideal (even if not always the reality) prior to the late 1960s. Contrary to those
who might argue that it was the "death of God" that accounts for the moral
incoherence of mainstream contemporary universities, Kronman argues
that it was the death of humanity. His solution is to resuscitate a robust "secular humanism," which, he argues, was what from the time of Charles Eliot
to the late 1960s provided a common ground for universities to explore the
meaning of life. That outlook, most clearly represented in "the tradition of
European arts and letters," had offered coherence in the absence of common
religious authority.[6] But the humanities helped destroy such humanism, first
by adopting the research ideal and then by adopting a superficial multiculturalism that made educators suspicious of Western ideals. Soon the laudable ideal of inclusion had come to mean epistemic inclusion that favored
the points of view of those who could claim to be previously excluded and
oppressed. That, in turn, was justified by "constructivism" or various "postmodern" views that saw truth as social constructions determined largely by
power. Lost in this method of inclusivism was any basis for looking for principles of common humanity that could provide common ground. Hence, the
universities, by trying to value every point of view equally, undercut the idea
that education ought to involve looking for universal principles that might
give individual and collective human life greater meaning and provide a basis
to constructively critique local prejudice.[7]

Columbia University's Andrew Delbanco, in *College: What It Was, Is, and
Should Be* (2012), shared many of Anthony Kronman's concerns that some
of the essential humane benefits of college education were in grave danger of
being lost. Yet he also wrestled with the fact that one of these ideals—"a sense
of ethical responsibility"— had helped create one of the greatest challenges to
preserving that ideal. That is that college education has become mass education, and rightly so. But proposals such as Kronman's, which in effect would
recover idyllic times when students had the leisure to reflect on the meaning

of life, involve a certain elitism. "For many more students," writes Delbanco, "college means the anxious pursuit of marketable skills in overcrowded, underresourced institutions, where little attention is paid to that elusive entity sometimes called the 'whole person.'" For others, the classroom exists only in cyberspace. He writes, "But it is a nightmare society that affords the chance to learn and grow only to the lucky few."[8]

The greatest culprit, according to Delbanco and to many other recent writers, is the "commodification" of higher education that is in the service of corporate capitalism. Our society, as has long been the case, is "dedicated to the one overriding purpose of economic expansion,"[9] and our universities are subordinated to that function. Such influences involve not only external corporate and government interests shaping universities through their funding, but also the internalization of the ideal by students and parents that the purpose of education is to advance economically within the system. As Delbanco points out, the corruption of universities by corporate interests has been a major theme in recent analyses of higher education as suggested by a host of book titles such as *Saving Higher Education in the Age of Money, Universities in the Marketplace: The Commercialization of Higher Education, Shakespeare, Einstein, and the Bottom Line: The Marketing of Higher Education,* and *University Inc.: The Corporate Corruption of Higher Education*—to name just a few.[10]

While those who see largely impersonal capitalist market forces that shape the culture as the greatest threat to humane education, a related diagnosis that became increasingly prominent in the 2010s sees the well-meant remedies for the division and inequalities of our society as having made the situation even worse. Although the commentaries on these issues are likewise vast, one useful entry into the discussion is William Egginton's *The Splintering of the American Mind: Identity Politics, Inequality, and Community on Today's College Campuses* (2018). Egginton, a professor of humanities at Johns Hopkins, sets the discussion of breakdown of community, of intellectual common ground, and even of communication in the universities in the context of the sharpening divisions in American society generally. He does not blame the current crisis primarily on the universities, but he sees them as not helping to resolve it either. Egginton regrets the displacement of the humane core of mid-twentieth-century education, not only for its edifying content, but more essentially because of its now-lost purpose of providing common ground for building civic society. In fact, he sees the redirection of the core as "necessary and beneficial" for the sake of women, gays, and minorities who

had "suffered generations of discrimination and violence." Yet he sees laudable efforts as having been "hijacked by the cult of the consumer and the ever-
increasing specialization of academic knowledge."[11] The consumer culture
feeds on an "ideology of extreme individualism." That leads to: "the idealiza-
tion of the individual, his or her racial, ethnic, or gender identity, and his or
her desires and rights as a consumer have been strengthened by the current
extremes of income inequality, by way of a they-have-theirs-so-I-should-
have-mine-too attitude." As a result, "our natural tendencies toward ethno-
centrism have become harder to overcome." What has been lost are some of
the central purposes of American education that characterized it from the
time of Jefferson through the mid-twentieth century. Those ideals involved
looking for a common humanity, learning how to communicate and understand each other across differences, contributing to building a civic society
by cultivating a common heritage, identity, and set of values, and cultivating
character and not just skills.[12]

Jonathan Haidt and Greg Lukianoff, in *The Coddling of the American Mind*
(2018), offer a complementary analysis. The good intentions of those who are
working for inclusiveness in higher education and in the wider culture, they
argue, are subverted by some bad ideas that have led to greater polarization.
One of these bad ideas is "safteyism" that encourages a "victimhood culture"
in which everyone has to be protected from offense. That, in turn, leads to
an academic culture in which, rather than students being encouraged to understand and appreciate perspectives differing from their own, students may
come to believe that they have a right not to be exposed to views that they regard as offensive or hurtful. Such attitudes are exacerbated by the human tendencies toward tribalism that have been heightened in recent years, in part by
electronic media and a polarized political culture. Meanwhile, identity politics has encouraged dividing the world between "victims and oppressors."
Students learn "to interpret the actions of others in the least generous way
possible." Even though Haidt and Lukianoff recognize that many of the underlying concerns are legitimate, the ability to distinguish those from the
frivolous is often lost in a culture in which students are encouraged to "always trust their feelings." According to Haidt and Lukianoff, "If someone
wanted to create an environment of perpetual anger and intergroup conflict,
this would be an effective way to do it."[13]

Haidt and Lukianoff, in much the same spirit as the other authors, believe
that at the core of university culture should be searches for truth, wisdom,
common humanity, and learning through trying to maximize opportunities

for free speech and open exchanges of opinion. If universities are to be meaningfully diverse institutions serving the welfare of the large society, they need to be places that cultivate learning to understand those with whom one differs, rather than simply try to silence them. The authors contrast current polarized identity politics with the "common humanity identity politics" of Martin Luther King Jr. King appealed not to difference but to "the shared morals and identities of Americans" and even, drawing on his religious commitments, referred to those whom he disagreed with as "brothers and sisters." Love and forgiveness rather than hate were to be essential components in reform. Rather than divide the world into good people versus evil people, say Haidt and Lukianoff, we need to recognize that "the line dividing good and evil cuts through the heart of every human being."[14]

One need not agree with all of these critiques drawn from this sampling of some prominent twentieth-first-century laments regarding the state of mainstream American universities to conclude that there is, at the least, a chorus of credible voices saying that universities have largely lost their way in what was once their central task. That task was to provide an education that would expose students to a variety of viewpoints while fostering critical perspectives that could help them sort out truth and error. The goal would be to serve students and the larger society by seeking both to understand common humanity and to appreciate difference in a context oriented toward seeking justice and cultivating virtues. Without doubt, all that still sometimes happens, thanks in part to authors such as those we have considered and many like them in the professoriate. Moreover, it should be said that in many respects contemporary universities *do* achieve the goal of serving society. For instance, much of university expansion over the past century has been in technological areas, medical schools, and specialized research in health-related studies. Other studies in the sciences and social sciences have provided invaluable resources for serving humanity and for understanding, utilizing, and protecting the natural order in countless ways. Much of the practical training in universities is also oriented toward improving the quality of life and serving others. In many such areas, American universities are the best in the world. And even in notorious episodes of ideological conflict, the excesses of a few should not judge the hundreds of American universities.

Even so, there is no denying that even the best of twenty-first-century American universities sometimes have been plagued by polarized, contending interest groups not open to listening to each other.[15] Genuine quests to seek truth and justice and to serve good purposes may be subverted by conflicting high ideals. Or they may be swamped and undermined by the necessities of serving the market in a materialistic, individualistic, hedonistic, consumerist, corporate-dominated, technological society.[16]

So how does the current situation relate to our historical narrative regarding the role of religion in the universities? First, it is helpful to consider the broader context. As described in the introduction to the present volume, we live in a postsecular age. That is not to say that, as a whole, secular viewpoints are necessarily diminishing and that religions are triumphing. Rather, it is to observe that, contrary to many mid-twentieth-century predictions, secularism is not steadily triumphing as religion inevitably recedes in the face of modernity. Religion, even some traditional forms of religion, seems to be here to stay, even as all sorts of secularism and secular outlooks also flourish in the contemporary world.

Second, although mainstream universities may be among the places in our culture where secular ideologies particularly flourish, the campus conflicts and choruses of dissatisfaction suggest that secularism itself is in disarray. It is no longer widely plausible to assert, as it was in the mid-twentieth century, that while religious ideologies are essentially irrational and sources of human conflict, rational, scientifically based, and humane secular ideologies offer the solutions for bringing people into agreement. Rather, competing secular ideologies are as much sources of conflict as are dogmatic religious beliefs. It is true that there are still sharp conflicts between some religious and some secular viewpoints, but those are only one small part of ideological disarray.

Third, the many laments in recent decades about the decline of the humanities bear on the consideration of religion in mainstream higher education. As we have seen, from the late nineteenth century through the 1960s, the humanities were often seen as the surrogate for religion as the provider of insight to the meaning and purposes of life. In the twenty-first century, thanks in part to their own deconstructive tendencies, the humanities are often seen as not serving such purposes or as central to higher education, and thus they have receded to marginal roles.[17]

That decline is also related to changing student perceptions of the purposes of higher education. As one recent lament observes, "In 1970, seven in 10 students thought it was very important or essential to 'develop a meaningful philosophy of life' through education, while about four in 10 (and five in 10 men) put a priority on using it to 'make more money.' By the mid-'80s, these ratios had flipped. Since then these ratios have flatlined." The author comments that "Of all the statistics on the humanities I've seen, I find this one the most depressing": that less than half of first-year college students "think highly enough of crafting a life philosophy in the course of their studies to muster the energy to fill out a bubble indicating as much."[18]

Still, despite some declines, the United States remains a place that includes relatively large percentages of religious believers, and so religion remains a significant, if diffuse, presence on campuses. American higher education is more diverse than it ever was, and that means its constituency is more diverse religiously than it ever was. Furthermore, students visiting from other countries or who are recent immigrants are also significant contributors to religious diversity. So mainstream universities, in fact, make room for and accommodate varieties of religious practices and outlooks, even if those religious interests operate largely independently of the universities' direct guidance.

Even the professoriate, though considerably less religious than the general American public, includes substantial percentages of the professedly religious. One careful survey in the early twenty-first century showed that at non-elite doctoral-granting universities, over half of the professors believe in God, even while almost another quarter are atheist or agnostic. At elite universities, the number of professed believers drops to about one-third, and the atheist/agnostic category is just over one-third. Of all professors, (including those at religiously affiliated schools), 27.3% were Roman Catholic, and 18.8% said that "born-again" Christian described them at least slightly. The percentages of atheists and agnostics, especially at elite schools, are much higher than in the general public, and the numbers who would affirm being "born again" are much lower.[19] Yet the percentages of believers are still substantial, so that no one group or set of groups, whether religious or nonreligious, can be said to hold a monopoly on higher education. In the multitude of voices and forces that compete to shape mainstream American academia, therefore, it is impossible to provide a precise overall characterization of the roles of religions and religious beliefs beyond that they are rarely a major influence.[20] So one can say that religion is often marginalized, especially in intellectual inquiry. Yet there is no one clearly defined place for religious beliefs, practices, and perspectives.

Despite the significant presence of religion in modern American higher education, some documented discrimination in the academic mainstream clearly exists against certain types of religious beliefs. Surveys have shown that close to half of academics in the social sciences and the humanities are willing to say that if they knew that a job candidate or a graduate school applicant was a fundamentalist or an evangelical, that would have some negative impact on their evaluation of that candidate. Such acknowledged biases against fundamentalists and evangelicals are higher than those against Mormons (still considerable) and far higher than those concerning mainline Protestants, Catholics, or Jews. Such attitudes vary somewhat across disciplines and are less pronounced among those in the hard sciences.[21] Moreover, some of the bias against fundamentalists or evangelicals is likely fueled in part by political biases. The rise of the religious right since the 1970s and white "evangelicals" becoming its most solid constituency have blurred the line between "fundamentalist" and "evangelical." Since academics, particularly in the social sciences and humanities, tend to be disproportionately liberal or Democratic, they likely perceive anyone who could be identified as fundamentalist or evangelical as perhaps bringing with them a Religious Right, "culture wars" agenda.[22] Such biases may have increased with the polarization related to the election of Donald Trump as president in 2016. The impact of such biases is, of course, very difficult to measure.

Acknowledging that there is some discrimination, especially against conservative white American religious groups, the biases are far from absolute, and the larger picture reveals that religious interests of almost every sort have made modest gains in the American academy since the 1970s. That is the conclusion of the recent sociological study by John Schmalzbauer and Kathleen A. Mahoney titled *The Resilience of Religion in American Higher Education* (2018). In an impressively thorough survey of the data from many studies, Schmalzbauer and Mahoney document their thesis that, contrary to the secularization thesis, religion has been remarkably resilient in the American academy.[23] In a sense, their study provides the sequel to the story told in the present volume. The difference is that my historical focus is on the often-ironic history of the informal Protestant establishment. I was also specifically interested in the questions of the degree to which Protestant Christianity did or did not provide normative influences, how much it was shaped by other cultural influences, and how it often combined with those related cultural influences in shaping mainstream American higher education. The narrative of that Protestant story essentially comes to an end by the 1970s with the informal disestablishment of mainline Protestantism.[24] Schmalzbauer and Mahoney's is a broader sociological study of the many ways that all sorts of religion has sprung back after disestablishment, often in the crevices, but springing back significantly nonetheless. Only a relatively small part of that story has any direct connection with the old mainline Protestant establish- ment. Various forms of Protestantism are, however, among the grassroots sorts of religion found on campuses.

Among the measures that Schmalzbauer and Mahoney use to gauge the resilience of religion is that of academic interest in studying about religion. Not only is the field of religious studies that emphasizes comparative reli- gion a flourishing discipline, but today religion is also a matter of growing interest in some other academic fields. For instance, in my own field of his- tory, the American Historical Association reported that in 2009 religious his- tory had become the most popular sub-field reported among its members.[25] One reason for such resurgence is simply the increasing prominence of re- ligion, especially of Islam, in world affairs since the fall of the Soviet Union and the corresponding increasing consciousness, especially since September 11, 2001, of the place of Islam in American life. Furthermore, in some fields such as history, political science, international studies, and the like that are shaped considerably by politics, the increase in direct influences of religion in American politics since the rise of the religious right has reinforced the point that, like it or not, religious forces remain prominent among those to be reckoned with.[26] Some of the increase is simply a matter of academic interest, but some of it comes from scholars who openly avow the perspectives of their own religious commitments.[27]

A significant index of religious resilience in recent decades is that of stu- dent religious expression and practice. Religion in the United States has flourished best when it emerged voluntarily from the "bottom up" rather than being imposed from positions of power. The lack of an effective reli- gious establishment, combined with a huge variety of religious beliefs, has helped foster the unusual vitality of religious groups in the United States. Those have been major factors in distinguishing the United States from other highly industrialized nations of the Western world, where religious prac- tice has dropped dramatically since early in the twentieth century. Not only have American revivalist groups of various races and ethnicities cultivated grassroots religious commitment, but also American immigrant groups have found the experience of being a minority in a diverse society as one leading them toward strengthening their religious faith as a voluntary choice. It is not surprising then, that the sequel to disestablishment of any privileged religion on campuses has been vitality in student religious expression, rather than its diminishment.

Christian campus ministries such as InterVarsity Christian Fellowship and Cru (formerly Campus Crusade for Christ) have grown significantly since the 1960s and enjoyed steady and substantial gains since the 1990s.[28] That growth has been fed in part by growing Asian-American populations on campuses. While such evangelical parachurch ministries, which combined include something over a quarter-million students, do not represent a large percentage of all students, they are a significant presence. Hundreds of thousands more students are served by denominational and local church ministries and by nationally unaffiliated campus evangelical organizations. Catholic Campus ministries and local churches touch comparable numbers. Something like 5.5 million students are Catholic. Of those at nonsectarian schools, about one-fifth of seniors report attending religious services regularly, and about half say they do so occasionally. About 15% of Catholic students participate in a campus-based religious group. Jewish, Muslim, and mainline Protestant groups have all experienced revitalization, especially since the 1990s.[29] At many schools, chaplains' offices that once were Protestant have been transformed into interfaith ministries, including support for a wide range of religious practices.[30] Altogether, even though something like three out of four university students are not actively practicing a religion, the substantial minority who are active offer some vital presences on campuses.[31] In 2007, toward the end of his long ministry as chaplain at Harvard, Peter Gomes, a Trinitarian Christian, remarked that on Harvard's campus "there is probably more active religious life now than there has been in 100 years." Observers at other campuses agreed that there had been an upturn in in religious interest in recent decades.[32]

One phenomenon that both points to the resilience of religion and adds to the ironies of the story told here is that however secularized and occasionally even anti-religious American higher education has become, there is still a positive correlation between college or university education and active religious affiliation. That is, the rate of decline in religious participation of Americans between the ages of 18 and 22 is higher among those who do *not* attend college than among those who do. Though in the twenty-first century there has been the well-known rise of the "nones" in that age group so that percentage of ages of college freshman with no religion rose from 15.4% in 1971 to 31% in 2016, university experience itself was not likely to weaken faith. College experience is more likely to liberalize students' faith to some degree, but also more likely to strengthen it. Only 14% of seniors said their faith had been weakened during the college years, while 38% reported it had been strengthened.[33]

Multiple reasons might be offered for this phenomenon. Sociologist Christian Smith, who has extensively studied the spiritual lives of young Americans, suggests several factors. Growing numbers of committed Protestant and Catholic faculty members who model relating faith to academic life may play a role. Further, the growth of intellectual relativism in some fields has undermined old positivist critiques of faith as being "unscientific." Or, ironically, a decrease in students seeing higher education as involving a quest for "the meaning of life" and an increase in seeing it as essentially instrumental for improving one's marketability may mean that faiths are less often undermined in the classroom. Further, as Smith himself has shown, students in recent decades tend to be quite conventional and not as rebellious against their parents' beliefs as is sometimes assumed. And in a culture that can be seen as "postsecular" rather than increasingly secular, there is not necessarily a perception that being less religious makes one more advanced and in step with the sophisticated spirit of the age.[34]

While religion clearly retains a visible presence on American university campuses, its relationship to the value and practice of "diversity" in mainstream higher education remains problematic. In principle, religion is recognized as a kind of diversity that ought to be accepted and honored on campuses. In practice, however, it is often neglected in diversity training and in related new general education requirements on many campuses that concentrate on diversity in race, gender, and sexuality. That is the finding of Eboo Patel, who, working from a Muslim perspective, has become one of the leading advocates for finding healthy ways to deal with religious diversity on campuses. Patel emphasizes the value of finding common ways that various religions can contribute to strengthening the civic order in a democracy that is committed to permitting religious diversity. Patel sees colleges and universities as "mini civil societies" so that they can be "key sites for building pluralism."[35] John Inazu, another advocate of protecting religious diversity on campus, is less optimistic that it is possible to find the "common good" that various religious and secular interest groups can agree on. He believes it is better to strengthen the law to ensure equal treatment.[36] Inazu, a legal scholar, has been a strong proponent of a "confident pluralism" that seeks equal protection of both religious and secular diversities in a genuinely pluralistic society.[37]

Among the unresolved issues on campus, and in society at large, are those concerning whether in the name of diversity some groups may be excluded for not being sufficiently diverse. A striking example of this paradox is that some Christian student organizations, such as InterVarsity Christian Fellowship and Young Life, have been denied recognition and access to university facilities at a number of campuses because they have required consent to a credal statement as a condition for leadership in the organization. School regulations against such practices have been difficult to sustain and have been withdrawn in some cases due to legal challenges. One issue is the problematic character of applying the same principle to every religious group, such as Muslim or Orthodox Jewish, or of requiring every organization dedicated to a specific purpose to be open to being led by those who might reject that purpose.[38] Another consideration is that if every organization were required to be diverse in exactly the same ways, then the diversity policies would be limiting the diversity among organizations.[39] In a sense it might be seen as a reversion to an establishment of an orthodoxy.

Further, the laudable ideal of promoting "diversity" itself involves a deeper problem. The goal of maximizing "diversity," like the ideal of "academic freedom," always involves limits. Every social group or institution rules out some sorts of behaviors, attitudes, beliefs, or identities as unacceptable. Practically speaking, defining what is not permitted becomes especially problematic when the behaviors or teachings of two otherwise acceptable groups may be offensive to each other. To what extent do religious or other private groups have the right to set their own rules even if those would be unacceptable or even offensive rules for the wider society? For instance, should Orthodox Jews, Muslims, Catholic, or fundamentalist groups be free to limit their clergy leadership to males? One of the first principles in maintaining a diverse civil society or institution is that people have to be taught how to live together with difference. Tolerance and diversity have to go hand in hand. Yet, given that in every society some types of behaviors will be ruled out for everyone, on what grounds ought administrators decide which to tolerate and which to exclude? What are the common principles to which they might appeal?

This is not the place to attempt to resolve such complex issues that can never be resolved to everyone's satisfaction. Nonetheless, observers such as Patel and Inazu are both correct in recognizing that a valuable part of the American heritage has been the ideal (however imperfectly realized) of tolerating religiously based diversity even if the larger community does not approve of the religious practices involved. That valued principle has to be weighed, of course, against other common principles and interests. Still, the religious identity of students is a diversity issue that is not going to go away and ought not be neglected. The operative goal ought to build campus communities that maximize tolerance and respect for deeply held differences.

Overall, then, we can say that religious beliefs and practices on American campuses continue to prove themselves to be meaningful and durable into the twenty-first century. While examples of anti-religious prejudices persist, there also remain many countervailing outlooks and practices. The ideological disarray of mainstream higher education seems to open up opportunities for religious expression in academia even in an era of overall cultural decline in percentages of religious practice. Moreover, increasing international student populations have provided a new source of religious vitality on campuses. Organized religions provide communities that can offer identity, support, fellowship, and purpose as alternatives to a larger culture where these values seem to be eroding. Mainstream university campuses, despite their well-documented flaws and challenges, continue to be places where such communities can flourish as minority viewpoints.

Epilogue

An Unexpected Sequel: A Renaissance of Christian Academia

> The obscurantism of the orthodox portion of Protestantism has created a cleavage between religion and education, particularly in the south, the middle west, and the far west. . . .
>
> The[se] culturally obscurantist versions of the Protestant faith are so irrelevant to religion in higher education that no policy in the academic program can hope to overcome the irrelevance.
>
> Reinhold Niebuhr, *The Contribution of Religion to Cultural Unity*, 1945[1]

By the 1970s, as we have seen, the centuries-old story of efforts to make Protestant Christianity integral to mainstream American higher education had come to an end.[2] During the ensuing decades some of the more widely shared ideals in universities, such as service to society and enriching human life, could be seen as including some Protestant DNA. A good bit of the idealism nonetheless had transformed itself into competing campus social-political ideologies. And the multiversities were increasingly being seen as valuable chiefly for resources fostering technological advance and teaching marketable skills rather than anything higher. As the twenty-first-century academic jeremiads on the decline of the humanities and of constructive civil discourse suggest, aspirations of universities to generate common ideals for society are generally seen as being in disarray.[3]

In the meantime, during that same era, there has been a sequel to the story of Christianity and American higher education that few in the mid-twentieth century would have predicted. Rather than a fading away, there has been a remarkable resurgence of self-consciously Christian teaching, learning, and scholarship. During the past half-century, colleges and universities with specifically Christian standards for their faculties have grown substantially both

The Soul of the American University Revisited. George M. Marsden, Oxford University Press. © Oxford University Press 2021. DOI: 10.1093/oso/9780190073312.003.0026

in size and in quality, even if collectively they still make up only a small portion of the American collegiate scene. Furthermore, university-level scholarship that is explicitly Christian has been burgeoning in recent decades not only in theology but also in a host of academic fields. And especially remarkable is that a significant segment[4] of this resurgence comes from among the heirs to what Reinhold Niebuhr wrote off as the hopelessly obscurantist "orthodox portion of American Protestantism."

In the mid-twentieth century, if the academic institutions and intellectual efforts of such "fundamentalists" or conservative evangelicals were noticed at all, they were likely to be regarded as the late flowering of nearly extinct species, rather than harbingers of a significant intellectual renewal movement. A telling example is the definitive study of American higher education, *The Academic Revolution*, by David Riesman and his Harvard colleague, Christopher Jencks, published in 1968. When Jencks and Riesman turned to "Protestant Denominations and Their Colleges," they first remarked that it was "perhaps a tribute to the present influence of academic professionalism" that they could postpone this topic until the eighth chapter: "A century ago this would have been chapter one." By the 1960s the great majority of formerly Protestant schools were dropping any denominational distinctives and "in part this was probably a matter of natural selection." "Colleges founded to preserve a particular kind of orthodoxy," Jencks and Riesman explained, "had a much lower life expectancy than colleges whose founders possessed a more expansive and more academic view of their role." As a matter of self-preservation, most colleges had to diversify their student bodies and prioritize professional, rather than religious, standards for their faculties.[5] Here was the secularization thesis in its classic form.

Still there were the "holdouts." These included such "remnants of pre-industrial America," as, for instance, The Brethren, the Adventists, the Mennonites, and the Church of God. And, of course, there were the Mormons, who had "never distrusted education in the way many other fundamentalist sects do."[6] Jencks and Riesman also saw the anticommunism of "the radical right" as accounting for a few Protestant colleges, such as Pepperdine in Southern California or Harding College in Arkansas. Otherwise, "very few Protestant colleges . . . admit that the substance of what they teach is influenced by ideological considerations."

To this last remark, Jencks and Riesman added a footnote pointing to Wheaton College in Illinois as "a partial exception." To the note they added, "There are a few other exceptions, such as Calvin College in Michigan and a number of Southern fundamentalist colleges of which Bob Jones University in South Carolina is probably the best known." Partisans of Wheaton or Calvin might have taken heart that they thus made it at least onto the low-altitude radar of the Harvard sociologists, which is more than could be said of quite a few other "evangelical" colleges, such as Westmont in California, Bethel in Minneapolis, Taylor in Indiana, Gordon in Massachusetts, or North Park in Chicago. But registering as such a blip at Harvard was hardly compensation for not only being classified with the "hold outs" but also being placed in the same sentence as strictly fundamentalist and notoriously racist Bob Jones University.[7] The praise could hardly have been fainter.

While Jencks and Riesman seemed to be intrigued by the possibility that someday a Catholic school might be able to be competitive with the better universities in "academic professionalism" while fusing that "with concern of ultimate social and moral importance,"[8] a groundswell of discussion of these very topics that was developing within the evangelical networks went unnoticed. Such commentary could be found in the circles associated with *Christianity Today*, the flagship magazine for those evangelicals sympathetic to Billy Graham who were trying to rebuild an intellectual presence. Wheaton College and to a lesser extent Calvin College were, indeed, key building blocks in that effort. Still, from the perspective of mainstream academia, these institutions were tainted with the heritage of fundamentalism and were "holdouts" on the way to extinction, rather than anything like heralds of something new.

William McLoughlin of Brown University, one of the most distinguished religious historians of the era, similarly interpreted the whole groundswell of evangelical and Pentecostal movements through the lens of the secularization thesis. In a 1967 essay titled "Is There a Third Force in Christendom?," McLoughlin responded to speculations that a reconfiguration of Christendom was appearing in which these new revivalist groups would be a major force in addition the long-standing Protestant/Catholic divide. In McLoughlin's view, these groups were "fringe sects" and, rather than having the potential to become a significant cultural movement, "appear to be the usual and inevitable emotional and institutional effluvia of a major alteration within Christendom."[9] So the modern world might be giving birth to something new, but it would be essentially the superficial side effects of adjustments to a progressive secularity.

We should not be surprised that Ivy League professors did not recognize that evangelical higher education and scholarship might be more than the last gasps for intellectual air of a dying movement. The background was the fundamentalist movement, which only a few decades earlier had led to separation from mainstream intellectual life, symbolized by rejection of biological evolution. Fundamentalists insisted on the supreme intellectual authority of the Bible, literally interpreted. Virtually everyone in the 1960s was aware of Billy Graham, and those informed on such matters would know that he had jettisoned some of the extreme separatist fundamentalism in favor of a broader evangelical revivalism. Still, the fundamentalist image was dominant. One of the most influential academic books of the 1960s was Richard Hofstadter's Pulitzer Prize–winning *Anti-intellectualism in American Life*. There Hofstadter, noting that Graham was one of "the most admired men" in America, offered as one of his opening "Exhibits" of "Anti-Intellectualism in Our Time," a lengthy quotation in which the evangelist condemned just about every trend and "ism" in the academic world. Hofstadter went on to anchor his historical analysis of American anti-intellectualism with three substantial chapters on the evangelical spirit, revivalism, and the fundamentalist revolt against modernity.[10]

Billy Graham was not opposed to careful intellectual inquiry as such. In fact, he expressed high regard for quality Christian scholarship and cultivated associations with some of the leading scholars who shared his theological outlook. He was at the same time an heir to a generation of fundamentalist hostility to the intellectual mainstream and so condemned most of the intellectual trends of the day. Furthermore, as a revivalist he was part of a populist heritage that thrived on simplistic formulas and might be properly classed as anti-intellectual. Yet, despite using some such rhetoric, as in his biblicist apocalyptic prediction of imminent doom preceding Christ's return to earth to set up a millennial kingdom, Graham was also promoting more substantial intellectual renewal among his massive constituency. He recognized that the fundamentalist heritage was intellectually deficient and believed that regaining scholarly credibility would in the long run be crucial to the witness of traditionalist Christianity.[11]

Among Graham's closest allies in this regard were a number of scholars at Fuller Theological Seminary, founded in 1947 in Pasadena, California. The vision for the seminary had come largely from Harold John Ockenga, who held a Ph.D. in philosophy and remained pastor of Park Street Church next to the Boston Common, even while he served as the new seminary's president in absentia. During the mid-1940s Ockenga had hosted a number of "scholar's conferences," in which he brought some of the few accomplished

A RENAISSANCE OF CHRISTIAN ACADEMIA 369

evangelical scholars to New England to discuss strategies for intellectual renewal.[12] Ockenga was also the founder of the National Association of Evangelicals in 1942, and he was the leading organizer of what he called the "New Evangelicals," a movement to renew fundamentalism. Following Billy Graham's sensational evangelistic success in Los Angeles in 1949, Ockenga provided the next venue for a highly successful Graham campaign in Boston that helped set the pattern for Graham's work in the next decades.

Ockenga's and Graham's point man for intellectual renewal was Carl F. H. Henry of Fuller Seminary. Henry earned a doctorate in philosophy at Boston University in addition to a Th.D. from Northern Baptist Seminary. Henry's first major publication was a substantial tome appearing in 1946 with the ambitious theme of *Remaking the Modern Mind*. A decade later, when Graham was looking for someone to edit a serious thought journal, Henry, who also had journalistic experience, was an obvious choice. Under Henry's leadership the well-funded new publication, *Christianity Today*, directed primarily at pastors, set a serious tone and published accessible articles by capable conservative theological scholars from the United States and Great Britain.

One of Carl Henry's priorities was to also establish "a great Christian university."[13] Henry, like Billy Graham, was a graduate of Wheaton College, widely regarded as the premier evangelical college. But, as he wrote to Graham in 1955, such schools were not training Christians to address "the cultural crisis, but have abandoned the effective articulation of Christianity in relation to the great cultural issues—education, economics, politics, art, and even theology—to non-evangelical groups." Rather, "their passion has been evangelism and missions, and Christian education in the narrow sense, but not really Christian education in the large."[14]

According to Henry, Wheaton, despite some capable professors, was still in the grip of a pietistic fundamentalist mentality. In 1943, under the presidency of a former missionary, the school had fired its best-known (though contentious) philosopher, Henry's former mentor, Gordon Clark. Further, it had disbanded the philosophy department, teaching the subject only under the auspices of the Bible department. According to Carl Henry, Wheaton also replaced required courses on ethics and theism with those on Scriptural memorization and evangelism.[15] The college had doubled the number of required Bible courses so that all students had the equivalent of a minor in Bible.[16]

In the light of such a state of affairs even at the preeminent evangelical college, Henry pressed hard for making a fresh start and establishing a

Christian University. By 1959, Graham was sufficiently intrigued to sponsor some meetings of evangelical leaders, potential donors, and a number of academics to explore the issue. The new school was to be called "Crusade University" and located near the cultural hub of New York City. Henry believed that the first step would be to found a liberal arts college, but with a strong enough faculty with Ph.D. s so that it could offer degrees right up to the Ph.D. level.[17] After that, a full range of other schools, such as education, business, engineering, law, and medicine, would eventually be added. Where the evangelical community would find the sorts of committed leading Christian scholars even to found a first-rate liberal arts college was not clear. The *New York Times* reported that the initial required investment would be about twenty million dollars.[18]

At a second meeting in October 1960, with a few more academics involved, the conversations faltered on an issue that Henry had thought could be sidestepped. Several of the participants, including one of the few with a university position, thought the school should maintain strict behavioral prohibitions against smoking, drinking, card playing, dancing, and movie attendance, as was standard at schools such as Wheaton. These were still major issues in many evangelical communities with a fundamentalist heritage. Others, who were more strictly Reformed, such as William Harry Jellema, an impressive philosopher from Calvin College, argued that it was arbitrary to single out these behavioral standards while neglecting other sins that might be just as damaging to the faith. Such an impasse was not in itself sufficient to doom the enterprise, but it was symptomatic of larger problems that kept potential major donors, who had their own agendas, from supporting such an ambitious but problematic enterprise.

Though the practical issues of finding sufficient faculty and funding were most likely the immediate cause of the demise of the Crusade University idea, the disagreement over behavioral standards pointed to a more basic problem in trying to mobilize American evangelicals behind such a cause: there was no single evangelical community that could set the standards for such an enterprise. Rather, evangelicalism was a loose coalition of a variety of generically related subgroups, each of which had its own doctrinal and behavioral standards, expectations, and peculiar concerns.[19] They might agree in their admiration for Billy Graham, but beyond that they often disagreed about their ways of defining the exact boundaries of the faith.

The state of evangelical higher education illustrated the point. One could identify scores of small denominational colleges and Bible institutes.

Virtually all of these had been shaped by the impulses of the fundamentalist era to defend the faith and to protect young people from the worst dangers of modern thought and mores. Each was sectarian in the sense of maintaining a distinct set of doctrines, practices, and behavioral standards. There were also a few denominationally independent colleges such as Wheaton or its smaller counterparts, Westmont on the West Coast and Gordon in New England. These schools required their faculties to subscribe to conservative evangelical or fundamentalist doctrinal statements and had strict behavioral codes prohibiting smoking, drinking, dancing, movie or theater attendance, and card playing. They might easily be viewed as leftovers from the fundamentalist era, and hardly a promising wave of the future. It is easy to understand why Reinhold Niebuhr (or Carl Henry, for that matter) would see them as culturally irrelevant, and David Riesman and Christopher Jencks would dismiss such evangelical colleges as a whole as "holdouts" from a bygone era.

Yet if we look more closely at the "possible exceptions" of the 1960s, Wheaton and Calvin (and some others might have been included), we can see that alongside their heritages of defensiveness from the fundamentalist era, there were already important signs of what would prove an academically impressive future. Wheaton in the 1960s was in the midst of perennial struggles with its fundamentalist heritage. A strict behavioral code and "pledge" from students and faculty to avoid smoking, drinking, dancing, card playing, and movies remained firmly in place. But the most conspicuous intellectual issue was the classic fundamentalist stance concerning evolution and Creation. One of the features of the "new evangelical" movement was that some evangelical scientists associated with The American Scientific Affiliation, founded in 1941 as an organization for conservative Bible-believing scientists, had been cautiously pushing toward making it allowable for evangelicals to hold to "theistic evolution." They argued that the Bible allowed some room for evolutionary explanations of the means God used to create, even if humans were in some sense a special creation. Some Wheaton professors were sympathetic to this cause, and one zoologist, Russell Mixter, in particular lightning rod.[20] Mixter's view, which he called "progressive creationism," was an especially cautious one, trying to fit evolutionary science with the Genesis accounts. Mixter and other sympathetic faculty members assured college leaders that they truly followed the biblical account, but that was not enough for the hardline fundamentalist critics of the college, including one who was a trustee. In 1961, the college accordingly added an addendum to its doctrinal standards stating that Adam and Eve were the first parents of the entire human race, "created by a direct act of God and not from previously existing forms of life." Despite subsequent faculty urging to remove the addendum, the trustees refused.[21]

As the faculty pushback suggests, Wheaton was, in fact, changing. Or one might say that the Wheaton of the future was beginning to take on a new life within the shell of its fundamentalist past. Many of the faculty and student body were looking for a richer Christian intellectual heritage. Yet the institution was still controlled by a Board of Trustees and a constituency susceptible to angry populist alarms over perceived deviations from the shibboleths of the fundamentalist era. That would long remain a feature of the school and, more broadly, a feature of white American evangelicalism. Even though parts of the many-sided movement, especially its academic centers, proved to be capable of remarkable intellectual renewal, that still left most others in the immense conglomeration untouched. Many in the populist constituencies that might provide money and sit on governing boards might also prefer to rely on more simplistic formulas regarding the Bible, science and Creation, America as a Christian nation, the coming millennium, personal behavior, and the like.[22]

A look at the work of two of the most influential Wheaton professors of the era can illustrate the direction in which things were heading. Clyde Kilby, professor of English, had as a young faculty member in the 1940s discovered the writings of C. S. Lewis and continued throughout his career to promote the British scholar and Christian apologist. Not only did he imbue a love of Lewis among a generation of Wheaton students, but also with his well-received 1964 volume, *The Christian World of C. S. Lewis*,[23] he helped reassure evangelicals that Lewis was, indeed, within the pale. That was not as easy as it might sound. In addition to smoking and drinking, Lewis did not hold that the Bible was without error in all its historical claims, believed God used evolution as a means of creation, had no time for fundamentalist premillennial views, and had a rather ambiguous view of hell. Though he had been a distinguished scholar and teacher at Oxford and Cambridge, Lewis would not have come close to being allowed to teach at Wheaton. Yet by 1965, Kilby had established a "C. S. Lewis Collection" at Wheaton, which, by the time of Kilby's retirement in 1981, had grown into the well-funded Marion E. Wade Center for research on Lewis and other British literary scholars. These included Owen Barfield, C. K. Chesterton, George MacDonald, Dorothy Sayers, J. R. R. Tolkien, and Charles Williams—none of whom would have been eligible to serve on the Wheaton faculty. Lewis had by this time become, next to Billy Graham, perhaps the leading saint in the evangelical hierarchy, and his books have remained perennial bestsellers in that subculture.[24]

During the 1950s and 1960s, Kilby's promotion of Lewis represented what proved to be a remarkably effective end run around the fundamentalist defenses. While at Wheaton Kilby was the principal agent for this move, it was more essentially, of course, Lewis's own winsome thoughtfulness, evident orthodoxy, evangelistic concern, and sincere piety that won so many thoughtful American evangelical followers. In a subculture dominated by populists and often-simplistic formulas, many Christians were looking for something with more intellectual depth. Lewis offered such depth while emphasizing that, rather than speak for any Christian sect, he hoped to represent "mere Christianity," that is, beliefs that had been common to virtually all Christian teachings throughout the ages. Essentially these teachings were drawn from the broadly Augustinian tradition that included both Catholics and Protestants and well over a millennium of theological riches.[25]

At the same time, Wheaton's other most popular professor, Arthur F. Holmes, was campaigning for renewal on another front. An émigré from Great Britain who had served in the Royal Air Force, Holmes received his A.B. in Bible from Wheaton in 1950. That same year, Wheaton asked him to stay on to teach philosophy, an offer that, as historian Michael Hamilton observes, "simultaneously demonstrated the faculty's high opinion of Holmes and its low opinion of the discipline of philosophy."[26] Due to earlier controversies, as Carl Henry had lamented, the Philosophy Department had been disbanded, and the subject was taught under the auspices of the Bible department. Holmes educated himself in the classic philosophical principles of the Reformed tradition and eventually, in 1957, earned his Ph.D. in philosophy from Northwestern University. In the meantime, he set about rebuilding the role of philosophy at Wheaton. Especially significant was that in 1955 he established an annual Wheaton Philosophy Conference that incorporated some notable guest speakers from beyond the evangelical circles. For instance, the French phenomenologist, Paul Ricour, gave the keynote address in 1960. The conference helped build a substantial network of Christian philosophers in the region and eventually would contribute to the establishment in 1978 of the widely influential Society of Christian Philosophers.

Not until 1967, however, after a painful struggle that included threats to resign did Holmes achieve his goal of re-establishing a separate Philosophy Department at Wheaton. Meanwhile, Holmes, who was a master teacher, was inspiring students with excitement for the discipline. That was especially significant, because Wheaton, unlike most other evangelical colleges, had a selective admissions policy and Graduate Record Exam scores well above national averages.[27] And because Wheaton was widely seen as the premier evangelical school, the top students included those who could have gone to college anywhere but chose Wheaton because of religious commitments. Holmes's larger goal was to inspire a generation of committed Christian students to provide alternative perspectives in the discipline—he said that his dream was to have a hundred Wheaton graduates who had earned Ph.D.s in philosophy. By 2017 that number had been surpassed, and a number of Wheaton graduates who themselves held university positions were educating more Christian philosophers.[28] In addition, Holmes probably helped motivate at least as many other students to go into academia in other disciplines.

One of the most significant dimensions of Holmes's work was that the annual Wheaton Philosophy Conference connected him with the philosophers at Calvin College in Grand Rapids, Michigan, where philosophy was already well on its way to becoming the preeminent discipline. Though Calvin had been founded as a preparatory school in 1876, it became a regular four-year college in 1920. In 1921 William Harry Jellema established the Philosophy Department. A brilliant teacher by all accounts, Jellema's impact on Calvin anticipated Arthur Holmes's later work at Wheaton and encountered some similar obstacles.

The Christian Reformed Church and Dutch immigrant community that maintained Calvin was deeply committed to preserving its distinctive theological religious heritage from American corruptions. The denomination was descended from a Dutch counterpart that had in the late nineteenth century, under the leadership of Abraham Kuyper, seceded from that country's Reformed state church. That heritage left the Dutch Americans with a strong concern for doctrinal correctness. Yet, unlike most of their doctrinally conservative American evangelical counterparts, rather than having a populist anti-intellectual heritage, they had a strong concern for education. Thus, they maintained their own Christian school system, and their concerns extended to higher education as well. In the Netherlands, Kuyper had founded and led a university as well as a denomination. He was an accomplished theologian and philosopher and became the progenitor of an influential school of Christian thought. He also emphasized the importance of wider Christian cultural engagement, himself serving as Prime Minister of the Netherlands from 1901 to 1905. Everything in life, Kuyper and his followers held, should be guided according to Christian principles, including education.

Deeply loyal to this heritage, the American-born and educated Jellema emphasized its positive dimensions as part of a broader heritage rooted in Augustinian thought and Christian humanism. The 1920s and 1930s, though, were not congenial times for such emphases in conservative American religious communities. Even though the Christian Reformed tended to be suspicious of what they regarded as the superficialities of the American revivalist traditions, the ethos of the national fundamentalist controversies reinforced the defensive side of their heritage, which emphasized the "antithesis" between Christian and non-Christian—and especially modern—attitudes. At Calvin in the 1920s, Jellema came under some scrutiny from theologians suspicious of his philosophical views. While he survived that, the atmosphere in the community was becoming increasingly restrictive. In 1928, the governing synod of the denomination doubled down on enforcement of prohibitions of "worldly amusements," including dancing, gambling, card playing, and movie or theater attendance. When in 1935, a new college president seemed preoccupied with enforcing ideological uniformity and strict behavioral rules, Jellema went into voluntary exile and accepted a position at Indiana University. In the meantime, however, he had inspired many of the best students at Calvin and so laid a foundation for intellectual renewal.[29]

After World War II the tide was turning in Grand Rapids in favor of the more positive side of the heritage. One of Jellema's protégés, Henry Stob, also an inspiring teacher, returned to the college in 1946 after war service to teach philosophy. The college was suddenly burgeoning with new students, many of them war veterans with broader outlooks. By 1948, Harry Jellema felt that the way was clear to return from his exile. During the next fifteen years there, even while tensions with militant conservatives persisted, Jellema was allied with increasing numbers of kindred spirits and former students on the faculty and administration. While not looking professionally much beyond the denomination, these were teachers who set high intellectual standards. While Calvin as a denominational school did not have selective admissions like Wheaton, it did benefit from intense denominational loyalty. So many of the most talented young people in a denomination with a heritage of intellectual and cultural engagement attended the college, and many of them were inspired to go on to graduate study and to return to their alma mater.

By the mid-1960s, had Riesman and Jencks looked at Calvin, they might have seen it as more than "a partial exception" to traditionalist Christian colleges considered to be fading holdouts. But the school was still so insular as to be largely unknown. Over 95% of its faculty were Calvin graduates.

Moreover, despite not having many of the behavioral restrictions of most evangelical colleges, it had other unusually restrictive requirements for faculty, including subscription to classic Reformed doctrinal statements, membership in the Christian Reformed Church, and educating children in Christian schools.

In the midst of such isolation, the annual Wheaton Philosophy Conferences were one small but notable step in bringing Calvin to have American reference points beyond strictly Reformed communities. William Harry Jellema, while at Indiana, had already been a significant influence on Carl Henry and had been enlisted by Harold John Ockenga for ongoing discussions of evangelical scholarly renewal. He was also, at least indirectly, an influence on Arthur Holmes. In any case, the interaction of increasing numbers of Calvin philosophers with their evangelical peers was a harbinger of what would become a remarkable renewal.

Two of Jellema's Calvin students of the early 1950s, Alvin Plantinga and Nicholas Wolterstorff, were especially influential in shaping that renewal. Plantinga, after a year of undergraduate study at Calvin, transferred to Harvard on a scholarship. But on his first spring break he was back at Calvin and sat in on a class taught by Harry Jellema, which convinced him to transfer back to Calvin. In 1954 he began graduate work at Michigan and then moved on to Yale, where he received his Ph.D. in 1957. After a time teaching at Wayne State University, he returned to Calvin in 1963 and stayed there until 1982, when he moved to the University of Notre Dame, where he remained until retiring in 2010. Wolterstorff graduated from Calvin in 1953, received his Ph.D. in philosophy at Harvard in 1956, served as an instructor in philosophy at Yale from 1957 to 1959, then returned to Calvin. He remained there thirty years before going back to Yale to complete his career as the Noah Porter Professor of Philosophical Theology.

In the decades beginning in the 1960s, Plantinga and Wolterstorff, together with William Alston and several other Christian philosophers at Calvin, developed a defense of Christian belief that came to be known as "Reformed epistemology." Plantinga, a powerful analytic logician, became the best-known articulator of this view. His fundamental argument sought to show that, contrary to many twentieth-century views and assumptions, belief in God is not irrational.[30] Wolterstorff, looking back from the twenty-first century, reflected more broadly on the implications of this sort of argument regarding the subject of the place of religion in modern universities. Wolterstorff began with Max Weber's 1918 pronouncements on "Science as a Vocation" as characteristic of what became a powerful motif of much of twentieth-century thought. Meaning by "science" most "academic learning," Weber insisted on the fact/value distinction. "Whenever the man of science introduces his own personal value judgment," Weber affirmed, "a full understanding of the facts *ceases*." Wolterstorff observed that when he was studying at Harvard in the 1950s, such views were still very much in the air. Specifically, "no one spoke of such things as feminist epistemology and black sociology. Had anyone proposed such a thing, her proposal would have been greeted with a blend of incomprehension, horror, and derision." But by the twenty-first century, such perspectives have become commonplace. Thanks to Thomas Kuhn, Hans-Georg Gadamer, and many others, most academics have come to accept that people conduct even their scientific investigations within a tradition. As Wolterstorff presents his own version of what is now a widely accepted position, our "reasoning is always functioning in the service of some particular faith or love, or in the service of some intuition or interpretation of how things are."[31] And along with Plantinga, he argues that belief God is not an irrational faith or love. Such arguments have altered the intellectual playing field in the past half-century or so. Even though in mainstream academia there may be as many or more prejudices against traditional religious perspectives as there ever were, the widely held twentieth-century argument that traditional religious viewpoints ought to be excluded as irrational is no longer viable. Wolterstorff quotes atheist Richard Rorty as stating, regarding the ideal of "basing our views on Enlightenment philosophy," that "the claim that in doing so we are appealing to reason, whereas the religious are being irrational is hokum."[32]

Wolterstorff (whose outlook is very close to that which informs the present volume) also points out that the idea that reason is always in the service of some faith or love is nothing new for Christians in the tradition of Augustine, whose "apothegm borrowed from Clement of Alexander declared *credo ut intelligam*, 'I believe in order that I may know.' Belief is the condition of knowledge, knowledge is the goal of belief."[33] And it can be added that this principle had been already preserved and articulated in the Reformed tradition as refracted through Abraham Kuyper and William Harry Jellema.

By the 1970s, the notion that Christianity provided the foundation for a robust and distinctive approach to higher education—along with its corollary that faith should be "integrated" with all of learning—was spreading widely among evangelical academics. Arthur Holmes was, for instance, an influential popularizer of the outlook, as the titles of his accessible books of the 1970s suggest: *Faith Seeks Understanding: A Christian Approach to Knowledge* (1971), *The Idea of a Christian College* (1975), and *All Truth Is God's Truth* (1977).[34] For many heirs to the fundamentalist heritage, the positive engagements with their disciplines encouraged by such approaches was something of a new departure. Even Carl Henry's efforts for evangelical academic renewal in the 1950s were often framed in combative apologetic terms. As historian Michael Hamilton has described it, he depicted "a Manichean world in which a David-sized evangelicalism was at that moment striking a telling intellectual blow against the Goliath of liberalism." In this view, liberalism included not only secularists but also most mainline Protestant and neo-orthodox scholarship. As a committee for the National Association of Evangelicals put it in 1951, they aspired "to carry the battle to the enemy."[35] By contrast, the new approach, even while starting from a point of faith that was a sharp alternative to most modern outlooks, was largely constructive in its long-term program. The "integration of faith and learning," instead of being a declaration of war on contemporary thought, meant that Christian scholars of many stripes should be earning their places among the diversity of competent voices in the academic mainstream. At the same time, they might bring insights from their academic disciplines to help provide perspectives and guidance for their own communities.

So far this story has been illustrated just through the intellectual opening of two leading schools and the development of some especially influential philosophical ideas. Arguably, these models became the most common ones in shaping other colleges and universities in the evangelical tradition. Yet given the many-sided nature of evangelicalism and its varieties of denominations and institutions, the whole story would be much more complex and lengthy. One could tell similar stories at scores of other evangelical schools and regarding a multiplicity of academic disciplines and involving differing theological traditions and philosophical perspectives.

This "opening of the evangelical mind"[36] that was emerging after the 1960s went hand in hand with social and demographic forces that were changing American evangelicalism and its institutions of higher education. The G.I Bill. and postwar boom in college enrollments had eventually produced more well-trained faculty for Christian colleges. In addition, schools that had been essentially Bible schools were transforming themselves into standard four-year liberal arts colleges. By the later 1960s, a second generation of students and potential scholars was arising who, affected by the spirit of the times, aspired to more positive cultural engagement. By the 1970s, even organizations associated with Billy Graham, such as the Congress on World Evangelicalism, were cautiously endorsing social justice as a goal.[37] Even though most rank-and-file American evangelicals remained deeply suspicious of the cultural mainstream, those aspiring to academic positions were more likely to see their callings as including using the best of the whole range of human thought to help Christians to better understand and influence their culture.

Furthermore, by the 1970s traditionalist or "evangelical" Protestantism was becoming the fastest growing part of American religion, increasing at the same time that mainline Protestantism was decreasing in numbers. Percentages of Americans seeking higher education, including among evangelicals, continued to grow. There was also a developing sense of traditionalist Protestant evangelicals, despite their many varieties, as being part of one movement. Accordingly, *Newsweek* declared 1976 "the year of the evangelical," in reference to the importance of that demographic for Democrat Jimmy Carter's presidential campaign.

That same year, as further evidence of a growing sense of commonality among evangelical educators, the presidents of thirty-eight Christian Colleges met to organize what became the Council for Christian Colleges & Universities (CCCU). The organization rapidly and steadily expanded after that. By 1988 it represented 77 member institutions, and by 2004 that number had climbed to 105, representing 27 denominations.[38]

The diverse constituencies of the schools making up the CCCU illustrate the varieties of approaches to what should be the distinguishing marks of Christian higher education. One important study in the 1990s of "models for Christian higher education" identified seven major Protestant approaches to higher education, in addition to Roman Catholic. Among the Protestants, the Mennonite schools represented the most distinct alternative. As one observer put it, while the Reformed tended to be cerebral, hoping to transform living by thinking, the Mennonites emphasized adopted a radically Christocentric lifestyle, hoping to transform thinking by living.[39] Schools in the various Wesleyan holiness traditions, such as the Nazarene, tended to emphasize more personal devotion, piety, and purity as disciplines of the faith. "Restorationist" schools, most notably in the Churches of Christ tradition, had a particularly strong heritage of emphasizing "the Bible alone" as a source of wisdom. As a result, Churches of Christ schools until the later twentieth century tended to avoid the study of the field of philosophy, on the grounds it involved largely worldly wisdom.[40] Many theologically conservative schools with Baptist heritages, especially those in the Southern Baptist tradition, tended to have similar, though less sharply defined, approaches. Often taking for granted the evangelical piety of students and faculty from the region, they provided and encouraged opportunities for evangelical worship and Bible study, and for making public Christian commitments.[41] Schools such as Wheaton that identified as interdenominational or "evangelical" tended to be mixes of traditions, including both the Reformed and pietistic. Lutheran schools have a heritage of distinguishing "two kingdoms," emphasizing more strongly than do the Reformed the essential incompatibility of Christian and worldly wisdom, so that the two are not so much to be integrated as to be brought into dialogue. Although a few Lutheran schools are affiliated with the CCCU, most identify more with more open mainline Protestant heritage.

During the same decades that schools from a variety of Protestant traditions were building alliances, much the same was happening among self-consciously "Christian" scholars in many of the academic disciplines. Typically by the late 1960s or 1970s, they would find that there were enough like-minded "evangelical" or traditionalist Protestant scholars in a discipline to found a "Christian" academic society. Thus were born organizations such as the Conference on Christianity and Literature, the Conference on Faith and History, the Christian Sociological Society, Association of Christian Economists, Christian Engineering Society, Christian Legal Society, and several others.[42] These societies not only encouraged their members to produce scholarship that would meet the highest standards of the discipline but also encouraged them to do so with self-consciously Christian outlooks and concerns. Such perspectives would not necessarily change the technical aspects of scholarship, but might reorient important dimensions of its purposes, guiding questions, underlying moral principles, and applications.

By far the most influential of these groups was the Society of Christian Philosophers. Organized in 1978, at the suggestion of William Alston, the organization soon published its own formidable journal, *Faith and Philosophy*. Its membership included Catholics as well as Protestants and eventually rose to some six hundred members. While, as already noted, it helped cleared the way for Christian thought more generally by offering critiques of contemporary thought that tried to exclude religious perspectives, the overall thrust of the many publications of its members was positive engagement with every aspect of the field.[43] One signal that its work was respected in the mainstream of American philosophers is that six of its presidents also served as regional presidents of the American Philosophical Association.[44] In other fields the impact on the profession was more limited, though there were a few significant entries into the mainstream here and there.

More broadly, the idea was spreading that self-consciously Christian scholar-teachers should be "integrating faith and learning" and seeking distinct "Christian perspectives" throughout the disciplines. That was becoming something of a mandate in many Christian academic circles. Faculty workshops and student orientations at Christian colleges typically stressed the centrality of faith integration. One small but representative evidence of this trend was that, beginning around 1990, Harper and Row began publishing a series of texts, coordinated by the CCCU, looking at various disciplines, including literature, history, and biology, business, music, and even mathematics, "through the eyes of faith."[45]

Despite these signs of renewal and progress, if we stop to consider the state of evangelical scholarship as it appeared in the early 1990s, it was not at all clear how far it might go. The best evidence of its limitations is found in the lament of one of the most astute evangelical observers, historian Mark Noll, in *The Scandal of the Evangelical Mind* (1994). The scandal of the evangelical mind, he declared bluntly, "is that there is not much of an evangelical mind."[46] Even though Noll, one of the products of Wheaton from the 1960s, was one of the leading figures who was showing that explicitly Christian scholarship could meet the highest academic standards, he did not think there was deep support in the community for that sort of intellectual enterprise. Anti-intellectualism was still strong in much of the evangelical community, and the simplistic shibboleths from the fundamentalist era still could inhibit the academic enterprise, even at places like Wheaton where he was teaching.

At the time, it seemed that the evangelical intellectual enterprise still needed further strengthening. With that in mind, Noll and some others helped initiate in the Pew Christian Scholars Programs. Begun in in 1990 and lasting through the decade, these provided, among other things, substantial funding for Christian research projects, not only for evangelical scholars but also for some Catholics and mainline Protestants.[47] The Pew Younger Scholars program, administered at the University of Notre Dame, offered generous fellowships to encourage some of the brightest Christian (mostly evangelical) college students to enter the top graduate programs in their fields.

At the same time, there were similar moves to promote more traditionalist Christian scholarship among mainline Protestants. The Lilly Foundation, headed by Robert Lynn, already in the 1980s had been supporting efforts of mainline schools and scholars to strengthen the explicitly Christian dimensions of their work. They also supported some evangelical initiatives, such as the Institute for the Study of American Evangelicalism at Wheaton. And Lynn was instrumental in enlisting the Pew Charitable Trusts to support other projects in Christian scholarship, including the original version of the present volume.[48] On the mainline Protestant side, Lutheran schools, especially Valparaiso University, provided leadership in the founding in 1991 of The Lilly Network of Church-Related Colleges and Universities. The Lilly Network has grown to include over one hundred schools. Many of these are schools also associated with the CCCU, but many others are mainline Protestant or Catholic. Over the years, the Lilly Network has promoted Christian academics, especially through a variety of fellowships, grants, and publications encouraging professors to view their teaching and scholarship as a Christian vocation.[49]

Such programs emerging in the 1990s proved to be of immense value in boosting the pace of self-consciously Christian engagement with the academy. They were, as it happened, also catching a wave that was already building. The combination of generations of rising numbers of college-educated evangelicals, the flourishing of Christian colleges, and the growth of campus ministries such as InterVarsity Christian Fellowship were helping to promote rising consciousness of the importance of Christian scholarly engagement.[50] In this decade, young evangelical scholars were crowding into graduate programs, especially those that had some specifically Christian dimension. As a result, CCCU institutions could choose among excellent candidates for faculty positions. So such schools could develop truly high-quality faculties with many excellent teachers comparable to those at selective liberal arts colleges. Some other traditionalist Protestant scholars were finding positions at more secular institutions. Whereas in the 1980s it was relatively rare for scholars in such traditions to publish with university presses, by the early 2000s one could point to considerable lists of such publications. During the same years, more Christian publishers were developing strong lines of academic scholarly publications.[51]

One concern, still being expressed in the early 1990s, as it had been since the 1950s, was the lack of a traditionalist Protestant university that was truly a research center for training future generations of evangelical scholars. Many of the schools in the CCCU already called themselves "universities," but none were offering doctoral programs that could compete with major research universities. The obstacles to establishing a high-quality university with such programs were considerable. Attempting to build it on a coalition of traditions would soon lead to the problem that Carl Henry had encountered of whose tradition would shape the policies. And in most fields, it would seem preferable to have the most talented evangelical students earn their credentials at the top universities rather than at a fledging second-tier institution, despite its Christian commitment.

The major response to these challenges was the transformation of Baylor University as it entered the new century. Founded in 1845, Baylor had long been a respectable but undistinguished Texas Baptist university. Its Christian character had been shaped largely by it being an institution of the Baptist General Convention of Texas, an affiliate of the Southern Baptist Convention. That meant, as had been true of most denominational colleges throughout American history, a reliance on leadership from its denomination and a self-selected predominance of faculty and students who were of its or similar religious persuasion. The Christian dimensions of the institution depended largely on the piety of administrators, faculty, and students and on chapel, Sunday services, and other religious activities to supplement academic study in a Christian atmosphere.

Part of the immediate impetus at Baylor to rethink what it meant to be a Christian university, rather than just a Baptist university, was the threat of a militant conservative or "fundamentalist" takeover. That was happening amid much turmoil at a number of Southern Baptist schools, and Texas Baptists feared that it could happen in their state also. Typically such takeovers involved imposing strict doctrinal standards in theology and mandating other conservative teachings, including a conservative evangelical political agenda. In order to avoid such a possibility, the Baylor Board of Trustees weakened its ties with the Texas Convention so as to ensure the school's virtual independence from denominational regulation. That formal severing of church ties had the paradoxical effect of prodding the Baylor leadership to explicitly address the question of what it meant for a school to be "Christian" as an intentional choice, rather than as simply assumed.

Borrowing largely from the Reformed precedents then current in many evangelical educational circles, Baylor's leaders explicitly made "the integration of faith and learning" a high priority.[52] Enlisting some core faculty behind this ideal, they looked to the University of Notre Dame, practically speaking, as a possible model. Notre Dame was maintaining its "Catholic character" by ensuring that at least half the faculty were Catholics. It also, as it happened, included a number of Reformed scholars on its faculty, most prominently Alvin Plantinga in Philosophy and historian Nathan Hatch, who was soon to become its provost. Also, by making some significant hires, especially targeting some leading Catholic scholars, Notre Dame was making significant progress in becoming a major research university. By the 1990s, one of Notre Dame's aspirations was to be ranked as high academically as it was in football. That goal was surpassed some years later, though due only partially to a rise in academic standing.

Baylor, being in Texas, did not lack for funds. That, combined with the new vision of its leadership, led to some major initiatives by the beginning of the twenty-first century. Specifically they made very attractive offers in order to induce quite a few well-known Christian scholars to come to Baylor as "distinguished and university professors" and to anchor some key graduate programs.[53] A number of the most influential of these had Wheaton connections, although Catholics and others pursuing explicitly Christian scholarship were included. Such aggressive hiring led to many internal tensions in the first decades of the century, particularly among those not happy with the privileging of explicitly Christian scholarship and creating a new elite level of professors. Still, although the path was never smooth, the initiative proved enough of a success that, even if the school still included faculty of a wide range of points of view, it could bill itself as "a private Christian university and a nationally ranked research institution."[54] Although Baylor built strong Christian-oriented graduate programs in a number of key areas, as was true of Christian scholarship more broadly, philosophy was the field where there was the greatest success. Professor C. Stephen Evans, who had been one of those whom Arthur Holmes at Wheaton had inspired to go on into graduate study, reported that within less than twenty years after his arrival at Baylor in 2001, they had placed more than fifty graduates of their doctoral program in faculty positions.[55]

Baylor's progress in promoting Christian perspectives on a wide range of topics, even amid internal dissension at times, was symptomatic of a much broader renewal movement in traditionalist Christian scholarship. Despite lingering examples of the sorts of anti-intellectualism that Noll had lamented in Scandal, the years spanning the turn of the century turned out to be a time of thriving for evangelical Protestant schools. During this time, schools associated with the CCCU became the fastest growing segment in American higher education.[56] Faculties at such schools almost universally became significantly stronger in their academic and scholarly credentials. Faculty members also were increasingly interchangeable at such schools, so that many of those schools that had been more sectarian and parochial became part of a broader community of renewed Christian thinking. Already by 2000, the advances were impressive enough for political scientist and journalist Alan Wolfe to publish a long essay in the *Atlantic* depicting "The Opening of the Evangelical Mind." Wolfe described the remarkable recovery that had taken place since the intellectual isolation of the fundamentalist era. He also affirmed that the renewal movement was of a quality as to deserve respect in the academic mainstream.[57]

In the years following the recession of 2008, CCCU institutions, despite their intellectual development, were also facing significant challenges. Their strength was that because of their religious commitments, they were schools in which the liberal arts, including the humanities, were oriented toward the big questions of life and of how to understand and serve the wider society. These were to provide the contexts for programs in the sciences and in professional fields. As in the rest of American higher education, however, the humanities were declining as the heart of higher education. Americans—evangelicals included—were increasingly viewing college and university education as an economic investment and as means to acquire practical skills that would lead to comfortable lifestyles. Seen in such a light, private schools, though they may have strong professional and scientific programs, were more costly than were state institutions that offered even more specialized programs. Furthermore, whatever the renaissance in Christian thought and its considerable impact on students and those who read the many publications, there is always considerable tension between the outlooks of scholars and the much larger constituencies of evangelical communities. In such communities there is much stronger preference for popular simplified formulas, such as regarding Creation science, the Christian origins of America, or authoritarian views of psychology and the family, rather than nuanced scholarship.[58] Some of the schools affiliated with the CCCU have also been hurt by the American political polarization of the era. Evangelical constituencies remained predominantly Republican and conservative, while faculties were more mixed, including not only political conservatives but also some prominent professors known for their emphases on social justice, equality of opportunity, antiracism, or care for the environment.[59] At any rate, while Christian colleges were on the whole flourishing in academic quality, like private colleges in general, their enrollments and growth had to some degree stagnated, and quite a few faced an uncertain future.[60] One symptom of the problem of finding numerically large audiences for nuanced Christian thought was that the leading intellectual journal of the movement, *Books and Culture*, never became financially self-sustaining and in 2016 was jettisoned by its sponsor, *Christianity Today*, after a run of twenty-one years.[61]

Even so, what developed in just a quarter century since Mark Noll lamented the "scandal of the evangelical mind" was truly remarkable. By 2020, the CCCU included more than 150 colleges and universities in the United States and Canada and more than 30 from another 18 countries around the world. That is one substantial piece of evidence that self-consciously "Christian scholars," mostly from evangelical traditions without strong intellectual heritages, have become one of the truly significant meaningfully interconnected and ethnically diverse interdisciplinary academic communities in the world. Explicitly Christian thought has been continuing to develop in many major disciplines, supported by societies of Christian scholars and academic journals.[62] Electronic media further facilitates rapidly growing worldwide connections. There is, as there always has been, an important British component in international evangelical thought. In fact, one of the factors that has helped overcome American sectarianism and give a wide variety of Christian scholars a sense of commonality has been a sensibility that C. S. Lewis called "mere Christianity": that is, one's primary identity as part of the long heritage of broadly orthodox Christianity in contrast to widely prevalent American "Bible alone" tendencies to ignore history and sectarian emphases on some exclusive tests for belonging, Furthermore, the international Christian academic community with such a sense of common identity now extends to almost every part of the world. Even as constituencies supporting such educational enterprises may be diminishing in the West, they are expanding in the majority world.[63]

The surge of evangelical Protestants earning doctorates since the 1980s has both strengthened CCCU schools and brought increasing numbers of self-consciously Christian scholars into pluralistic institutions. One twenty-first-century survey reported about one-fifth of the American professoriate identifying as "born again." That compares to about another fifth who identify as "atheist or agnostic," and still another fifth saying they are "spiritual but not religious." The rest express a variety of other religious or nonreligious outlooks. As in earlier times, the higher the prestige of the institution, the lower the religiosity.[64] And there remains some documented discrimination in hiring and graduate admissions if a candidate is known to be evangelical.[65] Nonetheless, campus ministries such as InterVarsity Christian Fellowship and some churches that serve campuses work to show that traditional faith is compatible with high academic standards. More than twenty major universities have nearby Christian study centers that encourage sophisticated integration of faith with learning and university life.[66] And there are numerous examples showing that when traditionalist Christian scholars do high-quality work, they will be accepted in university settings as readily as scholars of other persuasions. As Mark Noll remarks in *Jesus Christ and the Life of the Mind*, his more optimistic twenty-first-century sequel to *The Scandal of the Evangelical Mind*, among quite a few encouraging signs is that "while in 1960 there may have been a handful of leading scholars willing to identify as believers, now it would be impossible to list all such scholars in their many fields."[67] And because the conversation partners in these enterprises are often Christian thinkers in more churchly traditions, rather than the rank and file of more populist American evangelicals, Noll and a number of other scholars in recent years have questioned whether tagging the intellectual enterprise as basically "evangelical" is misleading and something like "Christian mind" would be more helpful.[68]

Noll, who completed his formal career at the University of Notre Dame, notes as one of the encouraging signs in recent decades the "growing cooperation with Catholic scholars."[69] That is, indeed, the case. Even though the two enterprises, Catholic and evangelical higher education, have followed very different trajectories over the past several generations, in recent decades there has substantial cooperation or at least borrowing. Despite differences in traditions, they often find they have far more similarities than differences.

Perhaps the most striking feature of Catholic higher education is its varieties. There are well over two hundred Catholic institutions, but it would take a substantial and detailed study to classify where they all stand on the question of what it means to be Catholic. Already in the 1960s Jencks and Riesman thought that most of the Catholic schools, despite their strongly evident parochialism at the time, "have moved toward the secular norm."[70] For that reason the sociologists believed that many Catholic schools would move more into the mainstream and some would even move into the top tiers. That has, indeed, happened. Yet most Catholic schools are run by various religious orders, and the degrees to which they have accepted "a secular norm" as opposed to remaining distinctively Catholic pretty much covers the spectrum of possibilities. That has led to considerable internal discussion as to what the "Catholic character" of a university properly involves.[71] As of the 2010s, of the 220 American Catholic institutions, 159 had established offices of mission and identity.[72]

Catholic schools, more than most Protestant institutions, typically have relied on a conspicuous religious presence in architecture, statuary, iconography, priests on the faculty, and opportunities for Catholic worship. In the mid-twentieth century, distinctly Catholic teaching was usually maintained through required theology and philosophy courses based on neo-Thomist principles.[73] Such schools allowed considerable room for the sciences and other more secular learning as developing largely independently of specific Catholic teachings, even if all learning might in some sense be seen as having a "sacramental dimension."[74] Unlike traditionalist Protestant schools of the CCCU variety, most Catholic institutions do not require of faculty members a commitment to Catholic faith. Sometimes the number of Catholics on the faculty has been only a relatively small minority. Furthermore, unlike more conservative Protestant constituencies and institutions, the outlooks of serious practicing Catholics come in a wide variety, from ultraconservative and traditionalist to highly liberal and progressive. These Catholics may worship together but seemingly disagree on just about everything else.

And if the twenty-first century is, indeed, a postsecular era, one implication is that the claims of strictly secularist outlooks have become less compelling. So, as in conservative Protestant circles, Catholic thought has established a solid place to flourish. It is not surprising, therefore, that some Catholics have become conversation partners with Protestants of comparable persuasions. Further, Catholic philosophers such as Alasdair McIntyre or Charles Taylor have, like some Protestant counterparts, gained respected standing in wider academic communities. Furthermore, as is true of traditionalist Protestantism, some of the most promising dimensions of recent developments are international. Among Catholics as well as Protestants, growth in the majority world has been immense, even while their counterparts have diminished numerically in the former Christendom. That has ensured a worldwide character in their intellectual communities. In recent decades Catholic and Protestant Christian scholars have frequently been conversation partners. And Catholic influences have often been considerable in shaping how some Protestants study the Bible, in their appreciation for the Church Fathers, in the ways they do theology, in practice the integration of faith and learning, and in spiritual practices and disciplines.

In conclusion, how is one to make sense of the varied, multifaceted, and uneven "renaissance" nature of Christian intellectual life and academia over the past few decades? Christendom, in the sense of being those parts of the world where Christianity has had an established place in the civil society, may be largely a distant memory or lost ideal. In the United States, and particularly in its institutions of higher education, such a notion was always a mixed blessing. It was a heritage that helped ensure that some high ideals would be part of the enterprise, but it was mixed with so many other interests and discriminatory—at times even exploitative—practices as to always provide at best a mixed blessing. At the heart of the problem, of course, is not just particular historical circumstances but the human condition and our well-proven ability to corrupt even the best human endeavors with selfish interests.

One lesson of the past would seem to be that Christian and other religiously based higher education is better off when it recognizes, as is easy to do in our postsecular age, that it is a minority enterprise in a richly diverse society. As such, it will not be able to impose its will on others, but, rather, its challenge will be to make itself so attractive in its practices and outlooks that, despite its inevitable imperfection, others will admire it and want to emulate some of its qualities. As Thomas Kuhn observes in *The Structure of Scientific Revolutions*, people are persuaded of the merits of an alternate view not so much by argument as by how that view works for its followers: "They can say: I don't know how the proponents of the new view succeed, but I must learn whatever they are doing, it is clearly right."[75]

Notes

Introduction

1. [Perry L. Glanzer, Nathan F. Alleman, and Todd Ream, *Restoring the Soul of the University: Unifying Higher Education in a Fragmented Age* (Dowers Grove, Ill.: InterVarsity Press, 2017), 322.

2. One early influential expression was Jurgen Habermas, "Secularism's Crisis of Faith: Notes on a Post-Secular Society," *New Perspectives Quarterly*, XXV (2008): 17–29. As applied to the present topic, see *The American University in a Postsecular Age*, Douglas Jacobsen and Rhonda Hustedt Jacobsen, eds. (New York: Oxford University Press), 2008.

3. Daniel T. Rodgers, *Age of Fracture* (Cambridge, Mass.: Harvard University Press, 2011, 99–110, provides an overview of the American reception of such views and puts them in the context of the general breakdown of hopes for cultural consensus that persisted through the 1950s. On the problem within those mid-century ideals, see George Marsden, *The Twilight of the American Enlightenment* (New York: Basic Books, 201

4. I have argued this point in the "Concluding Unscientific Postscript" of *The Soul of the American University* and also in its sequel, *The Outrageous Idea of Christian Scholarship* ((New York: Oxford University Press, 1997). I think the point is more widely acknowledged today.

5. See, for instance, George Yancey and David A. Williamson, *So Many Christians: So Few Lions, Is There Christianophobia in the United States?* (London: Rowman and Littlefield, 2015).

6. James Tunstead Burtchaell, *The Dying of the Light: The Disengagement of Colleges and Universities from Their Churches* (Grand Rapids, Mich.: Eerdmans, 1998), provides an informative history parallel to the present one, but emphasizing the theme of declension. C. John Sommerville, *The Decline of the Secular University* (New York: Oxford University Press, 2006), also frames his account frankly as a decline and offers some suggestions for renewal.

7. David Martin, *A General Theory of Secularization* (New York: Harper & Row, 1978).

8. Charles Dorn, *For the Common Good: A New History of Higher Education in America* (Ithaca, N.Y.: Cornell University Press, 2017), presents an alternative approach looking at a nice variety of schools, regions, and time periods.

9. See the chapter on the twenty-first century, this volume, for a summary and documentation of this trend.

10. See the concluding chapter of this volume regarding these developments.

11. Particularly, if readers should be interested in the role of religion in the founding eras at the University of California or Stanford, they should consult the earlier edition.

Prologue I

1. McGeorge Bundy, "The Attack on Yale," *Atlantic* 188 (November 1951), 50–52.
2. William F. Buckley Jr., "God and Man at Yale: Twenty-five Years Later," in *A Hymnal: The Controversial Arts* (New York: G. P. Putnam's Sons, 1975), 426. An internal Report of the Committee on Religious Life and Study, University Council, Charles P. Taft, Chairman, November 1, 1952, Yale University, A. Whitney Griswold Papers, also notes "some less attractive Catholic qualities" in Buckley's book and that Buckley omitted any mention of his Catholic affiliation.
3. Buckley, "God and Man at Yale," 424.
4. Some reviewers called Buckley to task for this confusion. Peter Viereck observed that it was "humorless, or else blasphemous, . . . to enshrine jointly as sacrosanct 'Adam Smith and Ricardo, Jesus and Saint Paul.'" The book, he thought, was the "product of narrow economic privilege." *New York Times Book Review,* November 4, 1951, 39. *Time,* while taking pleasure at seeing Yale squirm, referred snidely to "the brassy trumpet of a 25-year old alumnus" and also pointed out Buckley's "odd premise that Christianity and capitalism are, if not completely equal, at least inseparable." October 29, 1951, 57.
5. William F. Buckley Jr., *God and Man at Yale: The Superstitions of "Academic Freedom"* (Chicago: Henry Regnery, 1951), 3.
6. Quoted in Buckley, *God and Man,* 43.
7. Buckley, *God and Man,* 4, 8, the latter quoting a recent World Council of Churches formula.
8. Buckley, *God and Man,* 9, 10, 13, 18–19, 16, 25.
9. Ibid., 29.
10. Paul Blanshard's very popular *American Freedom and Catholic Power* (Boston: Beacon Press, 1949) was the best-known expression of this. The sentiments, however, often were founded deeply even among the progressives in the Protestant establishment. See chapter 19 of this volume.
11. Bundy, "The Attack on Yale." Randolph Crump Miller, "Review of *God and Man at Yale,*" *Churchman* 116 (January 15, 1952), 13.
12. Cf. George Marsden, *Reforming Fundamentalism: Fuller Seminary and the New Evangelicalism* (Grand Rapids, Mich.: Wm. B. Eerdmans, 1987).
13. Report of the Committee on Religious Life and Study, November 2, 1952, 1, 2, 5.
14. This is a summary of the account of "religion" in Merrimon Cuninggim, *The College Seeks Religion* (New Haven: Yale University Press, 1947), 247. Cuninggim was a recent Yale Ph.D. His views are discussed in more detail in this volume.
15. "Mainline Protestant" is here used in a descriptive, not a normative, sense and refers to denominations such as Methodist Episcopal, American Baptist, Presbyterian Church in the U.S.A., Congregationalists, Disciples, Episcopalian, and others associated with the National Council of Churches as distinct from more strictly evangelical, confessional, fundamentalist, pentecostal, or other sectarian groups that remained separatist.

16. Robert Wuthnow, *The Struggle for America's Soul: Evangelicals, Liberals, and Secularism* (Grand Rapids, Mich.: Wm. B. Eerdmans, 1989), 34–35.

17. "Report of the President's Advisory Committee," Henry Sloane Coffin, '97, Chairman, February 9, 1952, Yale University, A. Whitney Griswold Papers.

Prologue II

1. On Coffin, see Bradley J. Longfield, *The Presbyterian Controversy: Fundamentalists, Modernists, and Moderates* (New York: Oxford University Press, 1991), 77–103.

2. Episcopal Bishop Henry Knox Sherrill (Yale '11) made this comparison in recollections quoted in Ralph Henry Gabriel, *Religion and Learning at Yale: The Church of Christ in College and University, 1757–1957* (New Haven: Yale University Press, 1958), 209.

3. Laurence R. Veysey, *The Emergence of the American University* (Chicago: University of Chicago Press, 1965), 235.

4. W. H. Sallmon, "The Young Man's Christian Association," *Two Centuries of Christian Activity at Yale*, James B. Reynolds et al., eds. (New York: 1901), 225.

5. Brooks Mather Kelly, *Yale: A History* (New Haven: Yale University Press, 1974), reports that in 1901 the YMCAs at Yale College and at Yale's scientific school had a total membership of 1,000 out of a combined student body of 1800. A count in 1901 revealed that 63% of Yale's 1190 undergraduates were "church members," including 44 Catholics and 16 Jews. Of the 610 students at Yale's Sheffield Scientific School, 50% were members. Percentages in the medical and law schools were (significantly) 33% and 40%, while in the graduate school it was 69%. In Divinity it was 100%. *Two Centuries,* Appendix D (2).

6. George Wilson Pierson, *Yale College: An Educational History, 1871–1921* (New Haven: Yale University Press, 1952), 13.

7. James F. Findlay Jr., *Dwight L. Moody: American Evangelist, 1837–1899* (Chicago: University of Chicago Press, 1969), 350.

8. John R. Mott, Address at Yale Alumni Dinner, June 1899, quoted in H. P. Beach, "Yale's Contribution to Foreign Missions," in *Two Centuries,* 283.

9. H. B. Wright, "Recent Epochs of Christian Life," in *Two Centuries,* 111.

10. H. B. Wright, "Yale and the Northfield Student Conferences," in *Two Centuries,* 245. Cf. George M. Marsden, *Fundamentalism and American Culture: The Shaping of American Evangelicalism, 1870–1925* (New York: Oxford University Press, 2006 [1980]), for an account of this side of the Moody heritage.

11. W. S. Coffin, "Yale and the City of New Haven," in *Two Centuries,* 255–81.

12. Mott, quoted in *Two Centuries,* 283.

13. Wright, "Recent Epoches," in *Two Centuries,* 110. The Methodist group was absorbed in the association. A similar Catholic group was merged into a resident organization under the Dominican Fathers of New Haven.

14. Lyman Beecher, *The Autobiography of Lyman Beecher*, Barbara M. Cross, ed. (Cambridge, Mass.: 1961), Vol. I, 252–53.

15. George W. Pierson, *Yale: The University College, 1921–1937* (New Haven: Yale University Press, 1955), 84–86. Compulsory chapel continued at Yale until 1926.

16. Gabriel, *Religion and Learning,* 191–203.

17. Henry Davidson Sheldon, *Student Life and Customs* (New York, 1901), 285–86. Cf. Veysey, *The Emergence of the American University,* 280–81, for other evidence of a decline in atheism. Veysey attributes this to a growing indifference toward things religious generally. Much indifference toward things religious was, indeed, present on turn-of-the-century college campuses, as in other eras. However, the successes of counterefforts for voluntary religion were more pronounced during the Progressive era than at any other time.

18. Quoted from Moody (from the 1897–1898 school year), in *Two Centuries,* 115.

Prologue III

1. "Yale as a Battle Ground," *New York Times,* April 4, 1880, 1; "Two Parties at Yale," April 5, 1880, 1 ("White Czar" quotation).

2. "Yale College," editorial, *New York Times,* April 6, 1880, 4.

3. Harris E. Starr, *William Graham Sumner* (New York: Henry Holt, 1925), 136, 168 (from sermons preached in 1872).

4. *New York Times,* April 4, 1880, 1.

5. Harris E. Starr, *William Graham Sumner* (New York: Henry Holt, 1925), 543, cf. 541–42. Bruce Curtis, *William Graham Sumner* (Boston: Twayne, 1981), 25–42, provides a clear summary of Sumner's changing religious views. The following account is based largely on Starr, *Sumner,* 345–69, which reprints many of the original documents, and Burton J. Bledstein, "Noah Porter versus William Graham Sumner," *Church History* 43 (September 1974), 340–49.

6. Starr, *Sumner,* 136.

7. W. G. Sumner, "A Private and personal communication to the members of the Corporation and to the permanent officers of Yale College, New Haven, June 1881," reproduced in Starr, *Sumner,* 358–59.

8. Porter to Sumner, December 6, 1879, from Starr, *Sumner,* 346–47.

9. Ibid.

10. Bledstein, "Porter versus Sumner," 341.

11. Academic freedom was not yet established as a principle in American higher education, but its components were emerging as the rights of a professional to regulate one's own affairs. See the discussion of this dimension in Richard Hofstadter and Walter P. Metzger, *The Development of Academic Freedom in the United States* (New York: Columbia University Press, 1955), 335–38. Even at Johns Hopkins and Cornell, there were cases of faculty not hired because their religious views were considered too radical (340). Hiring and firing were two different matters, however.

Chapter 1

1. This subject has, of course, been treated by many authors. A classic and suggestive overview of the theme is E. Harris Harbison, *The Christian Scholar in the Age of the Reformation* (New York: Scribners, 1956).

2. This account comes most directly from John Van Engen's fine overview, "Christianity and the University: The Medieval and Reformation Legacies," in *Making Higher Education Christian: The History and Mission of Evangelical Colleges in America*, Joel A. Carpenter and Kenneth W. Shipps, eds. (Grand Rapids, Mich.: Christian University Press, 1987), 19–37.

3. The preceding paragraphs depend most directly on Van Engen, "Christianity and the University," 23–24. Cf. Samuel Eliot Morison, *The Founding of Harvard College* (Cambridge, Mass.: Harvard University Press, 1935), 18–39.

4. Quoted in Van Engen, "Christianity and the University," 27.

5. Harbison, *Christian Scholar*, 121.

6. Ibid., 113.

7. When asked about the usefulness of reason, he replied, "Reason corrupted by the Devil is harmful . . . but reason informed by the Spirit is a help in interpreting the Holy Scriptures. . . . Reason is of service of faith when it is enlightened, since it reflects upon things; but without faith it is of no use." Quoted in Harbison, *Christian Scholar*, 123.

8. Lewis W. Spitz, "The Importance of the Reformation for the Universities: Culture and Confession in the Critical Years," in *Rebirth, Reform and Resilience: Universities in Transition, 1300–1700*, James M. Kittleson and Pamela J. Transue, eds. (Columbus: Ohio State University Press, 1984), 42–67.

9. Perry Miller, *The New England Mind: The Seventeenth Century* (Boston: Beacon Press, 1939), explores the influence of the Renaissance on New England Puritanism.

10. Spitz, "The Importance of the Reformation," 53, points out that Melanchthon was instrumental in the reorganization of Wittenberg and in the establishment of a Lutheran university at Marburg in 1527, both of which became models of Protestant universities.

11. William J. Bouwsma, *John Calvin: A Sixteenth-Century Portrait* (New York: Oxford University Press, 1988), 14.

12. John Morgan, *Godly Learning: Puritan Attitudes towards Reason, Learning, and Education, 1560–1640* (Cambridge: Cambridge University Press, 1986), 43.

13. Spitz, "The Importance of the Reformation," 57.

14. Wilhelm Pauck, "The Ministry in the Time of the Continental Reformation," in *The Ministry in Historical Perspectives*, H. Richard Niebuhr and Daniel D. Williams, eds. (New York: Harper & Brothers, 1956), 147.

15. Van Engen, "Christianity and Universities," 34.

16. Lawrence Stone, "Introduction" and "The Size and Composition of the Oxford Student Body 1580–1900," in *The University in Society*, Vol. I, Lawrence Stone, ed. (Princeton: Princeton University Press, 1974), vii, 3–111.

17. Morison, *Founding of Harvard*, 359–63. One hundred were from Cambridge (35 from Emmanuel), 32 were from Oxford, and 8 were from non-English schools. Trinity College,

Cambridge, was also very important, with thirteen graduates in New England, including John Winthrop, Charles Chauncy (later president of Harvard), and John Cotton. Cotton, however, had moved from Trinity to Emmanuel, where he eventually became head lecturer.

18. On early Emmanuel, see Morgan, *Godly Learning*, 247–55.

19. Morison, *Founding of Harvard*, 331; this is the motto of the seal of the 1692 charter. The earliest design for a college seal, proposed in 1643, contained the motto *Veritas* but was never used or known again until the nineteenth century. *In Christi Gloriam* appeared on the seal of the 1650 charter.

20. For this point I am indebted to Glenn T. Miller, *Piety and Intellect: The Aims and Purposes of Ante-Bellum Theological Education* (Atlanta: Scholars Press, 1990), 125.

21. Oxford and Cambridge had been to this degree secularized by the Reformation; they passed from the under the aegis of the pope and Crown to the authority of the Crown alone, though they retained some degree of their medieval autonomy. Jurgen Herbst, "The First Three American Colleges: Schools of the Reformation," in *Perspectives in American History*, Vol. VII, Donald Fleming and Bernard Bailyn, eds. (Cambridge, Mass.: Charles Warren Center, Harvard University, 1974), 19–20.

22. Ibid., 78–52.

23. This point is illustrated by contrasting the developments in American higher education with those of the German universities arising out of the Lutheran Reformation. German Protestant universities in the nineteenth century were firmly established as agencies of the states, which maintained theological faculties as part of their broader religious establishments. In the United States, by contrast, churches and private corporations of Christians could maintain a controlling role, while colleges still served public functions. See Thomas Albert Howard, *Protestant Theology and the Making of the Modern German University* (New York: Oxford University Press, 2006).

24. Samuel Eliot Morison, *Harvard College in the Seventeenth Century*, Part I (Cambridge, Mass.: Harvard University Press, 1936), 305–19. Cf. Richard Hofstadter and Walter P. Metzger, *The Development of Academic Freedom in the United States* (New York: Columbia University Press, 1955), 86–91.

25. E.g., Morison, *Founding of Harvard*, 171–80.

26. Puritanism by this time had professionalized the clergy to the point of seldom ordaining men without university training. See Morgan, *Godly Learning*, 96. As "New England's First Fruits" put it in 1643, they were "dreading to leave an illiterate Ministry to the Churches, when our present Ministers shall lie in the Dust." From "New England's First Fruits," 1643, reproduced in Morison, *Founding of Harvard*, 432–33. Morison plays down the function of ministerial training, but Winthrop Hudson's response that Harvard was "little more than a theological seminary" seems too strong. See Winthrop S. Hudson, "The Morison Myth Concerning the Founding of Harvard College," *Church History* 8 (June 1939), 152.

27. This percentage of clergy was actually below that of Oxford and Cambridge. See Morison, *Founding of Harvard*, 247n.

28. "*Statutes of Harvard*, ca. 1646," in *American Higher Education: A Documentary History*, Vol. I, Richard Hofstadter and Wilson Smith, eds. (Chicago: University of Chicago Press, 1961), 8.

29. Morison, *Seventeenth Century*, Part I, 169–266.

30. Ibid., 268–72.

31. Ibid., 272–75.

32. Charles Chauncy, "A Commencement Sermon" (Cambridge, 1655), from excerpt in *The Puritans: A Sourcebook of Their Writings*, Vol. II, rev., Perry Miller and Thomas H. Johnson, eds. (New York: Harper & Row, 1963 [1938]), 706–7. Cf. Norman Fiering, *Moral Philosophy at Seventeenth-Century Harvard: A Discipline in Transition* (Chapel Hill: University of North Carolina Press, 1981), 19.

33. Miller and Johnson, *Puritans*, 706.

34. Cf. Fiering, *Moral Philosophy*, 26.

35. Ibid., 24–29.

36. Cf. Morgan, *Godly Learning*, 261–63.

Chapter 2

1. Disestablishment at the time of the American Revolution and defeat in the Civil War both severely limited the influence of Anglican William and Mary.

2. Increase Mather, Commencement Address (before 1697), quoted in Samuel E. Morison, *Harvard College in the Seventeenth Century* (Cambridge, Mass.: Harvard University Press, 1936), 167, cf. 224–27.

3. Quoted in Morison, *Harvard College*, 168.

4. Cf., Rick Kennedy, "The Alliance between Puritanism and Cartesian Logic at Harvard, 1687–1735," *Journal of the History of Ideas*, 51 (October–December 1990), 549–72.

5. Richard Warch, *School of the Prophets: Yale College, 1701–1740* (New Haven: Yale University Press, 1973), 10. I am relying on Warch as the most complete of many accounts of these developments.

6. Miller, *The New England Mind: From Colony to Province* (Cambridge, Mass.: Harvard University Press, 1953), presents a compelling dramatization of this crisis.

7. Warch, *School of the Prophets*, esp. 36. Their kin in the middle colonies, in fact, soon found that their harmony with their Scotch-Irish brethren in organizing a Presbyterian denomination was disrupted by differences of their English dissenter views of the place of creeds compared with the Scottish view, which was closer to the continental matter of requiring strict subscription.

8. Ibid., 96–117. Part of Increase Mather's problem as Harvard president was that he refused to move from Boston to Cambridge.

9. Edmund S. Morgan, *The Gentle Puritan: A Life of Ezra Stiles, 1727–1795* (New York: W. W. Norton, 1962), 36–37.

10. Frederick Rudolph, *The American College and University: A History* (New York: Vintage Books, 1962), 14. Richard Hofstadter and Walter P. Metzger, *The Development of Academic Freedom in the United States* (New York: Columbia

University Press), 133–34, make the point that the faculty lost the autonomy enjoyed by the English schools and the college was controlled by a board divided between clergy and lay members, reflecting its dual obligations to church and state.

11. Morgan, *Gentle Puritan*, 34–37, has a fine account of this episode. See also George Marsden, *Jonathan Edwards: A Life* (New Haven: Yale University Press, 2003), for a fuller account of Edwards's involvement.

12. Ibid., 39–40; Hofstadter and Metzger, *Academic Freedom*, 168–69.

13. Edwards, for instance, retained the dim view of his student days concerning the benefits of college education for piety. See *Some Thoughts Concerning the Present Revival of Religion in New England (1740)*, excerpt in Sol Cohen, ed., *Education in the United States: A Documentary History*, Vol. II (New York: Random House, 1974), 680–81.

14. Whitefield replied, saying that he was sorry, but he conceded nothing. Edward Wigglesworth, Hollis Professor of Divinity at Harvard, issued a careful rebuttal to Whitefield in 1745. Wigglesworth pointed out, for instance, that Tillotson had not been taken out of the library for nine years prior to Whitefield's first visit. Cohen, *Education*, 681. See also Hofstadter and Metzger, *Academic Freedom*, 161–63.

15. See documents in Richard Hofstadter and Wilson Smith, eds., *American Higher Education: A Documentary History* (Chicago: University of Chicago Press, 1961), 64–72. Clap obtained a charter for the college in 1745 and formulated at the same time the strictest laws for regulation of students' lives. Ibid., 49–61.

16. Morgan, *Gentle Puritan*, 104. The term Presbyterians used was "New Side."

17. Thomas Clap, *The Religious Constitution of Colleges* (New London, Conn., 1754), excerpt in Cohen, *Education*, 687–91.

18. Morgan, *Gentle Puritan*, 316–18. Louis Leonard Tucker, *Puritan Protagonist; President Thomas Clap of Yale College* (Chapel Hill: University of North Carolina Press, 1962), 232–62. Hofstadter and Metzger, *Academic Freedom*, 170–77.

19. Nine of the 12 clergy on the original board (of 23 total) were New Englanders. Douglas Sloan, *The Scottish Enlightenment and the American College Ideal* (New York: Teachers College Press, 1971), 58.

20. Hofstadter and Metzger, *Academic Freedom*, 116–17. At Rhode Island College, for instance, while Baptists were ensured control, an elaborate scheme was worked out to include fixed numbers of Quakers, Congregationalists, and Anglicans; "Charter of Rhode Island College (Brown University), 1764," in Hofstadter and Smith, *Documentary History*, 134–36.

21. "Samuel Johnson Advertises the Opening of King's College (Columbia), 1754," in Hofstadter and Smith, *Documentary History*, 110. Cf. 99–136 for valuable documents on sectarian rivalries of the era. Cf. Hofstadter and Metzger, *Academic Freedom*, 115–17, 144–51.

22. "Laws of Kings College, 1755," in Hofstadter and Smith, *Documentary History*, 117–21. Students at Kings were required to attend morning and evening prayers daily, and on Sunday they had to be present at the church designated by their parents or guardians.

23. Miller, *Revolutionary College*, 79–86, provides a helpful account of efforts to implement this approach.

24. See, for example, Gordon S. Wood, *The Creation of the American Republic, 1776–1787* (New York: W. W. Norton, 1969).

25. See Henry F. May, *The Enlightenment in America* (New York: Oxford University Press, 1976), for a particularly valuable account of the era.

26. Sloan, *Scottish Enlightenment*, 1–35. David Hume, of course, was an exception, neither defending Christianity nor gaining a university position.

27. Ibid., 36–72.

28. Garry Wills, *Inventing America: Jeffersons' Declaration of Independence* (Garden City, N.Y.: Doubleday, 1978), 176–80, 200–201. Wills also documents some of the other extensive Scottish influence. Small followed the Scottish method of vernacular lectures, rather than commentary on Latin texts. In addition, he helped add some new practical subjects and belles lettres to the curriculum.

29. Thomas Clap, *An Essay on the Nature and Foundation of Moral Virtue . . . for the Use of the Students at Yale-College* (New Haven, 1765), 41, 24, and passim. Cf. Tucker, *Puritan Protagonist*, 144–74. Lawrence A. Cremin suggests that Samuel Johnson, president of Kings, held a similar view. Johnson, a Yale graduate, was a leading tutor who joined Timothy Cutler in defecting to Anglicanism. He was an admirer of the philosophy of George Berkeley, which may have put him in a differing camp from the Scottish philosophers, but he was also an Arminian open to an expanded view of human ability. Lawrence A. Cremin, *American Education: The Colonial Experience, 1607–1783* (New York: Harper & Row, 1970), 461. Cf. Warch, *School of the Prophets*, 294.

30. Norman Fiering, *Moral Philosophy at Seventeenth-Century Harvard* (Chapel Hill: University of North Carolina Press, 1981), 102 and passim; *Jonathan Edwards's Moral Thought*, 3.

31. Fiering, *Moral Philosophy*, 296.

32. Quoted in Fiering, *Moral Philosophy*, 297.

33. Fiering, *Jonathan Edwards's Moral Thought*, 8.

34. Jonathan Edwards, *The Nature of True Virtue*, *The Works of Jonathan Edwards*, Vol. 8, *Ethical Writings*, John E. Smith, ed. (New Haven: Yale University Press, 1980) [1765]), 553.

35. Accordingly, he paired *The Nature of True Virtue* with a prior theological treatise, *Concerning the End for Which God Created the World*. These were originally published (posthumously) in 1765 under the lead title *Two Dissertations*.

36. Sloan, *Scottish Enlightenment*, 73–102, provides a most valuable account of Alison.

37. Ibid., 86–88.

38. "Ezra Stiles on Changes in the Yale Corporation, 1792," in Hofstadter and Smith, *Documentary History*, 164.

39. Hofstadter and Smith say, "No man then in academic life displayed more admirably the viewpoint of the American Enlightenment." Ibid., 159.

40. Morgan, *Gentle Puritan*, 318, 376–403. Paley's work was recently published (London, 1785). Paley was a Lockean who rejected the "moral sense" of the Scots, and his

influence in collegiate education paralleled that of the Scots. Paley was a "rational Christian" (of a broad nonsectarian sort) who saw Scripture as an important supplemental guide in making moral judgments, but he was also optimistic as to human ability to find moral truth though rational calculation. This combination of piety and reason, as well as Paley's simple, engaging style, contributed to the popularity of his text during the next half century. Eventually, by the pre–Civil War era, the rival Scottish moral philosophers had triumphed, though Paley's *Natural Theology; or, Evidences of the Existence and Attributes of the Deity Collected from the Appearance of Nature* (London, 1802) remained a standard text until the Darwinian era. It is important to keep in mind also that college teachers often used texts with which they disagreed as occasions for developing their own critical viewpoints. Stiles's successor, Timothy Dwight, for instance, used Paley but criticized him from a Calvinist perspective. See Stephen E. Berk, *Calvinism versus Democracy: Timothy Dwight and the Origins of American Evangelical Orthodoxy* (Hamden, Conn.: Archon Books, 1974), 84–85.

41. Quoted in Mark A. Noll, *Princeton and the Republic, 1768-1822: The Search for a Christian Enlightenment in the Era of Samuel Stanhope Smith* (Princeton: Princeton University Press, 1989), 43.

42. Ibid., 41, from Witherspoon's lectures. For an engaging explanation of Hutcheson's analysis of how human moral principles worked, see Wills, *Inventing America*, passim.

43. Helpful for understanding the changing spirit of eighteenth-century education is Robert Middlekauff, *Ancients and Axioms: Secondary Education in Eighteenth-Century New England* (New Haven: Yale University Press, 1963).

44. Quotation from Thomas Jefferson Wertenbaker in Noll, *Princeton and the Republic*, 52. Statistics from 171–72; public service, 135, 216–17.

45. Ibid., 203.

46. Benjamin Rush on Republican education, 1798, in Hofstadter and Smith, *Documentary History*, 170–71. Cf. Noll, *Princeton and the Republic*, 201, on Stanhope Smith's similar views.

47. Rush in Hofstadter and Smith, *Documentary History*, 171.

Chapter 3

1. Thomas Jefferson to Thomas Cooper, November 1, 1822, from selection *in* American Higher Education: A Documentary History, Vol. I, Richard Hofstadter and Wilson Smith, eds. (Chicago: University of Chicago Press, 1961), 395–96.

2. Jefferson to William Short, April 13, 1820, from excerpt in Robert M. Healey, Jefferson on Religion in Public Education (New Haven: Yale University Press, 1962), 236. Cf. equally vitriolic remarks to Cooper, March 13, 1820, excerpt on 235.

3. David C. Humphrey, *From King's College to Columbia 1746–1800* (New York: Columbia University Press, 1976), 269–82. A similar development took place in Pennsylvania in 1779, when the state took over the College of Philadelphia, renaming it the University

of Pennsylvania. In 1789 the school was returned to its original trustees under the direction of the Anglican provost William Smith, who had been displaced in 1779. The religious dimensions of this conflict, however, were less clear, since the college was always more secular than its counterparts, a factor that may have contributed to its languishing for a half-century after the Revolution. Edward Potts Cheyney, *History of the University of Pennsylvania, 1740-1940* (Philadelphia: University of Pennsylvania Press, 1940), 129-216.

4. Healey, *Jefferson on Religion*, 210-13. Philip Alexander Bruce, *History of the University of Virginia, 1819-1919*, Vol. I (New York: Macmillan, 1920), 45-55.

5. On Presbyterian college founding, see Howard Miller, *The Revolutionary College: American Presbyterian Higher Education, 1707-1837* (New York: New York University Press, 1976), esp. 123-28, 145-49.

6. University of North Carolina, Trustee Minutes, February 6, 1795. I am grateful to Roger Robins for his research on this topic. See also Donald Robert Come, "The Influence of Princeton on Higher Education in the South before 1825," *William and Mary Quarterly*, 3rd ser., 2 (October 1945), 378-87.

7. Kemp P. Battle, *History of the University of North Carolina*, Vol. I (Raleigh: Edwards & Broughton, 1907), 42, 240.

8. Quoted in Come, "Influence of Princeton," 395. By the end of Waddell's administration, even the Baptists were complaining that the school had been turned into a sectarian Presbyterian enterprise. Thomas G. Dyer, *The University of Georgia: A Bicentennial History, 1785-1985* (Athens: University of Georgia Press, 1895), 31-32.

9. When the Presbyterians asked for state support they emphasized the inclusive and nonsectarian nature of their enterprise. Miller, *Revolutionary College*, 149-59.

10. Jefferson to Plumer, July 21, 1816, quoted in *The Colleges and the Public, 1787-1862*, Theodore Rawson Crane, ed. (New York: Teachers College Press, 1963), 64. See also the views of Isaac Hill and William Plumer, in excerpts, 61-66. Also see Donald G. Tewksbury, *The Founding of American Colleges and Universities before the Civil War: With Particular Reference to the Religious Influences Bearing upon the College Movement* (New York, 1932), 148-52. Richard Hofstadter and Walter P. Metzger, *The Development of Academic Freedom in the United States* (New York: Columbia University Press, 1955), 219-20.

11. Hofstadter and Smith, *American Higher Education*, 202-19; for Webster defense and Marshall decision, quotation, 216. Historical debate about interpretations of the Dartmouth decision have centered around whether it was clearly a private versus public issue and about whether concerns for religious orthodoxy were primary in the dispute. See the "Forum" between John S. Whitehead and Jurgen Herbst, "How to Think about the Dartmouth College Case," *History of Education Quarterly* 26 (Fall 1986), 333-49.

12. Hofstadter and Metzger, *Academic Freedom*, 248-51. Cf. Miller, *Revolutionary College*, 236-44.

13. Quoted from Priestley's *Memoirs*, I:335, in Healey, *Jefferson on Religion*, 233. See also Dumas Malone, *The Public Life of Thomas Cooper, 1783-1839* (New Haven: Yale University Press, 1926), 234-47.

14. Cabell to Jefferson, August 5, 1821, quoted in Healey, *Jefferson on Religion*, 237.

15. Healey, *Jefferson on Religion*, argues for this interpretation, describing Jefferson as a "Unitarian evangelist" (244). Jefferson was convinced that religion was important to a republic but wanted it to be the right sort of religion, which he regarded as nonsectarian (257).

16. Jefferson et al., Report of the Rockfish Gap Commission (1818), reprinted in Hofstadter and Smith, *American Higher Education*, 193–99, quotation, 198. Cf. discussion in Healey, *Jefferson on Religion*, 217–19.

17. Healey, *Jefferson on Religion*, 239.

18. Report of Board of Visitors, University of Virginia, October 7, 1822, quoted in Healey, *Jefferson on Religion*, 220.

19. See D. C. Masters, *Protestant Church Colleges in Canada: A History* (Toronto: University of Toronto Press, 1966). The most notable example of this arrangement is at the University of Toronto.

20. As an alternative, James Madison, Jefferson's successor as rector, suggested a plan, eventually adopted, of having chaplains appointed yearly, rotating from the four major Protestant denominations. In 1859 Presbyterians explored starting a theological school at the university, but the Civil War deflected the plan. See Philip Alexander Bruce, *History of the University of Virginia, 1819–1919*, Vol. II (New York: Macmillan, 1920), 368–71.

21. Mark A. Noll, *Princeton and the Republic, 1768–1822* (Princeton: Princeton University Press, 1989).

22. For an interpretive overview, see Glenn T. Miller, *Piety and Intellect: The Aims and Purposes of Ante-Bellum Theological Education* (Atlanta: Scholars Press, 1990). By 1832 there were already twenty-two theological seminaries. See Lawrence A. Cremin, *American Education: The National Experience, 1783–1876* (New York: Harper & Row, 1980), 400.

23. Jefferson to Cooper, November 2, 1822, quoted in Healey, *Jefferson on Religion*, 224.

24. Quoted and summarized in Malone, *Cooper*, 342–43.

25. Dr. Cooper's Defense before the Board of Trustees of South Carolina College (1832), reprinted in Hofstadter and Smith, *American Higher Education*, 396–417.

26. Malone, *Cooper*, 360.

27. Hofstadter and Metzger, *Academic Freedom*, 269.

28. Henry F. May, *The Enlightenment in America* (New York: Oxford University Press, 1976), 307–36, provides an account of the decline of the skeptical Enlightenment, especially in the South.

29. Albea Godbold, *The Church College of the Old South* (Durham, N.C.: Duke University Press, 1944), 162.

30. Bruce, *University of Virginia*, Vol. III, 133–37; II, 368–69.

31. E.g., Malone, *Cooper*, 345 and passim.

Chapter 4

1. On the populist attacks, see Nathan O. Hatch, *The Democratization of American Christianity* (New Haven: Yale University Press, 1989), especially the appendix of anti-Calvinist verse, 227–43.

2. George M. Marsden, *The Evangelical Mind and the New School Presbyterian Experience* (New Haven: Yale University Press, 1970), discusses many of these trends.

3. The standard source is Donald G. Tewksbury, *The Founding of American Colleges and Universities before the Civil War: With Particular Reference to the Religious Influences Bearing upon the College Movement* (New York: Columbia University Teachers College, 1932), e.g., 16–28, 69. Tewksbury tabulated "permanent colleges" and their denominational affiliations. Natalie A. Naylor, "The Ante-Bellum College Movement: A Reappraisal of Tewksbury's Founding of American Colleges and Universities," *History of Education Quarterly* 13 (Fall 1973), 261–74, shows that Tewksbury's statistics, although useful for relative comparisons, are not complete. Also, she shows that the often cited 81% failure rate that Tewksbury reported is misleading since most of the failed colleges existed only on paper.

4. David B. Potts, "American Colleges in the Nineteenth Century: From Localism to Denominationalism," *History of Education Quarterly* 11 (Winter 1971), 363–80. Cf. Potts, *Baptist Colleges in the Development of American Society, 1821–1861* (New York: Garland, 1988).

5. On the general character of these colleges, see Douglas Sloan, "Harmony, Chaos, and Consensus: The American College Curriculum," *Teachers College Record* 73 (December 1971), 221–51; Lawrence A. Cremin, *American Education: The National Experience, 1783–1876* (New York: Harper & Row, 1980), 406–7. William C. Ringenberg, "The Old-Time College, 1800–1885," in *Making Higher Education Christian: The History and Mission of Evangelical Colleges in America*, Joel A. Carpenter and Kenneth W. Shipps, eds. (Grand Rapids, Mich.: Christian University Press, 1987), 77–97, is a useful overview. Also, see Albea Godbold, *The Church College of the Old South* (Durham, N.C.: Duke University Press, 1944).

6. Sloan, "Harmony, Chaos, and Consensus." Godbold, *Church College*, 126–27. On doxological science, see also Theodore Dwight Bozeman, *The Baconian Ideal and Antebellum American Religious Thought* (Chapel Hill: University of North Carolina Press, 1977), and Mark A Noll, "The Revolution, the Enlightenment, and Christian Higher Education in the Early Republic," in Carpenter and Shipps, *Making Higher Education Christian*, 56–76.

7. G. Stanley Hall, "Philosophy in the United States," *Mind* 4 (January 1879), 89–93.

8. Cf. Daniel Walker Howe's account of faculty psychology, *The Political Culture of the American Whigs* (Chicago: University of Chicago Press, 1979), 29.

9. "The Yale Report of 1828," reprinted in *American Higher Education: A Documentary History*, Vol. I, Richard Hofstadter and Wilson Smith, eds. (Chicago: University of Chicago Press, 1961), 279, 289.

10. Godbold, *Church College*, 128–39. Frederick Rudolph, *The American College and University: A History* (New York: Vintage Books, 1962), 79–84.

11. Cremin, *American Education,* 56–74, provides a convenient summary of the predominantly Presbyterian and Congregationalist voluntary crusades and their wide implications for both schooling and education at all levels.

12. James Findlay, "The SPCTEW and Western Colleges: Religion and Higher Education in Mid-Nineteenth Century America," *History of Education Quarterly* 15 (Spring 1977), 37–38.

13. Lyman Beecher, *A Plea for the West* (Cincinnati: Truman and Smith, 1835), 10–11, 17, and passim.

14. Ibid., 79–81, 124n.

15. For the best account of this outlook, see Howe, 1979, and "The Evangelical Movement and Political Culture in the North during the Second Party System," *Journal of American History* 77 (March 1991), 1216–39. Louise Stevenson, *Scholarly Means to Evangelical Ends: The New Haven Scholars and the Transformation of Higher Learning in America, 1830–1890* (Baltimore: Johns Hopkins University Press, 1986), makes some of the same points.

16. Bozeman, *Baconian Ideal,* esp. 3–31, 71–86.

17. The question of sectarianism was being sharply debated during this whole era. For instance, Philip Lindsley (1786–1855), president of the University of Nashville and a protégé of Princeton's Samuel Stanhope Smith, decried the pretensions of the scores of sectarian schools that were springing up in his region, because of both their educational superficiality and their claims to be nonsectarian: "I do not object to any sect's being allowed the privilege of erecting and maintaining, at their own expense, as many schools, colleges and theological seminaries as they please. But then, their sectarian views should be openly and distinctly avowed. Their purpose should be specified in their charters: and the legislature should protect the people from imposition. . . . Hitherto, almost every legislature has pursued an opposite policy, and has aided the work of deception, by enacting that, in the said sectarian institution, youths of all sects should be entitled to equal privileges" (Philip Lindsley, Baccalaureate Address, 1829, in Hofstadter and Smith, *Documentary History,* 234). Howard Miller, *The Revolutionary College: American Presbyterian Higher Education, 1707–1837* (New York: New York University Press, 1976, 242–46, 257–58), documents the constant debate over sectarianism, particularly when public funding was involved. Miller also argues, however, that the Presbyterians of the early nineteenth century had lost their broader nonsectarian version of the colonial era (284–85). It is probably more accurate to say that they *continued* to experience a deep tension between their sectarianism and their aspirations to lead in shaping a righteous republic.

18. Victor Roy Wilbee, "The Religious Dimensions of Three Presidencies in a State University: Presidents Tappan, Haven, and Angell at the University of Michigan," Ph.D. dissertation, University of Michigan, 1967, 24.

19. George Duffield et al., Report of Michigan Regents, December 20, 1841, Hofstadter and Smith, *Documentary History,* 437–38. Cf. Howard H. Peckham, *The Making of the University of Michigan, 1817–1867* (Ann Arbor: University of Michigan Press, 1967), 23–24. Political sectarianism complicated the issues at Michigan. The religious and political mix is illustrated through the case of the Rev. Daniel Denison Whedon, of

the Methodist Episcopal Church (and later a prominent biblical commentator), who in 1851 was dismissed by the regents of the university for opposing the extension of slavery. Specifically, Whedon was condemned for having "advocated the doctrine called, 'The Higher Law,' a doctrine which is unauthorized by the Bible, at war with the principles, precepts, and examples of Christ and His Apostles, subversive alike of Civil Government, civil society, and the legal rights of individual citizens, and in effects constitutes in the opinion of this Board a species of moral treason against the Government." From I. N. Demmon, ed., *University of Michigan Regents' Proceedings, 1837–1864*, 501–503, excerpted in Hofstadter and Smith, *Documentary History*, 439.

20. Thomas Reid, *Essays on the Intellectual Powers of Man* (Cambridge, Mass.: M.I.T. Press, 1969 [1785]), esp. xxxix, 614–43.

21. Cf. Henry F. May, *The Enlightenment in America* (New York: Oxford University Press, 1976).

22. For a fuller discussion of these views and their implications, see George M. Marsden, "The Collapse of American Evangelical Academia," in *Faith and Rationality: Reason and Belief in God*, Alvin Plantinga and Nicholas Wolterstorff, eds. (Notre Dame, Ind.: University Notre Dame Press, 1983), 219–64.

23. Mark Hopkins, *Evidences of Christianity* (Boston, 1876, [1846]), 97–98, 39.

24. Ibid., 75 and passim.

25. Francis Wayland, *Elements of Political Economy*, 2nd ed. (1852 [1837]), quoted in William G. McLoughlin, ed., *The American Evangelicals, 1800–1900: An Anthology* (New York: Harper & Row, 1968), 126.

26. On Nott and Wayland, see Frederick Rudolph, *Curriculum: A History of American Undergraduate Course of Study since 1636* (San Francisco: Jossey-Bass, 1977), 85–87, and Lawrence A. Cremin, *American Education: The National Experience, 1783–1876* (New York: Harper & Row, 1980), 273–79.

27. See Stewart Davenport, *Friends of Unrighteous Mammon: Northern Evangelicals and Market Capitalism 1815–1860* (Chicago: University of Chicago Press, 2008).

28. Wayland, *Elements of Political Economy* (Boston, 1860 [1837]'), iv and passim.

29. Howe, *What Hath God Wrought*, 288; Wayland quotes are from *The Duties of an American Citizen* (Boston, 1825), 19, 34, 44.

30. Adrian Desmond and James Moore, *Darwin: The Life of a Tormented Evolutionist* (New York: Warner Books, 1992), provide a compelling account of this motive and of the social dynamics associated with it in England.

Chapter 5

1. E.g., Carl Diehl, *Americans and German Scholarship* (New Haven: Yale University Press, 1978), passim; James Turner, "The Prussian Road to University? German Models and the University of Michigan, 1837–c. 1895," *Rackam Reports* (Ann Arbor: University of Michigan, 1989), 6–52; Laurence Veysey, *The Emergence of the American University* (Chicago: University of Chicago Press, 1965), 126–33.

2. Carl Diehl, *Americans and German Scholarship, 1770–1870* (New Haven: Yale University Press, 1978), 50–69, 148. See also Thomas Albert Howard, *Protestant Theology and the Making of the Modern German University* (New York: Oxford University Press, 2006), and Michael J. Hofstetter, *The Romantic Idea of a University: England and Germany, 1770–1850* (New York: Palgrave, 2001).

3. See James M. Turner, *Philology: The Forgotten Origins of the Modern Humanities* (Princeton: Princeton University Press, 2014).

4. Diehl, *Americans and German Scholarship*, 18. Cf. Konrad H. Jarausch, *Students, Society, and Politics in Imperial Germany: The Rise of Academic Illiberalism* (Princeton: Princeton University Press, 1982), 9. R. Steven Turner, "The Prussian University and the Research Imperative, 1806–1848," Ph.D. dissertation, Princeton University, 1973, 259–67, 273–77.

5. Fichte, "Concerning the Only Possible Disturbance of Academic Freedom," Rector address at Berlin University, October 19, 1811, quoted in Turner, "Prussian University," 268.

6. Victor Roy Wilbee, "The Religious Dimensions of Three Presidencies in a State University: Presidents Tappan, Haven, and Angell at the University of Michigan," Ph.D. dissertation, University of Michigan, 1967, 24.

7. He considered Hamilton, for instance, "the very highest authority on the subject" of educational reform. Henry P. Tappan, *The University: Its Constitution and Its Relations, Political and Religious: A Discourse, June 22, 1858* (Ann Arbor, 1858), 8.

8. Wilbee, "Religious Dimensions," Ph.D. dissertation, University of Michigan, 1967, 52–70.

9. Henry P. Tappan, *University Education* (New York, 1851), 61. Cf. 54–56 and 75 on Wayland's views.

10. Ibid., 65.

11. Ibid., 13–14.

12. Henry P. Tappan, "John Milton," unpublished manuscript, Tappan Papers, Michigan Historical Collections of the University of Michigan, 63, quoted in Wilbee, "Religious Dimensions," 75.

13. Turner, "Prussian University," 358, 429–30.

14. Turner, "Prussian Road to University?"

15. Tappan, *The University*, 5.

16. Wilbee, "Religious Dimensions," 59.

17. Tappan, *The University*, 20. Harvard, for instance, by this time was hiring some faculty on this basis but others on the more traditional informal and local criteria. See Robert A. McCaughey, "The Transformation of American Academic Life: Harvard University, 1821–1892," *Perspectives in American History* 8 (1974), 239–332.

18. Wilbee, "Religious Dimensions," 99, 108.

19. Howard H. Peckham, *The Making of the University of Michigan, 1817–1967* (Ann Arbor: University of Michigan Press, 1967), 38, 47.

20. Tappan, *The University*, 32–33.

21. Wilbee, "Religious Dimensions," 99. Tappan had already proposed such an arrangement before he went to Ann Arbor. *University Education*, 94.

22. Tappan, *The University*, 23–25. By the 1850s other colleges were being allowed formally to grant degrees as well. On background of religious issues see Wilbee, "Religious Dimensions," 1–51, 99, 120, and passim.

23. Wilbee, "Religious Dimensions," 61.

24. Tappan, *The University*, 32. The question of whether science might start with biblical data was being sharply debated at mid-century with respect to the science of geology, for instance, regarding the work of Taylor Lewis at Union College. See George Marsden, *The Evangelical Mind and the New School Presbyterian Experience* (New Haven: Yale University Press, 1970), 142–56.

25. Tappan, *The University*, 6.

26. Tappan, *University Education*, 27, 42, 39.

27. Ibid., 40.

28. Henry P. Tappan, *The Progress of Educational Development: A Discourse . . .*, June 25, 1855 (Ann Arbor, 1855), 22.

29. Peckham, *The Making of the University of Michigan*, 39–52.

Part II

1. Mark Noll, *The Civil War as a Theological Crisis* (Chapel Hill: University of North Carolina Press, 2006), 36–7.

Chapter 6

1. Quoted from David C. Lindberg and Ronald L. Numbers, "Beyond War and Peace: A Reappraisal of the Encounter between Christianity and Science," *Perspectives on Science and Christian Faith* 39(3, September 1987), 140–49.

2. "Prof. White on "The Battle-fields of Science," *The New York Tribune*, December 18, 1869, 4.

3. As quoted in Harold Y. Vanderpool, ed., *Darwin and Darwinism* (Lexington, Mass.: D. C. Heath), 91.

4. Andrew Dickson White, *Autobiography of Andrew Dickson White*, 2 vols. (New York, 1906, 1:279).

5. Earl Hubert Brill, "Religion and the Rise of the University: A Study of the Secularization of American Higher Education, 1870–1910," Ph.D. dissertation, American University, 1969, 50; Glenn C. Altschuler, *Andrew D. White—Educator, Historian, Diplomat* (Ithaca, N.Y.: Cornell University Press, 1979); Morris Bishop, *A History of Cornell* (Ithaca, N.Y.: Cornell University Press, 1962); Walter P. Rogers, *Andrew D. White and the Modern University* (Ithaca, N.Y.: Cornell University Press, 1942); and White, *Autobiography*.

6. Altschuler, *White*, 56.

7. Cornell to his wife, August 20, 1843, and April 2, 1854, quoted in Bishop, *Cornell*, 26–27.

8. Horace Greeley, "Address at the Laying of the Cornerstone of the People's College" (1858), quoted in Rogers, *White*, 9.

9. Rogers, *White*, 54–60.

10. Beecher, who was in her seventies, decided to enroll in a course at Cornell. When White informed Beecher that Cornell had no course open to women, she replied, "Oh that is quite all right Doctor White, in fact I prefer to take it with men." Kathryn Kish Sklar, *Catharine Beecher: A Study in American Domesticity* (New York: W. W. Norton, 1878), 258–59. More directly bringing the change was a promised donation if they did so. Andrea L. Turpin, *A New Moral Vision: Gender, Religion, and the Changing Purposes of American Higher Education 1837–1917* (Ithaca, N.Y.: Cornell University Press, 2016), 97–100.

11. White, "Inaugural Address," in *Account of the Proceedings of the Inauguration, October 7, 1868* (Ithaca, N.Y.: Cornell University, 1869), quoted in Bishop, *Cornell*, 190–91; Rogers, *White*, 73; and Brill, "Religion," 152.

12. Ezra Cornell, "Address at the Inauguration of Cornell University," quoted in Rogers, *White*, 73.

13. White to Willard Fiske, October 19, 1880, quoted in *White*, Rogers, 81.

14. Quoted in Bishop, *Cornell*, 191. Cf. 190–96.

15. Ibid., 192–39; Richard Hofstadter and Walter P. Metzger, *The Development of Academic Freedom in the United States* (New York: Columbia University Press, 1955), 340–41. Firing a Jew was, of course, easier than firing someone of Christian heritage, such as William Graham Sumner at Yale. On the other hand, White insisted that he would be glad to hire an academically qualified Buddhist; Laurence R. Veysey, "The Emergence of the American University, 1865–1910: A Study in the Relations between Ideals and Institutions," Ph.D. dissertation, University of California, Berkeley, 1961, 373n.

16. Quotations are from Veysey, "Emergence," 372–73, except for Sage proviso from Robert S. Shepard, *God's People in the Ivory Tower: Religion in the Early American University* (Brooklyn: Carlson Publishing, 1991), 19. In 1890 Sage also endowed an entire School of Philosophy, which included a professorship in the history and philosophy of religion and Christian ethics. This was one of the first positions in comparative religion in an American university. Christian ethics was added to accommodate the training of the first incumbent, the Rev. Charles Tyler, who had been pastor of Sage's Congregational church in Ithaca. Ibid., 18–20. James Turner, *Religion Enters the Academy* (Athens: University Georgia Press, 2011), provides a helpful overview of the emergence of the study of comparative religion in American universities.

Chapter 7

1. Louise L. Stevenson, *Scholarly Means to Evangelical Ends: The New Haven Scholars and the Transformation of Higher Learning in America, 1830–1890* (Baltimore: Johns Hopkins Press, 1986), 63–65. Much of the following account is indebted to Stevenson's insightful study.

2. Earl Hubert Brill, "Religion and the Rise of the University: A Study of the Secularization of American Higher Education, 1870–1910," Ph.D. dissertation,

American University, 1969, 60–61, 248. See 229–51, which provides an excellent account of the Yale struggles.

3. Ibid., 5–6.

4. Noah Porter, *The Elements of Moral Science: Theoretical and Practical* (New York: Charles Scribner's Sons, 1885).

5. Herbert W. Schneider, *A History of American Philosophy,* 2nd ed. (New York: Columbia University Press, 1963), 215.

6. Noah Porter, "The American Colleges and the American Public," *New Englander* 28 (January 1869), 81, 76, and passim, as summarized by Brill, "Religion," 238.

7. Noah Porter, "The American Colleges and the American Public," *New Englander* 28 (October 1869), 753–60.

8. Cf. Porter, "Inaugural Address," Yale College, October 11, 1871, quoted in Stevenson, *Scholarly Means,* 69.

9. For instance, President Theodore Dwight Woolsey of Yale in "The Religion of the Future," *New Englander* 28 (July 1869), 463–88, argued that, contrary to some recent claims, Christianity is the only religion capable of leading humanity to its ultimate progress.

10. Quoted in Alice Payne Hackett, *Wellesley: Part of American History* (New York: E. P. Dutton, 1949), 39. For a valuable account of women's higher education see Andrea L. Turpin, *A New Moral Vision: Gender, Religion and the Changing Purposes of American Higher Education, 1837–1919* (Ithaca, N.Y.: Cornell University Press, 2016). See also Helen Lefkowitz Horowitz, *Alma Mater: Design and Experience in the Women's Colleges from Their Nineteenth-Century Origins to the 1930s* (New York: Knopf, 1984).

11. Ibid., 42. For a critical view of Durant, his ties to the old-college ideal, and paternalism, see Patricia Palmieri, "Insipid Vita Nuova: Founding Ideals of the Wellesley College Community," *History of Higher Education,* 1983, 59–78.

12. Hackett, *Wellesley,* 31, 57, 151.

13. Andrea L. Turpin, *A New Moral Vision: Gender, Religion, and the Changing Purpose of American Higher Education, 1837–1917* (Ithaca, N.Y., Cornell University Press, 2016), provides the best account of these origins and of the role of religion in higher education. Her work might be read as a complement to the present work. See also Helen Lefkowitz Horowitz, *Alma Mater: Design and Experience in the Women's Colleges from Their Nineteenth-Century Origins to the 1930s* (New York: Knopf, 1984), for a perceptive overview of these developments.

14. Noah Porter, "The Christian College," address delivered at Wellesley College (Boston, 1880), 29–30.

15. For background on Porter and Yale, see Louise L. Stevenson, *Scholarly Means to Evangelical Ends: The New Haven Scholars and the Transformation of Higher Learning in America,* 1830–1890 (Baltimore: Johns Hopkins Press, 1986).

16. Ibid., 8, 21, 22.

17. Cf. Edmund S. Morgan, *The Puritan Dilemma: The Story of John Winthrop* (New York: Little, Brown, 1958).

18. Porter's wife Mary was a daughter of Yale Divinity School's famous Nathaniel William Taylor, who had been subjected to such attacks, especially by Old School Presbyterians and conservative Congregationalists.

19. Brooks Mather Kelley, *Yale: A History* (New Haven: Yale University Press, 1974), 241, points out that the disciplinary model of the Yale Report of 1828 to which Porter appealed was designed for an era when boys might enter college earlier and when some were graduating by age eighteen. By the 1870s the average entrance age was over eighteen.

20. Porter, "American Colleges," 762–67.

21. For example, David Starr Jordan, who became president of Stanford, described the clerical mind as irrevocably committed to untestable assumptions. From "The Church and Modern Thought," *Overland Monthly* 18 (1891), 392, cited in Richard Hofstadter and Walter P. Metzger, *The Development of Academic Freedom in the United States* (New York: Columbia University Press, 1955), 348. During the 1870s the *Index*, the journal of the American Liberal Union, edited by Francis E. Abbott, also pushed this interpretation. See Hofstadter and Metzger, *Academic Freedom*, 348–51.

22. In 1879 G. Stanley Hall wrote that "with comparatively few exceptions all the most competent teachers of natural or physical science either tacitly accept or openly advocate the fundamental principles of evolution. Even the most orthodox institutions are often no exception to this rule." "Philosophy in the United States," *Mind* 4 (January 1879), 101. On Yale see Hofstadter and Metzger, *Academic Freedom*, 332–33. Stevenson, *Scholarly Means*, 76–79.

23. Charles D. Cashdollar, *The Transformation of Theology, 1830–1890: Positivism and Protestant Thought in Britain and America* (Princeton: Princeton University Press, 1989), esp. 446.

24. Ibid.

25. Noah Porter, *The Human Intellect* (New York: Scribner, 1868), 661–62.

26. Noah Porter, "Herbert Spencer's Theory of Sociology," *Princeton Review*, ser. 4, 6 (September 1880), 295

27. This is the tone implied by Hofstadter and Metzger, who lump the Porter–Sumner controversy with repression of teaching of biological evolution (*Academic Freedom*, 336–38).

28. Henry Durand, "Bright College Years" (1881). From Judith Ann Schiff, "The Birth, Near Demise, and Comeback of 'Bright College Years,'" *Yale Alumni Magazine*, 63.3.

Chapter 8

1. Earl Hubert Brill, "Religion and the Rise of the University: A Study of the Secularization of American Higher Education, 1870–1910," Ph.D. dissertation, American University, 1969, 52–53.

2. D. G. Hart, "Faith and Learning in the Age of the University: The Academic Ministry of Daniel Coit Gilman," in *The Secularization of the Academy*, George M. Marsden and Bradley J. Longfield, eds. (New York: Oxford University Press, 1992), 16–17.

3. As D. G. Hart points out in "Faith and Learning," 107–45, Gilman and the persons in his generation whom he represented could be seen as harmonizers of science and religion in continuity with the antebellum evangelical harmonizers, as genuine affirmations of the Christian heritage, broadly conceived.

4. Trustee resolutions, October 8, 1867, Verne A. Stadtman, *The University of California, 1868–1968* (New York: McGraw Hill, 1970), 31.

5. Willey to Baldwin, September 1, 1869, in Stadtman, *University of California*, 36.

6. Freshmen were required to take twelve hours of Latin and Classical Greek in their first three years. Except for five hours of mental and moral philosophy, the rest of the curriculum was modern, including requirements in English, modern languages, mathematics, science, geography, drawing, and military science. "Schedule of Studies Pursued in University and Text Books used. Reported to President Durant, April 7, 1871," University of California archives, Box 12:2.

7. Winton U. Solberg, "The Conflict between Religion and Secularism at the University of Illinois, 1867–1894," *American Quarterly* 18 (1966), 189–90.

8. Gilman, "The University of California in Its Infancy," Inaugural, Nov. 7, 1872, in *University Problems in the United States* (New York 1898), 178.

9. Gilman, Inaugural, 178–97.

10. *Register of the University of California*, 1874, 105, from California Political Code (1874).

11. Gilman reply to Patterson (two printed pages) [1873]. Gilman cover letter of April 15, 1901, says he is not sure where it was published. Historical Pamphlets, vol. 1, university archives, Bancroft Library, University of California.

12. Gilman to White, 1874, quoted in Stadtman, *University of California*, 79.

13. I am indebted to D. G. Hart, "Faith and Learning in the Age of the University: The Academic Ministry of Daniel Coit Gilman," in *The Secularization of the Academy*, George M. Marsden and Bradley J. Longfield, eds. (New York: Oxford University Press, 1992), 107–45, for his valuable research and insights on Gilman.

14. Hugh Hawkins, *Pioneer, A History of the Johns Hopkins University, 1874–1889* (Ithaca, N.Y.: Cornell University Press, 1960), 4–5. Four of the other trustees were Episcopal and one was Presbyterian.

15. Gilman, "The Johns Hopkins University in Its Beginnings," in *University Problems in the United States* (New York, 1898), 39.

16. Reverdy Johnson, Jr., to Gilman, January 4, 1875, and Gilman to Johnson, January 30, 1875, quoted in Hawkins, *Pioneer*, 22.

17. Hawkins, *Pioneer*, 69–71.

18. *New York Observer*, September 21, 1876, quoted in Hawkins, *Pioneer*, 71.

19. *Christian Advocate*, September 22, 1876, 308, quoted in Earl Hubert Brill, "Religion and the Rise of the University: A Study of the Secularization of American Higher Education, 1870–1910," Ph.D. dissertation, American University, 1969, 166.

20. Quoted in Hawkins, *Pioneer*, 71.

21. Hawkins, *Pioneer*, 252. Gilman, "The Johns Hopkins University," 19.

22. Gilman, "The Johns Hopkins University," 14–15.

23. Hawkins, *Pioneer*, 253, cf. 179n. re another candidate's being questioned on his orthodoxy. G. Stanley Hall to Gilman, January 5, 1881, apparently in response to questioning, assured Gilman that he was far from being a philosophical materialist; quoted in Dorothy Ross, *G. Stanley Hall: The Psychologist as Prophet* (Chicago: University of Chicago Press, 1972), 138–39. Gilman's hiring of Hall suggests that he was not concerned with questions of orthodoxy.

24. Ibid., 238–39.

25. Laurence Veysey, *The Emergence of the American University* (Chicago: University of Chicago Press, 1965), 127.

26. See Richard Hofstadter and Walter P. Metzger, *The Development of Academic Freedom in the United States* (New York: Columbia University Press, 1955), 367–412, on similarities and difference to the German model.

27. Roy Steven Turner, "The Prussian Universities and the Research Ideal, 1806 to 1848," Ph.D. dissertation, Princeton University, 1973, 387–90.

28. In England the issue was resolved with the same distinction. The universities were declared public and formally secularized by legislation in the latter half of the nineteenth century, while colleges were designated as private and thus free to continue religious practices and to be the loci for building character, manliness, and other Christian virtues. The difference was that in England there was a real institutional distinction between a college and a university. A university was a degree-granting agency, whereas a college was a community of teachers and students and traditionally the principal locus for instruction. In the United States, on the other hand, the university was almost always considered the extension of a college so that it was more difficult for the character of the two to remain distinct. I am grateful to Sheldon Rothblatt for clarifying for me the English analogy. See also his *The Revolution of the Dons: Cambridge and Society in Victorian England* (London: Faber and Faber, 1968).

29. James Turner, "Secularization and Sacralization: Speculations on Some Religious Origins of the Secular Humanities Curriculum, 1850–1900," in Marsden and Longfield, *Secularization of the Academy*, 74–106.

30. Burton J. Bledstein, *The Culture of Professionalism: The Middle Class and the Development of Higher Education in America* (New York: W. W. Norton, 1976), x, 34.

31. See, for instance, Alvin Plantinga, "Methodological Naturalism?," *Perspectives on Science and Faith 49* (September 1997), 143–154. Plantinga argues that natural scientific inquiry does not require strict methodological naturalism and that it can be conducted just as well from the conscious perspective of metaphysical theism.

32. Gilman, "Johns Hopkins University," 18.

33. "Address by President D. C. Gilman, LL.D., of Baltimore," in *National Perils and Opportunities: The Discussions of the . . . Evangelical Alliance for the United States* (New York, 1887), 281, 283, cf. v–x. In an address before the Phi Beta Kappa Society of Harvard University, July 1, 1886, Gilman makes similar points; "The Characteristics of a University," in *University Problems*, 97.

Chapter 9

1. "Dissolving View; Rev. Dr. Horton's Opinion of Unitarianism," *Oakland Tribune*, December 17, 1888, contrasts an atmosphere favorable to religion at Michigan to that at Berkeley. Horace Davis, the Unitarian president, also appealed to aspects of the Michigan model. Davis repeated Gilman's suggestion for denominational houses, citing a "Hobart House," founded by Episcopalians in Ann Arbor. *Occident,* September 11, 1888, and *San Leandro Advertiser,* September 8, 1888. From newspaper clippings book in university archives, Bancroft Library, University of California at Berkeley.

2. "A Dissolving View; Rev. Dr. Horton's Opinion of Unitarianism," *Oakland Tribune*, December 17, 1888. "Dr. Horton's Scheme of a Presbyterian College," *Enquirer,* July 29, 1889.

3. Bradley J. Longfield, "From Evangelicalism to Liberalism: Public Midwestern Universities in Nineteenth-Century America," in *The Secularization of the Academy,* George M. Marsden and Bradley J. Longfield, eds. (New York: Oxford University Press, 1992), 46–73.

4. George P. Fisher to E. C. Walker, July 28, 1869, in *From Vermont to Michigan: Correspondence of James Burrill Angell: 1869–1871*, Wilfred B. Shaw, ed. (Ann Arbor, 1936), 70–71. Angell had also taught modern languages and literature at Brown prior to the Civil War.

5. James Burrill Angell, "Inaugural Address, University of Michigan" (1871), *Selected Addresses* (New York, 1912), 29.

6. Victor R. Wilbee, "The Religious Dimensions of Three Presidencies in a State University: Presidents Tappan, Haven, and Angell at the University of Michigan," Ph.D. dissertation, University of Michigan, 1967, 198–200. Cf. Winton U. Solberg, "Religion and Secularism at the University of Illinois, 1867–1894," *American Quarterly* 18 (1966), 187.

7. Wilbee, "Religious Dimensions," 201–2.

8. Michigan Legislature, *Legislative Journal, Daily Proceedings* (Lansing, 1873), as quoted (without original page numbers) in Wilbee, "Religious Dimensions," Appendix A, 217–20. Concluding statement from *Journal,* 1775, quoted in Wilbee, 203.

9. Angell to Peter Collier, September 28, 1871, in Shaw, *From Vermont to Michigan,* 292–93. Wilbee, "Religious Dimensions," 179–82. Morning chapel services finally ended in 1894, and all services ended in 1901 or 1902.

10. Wilbee, "Religious Dimensions," 205–6.

11. Angell to D. C. Gilman, October 23, 1885, quoted in Laurence Veysey, *The Emergence of the American University* (Chicago: University of Chicago Press, 1965), 75.

12. Angell, "Religious Life in Our State Universities," *Andover Review* 13 (April 1890), 365–72. Cf. Clarence Prouty Shedd, *The Church Follows Its Students* (New Haven, 1938), 11.

13. Student Christian Association, "Editor's Note," *Religious Thought at the University of Michigan* (Ann Arbor, 1893), iv.

14. V. M. Spalding, "How Has Biological Research Modified Christian Conceptions?" in *Religious Thought at Michigan*, 96–109. Though the preponderant tone of the volume is liberal, some authors appear more conservative; e.g., W. J. Hardman defends biblical miracles and sees archaeological evidence as confirming the historicity of Scripture. "The Methods of Science Applied to Christianity," 124–38 in *Religious Thought at Michigan*.

15. Francis W. Kelsey, "Primitive and Modern Christianity," in *Religious Thought at Michigan*, 19.

16. H. C. Adams, "Christianity as a Social Force," in *Religious Thought at Michigan*, 53. Cf. Angell, "The Old and the New Ideal of Scholars," Baccalaureate Address, June 18, 1905 (Ann Arbor, 1905), 8.

17. Angell, "Christianity and Other Religions Judged by Their Fruits," in *Religious Thought at Michigan*, 3–14.

18. John Dewey, "Christianity and Democracy," in *Religious Thought at Michigan*, 60.

19. Bruce Kuklick, *The Rise of American Philosophy: Cambridge, Massachusetts, 1860–1930* (New Haven: Yale University Press, 1977), 230–53, provides a valuable account of Dewey's journey and its relation to earlier New England theology. Steven C. Rockefeller, *John Dewey: Religious Faith and Democratic Humanism* (New York: Columbia University Press, 1991), is also valuable.

20. Dewey, "Christianity and Democracy," 60–69.

21. Adams, "Christianity as a Social Force," 51–59.

22. Richard Hofstadter and Walter P. Metzger, *The Development of Academic Freedom in the United States* (New York: Columbia University Press, 1955), 411–67.

23. In "The Expanding Power of Christianity," for instance, Angell talks about God as "a beneficent moral governor of the universe," the need for special revelation, "the plan of redemption" (though declining to discuss any theories of the atonement), and "the hope for immortal life" (though he is vague as to whether this is a quality of life or actual life after death.) *Religious Thought at Michigan*, 141–50.

24. Ibid. See also several baccalaureate addresses, all published in Ann Arbor: "Lesson Suggested by Christ's Life to the Scholar" (1903), "The Old and the New Ideal of Scholars" (1905), and "The Age of Quickened Conscience" (1908).

25. Angell, "Religious Life," 368–69.

26. Wilbee reports a survey at Michigan in 1881 that showed that "seventy per cent of the students and thirty-nine per cent of the faculty were not professing Christians." "Religious Dimensions," 206. Other reports suggest a rise in Christian belief in colleges during this era, though such a large change would seem remarkable.

27. Frank W. Kelsey, "State Universities and Church Colleges," *Atlantic Monthly* 80 (December 1897), 827. Jews were listed among "church members."

28. Ibid., 828. At this time Michigan had in all its schools 2263 men and 662 women students. The surveys included all schools and typically showed the proportion of church members "somewhat greater in the collegiate department than in the professional schools." However, at Michigan the medical school had the highest percentage of church members, suggesting perhaps that the ethos of the Michigan elite was still substantially Christian.

29. Quoted in Willian Carey Jones, *Illustrated History of the University of California* (San Francisco 1895), 101–2.

30. Elmer Ellsworth Brown, "Religious Forces in Higher Education," *Pacific Theological Seminary Publications,* No. 3, 4, quoted in Merrimon Cuninggim, *The College Seeks Religion* (New Haven: Yale University Press, 1947), 81. Brown's views of religion and its place in the university (Cuninggim, 81–82) are very similar to those expressed by Mary Gilmore. The architecture of Berkeley that emerged in the first half of the twentieth century argued for the same ideal. While the university itself was built in a massive classical style, it was surrounded by an array of churches, Ys, and theological seminaries.

31. James Angell, "Lessons Suggested by Christ's Life to the Scholar," Baccalaureate Address (Ann Arbor, 1903), 4–5. On the continuing New England influence, Samuel Haber, *Authority and Honor in the American Professions, 1750–1900* (Chicago: University of Chicago Press, 1991), 277, notes that, while the professoriate increased by four times from 1870 to 1900, it also became more predominantly of Congregational and Presbyterian background.

32. Ibid., 5. "But after all in every true scholar, the manhood is more than the scholarship.... It calls on the scholar as a man to dedicate all his powers and attainments to the good of his fellows." This passage suggests that "manhood" and "Manliness," so often used in this era, might have a connotation of the selflessness arising from recognizing one's common humanity. Angell illustrates this point with examples of service of women from the university.

33. John Dewey, "Reconstruction," *The Bulletin* 15 (May 1894), quoted in Wilbee, "Religious Dimensions," 207.

34. Dewey, "Christianity and Democracy," 68–69.

Chapter 10

1. This is more directly a paraphrase of Daniel Walker Howe, *The Unitarian Conscience* (Cambridge, Mass.: Harvard University Press, 1970), 300, alluding to comments in *The Education of Henry Adams* (1907).

2. Robert A. McCaughey, "The Transformation of American Academic Life: Harvard University, 1821–1892," in *Perspectives in American History,* Vol. VIII (1974), Appendix D, 327–32, provides a valuable profile of Harvard faculty from 1821 to 1892.

3. See Howe, *Unitarian Conscience.*

4. From Ware, "On the Formation of Christian Character," as summarized in Howe, *Unitarian Conscience,* 106–7.

5. Josiah Quincy, *The History of Harvard University* (Cambridge, Mass., 1840), Vol. 11, 444–46, from excerpt in *American Higher Education: A Documentary History,* Richard Hofstadter and Wilson Smith, eds. (Chicago: University of Chicago Press, 1961), Vol. I, 436.

6. This is an elaboration of points made in Richard Hofstadter and Walter P. Metzger, *The Development of Academic Freedom in the United States* (New York: Columbia University Press, 1955), 371–75.

7. Frederic Henry Hedge, "University Reform, an Address to the Alumni of Harvard, at Their Triennial Festival," *Atlantic Monthly* 18 (July 1866), 199–307, excerpt in Hofstadter and Metzger, *Academic Freedom*. See Hofstadter and Smith, *Documentary History*, Vol. II, 562–63. Eliot said much the same in his "Inaugural Address as President of Harvard College" (1869): "The worthy fruit of academic culture is an open mind, trained in careful thinking, instructed in the methods of philosophical investigation, acquainted in a general way with the accumulated thought of past generations, and penetrated with humility. It is thus that the university in our day serves Christ and the church." Eliot, *Educational Reform: Essays and Address* (New York, 1898), 8.

8. Hugh Hawkins, *Between Harvard and America: The Educational Leadership of Charles W. Eliot* (New York: Oxford University Press, 1972), 38. My primary debt for the overview of Eliot that follows is to Hawkins. Also see Earl Hubert Brill, "Religion and the Rise of the University: A Study of the Secularization of American Higher Education, 1870–1910," Ph.D. dissertation, American University, 1969; and Laurence Veysey, *The Emergence of the American University* (Chicago: University of Chicago Press, 1965).

9. Eliot, *Educational Reform*, 34.

10. Hawkins, *Eliot*, 166.

11. Emerson, "The American Scholar" (1837).

12. McCaughey, "Transformation," presents a thorough analysis of the rise of professionalism at Harvard. He argues that Eliot did not fully move away from hiring Unitarian gentlemen scholars (like himself) until around the late 1870s, when he was forced by the competition from Johns Hopkins into adopting more professional criteria.

13. Charles W. Eliot, "Liberty in Education" (Debate with James McCosh before the Nineteenth Century Club of New York, 1885), Eliot, *Educational Reform*, 142–43.

14. Ibid., 144

15. Ibid., 148.

16. Laurence Veysey, "The Emergence of the American University," Ph.D. dissertation, University of California, Berkeley, 1961, 411.

17. Charles W. Eliot, "New Education," *Atlantic Monthly*, 23, 216, quoted in Hawkins, *Eliot*, 53.

18. Charles W. Eliot, "Experience with a College Elective System" (1895), Eliot papers, quoted in Hawkins, *Eliot*, 94.

19. Brill, "Religion and the Rise of the University," 186–93, provides the best account of this.

20. Quoted in Bruce Kuklick, *The Rise of American Philosophy, Cambridge, Massachusetts 1860 to 1930* (New Haven: Yale University Press, 1977), 161. See also 161–62. I am most immediately dependent on Kuklick for much of this account. See also Louis Menand, *The Metaphysical Club* (New York: Farrar, Strauss, and Giroux, 2001), for an engaging account of the wider context.

21. Kuklick, *Rise*, esp. 565.

22. William James, "The Ph.D. Octopus" (1903), in *Memories and Studies* (Westport, Conn.: Greenwood Press, 1971 [1941]), 334.

23. Perhaps it is significant that the free-floating elective system went out of favor after the turn of the century at the same time as fewer disciplines seemed to be playing this quasi-spiritual and moral role.

24. James Turner, "Secularization and Sacralization: Speculations on Some Religious Origins of the Secular Humanities Curriculum, 1850–1900," in *The Secularization of the Academy,* George M. Marsden and Bradley J. Longfield, eds. (New York: Oxford University Press, 1992), 74–106.

25. Quoted from Ellery Sedgwick in Turner, "Secularization," 87. This account is drawn from Turner. See also Turner's *The Liberal Education of Charles Eliot Norton* (Baltimore: Johns Hopkins University Press, 1999).

26. Eliot, "What Place Should Religion Have in a College?" (unpublished reply to McCosh, 1886), Eliot papers, Harvard, quoted in Hawkins, *Eliot,* 129–30.

27. Eliot, Address at the Inauguration of Daniel C. Gilman as president of Johns Hopkins University, February 22, 1876, *Educational Reform,* 43.

28. Eliot, "Inaugural Address," 31.

29. Hawkins, *Eliot,* 191–96. The distance that Eliot had moved from evangelical Christianity is suggested by the remark of Billy Sunday that Eliot was "so lowdown he would need an aeroplane to get into hell." Upton Sinclair, *The Goose-Step: A Study of American Education* (Pasadena, Calif.: 1923), 103, quoted in Hawkins, 297.

30. Eliot, "The Religion of the Future" (1909), in *The Durable Satisfactions of Life* (New York, 1910), 172.

Chapter 11

1. Samuel Eliot Morison, *Three Centuries of Harvard* (Cambridge, Mass.: Harvard University Press, 1936), 362–63.

2. J. David Hoeveler Jr., *James McCosh and the Scottish Intellectual Tradition: From Glasgow to Princeton* (Princeton: Princeton University Press, 1981), 64.

3. Ibid., passim.

4. Ibid., 224.

5. Gary Scott Smith, *The Seeds of Secularization: Calvinism, Culture and Pluralism in America*, 1870–1915 (Grand Rapids, Mich.: Christian University Press, 1985), 94–111, esp. 98. See also David N. Livingstone, *Darwin's Forgotten Defenders: The Encounter between Evangelical Theology and Evolutionary Thought* (Grand Rapids, Mich.: William B. Eerdmans, 1987).

6. Andrew Dickson White, *A History of the Warfare of Science with Theology in Christendom* (New York, 1896), Vol. I, 80, cf. 412n. Cf. Hoeveler, *McCosh*, 278–79.

7. Hoeveler, *McCosh,* 239.

8. Ibid., 252–53, quotation, 252, is addressed to the trustees in 1885. McCosh did eventually take the lead in eliminating evening prayers, thus reducing the chapel requirement to once daily.

9. E.g., McCosh, *What an American University Should Be* (New York, 1885).

10. Eliot, "On the Education of Ministers," from the *Princeton Review,* May 1883, in Eliot, *Educational Reform: Essays and Address* (New York, 1898), 66–70.

11. Francis Patton, "On the Education of Ministers: A Reply to President Eliot," *Princeton Review,* 4th ser., 2 (July 1883), 48–66, quotations, 49 and 57.

12. Hoeveler, *McCosh,* 234–36. Porter was invited also but bowed out.

13. From a substantial abstract in "Religion in Colleges, Discussions by Drs. McCosh and Eliot," *New York Daily Tribune,* February 4, 1886, 3.

14. James McCosh, *What an American University Should Be,* 522, passim.

15. *New York Daily Tribune,* February 4, 1886, 3. McCosh, *Religion in a College: What Place it Should Have* (New York, 1886), Prefatory note, 3.

16. P. C. Kemeny, *Princeton in the Nation's Service: Religious Ideals and Educational Practice, 1868–1928* (New York: Oxford University Press, 1998). I also deal with it in some detail in the earlier version of *The Soul of the American University,* 196–235.

17. Wilson to Albert Shaw, November 3, 1890, *Papers of WW,* Vol. VII, 62. Quoted in Paul C. Kemeny, "President Francis Landey Patton, Princeton University and Faculty Ferment," *American Presbyterians: The Journal of the Presbyterian Historical Society* 69 (1991), 116.

18. James Mark Baldwin, *Between Two Wars, 1861–1921 Being Memories, Opinions and Letters Received* (Boston, 1926), Vol. I, 341. From Kemeny, unpublished draft of "Patton."

19. Thomas Jefferson Wertenbaker, *Princeton, 1746–1896* (Princeton: Princeton University Press, 1946), 374–75. This debate, in part, reflected a difference between the Old School and the New School Presbyterian heritages. The Old School thought that since consumption of alcohol was not forbidden in Scripture, such questions of personal behavior were matters of Christian liberty. Some of the seminary faculty joined in the petition for the liquor license. The complaints came primarily from former New School areas such as New York.

20. Patton, *New York Herald,* January 21, 1898, quoted in Wertenbaker, *Princeton,* 375.

21. Wilson to Frederick Jackson Turner, November 15, 1896, *The Papers of Woodrow Wilson,* Arthur S. Link, et al. eds. (Princeton: Princeton University Press, 1968–1994), Vol. X, 53.

22. Kemeny, *Princeton in the Nation's Service,* 113–115.

23. Kemeny, "Patton," 118.

24. Henry Wilkinson Bragdon, *Woodrow Wilson: The Academic Years* (Cambridge, MA: Haravard University Press, 1967), 272. Bragdon provides a helpful picture of changing campus life.

25. Ibid., 274–77.

26. Wilson, "Princeton in the Nation's Service," A Commemorative Address, October 21, 1896, *Papers of WW,* Vol. X, 11–31.

27. Wilson, "The 1905 Baccalaureate Sermon," reprinted in John M. Mulder, "Wilson the Preacher: The 1905 Baccalaureate Sermon," *Journal of Presbyterian History* 51 (1973), 275.

28. Quoted from Arthur Walworth, *Woodrow Wilson* (Boston, 1965), 84, in John M. Mulder, *Woodrow Wilson: The Years of Preparation* (Princeton: Princeton University Press, 1978), 178.

29. Ibid., 176–82. Mulder, "Wilson the Preacher."

30. Kemeny, "Patton," 118.

31. In their day the Princeton theologians were the most capable intellectually of the defenders of strict traditional biblical authority. But their intellectual position, based as it was on the heritage of Scottish Common Sense philosophy, also put them in a precarious position in relation to the contemporary modern scholarship. In brief, they insisted, that there was a common rationality that all humans should follow and that the basic Christian viewpoint could win the day on purely rational grounds. I have written about why that was a problem in *Understanding Fundamentalism and Evangelicalism* (Grand Rapids, Mich.: Wm. B. Eerdmans, 1991), 122–152.

32. Kemeny, *Princeton in the Nation's Service*, 160–163.

Chapter 12

1. James P. Wind, *The Bible and the University* (Atlanta: Scholars Press, 1987), 42, quoting Vincent in 1886. This account of Harper very closely follows Wind, 37–46, 105–9.

2. Quoted in ibid., 58.

3. Harper, "Editorial," *Biblical World* 3 (1894), 3, quoted in Stephen A. Schmidt, *A History of the Religious Education Association* (Birmingham, Ala.: Religious Education Press, 1983), 11.

4. Richard J. Storr, *Harper's University: The Beginnings* (Chicago: University of Chicago Press, 1966) 6–34.

5. For instance, Robert Herrick, *Chimes* (New York, 1926), 6; Storr, *Harper's University*, 210. Laurence Veysey, *The Emergence of the American University* (Chicago: University of Chicago Press, 1965), 31.

6. Thorstein Veblen, *The Higher Learning in America* (New York: Viking Press, 1935 [1918]), 225 and passim.

7. Upton Sinclair, *Goose-Step: A Study of American Education,* 2nd ed. (Pasadena, Calif., 1923 [1922]), 240–41. James P. Wind, *The Bible and the University* (Atlanta: Scholars Press, 1987), 147–61, helpfully summarizes these and a number of other assessments of the university.

8. Veysey, *Emergence*, 263–68, 342–56.

9. Veysey, *Emergence*, 368–79.

10. Cf. Samuel Haber, *Efficiency and Uplift: Scientific Management in the Progressive Era, 1890–1920* (Chicago: University of Chicago Press, 1964). Max Weber's observations in *The Protestant Ethic and the Spirit of Capitalism* (1905) makes the point of the affinities of Protestantism and the spirit of compulsive efficiency.

11. Wind, *The Bible and the University*, develops this point. I am much indebted to his insights. The tendency to eliminate religion as a major cultural interpreter appears already early in the twentieth century in the outlooks of observers such as Veblen and

Sinclair. They were preoccupied with the important insight of business dominance, a way of looking at things that was reinforced (notably in Sinclair's case) by the vogue of Marxist interpretation.

12. Quoted in Wind, *The Bible and the University*, 178.
13. Margaret Grubiak, *White Elephants on Campus: The Decline of the University Chapel in America, 1920–1960* (Notre Dame, Ind.: University of Notre Dame Press, 2014).
14. Gates to Mrs. J. D. Rockefeller, December 22, 1892, from Veysey, *Emergence*, 373n. Baptists predominated, with twenty-four Congregationalists and ten Presbyterians. (It was required that two-thirds of the trustees be Baptist.)
15. By 1903 a graduating class of 142 included 10 Jews and 8 Roman Catholics. Storr, *Harper's University*, 110.
16. From a statement in a presidential report, 1902, quoted in Storr, *Harper's University*, 185. See his useful account of religion at the university from which the present account is drawn (183–89).
17. Ibid., 92–93.Thomas Wakefield Goodspeed, *A History of the University of Chicago* (Chicago, 1916), 395.
18. Harper, "University and Religious Education," *The Trend in Higher Education* (Chicago, 1905), 58, 74–75.
19. Amos Alonzo Stagg to his family, January 20, 1891, from Storr, *Harper's University*, 179. See Stagg and Wesley Stout, *Touchdown!* (New York: Longmans, Green and Co., 1927), 110.
20. Veysey, *Emergence*, 276–77.
21. Stagg and Stout, *Touchdown!*, 147.
22. Harper, Decennial Report, July 1, 1902, in *The Idea of the University of Chicago: Selections from the Papers of the First Eight Chief Executives of the University of Chicago from 1891 to 1975*, William Michael Murphy and D. J. R. Bruckner, eds. (Chicago: University of Chicago Press, 1976), 7. The quotation continues: "The drawing of a narrower line than this would be fatal to the growth of the University. Here lies the distinction between a college and a university. The one may be controlled by the ecclesiastical or political spirit; the other may not be...."
23. William Rainey Harper, "America as a Missionary Field," in *Religion and the Higher Life: Talks to Students* (Chicago: University of Chicago Press, 1904), 175–84.
24. Willian Rainey Harper, "The University and Democracy," in *Trend in Higher Education*, 12.
25. Ibid., 21; cf. 1–34 and passim.
26. Quoted (without precise citation) in Robert M. Crunden, *Ministers of Reform: The Progressives' Achievement in American Civilization, 1889–1920* (Urbana: University of Illinois Press, 1984), 58.
27. John Dewey, "The Ethics of Democracy" (1888), quoted in Dorothy Ross, *The Origins of American Social Science* (Cambridge: Cambridge University Press, 1991), 163.
28. Crunden, *Ministers of Reform*, passim.
29. Jean B. Quandt, *From the Small Town to the Great Community: The Social Thought of Progressive Intellectuals* (New Brunswick, N.J.: Rutgers University Press, 1970), shows this ideal of community to be at the heart of the progressive vision (102–25 [on Dewey] and passim).

30. Cf. Crunden, *Ministers of Reform,* 200–224.

31. On Small's career, see Vernon K. Dibble, *The Legacy of Albion Small* (Chicago: University of Chicago Press, 1975).

32. Small, "Research Ideals," *Record* 10 (October 1905), 87, quoted in Storr, *Harper's University,* 159.

33. Benjamin G. Rader, *The Academic Mind and Reform: The Influence of Richard T. Ely in American Life* (Lexington: University of Kentucky Press, 1966), 2. See list of students, 26–27.

34. "Statement of Dr. Richard T. Ely," Report of the Organization of the American Economics Association (Baltimore, 1886), 18.

35. Cf. Thomas L. Haskell's discussion of these and other tendencies in *The Emergence of Professional Social Science: The American Social Science Association and the Nineteenth-Century Crisis in Authority* (Urbana: University of Illinois Press, 1977), 1–23. Robert C. Bannister, *Sociology and Scientism: The American Quest for Objectivity,* 1880–1940 (Chapel Hill: University of North Carolina Press, 1987), 32–63, provides a valuable discussion of Small's views, including his concept of objectivity. Cf. the discussion in Mary O. Furner, *Advocacy and Objectivity: A Crisis in the Professionalization of American Social Science, 1865–1905* (Lexington: University of Kentucky Press, 1975), 295–304. Also see Arthur J. Vidich and Sanford M. Lyman, *American Sociology: Worldly Rejections of Religion and Their Directions* (New Haven: Yale University Press, 1985), 178–94.

36. Ross, *Origins of American Social Science.* Ross acknowledges this connection in passing but misses the religious force of Protestant exceptionalism.

Part III

1. Julie Reuben, *The Making of the Modern University: Intellectual Transformation and the Marginalization of Morality* (Chicago, University of Chicago Press, 1996.

2. Andrew Jewett, *Science, Democracy, and the American University: From the Civil War to the Cold War* (Cambridge: Cambridge University Press, 2012).

3. Christian Smith, *The Sacred Project of American Sociology* (New York: Oxford University Press, 2014).

4. Roger L. Geiger, *The History of American Higher Education: Learning and Culture from the Founding to World War II* (Princeton: Princeton University Press, 2014), 365, 369.

5. Andrea L.Turpin, *A New Moral Vision: Gender, Religion, and the Changing Purposes of American Higher Education, 1837–1917* (Ithaca, N.Y.: Cornell University Press, 2016), 237. See also further chapters in this volume regarding women's higher education.

Chapter 13

1. Editor's note, Harold Bolce, "Blasting at the Rock of Ages," *Cosmopolitan* 46 (May 1909), 665.

2. Ibid., 665–76; Bolce, "Avatars of the Almighty," *Cosmopolitan 47* (July 1909), 209–18, and Bolce, "Christianity in the Crucible," *Cosmopolitan 47* (August 1909), 310–19.

3. Bolce, "Rallying Round the Cross," *Cosmopolitan 47* (September 1909), 492.

4. Valuable studies are Thomas H. A. LeDuc, *Piety and Intellect at Amherst College, 1865–1912* (New York: Columbia University Press, 1969); John Barnard, *From Evangelicalism to Progressivism at Oberlin College: 1866–1917* (Columbus: Ohio State University Press, 1969); David B. Potts, *Wesleyan University, 1831–1910: Collegiate Enterprise in New England* (New Haven: Yale University Press, 1992); and Earl Hubert Brill, "Religion and the Rise of the University: A Study of the Secularization of American Higher Education, 1870–1910," Ph.D. dissertation, American University, 1969.

5. The U.S. Census figures for 1910 indicate 346,000 undergraduates (up from 232,000 in 1900) and 9,000 graduate students at 951 institutions. The total number of students represents 5.12% of the U.S. population of 18- to 21-year-olds (up from 4.01% in 1900). In 1910 degrees in higher education were granted to 30,716 men and 9,039 women. Of these, 399 were Ph.D.s for men and 44 for women; United States Bureau of the Census, *Historical Statistics of the United States, Colonial Times to 1957* (Washington, D.C.: Government Printing Office, 1960), 210–12.

6. William A. Scott, "The Religious Situation in State Universities," *Biblical World 26* (July 1905), 25, cf. 20–24.

7. Wheeler to Stephens, February 22, 1916. Stephens Papers, University of California, Berkeley, in Henry F. May, "Two or Three Berkeleys: Competing Ideologies in the Wheeler Era, 1899–1919," paper presented to university history group, University of California, Berkeley, 1991, 10. I am grateful to May for pointing out this quotation and especially for much thoughtful advice and encouragement on this project.

8. This summary follows that of Philip Gleason, "American Catholic Higher Education: A Historical Perspective," in *The Shape of Catholic Higher Education*, Robert Hassenger, ed. (Chicago: University of Chicago Press, 1967), 15–53. Also valuable are the essays in Gleason, *Keeping the Faith: American Catholicism Past and Present* (Notre Dame, Ind.: University of Notre Dame Press, 1987).

9. Useful studies of this subject are John Tracy Ellis, *The Formative Years of the Catholic University of America* (Washington, D.C.: Catholic University of America Press, 1946); Patrick H. Ahern, *The Catholic University of America 1887–1896: The Rectorship of John J. Keane* (Washington, D.C.: Catholic University of America Press, 1948); and C. Joseph Nuesse, *The Catholic University of America: A Centennial History* (Washington, D.C.: Catholic University of America Press, 1900).

10. R. Scott Appleby, "*Church and Age Unite!" The Modernist Impulse in American Catholicism* (Notre Dame, Ind.: University of Notre Dame Press, 1992), offers a valuable account of Zahm as well as Catholic modernism generally.

11. Margaret Mary Reher, *Catholic Intellectual Life in America: A Historical Study of Persons and Movements* (New York: Macmillan, 1989), 95, 97. Gerald P. Fogarty, S.J., *The Vatican and the American Hierarchy from 1870 to 1965* (Collegeville, Minn.: Liturgical Press, 1982), who provides one of the most valuable accounts of the developments, heads his chapter: "Americanism Condemned: The End of Intellectual Life."

12. Gerald P. Fogarty, S.J., *American Catholic Biblical Scholarship: A History from the Early Republic to Vatican II* (San Francisco: Harper & Row, 1989), 83–116. Cf. Reher, *Catholic Intellectual Life*, 61–98.

13. Appleby, "Church and Age Unite," 230.

14. R. Laurence Moore, *Religious Outsiders and the Making of Americans* (New York: Oxford University Press, 1986), 49–71, summarizes some of these critiques and adds to them. See also Reher, *Catholic Intellectual Life*, 86–87; David J. O'Brien, *The Renewal of American Catholicism* (New York: Oxford University Press, 1972); and Philip Gleason, "Immigrant Assimilation and the Crisis of Americanization" (1969), in Gleason, *Keeping the Faith*, 58–81.

15. Quoted from Pius X, *Doctoris Angelici* (1914), in William M. Halsey, *The Survival of American Innocence; Catholicism in an Era of Disillusionment, 1920–1940* (Notre Dame, Ind.: University of Notre Dame Press, 1980), 141; see account, 140–41.

16. Cf. Halsey, *Survival*, 5.

17. Halsey argues that there was something of a renaissance, however.

18. John Tracy Ellis, *American Catholics and the Intellectual Life* (Chicago: Heritage Foundation, 1956), 47.

19. Ibid., 24, 31, 34, 47. Episcopalians and Presbyterians each had five to six times as many *Who's Who* listings, even though total Catholic populations outnumbered them by about twenty and eight times, respectively.

20. Cf. Philip Gleason, "Neoscholasticism as Preconciliar Ideology," *CCICA Annual 1988* (Catholic Commission on Intellectual and Cultural Affairs), 15–25.

21. Gleason, "Immigrant Assimilation," argues that such Americanization happened very quickly after the dependency on Thomism was broken after the 1950s: "What happened, in short, was that a campaign which was intended to increase the number of Catholic intellectuals had reached the point of denying that there could be such a thing as a Catholic intellectual" (76).

22. William P. Leahy, S.J., *Adapting to America: Catholics, Jesuits, and Higher Education in the Twentieth Century* (Washington, D.C.: Georgetown University Press, 1991), provides a valuable account.

23. Thorstein Veblen, *The Higher Learning in America: A Memorandum on the Conduct of Universities by Business Men* (New York, 1935 [1918]), remarks that "none but the precarious class of schools made up of the lower-grade and smaller of these colleges, such as are content to save souls alive without exerting any effort on the current of civilization, are able to get along with faculties made up exclusively of God-fearing men" (149).

24. Paul K. Conkin, *Gone with the Ivy: A Biography of Vanderbilt University* (Knoxville: University of Tennessee Press, 1985), 32. This account and the subsequent account concerning Vanderbilt depend on Conkin, which is one of the very best and most thorough of the university histories and is especially distinguished for integrating the place of religion into the story.

25. Ibid., 50–51, 60–63.

26. Ibid., 59.

27. Ibid., 76–84.

28. Ibid., 94–154.

29. Ibid., 151–56.

30. Ibid., 157–84.

31. For example, at Emory, Candler's initial million-dollar gift came with special emphasis on providing a church-directed alternative to secular education. Nonetheless, to pick some minor but indicative instances, the first on-campus dance was allowed in 1941 and compulsory chapel was discontinued in 1958, although the university continued to affirm its "Christian heritage." Thomas H. English, *Emory University, 1915-1965: A Semicentennial History* (Atlanta: Emory University Press, 1966), 61, 104. On Asa Candler's intentions see his letter of July 16, 1914, quoted in Henry Morton Bullock, *A History of Emory University* (Nashville: Parthenon Press, 1936), 285–88.

32. Harold F. Williamson and Payson S. Wild, *Northwestern University: A History 1850-1975* (Evanston, Ill.: Northwestern University Press, 1975), 110, cf. 103.

33. Harmon L. Smith, "Borden Parker Bowne: Heresy at Boston," in *American Religious Heretics: Formal and Informal Trials*, George H. Shriver, ed. (Nashville: Abingdon Press, 1966), 148–87; Stewart G. Cole, *The History of Fundamentalism* (Westport, Conn.: Greenwood Press, 1971 [1931]), 184–92; Robert E. Chiles, *Theological Transition in American Methodism: 1790-1935* (Nashville: Abingdon Press, 1965), 64–65, 70–71. For a conservative complaint, see L. W. Munhall, *Breakers! Methodism Adrift* (New York, 1913).

34. Andrew Carnegie, "A Confession of Religious Faith" (1902), quoted in Ellen Condliffe Lagemann, *Private Power for the Public Good: A History of the Carnegie Foundation for the Advancement of Teaching* (Middletown, Conn.: Wesleyan University Press, 1983), 11.

35. Henry S. Pritchett, "The Educated Man and the State," *Technology Review* 3 (1901), 41, quoted in Lagemann, *Private Power*, 29. Lagemann quotation characterizing Pritchett is from *Private Power*, 35.

36. Henry S. Pritchett, "A Woman's Opportunity in Business and the Industries, an Address Given at the Second Annual Commencement of Simmons College, Boston, June 12, 1907," quoted in Lagemann, *Private Power*, 22.

37. Henry S. Pritchett to Andrew Carnegie, November 16, 1905, quoted in Lagemann, *Private Power*, 37–38.

38. Lagemann, *Private Power*, 37–39.

39. Henry S. Pritchett, "The Policy of the Carnegie Foundation for the Advancement of Teaching," *Educational Review* 32 (June 1906), 86, 89. At that time there were listed 218 denominational schools with 2,802 professors, 58 state institutions with 1,461 professors, and 51 nondenominational with 1,944 professors, which altogether included "about one-half of the entire number of so-called higher institutions" (86). Catholic schools were among those apparently not considered. See Richard Hofstadter and Walter P. Metzger, *The Development of Academic Freedom in the United States* (New York: Columbia University Press, 1955), 361–62.

40. Pritchett, "The Relations of Christian Denominations to Colleges," *Educational Review* 36 (October 1908), 217–41.

41. The Carnegie Foundation for the Advancement of Teaching, *Second Annual Report of the President and Treasurer* (1907), 53–54, quoted in Hofstadter and Metzger, *Academic Freedom*, 362.

42. Quoted in Richard Wilson, ed., *Syracuse University*, Vol. III, *The Critical Years* (Syracuse, N.Y.: Syracuse University Press, 1989), 349.

43. Ibid., 251.

44. Inaugural of James R. Day as chancellor, Syracuse University, June 27, 1894, reprinted in W. Freeman Galpin, *Syracuse University*, Vol. II, *The Growing Years* (Syracuse, N.Y.: Syracuse University Press, 1960), Appendix, 488.

45. Ibid., 411–14, quotations from 412 and 414. Lagemann, *Private Power* 185–86, quotes other protests from Day. See 180–83 on Josiah Royce's objections to Carnegie's efforts at standardization.

46. Galpin, *Syracuse*, Vol. II, 469–77.

47. Ibid., 415–20.

48. These quotations are all cited without full references in Galpin, *Syracuse*, Vol. II, 415n. Letter of Rockefeller is from December 11, 1916.

49. W. P. Graham to Frank Collins, January 1, 1942, from excerpt in Galpin, *Syracuse*, Vol. II, vi.

50. Upton Sinclair, *Goose-step: A Study of American Education*, 2nd ed. (Pasadena, Calif., 1923 [1922]), 277–87.

51. Quoted without exact citation in Galpin, *Syracuse*, Vol. II, 25.

Chapter 14

1. James Leuba, *The Belief in God and Immortality: A Psychological, Anthropological and Statistical Study* (Chicago, 1921 [1916]) , 224, xviii.

2. Ibid., 252–53. These figures are from the second set of five hundred questionnaires that Leuba sent to scientists. The first set, worded slightly differently, yielded somewhat higher levels of belief but similar difference between the two groups (51% for "lesser" and 35.7% for "greater" regarding God and 66.5% for "lesser" and 38.8% for "greater" regarding immortality). Leuba used the second set of questions in surveying those of other disciplines.

   Leuba also compared the beliefs of biologists and physical scientists in these groups and discovered that biologists were substantially more likely to be skeptical, the most striking difference being that "greater" biologists were only about half as likely (16.9%) to affirm belief in a prayer-answering God as were the "greater" physicists (34.8%). Of "lesser" biologists, however, 39.1% affirmed this belief. These figures conflate the answers to the two surveys. Ibid., 255.

3. Ibid., 279. For sociologists Leuba compared academics with nonacademics in the field and found the nonacademics to be almost twice as likely as the academics to affirm the beliefs in question (263).

4. Ibid., 277.

5. Ibid., 280.

6. Ibid., 186, 201, 283–84.

7. Ibid., 212, cf. 185.

8. Ibid., 213, 215–16.

9. Ibid., 280, 282.

10. Ibid., 286–87.

11. Richard Hofstadter and Walter P. Metzger, *The Development of Academic Freedom in the United States* (New York: Columbia University Press, 1955), 468–90.

12. In the 1880s the debate on "academic freedom" had to do with Charles Eliot's introduction of the elective system for students. Laurence Veysey, *The Emergence of the American University* (Chicago: University of Chicago Press, 1965), 384–85. Cf., for example, Andrew F. West's attack on Eliot's views in "What Is Academic Freedom?" *North American Review* 140 (1885), 432–44, reproduced in Walter P. Metzger, ed., *The American Concept of Academic Freedom: A Collection of Essays and Reports* (New York: Arno Press, 1977).

13. Richard Hofstadter recognizes this in Hofstadter and Metzger, *Academic Freedom*, 240–42. See also chapter 3 of the present work.

14. Charles D. Cashdollar, *The Transformation of Theology, 1830–1890: Positivism and Protestant Thought in Britain and America* (Princeton: Princeton University Press, 1989), traces the spread of Comtean positivism during the intervening era.

15. Metzger, in Hofstadter and Metzger, *Academic Freedom*, 373, uses the term "sanctified." Cf. his account of *Lernfreiheit* and *Lehrfreiheit*, 386–407, on which my account principally depends. This interpretation is confirmed in Veysey, *Emergence*, 384–97; Charles E. McClelland, *State, Society and University in Germany, 1700–1914* (Cambridge: Cambridge University Press, 1980); and Fritz K. Ringer, *Education and Society in Modern Europe* (Bloomington: Indiana University Press, 1979). I am also indebted to Darryl G. Hart, my colleague on this project for a year, for his background work on this subject.

16. Hofstadter and Metzger, *Academic Freedom*, 387.

17. Vesey, *Emergence*, 400–6. Hofstadter and Metzger, *Academic Freedom*, 436–45. For a more detailed account of the role of religion at Stanford, see Marsden, *The Soul of the American University* (New York: Oxford University Press, 1994), 254–56.

18. See ibid., 390; cf. 367–412 for discussion of similarities and differences.

19. John Dewey, "Academic Freedom," *Educational Review* 23 (1902), 1, 3, reproduced in Metzger, *American Concept*.

20. Ibid., 8–13.

21. Ibid., 13–14.

22. Nicholas Murray Butler, "Academic Freedom," *Educational Review* 47 (March 1914), 291–94, reproduced in Metzger, *American Concept*.

23. Hofstadter and Metzger, *Academic Freedom*, 352. The percentage of clerical board members was 39.1% in 1860–1861, 23% in 1900–1901, and 7.2% in 1930–1931.

24. Ibid., 291.

25. Charles W. Eliot, "Academic Freedom," *Science* 26 (July 5, 1907), 2, reproduced in Metzger, *American Concept*.

26. John Mecklin, *My Quest for Freedom* (New York: Scribners, 1945), 132–34. David Bishop Skillman, *The Biography of a College: Being the History of the First Century of the Life of Lafayette College* (Easton, Penn., 1932), Vol. II, 49.

27. Skillman, *Biography of a College,* Vol. II, 119–37.

28. Mecklin, *Quest,* 1–148. Skillman, *Biography of a College,* Vol. II, 195.

29. Mecklin, *Quest,* 148–56. "The Case of Professor Mecklin: Report of the Committee of Inquiry of the American Philosophical Association and the American Psychological Association," *Journal of Philosophy, Psychology and Scientific Methods* 11 (January 1914), 75.

30. Mecklin *Quest,* 156–65. Skillman, *Biography of a College,* Vol. II, 194–99.

31. Letter of John M. Mecklin, September 11, 1913, *Journal of Philosophy, Psychology, and Scientific Methods* 10 (September 1913), 559–60. He addressed a similar letter to *Science,* which also took a leading role in fostering the organization of the AAUP.

32. "The Case of Professor Mecklin," *Journal of Philosophy, Psychology, and Scientific Methods* 11 (January 1914), 67–81.

33. Mecklin, *Quest,* 133–34. Cf. "The Case of Professor Mecklin," 74.

34. Skillman, *Biography of a College,* Vol. II, 198–203. In 1915 Warfield became president of Wilson College, a Presbyterian women's college in Chambersburg, Pennsylvania, where he served another lengthy tenure.

35. Hofstadter and Metzger, *Academic Freedom,* 472–74. The majority of cases had to do with dismissals that were alleged to be connected with a professor's political views. Religion cases, however, were the second leading concern. Among the half-dozen or so cases that were current at the time the AAUP was founded was one other having to do with religion in which a professor at Wesleyan University in Connecticut was dismissed, allegedly for remarks he made in a public speech opposing sabbatarianism. Ibid., 479.

36. Arthur O. Lovejoy, "Organization of the American Association of University Professors," *Science* 41 (January 29, 1915), 151–54.

37. John Dewey, "The American Association of University Professors: Introductory Address," *Science* 41 (January 29, 1915), 148–49.

38. Lovejoy, "Organization," 152; Dewey, "Introductory Address," 148.

39. "General Report of the Committee on Academic Freedom and Academic Tenure," presented at the Annual Meeting of the Association, December 31, 1915. Reproduced from *Bulletin of the American Association of University Professors,* 1 (1915), 17–43, in Metzger, *American Concept.*

40. James Day, "The Professors's Union," quoted in *School and Society* 3 (January 29, 1916), 175. John Dewey dismissed such views as "literally appalling when they come from the head of a university, for, acted upon, they mean the death of American scholarship." Dewey, "Is the College Professor a 'Hired Man'?," *Literary Digest* 51 (July 10, 1915), 65. Both quoted in Hofstadter and Metzger, *Academic Freedom,* 482.

41. "Report," Committee on Academic Freedom and Tenure of Office, *Bulletin* (Association of American Colleges) 3 (April 1917), 49–50.

42. By 1922 the AAC's Academic Freedom Commission had conceded most points to the AAUP, and in 1940 the AAC's approval was crucial to the canonization of the AAUP's 1940 report. Hofstadter and Metzger, *Academic Freedom*, 485–87.

43. Carol S. Gruber, "Mars and Minerva: World War I and the American Academic Man," Ph.D. dissertation, Columbia University, 1968, 96–101. Particularly revealing are attacks from the University of Chicago Divinity School on premillennial fundamentalists of Moody Bible Institute and elsewhere as unpatriotic. See George Marsden, *Fundamentalism and American Culture: The Shaping of American Evangelicalism 1870–1925* (New York: Oxford University Press, 1980), 146–48.

44. Gruber, "Mars and Minerva," 69–70, 80, 98, 106–9, 208.

45. Charles Beards to N. M. Butler, October 8, 1917, *Minutes of the Trustees of Columbia University* 38 (1917–1918), 89–90, reprinted inRichard Hofstadter and Wilson Smith, eds., *American Higher Education: A Documentary History,* II (Chicago: University of Chicago Press, 1961), 882. For accounts of the controversy see Gruber, "Mars and Minerva," 227–49, and Hofstadter and Metzger, *Academic Freedom,* 498–502. Two other Columbia professors resigned in the wake of the controversy.

46. AAUP, "Report of Committee on Academic Freedom in Wartime," 29–47, reproduced in Metzger, *American Concept.*

47. Lovejoy, letters to editor of *The Nation* 99 (September 24, 1914), 376, (November 5, 1914), 548, quoted in Gruber, "Mars and Minerva" 135. Ely, *The World War and Leadership in Democracy* (New York, 1918), ca. 18–34, quoted in Gruber, "Mars and Minerva," 116. For similar statements see Gruber, "Mars and Minerva," passim.

48. Gruber, "Mars and Minerva," 250–52. John R. Commons, another pioneer of American social science, was also an organizer of the petition drive.

49. For example, in the field of history Carl Becker and Charles Beard appreciated that the Enlightenment faith in objectivity could no longer be sustained, but they represented a minority in the field. See Peter Novick, *That Noble Dream: "The Objectivity Question" and the American Historical Profession* (Cambridge: Cambridge University Press, 1988). Furthermore, as progressive secularists, they were so much on the side of freedom that they were hardly going to challenge the Enlightenment basis for the recent definition of academic freedom.

    Probably most representative of the rationale for academic freedom in the interwar era was Arthur O. Lovejoy's article on the topic in the *Encyclopedia of the Social Sciences* (New York: Macmillan, 1930), Vol. I, 384–88, reproduced in Metzger, *American Concept,* which is an eloquent appeal to the ideal of universal "unbiased investigation and thought" serving the cause of "the intellectual life of a civilized society." Societies with only religiously defined schools would lack "adequate provision for the advancement of science."

50. Walter P. Metzger, "The 1940 Statement of Principles on Academic Freedom and Tenure," *Law and Contemporary Problems* 53 (Summer 1990), 3–77. On the legal standing of academic freedom see the entire issue of *Law and Contemporary Problems* and Walter P. Metzger, ed., *The Constitutional Status of Academic Freedom* (New York: Arno Press, 1977).

51. AAUP, "Academic Freedom and Tenure: 1940 Statement of Principles and [1970] Interpretive Comments," *AAUP Policy Documents and Reports* (Washington, D.C., 1973), reproduced in Metzger, *American Concept.*

Chapter 15

1. See George Marsden, *Fundamentalism and American Culture* (New York: Oxford University Press, 1992), 141–64.
2. Betty A. DeBerg, *Ungodly Women: Gender and the First Wave of American Fundamentalism* (Minneapolis: Fortress Press, 1990), emphasizes this theme.
3. "Education," *The Encyclopedia Americana, International Edition* (New York: Americana Corporation, 1963), Vol. IX, 635.
4. Premillennialists, who had much to do with organizing fundamentalism, believed that Jesus would soon return to judge corrupt civilization. See Marsden, *Fundamentalism,* 43–71.
5. "The Conference on Fundamentals," *Watchman-Examiner* (July 1, 1920), 839–40. Cf. Marsden, *Fundamentalism* 161–67. The committee's mandate, however, was weak, and its report, returned in 1921, essentially exonerated the schools and suggested that their doctrinal purity be secured by boards of trustees or by local Baptists and not by the convention. Agitation from the more extreme fundamentalists continued, however. Robert A. Ashworth, "The Fundamentalist Movement among the Baptists," *Journal of Religion* 4 (November 1924), 613–21.
6. Willard B. Gatewood Jr., *Preachers, Pedagogues and Politicians: The Evolution Controversy in North Carolina, 1920–1927* (Chapel Hill: University of North Carolina Press, 1966), 30–37.
7. Ferenc Morton Szasz, *The Divided Mind of Protestant America, 1880–1930* (Tuscaloosa: University of Alabama Press, 1982), 110–11.
8. William Jennings Bryan, *In His Image* (New York, 1923), 118–21, 133, 122, and passim.
9. Ibid., 122. Bryan, "The Fundamentals," *The Forum* 70 (July 1923), from excerpt in Willard B. Gatewood, ed., *Controversy in the Twenties: Fundamentalism, Modernism, and Evolution* (Nashville: Vanderbilt University Press, 1969), 136.
10. Ronald L. Numbers, *The Creationists* (New York: Knopf, 1991), 43.
11. Numbers's valuable account of these developments in *The Creationists* notes that such attacks often helped motivate fundamentalists.
12. Gatewood, *Preachers,* 30–37, 59–75.
13. On the history of religion at Duke I am especially grateful for the assistance of Bradley J. Longfield. See also Gatewood, *Preachers,* 77–79, 193, 197–98.
14. Gatewood, *Preachers,* 1–128, passim, esp. 17, 87, 100, 103–4, 108, 111.
15. L. L. Bernard, "The Development of the Concept of Progress," *Journal of Social Forces* 3 (January 1925), 209, 212; Harry Elmer Barnes, "Sociology and Ethics: A Genetic View of the Theory of Conduct," *Journal of Social Forces* 3 (January 1925), 214. Cf. Gatewood, *Preachers,* 114–15.
16. Gatewood, *Preachers,* 119n, 119.

17. Quoted in Gatewood, *Preachers*, 127.
18. W. H. Chase, "Address to Student Body," February 1925, University Papers. Quoted in Gatewood, *Preachers*, 137.
19. Gatewood, *Preachers*, 146–233 passim.
20. Joseph V. Denney, "Presidential Address," *Bulletin of the American Association of University Professors* 10 (February 1924), 26–28, reprinted in Gatewood, *Preachers*, 270–72.
21. "Report on the University of Tennessee," *Bulletin of the AAUP* 10 (April 1924), 21–68. Cf. *Bulletin of the AAUP* 11 (February 1925), 70. James Riley Montgomery, Stanley J. Folmsbee, and Lee Seifert Greene, *To Foster Knowledge: A History of the University of Tennessee, 1794–1970* (Knoxville: University of Tennessee Press, 1984), 186–88.
22. Report of Committee M, "Freedom of Teaching in Science," *Bulletin of the AAUP* 11 (February 1925), 93–95.
23. C. M. Richmond, "The Place of Religion in Higher Education in America," *Bulletin of the Association of American Colleges*, reprinted in *Bulletin of the AAUP* 11 (March–April 1925), 174.
24. Report on American Council on Education," *Bulletin of the AAUP* 11 (February 1925), 99–109.
25. Montgomery et al., *To Foster Knowledge*, 188.
26. Bryan, *In His Image*, 122.
27. Szasz, *Divided Mind*, 122–23.
28. W. W. Campbell, "Evolution in Education in California," *Science* 61 (April 3, 1925), reprinted in Gatewood, *Preachers*, 249.
29. Quoted in Gatewood, *Preachers*, 192. Cf. 191.
30. Lippmann, *American Inquisitors: A Commentary on Dayton and Chicago* (New York: Macmillan, 1928), 12–22, 37–49.
31. Editorial, "Academic Freedom Not Yet Achieved," *Christian Century* 40 (March 8, 1923), 292.

Chapter 16

1. United States Bureau of the Census, *Historical Statistics of the United States, Colonial Times to 1957* (Washington, D.C.: Government Printing Office, 1960), 210–11.
2. See, e.g., Paula S. Fass, *The Damned and the Beautiful: American Youth in the 1920s* (New York: Oxford University Press, 1977), 13–52.
3. *Church of the Holy Trinity v. United States*, 143 U.S. 457 (1892) at 471. In 1905 Brewer published his addresses as *The United States as a Christian Nation* (Philadelphia: John C. Winston Co., 1905). Quotation from Robert T. Handy, *Undermined Establishment: Church–State Relations in America, 1880–1920* (Princeton: Princeton University Press, 1991), 13 and passim.
4. Burton Confrey, "Secularism in American Higher Education," *Catholic University of America Educational Research Monographs* 6 (January 15, 1931), 47–127, provides a

compilation of "Constitutional Provisions, Statutes, and Legal Decisions Relating to the Secularization of Public Schools in the United States."

5. Handy, *Undermined Establishment,* 15–16, 45–48, 136–37.

6. Anson Phelps Stokes, *Church and State in the United States* (New York: Harper & Bros., 1950), Vol. 11, 621–22. Stokes reports that at Wisconsin there was even a serious debate in the Board of Regents in 1942 on the propriety of the university press publishing a book titled *The Religious Availability of God.*

7. Merrimon Cuninggim, *The College Seeks Religion* (New Haven: Yale University Press, 1947), 79–86.

8. Robert S. Shepard, *God's People in the Ivory Tower: Religion in the Early American University* (Brooklyn: Carlson, 1991), shows that the field of comparative religion, despite some fanfare around the turn of the century, did not catch on in colleges or universities. To the extent the subject was taught at all, it was usually under the auspices of theological seminaries. See this volume on academic study of the Bible, which fared somewhat better.

9. Cf. Darryl G. Hart, "American Learning and the Problem of Religious Studies," in *The Secularization of the Academy,* George M. Marsden and Bradley J. Longfield, eds. (New York: Oxford University Press, 1992), 202–3.

10. Handy, *Undermined Establishment,* 160. Confrey, "Secularism," provides a chart summarizing these and related provisions.

11. Charles Foster Kent, "The Undergraduate Courses in Religion at the Tax-Supported Colleges and Universities of America," *Bulletin of the National Council on Religion in Higher Education* 4 (1924), 1–34, presents the results of a survey conducted in 1922–1923 showing that typically a few courses in Bible were offered at state universities, enrolling from 5 to 10% of the student bodies. However, only 20 to 30% of teachers' colleges and agricultural colleges had any courses in religion, and municipal colleges and universities were even less likely to offer such courses. Only 7 of the 48 states had no tax-supported institution offering courses in religion. Another survey of 21 state universities and colleges (presumably of all varieties) in 1923–1924 showed that 6 offered undergraduate courses in Bible and religion, though none at the graduate level. Edward S. Boyer, "Religious Education in Colleges, Universities and Schools of Religion," *Christian Education* 11 (October 1927), 38.

12. From a 1904 committee report to the General Assembly of the Presbyterian Church in the U.S.A., cited in Clarence Prouty Shedd, *The Church Follows Its Students* (New Haven: Yale University Press, 1938), 14. Shedd surveys these developments and is the principal immediate source for the present account.

13. John Whitney Evans, *The Newman Movement: Roman Catholics in American Higher Education, 1883–1971* (Notre Dame, Ind.: University of Notre Dame Press, 1980,) is a valuable study of this work.

14. Shedd, *Church Follows Its Students,* 16, 26. Cuninggim, *College Seeks Religion,* 147. Cf. Mont Whitson, *The Work of a Bible Chair* (Lubbock, Tex.: College Christian Press, 1954); Charles Foster Kent, "Religion at a Great State University: Based on the University of Illinois Survey," *Bulletin of the National Council of Schools of Religion* 3 (1923); and Winton U. Solberg, "The Catholic Presence at the University of Illinois,"

Catholic Historical Review 76 (October 1990), 765–812. In 1937 Presbyterians reported receiving credit for courses at 22 of their 51 centers at all universities. Methodist Wesley Foundations were receiving credit at 14 of their 46 foundations. Shedd, *Church Follows Its Students, 130–31.*

15. Shedd, *Church Follows Its Students,* 190–95. On Kent's role see Seymour A. Smith, *Religious Cooperation in State Universities: An Historical Sketch* (n.p., 1957), 28, and Bradley Longfield, "'For God, for Country and for Yale': Yale, Religion and Higher Education between the World Wars," in Marsden and Longfield, *Secularization of the Academy,* 146–69. Milton D. McLean and Henry H. Kimber, *Teaching of Religion in State Universities: Descriptions of Programs in Twenty-Five Institutions* (Ann Arbor: University of Michigan Press, 1960), 109–13, has a useful summary of the evolution of the school, its gradual absorption into the university, and the redefinition of its goals ca. 1950 to general study and appreciation of religious values in human culture.

16. "Two Decades: The Story of the National Council on Religion in Higher Education (Founded by Charles Foster Kent), 1922–1941," *The Bulletin* 11 (May 1941), 12–13. The journals *Christian Education* and *Religious Education* published numerous articles on religion at state universities during this era.

17. Probably the most novel arrangement was at the University of North Dakota, which provided a variation on the Iowa arrangement but with only one denomination involved. There the Wesley Foundation started its own School of Religion and during the 1920s was recognized as essentially a college of the university. The school was run by the Methodist Episcopal Church, financed by voluntary contributions, yet its courses, which had the announced purpose of "the cultivation of religious idealism," were granted university credit and listed in the university catalog. In 1922–1923 Wesley College was offering nine courses enrolling about 145 in a university of 1,500 students. Herbert Leon Searles, "The Study of Religion in State Universities," *University of Iowa Studies in Character* 1 (ca. 1928), 86–87. Kent, "Undergraduate Courses," 12. North Dakota was thus following a Canadian model in which some church colleges and theological schools were affiliated with state-supported universities. See D. C. Masters, *Protestant Church Colleges in Canada: A History* (Toronto: University of Toronto Press, 1966). According to Masters, this arrangement did not do much to forestall secularization of Canadian universities because the theological positions of the church colleges liberalized in the twentieth century (209–11). Theological colleges are still affiliated, however, with some major Canadian universities, notably the University of Toronto.

18. Shedd, *Church Follows Its Students,* 205–11. Solberg, "Catholic Presence."

19. Searles, "Study of Religion," 16, indicates that this was the ideal at Iowa and in the movement generally.

20. McLean and Kimber, *Teaching of Religion,* 102–9. See their list of course offerings for 1957–1958, which have a strongly Christian tone (32–36).

21. Shedd, "Religion in State Universities," *Journal of Higher Education* 12 (November 1941), 408, quoted in Cuninggim, *College Seeks Religion,* 88. Statistics are from

Cuninggim, 146–47, 298–306. Among black colleges, 81% of private schools had departments of religion, but only 2 of 16 state schools had such offerings (304).

22. Shedd, *Church Follows Its Students,* 131, reporting that 10,245 of 279,802 students in tax-supported schools enrolled in religion courses in 1936.

23. Cuninggim, *College Seeks Religion,* 149. Quotation from William B. Huie, "How to Keep Football Stars in College," *Collier's* 107 (January 4, 1941), 20.

24. "Two Decades," 15, 36–37.

25. Cuninggim, *College Seeks Religion,* 94, and passim on administrative support. On the AAC, see Hart, "Religious Studies," 205–6. See also journals of these organizations such as *Religious Education, Christian Education,* the *Journal of Bible and Religion,* and the *Bulletin of the Association of American Colleges,* which are rich in materials on religion in higher education.

26. The Edward W. Hazen Foundation, *The Edward W. Hazen Foundation 1925–1950* (New Haven: Hazen Foundation, 1950).

27. During this era there was relatively little talk of relating Christianity to academic disciplines, although presumably that is one of the things Kent scholars were supposed to be doing. One exception is Charles Ellwood, who was brought to head the Sociology Department at the new Duke University after thirty years of teaching at Missouri. Ellwood saw sociology as a Christian mission for the benefit of democratic society. His views were thus much like those typical of leading figures in the field at the turn of the century. Under its founding president, William Preston Few, Duke University (formerly Trinity College), which had Methodist connections, was more explicit in its liberal Christian ideals than were most universities in the North. I am indebted to my colleague on this project, Bradley J. Longfield, for his "'*Eruditio et Religio*': Religion at Duke between the World Wars" (unpublished manuscript).

28. Robert L. Geiger, *To Advance Knowledge: The Growth of American Research Universities: 1900–1940* (New York: Oxford University Press, 1986), 108.

29. This is the major thesis of David O. Levine, *The American College and the Culture of Aspiration, 1915–1940* (Ithaca, N.Y.: Cornell University Press, 1986).

30. Cf. Frederick Rudolph, *Curriculum: A History of the American Undergraduate Course of Study since 1636* (San Francisco: Jossey-Bass, 1977), 245–55.

31. Levine, *American College,* 162.

32. Cuninggim, *College Seeks Religion,* 303–5. Kent, "Undergraduate Courses in Religion," 26.

33. Geiger, *To Advance Knowledge,* 232, 263.

34. Ibid., 166.

35. Robert L. Church, "Knowledge and Power: American Higher Education in the Twentieth Century: A Review Essay," *History of Education Annual* 7 (1987), 99. This remark is usually attributed to Robert Maynard Hutchins. On Hutchins, see chapter 20 of this volume.

36. Geiger, *To Advance Knowledge,* argues that this pragmatic character is a source of the vitality of American universities that contributed to their gaining world leadership in the twentieth century.

37. By 1930 the percentage of clergy on the boards of private institutions had dropped to 7, down from 30 in 1860. William Clyde DeVane, *Higher Education in Twentieth-Century America* (Cambridge, Mass.: Harvard University Press, 1965), 79.

38. Margaret M. Grubiak, *White Elephants on Campus: The Decline of the University Chapel in American, 1920–1960* (Notre Dame, Ind.: University of Notre Dame Press, 2014). As she points out, sometimes the Gothic ideal was applied to learning itself, as at the Sterling Memorial Library at Yale or the Cathedral of Learning at the University of Pittsburgh.

39. Fass, *The Damned and the Beautiful*, 17–25.

40. F. Scott Fitzgerald, *This Side of Paradise* (New York: Charles Scribner's Sons, 1948 [1920]), 58–59, as summarized and quoted in Helen Lefkowitz Horowitz, *Campus Life: Undergraduate Cultures from the End of the Eighteenth Century to the Present* (Chicago: University of Chicago Press, 1987), 125. Cf. Fass, *The Damned and the Beautiful*, 25–29.

41. James Bissett Pratt, "Religion and the Younger Generation," *Yale Review* 12 (1923), 594–96, 610.

42. Robert Cooley Angell, *The Campus: A Study of Contemporary Undergraduate Life in the American University* (New York: D. Appleton and Co., 1928), esp. 185–88. In an in-depth survey of seniors from the limited population of Reed College in Oregon, Helen Chambers Griffin summarized the following conclusions: "About four phases of religious thought there was little or no disagreement. First, Jesus is considered only human, but a great thinker and teacher. Second, the Bible is thought of in terms of historical and literary criticism. Third, these students believe that the miracles recorded in the Bible either did not happen, or they had natural causes. Fourth, to them no one religion contains all the elements of beauty and truth." Helen Chambers Griffin, "Changes in the Religious Attitudes of College Students," *Religious Education* 24 (February 1929), 160.

43. Angell, *Campus,* 162–63. *Yale Daily News,* April 21, 1926, 1.

44. For the latter see *Trinity Chronicle,* editorials, April 21, 1926, 2, and December 12, 1926, 2.

45. Angell, *Campus,* 2, 66–89.

46. "Religion on the Campus," *Christian Century* 42 (March 19, 1925), 370, found regular graduations in the correlations between wealth and lack of church attendance among students at the University of Michigan.

47. Horowitz, *Campus Life*, is particularly good in pointing out the diversities of subgroups on campuses. At the same time, her account of the interwar era is written as though religion was no presence on campuses, except in the distinction between Christians and Jews.

48. C. Howard Hopkins, *History of the Y.M.C.A. in North America* (New York: Association Press, 1951), 628, 645–46.

49. Ibid., 629, 521, 590. The YWCAs were more decentralized and apparently did not typically give up their evangelicalism quite so soon. I am grateful to Kathy Long for her work on this point.

50. Angell, *Campus,* 200–210.

51. "Religion on the Campus," 370. Horowitz, *Campus Life*, 118, 204, cf. 193–219.

52. News report, "Finds Student Y in Perilous Position," *Christian Century* 44 (June 23, 1927), 787–88.

53. Cuninggim, *College Seeks Religion*, 136.

54. Ibid., 134.

55. Longfield, "'For God, for Country, and for Yale,'" 147.

56. I am indebted to Jeffrey Trexler for making this point and providing documentation of it. See Jeffrey Alan Trexler, "Education with the Soul of a Church: The Yale Foreign Missionary Society and the Democratic Ideal," Ph.D. dissertation, Duke University, 1991.

57. We get a mixed picture of the impact of extracurricular religion at Yale by contrasting two volumes, Mrs. Howard Taylor's *Borden of Yale '09* (London: Religious Tract Society, 1927) and Owen Johnson's *Stover at Yale* (New York: F. A. Stokes, 1911). *Borden of Yale* is a sentimentalized biography of William Whiting Borden (1887–1913), who gave up a million-dollar inheritance to become a foreign missionary but died en route to the field. Borden is conservative religiously and complains of the liberalism of many of the chapel speakers, though approving of guests such as missionary promoters Robert Speer and John R. Mott. He was active in Dwight Hall and appreciative of a faculty-led Bible study. He also notes that the YMCA vice president was tapped to head Skull and Bones. At the same time he complains to his mother of the students, "The great majority smoke, go to the theater Saturday night and do their studying on Sunday. Rather a hopeless state of affairs!" (89). *Stover at Yale*, a fictional account of turn-of-the-century Yale, published in 1911, depicts a Yale in which religion is virtually absent. Dink Stover undergoes various "tests of manhood," which prove to be character building while helping him become a football hero and get into Skull and Bones.

58. *Yale Daily News*, November 2, 1925, 2. The editorials are summarized in Longfield, "'For God, for Country, and for Yale.'"

59. Quoted in Ralph H. Gabriel, *Religion and Learning at Yale: The Church of Christ in the College and University*, 1757–1957 (New Haven: Yale University Press, 1958), 2.

60. *Yale Daily News*, October 26, 1927, 1.

61. *Report of the President of Yale University for the Academic Year 1933–1934* (New Haven, 1934), 49, and James R. Angell, *American Education: Addresses and Articles* (New Haven: Yale University Press, 1937), 231–32, both quoted in Longfield, "'For God, for Country, and for Yale,'" 157–58.

62. Marion L. Burton, *Bulletin of the American Association of University Professors* 11 (January 1925), 172–74. This excerpt was incorrectly attributed to Richmond.

63. Charles A. Richmond and Marion L. Burton, "The Place of Religion in Higher Education," *Bulletin of the American Association of Colleges* 10 (1924), 90, 103–6.

64. See, for instance, "Character Education in American Colleges and Universities," in *1925–26 Year Book of the National Council on Religion in Higher Education* (Ithaca, N.Y., 1926). The University of Iowa School of Religion had an Institute of Character Research and in the later 1920s was publishing a periodical, *University of Iowa Studies in Character*.

65. John D. Rockefeller Jr., "Character," *Christian Education* 11 (April 1928), 417–20. John R. Hart Jr., "Methods of Developing Character in College," *Christian Education* 11 (April 1928), 426.

66. Henry Sloane Coffin, "Pillars of Religion in the Colleges," in *Religion in the Colleges*, Galen M. Fisher, ed. (New York: Association Press, 1928), 23. Cf. Galen M. Fisher, "An Appraisal of the Conference," ibid., x.

67. "College Heads Say Drinking Declines," *Christian Century* 43 (July 29, 1926), 1100; "Are College Girls Bad?" *Christian Century* 43 (September 30, 1926), 1189–90. Similarly, a report in the *Christian Century* on a late 1926 student conference on religion on campuses observed that the ethics of sex life was not discussed in student conventions a decade earlier but assured that "this does not mean that sex morality is at a lower ebb than hitherto. . . . The emancipation of woman and the freer association of the sexes has indeed complicated an age-old problem; but whatever the perils that may come out of this freedom, they are more than balanced by the greater measure of sincerity with which young men and women face the problem of establishing a wholesome family life." "The Religion of the Campus," 44 (January 13, 1927), 37.

68. By 1928, for instance, most major leaders concerned for religion on campuses had joined student opinion in being "strongly opposed to compulsory chapel." Fisher, *Religion in the Colleges*, xi.

69. "What Are Education's Ruling Concepts?" *Christian Century* 48 (February 11, 1931), 197–98.

70. E.g., William F. Anderson, "The Church College—Battleground of Freedom," *Christian Century* 51 (September 5, 1934), 1115–57; "Shackles for Scholars," *Christian Century* 51 (May 8, 1935), 293–94; "Liberalism Has a Citadel in the Universities," *Christian Century* 53 (July 1, 1936), 924.

71. T. T. Brumbaugh, "Religion Returns to the Campus," *Christian Century* 55 (April 20, 1938), 493–95.

72. Cuninggim, *College Seeks Religion*, 250, 259, 247.

73. Ruth Davies, "Are Students Losing Their Religion?" *Christian Century* 56 (June 14, 1939), 767–69. Dan Gilbert, *Crucifying Christ in Our Colleges* (San Francisco: Alex. Dulfer Printing Co., 1933), offers a fundamentalist view of the situation. Including documented accounts of what was taught in college texts, Gilbert presented case studies of students whose lives had been ruined by following the advice of Nietzsche or of contemporaries such as Bertrand Russell, who taught that humans were essentially animals. Such critiques apparently had negligible impact outside fundamentalist and perhaps Catholic circles.

Chapter 17

1. Marcia Graham Synnott, *The Half-Opened Door: Discrimination and Admissions at Harvard, Yale, and Princeton, 1900–1970* (Westport, Conn.: Greenwood Press, 1979), 130–33. Dan A. Oren, *Joining the Club: A History of Jews at Yale* (New Haven: Yale University Press, 1985), suggests relatively good acceptance of Catholics at Yale and

no evidence of admissions quotas. Nonetheless, Catholics were very underrepresented in the most prestigious secret societies and fraternities. Synnott shows that Princeton was admitting about 5 to 10% Catholics in the interwar era, (195). This is about the same percentage found at state universities. A survey in 1923–1924 showed about 5% of students self-identified as Catholics at state universities. Edward S. Boyer, "Religious Education in Colleges, Universities and Schools of Religion," *Christian Education 11* (October 1927), 27. Presumably that percentage grew during the interwar era.

2. Winton U. Solberg, "The Catholic Presence at the University of Illinois," *Catholic Historical Review* 76 (October 1990), 765–812.

3. Virginia Lieson Brereton, *Training God's Army: The American Bible School, 1880–1940* (Bloomington: Indiana University Press, 1990).

4. William C. Ringenberg, *The Christian College: A History of Protestant Higher Education in America* (Grand Rapids, Mich.: Christian University Press, 1984), provides a valuable overview of these developments.

5. Ibid., 138. At Wellesley, for instance, it had only been since 1912 that students had been allowed to travel on railroads or streetcars on Sundays without special permission, and in the 1920s Sunday mornings were to be observed as a quiet time. *Wellesley College News*, April 29, 1926, 5. Wellesley, perhaps because of its strong tradition of voluntary evangelicalism, had voluntary morning chapel. In 1922, in response to declining attendance, students debated whether to make it compulsory, but that plan was defeated. *Wellesley College News*, March 2 to March 23, passim. The college, however, continued to have required courses on the Bible into the 1960s.

6. Andrea Turpin, *A New Moral Vision: Gender, Religion, and the Changing Purposes of Higher Education*, 1837–1917 (Ithaca, N.Y.: Cornell University Press, 2016), esp. 265–271.

7. Raymond Wolters, *The New Negro on Campus* (Princeton: Princeton University Press, 1975), 313.

8. Synnott, *Half-Opened Door*, 83–84, 91, 133–35, 174–75, and passim.

9. Benjamin E. Mays, "The Religious Life and Needs of Negro Students," *Journal of Negro Education* 9 (July 1940), 332–36. Ringenberg, *Christian College*, 138.

10. Walter R. Chivers, "Religion in Negro Colleges," *Journal of Negro Education* 9 (January 1940), 5–12. Cf. Richard I. McKinney, "Religion in Negro Colleges," *Journal of Negro Education* 13 (Fall 1944), 509–18.

11. Wolters, *New Negro*, 29–69, 293–313.

12. Ibid., 70–71. The ratio is for 1925. The number of blacks attending colleges was expanding very rapidly in the 1920s, so this ratio was changing.

13. Howard University Catalogue 1898–1899, 57, 58–59.

14. Rayford W. Logan, *Howard University, 1867–1967* (New York: New York University Press, 1969), 151.

15. "The Howard University Self-Study," June 30, 1966 (unpublished university document), 50.

16. Wolters, *New Negro*, 73.

17. Ibid., 70–136.

18. I am indebted to Paul Kemeny for his work in charting the secularization of Howard, particularly in its formal statements, such as presidential inaugurals, and in internal reports.

19. Quoted in Wolters, *New Negro*, 83. Christopher Jencks and David Riesman, *The Academic Revolution* (Chicago: University of Chicago Press, 1977 [1968]), 406–79, provides a critical look at the state of African American higher education in the 1960s.

20. Gilbert Klaperman, *The Story of Yeshiva University: The First Jewish University in America* (London: Macmillan, 1969).

21. Israel Goldstein, *Brandeis University: Chapter of Its Founding* (New York: Bloch, 1951), provides the revealing perspectives of one of its founders. Goldstein also provides a summary of other efforts at Jewish higher education (1–5). Jencks and Riesman, *Academic Revolution*, 318–21, make some astute remarks about the similarities between dominant Jewish views and mainline Protestant views of higher education. Brandeis, they point out, aspired to be "separate but identical" (319). Edward S. Shapiro, *A Time for Healing: American Jewry since World War II* (Baltimore: Johns Hopkins Press, 1992), 71–76, discusses the criticisms of Yeshiva College and more recent debates regarding Brandeis's identity.

22. Susanne Klingenstein, *Jews in the American Academy 1900–1940: The Dynamics of Intellectual Assimilation* (New Haven: Yale University Press, 1991), illustrates this point, though she is asking a different set of questions.

23. Synnott, *Half-Opened Door*, 15–16.

24. Levine, *The American College and the Culture of Aspiration, 1915–1940* (Ithaca: University of Cornell Press, 1986), 136–61. Synnott, *Half-Opened Door*, passim.

25. Synnott, *Half-Opened Door*, 160–98, 218–25.

26. Oren, *Joining the Club*, 105–9. Even among fundamentalists, although there are clear instances of Christian religious justifications for anti-Semitism, there is also much evidence that dispensationalist teaching regarding the role of the Jews in the last days tempered grassroots anti-Semitism in America.

27. Ibid., 118–22. No Catholic held a full professorship at Yale College in this era, though after 1929 one of the graduate faculty did teach French at the college (357). Cf. Klingenstein, *Jews in the American Academy*, 102–3, for a slightly wider summary of trends.

28. James M. Turner, "Secularization and Sacralization: Speculations on Some Religious Origins of the Secular Humanities Curriculum, 1850–1900," in *The Secularization of the Academy*, George M. Marsden and Bradley J. Longfield, eds. (New York: Oxford University Press, 1992), 74–106.

29. Oren, *Joining the Club*, 121–22.

Chapter 18

1. See Clyde W. Barrow, *Universities and the Capitalist State: Corporate Liberalism and the Reconstruction of American Higher Education, 1894–1928* (Madison: University of Wisconsin Press, 1990), for a Marxist version of this point.

2. On the force of such principles in shaping modern institutions see Jacques Ellul, *The Technological Society* (New York: Vintage, 1964 [1954]). On the specifics see Roger L. Geiger, *To Advance Knowledge: The Growth of American Research Universities, 1900–1940* (New York: Oxford University Press, 1986).

3. Theodore Francis Jones, *New York University 1832–1932* (New York, 1933), 220–21, 193, quoted in David A. Hollinger, "Two NYUs and 'The Obligation of Universities to the Social Order' in the Great Depression," in *The University and the City,* Thomas Bender, ed. (New York: Oxford University Press, 1988), 254–55.

4. Hollinger, "Two NYUs," 251. This summary of the conference follows the themes of Hollinger's more detailed analysis.

5. James Rowland Angell, "The University Today: Its Aims and Province," in *The Obligation of Universities to the Social Order*, Henry Pratt Fairchild, ed. (New York: New York University Press, 1933), 20.

6. John Campbell Merriam, "Spiritual Values and the Constructive Life," in *Obligation of Universities,* 322, 327, 329.

7. Joseph Wood Krutch, *The Modern Temper: A Study and a Confession* (New York: Harcourt, Brace, & World, 1956 [1929]), 7, 16.

8. This image is borrowed from Henry F. May's monumental account of the beginnings of this intellectual revolution, just before World War I, *The End of American Innocence: A Study of the First Years of Our Time, 1912–1917* (New York: Alfred A. Knopf, 1959).

9. C. K. Ogden and I. A. Richards, *The Meaning of Meaning: A Study of the Influence of Language upon Thought and of the Science of Symbolism* (London: Trubner & Co., 1923), 228, quoted in Edward A. Purcell Jr., *The Crisis of Democratic Theory: Scientific Naturalism and the Problem of Value* (Lexington: University of Kentucky Press, 1973), 48. Another very valuable summary of these trends is found in Douglas Sloan, "The Teaching of Ethics in the American Undergraduate Curriculum, 1876–1976," in *Education and Values*, Douglas Sloan, ed. (New York: Teachers College Press, 1980), 191–254. Sloan documents, for instance, how in The Psychological Index the subject of Ethics has disappeared as a heading, and such topics are subsumed under "Social Functions of the Individual" (207n).

10. Einstein's relativity theory and Werner Heisenberg's uncertainty principle contributed to the sense that even common sense was unreliable. At the same time logicians demonstrated that even the most fundamental principles of Aristotelian logic, such as the law of noncontradiction or of the excluded middle, could be construed as merely assumptions, and other consistent logics could be constructed from alternative premises. Geometers likewise demonstrated that there could be non-Euclidean geometries that were as consistent with their premises as was classical geometry. Even the most obvious axioms of rationality were thus mere human constructions. Innovative social

scientists were soon speaking of "non-Euclidean" social or political theories, which became a useful metaphor for challenging any verity. Purcell, *Crisis*, 49–59.

11. Carl L. Becker, *The Heavenly City of the Eighteenth-Century Philosophers* (New Haven: Yale University Press, 1932), 14–15, 32, and passim.

12. Carl Becker, *Everyman His Own Historian: Essays on History and Politics* (Chicago: Quadrangle Books, 1966 [1935]), 233–35, 251.

13. Peter Novick, *That Noble Dream: The "Objectivity Question" and the American Historical Profession* (Cambridge: Cambridge University Press, 1988).

14. This point is developed persuasively in Douglas Sloan, *Faith and Knowledge: Mainline Protestantism and Twentieth-Century American Higher Education* (Philadelphia: Westminster Press, 1994).

15. Carl Becker himself offers a version of this in *Progress and Power* (New York: Random House, 1949 [1936]).

16. Ruth Benedict, *Patterns of Culture* (New York: Mentor Books, 1946 [1934]), 2, 8, 255, and passim.

17. John Dewey, *A Common Faith* (New Haven: Yale University Press, 1934), 51.

18. For this concise phrasing of the modern (and postmodern) moral predicament, I am indebted to Phillip E. Johnson, "The Creationist and the Sociobiologist: Two Stories about Illiberal Education," *California Law Review* 80 (July 1992), 1089.

19. John Barnard, *From Evangelicalism to Progressivism at Oberlin College: 1866–1917* (Columbus: Ohio State University Press, 1969).

20. Mary Ann Dzuback, *Robert M. Hutchins: Portrait of an Educator* (Chicago: University of Chicago Press, 1991), 3–20and passim, argues this point.

21. Purcell, *Crisis,* 140–41. See also relevant sections of Dzuback, *Hutchins*, and Harry S. Ashmore, *Unseasonable Truths: The Life of Robert Maynard Hutchins* (Boston: Little, Brown, 1989).

22. See, for instance, Mortimer J. Adler, *Philosopher at Large: An Intellectual Autobiography* (New York: Macmillan, 1977).

23. Quotations from Ashmore, *Unseasonable Truths,* 58, 59.

24. Ibid., 89. In a 1973 interview, from which this quotation is taken, Hutchins also remarked that he believed it was possible to maintain "those habits of having faith in one God, the Creator, or having faith in the immortality of the soul or any of the other central doctrines of religion" (idem). Neither of his recent biographers, Dzuback and Ashmore, provides any sustained account of his religious views during his years as university president.

25. Quoted from excerpt in Adler, *Philosopher at Large,* 162.

26. Purcell, *Crisis,* 31.

27. Adler, *Philosopher at Large,* 163–66, quotation from excerpt (163). Purcell, *Crisis,* 3.

28. Robert Maynard Hutchins, *The Higher Learning in America* (New Haven: Yale University Press, 1936), 31, 34–35, 48, 94–95, 106–7, 97, 119, and passim.

29. E.g., Henry Seidel Canby, "A Call for Aristotle," *Saturday Review* 14 (October 24, 1936), 10–11. Cf. Dzuback, *Hutchins,* 187.

30. Glenn Frank, "Toward an Ordered Learning," *Yale Review* 26 (December 1936), 393.

31. William M. Halsey, *The Survival of American Innocence: Catholicism in an Era of Disillusionment, 1920–1940* (Notre Dame, Ind.: University of Notre Dame Press, 1980), 15–117.

32. Sidney Hook, *Social Myths and Democracy* (New York, 1966), 76, originally published in *Partisan Review,* ca. 1938, quoted in Purcell, *Crisis,* 203. Purcell provides an excellent summary of the debates (esp. 117–58, 197–217). Merrimon Cuninggim, *The College Seeks Religion* (New Haven: Yale University Press, 1947), had a useful summary (96–122). R. Freeman Butts, *The College Charts Its Course: Historical Conceptions and Current Proposals* (New York: McGraw-Hill, 1939), 253–426, provides a contemporary summary from a progressive perspective.

33. *John Dewey: The Later Works, 1925–1953,* Vol. II, *1935–1937,* Jo Ann Boydston, ed. (Carbondale: Southern Illinois University Press, 1987), 392, 400, 401, 596. This exchange originally appeared in *Social Frontier* 3 as follows: John Dewey, "Rationality in Education" (December 1936), 71–73; Dewey, "President Hutchins' Proposals to Remake Higher Education" (January 1937), 103–4; Robert Maynard Hutchins, "Grammar, Rhetoric, and Mr. Dewey" (February 1937), 137–39; Dewey, "The Higher Learning in America" (March 1937), 167–69.

34. Van Wyck Brooks, "Conference on Science, Philosophy and Religion in Their Relation to the Democratic Way of Life," in *Science, Philosophy and Religion: A Symposium* (New York: Conference on Science, Philosophy and Religion . . . Inc., 1941), 1–4. Brooks's remarks echoed some of the same concerns expressed in the much-discussed recent essay by Archibald MacLeish, "The Irresponsibles," *The Nation,* May 18, 1940, also in MacLeish, *The Irresponsibles* (New York: Duell, Sloan and Pearce, 1940), 3–34.

35. Mortimer J. Adler, "God and the Professors," *Science, Philosophy and Religion,* 120–49.

36. Sidney Hook, "The New Medievalism," *New Republic* 103 (October 28, 1940), 602–3.

37. *Science, Philosophy and Religion,* esp. 19, 90–119, 162–83, 213, 56–75. After three annual conferences on "Science, Philosophy and Religion," conferences were held more or less annually through most of the 1950s, with subsequent gatherings in 1960 and 1966.

38. Bertrand Russell, *The Autobiography of Bertrand Russell, 1914–1944* (Boston: Little, Brown, 1951), 348.

39. Barry Feinberg and Ronald Kasrils, *Bertrand Russell's America, 1896–1945* (New York: Viking Press, 1973), 135–67. Quotation (153) from attorney Joseph Goldstein, Supreme Court, New York County, Appellate Division, *Papers on Appeal from Order,* in the matter of the application of Jean Kay against the Board of Higher Education of the City of New York, 40.

40. John Dewey and Horace M. Kallen, eds., *The Bertrand Russell Case* (New York: Da Capo Press, 1972 [1941]), 9, 38, and passim.

41. *The Scientific Spirit and Democratic Faith: Papers from the Conference on the Scientific Spirit and the Democratic Faith: Held in New York City, May, 1943* (New York: King's Crown Press, 1944): Edward C. Lindeman, "Introduction," x; Max C. Otto, "Authoritarianism and Supernaturalism," 18; Brand Blanshard, "Theology and the Individual," 76. Fundamentalists were mentioned several times as a threat, but unlike Catholic authors, they were not taken seriously enough to quote even for purposes of refutation. Alan Jacobs, *The Year of Our Lord 1943: Christian Humanism in an Age*

of Crisis (New York: Oxford University Press, 2018), provides an insightful account of the discussions on the future of civilization.

42. John Dewey, ed. *The Authoritarian Attempt to Capture Education: Papers from the 2d Conference on the Scientific Spirit and Democratic Faith* (New York: King's Crown Press, 1945): Sidney Hook, "Democracy and Education: Introduction," 10–12; Harry D. Gideonse, "Can Free Communication Be Achieved? Introduction," 31–34; Bruce Bliven, "Problems of the Press," 34–40; Bernard B. Smith, "Problems of the Radio," 40–49 and passim.

Chapter 19

1. Merrimon Cuninggim, *The College Seeks Religion* (New Haven: Yale University Press, 1947), 120–22, provides a bibliography of some of these works.
2. Ibid., 110–19, summarizes some of these.
3. *General Education in a Free Society: Report of the Harvard Committee* (Cambridge, Mass.: Harvard University Press, 1945), 71, 43, 39, 76, 174, 205, 76, 44, and 95.
4. Ibid., 216–17. Laurence Veysey, "Stability and Experiment in the American Undergraduate Curriculum," in *Content and Context: Essays on College Education* (New York: McGraw-Hill, 1973), esp. 50–53. Veysey points out that, rather than being invented at Columbia as is sometimes suggested, the concepts of great book and of Western civilization courses date back to before World War I and seem to have been pioneered at Berkeley (51). Douglas Sloan, "The Teaching of Ethics in the American Undergraduate Curriculum, 1876–1976," in *Education and Values,* Douglas Sloan, ed. (New York: Teachers College Press, 1980), 237–48, presents a very valuable account of this "General Education" movement, its inability to agree on the basis for the common values it was supposed to teach, and its decline by the late 1950s.
5. United States Bureau of the Census, *Historical Statistics of the United States, Colonial Times to 1957* (Washington, D.C.: Government Printing Office, 1960), 210. By 1954 some 30% of the eighteen- to twenty-one-year-olds were attending college.
6. *Higher Education for American Democracy, A Report of the President's Commission on Higher Education* (Washington, D.C.: Government Printing Office, 1947), Vol. I, 101, 25–36.
7. Ibid., 67, 49, and passim.
8. Robert M. Hutchins, "Double Trouble: Are More Studies, More Facilities, More Money the Key for Better Education?," *Educational Record* 39 (April 1948), 107–22. Reprinted in *Saturday Review of Literature,* July 17, 1948, under this title, reprinted in *Education for Democracy: The Debate over the Report of the President's Commission on Higher Education,* Gail Kennedy, ed. (Boston: D.C. Heath, 1952), 81–89.
9. *Higher Education*, Vol. I, 50.
10. Cf. Hutchins, "Double Trouble," 84.
11. *Higher Education*, Vol. I, 10.

12. T. R. McConnell, "A Reply to the Critics," in Kennedy, *Education for Democracy,* 110, quoting from C. J. Turk, "The Immediate Goals of Higher Education in America," *College and Church* 13 (1948), 13–16.

13. *Higher Education,* Vol. V, 65–68.

14. Allan P. Farrell, "Report of the President's Commission: A Critical Appraisal," *Journal of Educational Sociology* 22 (April 1949), 508–22, reprinted in Kennedy, *Education for Democracy,* 97–104, esp 101–2. This article refers to several others of the Catholic critiques.

15. Robert S. Lynd, "Who Calls the Tune?" *Journal of Higher Education* 19 (April 1948), 163–74, reprinted in Kennedy, *Education for Democracy,* 52–61, esp. 55.

16. *Higher Education,* Vol. I, 102.

17. William Clyde DeVane, *Higher Education in Twentieth-Century America* (Cambridge, Mass.: Harvard University Press, 1965), 127, 130.

18. Robert Wuthnow, *The Struggle for America's Soul: Evangelicals, Liberals, and Secularism* (Grand Rapids, Mich.: William B. Eerdmans, 1989), 34–35. Cuninggim, *College Seeks Religion.* Keith Hunt and Gladys Hunt, *For Christ and the University: The Study of InterVarsity Christian Fellowship of the U.S.A., 1940–1990* (Downers Grove, Ill.: Intervarsity Press, 1991).

19. Sir Walter Moberly, *The Crisis in the University* (London: SCM Press, 1949), 300–301 and passim. On the parallel between British and American developments see David Bebbington, "The Secularization of British Universities since the Mid-Nineteenth Century," in *The Secularization of the Academy,* George M. Marsden and Bradley J. Longfield, eds. (New York: Oxford University Press, 1992), 259–77.

20. Another source that, like the *Christian Scholar,* is filled with discussions of religion and higher education during this period is *Church and College,* the educational news bulletin of the Commission on Christian Higher Education of the Association of American Colleges.

21. These and other developments are documented in Douglas Sloan, *Faith and Knowledge: Mainline Protestantism and Twentieth-Century American Higher Education* (Philadelphia: Westminster Press, 1994). See also Erich A. Walter, ed., *Religion and the State University* (Ann Arbor: University of Michigan Press, 1958), which provides very intelligent discussions concerning many of the developments and challenges involved and itself is a mark of the high-water point reached in these campaigns.

22. In Foreword to R. H. Edwin Espy, *The Religion of College Teachers: The Beliefs, Practice, and Religious Preparation of Faculty Members in Church-Related Colleges* (New York: Association Press, 1951), vii.

23. Sloan, *Faith and Knowledge,* documents the temporary character of the revival.

24. *College Reading and Religion: A Survey of College Reading Materials* (New Haven: Yale University Press, 1948). The Edward W. Hazen Foundation, *The Edward W. Hazen Foundation 1925–1950* (New Haven: Hazen Foundation, 1950).

25. The Edward W. Hazen Foundation, *College Reading,* vi, ix; Robert L. Calhoun, "History of Philosophy," Ibid. 1–27; Theodore Spencer, "English Literature," Ibid.

172–73; Margaret Mead and Jean Rhys, "Cultural Anthropology," Ibid. 296; William A. Orton, "Economics," Ibid. 261.

26. Spencer, "English Literature," 181–82, cf. 165–66, referring to Margaret Mead, "How Religion Has Fared in the Melting Pot," in *Religion and Our Racial Tensions*, Willard L. Sperry, ed. (Cambridge, Mass.: Harvard University Press, 1945), 61–81.

27. The Hazen Foundation, 31–32.

28. Reinhold Niebuhr, *The Contribution of Religion to Cultural Unity* (New Haven: Hazen Pamphlets, 1945), 3–15.

29. Sloan's analysis in *Faith and Knowledge* is a most important one and complements the present account.

30. Ellen W. Schrecker, *No Ivory Tower: McCarthyism and the Universities* (New York: Oxford University Press, 1986), 104, 106, 111, cf. 31, 379, and passim.

31. Ibid., 117–25, 323–25.

32. Purcell, *Crisis*, 235–66.

33. That Catholicism was sometimes associated with the extreme forms of anticommunism only reinforced the point that Catholicism might threaten liberal culture. On McCarthyism and the Catholic connection see Donald F. Crosby, *God, Church, and Flag: Senator Joseph R. McCarthy and the Catholic Church, 1950–1957* (Chapel Hill: University of North Carolina Press, 1978).

34. Paul Blanshard, *American Freedom and Catholic Power* (Boston: Beacon Press, 1949), 85 and passim.

35. Paul Blanshard, *Communism, Democracy and Catholic Power* (Boston: Beacon Press, 1951), ix–x.

36. Quoted in Robert Moats Miller, *Bishop G. Bromley Oxnam: Paladin of Liberal Protestantism* (Nashville: Abingdon Press, 1990), 408.

37. Ad in *Christian Century* 62 (February 28, 1945), 287, quoted in Philip Gleason, "Pluralism, Democracy, and Catholicism in the Era of World War II," *Review of Politics* 49 (Spring 1987), 226n. Cf. Gleason's account, 211–14.

38. Charles Clayton Morrison, *Can Protestantism Win America?* (New York: Harper & Bros., 1948), 1, vii.

39. Gleason, "Pluralism," 226n.

40. Miller, *Oxnam*, 405.

41. Ibid., 404–5.

42. John Murray Cuddihy, *No Offense: Civil Religion and Protestant Taste* (New York: Seabury Press, 1978), argues this point impressively.

43. Gleason, "Pluralism," esp. 215. Cf. Gleason, "Pluralism and Assimilation: A Conceptual History," in *Linguistic Minorities, Policies and Pluralism*, John Edwards, ed. (London: Academic Press, 1984), 221–57; and Gleason, "American Identity and Americanization," in *Harvard Encyclopedia of American Ethnic Groups*, Stephan Thernstrom et al., eds. (Cambridge, Mass.: Belknap Press, 1980), 43–46.

44. Blanshard, *American Freedom*, 59–106.

45. Quoted from Dewey, *The Nation's Schools* (without further citation) in Blanshard, *American Freedom*, 106.

46. Conant, *Education and Liberty* (Cambridge, Mass.: Harvard University Press, 1953), 86. Cf. Gleason, "Pluralism," 216.

47. A comparable controversy took place at Princeton in 1954 when the Roman Catholic director of the Aquinas Foundation severely criticized the character of the Princeton departments of philosophy and religion. The Aquinas Foundation had been established at Princeton in 1952 with the avowed goal of "the rebirth of Christian culture in university life and thought," a goal that caused resentment among those who felt that "it presupposes a lack of Christian culture in Princeton University." George W. Elderkin, *The Roman Catholic Controversy on the Campus of Princeton University* (n.p., 1955–1958), in four parts. Quotations from Part I, 5. The controversy at Harvard in the late 1940s over the ultraconservative claims of Leonard Feeney, S.J., recounted in Cuddihy, *No Offense,* 49–64, also suggests some parallels.

48. Will Herberg, a Jewish scholar, presented a milder version of this point in a 1952 symposium in response to Margaret M. Wiley. Wiley, noting that twenty-five years earlier no one "could have predicted that by mid-century religion would have become a vital issue in higher education," was unhappy with the Christian biases of the religious revival and advocated finding the "spiritual underpinning for One World" through great literature. Herberg countered that, if anything, the leading promoters of religion in higher education were more in danger "of falling into formlessness and shallow eclecticism rather than flaunting a rigid and exclusive dogmatism." What the modern world needed was more particularistic biblical religion. Modern people, he argued, were prone to "demonic idolatries," especially totalitarianism. Is this country the danger was the idolatry of "secular humanism" in which "man becomes the measure of all things." Such philosophy, which talked of relativism but made humanity an absolute, was what "permeates so much of contemporary higher education." "Religion in Higher Education: A Journal Symposium," *Journal of Higher Education* 23 (October 1952), 350–58, 365–67.

49. Cf. Cuddihy, *No Offense,* esp. 11–23, where they are described as extensions of Protestant tendencies to insist that no institution should define a person's relationship to God.

Chapter 20

1. Robert Maynard Hutchins, quoted from *Time,* November 21, 1949, in Harry S. Ashmore, *Unseasonable Truths: The Life of Robert Maynard Hutchins* (Boston: Little, Brown, 1989), 300.

2. Hutchins, "The Spiritual Need for the Times," *Journal of Higher Education* 18 (May 1947), 325.

3. Ibid., 101.

4. Douglas Sloan, "The Teaching of Ethics in the American Undergraduate Curriculum, 1876–1976," in *Education and Values,* Douglas Sloan, ed. (New York: Teachers College Press, 1980), 191–254, provides a valuable summary of these trends as well as an

analysis of their limits. For instance, Sloan documents that by 1950, 60 percent of state university and land grant colleges were offering academic credit for instruction in religion and that number continued to grow for the next decade and a half. Such programs were the principal loci for teaching ethics in the curriculum during that era. By the 1970s, however, pressures to professionalize the academic study of religion had led to a reduction of its ethical concerns (248–51). Cf. D. G. Hart, "American Learning and the Problem of Religious Studies," in *The Secularization of the Academy*, George M. Marsden and Bradley J. Longfield, eds. (New York: Oxford University Press, 1992), 195–233. R. Laurence Moore, "Secularization: Religion and the Social Sciences," in *Between the Times: The Travail of the Protestant Establishment in America, 1900–1960*, William R. Hutchison, ed. (Cambridge: Cambridge University Press, 1989), 233–52, presents a valuable account of renewed concerns about relating ethical values to the study of social sciences during and after World War II. He concludes, however, that these efforts had little lasting impact and did not stem the tide of secularization. An interesting statement of the problem at the time is found in the title essay of Morton White, *Religion, Politics, and the Higher Learning* (Cambridge, Mass.: Harvard University Press, 1959), 93. White suggests "that any educational effort to nourish religious feeling or to stimulate religious action by trying to present an abstract essence of religion, conceived as the life of feeling and willing (as opposed to knowing), will fail. From this I conclude that we should not make the effort in colleges which are not religious institutions, and that we become frankly sectarian in our teaching of religion and therefore limit higher religious instruction to the divinity schools; since divinity schools are more properly devoted to the *study and the propagation* of religions conceived as total ways of life, knowledge, emotion, and action."

5. John Henry Newman, *The Idea of a University* (Notre Dame, Ind.: University of Notre Dame Press, 1982 [1873, 1852]), 14–74.

6. A striking example is how little is said of theology in Jaroslav Pelikan's *The Idea of the University: A Reexamination* (New Haven: Yale University Press, 1992), even though Pelikan is a theologian and frames the book as a dialogue with Newman. Cf. my review essay, "Christian Schooling: Beyond the Multiversity," *Christian Century* 109 (October 7, 1992), 873–75.

7. Nathan M. Pusey, "A Faith for These Times," in *The Age of the Scholar: Observations on Education in a Troubled Decade* (Cambridge, Mass.: Harvard University Press, 1963), 7–8.

8. "Pusey's Divinity School Policy Criticized," letter to the editor, *Harvard Crimson*, March 3, 1956, 4. "Panel Disagrees on 'Commitment' of Faculty in 'Secular' University," *Harvard Crimson*, April 29, 1958, 1.

9. Nathan M. Pusey, "The Christian Tradition," letter to the editor, *Harvard Crimson*, April 9, 1958, 2.

10. At Harvard and elsewhere during the 1950s there was some controversy when athletic teams began to disregard the Protestant tradition of not playing or practicing on Sundays.

11. *Harvard Crimson*, April 18, 1958, 1; April 23, 1958, 1. Miller's viewpoint is based on his writing and oral tradition, consistent with the evidence. Other *Crimson* articles

on the controversy can be found in the following issues from 1958: March 28, April 8, 9, 10, 11, 12, 14, 15, 16, 17, 18, 19, 21, 23, 26, 29, May 19, 20, and June 9. An approximate survey of religious affiliations of Harvard undergraduates for 1956 showed 25% Jewish, 14% Catholic, 40% Protestant (Episcopal with the largest representation, 14.5%), 10% other, and 11% none. *Harvard Crimson,* March 28, 1958, 5.

12. Will Herberg, "The Making of a Pluralistic Society—A Jewish View," in *Religion and the State University,* Erich A. Walter, ed. (Ann Arbor: University of Michigan Press, 1958), 37–40.

13. John Courtney Murray, S.J., "The Making of a Pluralistic Society—A Catholic View," in Walter, *Religion,* 16, 22.

14. Roland H. Bainton, "The Making of a Pluralistic Society—A Protestant View," in Walter, *Religion,* 47.

15. William K. Frankena, "A Point of View for the Future," in Walter, *Religion,* 299, 305, and 295–309 passim. Mill quotation from his inaugural address as rector of St. Andrews University (299).

16. This is evident in Milton D. McLean and Harry H. Kimber, *Teaching of Religion in State Universities: Description of Programs in Twenty-five Institutions* (Ann Arbor: Office of Religious Affairs, University of Michigan, 1960).

17. This account depends largely on D. G. Hart, "Problem of Religious Studies," in Marsden and Longfield, *Secularization of the Academy,* 194–233. Also see Sloan, "The Teaching of Ethics," 248–51.

18. Hart, "Religious Studies." For valuable contemporary assessments of the trend see Paul Ramsey and John F. Wilson, eds., *The Study of Religion in Colleges and Universities* (Princeton: Princeton University Press, 1970). The acronym of the National Association of Bible Instructors (NABI) was a play on the Hebrew word for prophet.

19. Dorothy C. Bass, "Revolutions, Quiet and Otherwise: Protestants and Higher Education during the 1960s," in *Caring for the Commonweal: Education for Religious and Public Life,* Parker J. Palmer et al., eds. (Macon, Ga.: Mercer University Press, 1990), 222.

20. Cf. Grant Wacker, "A Plural World: The Protestant Awakening to World Religions," in Hutchison, *Between the Times,* 253–77. One sign of the times, for instance, was that the "Yale-in-China" program, which since early in the century had maintained a Christian college on the mainland as part of its educational mission, now reopened in Hong Kong on a purely secular basis. At home, the Yale board still included some of the men who had been shaped by pre–World War I missionary enthusiasm. Now, however, they were convinced that the Christian spirit of their cultural mission for international understanding was best expressed by dropping explicit references to Christianity. Jeffrey Alan Trexler, "Education with the Soul of a Church: The Yale Foreign Missionary Society and the Democratic Ideal," Ph.D. dissertation, Duke University, 1991.

21. David Riesman, *Constraint and Variety in American Education* (Lincoln: University of Nebraska Press, 1956), 25–52.

22. Philip E. Jacob, *Changing Values in College: An Exploratory Study of the Impact of College Teaching* (New York: Harper & Brothers, 1957), helped fuel the worry over conformism of college students during this time. Cf. the response of Allen H. Barton, *Studying the Effects of College Education: A Methodological Examination of Changing Values in College* (New Haven: Hazen Foundation, 1959). Barton quotes approvingly the concern of Theodore M. Greene, *Liberal Education Reexamined* (New York: Harper, 1943), regarding provincialism of students: "A person is provincial in his thinking if his outlook is restricted, either historically or systematically or geographically" (17). Kenneth A. Feldman and Theodore M. Newcomb, *The Impact of College on Students* (San Francisco: Jossey-Bass, 1969), another follow-up to Jacobs, develops a negative "authoritarian category that would include traditional religion" (Vol. I, 30–31). Theodore W. Adorno et al., *The Authoritarian Personality* (New York: Harper & Brothers, 1950), developed an "F-scale" on authoritarianism used in some studies of college students. Cf. Barton, *Effects*, 86–87.

23. The most comprehensive of these was Manning M. Pattillo Jr., and Donald M. MacKenzie, *Church-Sponsored Higher Education in the United States, Report of the Danforth Commission* (Washington, D.C.: American Council on Education, 1966).

24. Christopher Jencks and David Riesman, *The Academic Revolution* (Chicago: University of Chicago Press, 1968), 327, 332.

25. This is the conclusion of Bass, "Revolutions," 214–15, and of Robert Wood Lynn, "'The Survival of Recognizably Protestant Colleges': Reflections on Old-line Protestantism, 1950–1990," in Marsden and Longfield, *Secularization of the Academy*, 170–94, esp. 183, regarding Kenneth Underwood, *The Church, the University, and Social Policy: The Danforth Study of Campus Ministries* (Middletown, Conn.: Wesleyan University Press, 1969). Douglas Sloan, "The American Theological Renaissance" (an early draft of *Faith and Knowledge: Mainline Protestantism and Twentieth-Century Higher Education* [Philadelphia: Westminster Press, 1994 (forthcoming)]), 61–69, comes to a similar conclusion. By the late 1960s, he says, the slogan of three decades in the Student Christian Movement, "Let the University be the University," had shifted from a challenge to include Christian concerns to mean "Let the university be the university—as it is."

26. J. Edward Dirks, "About the Journal" (Editor's Preface), *Christian Scholar* 36 (1953), 3, 4. The first quotation is from J. V. Langmead Casserley, *The Retreat from Christianity in the Modern World* (London: Longmans, Green, 1952), 91. The *Christian Scholar* succeeded *Christian Education*. Cf. Sloan, "American Theological Renaissance," 1, 26.

27. "An Ending Not an End," *Christian Scholar* 50 (Winter 1967), 341, and "Announcing: SOUNDINGS: A Journal of Interdisciplinary Studies," *Christian Scholar* 50 (Winter 1967). Cf. Sloan, "American Theological Renaissance," 1, 26.

28. Harvey Cox, *The Secular City: Secularization and Urbanization in Theological Perspective*, rev. ed. (New York: Macmillan, 1965), 193–94, 217–37.

29. Such theological trends were already strong by the time Cox wrote. See Bass, "Revolutions," 209.

30. For a critical view of these developments see Leonard I. Sweet, "The 1960s: The Crises of Liberal Christianity and the Public Emergence of Evangelicalism," in *Evangelicalism*

and Modern America, George Marsden, ed. (Grand Rapids, Mich.: Wm. B. Eerdmans, 1984), 29–45.

31. This account follows closely that of Bass, "Revolutions," esp. 218–19, from which the quotations are taken.

32. I am grateful to Sloan, "American Theological Renaissance," 64–65, for this insight.

33. Robert Wuthnow, *The Struggle for America's Soul: Evangelicals, Liberals, and Secularism* (Grand Rapids, Mich.: William B. Eerdmans, 1989), 34–35.

34. *1986–87 Fact Book on Higher Education*, Cecilia A. Ottinger, comp. (New York: American Council on Education, 1987), chart 73.

35. Cf. Bass, "Revolutions," 212, and Clark Kerr, *The Uses of the University* (New York: Harper & Row, 1963).

36. Martin Trow, "Reflections on the Transition from Mass to Universal Higher Education," in *The Embattled University*, Stephen R. Graubard and Geno Ballotti, eds. (New York: George Braziller, 1970), 1–42.

37. Francis Oakley, *Community of Learning: The American College and the Liberal Arts Tradition* (New York: Oxford University Press, 1992), 73–104, offers revealing statistics documenting government expansion and vast increases in two-year colleges, community colleges, and higher education outside the humanities since the 1960s. For instance, in 1960 one in six faculty members taught at a liberal arts college, whereas by 1980 only one in twelve did (98).

38. Theodore Roszak, The Making of a Counter Culture: Reflections on the Technocratic Society and Its Youthful Opposition (Garden City, N.Y.: Doubleday, 1969), 205–38.

39. For example, Jill Conway, "Styles of Academic Culture," in Graubard and Ballotti, *Embattled University*, 43–55.

40. Clark Kerr, "The Carnegie Policy Series, 1967–1979: Concerns, Approaches, Reconsiderations, Results," in *The Carnegie Council on Policy Studies in Higher Education: A Summary of Reports and Recommendations* (San Francisco: Jossey-Bass, 1980), 2–3.

41. Duke University and David Goldstein, "Crossing Boundaries: Interdisciplinary Planning for the Nineties: Duke University Self-Study," (Durham, N.C.: Duke University, 1988), 3–4.

42. This statement is found on a plaque at the center of the West Campus, Duke University.

43. N. J. Demerath, III, "Cultural Victory and Organizational Defeat in the Paradoxical Decline of Liberal Protestantism," *Journal for the Scientific Study of Religion*, 34(4) (December, 1995), pp. 458-469.

44. It would have something to do with the tendency for higher education to somewhat liberalize the outlooks of students who are religious.

45. Christian Smith, *Souls in Transition: The Religious and Spiritual Lives of Emerging Adults* (New York: Oxford University Press, 2009), 288–289.

46. Brad Gregory, *The Unintended Reformation: How a Religious Movement Secularized Society* (Cambridge, Mass.: Harvard University Press, 2012). Patrick Deneen, *Why Liberalism Failed* (New Haven: Yale University Press, 2019).

47. I explore these paradoxes in *Religion in American Culture: A Brief History* (Grand Rapids, Mich.: Eerdmans, 2018).

48. David Brooks, *The Second Mountain: The Quest for the Moral Life* (New York: Random House 2019), 297.

49. David A, Hollinger, "Toward a Postethnic Perspective," *Postethnic America: Beyond Multiculturalism* (New York: Basic Books, 1995), 105–130.

50. Brooks, *Second Mountain*, 297–300.

51. For instance, Jonathan Haidt, *The Righteous Mind: Why Good People Are Divided by Politics and Religion* (New York: Random House, 2012), 156–163 and *passim*, presents a social evolutionary argument for this point, which is also made in classic Christian theology as in *Augustine's City of God*, for instance.

52. Putnam as summarized by Kevin Den Dulk, "Isolation and the Prospects for Democracy: The Challenge of the Alienated," *Comment*, 36 (2) (Summer 2018), https://www.cardus.ca/comment/article/isolation-and-the-prospects-for-democracy/#

Chapter 21

1. One exception is Steven Britt, *Two Cheers for Higher Education: Why American Universities Are Stronger than Ever—and How to Meet the Challenges They Face* (Princeton: Princeton University Press, 2019). His positive assessments are based mostly on quantitative data.

2. John Thelin, *A History of American Higher Education*, 3rd edition (Baltimore: Johns Hopkins University Press, 2019, writes that since many influential persons say higher education should be run like a business, "I have taken that to heart" in adding material on the twenty-first century, and "my reading and research leaned increasingly toward the economics of higher education," xvii. Cf. Roger L. Geiger, *American Higher Education since World War II: A History* (Princeton: Princeton University Press, 2019), who says much the same (313). Geiger provides a dispassionate analysis of the economic dimension of higher education, its changing demographics, and its usefulness for career preparation and serving society. Nonetheless, he sees diversity efforts as ironically leading to the "balkanization" of campuses (352), "campus life less diverse for most students" (352) and "groupthink" that discouraged disinterested study and would not allow challenges to prevailing political orthodoxies, (353–54).

3. William Egginton, *The Splintering of the American Mind: Identity Politics, Inequality, and Community on Today's College Campuses* (New York: Bloomsbury Publishing, 2018). "The Academy Is Largely Responsible for Its Own Peril," (Interview with Jill Lepore), *Chronicle Review,* Nov. 30, 2018, B6–B9.

4. Perry L. Glanzer, Nathan F. Alleman, and Todd Ream, *Restoring the Soul of the University: Unifying Christian Higher Education in a Fragmented Age* (Downers Grove, IL: InterVarsity Press, 2017), 1–13, provides a helpful overview of the perceptions of the crisis and offers further bibliography, 325, n4. An earlier volume, *What's Happened*

to the Humanities? Alvin Kernan, ed. (Princeton: Princeton University Press, 1997), includes an impressive lineup of distinguished authors.

5. Harry R. Lewis, *Excellence without Soul: How a Great University Forgot Education* (New York: PublicAffairs, 2006), xiv (quotation), 82–3, 2–3, and passim.

6. Anthony Kronman, *Education's End: Why Our Colleges and Universities Have Given Up on the Meaning of Life* (New Haven: Yale University Press, 2007), 237, 83 (quotation).

7. Ibid., 162–63, 137–38. In his more recent book, *The Assault on American Excellence* (New York: The Free Press, 2019), Kronman brings many of these same critiques up to date. He particularly analyzes the campus "free speech" controversies, arguing that that in the standoffs between the two camps of "speech hurts and offends" and "speech liberates," both sides get it wrong" (15). He also dwells on the wider implications for American culture, arguing that we can learn from some of the best thinkers of the past that "aristocratic" ideals of excellence can benefit the whole society.

   Daniel T. Rodgers, *Age of Fracture* (Cambridge, Mass.: Harvard University Press, 2011), offers a valuable broader intellectual history of such developments in the late twentieth century.

8. Andres Delbanco, *College: What It Was, and Should Be* (Princeton: Princeton University Press, 2014), 3, 7.

9. Ibid., 135, quoting Michael Young, *The Rise of Meritocracy, 1870–2033* (London: Penguin Books, 1961), 92.

10. Ibid., 143. Cf. his note 207. One influential more recent book is Elizabeth Armstrong and Laura Hamilton, *Paying for the Party: How College Maintains Inequality* (Cambridge, Mass.: Harvard University Press 2013), an ethnographic study of how economic inequalities are perpetuated in the ways they directly influence the lives of university students. Delbanco might have added Frank Donoghue, *The Last Professors: The Corporate University and the Fate of the Humanities* (New York: Fordham U. Press, 2008,) xv, which deplores "the oppressive signifi-cance of the corporate vocabulary of efficiency, productivity, and usefulness." Richard Arum and Josipa Roksa, *Academically Adrift: Limited Learning on College Campuses* (Chicago: University of Chicago Press, 2011), provides documentation of trends in learning.

11. William Eddinton, *The Splintering of the American Mind: Identity Politics, Inequality, and Community on Today's College Campuses* (New York: Bloomsbury Publishing, 2018), 14.

12. Ibid., 156, 157, 161–224.

13. Jonathan Haidt and Greg Lukianoff, in *The Coddling of the American Mind* (New York: Penguin Press, 2019), quotations from 57, 51, 33, 46.

14. Ibid., 243.

15. Among the recent books on this topic are John Palfrey, *Safe Spaces, Brave Spaces: Diversity and Free Expression in Education* (Cambridge, Mass.: MIT Press, 2017); Erwin Cherminsky and Howard Gillman, *Free Speech on Campus* (New Haven: Yale University Press, 2017); Michael S. Roth, *Safe Enough Spaces: A Pragmatist's Approach to Inclusion, Free Speech, and Political Correctness on College*

Campuses (New Haven: Yale University Press, 2019); Ulrich Baer, *What Snowflakes Get Right: Free Speech, Truth, and Equality on Campus* (New York: Oxford University Press, 2019); and Donald Alexander, *Free Speech and Liberal Education: A Plea for Intellectual Diversity and Tolerance* (Washington, D.C.: Cato Institute, 2020).

16. Roger L. Geiger in his comprehensive survey, *American Higher Education since World War II: A History* (Princeton: Princeton University Press, 2019), 313, observes that twenty-first-century universities are "more oriented toward relations with the commercial economy . . . more driven by markets and less by governments. More dependent on private-sector resources, it became increasingly responsive to consumers." Higher education serves a wider variety of students than ever, but the "overall effect" of identity politics "was to balkanize campuses" (351); "The politicization of the American universities in the 2010s was the most extreme since the 1960s" (366). At the same time a university degree is a chief predictor of individual success: "And as the chief repository of advanced knowledge, universities [created and preserved] a large share of the intellectual resources of our civilization" (313).

17. In early 2020 the *Chronicle of Higher Education* collected under the title "Endgame" fourteen essays from the previous year dealing with the ongoing "collapse" of literary studies: http://connect.chronicle.com/rs/931-EKA-218/images/ChronicleReview_Endgame.pdf. As *New York Times* columnist Russ Douthat observed, one parallel being drawn is the earlier decline of religion in higher education: "The Academic Apocalypse: The Crisis in English Departments Is Also a Crisis of Faith," New York Times, January 11, 2020.

18. Benjamin Schmidt, "The Humanities Are in Crisis," *The Atlantic*, August 23, 2018, https://www.theatlantic.com/education/archive/2018/08/the-humanities-face-a-crisisof-confidence/567565/ Cf. Alexander W. Astin et al., *The American Freshman: Thirty Year Trends, 1966–1996* (Los Angeles: Higher Education Research Institute, Graduate School of Education & Information Studies, University of California, Los Angeles, 1997), 12–15.

19. Neil Gross and Solon Simmons, "The Religious Convictions of College and University Professors," in Jacobsen and Jacobsen, eds., *The American University in a Postsecular Age*, 24–25. Cf. John Schmalzbauer and Kathleen A. Mahoney, *The Resilience of Religion in American Higher Education* (Waco: Baylor University Press, 2018) [Cited as hereafter as Resilience], 52.

20. Excepting in some Catholic universities that are now seen as mainstream.

21. George Yancey, *Compromising Scholarship: Religious and Political Bias in American Higher Education* (Waco: Baylor University Press, 2011), esp. 85–124.

22. On political attitudes of professors, see also Neil Gross, *Why Are Professors Liberal and Why Do Conservatives Care?* (Cambridge, Mass.: Harvard University Press, 2013). Gross emphasizes self-selection, that is, that people who are liberal and not narrowly religious tend to go into certain academic fields. But Yancey's study shows that bias is also sometimes a factor, including one that might inhibit people from selecting certain sorts of academic professions. Cf. Yancey's paper critiquing Gross's book, George Yancey, "Both/and Instead of Either/Or," *Society* 52 (February, 2015), 23–27.

23. They see the early 1970s as a "nadir for religion on campus as Protestant influence waned," *Resilience*, 6.

24. Though it is possible, as considered earlier, to argue for residual liberal Protestant influences among the forces shaping more recent ideals of inclusion and equal treatment for groups previously left out.

25. "Robert B. Townsend, "A New Found Religion? The Field Surges among AHA Members," *Perspective on History*, December 2009. https://www.historians. org/publications-and-directories/perspectives-on-history/december-2009/ a-new-found-religion-the-field-surges-among-aha-members

26. *Resilience*, 27–28, 33–41.

27. *Resilience*, 28–32, 41–44. And see the Epilogue to the present volume.

28. See John G. Turner, *Bill Bright and Campus Crusade for Christ: The Renewal of Evangelicalism in Postwar America* (Chapel Hill: University of North Carolina Press, 2008).

29. *Resilience*, 106–127.

30. Frederick Houk Borsch, *Keeping Faith at Princeton: A Brief History of Religious Pluralism at Princeton and Other Universities* (Princeton: Princeton University Press, 2012), offers a thoughtful and informative account of this transition, based largely on his own long experience at Princeton.

31. *Resilience*, 131, and 79% of undergraduates say they believe in God and 69% say that they pray.

32. Alan Finder, "Matters of Faith Find a New Prominence on Campus," *New York Times*, May 2, 2007, https://www.nytimes.com/2007/05/02/education/02spirituality.html. Gomes was also widely credited with remarking that there was probably more evangelical Christianity in Harvard Yard than at any time since the eighteenth century.

33. *Resilience*, 131. On the "nones" and the overall decline of American religious affiliation, see *Resilience*, 165–166. Since mainline Protestants have declined precipitously in this era and evangelical groups only slightly, the rise of the "nones" seems likely related to less residual denominational loyalties among those with mainline heritage, So that in the 1960s those who were not active in churches might report being "Methodist," "Disciples," or "United Church of Christ," in the twenty-first century their descendants check "none."

34. Christian Smith, *Souls in Transition: The Religious and Spiritual Lives of Emerging Adults* (New York: Oxford University Press, 2009), 248–251.

35. Eboo Patel, *Out of Many Faiths: Religious Diversity and the American Promise* (Princeton: Princeton University Press, 2018) 28–29. Also, Patel, "Faith Is the Diversity Issue Ignored by Colleges. Here's Why It Needs to Change," *Chronicle of Higher Education* (November 2018), A36.

36. John Inazu, "Hope without a Common Ground," (a response to Patel), *Out of Many Faiths*, 133–150.

37. John d. Inazu, *Confident Pluralism: Surviving and Thriving through Deep Difference* (Chicago: University of Chicago Press, 2016).

38. *Resilience*, 133. The InterVarsity website provides a list of the bans and reversals at ten schools or university systems as of the end of 2018: https://intervarsity.org/campus-access-issues

39. For a list of campus controversies and legal rulings over this issue involving InterVarsity, see "Legal Issues" on their website (assessed November 19, 2019) https://intervarsity.org/about-us/press-room/campus-access-issues/legal-challenges

Epilogue

1. Reinhold Niebuhr, *The Contribution of Religion to Cultural Unity* (New Haven: Hazen Pamphlets, 1945), 13.

2. The exceptions would be the continued presence of a divinity schools on the campuses of a number of leading private universities. These do not have a lot to do with shaping their universities as a whole, but they do sustain an intellectually substantial Christian presence.

3. See the works cited in the chapter on the twenty-first century (chapter 21).

4. Other substantial portions of explicitly Christian academic work is found among mainline Protestants and Catholics. But these developments, while significant, are not surprising as historical phenomena, given the strong institutional and intellectual heritages of these traditions.

5. Christopher Jencks and David Riesman, *The Academic Revolution* (Chicago: University of Chicago Press, 1977 [1968]), 312, 327.

6. Ibid., 331.

7. Ibid., 332n.

8. Ibid., 405.

9. William G. McLoughlin, "Is There a Third Force in Christendom?" *Daedalus* 96(1) (Winter 1967), 45.

10. Richard Hofstadter, *Anti-Intellectualism in American Life* (New York: Vintage Books, 1963 [1962]), 15, 55–141.

11. For engaging portraits of Graham see Grant Wacker, *America's Pastor: Billy Graham and the Shaping of a Nation* (Cambridge, Mass.: Harvard University Press, 2014, and Grant Wacker, *One Soul at A Time: The Story of Billy Graham* (Grand Rapids, Mich.: William B. Eerdmans, 2019).

12. On Fuller's early years and efforts at intellectual renewal see George Marsden, *Reforming Fundamentalism: Fuller Seminary and the New Evangelicalism* (Grand Rapids, Mich.: Wm. B. Eerdmans, 1986).

13. Carl F. H. Henry to Billy Graham, October 16, 1955, quoted in Owen Strachan, *Awakening of the Evangelical Mind: An Intellectual History of the New-evangelical Movement* (Grand Rapids, Mich.: Zondervan, 2015), 135. Strachan provides a valuable account of all these developments involving Ockenga, Henry, Graham, and their associates.

14. Carl F. H. Henry to Billy Graham, Oct. 8, 1955, quoted in Strachan, *Awakening*, 130–31.

15. Carl F. H. Henry, *Confessions of a Theologian: An Autobiography* (Waco, Tex.: Word Books, 1986), 67.
16. Michael S. Hamilton, "The Fundamentalist Harvard: Wheaton College and the Continuing Vitality of American Evangelicalism, 1919–1965," Ph.D. dissertation, University of Notre Dame, 1994, Vol. III, 50 (from Hamilton's digital version.)
17. Strachan, *Awakening*, 135.
18. *New York Times*, May 5, 1960, A5, cited in Strachan, *Awakening*, 144,
19.. Cf. Strachen, *Awakening*, 145–8.
20. Mixter edited a duly cautious volume *Evolution and Christian Thought* (1959) (Carl Henry wrote the concluding essay) that, despite some rumblings, won acclaim in the evangelical world. Ronald L. Numbers, *The Creationists: The Evolution of Scientific Creationism* (New York: Alfred A Knopf, 1994), 181.
21. Adam Laats, *Fundamentalist U: Keeping the Faith in American Higher Education* (New York: Oxford University Press, 2018), 245–254, quotation 252; Hamilton, "Fundamentalist Harvard," Vol. V, 11–15; Numbers, *Creationists*, 182–183. Laats provides a valuable account of the continuing influences of fundamentalist heritages on various evangelical or fundamentalist colleges into the twenty-first century. Another important study is Molly Worthen, *Apostles of Reason: The Crisis of Authority in American Evangelicalism* (New York: Oxford University Press, 2014), which offers a well-informed interpretation of evangelical thought since the mid-twentieth century.
22. See Randall J. Stephens and Karl W. Giberson, *The Anointed: Evangelical Truth in a Secular Age* (Cambridge, Mass.: Harvard University Press, 2011), regarding how such preferences continue.
23. Clyde Kilby, *The Christian World of C. S. Lewis* (Grand Rapids, Mich.: Eerdmans, 1964).
24. Cf. George Marsden, *C. S. Lewis's MERE CHRISTIANITY: A Biography* (Princeton: Princeton University Press, 2018).
25. Cf. ibid., 153–188.
26. Hamilton, "Fundamentalist Harvard," Vol. 5, 17.
27. Morris Keeton [and] Conrad Hilberry, *Struggle and Promise: A Future for Colleges* (New York: McGraw, 1969), 22.
28. https://magazine.wheaton.edu/stories/2017-winter-the-arthur-holmes-hundred
29. Calvin's history is found in a number of places including John J. Timmerman, *Promises to Keep: A Centennial History of Calvin College* (Grand Rapids, Mich.: Wm. B. Eerdmans, 1975). I have also benefited from early drafts of a projected history of Calvin by Michael Hamilton, furnished by the author.
30. For a concise summary of his argument see the speech by Alvin Plantinga on Receiving the Templeton Prize, the Field Museum, Chicago, September 24, 2017, https://www.templetonprize.org/laureate-sub/plantinga-acceptance-speech/.
31. Nicholas Wolterstorff, *Religion in the University* (New Haven: Yale University Press, 2019), 10, 48–49, 118.
32. Ibid., 113–14, quoting Richard Rorty, *Philosophy and Social Hope* (London: Penguin books, 1999), 172.
33. Ibid., 58.

34. Arthur Holmes was, for instance, an influential popularizer of the outlook, as the titles of his accessible books of the 1970s suggest: *Faith Seeks Understanding: A Christian Approach to Knowledge* (1971), *The Idea of a Christian College* (1975), and *All Truth Is God's Truth* (1977) (all, Grand Rapids, Mich.: Eerdmans).

35. Michael S. Hamilton, "Whoring after the Gods of Babylon or Pining for the Fleshpots of Egypt?," *Fides et Historia* 48(1) (Winter/Spring 2016), 120.

36. Wolfe, "The Opening of the Evangelical Mind," *Atlantic,* October 2000. And see note 57 in this chapter.

37. David R. Swartz, *Moral Minority: The Evangelical Left in an Age of Conservatism* (Philadelphia: University of Pennsylvania Press, 2012), provides the best account of these trends that involved quite a few, mostly younger, faculty at theologically conservative Christian colleges.

38. William Ringenberg, *The Christian College: A History of Protestant Higher Education in America* (Grand Rapids, Mich.: Baker Academic, 2006), 211. Ringenberg offers a valuable history. Though he emphasizes CCCU schools in his account of recent times, he notes that as of the early twenty-first century the U.S. Department of Education identified approximately nine hundred religiously affiliated colleges and universities. As Ringenberg, observes (211), Robert Benne's typology in *Quality with Soul: How Six Premier Colleges and Universities Keep Faith with Their Religious Traditions* (Grand Rapids: Eerdmans, 2001), is especially helpful in sorting degrees of pluralism and secularization and varieties of ways of relating to religious heritages.

39. *Models for Christian Higher Education: Strategies for Success in the Twenty-First Century,* Richard T. Hughes and William B. Adrian, eds. (Grand Rapids, Mich.: Eerdmans, 1997), 6, quoting "a Mennonite scholar."

40. Richard T. Hughes, "What Can the Church of Christ Tradition Contribute to Christian Higher Education?" in *Models,* 408.

41. Cf. Models, 8.

42. InterVarsity Graduate and Faculty Ministries: Christian Professional and Academic Societies, lists about forty of these as of 2019: https://gfm.intervarsity.org/resources/christian-professional-and-academic-societies. Some of these included Catholics, though Catholics tended to have their own older organizations.

43. A sampling of outlooks among distinguished Christian philosophers can be found in *Philosophers Who Believe: The Spiritual Journeys of Leading Christian Thinkers,* Kelly James Clark, ed. (Downers Grove, Ill.: InterVarsity Press, 1993.

44. https://www.societyofchristianphilosophers.com/content.aspx?page_id=22&club_id=560358&module_id=340659 and https://www.apaonline.org/page/presidents

45. E.g., Susan Van Zanten, *Literature through the Eyes of Faith* (San Francisco: Harper and Row, 1989). Another sampling of Christian perspectives among professors of various disciplines is found in *Professors Who Believe: the Spiritual Journeys of Christian Faculty,* Paul M. Anderson ed. (Downers Grove, Ill.: InterVarsity Press, 1998).

46. Mark Noll, *The Scandal of the Evangelical Mind* (Grand Rapids, Mich.: Eerdmans, 1994), 3.

47. Steven Patrick Miller, *The Age of Evangelicalism: America's Born-Again Years* (New York: Oxford University Press, 2014), 98–99.

48. The multi-year project that resulted in, among other things, *The Soul of the American University* (1994), was one of the first such projects funded by Pew as brokered by Lynn.

49. https://www.lillyfellows.org/media/1581/lilly-network-benefits-flyer.pdf

50. David C. Mahan and C. Donald Smedley, "University Ministry and the Evangelical Mind," *The State of the Evangelical Mind: Reflections on the Past, Prospects for the Future*, Todd C. Ream, Jerry Pattengale, and Christopher J. Devers, eds. (Downers Grove, Ill.: InterVarsity Press 2018), 59–100, provides a helpful overview of the impact of these ministries.

51. Mark A. Noll, "Evangelical Intellectual Life: Reflections on the Past," in *State of the Evangelical Mind*, 27–28, reviews the dramatic rise in university press publications at Wheaton College.

52. Donald D. Schmeltekopf, *Baylor at the Crossroads: Memoirs of a Provost* (Eugene, Oreg.: Cascade Books, 2015), 14–16. Schmeltekopf provides a valuable insider's account of all these developments.

53. Ibid., 63–69.

54. https://www.baylor.edu/about/ (January 13, 2020).

55. Personal correspondence of Evans with the author. And see https://www.baylor.edu/philosophy/index.php?id=924790 for details (January 13, 2020).

56. Ringenberg, *Christian College*, 209, reports "an enrollment increase of 67.3% for the CCCU institutions and 2.1% for all colleges and universities for the 1992–2002 decade."

57. Alan Wolfe, "The Opening of the Evangelical Mind," *Atlantic*, October 2000, https://www.theatlantic.com/magazine/archive/2000/10/the-opening-of-the-evangelical-mind/378388/

58. Randall J. Stephens and Karl W. Giberson, *The Anointed: Evangelical Truth in a Secular Age*, provides a valuable account of the continuing preferences for such simple formulas rather than the more complex results of academic scholarship.

59. Liberty University is the most significant alternative. Not a member of the CCCU, it has become the largest explicitly Christian university by embracing its fundamentalist heritage (though they no longer use the term "fundamentalist"), especially in combative politics and also in developing impressive online learning. For this side of the evangelical educational heritage see Laats, *Fundamentalist U*.

60. John McGee, *Breakpoint: The Changing Marketplace for Higher Education* (Baltimore: The Johns Hopkins University Press, 2015), provides a helpful overview of such challenges. Todd C. Ream, Jerry Pattengale, and Christopher J. Devers, in their "Introduction" to *State of the Evangelical Mind*, esp. 9–13, offer an overview of challenges facing CCCU schools in recent years.

61. "Books and Culture Ends Twenty-one Year Run," *Christianity Today* News Release, October 2016, https://www.christianitytoday.org/media-room/news/2016/books-cultures-ends-21-year-run.html. Meanwhile CCCU institutions have long sustained a more strictly academic interdisciplinary journal, *Christian Scholar's Review*, founded in 1970 as one of the first efforts to rebuild evangelical intellectual culture.

62. John Schmalzbauer and Kathleen A. Mahoney, *The Resilience of Religion in American Higher Education* (Waco: Baylor University Press, 2018), which provides valuable overviews and documentation of these developments, says (22) "over fifty religious scholarly organizations foster the integration of faith and learning." At the same time, since one of the strengths (as well as financial necessities) of CCCU schools is that they are primarily teaching institutions, their faculty members are still often frustrated by lack of time and encouragement for new research and writing. Schmalzbauer and Mahoney (83) note that as of 2010, faculty members at CCCU schools were publishing significantly less than counterparts at secular institutions.

63. See, for example, the networks of institutions and scholars connected with the International Network for Christian Higher Education (INCHE).

64. Schmalzbauer and Mahoney, *Resilience*, 52.

65. See, for instance, George Yancey, *Compromising Scholarship: Religious and Political Bias in American Higher Education* (Waco: Baylor University Press, 2010.)

66. The Consortium of Christian Study Centers listed a total of twenty-nine affiliated institutions as of November 19, 2019: https://studycentersonline.org/membership/member-study-centers/. For the history of these see, Charles E. Cotherman, *To Think Christianly: A History of L'Abri, Regent College, and the Christian Study Center Movement* (Downers Grove, Ill.: InterVarsity Academic, 2020).

67. Noll, *Jesus Christ and the Life of the Mind* (Grand Rapids, Mich.: Eerdmans, 2011), 156. Sociologist D. Michael Lindsay, *Faith in the Halls of Power* (New York: Oxford University Press, 2007), 75–116, documents some advances of evangelicals in mainstream academia,

68. Noll, "Reflections," in *State of Evangelical Mind*, 30–31. In the same volume, James A. K. Smith, "The Future Is Catholic: The Next Scandal of the Evangelical Mind," 141–160, and Mark Galli, "The Ongoing Challenge to the Evangelical Mind," 161–172, offer particularly helpful reflections on this question. The prominent role of the more churchly Reformed in American "evangelical" intellectual life plays a role in building such affinities.

69. Noll, *Jesus Christ and the Life of the Mind*, 158. Also significant are interactions with mainline Protestant intellectual communities. Twenty-first-century evangelicals have conversation partners, especially with those in what might be called chastened liberal camps that are found in some prominent university divinity schools and theological seminaries or in the Lilly network of colleges and universities.

70. Jencks and Riesman, *Academic Revolution*, 399.

71. For instance, *The Challenge and Promise of a Catholic University*, Theodore M. Hesburgh, C. S. C., ed. (Notre Dame, Ind.: University of Notre Dame Press, 1994).

72. Schmalzbauer and Mahoney, *Resilience*, 76.

73. For this history see Philip Gleason, *Contending with Modernity: Catholic Higher Education in the Twentieth Century* (New York: Oxford University Press, 1995).

74. See Monika K. Hellwig, "What Can the Roman Catholic Tradition Contribute to Christian Higher Education?," *Models for Christian Higher Education*, 13–23. See also for some of the varieties in Catholic higher education.

75. Thomas S. Kuhn, *The Structure of Scientific Revolutions*, 2nd edition enlarged (Chicago: University of Chicago Press, 1970 [1962]), 203.

Index

For the benefit of digital users, indexed terms that span two pages (e.g., 52–53) may, on occasion, appear on only one of those pages.

Abbot, Lyman, 182–83
abstinence, 168–69
Adams, Henry C., 147–48, 151
Addams, Jane, 184–85
Adler, Felix, 107
Adler, Mortimer, 299, 300–1, 304, 306–7, 308
  professoriate attacked by, 305–6
African-Americans, 249, 282–84, 377
  Christianity in colleges of, 261, 270, 282–84
  college attendance of, 437n.12
  discrimination against in universities, 192, 282, 312, 325–26
  and Princeton, 282
  schools established by, 283–84
agnosticism, 21, 114, 167, 193–94, 253
  and Darwinism, 19–20, 114, 126
Alison, Francis, 57–58, 59
Allport, Gordon, 318
Alston, William, 376–77, 381–82
American Academy of Religion (AAR), 335–36
American Association of University
  and academic freedom, 219–20, 222, 223, 225–26, 234, 235–36, 238, 250–51, 322
  Communist party membership viewed by, 322–23
  critics of, 234–35
  founding of, 219–20, 221–22, 231
  on the function of the university, 222–23
  Professors (AAUP), 231–35
  and religiously defined schools, 235, 252, 273
  and World War I, 235–37, 238

American Council on Education, 251, 262
American Economics Association (AEA), 186, 221–22, 234
American Historical Association, 295, 359
American Missionary Association, 283
American Philosophical Association, 229–30, 380–81
American, Psychological Association, 229–30
American Revolution, 47, 53, 63–64, 79–80, 82, 170–71
American Scientific Affiliation, 372
Ames, William, 36, 39, 41
Amherst, 195, 270
Andover Theological Seminary, 69–70, 85, 146
Angell, James Burrill, 137–38, 189
  And Christianity, 144, 148, 149–50
  and the University of Michigan, 137–39, 140–42, 149–50
  and voluntary religion, 143, 148, 229, 292–93
Angell, James Rowland, 229, 270, 271, 292–93
Anglicanism and the Anglicans, 46, 47, 50, 52, 53, 54, 63–64, 65, 102, 253
  defectors to, 46–47, 52
anticommunism, 321–23, 366, 444n.33
anti-Semitism, 286–89, 438n.26, *See also* Jews and Judaism
Aquinas, Thomas, 29, 40–41, 200, 279, 299, 303, 311, 445n.47, *See also* Thomism
  and reason, 30–31, 302, 303

Aristotle, 57–58, 299, 302
  in university curriculum, 31, 32–33, 40,
    41, 43–44, 56–57
  and virtue, 56
Arminians, 46, 55, 399n.29
Association of American Colleges (AAC),
    234–35, 238, 250–51, 262, 272
atheism, 9, 10, 15, 112–13, 114, 116,
    164, 241–42, 394n17
Auburn Theological Seminary, 91
Augustine, 6–7, 30–31, 41, 227, 294, 377
"Authoritarian Attempt to Capture
    Education," 308, 324
Ayer, A. J., 293–94

Bacon, Francis, 84, 112, 128–29, 231–32
  and American Protestantism, 80, 83–
    84, 94–95
Bainton, Roland, 334–35
Baldwin, James Mark, 168
Bancroft, George, 94, 153
Baptists, 12, 37–38, 45, 249–50, 257–58
  antievolution among, in North
    Carolina, 246–48
  colleges of, 51, 63–64, 74, 85, 203, 280–
    81, 379–80, 383
  and the separation of church and
    state, 247–48
  and the University of Chicago, 175–76,
    179, 299
Barnes, Harry Elmer, 248–49
Barth, Karl, 296
Bass, Dorothy, 340
Baylor University, 383–85
Beard, Charles, 236, 295, 428n.49
Becker, Carl, 294–95, 428n.49
Beecher, Catharine, 105, 113–14,
    408n.10
Beecher, Lyman, 19, 80
  and education in the West, 78–79,
    80, 81–82
Bemis, Edward W., 186, 221–22
Benedict, Ruth, 296–98
Berkeley, Bishop George, 50, 399n.29
Bernard, L. L., 248–49
Bertocci, Peter, 318
Bible, 21–22, 83–84, 86, 151, 199, 273,
    280–81, 386

authority of, debated, 4–5, 66, 94, 123,
    143–45, 152, 242–43, 245–180, 320,
    367–68, 372–73, 379–80
  in the curriculum, 39, 40–41, 66, 94,
    113, 172–73, 175–29, 189, 207–8,
    248, 249–50, 257, 258–59, 260–62,
    266, 268, 280, 369
  scientific study of, 145, 204, 206–7, 251–
    52, 371–72
biological evolution. See Darwinism;
    evolution
Birge, Edward A., 244
Blanshard, Brand, 11–12, 307–8
Blanshard, Paul, 324, 326, 391n.10
Bledstein, Burton J., 131–32
Boas, Franz, 296, 304
Bolce, Harold, 193–95, 215
Bonhoeffer, Dietrich, 339
Borden, William Whiting, 435n.57
Boston University, 203, 207, 369
Bowne, Borden Parker, 207–8
Brainerd, David, 48
Brandeis University, 285, 438n.21
Briggs, Charles, 226–27
Britain, 47, 53–54, 126, 369, 373
Brooks, Van Wyck, 304, 441n.34
Brown, Elmer Ellsworth, 292–93,
    415n.30
Brownson, Orestes, 198
Brown University (Rhode Island College),
    85, 367, 398n.20
  interdenominational rivalries
    at, 51–52
Brumbaugh, T. T., 275–76
Bryan, William Jennings, 246, 247–48,
    252–53, 254
  antievolutionism of, 244–46, 249, 251–
    52, 272–73
Bryn Mawr College, 215, 218–19
Buchanan, James, 105
Buckley, William F., Jr., 17, 23–24, 25–
    26, 326–28
  Yale criticized by, 9, 10, 11, 12–14,
    15, 326–28
Bundy, McGeorge, 9, 13
Burton, Marion L., 273
Bushnell, Horace, 121–22
Butler, Joseph, 83–84

Butler, Nicholas Murray, 209,
    224–26, 236

Cabell, Joseph, 68, 69
Caldwell, Joseph, 66
Calhoun, Robert, 11, 318
California, 122–23, 138–39, 151–52, 366.
    See also University of California
Calvin College (University), 366–67,
    370, 374
Calvin, John, 33, 63
Calvinism, 33, 40, 46, 56, 64, 69–70, 73, 80.
    See also Protestantism: Reformed
    compared to Jesuits, 79
    and Dewey, 146
    at Harvard, 26, 49, 154
    Jefferson's attacks on, 63, 70–71, 73
    and the Puritans, 79
    teachings, 33, 37, 40–41, 73
    and the Unitarians, 73, 152–53, 167
Cambridge University, 35–36, 45, 47, 48–
    50, 53–54, 156, 372–73
    dissenting sects excluded from,
    45, 47, 80
    Emmanuel College of, 35–36, 39
Canada, 69, 209, 386, 432n.17
Candler, Asa, 206
Candler, Warren, 205–6
capitalism, 176, 177, 211–12, 213–14,
    346–47, 353
Carlson, Anton J., 300–1
Carnegie, Andrew, 208–9
Carnegie Commission on Higher
    Education, 343
Carnegie Council on Policy Studies in
    Higher Education, 343
Carnegie Foundation, 206, 209, 210,
    211, 212
Carnegie Foundation for the
    Advancement of Teaching, 208,
    424n.39
Carnegie Institution, 292–93
Carnegie Pension Fund of, 209, 210
Carver, Thomas Nixon, 186
Cashdollar, Charles, 117–18
Catholicism and Catholics, 13–14, 34–35,
    40–41, 78–79, 151, 258, 304
    and academic freedom, 12, 79

academic writings of, 318–19
Americanists, 197–202
and authority, 32, 79, 196–202, 307–8,
    313, 324
and the common schools, 78–79, 93–94
criticized by progressive
    secularists, 306–8
and fascism, 13–14, 302–3, 325–26
funding for schools of, 314–15
and intellectual inquiry, 79, 198–202
and modernism, 199, 200
neo-Thomist revival of, 302–3 (see also
    Thomism)
in non-Catholic universities, 123, 142,
    148, 151, 172, 180–81, 260, 279–80,
    288–89, 436–37n.1, 447n.13
and pluralism, 306–8, 311–12, 326
population of, 201–2, 256
Protestant domination of education
    viewed by, 13–14, 225, 256,
    321, 326–28
schools of, 74, 196–202, 214, 279, 310,
    326, 333
viewed by Protestants, 13–14, 79, 180,
    201–2, 214, 220, 254, 302–3, 307–8,
    324–26, 334, 444n.33
in Who's Who in America, 201–2
Catholic University of America, 196–97
Cattell, J. McKeen, 236
Central College, 68
Channing, William Ellery, 103–4
chapel attendance, 4, 19, 52, 71–72, 75, 93,
    97, 106–7, 123, 127–28, 141, 156, 165,
    166, 168, 172, 180, 191, 256–57, 270,
    271, 280, 281,
    282–84, 287
Chase, Harry W., 247–48, 249–50
Chauncy, Charles, 40, 54–40, 59,
    395–96n.17
Chautauqua movement, 175–76, 186
Christian Century, 254, 274, 275, 325, 331–
    32, 436n.67, 436n.73
Christianity, 181–82, 214, 256.
    See also Church and state;
    individual denominations;Religion
    in American universities, 10, 93–95,
    135, 189, 213–14, 271–73, 275–76,
    317–18, 331

Christianity (*cont.*)
  and culture, 14, 26, 55–56, 111–12, 144,
    186–87, 288–89, 291, 296–98, 306,
    310–11, 320
  definition of, 14, 135, 139, 147, 173,
    270, 327
  and the future of civilization, 10–11,
    17–18, 75, 111–12, 346, 409n.15
  heritage of, dropped by universities,
    336–41, 447n.20
  liberal, 64, 111, 133, 134–35, 141, 143,
    151, 181–82, 208, 287–88 (*see also*
    Protestantism: liberals of)
  and morality, 56–57, 60–61, 73, 144,
    147, 180, 331
  and pagan learning, 30–31
  reason and faith debated by, 30–31, 83
  subversion of, in universities, 10
Christian Scholar, 317–18, 338
church and state, 37–38, 41–42, 78–79,
    122, 138, 141, 197–98, 247–48, 255,
    256–57, 260–61, 325. *See also* United
    States Supreme Court
  departments of religion on, 261
Churches of Christ, 379–80
City College (of New York), 306–7
civil war, 77, 93, 97, 102, 103, 137–38, 163–
    64, 203–4, 256, 291
  and the universities, 71–72, 97, 99, 283,
    402n.20
Clap, Thomas, 47–48, 49–50, 55–56, 57–
    58, 229
Clark, Gordon, 369
Clark, Tom, 336
Clark University, 176
Clarke, Samuel, 49, 56–57
clergy, 4, 45–46, 117, 195, 313
  at American universities, 36–37, 38–39,
    45–46, 47–48, 50, 51–52, 65, 75, 77,
    97, 100, 109, 113, 116, 163–64, 172–
    73, 224–25
  education of, 34–35, 39, 63, 97, 102, 153,
    165, 194–95, 247
Cleveland, John and Ebenezer, 49
Cocker, Benjamin F., 139–40
Coe, George E., 193–94, 197
Coffin, Henry Sloane, 17–18, 19, 173, 189,
    270, 273–74, 304, 321, 325–26

  and Buckley's criticism of Yale, 9, 15, 17
Cohen, I. Bernard, 332–33
cold war, 34, 52, 315–16, 322
College of California, 122–23. *See also*
    University of California
College of New Jersey. *See* Princeton
    University
College of Philadelphia. *See* University of
    Pennsylvania
College of South Carolina, 70–71
colleges, 80, 110–16, 129–31, 142, 195,
    233, 262
  becoming universities (*see* Universities,
    American: colleges replaced by)
  Catholic. *See* Catholicism and Catholics:
    schools of
  purpose of, 78, 110–11, 116, 410n.19
Columbia University (King's College), 65,
    224, 234, 236
  and the Anglicans, 54, 64
  moral order maintained at, 52, 55–56
  and the Presbyterians, 52, 63–64
Columbia Theological Seminary, 247
Commons, John R., 186, 213–14, 221–22
common schools, 78–79, 93–95
Common Sense philosophy, 82–87, 89, 91,
    152, 163, 419n.31
  and science, 82–87
communism, 9, 321–23, 324
Comte, Auguste, 21, 112, 117–19
Conant, James Bryant, 322, 326
confessionalism, 26, 34, 37–38, 45, 163–
    64, 339
Congregationalists, 12, 45, 51, 64, 73, 79,
    80, 82, 175–76
  and biblical authority, 45
  liberal progressive, 121–22, 125,
    141, 146
  and the Presbyterians, 64, 69–70, 77–78,
    80, 81–82, 137, 175–76
  schools founded by, 51, 63, 66–67, 69–
    70, 74, 81, 122, 175–76, 203
  and universities, 12, 47–48, 121, 283–84
  at Yale, 12, 47–48, 121
Conkin, Paul, 203–4
Cooper, Thomas, 63, 68, 70–71, 72, 215–16
Cornell, Ezra, 104–6
Cornell University, 101, 102–3, 117, 179

and academic freedom at, 147–48
founding of, 92–93, 104–5, 109, 176
nonsectarianism at, 106–7, 210–11
Council for Christian Colleges &
Universities (CCCU), 379–80, 381–
83, 384–87, 388
Council of Church Boards of Education,
262, 273–74
counterculture movement, 336, 340,
341, 342–43
Cox, Harvey *(The Secular City)*, 338–40
Cremin, Lawrence A., 399n.29
Crunden, Robert, 184–85
culture, Western, 144, 291, 297, 310–11
Cuninggim, Merrimon, 261–62, 276,
317, 340–41
curriculum, 158–59, 227–28, 263. *See also*
individual universities
the Bible in, 113, 172, 189, 259
in Catholic colleges, 196–97
and the classics, 59, 76–77, 85, 98, 109,
151, 197
core requirements in, 311
and great books, 299, 300–1, 309–
10, 311
and Melanchthon, 32–33
in the mid-nineteenth century, 76–
77, 97–98
and moral philosophy, 54, 75, 131, 331
and pagan authors, 40–42
religion in, 135, 181, 256–57, 304,
318, 331
scientific or practical offerings in, 54–
55, 97–98
and theology, 54–55, 97–98, 131
Cutler, Timothy, 46–47, 50, 52, 399n.29

Dana, Henry Wadsworth Longfellow, 236
Danforth Foundation, 340–41
Darrow, Clarence, 251
Dartmouth College, 51, 66–67, 270
Darwin, Charles, 22, 164
Darwinism, 117–18, 163. *See also*
evolution
and agnosticism, atheism, and
and biblical authority, 143, 145, 245–46
and Catholics, 200
debated at Harvard, 157

materialism, 19–20, 126, 242–43, 252
and the Methodists, 204
Davenport, James, 48
Davie, William, 66
Davies, Ruth, 276–77
Davis, Horace, 413n.1
Dawson, Christopher, 201
Day, James R., 210–14, 234–35, 256–57
Debs, Eugene, 224–25
Deists, 58, 64, 268
Delbanco, Andrew, 352–53
democracy, 146–47, 291, 318–19. *See also*
culture, Western
and Christianity, 180, 183–85, 252, 327
and education, 309–10, 313–15, 320
Protestant commitment to, 186–87,
316, 320
and science, 234, 310
Democrats, 66–67, 81–82, 95, 123, 340–
41, 357–58, 379
Denny, Joseph V., 250
Dewey, John, 227–28, 229, 248, 307,
308, 329
A Common Faith, 297–98
and the AAUP, 222, 231–32
and academic freedom, 326
and Hutchins, 300, 302–3, 306
at Johns Hopkins, 146
religious beliefs of, 145–47, 150, 184–
85, 298, 310–11
and science, 150, 185, 321
students of, 270, 292–93
theories of education held by, 12, 184–
85, 190, 231–32, 298, 312–13, 326
—— at University of
Michigan, 145–47
and World War I, 236
Dinsmore, Charles, 248
Disciples of Christ, 258–59, 260
disestablishment of Christianity, 4, 5–6,
19, 358–59
divinity schools and theological
seminaries, 11, 34–35, 69–70, 73, 97,
206, 256–57, 263
Dixon, A. C., 243–44, 246, 247–48
Drummond, Henry, 18
Duffield, George, 81–82
Duke, James B., 247

Duke University (Trinity College), 203,
   246–47, 267, 276, 344–45, 433n.27
Dunster, Henry, 37–38, 40, 106
Durant, Henry and Pauline, 113–14
Dutch Reformed, 51–52, 65–66, 374
Dwight, Timothy, 77, 78
Dwight Hall (Yale), 12, 17, 19, 181–82, 270

Earp, Edwin L., 194
education, 98, 243, 263, 329. See also
   Universities, American
   and character, 121–22, 128–29, 287
   and democracy, 305, 309–10, 313–
   141, 320
   function and purpose of, 76, 110–11,
   287, 303, 310–11, 329
   graduate and professional, 128–32
   and religion, 29, 148–50, 215–19, 224–
   25, 255, 262, 264, 310–11
   and republican virtue, 56, 60
   and science, 131, 134, 150, 295, 296,
   298, 309–10 (see also Darwinism;
   evolution)
Edwards, Jonathan, 46–47, 48, 51, 55–56,
   57–58, 59, 77, 91, 163
Egginton, William, 353–54
Einstein, Albert, 304, 306, 439–40n.10
Eliot, Charles, 189, 208–9, 311
   and academic freedom, 166
   debates with McCosh of, 166–67
   and the education of clergy, 165
   and Harvard, 109, 151–52, 154–58, 189
   and nonsectarianism, 166–67
   and religion, 159–60, 165–66, 331–32
Eliot, T. S., 293
Ellis, John Tracy, 201–2
Ellwood, Charles, 433n.27
Ely, Richard T., 186, 234
   and patriotism, 235–36, 237
   students of, 186, 221–22
Emerson, Ralph Waldo, 89, 154, 208
Emmott, George, 128
Emory, 203, 206
England, 35, 36, 40, 45, 47, 54, 79–80, 83,
   101, 102, 326, 331, 412n.28. See also
   Britain educational institutions in;
   Cambridge University; Oxford
   University

English Student Christian
   Movement, 317
Enlightenment, 58, 71–72, 77, 97–98,
   152, 294
   American, 60
   and the American
   Revolution, 53, 64, 82
   and a nonsectarian public education
   system, 82, 86
   and science, 145, 153, 200–1,
   220, 295–96
   in Scotland, 43–44, 83
   Episcopalians, 12, 69–70,
   142, 258, 423n.19. See also
   Anglicanism and the Anglicans:
   and universities
Evangelical Alliance, 133
evangelicalism and evangelism, 18–19,
   134, 146
   and American universities, 18, 77, 81–
   82, 151
   and biblical authority, 246
   and liberal Protestants, 252
   modern view of, 357–58
   revival of, in 1950s, 317–21
   and scientific
   authority, 86, 128–29
   at Yale, 10, 17–18, 19
Evans, C. Stephen, 384
Everett, Edward, 153
evolution, 157, 243–44, 252–53, 254. See
   also Darwinism
   and biblical authority, 164, 198–99, 204,
   242–43, 245–46, 252, 371–73
   teaching of, 117–18, 213–14, 223,
   228, 243, 244, 246, 247, 249–50,
   251, 253–54

faculty, 131, 234, 250, 305
   and academic freedom, 215, 222, 225–
   26, 238
   Catholic, 172, 361
   Christian, at secular institutions, 338
   freedom of speech for, 220–21,
   223, 234
   at Harvard, 49, 151, 153, 332
   hiring of, 71–72, 115, 172, 219–20, 288,
   337, 384, 386–87

influence on students of, 243, 273–74
Jewish, 288
at Princeton, 168–70
professionalization of, 229 (*see also*
    Universities, American:
    professionalism of
    religious tests for)
traditional Christianity viewed by, 216–
    19, 232–33, 234–35, 245, 284
at the University of
    Chicago, 181–83
and World War I, 236–38
at Yale, 287–88
Faculty Christian Fellowship,
    317–18, 338
Farrell, Allan P., 314–15
fascism, 13, 302–4, 325–26
Federal Council of Churches, 258–
    59, 321–22
Fermi, Enrico, 304
Few, William Preston, 246–47, 433n.27
Fey, Harold E., 325
Fichte, Johann Gottlieb, 90–91
Finkelstein, Louis, 304, 305, 306
Finley, John H. Jr., 332–33
Finney, Charles, 113–14, 298–99
Fisher, George P., 137–38
Fisk University, 283
Fitzgerald, F. Scott, 265, 293
Ford Foundation, 329
Fosdick, Harry Emerson, 304
Franeker University, 36
Frank, Glenn, 302
Frankena, William, 334–35
Franklin, Benjamin, 57–58
Frazier, E. Franklin, 284
Freedmen's Bureau, 283
French Revolution, 64–65
fundamentalism and
    fundamentalists, 18, 272,
    297–98, 324
and academic freedom, 241, 250
and antievolution, 242–50
criticized by progressive
    secularists, 307–8
excluded from universities, 323–24
and religion and education, 252, 253–
    54, 255, 280–81

schools established by, 280–81
viewed by mainline Protestants, 252–53,
    307–8, 334

Galileo, 71, 204
General Education in a Free Society. *See*
    Harvard Report
geology, 204
Germany, 83, 156, 185–86, 243–44. *See
    also* Prussia
academic freedom in, 94–95,
    129, 219–26
and American education, 89, 128–29,
    153, 154, 156, 241–42
Americans studying in, 89–93, 104,
    109–10, 116, 128–29, 144–45, 153,
    156, 186, 205, 220–21,
    226–27, 237
education in, 90–92, 128–29
historical criticism of Christianity
    in, 144–45
idealism in, 90, 154, 156, 220–21
and World War I, 235–36, 237–
    38, 241–42
Gibbons, James, 199
Gilkey, Charles W., 299–300
Gilman, Daniel Coit, 130–31, 142, 189
at Johns Hopkins, 117, 125–29, 133–
    34, 159
nonsectarianism of, 121–22, 124
and religion and science, 133–34
religious outlook of, 121–22
and the University of California, 122,
    123, 125, 126, 127
and the Yale presidency, 109
Gilmore, Mary Hawes, 148–49
Gilson, Etienne, 201, 306
Gleason, Philip, 326
God and Man at Yale (Buckley), 9, 58
Goose-Step: A Study of American
    Education (Sinclair),
    177–78, 213
government. *See* church and state
Graham, Billy, 317, 367–70, 372–
    73, 378–79
Great Awakening, 48, 49, 52, 77
Greeley, Horace, 105
Greene, T. M., 11

Griffin, Helen Chambers, 434n.42
Griswold, A. Whitney, 15, 391n.2

Hadley, Arthur Twining, 209, 270
Haidt, Jonathan, 354–55
Haight, Henry, 123
Hall, G. Stanley, 76
    students of, 215, 247
Ham, Mordecai, 246
Hamilton, Michael, 373, 377–78
Hamilton, Sir William, 91, 163
Hampden-Sydney College, 65–66
Harbison, E. Harris, 32
Harnack, Adolf von, 237
Harper, William Rainey, 175–87, 197,
        209, 266
    and academic freedom, 223
    and Bemis, 221–22
    and biblical study, 175–76, 179, 181,
        189, 257
    and the Chautauqua movement, 175–
        76, 186
    college affiliated program of, 176–
        77, 262
    compared to Hutchins, 298–99
    and organization, 175–76, 179
    Religious Education Association
        founded by, 262
    and Rockefeller, 175–77
    Trend in University Education, 183–84
    and the university as a church
        community, 180–81, 189
Hart, D. G., 125, 411n.3
Harvard, John, 36
Harvard Divinity School, 331–32, 338–39
Harvard Report (General Education in a
        Free Society), 309, 310–11, 312
Harvard University (Harvard College), 35,
        43–45, 97, 151–53
    chapel, 156, 287, 332–33
    church and state served by, 36, 37, 38
    clergy trained at, 38, 153
    cultural idealism at, 153, 159–61
    curriculum at, 39–42, 43–44
    elective system at, 151–52, 155, 158
    minorities at, 282, 287, 332–33
    nonsectarianism at, 106, 159–60, 166
    philosophy at, 43–44, 152–53

and Princeton, 163, 166–67
    religion at, 45–46, 49, 69–70, 151–52,
        153, 154, 156, 332–33
    transformation into university
        of, 151–53
    and the Unitarians, 151–53
Hatch, Nathan, 383–84
Haverford College, 125–26
Hazen Foundation, 262, 318, 319
Heavenly City of the Eighteenth-Century
        Philosophers, The (Becker), 294
Hedge, Frederic Henry, 153
Hegel, George Wilhelm Friedrich, 89, 90,
        146–47, 185
Heisenberg, Werner, 439–40n.10
Hemingway, Ernest, 293
Henderson, Charles R., 180–81
Henry, Carl, 369–71, 373, 376, 377–
        78, 382–83
Herberg, Will, 333, 334–35, 445n.48
Higher Education for American Democracy.
        See Report of the President's
        Commission on Education
high school, 243, 252
Hilgard, E. W., 141
Hillel Foundations, 12, 258
Hobart College (Geneva College),
        33, 103–4
Hocking, William E., 304
Hodge, Archibald Alexander, 164
Hodge, Charles, 163–64
Hofstadter, Richard, 71, 367–68
Holley, Horace, 67
Hollinger, David, 292–93, 345–46, 348
Holmes, Arthur, 373–74, 384
Holmes, Oliver Wendell Jr., 163, 299
Hook, Sidney, 302–3, 305–6, 308, 322
Hopkins, C. Howard, 268–69
Hopkins, Johns, 125
Hopkins, Mark, 84, 86–87, 99
    on Christianity and science, 84
Horton, Francis, 137, 140
Howard University, 283–84
Howe, Daniel, 86
Howe, Frederic C., 186
Howe, Mark DeWolfe Jr., 332–33
Howison, George Holmes, 193–94
Hudson, Winthrop, 396n.26

Hull-House, 184–85, 186
humanism, 33, 34, 106–7, 184, 292, 352,
    445n.48
Hume, David, 53–54, 83
Hutcheson, Francis, 53–54, 55, 56–58, 59
Hutchins, Robert Maynard, 298, 308,
    313, 315–16
  and the conference on "Science,
    Philosophy and Religion," 304–8
  criticism of, 302–3, 306
  and higher education, 300–3, 306,
    311, 329–30
  religious views of, 299–300
Hutchinson, Anne, 38
Huxley, Thomas H., 22, 101, 102, 112, 114,
    126, 127
  lecture at Johns Hopkins by, 126–27

idealism, 99, 118, 146, 158
  and Christianity, 159
  and education, 91–92, 128–29, 153
  evolutionary, 194, 195
  German, 90, 154, 156, 220–21
Indiana University, 375
individualism, 10, 52–53, 154, 176, 182–
    83, 184, 345–47, 353–54
industrialization, 1, 4–5, 86, 99, 102, 105,
    131–32, 133, 147, 209, 243, 292, 359
InterVarsity Christian Fellowship, 317,
    360, 362, 382, 386–87
Ireland, John, 198

James, William, 151, 157–58, 193–94, 227,
    270, 300
  and Darwinism, 157
  and psychology, 157
Jebb, John, 65
Jefferson, Thomas, 54. See also
    Jeffersonians
  and education, 66–67, 149–50, 215–16,
    220, 353–54
  and the Presbyterians, 63, 65–66, 68
  and reason and popular rule, 66–67,
    70, 253
  views on religion of, 68, 149–50, 151,
    215–16, 253
  and Virginia's state university, 65–66,
    68–69, 71–72, 220

Jeffersonians, 71, 73, 149–50. See also
    Jefferson, Thomas
  and academic freedom, 220
  and science, 86, 220
  and sectarianism, 80, 93–94,
    124, 258–59
  state education program of, 64–67, 72, 81
Jellema, William Harry, 370, 374, 375
Jencks, Christopher, 337–38, 366–67, 370–
    71, 375–76, 387
Jesuits, 11–12, 63, 70–71, 79, 280
Jewish Theological Seminary, 304, 305–6
Jews and Judaism, 138, 228
  in American education, 148, 259, 285–
    89, 333, 334
  American higher education accepted
    by, 285
  campus ministries established by,
    12, 258
  and the conference on "Science,
    Philosophy and Religion," 303–8
  discriminated against, at universities,
    224–25, 268, 285–89, 312, 325–26
  and Harvard, 151, 287
  hired at Cornell, 107
  and pluralism, 311–12, 325–26, 330
  and Princeton, 172, 287
  and the University of Chicago, 179,
    180–81, 182–83
  at Yale, 287–88
Johns Hopkins University, 117, 125–32,
    176, 231
  religion at, 125–27
  and the research ideal, 149, 179, 181
  voluntary chapel at, 127–28
Johnson, Samuel, 52, 399n.29
Jones, Theodore Francis, 292–93
Jordan, David Starr, 193–94, 209, 410n.21
Journal of Social Forces, 248–49
Joynes, Edward S., 204–5
Judeo-Christian Western heritage, 289, 330

Kallen, Horace Meyer, 307
Kant, Immanuel, 76, 91, 163
  and reality creatively defined by the
    intellect, 90, 153, 157
Keane, John, 197–99, 201–2
Kellogg, Martin, 123

Kelsey, Francis W., 144
Kent, Charles Foster, 259, 262, 433n.27
Kerr, Clark, 341–42, 343
Kilby, Clyde S, 372–73
King, Martin Luther, 317, 348, 354–55
King's College. *See* Columbia University
Kirkland, James Hampton, 205, 206, 214
Kronman, Anthony, 352–53
Krutch, Joseph Wood, 293
Kuhn, Thomas, 377, 389
Kuklick, Bruce, 416n.20
Kuyper, Abraham, 374, 377

Lafayette College, 225–27, 228–31, 233
LaFollette, Robert, 237
Lagemann, Ellen Condliffe, 208–9
Lane Theological Seminary, 78
languages, 30–31, 32–33, 34, 39,
in Catholic colleges, 196–97
Latourette, Kenneth, 11
LeConte, John and Joseph, 123, 143–44
Leland Stanford Junior University. *See*
　　Stanford University
Leo XIII, Pope, 197–98, 200
Leuba, James, 215–19, 232–33, 239, 245,
　　247–53, 425n.2
Leverett, John, 44–45
Lewis, C S. 372–73, 386
Lewis, Harry, 351–52
Lilly Network of Church-Related Colleges
　　and Universities, 381–82
Lincoln, Abraham, 101, 105, 123, 137–
　　38, 144–45
Lippmann, Walter, 253
Lovejoy, Arthur O., 229–30, 322
　　and AAUP, 231, 233, 235–36, 237, 322
　　and World War 1, 236, 237
Lovett, Sidney, 287–88
Low, Frederick, 123
Lowell, Lawrence Abbot, 282
Lukianoff, Greg, 354–55
Luther, Martin, 32–33, 34, 94–95, 311
Lutherans, 12, 33, 69–70, 258, 280–81
Lynd, Robert S., 315

McCarthy, Joseph and McCarthyism, 9,
　　219–20, 321–23
McConnell, T. R., 314

McCorkle, Samuel F., 66
McCosh, James, 163–65, 166–68
　　and Common Sense, 163
　　debates with Eliot, 166–67
　　and evolution, 163
　　and religion and the university, 163–
　　65, 166–67
McCracken, Stephen B., 138, 141
McGuffey, William H., 71–72
MacIntosh, Douglas, 304
Mackay, John, 304
McLoughlin, William, 367
McNair, John Calvin, 248
Madison, James, 59–60, 402n.20
Mahoney, Kathleen A., 358–59
Marshall, John, 67, 220, 295–96, 323–24,
　　419–20n.11
Marxism and Marxists, 1, 220, 295–96,
　　323–24, 419–20n.11
materialism, 200, 245, 275. *See also*
　　naturalism
　　and science and evolution, 194, 198–99,
　　207, 241–43, 252
　　and the universities, 208, 318, 326–27
Mather, Cotton, 45–46, 106
Mather, Increase, 43–46
Mathews, Shailer, 193–94, 235–36, 248–33
Melanchthon, Philip, 32–33, 283, 432n.17
Methodist Episcopal Church, 203–4, 207–
　　8, 209–10, 283, 392n15, 404–5n.19,
　　432n.17
Methodists
　　and Duke University, 267, 344–45
　　and Northwestern University, 175–76,
　　193–94, 203, 206–7
　　schools established by, 74, 175–76, 193–
　　94, 203–14
　　Southern, 203–4, 206
　　and Syracuse University, 193–94, 210–
　　11, 212–14, 256–57
　　and universities, 126–27, 260–61, 283
　　viewed by Presbyterians and
　　Congregationalists, 80
　　at Yale, 12, 19
Middle Ages, 26, 29, 30, 34–35, 151, 220–
　　21, 270, 294
Mill, John Stuart, 112, 163, 311, 334–35
Miller, Perry, 332–33

Mivart, St. George, 198
Mixter, Russell, 372
Moberly, Walter, 317–18, 338–39
modernism, 17, 199, 200
Moody, Dwight L., 113, 142, 148, 191
    on Yale, 18, 20, 189
Moody Bible Institute, 280–81, 428n.43
Moore, Frederick W., 206
moral philosophy, 82, 97–98, 143, 158
    in college curricula, 75, 109, 110, 141,
        186, 256, 331
    and moral order, 52, 53, 75
    Scottish, 54–55
    and the service of the republic, 57–61
    social sciences arising out of, 55–57,
        142, 147
    and Wayland, 84
moral science. See moral philosophy
Morgan, Edmund S., 46–47
Morgan Park Theological Seminary, 176
Morison, Samuel Eliot, 37–38, 396n.26
Morrill Land Grant Act, 102–3, 105, 122
Morris, George Sylvester, 146
Morrison, Cameron, 246, 247–48
Morrison, Charles Clayton, 325–26
Mott, John R., 18, 19, 435n.57
Münsterberg, Hugo, 151
Murray, John Courtney, 333–35
Muste, A. J., 304

National Association of Bible Instructors,
    262, 335–36
National Council of Churches, 317–18,
    321–22, 325, 337–38, 392n15
National Council on Religion and Higher
    Education, 259–60
National Defense Education Act, 315–16
National Security League, 235–36
National Student Christian Federation,
    338–39, 340–41
naturalism, 2, 293, 320, 333
    evolutionary, 157, 159
    methodological, 132–35
    scientific, 22, 23–24, 145, 300–1
Neal, John R., 251
neo-orthodoxy, 296, 320, 377–78
Nevins, Allan, 304
New England, 45, 54–55

education in, 29, 36, 43, 80
    emigration of university men to, 35
New Lights, 48, 50, 54–55, 77. See also
    evangelicalism and evangelism
    and Princeton, 48–49, 51, 59
Newman, John Henry, 330–32
Newton, Isaac, 56–57, 59
New York State, 64, 65, 77, 103–4,
    212, 256–57
Niebuhr, H. Richard, 296, 346
Niebuhr, Reinhold, 296, 317, 320–21, 349,
    365–66, 370–71
Nietzsche, Friedrich Wilhelm, 243–44,
    245, 436n.73
Noll, Mark A., 381, 384–85, 386–87
Northwestern University, 175–76, 193–94,
    203, 206–7, 246–47, 373
Norton, Charles Eliot, 159
Nott, Eliphalet, 85, 91

Oberlin College, 113–14, 195, 298–99
O'Brien, John, 279–80
Ockenga, Harold J., 368–69, 376
Odum, Howard W., 248–49
Old Lights, 48, 49–50, 59
Otto, Max, 307–8
Oxford University, 35–36, 48–49, 53–
    54, 156
    dissenting sects excluded from, 45,
        47, 49–50
Oxnam, G. Bromley, 324, 325–26

Pace, Edward A., 200
pagans, 30, 40, 45. See also Aristotle
Paine, Thomas, 215–16, 252–53
Paley, William, 58, 75, 83–84, 399–400n.40
Parker, Theodore, 103–4, 207
Parrington, Vernon L., 318–19
Patten, Simon, 194
Patton, Francis L., 164, 172–73
    religious views of, 165–66, 167–68
    and Princeton, 168–70, 172
Patton, George, 172–73
Peale, Norman Vincent, 317
Pearson, Charles W., 206–7
Peirce, Charles Sanders, 231–32
Pelikan, Jaroslav, 446n.6
Pentecostals, 224–25

Phi Beta Kappa Society, 225
philosophy, 43–44, 45, 152, 318–19. *See also* moral philosophy
pietism, 52–53
Pius X, Pope, 199
Plantinga, Alvin, 376–77, 383–84
Plato, 40, 41, 43–44, 56–57, 76, 299, 302, 303
Plumer, William, 66–67
pluralism, 35–36
   criticism of American, 333
   in United States, 326, 337
Poels, Henry A., 199
Pohle, Joseph, 198
Poole, David Scott, 249–50
Porter, Noah, 22–23, 109–10, 115, 121, 128, 129–30, 137
   The Human Intellect, 118
   on religion and college, 22, 23, 25, 110–12, 114, 118
   and Sumner, 21–24, 112–13, 117, 118, 121
positivism, 21, 117–18, 200–1, 305, 333
Poteat, William, 243–44, 246, 248, 249–50
Pound, Roscoe, 248
Pratt, James Bissett, 265
Presbyterians, 45. *See also* Calvinism; Protestantism
   and abstinence, 168–69
   and American education, 54, 63–64, 122
   antievolutionism among, in North Carolina, 247–48
   and biblical authority, 172–73
   at Columbia University, 65
   and the Congregationalists, 64, 77–78, 79, 81–82
   criticism of, 63–64, 66, 68, 70–71
   and the Jeffersonian state educational programs, 65, 66, 68, 71–72
   and Lafayette College, 226–27, 230, 231
   New School, 81, 91, 103–4, 163–64
   Old School, 81–82, 83, 163–64, 171, 226–27
   and Princeton, 69–70, 163–64, 165, 168–69
   schools founded by, 51, 52, 54, 57–58, 66, 69–70, 74, 80, 203

Scottish and Scotch-Irish, 53–54, 59, 81–82
   sectarianism of, 63, 81
   and the separation of church and state, 248
   and universities, 126, 197
   and the University of Michigan, 142
   and the University of North Carolina, 247, 260–61
Price, Richard, 65
Priestley, Joseph, 65, 68
Princeton University (College of New Jersey), 71, 55, 59–60, 66, 163
   board of, 51
   criticism of, 445n.47
   and Darwinism, 163, 164
   founding by New Light clergy of, 48–50, 51, 377
   and Harvard, 163, 166–67
   and minorities, 282, 287
   moral philosophy at, 59, 172
   and the Presbyterians, 69–70, 163–64, 168
   public served by, 69–70, 170–71, 189
   religion at, 60, 163–65, 445n.47
   and science, 164–66, 171–72
   social elitism at, 287–88
   transformation into university of, 163, 164–65
Princeton Theological Seminary, 163–64, 282
   founding of, 69–70, 163–64
   Warfield at, 226–27
Pritchett, Henry Smith, 208–10, 211
professors. *See* faculty
Progressive era, 222, 281–82, 394n17
progressivism, 109–10, 165, 220–22
   and academic freedom, 215, 225
   and secularism, 193–94, 302–3
   and social idealism and activism, 184–85
prohibition and temperance, 197, 241–42, 255, 272, 275
   and campus drinking, 267, 274
Protestantism, 31–32, 52, 145, 288.
   See also Christianity; *individual denominations*; Religion

and academic freedom, 152–53, 321–22, 327–28
activism in, 195, 258
and the Bible, 66, 175–76
and calling, 43
Catholicism viewed by (see Catholicism)
and Catholics: viewed by Protestants
and character, 273–74
Christianity defined by, 14
college attendance of, 195–96, 341
and the conference on "Science, Philosophy and Religion," 304–6
conservatives of, 220, 241, 242–43, 245, 252, 254 (see also Evangelicalism and evangelism; fundamentalism and fundamentalists)
cultural dominance of, 13, 25–27, 129–30, 180, 201–2, 243–44, 254, 324
demise of dominance of, 311–12, 336 (see also pluralism)
and democracy, 13, 186–87, 316, 320
and education, 2, 4, 9, 13, 32, 34, 41–42, 65, 83, 255, 263, 313
and efficiency, 209
establishmentarian outlook of, 13–14, 114–15, 336, 339
and evangelism, 17, 18 (see also evangelicalism and the evangelism)
and freedom, 79–80, 94–95, 186–87
and the future of civilization, 79–80, 285–86, 345
and ideals for the nation, 180, 316
liberals of, 148, 166, 172, 189, 195, 241–42, 245, 252, 255, 260, 267, 274–75, 286, 287–89, 306, 310–11, 320, 325, 329, 346, 349
low-church, 180, 182–83
mainline, 14, 17, 271–72, 318, 324, 337–38, 339, 347, 358–59, 379
nonsectarian, 81, 107–8, 169
and public education, 80, 81, 82–83
Reformed, 45–46, 73 (see also Congregationalists; Presbyterians)
schools established by, 97–98, 99, 148, 275, 288, 310, 337, 366 (see also individual denominations)

and science (see science: and Protestantism)
and the universities, 94–95, 97, 178, 235, 259, 280, 285–86, 288–89, 310, 336
Protestants United, 325–26
Prussia, 88 , 104, 106, 107, 108
psychology, 131, 157, 168, 215, 216–17, 218, 223, 227–28, 245, 247, 270, 318, 385–86
Puritans, 31–32, 49, 77, 79, 115, 152, 163
authority for, 38, 40, 41–42, 52
and democracy, 318–19
and education, 33, 39, 38–39, 40, 41–42, 43
and a national covenant of, 241
sacredness of all life for, 38–39, 40
sectarianism of, 106, 115, 297
Pusey, Nathan M., 331–33

Quakers, 125–26, 398n.20
Quincy, Josiah, 152–53

racism, 283–84, 285–87, 296–97, 325–26, 337, 385–86
and education, 31–35, 37–38, 156
English, 35–36
Reformation, 29, 79, 139, 152–53, 196
and universities, 13, 312, 340
Reid, Thomas, 53–54, 83
relativism, 153, 295, 296, 361, 445n.48
religion, 145–46, 228, 247–48, 342–43.
    See also Christianity; church and state; individual denominations; Protestantism
and character, 273–74
and college attendance, 341–42
comparative, 296–97, 336, 359, 408n.16
decline of, in public life, 14, 189–90
departments of, established in universities, 3, 259–61, 263, 317–18, 330, 335
disestablishment of, 4, 5–6, 19, 359
and education, 130–31, 215–19, 224, 444n.45
and intellectual inquiry, 6, 97–98, 225, 357
non-Western, 336
professionalization of studies on, 335–36, 445n.48

religion (*cont.*)
  and the public school system, 335
  revival of, in 1950s, 317–21, 326–27,
    330, 444n.45
  and science, 130, 131–32, 150,
    220, 252, 273, 306 (*see also*
    methodological secularization)
  and social class, 268, 270
  and the university, 1–2, 3–4, 131–32,
    195, 202, 319–21, 326–27, 330, 333–
    34 (*see also* Universities, American)
Religious Education Association, 262
Renan, Ernst, 145
Report of the President's Commission on
    Education, 312
Republican Party, 61, 95
  and national industrial and moral
    development, 99, 105, 220–21
Rhode Island College. *See* Brown
    University
Rice, John, 68
Richmond, C. A., 272, 435n.62
Riesman, David, 337–38, 366–67, 370–71,
    375–76, 387
Robert Elsmere (Ward), 137
Robinson, James Harvey, 250
Rockefeller, John D., 211–12, 273–74
  and Day, 212, 213–14
  research funded by, 262, 264
  and the University of Chicago, 175,
    176, 264
Roman Catholicism. *See* Catholicism
romanticism, 89
Roosevelt, Theodore, 211–12
Ross, Dorothy, 186–87
Ross, Edward A., 186, 193–94, 221–22
Roszak, Theodore, 342
Royce, Josiah, 151, 158, 193–94
Rush, Benjamin, 60
Russell, Bertrand, 306–7, 318–19, 436n.73
Rutgers College, 51

Sage, Henry W., 147–48
Sage, Russell, 107
St. Andrews University, 208, 447n.15
Santayana, George, 151
Schmalzbauer, John, 358–59
schools of religion, 259–61, 275–76

science, 85, 90, 208–9, 245–46, 253–54
  and academic freedom, 165, 223, 238
  and the American university, 110–11,
    116, 117, 180, 285–86, 291, 292
  authority of, 86, 97–98, 297–98
  and biblical authority, 94
  and Catholicism, 197, 200–1
  and Christianity, 83–84, 111–12,
    118–19, 129–31, 133, 143–44, 145,
    189–90, 194
  and Common Sense, 82, 83–84
  and communitarian values, 185
  and democracy and freedom, 234,
    310, 321
  and the Enlightenment, 145, 153, 200–
    1, 220, 295–96, 428n.49
  and evangelicalism, 86, 134–35
  and materialism, 194, 207
  and nonsectarianism, 82, 103–4,
    111, 129–30
  and Protestantism, 80, 114–15, 306–
    7, 320
  and religion, 129–30, 131–33,
    150, 220, 252, 273, 306 (*see also*
    methodological secularization)
  religion precluded by (*see* positivism)
  reverence for, 97–98, 101, 134, 153, 317
  and spiritual values, 292–93,
    439–40n.10
  and truth, 234, 292–93, 439–40n.10
  and Wilson's beliefs, 171–72
"Science, Philosophy and Religion,"
    304, 306
"Scientific Spirit and Democratic
    Faith," 307–8
Scopes, John, 251
Scotland, 53–55, 91, 94–95, 145
  Common Sense philosophy and
    American national outlook,
    82, 83–84
  See also Common Sense philosophy;
    Universities, Scottish
sectarianism, 18–19, 56, 310, 404n.17
  in American universities, 67, 256–57
    (*see also under individual universities*)
  and Congregationalists, 80, 81–82
  and the Jeffersonians, 81, 93–94,
    124, 258–59

and the Presbyterians, 404n.17 n.17,
    63, 80–82
and the Puritans, 106, 115, 297
and science, 103, 111
Secular City, The (Cox), 338–39
secularism, 1, 14, 114, 194, 276, 314–15,
    325, 326–27, 333, 334–35, 339–
    40, 356
secularization, 1, 3, 65–66, 255, 257,
    265, 276, 338–39, 432n.17. *See also*
    methodological secularization
Seligman, Edwin R. A., 234, 236
Seymour, Charles, 10, 11
Shaftesbury, Earl of, 56–57
Shaw, Albert, 186
Shedd, Clarence P., 261–62, 317–18,
    431n.12
Sheen, Fulton J., 308, 317
Sheffield Scientific School (Yale), 109–
    10, 141
Sheldon, Henry Davidson, 19–20
Sinclair, Upton, 177–78, 192, 213,
    419–20n.11
slavery, 71, 81–82, 99–100, 146–47,
    404–5n.19
Sloan, Douglas, 321
Small, Albion W., 185–87, 193–94
Small, William, 54
Smith, Adam, 53–54, 85, 311, 391n.4
Smith, George Adam, 18
Smith, Preserved, 196
Smith, Samuel Stanhope, 60, 69–70,
    404n.17
Smith, William, 57–58, 400–1n.3
social gospel, 147–48, 244, 268–69
socialism, 213–14, 222
Society of Christian Philosophers,
    373, 380–81
Society for Religion and Higher
    Education, 338
Society for the Promotion of Collegiate
    and Theological Education at the
    West (SPCTEW), 78
sociology, 22, 23, 117–18, 119, 158,
    185–87, 190, 193–94, 223, 376–77,
    433n.27
Soper, Edmund D., 246–47
Sorokin, Pitirim, 304, 306

Soundings: A Journal of Interdisciplinary
    Studies, 338
Southern Methodist University, 203,
    204, 206
Spalding, V. M., 143–44, 414n.14
Speer, Robert, 435n.57
Spencer, Herbert, 21, 22–24, 112, 117, 118
Spencer, Theodore, 319
sports, 181–82, 190–91, 205, 267
Sprowls, J. W. 250
Stagg, Amos Alonzo, 18, 19, 181–
    83, 315–16
Stanford, Jane Lathrop, 221–22
Stanford, Leland, 221–22
Stanford University, 176, 193–94, 221–22
state universities. *See also* church and state
    departments of religion on
    religion in curriculum at, 225, 255,
    256–58, 335
Stein, Gertrude, 293
Stephens, George Herbert, 227
Stephens, Henry Morse, 196
Stiles, Ezra, 58, 59, 77
Stiles, Isaac, 46–47, 48
Stokes, Anson Phelps, 270
Stone, Lawrence, 35
Stowe, Harriet Beecher, 73
Strauss, David Friedrich, 145
students
    alcohol consumption of, 95, 168–69,
        182, 255, 265, 267, 274
    attitude toward religion of, 266, 272,
        276–77, 434n.42
    behavior of, on campuses, 97, 255, 267,
        274, 435n.57
    church membership of, 195–96 (*see also*
        chapel attendance)
    diversity of, 264–65, 279–89
    fraternities and sorority membership
        of, 267–68
Students for Democratic Society (SDS), 418
Student Volunteer Movement, 18,
    148, 268–69
Sumner, William Graham, 21–24, 25, 109,
    112–13, 117–19, 193–94, 408n.15
Sunday, Billy, 246, 247, 417n.29
Swift, Harold, 299
Swing, David, 165

Syracuse University, 193–94, 203, 204, 210–11, 212–14, 221–22, 256–57

Tappan, Henry P., 91–94, 95, 103–4, 107–8, 109–10, 113–14, 128
Tennent, Gilbert, 48, 51
theism, 112, 114, 118–19, 184–85, 228, 245–46, 369, 412n.31
theological seminaries. See divinity schools and theological seminaries
theology, 32–33, 45, 54–55, 109–10, 338–39
  and education, 34, 69, 97–98, 112, 129–31, 225, 302, 330–31
  German, 241
  professionalization of, 116–17
  as queen of the sciences, 31, 34, 44–45
  and science, 101, 331
  training in, 69–70 (see also Divinity schools and theological seminaries)
Thomism, 200–2. See also Aquinas, Thomas
Ticknor, George, 153
Tillich, Paul, 304
Tillotson, John, 49
totalitarianism, 275, 291, 298, 308, 329–30, 445n.48
  and Catholicism, 302–3, 324
Transcendentalism, 89, 90, 155, 321, 327
Transylvania University, 67
Trinity College. See Duke University
Truman, Harry S., 312
Tufts, James F., 184–85, 227–28, 229
Turner, Frederick Jackson, 169
Turner, James, 288
Twain, Mark, 122
Tyler, Charles, 408n.16

Underwood, Kenneth, 341
Union College, 85, 91, 405n.24
Union Theological Seminary, 17, 298–99
Unitarians, 83, 104–5, 152–53, 154, 201–2, 220
  and the Calvinists, 73, 152–53, 167
  and Harvard, 69–70, 151, 152, 416n.12
  schools established by, 69–70, 80
  and the universities, 93–94, 137, 142, 151, 250

United Church of Christ, 453n.33, See also Congregationalists
United States Supreme Court, 67, 256, 336
Universalists, 93–94
Universities, 30–31, 90–91, 94
  American (see Universities, American)
  Canadian, 432n.17
  English, 35, 94, 170, 182–83
  European, 92–93, 94
  German, 89–90, 91–92, 104, 128–29, 153, 182–83, 220–21
  Scottish, 53–55, 58, 83, 397n.7
  women's (see Women's colleges)
Universities, American. See also academic freedom; education; individual colleges and universities; state universities
  absence of centralized control or ideological center on, 98, 246, 264
  attendance at, 195–96, 255, 263, 309, 311–12
  bureaucratic organization and principles of, 178, 264, 292, 419–20n.11
  Catholic (see Catholicism and Catholics: schools of)
  and character, 14, 106–7, 111, 152–53, 155, 171, 287
  and Christianity (see Christianity)
  colleges replaced by, 98–100, 112, 117, 121
  criticism of, 177–78, 194–95
  definition of, 219–20, 222, 224, 285, 334–35
  distinction between colleges and, 111, 412n.28
  as established state religious organizations, 47, 63, 69–70
  expansion of, 263–64, 341–42, 355
  faculty of (see faculty)
  and freedom, 116, 155, 157, 180, 275, 285–86, 301 (see also Democracy)
  and free enterprise, 74–75, 97–98, 180, 215
  function and purpose of, 78, 97–98, 131–32, 155, 233–34, 309, 343–44

funding of, 264, 316, 341–42 (*see also*
   Catholicism
   and Catholics:
   funding for schools of)
ideals of, 285–86, 292, 345
models for, 32–33, 37, 53–54, 83
as multiversities, 341–45
nonsectarianism in, 74–75, 111–16,
   206–7, 209–10, 288–89, 333
and politics, 341, 342
practical, 6–7, 341–42, 351, 385–86
professionalization of, 2, 73, 91–
   93, 109–10, 128, 131–32, 229,
   235, 263, 301 (*see also* faculty:
   professionalization of)
and public service, 41–42, 74–75, 98,
   131–32, 209–10, 288–89, 292–93,
   316, 337, 345
religion declining in, 1–2, 20, 24, 25–27,
   224–25, 265, 394n17
and research, 23–24, 128–29, 149, 179,
   262, 264, 292, 315–16, 352
revivals at, 6, 18, 77, 78, 142, 283–84,
   317, 330
sectarianism in, 67–68, 256
social elitism in, 178, 287–88, 312
tolerance and diversity at, 51–52, 323
underrepresentation of groups in, 148,
   175, 279–89, 323
voluntary religion at, 148–50
University Christian Movement
   (UCM), 340–41
University of Berlin, 89, 104, 109–10, 116
University of California, 122–24, 125–
   26, 137, 148–50, 183–84, 196,
   262, 322–23
architecture of, 415n.30
University of Chicago, 150, 175–86,
   262, 315–16
architecture of, 180
and the Baptists, 175–76, 179, 299
Hutchins at, 299–300, 305
and Rockefeller, 175, 176, 177, 180
sports at, 181–83
University of Chicago Divinity
   School, 235–36
University of Illinois, 123, 260,
   264, 279–80

University of Iowa, 259, 435n.64
University of Kansas, 148, 258–59
University of Michigan, 92–94, 103, 104,
   137–38, 150, 262, 267
Bible studied at, 185
as model, 123, 137, 142, 258
religious activities of students at, 142,
   143, 145–47, 266, 414n.28,
   415n.32
Religious Thought at the University of
   Michigan, 143–50
sectarianism at, 103, 404–5n.19
University of Nashville, 404n.17
University of North Carolina, 246, 247,
   260–61, 281
University of North Dakota, 432n.17
University of Notre Dame, 198–99, 279–
   80, 376, 381, 383–84, 387
University of Pennsylvania (College of
   Philadelphia), 51, 52, 57–58, 63–64,
   194, 400–1n.3
University of South Carolina, 68,
   123, 256
University of Tennessee, 251
University of Toronto, 432n.17
University of Vermont, 137–38, 146
University of Virginia, 26, 63, 71–72, 220,
   253, 258–59
University of Washington, 148
University of West Virginia, 148
University of Wisconsin, 221–22, 244,
   307–8, 439n.1

Valparaiso University, 381–82
Vanderbilt University, 176, 203, 204–7,
   209–10, 214
Vassar College, 113–14, 270
Veblen, Thorstein, 177–78, 192, 419–
   20n.11, 423n.23
Veysey, Laurence, 178–79, 394n17
   408n.15, 442n.4
Viereck, Peter, 391n.4
Vietnam War, 336, 340, 342
Vincent, George E., 186
Virgil, 33
virtue
   Aristotelian, 56
   and intellectual cultivation, 85

virtue (*cont.*)
  and moral philosophy, 56–57
  republican, 60–61

Waddell, Moses, 66, 112
Wake Forest College, 243–44, 246, 249–50
Ward, Mrs. Humphrey, 137
Ware, Henry, 69–70, 152–53
Warfield, Benjamin Breckinridge, 164, 226–27
Warfield, Ethelbert, 226–30, 231, 235
Wayland, Francis, 84–87, 89, 99–100, 104, 137–38
  compared to other educators, 91
  Political Economy, 85
Weber, Max, 346–47, 376–77, 419–20n.11
Webster, Daniel, 67
Weiss, Paul, 11–12
Wellesley College, 113, 437n.5
Wesleyan University, 427n.35
Wesley College, 432n.17
Western College Society. See
  Society for the
  Promotion of Collegiate and
  Theological Education at the West
Westminster Confession of Faith, 46
Wheaton College, 366–67, 369, 370–74, 375, 376, 379–80, 381–82, 384
Whedon, Daniel Denison, 404–5n.19
Wheeler, Benjamin Ide, 196
Wheelock, John, 66–67
Whigs, 60, 85, 86, 101–2, 111–12, 114–15
  cultural ideal of, 79–82, 110, 111, 220–21
  and education, 73, 74, 80, 107–8
  freedom supported by, 115, 186–87, 302–3
White, Andrew Dickson, 175, 193–94, 307
  and Christianity, 103–4, 106, 107–8, 189
  Cornell University founded by, 23, 92–93, 102–3, 104–6, 117
  and Gilman, 104, 121, 124
  History of the Warfare of Science with Theology in Christendom, 101, 164, 204, 307
  and minorities at Cornell, 107, 409n.10, 409n.15
  on science, 101–2, 111

sectarianism opposed by, 115, 103–4, 106, 121
  and Tappan, 92–93, 101–2, 103, 104
White, Morton G., 332–33
Whitefield, George, 48–49
Who's Who in America, 201–2
Wigglesworth, Edward, 398n.14
Wiley, Margaret M., 445n.48
Willett, Herbert B., 193–94
William and Mary, College of, 43, 47, 54, 63–64, 65–66
  as a state religious organization, 26, 397n.1
Williams College, 84, 265, 270
Wilson, Woodrow, 167–68, 172, 173, 178–79, 189, 197, 209, 235–36, 241, 316
  conception of university held by, 189
  "Princeton in the Nation's Service," 170–71
  religious views of, 171, 172
  and the scientific ideal, 171
  and social elitism at Princeton, 172–73, 287
  and Turner, 169
  and West's graduate college at Princeton, 170–71
Wilson College, 427n.34
Winchell, Alexander, 204, 210
Winthrop, John, 395–96n.17
Wisconsin, 80, 256, 257
Witherspoon, John, 59–60, 66, 163, 168
Wittenberg, 32–33, 395n.10
Wolterstorff, Nicholas, 376–77
women, 422n.5 n.5, 113, 196, 262
  at Cornell University, 408n.10 n.10, 105
  education of, 38, 113–14, 148, 190–91, 281–82, 297, 315–16 (*see also* Women's colleges)
  and religion, 144, 148, 154, 218, 262, 269, 415n.32, 436n.67
  rights of, 241–42, 244, 255, 274, 281–82, 297, 353–54
Women's colleges, 114, 190–91, 281
Woodrow, James, 247
Woolsey, Theodore Dwight, 23, 109, 409n.9
World's Christian Fundamentals Association, 243–44, 246

World War I, 195, 196–97, 241, 243, 262, 263, 276, 280, 282, 285–86, 288–89, 293, 295–96, 318–19, 332–33, 447n.20
and academic freedom, 235–36, 238
World War II, 421n.4 n.4, 445n.4 n.4, 282, 285, 303–4, 307–8, 311–12, 315, 316, 375
and religion, 13, 14, 276, 317, 318–19

Yale, Eli, 47
Yale Christian Association. *See* Dwight Hall
Yale Corporation, 23–24, 58, 109, 270, 271
Yale Report, 76, 410n.19
and the classics, 110–11
Yale University (Yale College), 9–15, 17–20, 21–22, 23–24, 25, 26, 43, 45–46, 49–50, 55–58, 103–4, 109–11, 113, 114, 115–16, 117–18, 119, 175, 267, 270–71, 326–27, 408n.15
and the Bible, 21–22, 175–76
Catholics at, 9, 12, 391n.5, 393n13, 436–37n.1, 438n.27
chapel attendance at, 19, 270–71, 287
criticized by William F. Buckley, Jr., 9–15, 17, 25, 326–28
curriculum at, 21, 23, 58 (*see also* Yale Report)
evolution taught in, 117–18

football at, 17, 19, 181–82, 190–91
foreign missionary work of, 18–19, 20
minorities at, 282–83, 286–89
as model, 76, 77
religion at, 10, 11, 15, 17–19, 20, 21, 25, 58, 77, 109, 114, 189, 270, 287–88, 326–27, 435n.57, 447n.20
sectarianism at, 46–50, 51, 52–53, 55–56
Sheffield Scientific School at, 393n.5 n.5, 109–10, 122, 141
Yeshiva College, 285
Young Men's Christian Association (YMCA), 142, 257–58, 262, 339
at Cornell, 106–7
evangelism of, 12, 180–81, 268, 269–70
and Johns Hopkins, 127–28
membership in, 190–91, 196, 268–69
and social gospel, 268–69
at the University of Michigan, 93
at Vanderbilt, 205
at Yale. 391n.5 (*see also* Dwight Hall)
Young Women's Christian Association (YWCA), 142, 180–81, 190–91, 196, 257–58, 339
evangelism of, 268–69

Zahm, John, 198–99
Zwingli, Ulrich, 33, 34